# SICILY

**VIRGINIA MAXWELL**
**DUNCAN GARWOOD**

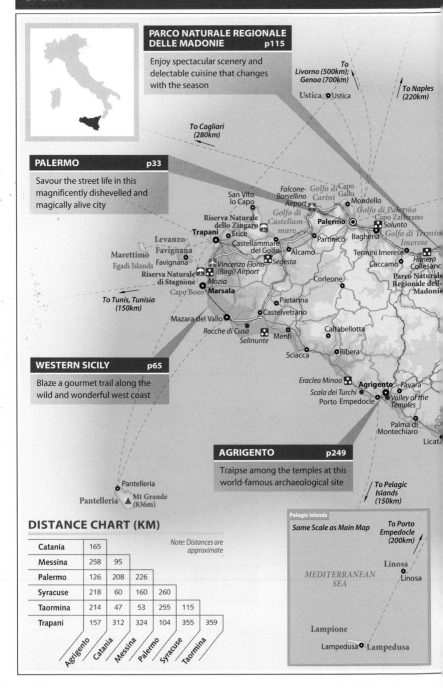

**PARCO NATURALE REGIONALE DELLE MADONIE** p115

Enjoy spectacular scenery and delectable cuisine that changes with the season

To Livorno (500km); Genoa (700km)

To Naples (220km)

Ustica • Ustica

To Cagliari (280km)

**PALERMO** p33

Savour the street life in this magnificently dishevelled and magically alive city

Falcone-Borsellino Airport

San Vito lo Capo

*Golfo di Carini* Capo Gallo

Mondello

*Golfo di Palermo* Capo Zafferano

**Palermo** ◉ Solunto

*Golfo di* *Castellam mare*

Riserva Naturale dello Zingaro

**Trapani** • Erice

Castellammare del Golfo

Partinico

Bagheria *Golfo di Termini Imerese*

Termini Imerese

Himera Collesano

Caccamo

**Levanzo**

**Marettimo**

**Favignana**

Egadi Islands Favignana

Alcamo

Segesta

Vincenzo Florio (Birgi) Airport

Riserva Naturale di Stagnone

*Mozia*

Capo Boeo **Marsala**

Corleone

*Parco Naturale Regionale delle Madonie*

To Tunis, Tunisia (150km)

Partanna

Castelvetrano

Mazara del Vallo

*Rocche di Cusa*

Selinunte

Menfi

Caltabellotta

Sciacca

Ribera

**WESTERN SICILY** p65

Blaze a gourmet trail along the wild and wonderful west coast

Eraclea Minoa

*Scala dei Turchi*

Porto Empedocle

**Agrigento** Favara

*Valley of the Temples*

Palma di Montechiaro

Licata

**AGRIGENTO** p249

Traipse among the temples at this world-famous archaeological site

To Pelagic Islands (150km)

Pantelleria

**Pantelleria** ▲ Mt Grande (836m)

## DISTANCE CHART (KM)

| Pelagic Islands | |
| --- | --- |
| *Same Scale as Main Map* | To Porto Empedocle (200km) |
| *MEDITERRANEAN SEA* | Linosa Linosa |
| Lampione | |
| | Lampedusa Lampedusa |

| | | | | | | |
| --- | --- | --- | --- | --- | --- | --- |
| Catania | 165 | | Note: Distances are approximate | | | |
| Messina | 258 | 95 | | | | |
| Palermo | 126 | 208 | 226 | | | |
| Syracuse | 218 | 60 | 160 | 260 | | |
| Taormina | 214 | 47 | 53 | 255 | 115 | |
| Trapani | 157 | 312 | 324 | 104 | 355 | 359 |
| | Agrigento | Catania | Messina | Palermo | Syracuse | Taormina |

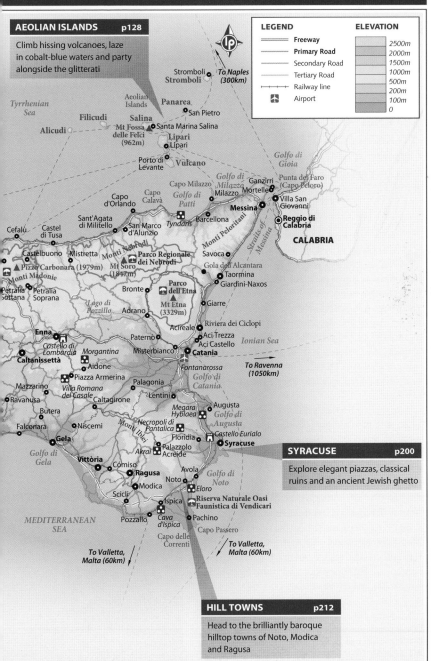

0 ——— 50 km
0 ——— 25 miles

**AEOLIAN ISLANDS**   p128

Climb hissing volcanoes, laze
in cobalt-blue waters and party
alongside the glitterati

**LEGEND**

===== Freeway
—— Primary Road
—— Secondary Road
—— Tertiary Road
+—+—+ Railway line
✈ Airport

**ELEVATION**

2500m
2000m
1500m
1000m
500m
200m
100m
0

*Tyrrhenian
Sea*

Stromboli • *To Naples
Stromboli*  (300km)

*Aeolian
Islands*  **Panarea**
• San Pietro

**Filicudi**  **Salina**
**Alicudi** ○—— Mt Fossa •○ Santa Marina Salina
delle Felci   **Lipari**
(962m)  • Lipari

Porto di • **Vulcano**
Levante

*Golfo di
Gioia*

Capo Milazzo  *Golfo di*  Ganzirri • Punta del Faro
Capo   *Milazzo*  Mortelle•  (Capo Peloro)
Capo  Calavà  *Golfo di*  • Milazzo
d'Orlando •  *Patti*  **Messina** ○

Sant'Agata •  ○  **Villa San
di Militello** San Marco  *Tyndaris*  Giovanni**
Cefalú  d'Alunzio  Barcellona  ○ **Reggio di
Castel  Calabria**

Castelbuono  Mistretta  *Monti Nebrodi*  Savoca ○  **CALABRIA**
▲ Pizzo Carbonara (1979m)  Mt Soro  Gola del'Alcantara
*Monti Madonie*  (1847m)  Taormina •
Petralia  **Parco
Sottana**  Petralia  **Bronte** •  **dell'Etna**  Giardini-Naxos
Soprana  *Lago di
Pozzillo*  **Mt Etna**  • Giarre
Adrano •  (3329m)

Acireale •  • Riviera dei Ciclopi
**Enna** ○  Paternò ○  Aci Trezza
Castello di  Misterbianco •  Aci Castello  *Ionian Sea*
**Caltanissetta**  **Lombardia**  Morgantina  ○ **Catania**

• Aidone  *Fontanarossa*
Piazza Armerina  *Golfo di*  **To Ravenna**
Mazzarino  Palagonia  *Catania*  (1050km)
Villa Romana  • Caltagirone
Ravanusa •  del Casale  Lentini •
Butera  **Megara**  *Golfo di*
Falconara •  ○ Niscemi  *Monti Iblei*  **Hyblaea**  *Augusta*
**Gela**  Necropoli di  • Floridia  **Castello Eurialo**
*Golfo di*  Pantalica  **Palazzolo**  ○ **Syracuse**
*Gela*  **Vittòria**  Akrai • Acreide
• Comiso  Avola •  *Golfo di*  **SYRACUSE**   p200
**Ragusa**  Noto •  *Noto*
Modica  • Eloro  Explore elegant piazzas, classical
Scicli  ruins and an ancient Jewish ghetto
*MEDITERRANEAN
SEA*  • Ispica  **Riserva Naturale Oasi
Faunistica di Vendicari**
Pozzallo  *Cava
d'Ispica*  • Pachino
Capo delle  Capo Passero
Correnti

*To Valletta,
Malta (60km)*  *To Valletta,
Malta (60km)*

**HILL TOWNS**   p212

Head to the brilliantly baroque
hilltop towns of Noto, Modica
and Ragusa

# INTRODUCING
# SICILY

**JUST WHEN YOU THINK YOU'VE LEARNED EVERYTHING THERE IS TO KNOW ABOUT ITALY, ALONG COMES SICILY AND BLOWS AWAY YOUR CERTAINTIES.**

This truly is an island of contradictions. The land is arid, yet everywhere you go food markets showcase lush, locally grown fruits, freshly gathered nuts, sun-ripened vegetables and pungent mountain cheeses. The surrounding seas have been depleted over the centuries, but are still able to meet the insatiable local appetite for fresh seafood. Its people, subjected to wave upon wave of foreign invasion over the centuries, are still quick to offer a warm welcome to visitors.

And the contradictions don't stop there. Though Sicily's history is fantastically rich, its modern disrepair is infamous – nearly as infamous, in fact, as its enslavement to the Mafia. Like it or not (and most Sicilians are firmly in the latter camp), these realities throw a shadow over the island as foreboding as the smoke issuing from its famously active volcanoes. The miracle is that even they cannot take the lustre off this Mediterranean jewel – its Arab-influenced culture and cuisine, ancient archaeological sites, flamboyant baroque cities and stunning natural landscapes make sure of that.

CEFALÙ

PALERMO

TOP The postcard-perfect seafront of Cefalù (p110)
BOTTOM LEFT Palermo's Arab Norman–style cathedral (p45)
BOTTOM RIGHT The evocative saltpans and windmills of Saline di Trapani, on the road to Marsala (p86)

SALINE DI TRAPANI

SYRACUSE

CACCAMO

**SYRACUSE**

**SALINA**

**TOP LEFT** Syracuse's idyllic harbour (p200) **TOP RIGHT** The imposing Duomo in Ortygia, Syracuse (p202) **BOTTOM LEFT** The striking castle and cathedral atop the ancient town of Caccamo (p114) **BOTTOM CENTRE** Sunset aperitivi on Salina, Aeolian Islands (p147) **BOTTOM RIGHT** Spectacular views from Chiesa di San Giovanni in Erice (p79)

**ERICE**

# GETTING STARTED

## SICILY

## WHAT'S NEW?

* Palermo's super-stylish Museum of Contemporary Art (p46)

---

* A totally refurbished ex-hibition space at Mozia's Whitaker Museum (p86)

---

* The opening of two new craters on the summit of Stromboli (p156)

---

* Exciting archaeological finds at the ancient Greek city of Morgantina (p243)

---

* An arty *agriturismo* (farm stay) in Butera (p319)

## CLIMATE: PALERMO

Average Max/Min

°C  °F  **Temp/Humidity**  %          in       **Rainfall**       mm

## PRICE GUIDE

|                | BUDGET | MIDRANGE | TOP END |
|----------------|--------|----------|---------|
| **SLEEPING**   | <€80   | €80-200  | >€200   |
| **EATING**     | <€20   | €20-40   | >€40    |
| **GLASS OF WINE** | €2  | €3       | €4      |

TOP The cloister at Cattedrale di Monreale, Monreale (p60) BOTTOM LEFT Ancient Greek ruins in Selinunte (p94) BOTTOM RIGHT A charming Ragusa street (p222) FAR RIGHT Views from Lipari to Vulcano (p143)

## ACCOMMODATION

The style of accommodation you choose will often be dictated by the destination. In Palermo and the Aeolians, boutique options are gaining popularity, offering stylish decor and high levels of service. In other cities and towns, family-run *pensioni* (guesthouses), B&Bs and apartments reign supreme. Most options are in the midrange category. In rural areas, *agriturismi* (working farms or country houses offering rooms) are beginning to appear, bringing much-needed employment to local communities and allowing visitors to explore the countryside slowly and in great style. For more information, see p302.

## MAIN POINTS OF ENTRY

**FALCONE-BORSELLINO AIRPORT** (PMO; ☎ 091 702 01 11; www.gesap.it) Aka Palermo airport or Punta Raisi. Flights from Tunisia, Spain, Pantelleria and other Italian cities.

**FONTANAROSSA AIRPORT** (CTA; ☎ 095 723 91 11; www.aeroporto.catania.it) Located in Catania, this is Sicily's major hub for both international and domestic flights.

**VINCENZO FLORIO AIRPORT** (TPS; ☎ 0923 84 25 02; www.airgest.it) Located in Trapani and commonly referred to as Birgi airport. Flights from Pantelleria and other Italian and European cities.

## THINGS TO TAKE

* Picnic-friendly pocket knife with corkscrew
* Sunglasses, a hat and something to cover shoulders when visiting churches
* Sturdy walking shoes to combat cobbles and country paths
* A detailed driving map
* Mosquito repellent (they can be a pest in summer)

WAYNE WALTON

## WEBLINKS

**BEST OF SICILY** (www.bestofsicily.com) Comprehensive coverage of the island.

**PRESS SICILIA** (www.press.sicilia.it, in Italian) Useful database of press articles.

**SICILIA ONLINE** (www.siciliaonline.it, in Italian) Info about events and tourism.

**SICILY FOR TOURISTS** (www.regione.sicilia.it/turismo) Sicily's official online tourism portal.

**SICILY WEB** (http://sicilyweb.it) Information about history and culture.

WAYNE WALTON

# FESTIVALS & EVENTS

## SICILY

## JANUARY/FEBRUARY

### CARNEVALE

During the week before Ash Wednesday, many towns stage carnivals. The most flamboyant festivities are in Sciacca (www.carnevaledisciacca.it, in Italian) and Acireale (www.carnevaleacireale.com).

### FESTA DI SANT'AGATA

**CATANIA**
One million Catanians follow a silver reliquary of St Agata through the city's main streets during this festival, which takes place from 3 to 5 February and is accompanied by a spectacular fireworks display (http://mediaonline.it/catania/agata.htm; see p181).

### SAGRA DEL MANDORLO IN FIORE

**AGRIGENTO**
Open-air performances of drama and music are held among the almond blossoms in the Valley of the Temples. The event takes place on the first Sunday in February (www.mandorloinfiore.net, in Italian).

## MARCH/APRIL

### PASQUA (EASTER)

Holy Week in Sicily is marked by solemn, slow-moving processions and passion plays. The most famous are in Trapani, Enna, Lipari and Erice.

## MAY/JUNE

### INFIORATA

**NOTO**
To celebrate the arrival of spring, Noto decorates its streets with colourful floral designs. Held around the third Sunday in May (www.infiorata.info).

### LA MATTANZA

**FAVIGNANA**
Tourists flock to this Egadi island between 20 May and 10 June to witness its ritual slaughter of bluefin tuna (see p84).

### TAORMINA FILM FEST

Hollywood big shots arrive in Taormina in mid-June for six days of film screenings and press conferences at the Teatro Greco (www.taorminafilmfest.it).

**TOP** Carnevale entertainment in Castelbuono (p116) **RIGHT** Crowds celebrate the patron saint of Catania during Festa di Sant'Agata (p181)

## JULY/AUGUST

### FESTINO DI SANTA ROSALIA

**PALERMO**

The capital celebrates its patron saint from 10 to 15 July with music, dancing and a parade of relics.

### TAORMINA ARTE

Opera, dance and theatre performances are staged at the Teatro Greco during July and August (www.taormina-arte.com, in Italian).

### PALIO DEI NORMANNI

**PIAZZA ARMERINA**

This medieval pageant, held between 13 and 14 August, commemorates Count Roger's taking of the town from the Moors in 1087 (p242).

## SEPTEMBER

### FESTIVAL INTERNAZIONALE DEL CUSCUS

**SAN VITO LO CAPO**

The island's heritage is showcased alongside one of its favourite dishes in this six-day festival (p72; www.couscousfest.it).

## DECEMBER

### FESTA DI SANTA LUCIA

**SYRACUSE**

The city's patron saint is commemorated with events such as a procession from the cathedral to Piazza Santa Lucia and fireworks. Held between 13 and 20 December.

### NATALE

During the weeks preceding Christmas, many churches set up cribs or Nativity scenes known as *presepi;* these are particularly notable in Caltagirone and Erice.

DANIELE LA MONACA/TIPS ITALIA/PHOTOLIBRARY

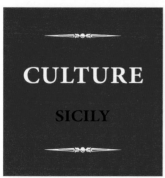

# CULTURE

## SICILY

## FILMS

**KAOS** (Paolo & Vittorio Taviani, 1984) Visually arresting film based on four stories by Luigi Pirandello.

**LA TERRA TREMA** (Luchino Visconti, 1948) Masterful adaptation of Giovanni Verga's 1881 novel *I Malavoglia*.

**THE GODFATHER TRILOGY** (Francis Ford Coppola, 1972–90) Saga of an American Mafia family that achieved box-office results nearly as big as those of *Ben Hur*.

**CINEMA PARADISO** (Giuseppe Tornatore, 1988) See it and weep (lots).

**STROMBOLI** (Roberto Rossellini, 1950) Neorealist drama mainly remembered for the affair between its director and leading lady.

## THE LEOPARD

Written by Giuseppe Tomasi di Lampedusa and published posthumously in 1958, *Il Gattopardo* (The Leopard) is generally considered to be the greatest Sicilian novel ever written. The story of an ageing aristocrat grappling with the political and sociological changes that are being brought to the island by the Risorgimento, it is set in an era and milieu that Lampedusa, the last of a long line of minor princes in Sicily, evokes magnificently. Faced with choosing between tradition and modernity, the book's central character takes the only honourable path (for him) and opts for tradition, thus signing the warrant for his family's loss of wealth, power and influence. Unusually, the 1963 cinematic version made by director Luchino Visconti – himself a member of the Italian aristocracy – is as critically acclaimed as the original. For more info, see p287 and p289.

TOP Palermo's grand Teatro Massimo (p53) BOTTOM Exhibits at Museo Archeologico Regionale in Palermo (p47) RIGHT *Passeggiata* in Taormina (p168) FAR RIGHT Teatro Greco during Taormina's Film Fest (p169)

## TOP MUSEUMS

**MUSEO ARCHEOLOGICO REGIONALE, PALERMO** The cream of Sicily's archaeological artefacts under one roof (p47).

-------------------------------------------------------------------------------------

**MUSEO ARCHEOLOGICO, AGRIGENTO** Amazing artefacts from Agrigento and Akragas (p257).

-------------------------------------------------------------------------------------

**MUSEO ARCHEOLOGICO EOLIANO, LIPARI** One of Europe's best collections of prehistoric and classical-era artefacts (p136).

-------------------------------------------------------------------------------------

**MUSEO ARCHEOLOGICO PAOLO ORSI, SYRACUSE** Sicily's largest archaeological collection (p206).

## DON'T MISS EXPERIENCES

★ Literary pilgrimages – check out Pirandello's birthplace (p261), Camilleri's *Inspector Montalbano* settings (p198 and p217) and di Lampedusa's haunts (p52)

-------------------------------------------------------------------------------------

★ *Passeggiata* – join the locals on their evening promenade in Lipari (p136)

-------------------------------------------------------------------------------------

★ Hilltop towns – hop from one mountain eyrie to the next in the southeast (p212) and in the Madonie mountains (p120)

-------------------------------------------------------------------------------------

★ *Agriturismi* – stay in a rural getaway (p302)

-------------------------------------------------------------------------------------

★ Open-air concerts – spend summer nights watching film, music and theatre under the stars in Taormina (p172) and Palermo (p53)

-------------------------------------------------------------------------------------

★ Aperitivo – people-watch from a cafe (p202)

-------------------------------------------------------------------------------------

★ Film sets – see where *The Godfather* trilogy, *Cinema Paradiso* and other classic films were shot (p290)

## BOOKS

**I MALAVOGLIA** (Giovanni Verga, 1881) An Italian literary masterpiece.

-------------------------------------------------------------------------------------

**MIDNIGHT IN SICILY** (Peter Robb, 1996) Disturbing but fascinating portrait of postwar Sicily.

-------------------------------------------------------------------------------------

**ON PERSEPHONE'S ISLAND** (Mary Taylor Simeti, 1986) Insightful personal memoir.

-------------------------------------------------------------------------------------

**THE DAY OF THE OWL** (Leonardo Sciascia, 1961) Social and political commentary disguised as crime fiction.

-------------------------------------------------------------------------------------

**THE SILENT DUCHESS** (Dacia Maraini, 1990) Feminist-flavoured historical novel set in 18th-century Palermo.

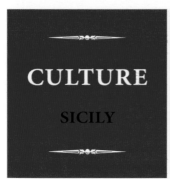

JOHN ELK III

# CULTURE

## SICILY

## LIVE MUSIC

**ESTATE CATANESE**
(www.comune.catania.it/eventi/
estate-catanese, in Italian) Summer
program of performances in
Catania.

----

**WOMAD SICILY**
(www.womad.org/festivals/sicily) September sees world music showcased in Palermo.

----

**GIUSEPPE SINOPOLI**
**FESTIVAL** (www.sinopoli
festival.it) Classical music in
Taormina's Teatro Greco and
other venues in October.

----

**SICILY JAZZ AND MORE**
(www.brassgroup.com) Performers
take the stage in Catania in
November.

## TOP ART GALLERIES

**GALLERIA REGIONALE DELLA SICILIANA,**
**PALERMO** Home to works dating from the
Middle Ages to the 18th century (p50).

----

**GALLERIA D'ARTE MODERNA,**
**PALERMO** Sicilian paintings and sculptures
from the 19th and 20th centuries (p51).

----

**MUSEO REGIONALE D'ARTE MEDIO-**
**EVALE E MODERNA** Impressive collection of
sculptures, paintings and applied arts (p205).

----

**MUSEO REGIONALE, MESSINA** Paintings by
Caravaggio and home-town boy Antonello da
Messina (p166).

----

**MUSEO D'ARTE CONTEMPORANEA**
**DELLA SICILIA (RISO), PALERMO** A new
contemporary art museum hosting temporary
exhibitions (p46).

## ANTONELLO DA MESSINA

The first – some would say only – great Sicilian painter was Antonello da Messina
(1430–79). In *The Lives of the Artists* (1550), Vasari described da Messina as 'a
man well skilled in his art' and claimed that he was the first Italian painter to use
oil paint, a technique he had learned in Flanders. Only four of his luminous paintings are in Sicily: *Annunziata* (The Virgin Annunciate, 1474–77) in Palermo (p50);
*Ritratto di un uomo ignoto* (Portrait of an Unknown Man, 1465) in Cefalù (p112);
*L'Annunciazione* (Annunciation, 1474) in Syracuse (p205); and *San Gregorio* (St
Gregory, 1473) in Messina (p166). For more on Sicilian art, see p97.

----

**TOP** Magnificent mosaics adorn Palazzo dei Normanni's Cappella Palatina in Palermo (p43) **RIGHT** Ancient
treasures on display at Museo Archeologico Regionale in Palermo (p47)

## SICILIAN BAROQUE

After being devastated by an earthquake in 1693, Sicily was presented with an opportunity to redesign many of its cities and experiment with a new architectural style that was taking Europe by storm: the baroque. A backlash against the pared-down classical aesthetic of the Renaissance, this new style was dramatic, curvaceous and downright sexy – a perfect match for Sicily's unorthodox and exuberant character. Aristocrats in towns such as Noto, Modica, Ragusa, Catania and Syracuse rushed to build baroque palazzi (palaces), many decorated with the grotesque masks and putti that had long been a hallmark of the island's architecture. Even the church got into it, commissioning ostentatious churches and oratories aplenty. For more on Sicilian architecture, see p97.

## DOS & DON'TS

⋆ Avoid discussing the *Lega Nord* (Northern League) or the Mafia, as these can be touchy subjects.

---

⋆ Take *dolcetti* (sweet biscuits or cakes) if you are invited into a local home.

---

⋆ Cover up when visiting a church – singlets, shorts, miniskirts and plunging necklines are forbidden.

---

⋆ Never intrude on a mass or service in a church.

---

⋆ Take official opening hours and timetables with a grain of salt – Sicilians are notoriously unpunctual.

# FOOD & DRINK

## SICILY

## STREET FOOD

**ARANCINE** Rice balls stuffed with meat or cheese, coated with breadcrumbs and fried.

----

**CALZONE** A pocket of pizza-like dough baked with ham, cheese or other stuffings.

----

**CROCCHÉ** Fried potato dumplings made with cheese, parsley and eggs.

----

**PANE CON LA MILZA** A bread roll (bun) filled with calf's spleen, *caciocavallo* cheese, a drizzle of hot lard and a squeeze of lemon juice.

----

**PANELLE** Fried chickpea-flour fritters often served in a roll.

----

**SFINCIONE** A local form of pizza made with tomatoes, onions and (sometimes) anchovies.

----

**STIGGHIOLA** Seasoned and barbecued lamb or kid intestines served on a skewer.

## SICILIAN SWEET TREATS

Most traditional Sicilian dishes fall into the category of *cucina povera* (cooking of the poor), featuring cheap and plentiful ingredients such as pulses, vegetables and bread. Supplemented by fish (locally caught and still relatively inexpensive), this diet is still widely embraced today, but differs in one major respect to that of previous generations – the inclusion of decadent desserts. The two most beloved of these are *cassata siciliana* (a mix of ricotta, sugar, candied fruit and chocolate that is flavoured with vanilla and maraschino liqueur, encased by sponge cake and topped with green icing) and *cannoli* (crisp tubes of fried pastry dough filled with creamy ricotta and candied fruit and decorated with a maraschino cherry and grated chocolate). You'll find both on restaurant menus throughout the island. To discover more about these and other sweet treats, see p297.

TOP Fresh delights at Mercato del Capo, Palermo (p57) **BOTTOM** Barrels of dessert wine in Marsala (p87)
**RIGHT** Dusk dining in Piazza del Duomo, Cefalù (p110) **FAR RIGHT** Fish couscous, a speciality in Trapani (p76)

## TOP RESTAURANTS

**PICCOLO NAPOLI, PALERMO** A traditional trattoria serving Palermo's best seafood (p57).

**LA BETTOLA, MAZARA DEL VALLO** Refined seafood dishes that are as fresh as they are delectable (p93).

**RISTORANTE LA MADIA, LICATA** Exciting modern Sicilian cuisine that showcases the best regional produce (p268).

**RISTORANTE DUOMO, RAGUSA** Faultlessly cooked and presented Sicilian classics (p226).

STEPHEN SAKS

OLIVER CIRENDINI

## DON'T MISS EXPERIENCES

★ Dessert wines – skip straight to the dessert course so that you can order a glass of Marsala, Moscato or Malvasia

★ Honey tasting on Etna – sample mountain honey made from orange blossom, chestnuts and lemons (p192)

★ *Brioche con gelato* – where else is it acceptable to eat an ice-cream sandwich for breakfast?

★ *Seltz* – get a fizzy lift from a traditional Catanese soft drink (p183)

★ Porcini mushrooms – head to the Madonie mountains to feast on freshly gathered fruits of the forest (p115)

★ *Cuscus trapanese* – Trapani's North African–influenced fish dish is so good it has its own festival (p72)

## LOOK OUT FOR

**INTERDONATO LEMONS** Natural hybrid of lemon and citron with a slightly bitter taste.

**ALMONDS FROM NOTO** Intense and aromatic nuts from ancient trees.

**PISTACHIOS FROM BRONTE** Emerald-green nuts with an unctuous texture and intense flavour.

**BLACK PORK FROM THE NEBRODI MOUNTAINS** Can be enjoyed in succulent ham, sausages and bacon.

**CAPERS FROM SALINA** Known for their firmness, perfume and uniform size.

# FOOD & DRINK

## SICILY

## FOOD GUIDES

**OSTERIE D'ITALIA** (Slow Food Editore; in Italian) Lists eateries that use regional products and are influenced by local food traditions.

**ALBERGHI & RISTORANTI ITALIA** (Michelin) The one that gets all the press.

**RISTORANTI D'ITALIA** (Gambero Rosso; in Italian) Italy's version of the Michelin guide.

**BAR D'ITALIA** (Gambero Rosso; in Italian) Rates bars and cafes according to their atmosphere and quality of coffee.

## COFFEE, SICILIAN STYLE

Sicilians take their coffee seriously, and order it in the following ways.

**ESPRESSO** A tiny cup of very strong black coffee; usually called a *caffè* or *caffè normale*.

**CAFFÈ MACCHIATO** An espresso with a dash of milk.

**CAPPUCCINO** Espresso topped with hot foaming milk; only drunk at breakfast or in the mid-morning.

**CAFFÈ LATTE** Coffee with milk that is steamed but not frothed; an extremely milky version is called a *latte macchiato* (stained milk). Again, only drunk in the morning.

**CAFFÈ FREDDO** The local version of an iced coffee.

## CERASUOLO DI VITTORIA

The prestigious appellation DOCG *(Denominazione di Origine Controllata e Garantita)* is awarded to Italian wines that meet strict requirements regarding production area, grape varietals, viticultural and bottling techniques and quality. There are currently around 40 DOCGs in Italy, but only one from Sicily: Cerasuolo di Vittoria. Produced in Caltanissetta, Catania and Ragusa, this wine is a medium-bodied blend of plummy Nero d'Avola and aromatic Frappato grapes and is equally at home accompanying fish, meat or cheese. Among the best-known producers are COS, Planeta, Valle dell'Acate, Terre di Giurfo, Gulfi and Fuedo di Santa Tresa. For more on Sicilian wine, see p298.

TOP Sicily is famous for its delicious *cannoli* (p297) RIGHT La Pescheria, Catania's bustling fish market (p177)

## THE ARK OF TASTE

The Ark of Taste is an international catalogue of endangered food products drawn up by the Slow Food Foundation for Biodiversity. It aims to protect indigenous edibles threatened with extinction by industrialisation, globalisation, hygiene laws and environmental dangers, and actively encourages their cultivation for consumption. Foods included in the list must be culturally or historically linked to a specific region, locality, ethnicity or traditional production practice, and must also be rare. There are 47 Sicilian foods on the list, ranging from the Ustica lentil to Trapani artisan sea salt and the Monreale white plum. For a full list, go to www.fondazioneslowfood.com/eng/arca/lista.lasso. For more on Slow Food, see p293.

## SICILIAN FAVOURITES

★ *Pasta alla Norma* – pasta with tomato, eggplant, basil and salty ricotta cheese

-----

★ *Caponata* – cooked vegetable salad made with tomatoes, eggplant, celery, capers, olives and onions

-----

★ *Frutta di Martorana* – marzipan pastries coloured and shaped to resemble real fruit; also called *pasta reale*

-----

★ *Pasta con le sarde* – pasta with sardines, fennel, pine nuts and raisins

-----

★ *Involtini di pesce spada* – swordfish rolls stuffed with breadcrumbs, currents and pine nuts

MICHAEL GEBICKI

# OUTDOORS

## SICILY

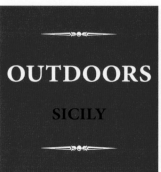

DIANA MAYFIELD

## TOP TREKS

**PIANO BATTAGLIA** Walk among the wildflowers in the Parco Naturale Regionale delle Madonie (p119).

**MT ETNA** Hike the picturesque northern slopes of the famous volcano (p192).

**VULCANO** Climb the short but steep path to the steaming rim of an active volcano's crater (p143).

**RISERVA NATURALE DELLO ZINGARO** Hike the coastal path between Scopello and San Vito lo Capo (p71).

**STROMBOLI** Complete the demanding six-hour guided walk up to the summit (p155).

**VALLE DELL'ANAPO** Take a gentle walk through an unspoiled valley (p214).

**RISERVA NATURALE TORRE SALSA** Admire sweeping panoramic views of the surrounding mountains and coast (p261).

## REGIONAL PARKS

There are no national parks in Sicily, but there are many protected natural landscapes. The largest and most significant of these are the Parco Naturale Regionale delle Madonie (p115), Parco Fluviale dell'Alcantara (p162), Parco Regionale dei Nebrodi (p122) and Parco dell'Etna (p189). Each offers the visitor a very different experience. In the Parco dell'Etna, for instance, you can taste homegrown wine and honey on the volcano's slopes as well as trekking to the crater; in the Parco Fluviale dell'Alcantara, you can swim, picnic, ride quad bikes, hike or canyon. The parks are large, and each deserve a few days of exploration; fortunately, all offer plenty of places to sleep and eat.

Sicily also has 79 regional nature reserves, six marine protected areas and one protected wetland. For information about visiting these protected natural landscapes, go to www.parks.it.

DALLAS STRIBLEY

TOP Barren and brooding Mt Etna (p189) **BOTTOM** Bathers relax in Vulcano's muddy waters (p144) **RIGHT** A glorious cove in Riserva Naturale dello Zingaro (p71) **FAR RIGHT** Hikers approach Mt Etna's summit (p189)

## TOP BEACHES

**FORGIA VECCHIA, STROMBOLI** Relax on this black volcanic beach (p157).

---

**CAMPOBIANCO, LIPARI** Slide down natural pumice chutes into crystalline azure waters (p139).

---

**SAN VITO LO CAPO** Join the sun-worshippers on this crescent-shaped sandy beach (p72).

---

**SPIAGGIA DEI CONIGLI, LAMPEDUSA** Visit one of the Mediterranean's finest beaches (p262).

## DON'T MISS EXPERIENCES

- ★ Diving and snorkelling – explore the underwater worlds of Lipari (p140), Ustica (p63) or Isola Bella (p171)

---

- ★ Volcano viewing – watch Stromboli's nocturnal fireworks from the summit or on a boat (p155)

---

- ★ Cycling – use peddle power to explore the Mt Etna area (p193)

---

- ★ Guided nature walks – join local naturalists on a walk around the Syracusan countryside (p208) or on the slopes of Etna (p193)

---

- ★ Mud baths – wallow in the mud at Vulcano (p144) or Eraclea Minoa (p262)

---

- ★ Sailing trips – explore the coastlines and hidden coves of Lipari, Alicudi and Filicudi by boat (p128)

## DRIVING TOURS

Tour striking landscapes, sampling great regional food and wine as you go.

- ★ **THE MONTI MADONIE** Admire medieval villages and majestic mountain scenery (p120).

---

- ★ **ETNA'S WESTERN FLANK** Pass Norman castles and pistachio groves (p190).

---

- ★ **BAROQUE TOWNS** Discover Unesco-listed hilltop towns (p212).

---

- ★ **ENNA TO ETNA** Traverse an undulating landscape of sun-baked hills (p232).

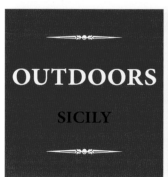

DALLAS STRIBLEY

# OUTDOORS

## SICILY

## URBAN ESCAPES

**ORTO BOTANICO, PALERMO** A tranquil botanical garden in the midst of the city's chaos (p53).

---

**VILLA COMUNALE, TAORMINA** Superb views, shady paths and botanical species galore (p171).

---

**VILLA BELLINI, CATANIA** This charming retreat in the centre of the city is named after the great composer (p177).

---

**LATOMIA DEL PARADISO, SYRACUSE** An ancient limestone quarry pitted with caves and full of orange and olive trees (p206).

## MARINE RESERVES

Sicily has six *area marina protetta* (protected marine reserves).

**ISOLE PELAGIE** (www.isole-pelagie.it, in Italian) Includes the three islands of the Pelagic archipelago: Lampedusa, Lampione and Linosa.

---

**ISOLE CICLOPI** (www.isoleciclopi.it, in Italian) On the Riviera dei Ciclopi outside Catania.

---

**CAPO GALLO** (www.ampcapogallo-isola.org, in Italian) In the Tyrrhenian Sea.

---

**ISOLA DI USTICA** (www.ampustica.it, in Italian) Around the island of Ustica.

---

**PLEMMIRIO** (www.plemmirio.it) The waters off Syracuse.

---

**ISOLE EGADI** (www.ampisoleegadi.net, in Italian) Includes the islands of the Egadi archipelago: Favignana, Levanzo, Marittimo and Formica.

## WORLD HERITAGE LANDSCAPE

The Aeolian Islands *(Isole Eolie)* is one of only two Italian natural landscapes included on the World Heritage list (the other is the Dolomites). Unesco's citation describes the Aeolians as providing an outstanding record of volcanic island building and destruction, and ongoing volcanic phenomena. It also notes that the islands have played a vitally important role in the education of vulcanologists for more than 200 years.

It's not only vulcanologists who are fascinated by these volcanic islands, though. Tourists from around the world flock here in summer to take advantage of the great hiking, swimming, snorkelling, diving and boating on offer. For more info, see p128.

---

TOP Stromboli's Sciara del Fuoco steams with fresh lava flow (p156) RIGHT Snorkelling in the azure shallows off Lido Burrone, Favignana, in the Egadi Islands (p83)

## WHEN TO GO?

If you're keen to go hiking while you're in Sicily, the best time is spring, when the wildflowers are in bloom and the landscape retains the rich, green flush it has acquired over winter. Try to avoid the busy Easter week if possible.

If you're planning to walk in mountain areas, the most pleasant time to do so is during summer. Remember, though, that August is the month when most Italians take their holidays and the trails can get very busy.

All beach and underwater activity kicks off at Easter and goes until September. Try to go in June – in July and August the coastline and smaller islands are unpleasantly busy.

## BIRD-WATCHING DESTINATIONS

⋆ Riserva Naturale dello Zingaro – has over 40 species, including the rare Bonelli eagle (p71)

---

⋆ Parco Regionale dei Nebrodi – the park is home to golden eagles, griffin vultures and falcons (p122)

---

⋆ Island of Mozia – this tiny island is a haven for many species (p86)

---

⋆ Riserva Naturale Oasi Faunistica di Vendicari – wetlands where flamingos, herons, spoonbills, ducks and collared pratincoles are found (p219)

---

⋆ Lingua – Salina's lagoon attracts huge numbers of migrating birds in April (p148)

DALLAS STRIBLEY

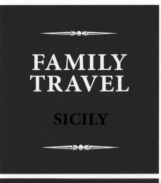

# FAMILY TRAVEL

## SICILY

## TOP ACTIVITIES

**FOSSA DI VULCANO** Follow the pongy path to the steaming crater of this volcano (p143).

**CABLE CAR TO ERICE** Take the kids on a steep ride to the hilltop town of Erice (p79).

**GROTTA DEL BUE MARINO** Visit Filicudi's spectacular sea cave by boat (p153).

## DON'T MISS EXPERIENCES

★ Farm stays – enjoy animals, swimming pools and lots of space while staying in an *agriturismo* (p302)

★ *Passeggiata* – search out carousels, cafes and convivial company of every age

★ Gelato – kids love the local ice cream, especially for breakfast!

★ Puppet theatre – watch brave knights defeat evil monsters in a traditional puppet play in Palermo (p52) and Acireale (p186)

★ *Granita* – there's nothing more refreshing (and yummy) than a crushed-ice drink on a hot day

★ Castles – storm the ramparts of Norman castles across the island (p104)

## TRAVEL WITH CHILDREN

Families are welcomed with open arms in Sicily. Restaurants, cafes and hotels are extremely family friendly, as are museums, galleries and archaeological parks. Admission to many cultural sites is free for under 10s or under 18s (particularly EU citizens). In restaurants, high chairs are usually available and it's perfectly acceptable to order a *mezza porzione* (half-serve) for little ones. On trains, the *offerte familia* allows a discount of 50% for children under 12 and 20% for other family members if you are travelling in a group of three to five people (see www.trenitalia.com for conditions). For tips on travelling with kids, grab a copy of Lonely Planet's *Travelling with Children*.

TOP Local boys play football in the alleyways of Palermo, which are great places to stroll (p40)

# CONTENTS

# THE AUTHORS

## VIRGINIA MAXWELL

**Coordinating Author, Palermo, Western Sicily, Tyrrhenian Coast**

While working as a publishing manager at Lonely Planet, Virginia decided that she'd be happier writing guidebooks rather than commissioning them. Since then, she's contributed to six of Lonely Planet's Italy titles, as well as to a host of magazines and websites. For this edition of *Sicily* she travelled across the island with her partner Peter and son Max, both of whom were supportive of her quest to find Sicily's best *cannolo*.

## DUNCAN GARWOOD

**Art & Architecture, Aeolian Islands, Ionian Coast, Syracuse & the Southeast, Central Sicily, Mediterranean Coast**

Since moving to Italy more than 10 years ago, Duncan has travelled the length and breadth of the country numerous times, contributing to a raft of Lonely Planet Italy titles as well as several newspapers and magazines. This was his second research trip to Sicily, a region whose beauty, drama and complexity he finds endlessly fascinating. He currently lives in the Alban hills just outside Rome with his Italian wife and two bilingual kids.

## LONELY PLANET AUTHORS

Why is our travel information the best in the world? It's simple: our authors are passionate, dedicated travellers. They don't take freebies in exchange for positive coverage so you can be sure the advice you're given is impartial. They travel widely to all the popular spots, and off the beaten track. They don't research using just the internet or phone. They discover new places not included in any other guidebook. They personally visit thousands of hotels, restaurants, palaces, trails, galleries, temples and more. They speak with dozens of locals every day to make sure you get the kind of insider knowledge only a local could tell you. They take pride in getting all the details right, and in telling it how it is. Think you can do it? Find out how at lonelyplanet.com.

# ITINERARIES

## ONLY THE BEST

### TWO WEEKS // AROUND THE ISLAND // 968KM

Fly into Palermo, Trapani or Catania and pick up a hire car to begin your circumnavigation of the island. Your destinations should be the same regardless of where you start: Agrigento, the Val di Noto, Syracuse, the Aeolian Islands, Palermo and Marsala. From

Catania, for instance, you could head south to Syracuse (p200) and follow our driving tour of baroque towns (p212) such as Noto, Modica and Ragusa in the Unesco-listed Val di Noto, an enchanting area in the island's southeast. Continue west to explore the evocative temples at Agrigento (p254) and then follow the coastline to Marsala (p87). From there, take the autostrada to Palermo (p33), where you can explore the crumbling but magnificent streets and indulge in the city's inviting cafe culture before taking a ferry to the Aeolian Islands (p128) for some sun, swimming and volcano climbing.

# WORLD HERITAGE SITES

### SEVEN TO 10 DAYS // CATANIA TO AGRIGENTO // 502KM

The devastating earthquake of 1693 may have wrought havoc on the island, but it also led to the creation of some of its greatest treasures: the late-baroque towns of the Val di Noto. Start your exploration of these Unesco-listed urban landscapes in Catania

(p176) and then follow the trail to Caltagirone (p243), Palazzolo Acreide (p214), Ragusa (p223), Modica (p220), Scicli (p222) and Noto (p216). After this overdose of ostentation, the austere Necropoli di Pantalica (p214) outside Ferla and Parco Archeologico della Neapolis (p205) in Syracuse will provide the perfect antidote. The trail ends at the most magnificent archaeological site in Sicily: Agrigento's Valley of the Temples (p254), with its five Doric structures spectacularly perched on a ridge near the Mediterranean coast.

# WILD ABOUT THE WEST

### 10 DAYS // PALERMO TO SELINUNTE // 197KM

Wend your way west from Palermo, heading along the A29 autostrada (motorway) to the splendidly sited temple and amphitheatre at Segesta (p78) and continuing on to the foodie mecca of Trapani (p73) to sample its unique Arabian-influenced cuisine.

From here, take the funicular to medieval Erice (p79) and visit the Phoenician site of Mozia (p86) before continuing along the Via del Sale (Salt Road) to elegant Marsala, where you should taste-test some of the town's famous sweet wine at Cantine Florio (p90). Continue south via the Arab-accented town of Mazara del Vallo (p91) and finish your trip at the ruins of the Greek city of Selinunte (p94) before taking the A29 back to Palermo or moving on to Agrigento.

ITINERARIES

# VILLAS & VIEWS

## ONE WEEK // CEFALÙ TO PIAZZA ARMERINA // 167KM

Kick off in postcard-perfect Cefalù (p110), where you can visit its splendid cathedral and climb to the ruins of a Norman citadel, before heading into the heart of the Parco Naturale Regionale delle Madonie (p115), a magnificent natural landscape dotted

with medieval hilltop towns and restaurants serving tasty regional cuisine. Follow our driving tour (p120) as far as Petralia Sottana (p118), and then head to the sunscorched centre at Enna (p232) to admire the views from the heavily fortified walls of the Castello di Lombardia (p235). Your final destination will be the 4th-century Villa Romana del Casale (p238) near Piazza Armerina, a lavish Roman villa decorated with the finest Roman floor mosaics in existence.

# ISLANDS & VOLCANOES

## ONE WEEK TO 10 DAYS // CATANIA TO THE AEOLIANS // 221KM

Start in Catania (p176), a city built of lava. From here, make the ascent up Sicily's most famous sight, Mt Etna (p189), from whose lofty heights the Cyclops hurled his stones at the fleeing Odysseus – you can still see their jagged forms along the dramatic

Riviera dei Ciclopi (p186), a stretch of coastline where traditional fishing villages have been reinvented as summer resorts in recent years. Follow our driving tour (p190) of the volcano's western flank and then head to Milazzo (p125), from where you can take a ferry to Lipari (p129), the largest of the Aeolian Islands. From here, nature lovers can island-hop to Salina (p147), while volcano enthusiasts can climb Fossa di Vulcano (p143) and Stromboli (p155).

ITINERARIES

# BEACH HOPPING

### 10 DAYS // PALERMO TO ACI CASTELLO // 666KM

Unpack your beach towel for the first time at Mondello (p60), Palermo's summer playground, before heading to the stunning Golfo di Castellammare (p70), where you'll find the popular beaches of Castellammare del Golfo (p70) and San Vito lo

Capo (p72). Continuing down the west coast, you'll eventually reach Eraclea Minoa (p262), with its twin attractions of a fabulous beach and an archaeological site. Next, make your way to the east coast. You'll encounter plenty of swimming possibilities along the way, including the stunning Scala dei Turchi (p262), the isolated beaches of the Riserva Naturale Oasi Faunistica di Vendicari (p219) and the blue waters at Aci Castello (p188), where a Norman castle broods over the beach scene.

# GASTRONOMIC GALLIVANT

### 10 DAYS // TRAPANI TO TAORMINA // 445KM

Take your appetite for top food and wine to Trapani (p73), where you can feast on *cuscus trapanese* and *busiate con pesto* before following the Strada del Vino e dei Sapori Erice DOC wine route (p79), sampling pastries from Erice's Maria Gram-

matico (p82) and sipping Marsala wine (p91) along the way. Next, make a pilgrimage to Licata's La Madia (p268), often described as Sicily's best restaurant, and to romantic Ragusa, where you can eat at Michelin-starred establishments such as Ristorante Duomo (p226) and Locanda Don Serafino (p226). Finish up in trendy Taormina (p168), which is another centre of fine dining on the island.

PALERMO

# 3 PERFECT DAYS

❦ DAY 1 // **THE BAROQUE CITY**
Start in the baroque heart of the city, the Quattro Canti (p41), then make your way to the gorgeous oratories and churches of the Tesori della Loggia (p47). After digesting so much over-the-top decoration, it may then be time to digest some simple Palermitan food – Casa del Brodo (p57) and Trattoria Primavera (p58) are both nearby. After lunch, visit the ostentatious Chiesa del Gesù (p43), walk past the crumbling baroque palazzos of the Kalsa district (p50) and finish at atmospheric Kursaal Kalhesa (p52) for a drink.

❦ DAY 2 // **BYZANTINE TREASURES**
After visiting the medieval church of La Martorana (p42), walk through the bustling Mercato di Ballarò (p57) to Caffetteria Massaro (p56) for a mid-morning snack. Nearby Palazzo dei Normanni (p43) is your next stop. You'll probably decide that it would be impossible to create a more magnificent interior than that of its Cappella Palatina, but the Cattedrale di Monreale (p60), your next destination, may make you think again. Returning to Palermo, swap the medieval for the modern and enjoy an aperitivo at Pizzo & Pizzo (p58) and dinner at Cucina (p57).

❦ DAY 3 // **HEDONISTIC PALERMO**
It's time to indulge in a little R&R. Wander through the Mercato del Capo (p57), have a break at Cappello Pasticceria (p56) and then enjoy a long lunch at Piccolo Napoli (p57), Palermo's best seafood restaurant. Afterwards, spend a few hours on the beach at Mondello (p60). At night, mingle with society types at the opera (p53).

PALERMO

**PALERMO**

**QUATTRO CANTI**    p41

Find your geographical bearings at the city's baroque crossroads

**I TESORI DELLA LOGGIA**    p47

Admire baroque stuccowork and paintings in this cluster of churches and chapels

**VILLA MALFITANO**    p55

Explore the villa and garden of this charming belle époque estate

0    0.5 miles

0    1 km

*Golfo di Palermo*

Ferries & Hydrofoils to Ustica (60km); Aeolian Islands (110km)

*La Cala*

Via della Cala

Via Emanuele

Foro

I Tesori della Loggia

Vucciria

Via Roma

Via Cavour

Via Mariano Stabile

Via Enrico Amari

Corso Domenico Saina

To Mondello (9km)

Piazza Sturzo

Via Ruggero Settimo

Piazza Giuseppe Verdi

**Viale della Libertà**

Piazza Castelnuovo

**NEW CITY P54**

Via Volturno

Via Dante

Giardino Inglese

To Pasticceria Alba (1km);
Parco della Favorita (1.5km);
Teatro della Verdura (3km);
Falcone-Borsellino Airport (25km)

Via Emanuele Notabartolo

Via Malaspina

Villa Malfitano

Corso Camillo Finocchiaro Aprile

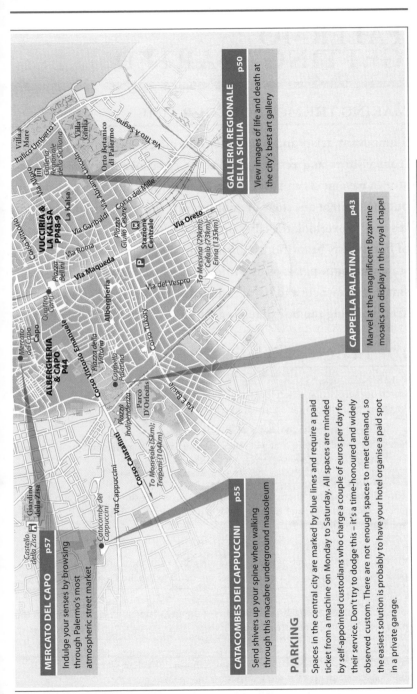

**GALLERIA REGIONALE DELLA SICILIA**    p50

View images of life and death at the city's best art gallery

**CAPPELLA PALATINA**    p43

Marvel at the magnificent Byzantine mosaics on display in this royal chapel

**MERCATO DEL CAPO**    p57

Indulge your senses by browsing through Palermo's most atmospheric street market

**CATACOMBES DEI CAPPUCCINI**    p55

Send shivers up your spine when walking through this macabre underground mausoleum

## PARKING

Spaces in the central city are marked by blue lines and require a paid ticket from a machine on Monday to Saturday. All spaces are minded by self-appointed custodians who charge a couple of euros per day for their service. Don't try to dodge this – it's a time-honoured and widely observed custom. There are not enough spaces to meet demand, so the easiest solution is probably to have your hotel organise a paid spot in a private garage.

PALERMO

# PALERMO
## GETTING STARTED

PALERMO

## MAKING THE MOST OF YOUR TIME

Flamboyant, feisty and full of life, Palermo evokes a strong response from visitors and residents alike. Its car-choked streets, rubbish-strewn pavements and decrepit infrastructure cause everyone to pull out their hair at one stage or another (pity the poor Palermitans), but it's easy to overlook the city's problems when you enter a church full of luminously beautiful Byzantine mosaics, wander along a street of stately baroque palazzos or witness the genial banter between street-smart stall owners and bargain-hunting housewives at a street market. Exploring can be exhausting, but it's well and truly worth it.

## TOP TRAILS

### ❦ BAROQUE BEAUTIES
Search out spectacular examples of Sicilian baroque architecture by wandering around the Quattro Canti (p41) and through the Vucciria (p46) and Kalsa (p50) districts.

### ❦ GIUSEPPE DI LAMPEDUSA'S PALERMO
Sign up for a walking tour that will introduce you to the life, novels and local haunts of the great Sicilian novelist (p52).

### ❦ OPERA DEI PUPI
Learn all about Sicily's unique and endearing art form by visiting the Antonio Pasqualino Museum (p51) and then see these manic marionettes in action at Teatro dei Pupi Cuticchio (p52).

### ❦ SICILIAN PASTRIES
There are plenty of options if you are on a mission to find the island's best *cannolo* (pastry shell filled with sweet ricotta) – see our guide to the city's top-five cafes (p56).

### ❦ STREET MARKETS
Spend a morning investigating the delights of the city's famous fresh produce markets (p57) – making sure you taste as you go!

### ❦ VINCENZO BELLINI'S CITY
Pay tribute to the great Sicilian-born opera composer – explore Piazza Bellini (p42) and then attend an opera at the Teatro Massimo (p53).

# GETTING AWAY FROM IT ALL

When you're feeling overwhelmed by this chaotic and cacophonous city, there are some great getaways:

- ★ **Orto Botanico di Palermo** Shelter from the traffic, crowds and street noise at this tranquil botanic garden (p53).

- ★ **Solunto** Enjoy magnificent views over the Tyrrhenian Sea from the oft-deserted ruins of this hilltop Roman town (p62).

- ★ **Ustica** Catch a ferry to one of the Mediterranean's top dive spots and explore its magnificent underwater world (p63).

- ★ **Villa Malfitana** Wander through the serene salons and gardens of this belle époque mansion (p55).

# UNUSUAL ATTRACTIONS

The province of Palermo has more than its fair share of weird and wonderful things to see and do:

- ★ **Catacombs dei Cappuccini** Experience the macabre fascination of this resting place for the city's dead (p55).

- ★ **Centro Internazionale di Documentazione sulla Mafia e Movimento Antimafia** This moving and informative anti-Mafia museum in Corleone is worth a trip from town (p62).

- ★ **Panino con la milza** Try Palermo's smelliest snack at one of the city's oldest eateries, Antica Focacceria di San Francesco (p50).

- ★ **Hammam** Help the Arab legacy live on at this North African–style spa (p55).

# TOP EATING EXPERIENCES

**CAPPELLO PASTICCERIA**
Come here for cakes that are both beautiful to look at and delicious to eat (p56).

**CUCINA**
Inexpensive nouvelle Palermitan cuisine that the city's arty types are happy to queue for (p57).

**PICCOLO NAPOLI**
Palermo's best seafood place serves ultra-fresh fish to an army of regulars (p57).

**PIZZO & PIZZO**
Classy *enoteca* (wine bar) known for its sensational wine list, buzzy atmosphere and tasty antipasti platters (p58).

**TRATTORIA IL MAESTRO DEL BRODO**
No-nonsense food straight from the market stalls of the Vucciria to the table (p58).

# RESOURCES

- ★ **Agenda Turismo: Palermo Provincia** A useful free booklet available from tourist information booths.

- ★ **Palermo Tourism** (www.palermotourism.com) Official tourist information for Palermo and its province.

- ★ **Riso** (www.palazzoriso.it) Exhibition program of the city's premier contemporary arts museum.

- ★ **See Palermo** (www.seepalermo.com) Useful information about the city and surrounds.

- ★ **Teatro Massimo** (www.teatromassimo.it) Book opera and ballet tickets pre-trip.

# INTRODUCING PALERMO

pop 659,433

**Sicily's main city is draped in a mantle of unpredictability and adventure: its streets are chaotic, its buildings are magnificently dishevelled and its residents – all of whom have a penchant for rule bending and a healthy suspicion of outsiders – can be an inscrutable lot. To gain an initial understanding of the city's unique culture, start by wandering the streets of the old city. The mix of architectural styles in the building stock points to the wave upon wave of invaders who have claimed the city as their own, as does the look of the locals. Put simply, there's no one style or people in this urban melting pot, and there never has been.**

The city looks old for a reason – it is. Nearly 3000 years old, at that. It started life as a huddle of Phoenician stores on a peaceful bay surrounded by the fertile Conca d'Oro, a prime piece of real estate that long made it a target for Sicily's colonisers. As the Carthaginians and Greeks began to flex their territorial muscles, the little depot grew in strategic and economic importance, eventually becoming known as Panormus (the Greek word for port).

Conquered by the Arabs in AD 831, the port flourished and became a very fine city. So much so that when the Normans invaded in 1072, Roger I (1031–1101) made it the seat of his kingdom, encouraging the resident Arabs, Byzantines, Greeks and Italians to remain. In Sicily, the Normans found their longed-for 'kingdom of the sun' and under their enlightened rule Palermo became the most cultured city of 12th-century Europe.

The end of Roger's line (with the death of William II in 1189) was to signal a very long and terminal decline of the city. A series of extraordinary and often bloody political struggles saw the island pass from German (Hohenstaufens) to French (Angevins) to Spanish (Aragonese) and English rule. None of these powers – who were nearly always uninterested and removed from Palermo – could regain the splendour of the Norman era. The only physical change to the city occurred under the Spaniards, with the imposition of a rational city plan that disguised the original Moorish layout. If you see the city from an altitude, you'll notice the baroque domes rising like islands above a sea of alleyways.

Industrial entrepreneurs such as the Florios and the Whitakers gave the city a brief flash of brilliance in the pre-WWI period by dressing it in the glamorous and decadent Liberty (Italian art nouveau) style, resulting in Palermo's final belle époque. But two world wars and massive material damage sank the city into despair and disrepair. At the end of 1945, the city was flooded by hundreds of impoverished rural labourers and gripped by Mafia violence.

The middle classes moved out into newly built housing estates, escaping the new wave of violence (and the bad plumbing). By the 1980s the city was virtually a European pariah, notching up weekly murders. After the Mafia super-trials of the 1990s, Palermo slowly began to emerge from its troubled past and city authorities embarked upon an ambitious program of revitalisation. Walk through the ancient quarters of La Kalsa, Vucciria and Albergheria today and you will notice restoration projects galore, signalling the fact that this great

## ACCOMMODATION

There are plenty of accommodation choices in and around Palermo; many tend to be at the upper end of the budget scale. Here are some standout options:

★ In the heart of the Kalsa, **Al Giardino Dell'Alloro** (p303) offers slightly racy art and a tranquil garden setting.

★ **BB22** (p303) is a stylish and ultra-friendly option in one of the Vucciria's most atmospheric pockets.

★ A grande dame of Palermo's hotels, **Grand Hotel et des Palmes** (p304) is wearing her age supremely well.

★ **Quintocanto Hotel & Spa** (p304) is a chic, centrally located choice with the added bonuses of a wellness centre and restaurant.

★ In an old train station near Corleone, **Antica Stazione Ferrovia di Ficuzza** (p304) houses a delightful hotel and acclaimed restaurant.

For more information on places to stay in Palermo, see p303.

PALERMO

city is working towards reclaiming its proud past and forging a prosperous future.

## ESSENTIAL INFORMATION

**EMERGENCIES //** Ambulance ( ☎ 118 or ☎ 091 666 55 28) Hospital (Ospedale Civico; Map p44; ☎ 091 666 11 11; Via Carmelo Lazzaro) Police ( ☎ emergency 113); Questura (Map p44; ☎ 091 21 01 11; Piazza Vittoria); foreigners office ( ☎ 091 672 51 11; Via San Lorenzo)

**TOURIST INFORMATION //** Central Tourist Office (Map p54; ☎ 091 605 83 51; www.palermo tourism.com; Piazza Castelnuovo 34; ☺ 8.30am-2pm & 2.30-6.30pm Mon-Fri) Sicily's regional tourist office is thin on personal help, but offers a few brochures on Palermo as well as the *Agenda Turismo,* published annually and containing listings for museums, cultural centres, tour guides and transport companies. City Information Booths ( ☺ usually 9am-1pm & 3-7pm); Piazza Bellini (Map p48); Piazza Castelnuovo (Map p54); Piazza della Vittoria (Map p44); Via Cavour (Map p54) Falcone-Borsellino Airport Information Office ( ☎ 091 59 16 98; in downstairs hall; ☺ 8.30am-7.30pm Mon-Sat)

## ORIENTATION

Palermo is large but easily walkable – if you can brave crossing the street, that is. Via Maqueda is its central street, extending from the train station in the south and then changing name to Via Ruggero Settimo at Piazza Giuseppe Verdi, the gateway to the new city. At Piazza Castelnuovo, it continues into Viale della Liberta, a grand boulevard lined with 19th-century apartment blocks.

Via Maqueda is bisected by Corso Vittorio Emanuele, running east to west from the port of La Cala to the cathedral and Palazzo dei Normanni. The intersection of Via Maqueda and Corso Vittorio Emanuele, known famously as the Quattro Canti (Four Corners), divides historic Palermo into four traditional quarters: La Kalsa (east), Vucciria (north), Il Capo (west) and Albergheria (south). These quarters contain the majority of Palermo's sights.

Parallel to Via Maqueda is another major street, Via Roma. A one-way system

PALERMO

moves traffic north up Via Roma from the train station and south down Via Maqueda.

# WALKING TOUR

**Distance: 2.5km**
**Duration: six hours (including lunch and museum visits)**

Central Palermo is dense but compact, so is best explored on foot. This tour covers the eastern half of the city and the labyrinthine alleys of La Kalsa.

Start at Piazza Giuseppe Verdi, dominated by the neoclassical **Teatro Massimo** (1; p53). Facing south, turn left down Via Bara all'Olivella to arrive at the **Museo Archeologico Regionale** (2; p47), which houses one of southern Italy's finest collections of classical art.

Next, head southeast down Via Monteleone towards Via Roma. Walk along Via Roma and then take the steps alongside the Chiesa di Sant'Antonio, which should bring you into the heart of **Mercato della Vucciria** (3; p57). Consider having lunch somewhere around the market – Casa del Brodo (p57) and the Trattoria Il Maestro del Brodo (p58)

are highly recommended, and one of the city's most famous eateries, the Antica Focacceria di San Francesco (p50), is only a short walk away.

From the market, cross into Via Alessandro Paternostro to arrive at the pretty Piazza San Francesco d'Assisi. Look into the **Oratorio di San Lorenzo** (4; Via dell'Immacolatella; admission free; ⊘ 9am-5pm Mon-Sat), built in 1569 by the Compagnia di San Francesco, then visit the 13th-century **Chiesa di San Francesco d'Assisi** (5; Piazza San Francesco d'Assisi; admission free; ⊘ 7am-noon & 4-6pm) to admire its rose window and decorations by Giacomo Sarpotta and members of the Gagini family. Don't miss the Renaissance elegance of the church's Cappella Mastrantonio, designed by Francesco Laurana and Pietro Bonitate in 1468.

Heading east on Via Merlo will bring you to the 18th-century **Palazzo Mirto** (6; ☎ 091 616 75 41; Via Merlo 2; adult/child €5/2.50; ⊘ 9am-6.30pm Mon-Sat, 9am-1pm Sun), a fine if relatively modest example of a Palermitan palazzo whose most notable feature is a charming *Salottino Cinese* (Chinese Salon) decorated with black lacquer, silken wallpaper and a painted ceiling.

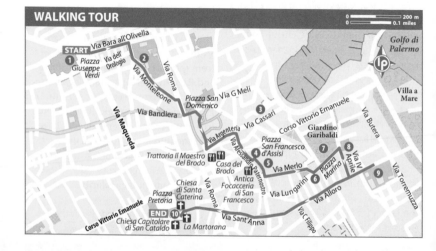

**WALKING TOUR**

Next, make your way to Piazza Marina, flanked by the Giardino Garibaldi (7), a fenced formal garden that is home to the city's oldest tree, a venerable 25m-high *ficus benjamina* (weeping fig) that is over 150 years old. The piazza has witnessed its fair share of bloody executions – unsurprising given that the largest palazzo here, the imposing 14th-century Palazzo Chiaromonte Steri (8; ☎ 091 607 53 06; www.federicosecondosrl.it, in Italian; Piazza Marina 61; adult/concession €5/3; ☉ 9am-1pm & 2.30-6.30pm Tue-Sat, 10am-2pm Sun) was the headquarters of the Inquisition. It's now a campus of the University of Palermo.

Enter Via del IV Aprile in the southeast corner of the square and walk south. This should bring you to Via Alloro, where a left turn leads to the splendid Galleria Regionale della Sicilia (9; p50).

Exiting the gallery, head west along Via Alloro, then cross Via Roma to reach Piazza Bellini (10), home to three of the city's most distinctive buildings: the Chiesa di Santa Caterina (p42), La Martorana (p42) and the Chiesa Capitolare di San Cataldo (p42).

# EXPLORING PALERMO

Though there are a couple of world-class museums, a sprinkling of historic palaces as well as a bevy of notable baroque churches to visit, your most uplifting and engaging experiences will come courtesy of a walk through the city's streets.

Join the *passeggiata* (evening stroll), enjoy a coffee on the terrace of an historic cafe, plunge into the maelstrom of a Palermitan street market and wander past a seemingly never-ending procession of building facades that are as grimy and crumbling as they are magnificent.

Most museums offer a discounted entry price for EU citizens under the age of 18 and over the age of 65.

## AROUND THE QUATTRO CANTI

The busy intersection of Corso Vittorio Emanuele and Via Maqueda marks the Quattro Canti (Four Corners; Map p48), the centre of Palermo. This intersection is surrounded by a perfect circle of curvilinear facades that disappear up to the blue vault of the sky in a clever display of perspective. It is known locally as *Il Teatro del Sole* (Theatre of the Sun) as each facade is lit up in turn throughout the course of the day.

### ♥ PIAZZA PRETORIA // OGLE OSTENTATIOUS BUILDINGS AND SOME NAUGHTY SCULPTURES

This piazza (Map p48) is fringed by imposing churches and buildings, but is visually dominated by the over-the-top Fontana Pretoria (Map p48), one of the city's major landmarks. The fountain's tiered basins ripple out in concentric circles and are crowded with nude nymphs, tritons and river gods that leap about the water. Designed by the Florentine sculptor Francesco Camilliani between 1554 and 1555 for the Tuscan villa of Don Pedro di Toledo, it was bought by Palermo in 1573 in a bid to outshine the newly crafted Fontana di Orione installed in Messina. Proudly positioned in front of the Palazzo Pretorio (Municipal Hall; Map p48), the fountain's flagrant nudity and leering nymphs proved a bit much for Sicilian churchgoers attending the grandly formal Chiesa di San Giuseppe dei Teatini (Map p48) on the opposite side of Via Maqueda, and they prudishly dubbed it the *Fontana della vergogna* (Fountain of Shame).

PALERMO

PALERMO

### ☙ PIAZZA BELLINI // WHERE BYZANTINE UNDERSTATEMENT MEETS BAROQUE EXCESS

The disparate architectural styles and eras of the buildings adorning this magnificent **piazza** (Map p48) should by rights be visually discordant, but in fact contribute to a wonderfully harmonious public space. On the northern side of the piazza is the **Chiesa di Santa Caterina** (Church of Saint Catherine; Map p48; ☎ 338 7228775; admission €2; ✷ 9.30am-1pm & 3-7pm Mon-Sat, 9.30am-1.30pm Sun Apr-Nov, 9.30am-1.30pm daily Dec-Mar), one of Palermo's most ornate baroque churches. Built between 1566 and 1596, its interior was embellished with a surfeit of marble in the 18th century, and many of the smooth white statues, gilded stucco and whirling frescoes were also added in this period. Look out for the carved marble presbytery, the main altar's silver angels and the statue of St Catherine in the right transept, which was carved by Antonello Gagini in 1534.

Opposite Santa Caterina, on the southern side of the piazza, is **La Martorana** (Chiesa di Santa Maria dell'Ammiraglio; Map p48; Piazza Bellini 3; donation requested; ✷ 8.30am-1pm & 3.30-5.30pm Mon-Sat Nov-Feb, 8.30am-1pm & 3.30-7pm Mon-Sat Mar-Oct, 8.30am-1pm Sun all year, mass daily at 10am), the city's most famous – and luminously beautiful – medieval church. This 12th-century structure was endowed by King Roger's Syrian emir, George of Antioch, and was originally planned as a mosque. Delicate Fatimid pillars support a domed cupola depicting Christ enthroned amid his archangels, while Arabic script endlessly repeats the name of Allah. The interior is best appreciated in the morning, when sunlight illuminates magnificent Byzantine mosaics.

In 1433 the church was given over to a Benedictine order of nuns founded by Eloisa Martorana (hence its nickname), who tore down the Norman apse, reworked the exterior in a fussy baroque fashion and added their own frescoed chapel – sadly destroying some of the wonderful mosaic work in the process. Two of the original mosaics to survive are the portrait of George of Antioch, crouched behind a shield at the feet of the Virgin Mary, and one of Roger II receiving his crown from Christ (the only portrait of him to survive in Sicily).

Mussolini returned the church to the Greek Orthodox community in 1935, and the Greek Mass is still celebrated here.

Next to La Martorana, the small pink-domed **Chiesa Capitolare di San Cataldo** (Church of Saint Cataldo; Map p48; Piazza Bellini 3; admission €1.50; ✷ 9am-3.30pm Mon-Fri, 9am-12.30pm Sat, 9am-1pm Sun) is almost bare inside. The building was founded in the 1150s by Maio of Bari (William I's emir of emirs, or chancellor) but Maio's murder in 1160 meant it was never finished – hence the lack of adornment within. It's not really worth paying the admission price as the main interest lies in the exterior, which illustrates perfectly the synthesis of Arab Norman architectural styles.

The eastern side of the piazza is adorned by the delightful **Teatro Bellini** (Bellini Theatre; Map p48), built in the late 19th century and named after the great Sicilian-born opera composer, Vincenzo Bellini. Sharing the theatre building is **Café/Pizzeria Bellini** ( ☎ 091 616 56 91; www.pizzeriabellini.it; Piazza Bellini 6; pizzas €4.50-10; ✷ closed Mon), whose outdoor tables command a wonderful view of the piazza. The pizzas aren't half bad, either.

### ❧ CHIESA DEL GESÙ // A BLAST OF BAROQUE COURTESY OF THE JESUITS

Also known as Casa Professa, Palermo's recently restored Jesuit church (Map p44; Via del Ponticello; admission free; ✆ 7-11.30am & 5-6.30pm Mon-Sat, 7am-12.30pm Sun, closed all afternoons Aug) was built in the 16th century and its interior was decorated over the next 200 years with no cost (or inclination towards ostentation) spared. It's a veritable blizzard of baroque, with inlaid marble and sculptures galore. Don't miss the nave chapels and the Pietro Novelli paintings in the second chapel off the right aisle.

## ALBERGHERIA

Once inhabited by Norman court officials, Albergheria has been a poor and ramshackle quarter since the end of WWII – indeed, you can still see wartime bomb damage scarring some buildings. The area is now home to a growing immigrant population that has revitalised the streets with its aspirations. It is also the location of Palermo's busiest street market, the Mercato di Ballarò (p57).

### ❧ PALAZZO DEI NORMANNI // MARVEL AT MOSAICS IN A MAGNIFICENT MEDIEVAL COURT

West along Corso Vittorio Emanuele, past the waving palms in Piazza della Vittoria and through the monumental Porta Nuova, built to celebrate the arrival of Carlos V in Palermo in 1535 after a victory over the Tunisians, rises the fortress-like Palace of the Normans (Palazzo Reale; Map p44; ✆ 091 626 28 33; Piazza Indipendenza 1; admission incl Cappella Palatina adult/concession €8.50/6.50; ✆ 8.30am-noon & 2-5pm Mon, Fri & Sat, 8.30am-12.15pm Sun). Once the centre of a magnificent medieval court, the palace is now the seat of the Sicilian parliament. Four days per week parliamentarians vacate the building, allowing visitors access to the Sicilian parliamentary assembly and to the sumptuous Sala di Ruggero II, the king's former bedroom, which is decorated with stunning mosaics of Persian peacocks and exotic leopards.

### Cappella Palatina

Downstairs, just off the palace's three-tiered loggia, is Palermo's premier tourist attraction, the Palatine Chapel (Map p44; ✆ 8.15am-5pm Mon-Sat, 8.15-9.45am & 11.15am-12.15pm Sun), designed by Roger II in 1130. This is one of Sicily's major tourist sites, so be prepared to queue to enter and once inside don't let the attendants hurry you through. Note that you will be refused entry if you are wearing shorts, a short skirt or a low-cut top – uncovered navels are also forbidden.

Recently unveiled after a painstaking five-year restoration, the chapel's well-lit interior is simply extraordinary. Every inch is inlaid with precious marbles and exquisite mosaics, giving the space a lustrous, jewel-like quality. The mosaics were mainly the work of Byzantine Greek artisans brought to Palermo by Roger II in 1140 especially for this project, and are incredibly sophisticated. They capture expressions, detail and movement with extraordinary grace and delicacy, and sometimes with enormous power – as evidenced by the depiction of Christ the Pantocrator and Angels on the dome. The bulk of the mosaics recount the tales of the Old Testament, but other scenes recall Palermo's pivotal role in the Crusades. Some of the mosaics are later and less-assured additions (eg the Virgin and Saints in the main apse under Christ the Pantocrator) but fortunately this doesn't impact adversely on the overall achievement.

PALERMO

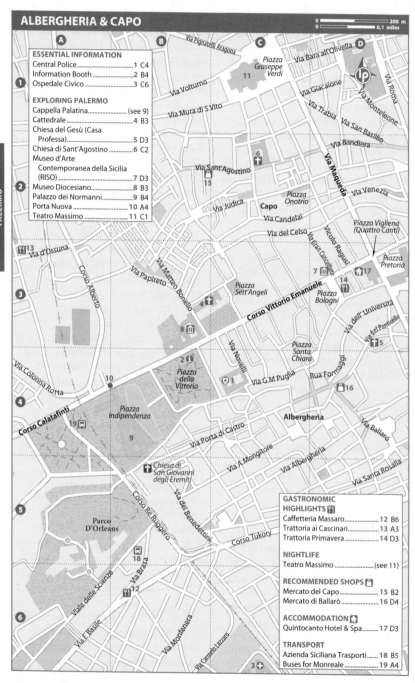

## ALBERGHERIA & CAPO

0 ————————— 200 m
0 ————————— 0.1 miles

It's not only the mosaics you should be gazing at – don't miss the painted wooden ceiling featuring *muqarnas* (a decorative device resembling stalactites), a masterpiece of honeycomb carving that is unique in a Christian church (and, many speculate, a sign of Roger II's secret identity as a Muslim). The walls are decorated with handsome marble inlay that displays a clear Islamic aesthetic, and the carved marble in the floor is breathtaking: marble was as precious as gems during the 12th century, so the value this floor had at the time is almost immeasurable by today's standards.

Note that if you visit the chapel on a day when the rest of the palazzo is closed, the entry price is reduced to €7/5 per adult/concession.

## CAPO

Bordering the Albergheria quarter, Il Capo is another web of interconnected streets and blind alleys. As impoverished as its neighbour, it too has a popular street market, the Mercato del Capo (p57), which runs the length of Via Sant'Agostino and terminates at Porta Carini. The centrepiece of the quarter is the imposing monastery of **Chiesa di Sant'Agostino** (Church of Saint Augustine; Map p44; Via Sant'Agostino; admission free; 8am-noon & 4-6pm Mon-Sat, 8am-noon Sun), which ran the region in medieval times.

### ❦ CATTEDRALE // A REPOSITORY OF NORMAN KINGS AND PRECIOUS ARTWORKS

The Normans converted plenty of mosques and palaces when they assumed power in Sicily, giving rise to the Arab Norman style that is unique to the island. Chief among these is Palermo's **Cathedral** (Map p44; ☎ 091 33 43 73; www.cattedrale.palermo.it, in Italian; Corso Vittorio Emanuele; admission free; 9.30am-1.30pm & 2.30-5.30pm Mon-Sat Nov-Feb, 9.30am-5.30pm Mon-Sat Mar-Oct, 8am-1.30pm & 4.30-6pm Sun & public holidays all year), an extraordinary amalgam of ziggurat crenellations, majolica cupolas, geometric patterns and blind arches. While impressive, the building has aesthetically suffered somewhat from the many reworkings during its history (pick from Arab Norman, Catalan Gothic, Gothic and neoclassical).

Construction began in 1184 at the behest of Palermo's archbishop, Walter of the Mill (Gualtiero Offamiglio), an Englishman who was tutor to William II. Walter held great power and had unlimited funds at his disposal, but with the construction of the magnificent cathedral at Monreale he felt his power diminishing. His solution was to order construction of an equally magnificent cathedral in Palermo. This was erected on the location of a 9th-century mosque (itself built on a former chapel), and a detail from the mosque's original decor is visible at the southern porch, where a column is inscribed with a passage from the Koran. The cathedral's proportions and the grandeur of its exterior became a statement of the power struggle between Church and throne occurring at the time, a potentially dangerous situation that was tempered by Walter's death (in 1191), which prevented him from seeing (and boasting about) the finished building.

Since then the cathedral has been much altered, sometimes with great success (as in Antonio Gambara's 15th-century three-arched portico that took 200 years to complete and became a masterpiece of Catalan Gothic architecture), and sometimes with less fortunate results (as in Ferdinando Fuga's clumsy dome, added between 1781 and 1801).

PALERMO

Thankfully Fuga's handiwork did not extend to the eastern exterior, which is still adorned with the exotic interlacing designs of Walter's original cathedral. The southwestern facade was laid in the 13th and 14th centuries, and is a beautiful example of local craftsmanship in the Gothic style. The cathedral's entrance is through the three magnificent Catalan Gothic arches built by Gambara in 1426, which is fronted by gardens and a statue of Santa Rosalia, one of Palermo's patron saints. A beautiful painted intarsia decoration above the arches depicts the tree of life in a complex Islamic-style geometric composition of 12 roundels that show fruit, humans and all kinds of animals. It's thought to date back to 1296.

Although impressive in scale, the interior is a sadly unflamboyant resting place for the royal Norman **tombs** (admission €1; 9.30am-1.30pm Mon-Sat), which contain the remains of two of Sicily's greatest rulers, Roger II (rear left) and Frederick II of Hohenstaufen (front left) as well as Henry VI and William II. Halfway down the right aisle is a **treasury** (admission €2; 9.30am-1.30pm Mon-Sat), whose most extraordinary exhibit is the fabulous 13th-century crown of Constance of Aragon (wife of Frederick II), made by local craftsmen in fine gold filigree and encrusted with gems.

### Museo Diocesiano

Next to the cathedral is the **Diocesan Museum** (Map p44; ☎ 091 607 71 11; www.diocesipa.it, in Italian; Via Matteo Bonello 2; adult/child under 6yr/over 65yr & child 6-17yr €4.50/free/3; 9.30am-1.30pm Tue-Fri, Sun & holidays, 10am-6pm Sat), which houses an important collection of artworks from the cathedral and from city churches destroyed during WWII. The 15th-century frescoes are a highlight, as are the Byzantine paintings

and icons, among which is the beautiful 1171 *Madonna della perla,* salvaged from the ruins of the church of San Nicoló Reale. Seek out the room dedicated to the 17th-century Sicilian painter Pietro Novelli (1603–47), who was one of the region's finest and served as a court painter to Spain's ruler, Philip IV. Much influenced by Anthony Van Dyck and Raphael, Novelli often portrayed himself in his chiaroscuro works.

Note that the ticket price also includes entry to the cathedral's tombs and treasury.

### ♥ MUSEO D'ARTE CONTEMPORANEA DELLA SICILIA (RISO) // **CONTEMPLATE THE CUTTING EDGE IN HISTORIC SURROUNDS**

The newest addition to Palermo's portfolio of art galleries is the **Museum of Contemporary Art** (Map p44; ☎ 091 32 05 32; www.palazzoriso.it; Palazzo Riso, Corso Vittorio Emanuele 365; adult/over 60yr & child under 18yr/concession €5/free/3; 10am-7.30pm Sat, Sun & Tue-Wed, 10am-9.30pm Thu & Fri), housed in a restored 18th-century neoclassical palazzo on the Corso. Its curators work with other city and regional institutions to provide alternative interpretations of Sicily's artistic heritage and to stage challenging international survey shows. The complex's stylish ground-floor cafe and bookshop are popular meeting places for avant-garde types.

## VUCCIRIA

The shabby Vucciria neighbourhood is known throughout Sicily for its Mercato della Vucciria (p57), the inspiration for Sicilian painter Renato Guttuso's most important work, *La Vucciria* (1974), described by writer Leonardo Sciascia as 'a hungry man's dream'.

Once the heart of poverty-stricken Palermo and a den of crime and filth, the Vucciria illustrated the almost medieval chasm that existed between rich and poor in Sicily up until the 1950s. Though it's still quite shabby, the quarter is one of Palermo's most fascinating areas to explore, with most of its interesting buildings in the vicinity of the imposing 17th-century Chiesa di San Domenico (Church of Saint Domenic; Map p48; ☎ 091 58 91 72; Piazza San Domenico; admission free; ⏰ 9.30am-noon Tue-Sat).

### 💖 MUSEO ARCHEOLOGICO REGIONALE // UNCOVER A RICH ARCHAEOLOGICAL CACHE

One of the most important museums of its kind in Europe, Sicily's Regional Archaeological Museum (Map p48; ☎ 091 611 68 05; Piazza Olivella 24) was closed for a major renovation when this book was being researched. When it reopens, it will display treasures including a Phoenician sarcophagi from the 5th century BC, 10,000 Etruscan artefacts, Greek carvings from Selinunte and Himera, the Hellenistic *Ariete di bronzo di siracus* (Bronze Ram of Syracuse), Etruscan mirrors, the largest collection of ancient anchors in the world, and finds from archaeological sites throughout the island.

### 💖 I TESORI DELLA LOGGIA // VISIT FIVE ARCHITECTURAL & ARTISTIC GEMS

The Treasures of the Loggia (Map p48; ☎ 091 843 16 05; www.tesoridellaloggia.it; adult/child under 7yr/child 7-17yr/concession €5/free/1/4; ⏰ 9am-1pm Mon-Sat) shouldn't be missed. The name is taken from the area behind the Chiesa di San Domenico, which is called La Loggia because it once had at its centre a loggia occupied by merchants and bankers from Genoa. One ticket (available from the Oratorio del Rosario in Santa Cita in Via Valverde) allows entrance to all five churches and chapels.

### Oratorio del Rosario in San Domenico

This small chapel (Map p48; Largo Cavalieri di Malta) was commissioned by the Society of the Rosary of San Domenico and is dominated by Anthony Van Dyck's fantastic blue-and-red altarpiece, *The Virgin of the Rosary with St Dominic and the Patronesses of Palermo*. Van Dyck left Palermo in fear of the plague, and painted the work in Genoa in 1628. Giacomo Serpotta's stuccowork (1710–17) is some of the most amazing you'll see; his elaborate work, vivacious and whirling with figures, brought rococo to Sicilian churches. Serpotta's name meant 'lizard' or 'small snake', and he often included one of the reptiles in his work as a sort of signature – see if you can find one here!

### Chiesa di Santa Cita

The 14th-century Church of Saint Cita (Map p48; Via Valverde) is named after the tired patron saint of domestic servants. The Dominican priests who acquired the church in the 16th century came up with the clever idea of allowing rich families to bury their dead here, thus both collecting income for the priests' monastery and endowing the church with particularly lavish funerary chapels. There are also some sculptures by Antonio Gagini.

### Oratorio del Rosario in Santa Cita

Serpotta's breathtaking stuccos are also on show in Santa Cita's 17th-century chapel (Map p48; Via Valverde), which adjoins the church. Indeed, this is where his work is at its best. The elaborate *Battle of Lepanto* on the entrance wall, depicting the Christian victory over the Turks, is framed by stucco drapes held by hundreds of naughty cherubs who were modelled on Palermo's street urchins.

PALERMO

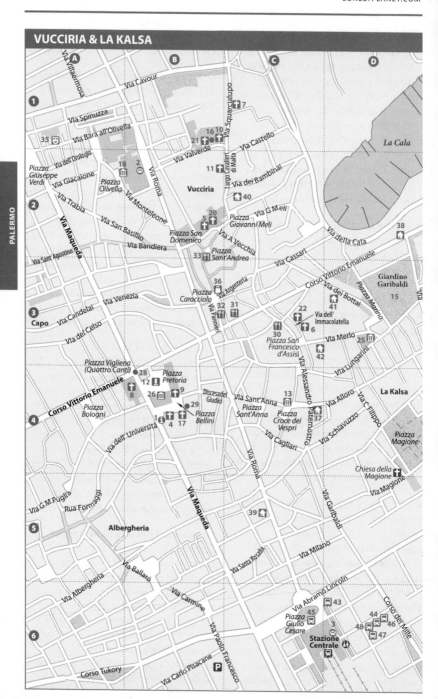

# VUCCIRIA & LA KALSA

La Cala

Vucciria

Giardino Garibaldi

Capo

Piazza Vigliena (Quattro Canti)

Corso Vittorio Emanuele

La Kalsa

Piazza Magione

Chiesa della Magione

Alberghiera

Stazione Centrale

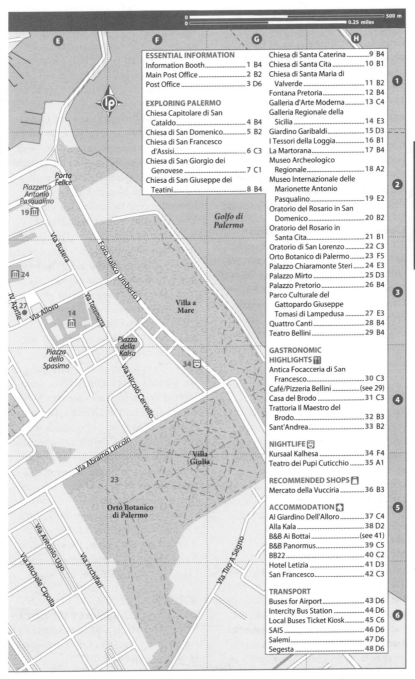

PALERMO

## Chiesa di San Giorgio dei Genovese

The extremely elegant Renaissance-style facade of the Church of Saint George of the Genoese (Map p48; Via Squarcialupo) is one of La Loggia's major adornments. The church was built between 1575 and 1591 to a design by Piedmontese architect Giorgio di Faccio and its interior is as pleasing as its exterior, featuring Corinthian tetrastyle columns and a gravestone-laden marble floor. During the WWII Allied bombing of Palermo, the entire area around the church was flattened but it was miraculously spared.

## Chiesa di Santa Maria di Valverde

The 14th-century Carmelite Church of Saint Mary in Valverde (Map p48; Largo Cavalieri di Malta) underwent a lavish transformation in 1633 courtesy of wealthy Genovese Camillo Pallavicino, whose only daughter had entered the convent of Valverde. It is graced by *The Madonna of Mount Carmel with Saints,* painted by Pietro Novelli in 1640.

## LA KALSA

Plagued by poverty, La Kalsa has long been one of the city's most notorious neighbourhoods. However, a recent program of urban regeneration has resulted in many of its long-derelict palazzos being restored and these are rapidly being turned into museums, boutique hotels and upmarket residential accommodation.

### ❧ GALLERIA REGIONALE DELLA SICILIA // VIEW MAGNIFICENT IMAGES OF LIFE AND DEATH

The accolade of Palermo's best art gallery has long been bestowed on the Sicilian Regional Gallery (Map p48; ☎ 091 623 00 11; www.regione.sicilia.it/beniculturali/palazzoabatellis; Palazzo Abatellis, Via Alloro 4; adult/child & over 65yr/ concession €8/free/4; ☺ 9am-12.30pm Tue-Sat), and

it is well deserved. Housed in a gorgeous Catalan Gothic palazzo sensitively transformed into an exhibition space in 1957 by Carlo Scarpa, one of Italy's leading architects, it is full of treasures and paintings dating from the Middle Ages to the 18th century.

The gallery gives a great insight into Sicilian painting – an art form sadly lacking in merit over more recent decades – and numbers among its treasures the *Trionfo della morte* (Triumph of Death), a magnificent fresco. Mounted on his wasted horse, demonic Death wields a wicked-looking scythe, leaping over his hapless victims (notably the vain and pampered aristocrats of Palermo) while the poor and hungry look on from the side. The huge image, carefully restored, has sensibly been given its own space on the ground level to maximise its visual impact.

Other treasures include Antonello da Messina's much-loved panel of the *Annunziata* (The Virgin Annunciate; 1474–77) in Room 10. It is interesting to see Messina's work alongside the sculptures of Francesco Laurana, most notably his exquisite bust of *Eleonara d'aragona* (Eleanor of Aragon; 1475), which is exhibited in Room 4. Both artists specialise in an economy of detail that lends their paintings and sculptures a perfect stillness that sets them apart from those of their contemporaries.

Also look out for Antonello Gagini's statue of the *Madonna del riposo* (Madonna of the Good Rest; 1528) in Room 5 and Mario di Laurito's *La visitazione* (The Visitation; 1526–36) in Room 7.

### ❧ ANTICA FOCACCERIA DI SAN FRANCESCO // SAMPLE PALERMITAN STREET FOOD IN A FAMOUS EATERY

Map p48; ☎ 091 32 02 64; Via Alessandro Paternostro 58; ☺ closed Tue Oct-May

This historic focacceria opposite the Chiesa di San Francesco d'Assisi first opened its doors in 1834 and is known for its *panino con la milza* (veal spleen boiled in lard and eaten in a brioche-type roll with an optional squeeze of lemon or smear of ricotta). If you can't stomach the idea of spleen, fear not – you can choose to sample another Palermitan snack, *panelle* (chickpea fritters), instead.

### ❤ GALLERIA D'ARTE MODERNA // APPRECIATE 19TH- AND 20TH-CENTURY SICILIAN ART

A strong runner-up in the best gallery stakes, Palermo's **Gallery of Modern Art** (Map p48; ☎ 091 843 16 05; www.galleriadarte modernapalermo.it; Via Sant'Anna 21; adult/child under 18yr/student & over 60yr €7/free/5; ⊙ 9.30am-5.30pm Tue-Sun) is set in a sleekly renovated palazzo and is home to a collection that ranges from 19th-century monumental historical genre paintings to Futuristic romps from the early 20th century. Divided over three floors, the collection is dedicated largely to Sicily and Palermo in its subject matter, and has a number of highlights, including Erulo Eroli's *I vespri siciliani* (Sicilian Vespers; 1890–91) on the ground floor, which depicts a famous incident from Sicily's history when the locals revolted in 1282 against the Angevin forces occupying the island.

Major works displayed on the 1st floor include Paolo Vetri's Impressionist-style *Fanciulla che esce dal bagno* (Girl Getting Out of Bath; 1870–73) and the paintings of Michele Catti (1855–1914), whose large canvases portray moody scenes of fin-de-siècle life in Palermo's streets; his *Ultime foglie* (Last Leaves; 1906) is a beautiful image of a wet Viale della Libertà on a late autumn day. The 2nd floor hosts a survey of the first few decades of Italian 20th-century art and includes some striking works, including Felice Casorati's *Gli scolari* (The Pupils; 1927–28) and Lia Pasqualino Noto's *L'infermiera* (The Nurse; 1931).

The gallery is wheelchair accessible and has computer terminals offering online jigsaw puzzles of works from the collection that children will love. Hire of a useful audioguide to the collection costs €4.

### ❤ MUSEO INTERNAZIONALE DELLE MARIONETTE ANTONIO PASQUALINO // LEARN ALL ABOUT PALERMO'S TRADITIONAL PUPPET THEATRE

Established by the Association for the Conservation of Folk Traditions of Palermo, the **Antonio Pasqualino International Marionette Museum of Palermo** (Map p48; ☎ 091 32 80 60; www.museomari onettepalermo.it, in Italian; Piazzetta Antonio Pasqualino 5, off Via Butera; adult/concession & child €5/3; ⊙ 9am-1pm & 3.30-6.30pm Mon-Fri, 9am-1pm Sat) is home to a collection of over 4000 marionettes, puppets, glove puppets and shadow figures from Palermo, Catania and Naples, as well as from far-flung places such as China, India, southern Asia, Turkey and Africa. They take puppeteering seriously here, researching the art form, providing informative labelling alongside museum exhibits and hosting the annual **Festa di Morgana** (www.festivaldimorgana.com), when puppeteers from all over the world converge on the museum for lectures and performances.

The museum hosts **puppet shows** (adult/child €6/4) on occasional Sundays at 5.30pm in autumn and winter. These are staged on the top floor of the museum in a beautifully decorated traditional theatre complete with a hand-cranked music machine.

## PALERMO'S OPERA DEI PUPI

Sicily's most popular form of traditional entertainment is the *opera dei pupi* (rod-marionette theatre), and the best place to attend a performance is in Palermo.

Marionettes were first introduced to the island by the Spanish in the 18th century and the art form was swiftly embraced by locals, who were enthralled with the re-enacted tales of Charlemagne and his heroic knights Orlando and Rinaldo. Effectively the soap operas of their day, these puppet shows expounded the deepest sentiments of life – unrequited love, treachery, thirst for justice and the anger and frustration of the oppressed. Back then, a puppet could speak volumes where a man could not.

There are traditionally two types of *opera dei pupi* in Sicily: Palermitan (practised in Palermo, Agrigento and Trapani) and Catanese (in Catania, Messina and Syracuse). Carved from beech, olive- or lemon-tree wood, the marionettes stand some 1.5m high, have wire joints and wear richly coloured costumes. The knights are clad in metal suits of armour that make the figures shine and resonate when they engage in swordfights with bloodthirsty Saracen warriors or mythical monsters.

Good puppeteers are judged on the dramatic effect they can create – lots of stamping feet, thundering and a gripping running commentary – and on their speed and skill in directing the battle scenes. Nowadays the *opera dei pupi* has been relegated to folklore status, maintained by a few companies largely for the benefit of tourists and children. The best places to attend a performance are at the **Museo Internazionale delle Marionette Antonio Pasqualino** (p51) or at the **Teatro dei Pupi Cuticchio** (Map p48; ☎ 091 32 34 00; www.figlidartecuticchio.com; Via Bara all'Olivella 95; adult/child €8/5), a company run by the Associazione Figli d'Arte Cuticchio (check website for performance times). You can also purchase marionettes at the association's shop opposite the theatre.

❦ **PASSEGGIATE TOMASIANE ITINERARI STORICO LETTERARI //**
**TRACK A LITERARY LEOPARD AROUND TOWN**

Run by the Parco Culturale del Gattopardo Giuseppe Tomasi di Lampedusa (Map p48; ☎ 091 616 07 96; www.parcotomasi.it; Vicolo della Neve, off Via Alloro), these two-hour literary walks (per small group €40; ⏲ 2.30pm Sun) are led by English-speaking Lampedusa expert Michele Anselmi, who talks about the life and masterwork of Sicily's most famous novelist before embarking on a tour of the Kalsa district and discussing the history of Palermo's ties with Lampedusa's great novel *Il Gattopardo* (The Leopard). The organisation also runs a cafe (⏲ 11am-9pm Wed-Fri & Sun-Mon,

6pm-1am Sat) that hosts music or literary events once a week (usually on Saturday evenings).

❦ **KURSAAL KALHESA //** ENJOY **A COCKTAIL IN PALERMO'S MOST ATMOSPHERIC BAR**

The bar of choice for the city's avant-garde, Kursaal Kalhesa (Map p48; ☎ 091 616 22 82; www.kursaalkalhesa.it, in Italian; 21 Foro Italico Umberto I; cocktails €6; ⏲ noon-3pm & 6pm-1.30am Tue-Fri, noon-1.30am Sat & Sun) occupies the remnants of a handsome early-19th-century palace, built into the city walls next to the monumental 16th-century Porta dei Greci e dei Bastioni (Door of the Greeks and Bastions). Come in the evening to recline on silk-covered divans beneath soaring vaulted ceilings and enjoy your choice from an extensive drinks list and tempting bar menu while listening to live music or mood-driven choices spun by the in-house DJ.

## 🏛 ORTO BOTANICO DI PALERMO //
### ESCAPE THE CITY'S CHAOS AT THIS TRANQUIL HAVEN

First opened in 1795, the city's **Botanical Garden** (Map p48; ☎ 091 623 82 41; www.ortobotanico.palermo.it; Via Abramo Lincoln 2b; adult/child under 10yr/concession & child 10-16yr €5/1/3; 🕙 9am-8pm May-Aug, 9am-7pm Apr & Sep, 9am-6pm Mar & Oct, 9am-5pm Nov-Feb, till 2pm Sun Nov-Feb) is a tropical paradise featuring massive fig trees, tall palms, dazzling hibiscus bushes and handsome neoclassical buildings and sculptures. There is an avenue of bizarre-looking bottle, soap and cinnamon trees, as well as coffee trees, papaya plants and sycamores. Beware the mosquitoes at dusk, though.

## THE 19TH-CENTURY CITY

North of Piazza Giuseppe Verdi, Palermo's streets widen, the buildings lengthen, and the shops, restaurants and cafes become more elegant (and more expensive). Glorious neoclassical and Liberty examples from the last golden age in Sicilian architecture give the city an exuberant and grandiose feel that contrasts with the narrow, introspective feel of the historic quarter.

## 🏛 TEATRO MASSIMO //
### MAKE AN OPERATIC ENTRANCE AT THIS FAMOUS THEATRE

Built between 1875 and 1897 to celebrate the unification of Italy, the **Teatro Massimo** (Map p48; ☎ 06 48 07 84 00, toll free 800 907080; www.teatromassimo.it; Piazza Giuseppe Verdi 9; tickets €25-125; 🕙 ticket office 10am-3pm Tue-Sun) has become a symbol of the triumph and tragedy of Palermo itself. It's the third-largest 19th-century opera house in Europe (only the Paris and Vienna Opera Houses are larger) and its long history is symptomatic of the conflicting powers that struggle for supremacy in Palermo society – civic pride and cultural creativity pitted against sinister bureaucracy and Mafia control (which is said to have been responsible for the extraordinary 24 years it took to restore the theatre). Appropriately, the closing scene of Francis Ford Coppola's *The Godfather III* – with its visually stunning juxtaposition of high culture and low crime, drama and death – was filmed here.

The building was designed by Giovanni Basile, Palermo's most popular architect in the years preceding WWI. In addition to the theatre, he also designed the two kiosks in front of it, which now sell newspapers, tobacco and magazines.

Operas, ballets and concerts are staged here between September and June. In July and August, the theatre closes and artistic action moves to the outdoor **Teatro di Verdura** (off Map p34; ☎ 091 688 41 37; Viale del Fante) in the grounds of the 18th-century Villa Castelnuovo, located next to the Parco della Favorita, 3km north of the centre.

Those who aren't able to attend a performance at the opera house but who wish to view the building's interior can instead take a guided 25-minute **tour** ( ☎ bookings 091 609 08 31; adult/child under 6yr/concession €5/free/3). These run between 10am and 2.30pm from Tuesday to Sunday.

The Teatro Massimo isn't the city's only great theatre. The nearby **Teatro Politeama Garibaldi** (Map p54; ☎ 091 58 80 01; Piazza Ruggero Settimo) was designed in classical form by Giuseppe Damiani Almeyda between 1867 and 1874 and so dominates Piazza Ruggero Settimo that many Palermitans refer to the square as

PALERMO

# NEW CITY

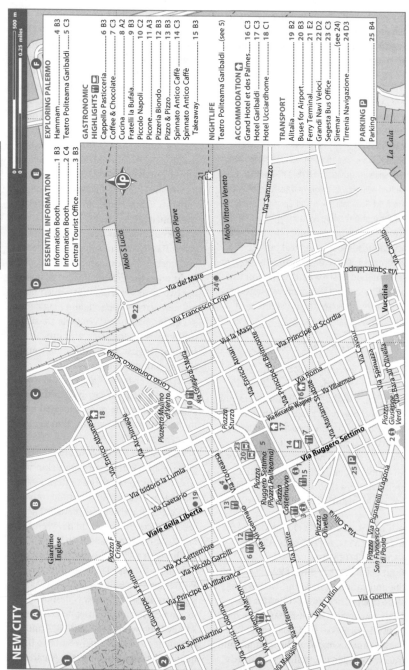

Piazza Politeama. The theatre hosts performances of symphonic and chamber concerts, jazz and occasional contemporary music.

### ☙ HAMMAM // SURRENDER TO THE STEAM IN A TURKISH BATH

The Islamic heritage of the city is brought to the fore at one of its most sybaritic attractions, **Hammam** (Map p54; ☎ 091 32 07 83; www.hammam.pa.it; Via Torrearsa 17d; admission €40; ☿ men 2-9pm Tue & Thu, 10am-8pm Sat, women 2-9pm Mon & Wed, 11am-9pm Fri). This modern affair features a lavish marble-faced bath hall, brick-domed steam room and spacious changing rooms. All the kit you need is supplied: black olive soap, *ghassoul* (a mixture of clay mud, rose petals and lavender) and henna for softening the skin. You'll need to fork out €10 to buy your own glove and slippers, which for hygiene reasons can't be borrowed.

After your scrub you can indulge in any number of massages and therapies, which range in price from €40 to €60, or you can simply relax with a mint tea and Arabian sweets in the cooling-off room or cafe.

Note that between December and March the hammam's opening hours vary slightly – it's open for women on Sundays between 2pm and 8pm and is closed on Mondays.

## OUTSIDE THE CITY CENTRE

### ☙ CATACOMBES DEI CAPPUCCINI // EXPERIENCE THE CITY'S MOST MACABRE TOURIST ATTRACTION

The compellingly creepy **Capuchin Catacombs** (Map p34; ☎ 091 652 41 56; Piazza Cappuccini 1; admission €3; ☿ 9am-noon & 3-5pm, closed Sun afternoon in winter) hold the mummified bodies of some 8000 Palermitans who died in the 19th and 20th centuries.

Originally the preserve of monks, the catacombs were eventually opened to a select and moneyed few who made substantial donations of land or money to the monastery. For their pains, these lucky individuals were laid out 'to drain' – ugh – after death, before being washed with vinegar, and powdered with arsenic and milk of lime. They were then dressed in their Sunday best and propped up in their very own niche like truly scary artworks.

Earthly power, sex, religion and professional status are rigidly distinguished here. Men and women occupy separate corridors, and within the women's area there is a first-class section for virgins. The most disconcerting sight is the near-perfectly preserved body of Rosalia Lombardo (just follow the signs for *bambina* or 'baby girl'), who died at the tender age of two in 1920.

Note that no photos are allowed. To get here, it's a 30-minute walk west up Corso Vittorio Emanuele, into Via Cappuccini after Piazza Indipendenza and then north into Via Ippolito Pindemonte to reach Piazza Cappuccini.

### ☙ VILLA MALFITANO // SEE WHERE BELLE ÉPOQUE PALERMITANS FROLICKED AND FLIRTED

A showcase of Liberty architecture, this delightful **villa** (Map p34; Via Dante 167; adult/student & child €5/3; ☿ 9am-1.30pm Mon-Sat) was built in 1886 by Joseph Whitaker, a member of the entrepreneurial English business dynasty that made a fortune in the Marsala trade in Sicily in the 19th century. Joseph and his wife Tina were leading figures in Palermo's high society and entertained their belle époque buddies here in lavish style, even hosting King Edward VII in 1907 and George V in 1925. Set in a 9-hectare (22 acre)

PALERMO

## TOP **FIVE**

### CAFES

Palermo is justly famous for its cafe society. To indulge in an excellent espresso accompanied by a creamy *cannolo* or decadently sweet *cassata*, head to the following:

★ **Pasticceria Alba** (off Map p34; ☎ 091 30 90 16; Piazza Don Bosco 7; ⏱ 7am-11pm Tue-Sun)
Aficionados insist that the city's best coffee is served here, and they're equally evangelical about Alba's extremely more-ish *arancine* (rice balls).

★ **Caffetteria Massaro** (Map p44; ☎ 091 42 05 86; Via Brasa 6-8; ⏱ 7am-4pm Mon-Fri, 7am-noon Sat) Pop into this Palermitan institution before or after visiting the nearby Palazzo dei Normanni. The cake display includes temptations galore and there's also a huge array of *panini* and other snacks to choose from.

★ **Cappello Pasticceria** (Map p54; ☎ 091 611 37 69; Via Niccoló Garzilli 10; ⏱ 7am-9.30pm Thu-Tue) The chocolates and cakes here are true works of art, as beautiful to look at as they are delicious to eat. Join the city's fashionistas in indulging in an afternoon treat or two in the boudoir-style salon at the back of the shop.

★ **Coffee & Chocolate** (Map p54; ☎ 091 32 92 20; Via Principe di Belmonte 108; ⏱ 7am-9pm Mon-Fri, 7am-midnight Sat, closed Aug) Like Fred and Ginger, coffee and chocolate belong together. Sample them here and you'll be dancing out of the door.

★ **Spinnato Antico Caffé** (Map p54; ☎ 091 32 92 20; Via Principe di Belmonte 107-15; ⏱ 7am-1am) The city's most famous and sophisticated cafe. Its **takeaway outlet** (Map p54; Piazza Castelbuono) sells treats to go or you can scoff while standing at the bar.

formal garden planted with rare and exotic species, the villa is most notable for its whimsical interior decoration, which features delights such as a 'Summer Room' with walls painted to resemble a conservatory, and a music room draped with 15th-century tapestries illustrating the *Aeneid*. To get here, it's a 20-minute walk west up Via Dante from Piazza Castelnuovo.

## FESTIVALS & EVENTS

**Festino di Santa Rosalia** Palermo's biggest annual festival celebrates Santa Rosalia, the patron saint of the city. The saint's relics are paraded through the city amid four days of fireworks and partying; 10 to 15 July.

**Provincia in Festa** Two months of art, music and sport events; August and September.

## GASTRONOMIC HIGHLIGHTS

Palermitans generally dine late and although kitchens open around 7.30pm, you'll eat alone if you get to a restaurant before 9.30pm, particularly in summer.

Local specialities in Palermo include *bucatini con le sarde* (pasta mixed with sardines), *babbaluci* (a street snack consisting of baby snails marinated in virgin olive oil, chopped fresh parsley and garlic), *calzoni* (a street snack of deep-fried pockets of dough that are filled with meat or cheese) and *frutta martorana* (colourfully decorated marzipan modelled into fanciful shapes and named after the convent of La Martorana).

## CASA DEL BRODO €

Map p48; ☎ 091 32 16 55; Corso Vittorio Emanuele 175; meals €20; closed Tue

This old-school trattoria (informal restaurant) has had soup as its speciality for more than a century. Its *tortellini in brodo* (tortellini pasta in broth) is truly restorative after a hard day's sightseeing and is fortunately included in one of the two well-priced set-priced menus (€16 and €18) offering two courses, water and wine. Don't get it confused with the nearby Trattoria Il Maestro del Brodo (p58).

## CUCINA €

Map p48; ☎ 091 626 84 16; Via Principe di Villafranca 54; meals €15; closed Sun & two weeks in Aug

This chic eatery offers a welcome alternative to the battalions of Palermitan restaurants offering identical menus (*involtino*, anyone?). Well-executed modern Italian cuisine is on offer here and dishes are light, fresh and flavoursome. The loyal clientele of art, design and media professionals queue for lunch but book for dinner – you should do the same.

## PICCOLO NAPOLI €€

Map p54; ☎ 091 32 04 31; Piazzetta Mulino al Vento 4; meals €30; lunch Mon-Sat, dinner Fri & Sat

Known throughout the city for its spectacularly fresh seafood, delectable olives and excellent house wine, Piccolo Napoli is one destination that serious foodies shouldn't miss. Nibble on some olives while perusing the menu for a pasta dish that takes your fancy and then head to the seafood display (often still wriggling) to make your choice of a *secondo* (second course). The atmosphere is bustling and the genial owner greets most customers by name – a clear sign that once sampled, the food here exerts a true siren's call. Slow Food recommended.

PALERMO

## STREET MARKETS

Palermo's historical ties with the Arab world and its proximity to North Africa are reflected in the noisy street life of the city's ancient centre, and nowhere is this more evident than in its markets.

Each of the four historic quarters of Palermo has its own market, but the Vucciria, Ballaró and Capo are the 'Big Three' in terms of popularity and history.

The Mercato della Vucciria (La Vucciria; Map p48; Piazza Caracciolo) is the most dishevelled of the three, with rough-edged customers, carts selling street snacks, a small number of produce stalls and often-grumpy stallholders. The Mercato di Ballarò (Map p44; streets around Via Ballarò) is filled with stalls displaying household goods, clothes and foodstuffs of every possible description – this is where many Palermitans do their daily shop. The Mercato del Capo (Map p44), which extends through the tangle of lanes and alleyways of the Albergheria and Capo quarters respectively, is the most atmospheric of all. Here, meat carcasses sway from huge metal hooks, glistening tuna and swordfish are expertly dismembered, and anchovies are filleted. Long and orderly lines of stalls display pungent cheeses, tubs of plump olives and a huge array of luscious fruits and voluptuous vegetables.

The markets open from 7am to 8pm Monday to Saturday (until 1pm on Wednesday), although they are busier in the morning. Remember: keep an eye on your belongings while exploring.

### PIZZERIA BIONDO €

Map p54; ☎ 091 58 36 62; Via Nicolò Garzilli 27; pizzas €5-12; ☽ dinner Thu-Tue, closed Aug–mid-Sep

This long-standing favourite has managed to hold its own against the considerable competition posed by the nearby branch of the excellent Fratelli la Bufala chain. Sit in the simple dining room or claim a table on the street to enjoy your choice of pizza from a huge menu. Be warned that Trattoria Biondo around the corner (owned by the same people) is overpriced considering the average quality of its food.

### PIZZO & PIZZO €€

Map p54; ☎ 091 601 45 44; Via XII Gennaio 1-5; ☽ closed Sun

Patrons intending to limit their stay at this sophisticated wine bar to a quick pre-dinner drink inevitably find their best-laid plans overturned. Enticed by an extensive and excellent list of wines by the glass, a buzzing atmosphere and a top-notch array of cheeses, cured meats, foie gras and smoked fish, most end up settling in for the night. It shares the honour of being known as Palermo's best *enoteca* with nearby Picone (Map p54; ☎ 091 33 13 00; Via G Marconi 36; ☽ closed Sun).

### SANT'ANDREA €€

Map p48; ☎ 091 33 49 99; Piazza Sant'Andrea 4; meals €30; ☽ dinner Mon-Sat

Hidden in the heart of the Vucciria, this stylish restaurant serves market-fresh food to an accompaniment of soft jazz and the contented chatter of diners. Our advice is to order conservatively – when we last visited, the mixed antipasto and the pasta with prawns and orange oil were delicious, but other choices featured flavour combinations that were overly ambitious and didn't really work. A regular haunt of Peter Robb while he

researched *Midnight in Sicily*, it continues to host writers and other arty types.

### TRATTORIA AI CASCINARI €

Map p44; ☎ 091 651 98 04; Via D'Ossuna 43-45; meals €25; ☽ lunch Tue-Sun, dinner Thu-Sat

With its bustling atmosphere, gingham tablecloths and charming management, Ai Cascinari is an ideal example of a neighbourhood trattoria. It's almost obligatory to start with the *antipasti misti* (mixed appetisers), but there's plenty of choice when it comes to the other courses, including excellent *involtini* (meat rolls) and unusual vegetarian options. Note that credit cards aren't accepted. Slow Food recommended.

### TRATTORIA IL MAESTRO DEL BRODO €€

Map p48; ☎ 091 32 95 23; Via Pannieri 7; meals €25; ☽ lunch Tue-Sun, dinner Fri & Sat

Another Slow Food–recommended eatery, this no-frills place in the Vucciria offers a sensational antipasto buffet (€5), delicious soups and an array of ultra-fresh seafood. Waiters are friendly and the quality of the food is a cut or two above that of neighbouring restaurants.

### TRATTORIA PRIMAVERA €€

Map p44; ☎ 091 32 94 08; Piazza Bologni 4; set menu €25; ☽ lunch & dinner Tue-Sat, lunch Sun

Take a healthy appetite if you plan to order the set menu at this unpretentious Slow Food favourite. You'll kick off with a huge array of flavoursome antipasti (including delicious caponata and aubergine/eggplant parmigiana) and then order your choice of *primo* and *secondo* – the fish dishes are particularly tasty. With a finale of fruit and including wine, water and cover charge, it's a huge bargain. Those with more modest appetites can order à la carte. Slow Food recommended.

# TRANSPORT

## TO/FROM THE AIRPORT

**AIRPORT //** Falcone-Borsellino Airport (off Map p34; ☎ 091 702 01 11; www.gesap.it) is at Punta Raisi, 30km west of Palermo on the A29 motorway.

**BUS //** Prestia e Comandè ( ☎ 091 58 63 51; www.prestiaecomande.it, in Italian) runs a half-hourly bus service between 5am and 11pm that transfers passengers from the airport to the centre of Palermo, dropping people off outside the Teatro Politeama Garibaldi (Map p54) and the train station (Map p48). To find the bus, follow the signs past the downstairs taxi rank and around the corner. Tickets for the journey, which takes anywhere from 35 to 50 minutes depending on traffic, cost €5.80 and are purchased on the bus. Return journeys to the airport run with the same frequency and pick up at the same points. This is definitely the best way to travel to Palermo from the airport. Segesta (Map p48; ☎ 091 616 79 19; www.segesta.it, in Italian) runs a service to Trapani (€7.30, 1¾ hours, three daily) and Societá Autolinee Licata (SAL; ☎ 0922 401 360; www.autolineesal.it, in Italian) runs a service to Agrigento (€9.10, 2¼ hours, two daily).

**CAR //** All the major car-hire companies are represented at the airport.

**TAXI //** There is a taxi rank outside the arrivals hall and the set fare to/from central Palermo is €45.

**TRAIN //** The Trinacria Express ( ☎ 091 704 40 07) runs between the airport and the train station. The journey takes 45 minutes and costs €5.50. Trains depart from the train station every 20 to 65 minutes from 4.45am to 8.09pm; from the airport they depart from 5.54am to 10.05pm.

## GETTING AROUND

**BOAT //** Palermo's port (Map p54; ☎ 091 604 31 11) is located off Via Francesco Crispi. Ferries depart here for Cagliari, Civitavecchia, Genoa, Livorno, Malta, Naples, Salerno, Tunis and Ustica; see p332 for details.

**BUS //** Bus offices and departure points are located on or near Via Paolo Balsamo, east of the train station. Cuffaro ( ☎ 091 616 15 10; www.cuffaro.info) runs services to Agrigento (€8.10, two hours, nine daily Monday to Saturday, three Sunday). SAIS (Map p48; ☎ 091 704 12 11; www.saistrasporti.it, in Italian) runs between two and three services per day to Petralia Soprana (€9.40), Petralia Sottana (€9.40) and Polizzi Generosa (€8.50) in the Madonie mountains as well as services to Cefalù (€5.40, one hour, four daily), Corleone (€4.50, one hour and 20 minutes, three daily), Enna (€9.40, 1¾ hours, up to seven daily Monday to Friday, four Saturday) and Catania (€14.20, 2½ hours, 13 daily Monday to Saturday, nine Sunday). Salemi (Map p48; ☎ 0923 98 11 20; www.autoservizisalemi.it, in Italian) runs a service to Mazara del Vallo (€8.30, 2½ hours) and Marsala (€8.80, 2½ hours) that departs every hour between 6.15am and 9.15pm (fewer on Sundays and holidays). It's also the agent for Azienda Siciliana Trasporti (AST; www.aziendasicilianatrasporti.it, in Italian) services to Ragusa (€12.80, four hours, four per day Monday to Saturday, two on Sunday). Segesta (Map p48; ☎ 091 616 79 19; www.segesta.it, in Italian) runs services to Trapani (€8.60, two hours, at least every hour between 6am and 9pm) and Rome (€33, 12 hours, one daily). It's also the agent for the Interbus (www.interbus.it, in Italian) service to Syracuse (€13, 3¼ hours, two daily Monday to Saturday, three Sunday).

**CAR & MOTORCYCLE //** Palermo is accessible on the A20-E90 toll road from Messina, and from Catania (A19-E932) via Enna; the second route is quicker. Trapani and Marsala are also easily accessible from Palermo by motorway (A29), while Agrigento and Palermo are linked by the SS121/189, a good state road through the interior of the island.

**PARKING //** When making a booking, ask your hotel to organise a parking space. Alternatively, you'll need to try and find a park on the city's streets or piazzas. Spaces are marked by blue lines and you must get a ticket from a machine on every day except Sunday. All spaces are minded by self-appointed custodians who charge a couple of euros per day for their service. Don't try to dodge this — it's a time-honoured and widely observed custom.

**PUBLIC TRANSPORT //** Palermo's orange AMAT buses ( ☎ 848 800817; www.amat.pa.it, in Italian) are overcrowded and slow due to the city's appalling traffic. Ask at the tourist booths for a leaflet detailing the different lines; most stop at the train station. Tickets

PALERMO

should be purchased before you get on the bus and are available from tobacconists or the booths at the terminal. They cost €1.20 (€1.60 if purchased from the bus driver) and are valid for 90 minutes. Once you get on the bus you need to validate the ticket in the orange machine, which prints a 'start' time on it.

**TRAIN //** Regular services leave from the train station (Map p48; ☎ ticket office 091 603 11 11; ◷ 5.30am-8.40pm) to Messina (from €11.45; three to 3½ hours, hourly), Catania (from €14.95, 4½ to 6¾ hours, eight daily) and Agrigento (€7.90, 2¼ hours, nine daily), as well as to nearby towns such as Cefalù (from €4.90, 45 minutes to 1¼ hours, 13 daily). There are also Intercity trains to Reggio di Calabria, Naples and Rome. Inside the station, there are ATMs, toilets and left-luggage facilities (first hour €4, next 11 hours €0.60 per hour, all subsequent hours €0.20 per hour; ◷ 7am-11pm).

# AROUND PALERMO
· · · · · ·

Palermo is in turn exhilarating and exhausting, and after a few days visitors often find that they need a respite from its noisy, dirty and crowded streets. Fortunately, there are plenty of options available for an easy urban escape.

## MONDELLO

In the summer months, it sometimes seems as if the entire city population has packed a beach towel, iPod and a pair of D&G shades and decamped to this popular beach resort only a 20-minute drive from the centre of town.

Originally a muddy, malaria-ridden port, Mondello (off Map p34) only really became fashionable in the 19th century, when the city's elite flocked here in their carriages, thus warranting the huge Liberty-style pier that dominates the seafront and kicking off a craze for building opulent summer villas. Most of the beaches are private (two loungers and an umbrella cost around €10 per day), but there is also a wide swath of public beach crammed with swimmers, pedalos and noisy jet skis.

Seafood restaurants and snack stalls have colonised the lido (Viale Regina Elena) and the main piazza hosts numerous cafes with outdoor seating. One of Sicily's trendiest restaurants, Bye Bye Blues ( ☎ 091 684 14 15; www.byebyeblues.it; Via del Garofalo 23; meals €50; ◷ dinner Thu-Tue, closed most of Jan), is located a few streets back from the beach, and the less sophisticated but always reliable trattoria/pizzeria Da Peppino ( ☎ 091 45 49 75; Via Torre di Mondello 36; meals €25) has a plumb position next to the historic tower on the lido.

To get here on public transport, take AMAT bus 806 (€1.20, 20 minutes, every 20 to 30 minutes between 4am and 11.30pm, fewer services on Sunday) from Piazza Politeama (Piazza Ruggero Settimo; Map p54).

## MONREALE

Inspired by a heavenly vision of the Virgin and driven by earthly ambition, William II set about building the sumptuous Cattedrale di Monreale ( ☎ 091 640 44 13; Piazza Duomo; admission to cathedral free, north transept €1.50, terraces €1.50; ◷ cathedral 8am-6pm, north transept 9am-12.30pm & 3.30-5.30pm), 8km southwest of Palermo. Living in the shadow of his grandfather, Roger II – who was responsible for the cathedral in Cefalù and the Cappella Palatina – and vying with Walter of the Mill, who was overseeing construction of a grand Duomo in Palermo, William was determined that his cathedral should be the biggest and best of all. The result was Monreale, considered to be the finest example of Norman architecture in Sicily. The mosaicists were from Sicily and Venice, but the stylised influence of the Byzan-

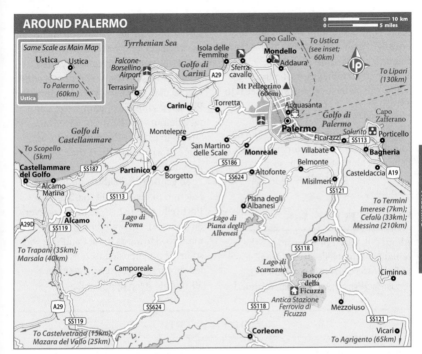

**AROUND PALERMO**

Same Scale as Main Map

Tyrrhenian Sea

Ustica
Ustica
To Palermo (60km)
Ustica

Falcone-Borsellino Airport
Terrasini

Isola delle Femmine
Golfo di Carini
A29
Sferracavallo
Capo Gallo
To Ustica (see inset; 60km)
Mondello
Addaura
Mt Pellegrino (606m)

Golfo di Castellammare
To Scopello (5km)

Montelepre
Carini
Torretta
Acquasanta
Palermo
Golfo di Palermo
Solunto
Porticello
Capo Zafferano

Castellammare del Golfo
SS187
Partinico
San Martino delle Scale
SS186
Monreale
Villabate
Ficarazzi
SS113
Bagheria

Alcamo Marina
SS113
Borgetto
SS624
Altofonte
Belmonte
Misilmeri
SS121
Casteldaccia
A19

A29D
Alcamo
SS119
Lago di Poma
Piana degli Albanesi
Lago di Piana degli Albanesi

To Trapani (35km); Marsala (40km)

To Termini Imerese (7km); Cefalù (33km); Messina (210km)

Camporeale
Lago di Scanzano
Marineo
SS118

A29
SS624
Bosco della Ficuzza
Antica Stazione Ferrovia di Ficuzza
SS118
Mezzoiuso
SS121
Ciminna

SS119
To Castelvetrano (15km); Mazara del Vallo (25km)
Corleone
To Agrigento (65km)
Vicari

0   10 km
0   5 miles

tines pervades their work. Completed in 1184 after only 10 years' work, the mosaics are an articulate and fitting tribute to William's ambition and to the grandeur of Sicilian culture at that time.

The interior is one of the most impressive creations of the Italian Middle Ages. A catalogue of shimmering mosaics depicts Old Testament stories, from the creation of man to the Assumption, in 42 different episodes. The beauty of the mosaics cannot be described – you have to see for yourself Noah's ark perching atop the waves or Christ healing a leper infected with large leopard-sized spots. The story of Adam and Eve is wonderfully portrayed, with a grumpy-looking, post-Eden-eviction Eve sitting on a rock while Adam labours in the background. The large mosaic of Christ, covering the dome, is stunning. Binoculars make viewing the mosaics much easier, although they are just as impressive to the naked eye. Take some €1 coins to illuminate the ill-lit mosaics in the apses. For a guide to the various scenes, print out the handy key and map at www.seepalermo.com/monrealekeyprint.htm.

Outside the cathedral is the entrance to the **cloister** (adult/EU citizen under 18yr & over 65yr/EU student 18-25yr €6/free/3; ⏰ 9am-6.30pm Tue-Sun), which illustrates William's love of Arab artistry. This tranquil courtyard is an ode to Orientalism, with elegant Romanesque arches supported by an array of slender columns alternately decorated with shimmering mosaic patterns. Each capital is different, and taken together they represent a unique sculptural record of medieval Sicily. The capital of the 19th column on the west aisle depicts William II offering the cathedral to the Madonna.

There are no eateries of note in Monreale. Your best option is probably Taverna del Pavone ( ☎ 091 640 62 09; www.taverna delpavone.eu; Vicolo Pensato 18; meals €26; ☾ lunch & dinner Tue-Sun). Exiting the cathedral, walk left up the main street and you'll see it in a small piazza on the right.

To reach Monreale, take bus 389 (€1.20, 30 to 40 minutes, every 25 to 60 minutes) from Piazza Indipendenza in Palermo (Map p44). The bus will drop you off outside the cathedral in Piazza Duomo.

## SOLUNTO

About 20km east of Palermo are the remains of the Hellenistic Roman town of Solunto ( ☎ 091 90 45 57; admission €2; ☾ 9am-6pm Mon-Sat, 9am-1pm Sun), founded in the 4th century BC on the site of an earlier Phoenician settlement. Although the ancient city is only partially excavated, the ruins are beautifully sited on the slopes of Monte Catalfano, with spectacular sea views. Wander along the Roman *decumanus* (main street), and take detours up the steep, paved side streets to explore the ruined houses, some of which still sport their original mosaic floors.

To get there, take the train from Palermo to the Santa Flavia-Solunto-Porticello stop (€2.10, 20 minutes, every 30 minutes). After alighting, follow the main road towards the sea and you will soon see a signposted turn-off to your left. From there, the ancient city is a 30-minute steep uphill walk.

---

### ∼ WORTH A TRIP ∼

Having suffered centuries of poverty and possessing a well-documented history as a Mafia stronghold, the town of **Corleone** – 60km from Palermo and best known through Francis Ford Coppola's classic *Godfather* trilogy –has been trying to reinvent itself over the recent decade. It is now home to the **Centro Internazionale di Documentazione sulla Mafia e Movimento Antimafia** ( ☎ 091 845 242 87; Via Orfanotrofio 7; admission €5; ☾ tours summer 10.30am, 11.30am, 12.30pm, 3.30pm, 4.30pm & 5.30pm Mon-Fri, no morning tours in winter), an absorbing and extremely moving anti-Mafia museum located in a small cobbled street off Piazza Garibaldi. The centre aims to promote speaking out against organised crime rather than succumbing to the Mafia-promoted culture of *omertà* (silence).

English-speaking tour guides recount the terrifying history of the local Mafia but focus on the brave efforts of anti-Mafia campaigners and judges. A huge 'No Mafia' sign greets visitors at the entrance, as does a quote from murdered anti-Mafia judge Giovanni Falcone: 'It's necessary to keep up your duty to the end at all costs, however hard may be the sacrifice to bear, because this is the essence of human dignity'. Three rooms are visited: the first holds the documents from the maxi trials of 1986–87; the second exhibits photographs by photojournalist Letizia Battaglia, who documented Mafia crimes in the 1970s and 1980s; and the third displays photographs of Mafia bosses, the men of justice who fought them and people who have lost loved ones.

AST buses travel between Corleone and Palermo (€4.50, one hour and 20 minutes, three daily). If you decide to eat here or stay the night in the area, the best option is Antica Stazione Ferrovia di Ficuzza (p304).

# USTICA

**pop 1330**

This tiny island floats alone almost 60km north of Palermo in the Tyrrhenian Sea. Part of the Aeolian volcanic chain, the land mass is actually the tip of a sub-merged volcano. Its black volcanic-rock landscape is sprinkled with blazing pink-and-red hibiscus flowers and prickly green cacti, the shoreline is littered with dramatic grottoes and the surrounding waters – protected within a *Riserva Naturale Marina* (Marine Reserve) – are kept sparklingly clean by an Atlantic current and are thus replete with fish and coral.

Palermitans flock here in July and August for their summer holidays – consider visiting in June and September to appreciate the dramatic coastline and grottoes without the crowds. Note that between October and Easter most of the island's restaurants and accommodation options close down during the week and ferry services from the mainland can be cancelled in bad weather.

The headquarters of the **Marine National Park** ( ☎ 091 844 94 56; Piazza Umberto 1) can advise on practicalities, activities, boat trips and dive centres.

## EXPLORING USTICA

### ❧ SCUBA DIVING & SNORKELLING // TAKE TO THE DEEP BLUE WATERS

Divers from all over the world come to Ustica between May and September to explore its magnificent underwater sites. Highlights include the underwater archaeological trail off Punta Cavazzi, where artefacts including anchors and Roman amphorae can be admired. Other popular dive sites are the Scoglio del Medico, an outcrop of basalt riddled with caves and gorges that plunge to great depths; and Secca di Colombara, a magnificent rainbow-coloured display of sponges and gorgonias. There are plenty of dive centres that offer dive itineraries and hire equipment; see www.ampustica.it for a list.

The Marine Reserve is divided into three zones. Zone A extends along the west flank of the island from Cala Sidoti to Caletta and as far as 350m offshore (marked with special yellow buoys): you can swim within its boundaries but fishing and boating are prohibited. Two of the island's most beautiful natural grottoes – the Grotta Segreta (Secret Grotto) and the Grotta Rosata (Pink Grotto) – are located here.

Zone B extends beyond Zone A from Punta Cavazzi to Punta Omo Morto; swimming and underwater photography are permitted within its boundaries, as is hook-and-line fishing. Zone C applies to the rest of the coast; swimming and boating are allowed and national fishing regulations apply. Always check your itinerary with a dive centre or the Marine National Park headquarters before you dive.

Those who are keen to observe the underwater world but don't wish to dive or snorkel can hop aboard a glass-bottomed Acquario Motorship; ask at the Marine National Park office for details.

### ❧ HIKING THE ISLAND // SEEK OUT SPECTACULAR VIEWS AND A TEMPTING ROCK POOL

Ustica is only 8.7 sq km in area, so it's easy to explore on foot. There are a number of walking trails, the most scenic of which passes through pine woods to the summit of **Guardia di Mezzo** (248m), before descending to the best part of the coast at **Spalmatore**, where it's possible to swim in natural rock pools. Other walking paths go to the Rocca della Falconiera, a defensive tower above the church; to the lookout point above the lighthouse at Punta Omo Morto; and to the Torre Santa Maria, a Bourbon-era tower that houses a small archaeological museum. Ask at the Marine National Park office for directions.

## GASTRONOMIC HIGHLIGHTS

❦ AL CLELIA DELL'HOTEL CLELIA €€
☎ 091 844 90 39; www.hotelclelia.it; Via Sindaco I 29; meals €30; ⊙ closed Sep-Apr
Ustica's best eatery is located on the top floor of one of its most popular hotels, with charming views of the sea and village rooftops. Unsurprisingly, fish is the house speciality – the fish couscous is particularly renowned. For dessert, there is usually a choice of *gelati* made daily using organic island-grown fruits.

## TRANSPORT

**BOAT** // Siremar ( ☎ 091 58 24 03; www.tirrenia.it/it/siremar, in Italian) operates a year-round car-ferry service between Ustica and Palermo (€19.85 one way, 2½ hours, two daily), and additional hydrofoils run from June to September (€23.05 one way, 1¼ hours, two daily). Ustica Lines ( ☎ 0923 87 38 13; www.usticalines.it) runs a Trapani–Favignana–Ustica–Naples hydrofoil service from June to the end of September up to four days per week. The journey from Naples to Ustica takes four hours and costs €72.40 one way.

PALERMO

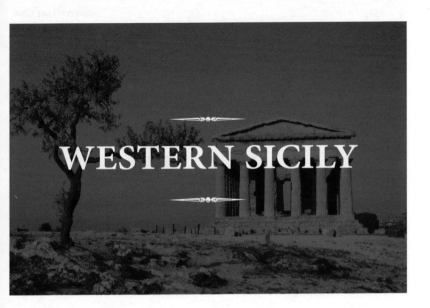

# WESTERN SICILY

## 3 PERFECT DAYS

**☙ DAY 1 // UP IN THE CLOUDS**
Climb aboard the funicular for a ride up the legendary mountain of Eryx. At the summit you'll find one of Sicily's most enchanting medieval towns, Erice (p79). Wander the winding alleyways, making sure you stop for a sugar fix at Maria Grammatico (p82) and to admire the magnificent panorama from the town's ruined castle. Returning down the mountain for dinner, head to Trapani (p73), a gastronomic gem where some of Sicily's best restaurants (p76) await you.

**☙ DAY 2 // MARVELLOUS MARSALA**
Home to friendly locals, a well-preserved historical centre and the island's most famous wine, the town of Marsala (p87) is one of the must-see destinations on this coast. Spend the morning touring Cantine Florio (p90) and then dedicate the afternoon to exploring the ancient island settlement of Mozia (p86), a short drive away along the famous Via del Sale (Salt Road). Return to Marsala to join the *passeggiata* (evening stroll) down Via XI Maggio before kicking on to La Sirena Ubriaca (p90) for an aperitivo and Osteria Il Gallo e l'Innamorata (p90) for dinner.

**☙ DAY 3 // A DAY IN THE SOUTHWEST**
Overlooking the vast expanse of the Mediterranean Sea, the archaeological site at Selinunte (p95) amply rewards those who make the effort to visit. Spend the morning exploring the evocative ruins of this ancient Greek city before heading towards the nearby town of Mazara del Vallo (p91) for lunch at La Bettola (p91), a walk around the atmospheric kasbah and a visit to the fascinating Museo del Satiro (p92).

# WESTERN SICILY

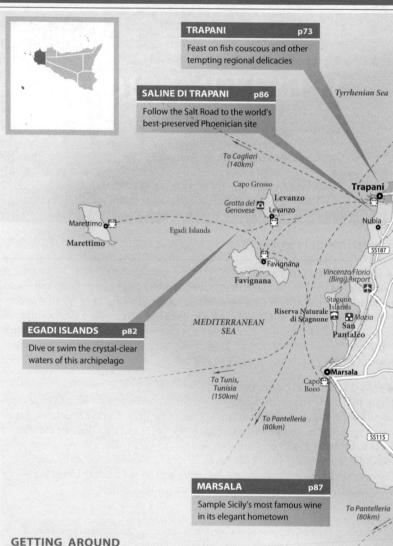

**TRAPANI**　　　　**p73**

Feast on fish couscous and other tempting regional delicacies

**SALINE DI TRAPANI**　　**p86**

Follow the Salt Road to the world's best-preserved Phoenician site

*Tyrrhenian Sea*

To Cagliari
(140km)

Capo Grosso

*Grotta del
Genovese*　　**Levanzo**
　　　　Levanzo

**Trapani**

Nubia

Marettimo

*Egadi Islands*

**Marettimo**

SS187

Favignana

**Favignana**

*Vincenzo Florio
(Birgi) Airport*

Stagone
Islands

Riserva Naturale
di Stagnone　　Mozia

*MEDITERRANEAN
SEA*

**San
Pantaleo**

**EGADI ISLANDS**　　**p82**

Dive or swim the crystal-clear waters of this archipelago

**Marsala**

To Tunis,
Tunisia
(150km)

Capo
Boeo

To Pantelleria
(80km)

SS115

**MARSALA**　　　**p87**

Sample Sicily's most famous wine in its elegant hometown

*To Pantelleria
(80km)*

## GETTING AROUND

The best way to explore this corner of Sicily is by car, although most destinations are accessible by bus and/or train. The A29 autostrada cuts through the interior from Palermo to Mazara del Vallo and the SS115 snakes along the coastline – unfortunately, neither is particularly picturesque. Ferries ply the waters between Trapani and the Egadi Islands all year; in summer there are also services between Marsala and the Egadis.

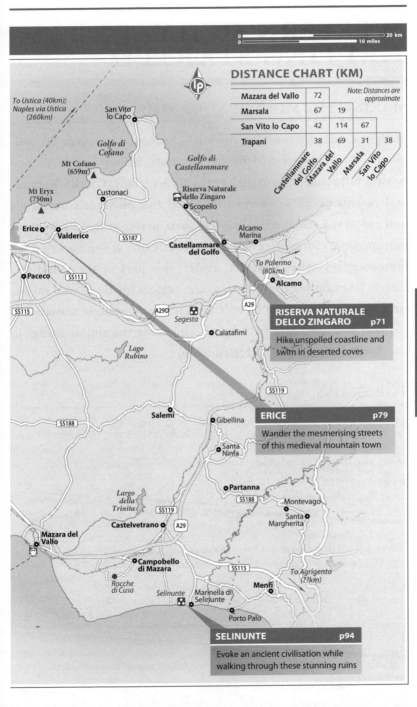

## DISTANCE CHART (KM)

| | Castellammare del Golfo | Mazara del Vallo | Marsala | San Vito lo Capo |
|---|---|---|---|---|
| Mazara del Vallo | 72 | | | |
| Marsala | 67 | 19 | | |
| San Vito lo Capo | 42 | 114 | 67 | |
| Trapani | 38 | 69 | 31 | 38 |

*Note: Distances are approximate*

**RISERVA NATURALE DELLO ZINGARO**   p71

Hike unspoiled coastline and swim in deserted coves

**ERICE**   p79

Wander the mesmerising streets of this medieval mountain town

**SELINUNTE**   p94

Evoke an ancient civilisation while walking through these stunning ruins

**WESTERN SICILY**

# WESTERN SICILY
## GETTING STARTED

## MAKING THE MOST OF YOUR TIME

Sicily's windswept western coast has beckoned invaders for millennia. Its richly stocked fishing grounds, hilltop vineyards and coastal saltpans were coveted by the Phoenicians, Greeks, Romans and Normans, all of whom influenced the province's landscape and culture. Even the English left their mark, with 18th-century entrepreneurs lured here and made rich by one of the world's most famous sweet wines, Marsala. Today, this part of the island is a largely unexploited tourism treasure, perfect for those who savour slow travel. Come here to visit ancient ruins, sample sensational seafood and meet laid-back locals who value the simple things in life: food, wine, family and friendship.

## TOP TRAILS

### ❦ MARSALA WINE
When John Woodhouse concocted his famous formula for exporting Marsala wine in the 18th century, he assured this local tipple a worldwide reputation. Learn all about its complex history and composition by touring Marsala's Cantine Florio (p90).

### ❦ SALT
Salt comes in piles rather than pinches here. See evidence of a still-buoyant ancient industry by following the Via del Sale (Salt Road) between Trapani and Marsala (p86).

### ❦ SWEET TEMPTATIONS
This part of the island is famous for its cakes, pastries and *gelato*. To understand why, sample the decadently delicious offerings at our top-five *pasticcerie* (p87).

### ❦ TUNA
For centuries, the bluefin tuna has propped up the local economy and dominated the regional cuisine. Visit the island archipelago where it has always reigned supreme (p82).

### ❦ WINE ROUTES
Marsala isn't the only local drop worth sampling – the local Erice DOC is eminently quaffable, too. To investigate fully, sign up for a guided tour of the Strada del Vino e dei Sapori Erice DOC (p79).

# GETTING AWAY FROM IT ALL

★ **Explore Mozia** Once home to a thriving Phoenician settlement, this tiny island in the Riserva Naturale di Stagnone now hosts bird life, archaeological remnants and the occasional tourist (p86).

★ **Seek out Segesta** Your first sight of the majestic temple hidden in its little-visited mountain valley is sure to form a lasting memory (p81).

★ **Picnic at Rocche di Cusa** History will be your only companion at this ancient Greek quarry near Selinunte (p94).

★ **Hike the Riserva Naturale dello Zingaro** Follow the coastal path between Scopello and San Vito lo Capo, enjoying a swim or two in deserted coves along the way (p71).

# BEST BEACHES

The best beaches on the west coast are found around the Golfo di Castellammare and on the Egadi Islands.

★ **Cala Minnola** Swim in the crystal-clear waters at this pebbled bay on the island of Levanzo (p85).

★ **Castellammare del Golfo** Sandy beaches and excellent restaurants make this fishing village a popular holiday destination (p70).

★ **Lido Burrone** This broad swath of beach is the most popular spot on the holiday island of Favignana (p83).

★ **San Vito lo Capo** A crescent-shaped beach and an obsession with couscous are the hallmarks of this resort (p72).

# TOP EATING EXPERIENCES

❦ **AL SOLITO POSTO**
Regional specialities dominate at this wildly popular Trapanese trattoria (p77).

❦ **CANTINA SICILIANA**
Home to Trapani's most famous seafood couscous (p77).

❦ **LA BETTOLA**
This Mazara del Vallo restaurant is one of Sicily's best (p93).

❦ **OSTERIA IL GALLO E L'INNAMORATA**
Come here for the most authentic and delicious *scaloppine con marsala* you'll ever eat (p90).

❦ **OSTERIA LA BETTOLACCIA**
Refined cuisine and pleasant surrounds in Trapani's Historic Centre (p77).

# RESOURCES

★ **EgadiWeb** (www.egadiweb.it) Guide to the Egadi Islands.

★ **Riserva Naturale dello Zingaro** (www.riservazingaro.it, in Italian) Official site of the Zingaro nature reserve.

★ **Selinunte On Line** (www.selinunte.net) Information about the archaeological park and Marinella di Selinunte.

★ **Strada del Vino e dei Sapori Erice DOC** (www.stradavinomarsala.it) All about the wine route.

★ **Trapani Welcome** (www.trapaniwelcome.it) Detailed information about the entire province.

**WESTERN SICILY**

# GOLFO DI CASTELLAMMARE

· · · · · ·

This gulf outside Palermo is as far west as many Sicilians will ever get, and even then, most locals have only visited its beaches. Those prepared to be a bit more adventurous will discover the unspoiled Zingaro nature reserve, quaint settlements built around historic *baglios* (manor houses) and *tonnare* (tuna-processing plants), and a coastal landscape dotted with tempting swimming coves. Added to all this are the ancient ruins of Segesta (p81), which are only a short drive inland.

## CASTELLAMMARE DEL GOLFO

pop 14,863

The stunning promontory between Castellammare del Golfo and Monte Cofano (659m) is perhaps the most beautiful in all of Sicily. At its heart lies the fishing village of Castellammare del Golfo, founded by the Elymians as the port for the city of Segesta (p81). It has a pleasant harbour that is overlooked by the remains of a much-modified Saracen castle and surrounded by sandy beaches, making it a hugely popular summer holiday destination.

Castellammare del Golfo is only 26km from Sicily's main airport, and many travellers choose to stay here rather than in Palermo after arriving or before departing from the island.

### GASTRONOMIC HIGHLIGHTS

☙ AL RISTORANTINO DEL MONSÙ €€
☎ 0924 53 10 31; Via Pisani 2; meals €30; ⊙ closed Mon & 2 weeks in both Feb & Nov
One of two restaurants in the village with a Slow Food Movement recommenda-

tion, Del Monsù has a panoramic terrace overlooking the harbour and a menu dominated by seafood dishes such as *busiate con bottarga di tonno e gamberi rossi* (fresh local-style pasta with cured fish roe and red prawns), *cuscus al nero di sepia* (couscous with black squid ink) and *pesce spada alla pantesca* (swordfish with cherry tomatoes, capers and olives).

☙ RISTORANTE DEL GOLFO €€
☎ 0924 3 02 57; Via Segesta 153; meals €35; ⊙ closed Tue (except in summer)
The town's other Slow Food favourite serves classic Sicilian dishes such as *sarde in agrodolce* (sardines in a sweet and sour sauce), *fettuccine con bottarga e zucchine* (pasta with cured fish roe and courgettes/zucchinis) and simply prepared *gamberi imperiali* (king prawns). If you're lucky, *cassatedde* (deep-fried pastries filled with ricotta) will be on the dessert menu.

☙ TROPICAL BAR €
☎ 0924 3 29 80; www.tropicalbar.info; Via Umberto I, 2; ⊙ closed Mon
Castellammare's best cafe is known for its excellent coffee, home-made *cornetti* (croissants), delectable Sicilian pastries (love those *cassatedde* with ricotta and honey!) and refreshing *gelato*. It also offers a *tavola calda* (selection of hot savoury snacks).

### TRANSPORT

**BUS //** Buses depart from Via della Repubblica. Autoservizi Russo ( ☎ 0924 3 13 64; www.russoautoservizi.it) runs services to Piazza Marina in Palermo (€5.20, 1¼ hours, six daily Monday to Saturday, extra services in July and August), as well as services to Scopello (€2.10, 10 minutes, four daily). Azienda Siciliana Trasporti (AST; ☎ 840 110323; www.aziendasicilianatrasporti.it, in Italian) runs a regular service to Trapani (€3.90, five daily Monday to Saturday); there's also a Sunday service from June to September.

**TRAIN //** The train station is an inconvenient 3km out of town, although there is a shuttle bus (€1.50). There are frequent trains from Palermo (€5.50, 1¾ hours, nine daily) and Trapani (€4.40, 50 minutes, four daily).

# SCOPELLO

The hamlet of Scopello couldn't be any more charming if it tried. Built around an 18th-century *baglio* fortified with a high wall and huge gates, its white houses and smooth-stone streets look like they belong in a 1950s Italian movie. In fact, the historic *tonnara* on the shore below is a popular film location – the 2004 Hollywood blockbuster *Ocean's Twelve* was filmed here, as was an episode of the *Inspector Montalbano* TV series (see p289).

There's nothing to do in Scopello except enjoy a coffee at the cafe on the main piazza or swim in one of the most idyllic coves on the island, which is next to the *tonnara*. Flanked by two tall rocks, one of which is crowned by a medieval tower, the cove has incredibly blue waters and a rough-pebbled shore. Note that it is officially only for the use of guests at the *tonnara* (see p305), although locals seem to take little notice of the 'Private Property' signs.

Try to avoid Scopello in August, when it becomes unpleasantly crowded.

## GASTRONOMIC HIGHLIGHTS

If you're staying at Pensione Tranchina (p305), make sure that you take advantage of its highly regarded dinners. Unfortunately, it doesn't cater for non-guests.

### ☙ BAR PASTICCERIA SCOPELLO €
☎ 0924 54 11 49; Via Diaz 13
This tempting *pasticceria* sells a huge range of Sicilian sweet treats and is the

town's social epicentre. Claim one of its outdoor tables and settle back for a session of people-watching fuelled by coffee and cake or a refreshing fruit-based *gelato* or *granita* (crushed-ice drink).

## TRANSPORT

**BUS //** AST runs a service to/from Trapani (€3.60, 1¼ hours, two daily). Autoservizi Russo buses run between Castellammare del Golfo and Scopello (€2.10, 10 minutes, four daily).

# AROUND SCOPELLO

### ☙ RISERVA NATURALE DELLO ZINGARO // HIKE INLAND TRAILS OR DIVE WRECK-FILLED WATERS
Saved from development by local protests, the tranquil **Riserva Naturale dello Zingaro** ( ☎ 0924 3 51 08; www.riserva zingaro.it, in Italian; adult/over 65yr & child under 10yr/child 10-14yr €3/free/2; ☺ 7am-9pm Apr-Sep, 8am-4pm Oct-Mar) is the star attraction on the gulf.

Zingaro's 7km of wild coastline is a haven for the rare Bonelli eagle, along with 40 other bird species and 700 plant varieties, some unique to this stretch of coast. Mediterranean flora dusts the hillsides with wild carob and bright yellow euphorbia, and hidden coves provide excellent swimming spots. **Cetaria Diving Centre** ( ☎ 0924 54 11 77; www.cetaria. com; Via Marco Polo 3) in Scopello organises guided dives in the waters off the nature reserve between April and October, visiting underwater caves and two shipwrecks; it also offers boat excursions with snorkelling.

The main entrance to the park is 2km from Scopello. A walk up the coast between the San Vito lo Capo and Scopello entrances will take about four hours along a clearly marked track (note that the San Vito entrance is 20km from the

WESTERN SICILY

town of San Vito lo Capo and there is no public transport). There are also several trails inland, which are detailed on the free maps available at the information offices at the park's two entrances. You can also download these from the website.

Baglio La Luna ( ☎ 335 8362856; www.bag liolaluna.com; d €80-140; ☺ Apr-Nov; ℗ ), a B&B on the edge of the park overlooking the gulf, can organise guided walks, bicycle excursions and cooking classes featuring local products.

# SAN VITO LO CAPO

pop 4108

Occupying the tip of the promontory is the seaside town of San Vito lo Capo, full of beachcombers and sun worshippers in summer but akin to a graveyard in winter. The town is renowned for its crescent-shaped sandy beach, but its most noteworthy sight is the fortress-like 13th-century Chiesa di San Vito, about halfway down Via Savoia.

## ♥ FESTIVAL INTERNAZIONALE DEL CUSCUS // SPICE UP YOUR HOLIDAY AT THIS UNIQUE CULTURAL FESTIVAL

San Vito is well known for its fish couscous, which is celebrated at this six-day event (www.couscousfest.it), held in September each year. The festival isn't just about the famous North African dish – it's marketed as a festival of cultural integration and hosts musicians and chefs from around the world. Highlights include a couscous cook-off (Italy against teams from other countries), free World Music concerts, and couscous workshops given by chefs from San Vito, Trapani and North Africa. There are also plenty of tasting opportunities.

## GASTRONOMIC HIGHLIGHTS

### ♥ AL RITROVO €€

☎ 0923 97 56 56; www.alritrovo.it; Viale Cristoforo Colombo 314; meals €30; ☺ closed 2 weeks in both Nov & Jan

Couscous features on the menu here (as it does at practically every other eatery in town), but there's also a good range of seafood and meat alternatives. The house speciality is *fritto misto* (mixed fried seafood), which you can wash down with a selection from the excellent wine list. There are also 13 rooms with modern decor (€48 to €93 per person with breakfast and dinner).

### ♥ POCHO €€

☎ 0923 97 25 25; www.pocho.it; meals €30; ☺ lunch Sun & dinner Wed-Mon, closed Oct-Mar

This hotel restaurant is set in the small village of Makari, overlooking the Isulidda beach 2km from San Vito. In warm weather, guests are seated on a terrace with panoramic views of the Golfo di Cofano. The delicious menu, which changes daily, leans heavily towards seafood-based local specialities such as fish couscous. It's worth considering a stay of a few days in the comfortable hotel (singles with breakfast and dinner €115 to €160, doubles €150 to €210), which has 12 rooms and an impressive pool terrace. Note that from mid-June to mid-September the restaurant is open every evening but is closed for Sunday lunch.

### ♥ THÀAM €€

☎ 0923 97 28 36; www.sanvitoweb.com/thaam, in Italian; Via Duca degli Abruzzi 32; meals €35; ☺ closed Wed in winter

A North African theme is evident in both menu and decor at this popular restaurant, which dishes up fish and chicken couscous beneath tented canopies on the street. It also offers attractively decorated rooms (€60 to €120) year round.

## ACCOMMODATION

There are fewer accommodation options on the west coast than on the rest of the island, and during the summer months most of these are busy – make sure you book well in advance. The following are four choices worth considering:

★ **Albergo Egadi** (p306) is a stylish option on the Egadis.

★ A Marsala charmer, **Hotel Carmine** (p307) is one of the best midrange hotels in Sicily.

★ Comfortable rooms and a family-friendly atmosphere are features at **Hotel San Domenico** (p306) in Erice.

★ Expect a warm welcome and excellent food at **Pensione Tranchina** (p305) in Scopello.

For a full list of accommodation options, see p305.

### TRANSPORT

**BUS //** Buses arrive at/depart from Via Piersanti Mattarella, just near the beach and parallel to Via Savoia – look for street signs marking the stops. AST services travel between San Vito lo Capo and Trapani (€3.70, 1½ hours, eight daily Monday to Saturday, four Sunday) and Autoservizi Russo travels to/from Palermo's Piazza Marina (€7.90, 2½-3¼ hours, three daily).

# TRAPANI
· · · · · ·

**pop 70,648**

Hugging the harbour where Peter of Aragon landed in 1282 to begin the Spanish occupation of Sicily, the sickle-shaped spit of land occupied by Trapani's Old Town once sat at the heart of a powerful trading network that stretched from Carthage to Venice. Traditionally the town thrived on coral and tuna fishing, with some salt and wine production. Over the past century, there has been much construction here – most of it unattractive – and it is often alleged that this is the result of healthy injections of Mafia-laundered money into the local economy. The busy port is the main embarkation point for the Egadi archipelago and the remote Moorish island of Pantelleria, as well as an embarkation point for ferries to Tunisia.

## ESSENTIAL INFORMATION

**EMERGENCIES //** Hospital (Ospedale Sant'Antonio Abate; ☎ 0923 80 94 50; Via Cosenza; ⊙24hr) Police (Questura; ☎ 0923 59 81 11; Piazza Vittoria Veneto; ☎ 24hr)

**TOURIST INFORMATION //** Tourist Office ( ☎ 0923 54 55 08; www.trapaniwelcome.it; Via San Francesco d'Assisi 27; ⊙8am-2pm) Tourist Information Point ( ☎ 0923 2 90 00; Piazzetta Saturno; ⊙8am-8pm Mon-Sat, 9am-noon Sun Mar–mid-Nov) Offers bike sightseeing tours, bike rental, maps, tour guides and guided trekking.

## ORIENTATION

Trapani is narrow and relatively compact, bordered on either side by the sea. It is split between the New City, which runs east from Via XXX Gennaio, and the Historic Centre, which occupies the promontory and incorporates the port. The city's main boulevard, Via Giovanni Battista Fardella, forms the spine of the New City. The main bus station is on Piazza Montalto and the train station is around the corner on Piazza Umberto I.

## LA PROCESSIONE DEI MISTERI

Since the 18th century, the citizens of Trapani – represented by 20 traditional *maestranze*, or guilds – have begun a four-day celebration of the Passion of Christ on the Tuesday before Easter Sunday by parading a remarkable, life-sized wooden statue of the Virgin Mary through the town's streets. Over the course of the next three days, nightly processions of the remaining *Misteri* (life-sized wooden statues) make their way through the old quarter and port to a specially erected chapel in Piazza Lucatelli, where the icons are stored overnight. Each procession is accompanied by crowds of locals and a Trapanese band, which plays dirges to the slow, steady beat of a drum.

The high point of the celebration is on Friday afternoon, when the 20 guilds emerge from the Chiesa del Purgatorio and descend the steps of the church, carrying each of the statues, to begin the 1km-long procession up to Via Giovanni Battista Fardella; the procession then returns to the church the following morning. The massive crowds that gather to witness the slow march often reach a peak of delirious fervour that is matched only by that of the Semana Santa parades in Seville, Spain.

To witness the procession, you'll need to book your accommodation well in advance. At other times, the figures are on display in the Chiesa del Purgatorio. For more information, check out www.processionemisteritp.it (in Italian, Spanish and French only).

# EXPLORING TRAPANI

❤ **THE OLD TOWN // APPRECIATE THE BAROQUE BACKDROP DURING AN EVENING STROLL**
Although the narrow network of streets in Trapani's Historic Centre is Moorish, the city takes most of its character from the fabulous 18th-century baroque of the Spanish period. A catalogue of examples can be found down pedestrianised Via Garibaldi, most notably the **Palazzo Riccio di Morana** and **Palazzo Fardelle Fontana**. The best time to walk down here is in the early evening, when the *passeggiata* is in full swing.

Another busy place during *passeggiata* is Corso Vittorio Emanuele, which is punctuated by the huge **Cattedrale di San Lorenzo** (Corso Vittorio Emanuele; admission free; ☺ 8am-4pm), with its baroque facade. At the east end of the corso is another baroque confection, the **Palazzo Senatorio**.

Towards the port, on Piazzetta Saturno, is the 14th-century **Chiesa di Sant'Agostino** (admission free; ☺ 8am-1pm), its austerity relieved only by its fine Gothic rose window and portal. Nearby stands something altogether more ornate, the Catalan Gothic **Chiesa di Santa Maria del Gesù** (Via San Pietro; admission free; ☺ 8am-1pm), which houses the exquisite *Madonna degli angeli* (Madonna of the Angels), a glazed terracotta statue by Andrea della Robbia.

❤ **CHIESA DEL PURGATORIO // LEARN ALL ABOUT TRAPANI'S FAMOUS MISTERI PROCESSION**
Off Vittorio Emanuele, south along Via Generale Dom Giglio, is this small church ( ☎ 0923 43 22 00; Via San Francesco D'Assisi; admission €1; ☺ 4-6.30pm) housing the 18th-century *Misteri* – 20 life-sized wooden figures depicting the story of Christ's Passion that are paraded throughout Trapani's streets every Easter. Some of

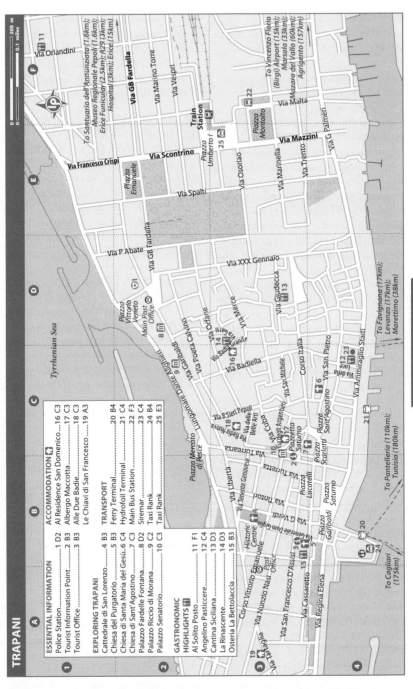

# TRAPANI

WESTERN SICILY

the statues are originals; others are copies of statues destroyed during Allied bombing of the town in WWII or irreparably damaged after being dropped by their bearers during a procession (the statues are heavy and unwieldy, and mishaps sometimes occur).

Each statue was commissioned and is now carried by members of a particular profession: *Jesus Before Hanna* was commissioned by the Land Surveyors and Tanners Guild and is now carried by greengrocers; *Jesus Before Herod* was commissioned by the Millers and Corn Sievers Guild and is now carried by fishmongers. Many are still being carried by the guilds that commissioned them: *The Crowning with Thorns* by the Millers and Bakers Guild and *The Whipping* by the Bricklayers and Stonemasons Guild. One of the figures – *The Ascent of Calvary* – isn't claimed by a particular guild but is instead accompanied by people with no guild affiliation. Each figure comes with an informative explanatory panel in English and Italian.

### ❦ SANTUARIO DELL'ANNUNZIATA // PAY HOMAGE TO THE MADONNA OF TRAPANI

This 14th-century basilica (Basilica Maria SS Annunziata; ☎ 0923 53 91 84; www.madonnaditrapani. com, in Italian; Via Conte Agostino Pepoli 178; admission free; ◷ 8am-noon & 4-7pm) is in the New City, a short bus ride along Via Giovanni Battista Fardella (bus 25, 26, 28 or 30) or a 45-minute walk from the Historic Centre. Remodelled in baroque style in the 17th century, the church retains its original Gothic rosette and doorway and is dedicated to the Madonna of Trapani, patron saint of the city and traditional protector of seafarers. The Cappella della Madonna behind the high altar contains a venerated marble sculpture of the Ma-

donna, thought to have been carved by Nino Pisano. Her image is also prominent in two other chapels: the 16th-century Cappella dei Marinai (Seamen's Chapel) and 15th-century Cappella dei Pescatori (Fishermen's Chapel).

### ❦ MUSEO REGIONALE AGOSTINO PEPOLI // GAWK AT SOME GLORIOUSLY GAUDY ARTWORKS

The former Carmelite monastery next to the Santuario dell'Annunziata now houses the Pepoli National Museum ( ☎ 0923 55 32 69; www.regionale.sicilia.it/beniculturali; Via Conte Agostino Pepoli 180; adult/child & over 65yr €4/free; ◷ 9am-1.30pm Tue-Sat, 9am-12.30pm Sun), a collection of local arts and crafts, paintings, sculptures and decorative art. The most interesting exhibits are those that were in the collection of Conte Pepoli, who made it his business to salvage much of Trapani's local arts and crafts, not least the garish coral carvings that were all the rage in Europe before the banks of coral off Trapani and San Vito lo Capo were decimated. Don't miss Andrea Pipa e Aiuti's gaudy 18th-century *presepe* (Nativity scene or crèche) made of alabaster, coral, shells and other marine material, or the significantly less ornate but far more beautiful coral carvings by Fra Matteo Bavera. Other highlights include an extraordinary *cassetta reliquiaria* (relic box) from the workshop of Alberto and Andrea Tipa and remnants of painted tile pavements from the Chiesa di Santa Maria delle Grazia (featuring fishing scenes) and the Chiesa di Santa Lucia (with scenes of Trapani's city centre).

## GASTRONOMIC HIGHLIGHTS

Trapani's unique position on the sea route to Tunisia has made couscous (or *cuscus,* as they spell it here) something of a speciality, particularly when served *alla trapanese* (in a soup of fish, garlic, chilli, tomatoes, saffron, cinnamon and nutmeg). Another irresistible staple is *pesto alla trapanese* (pesto made from fresh tomatoes, basil, garlic and almonds), eaten with *busiate,* a small hand-twirled pasta.

### ☙ AL SOLITO POSTO €€

☎ 0923 2 45 45; www.trattoria-alsolitoposto.com, in Italian; Via Orlandini 30a; meals €28; ✆ closed Sun & 15-31 Aug

Tucked at the end of Via Orlandini, this wildly popular trattoria is a well-deserved wearer of the Slow Food Movement badge. The *busiate con pesto alla trapanese* is the best in town and all of the seafood dishes are fresh and flavoursome – opt for tuna from May to June and swordfish or other species at other times of the year. It's wise to book in advance.

### ☙ ANGELINO PASTICCERE €

☎ 0923 2 69 22; www.angelino.it; Via Ammiraglio Staiti 87; ✆ closed Wed

You'll need to fight your way to the bar at this frantically busy cafe opposite the hydrofoil dock. It serves the best coffee in Trapani, and also offers a selection of delicious cakes, pastries (try a *bombolone di ricotta;* doughnut with sweet ricotta filling) and savoury snacks such as *arancine* (fried rice balls).

### ☙ CANTINA SICILIANA €€

☎ 0923 2 86 73; www.cantinasiciliana.it, in Italian; Via Giudecca 36; meals €28

Hidden in the old Jewish ghetto, this Slow Food favourite is known throughout the island for its simple but delicious dishes such as *sarde allinguate* (fried filleted sardines) and *busiate con pesce spada e melanzane* (busiate with swordfish and aubergine/eggplant). The *sec-*

*ondi* (second course) menu is dominated by seafood (including an expertly spiced *cuscus alla trapanese*), but there are a few token meat dishes, too. The restaurant runs the *enoteca* (wine bar or shop) next door, so it's not surprising that the wine list is excellent – if you're lucky, genial owner Pino Maggiore might offer you a complimentary glass of Passito di Pantelleria (sweet wine from the island of Pantelleria) with your dessert.

### ☙ LA RINASCENTE €

☎ 0923 2 37 67; Via Gatti 3; ✆ 9am-1pm & 3-7pm Thu-Tue

If you're keen to see how Sicilian sweets such as *cassata* and *cannoli* are made, head to this fabulously atmospheric *pasticceria* in the heart of the Old City. Signore Costadura and his assistant work in the shop's old-fashioned open kitchen using only the best ingredients, creating exquisite cakes, biscuits and *gelato* for their fervently loyal clientele.

### ☙ OSTERIA LA BETTOLACCIA €€€

☎ 0923 2 16 95; Via Generale Enrico Fardella 25; meals €40; ✆ closed Sat & Sun lunch all year & Sun dinner Nov-Easter

This is a great place to try couscous, prepared with a generous allocation of seafood and large enough for two to share. But the pleasant surprises don't stop there – the tempting menu showcases a selection of dishes that are far more refined in execution than is usual in Sicily. Highlights of a recent visit included *trancio di pesce spada in salsa di agrumi* (swordfish fillet in a citrus fruit sauce) and *tagliata di vitello in aceto blasamico e radicchio* (veal fillet served with balsamic vinegar and radicchio) – both perfectly cooked and beautifully presented. It's another favourite of the Slow Food Movement.

# TRANSPORT

## TO/FROM THE AIRPORT

**AIRPORT //** Sicily's third-busiest airport, Vincenzo Florio airport ( ☎ 0923 84 25 02; www. airgest.it), is 15km south of Trapani at Birgi and is commonly known as Birgi airport. Air One (www. alitalia.com/ap_it) flies to/from Milan; Meridiana fly (www.meridiana.it) travels between Birgi and Pantelleria; and Ryanair (www.ryanair.com) flies to/from destinations including Dublin, London, Madrid, Paris, Rome and Stockholm as well as a number of Italian cities.

**BUS //** AST buses (€4.50, 20 minutes, 17 daily) leave for the airport from the port and then the main bus station on Piazza Montalto approximately every hour from 5am to 11pm. Salemi ( ☎ 0923 98 11 20; www. autoservizisalemi.it) runs between one and five services from Monday to Saturday between the airport and Marsala (€3.90, 45 minutes) and also runs between one and five services from Monday to Saturday to Palermo (€8.80, two hours). The timetable depends on the time of year, with more services in summer. Terravision ( ☎ 0923 98 11 20; www.terravision.eu) operates buses between the airport and Palermo's Piazza Politeama and train station (€12, two hours, six to eight daily), stopping at Trapani's port and main bus station (€8 one way, €12 return) en route.

**TAXI //** A taxi between Birgi and Trapani costs approximately €35.

## GETTING AROUND

**BOAT //** Trapani's ferry terminal ( ☎ 0923 54 54 11) is opposite Piazza Garibaldi. For hydrofoils you will need to head east down Via Ammiraglio Staiti. Grimaldi Lines ( ☎ 081 496444; www.grimaldi -ferries.com) runs a service to Tunis in Tunisia (€85, nine hours, one per week). Siremar ( ☎ 892 123; www. siremar.it, in Italian; Via Ammiraglio Staiti 61) runs hydrofoils to Favignana (€9.80, 40 minutes), Levanzo (€9.80, 20 minutes) and Marettimo (€17.30, 1½ hours). It also runs a daily ferry to Pantelleria (€39.50, five hours, daily June to September and Sunday to Friday for the rest of year). Tirrenia ( ☎ 892 123; www.tirrenia.

it) runs a ferry service to Cagliari on Sardinia (€43 to €82 depending on class and season, 10 hours, one weekly). Ustica Lines ( ☎ 0923 87 38 13; www.usticalines. it; Via Ammiraglio Staiti 23) runs regular hydrofoils to Favignana (€9.80, 40 minutes, 11 daily), Levanzo (€9.80, 20 minutes, 10 daily) and Marettimo (€17.30, 1½ hours, two daily), as well as summer-only services to Ustica (€26.40, 2½ hours, four weekly) and Naples (€89.40, 6¾ hours, three weekly). Get tickets at the hydrofoil terminal. Add €1.50 to all Ustica and Siremar ticket prices if you book via the website or an agent.

**BUS //** All intercity buses arrive and depart from the main bus station (Piazza Montalto). Tickets can be bought from the bar in the station building. AST serves Erice (€2.10, 50 minutes, eight daily Monday to Saturday, four Sunday), San Vito lo Capo (€3.70, 1½ hours, eight daily Monday to Saturday, four Sunday), Marsala (€2.60, 40 minutes, one daily) and Mazara del Vallo (€5.40, 1¾ hours, one daily). Autoservizi Tarantola ( ☎ 0924 3 10 20; www.tarantolabus. it) operates a service to Segesta (€4.20, 50 minutes, four to five daily) and Lumia ( ☎ 0922 2 04 14; www.autolineelumia.it, in Italian) operates services to Agrigento (€11.30, four hours, three daily Monday to Saturday, one on Sunday). Segesta ( ☎ 091 616 79 19; www.segesta.it, in Italian) runs express buses connecting Trapani with Palermo (€8.60, two hours, at least every hour between 6am and 9pm). Note that all services decrease dramatically on Sundays, as well as on public holidays and in the low season (October to May).

**PARKING //** There are plenty of parks at the port and near the train station. Purchase tickets from the machines on the street (€0.60 per hour, €0.30 for fourth or successive hours).

**PUBLIC TRANSPORT //** Tickets for local ATM buses cost €1 and are valid for 90 minutes; buy them from *tabacchi* (tobacco shops). The Trapani Welcome Card (€8.80), available at the tourist information office and some hotels, covers one return trip on the Erice funicular and one three-day local bus pass.

**TRAIN //** Trapani is linked to Palermo (€7.70, 2½ hours, five daily), Marsala (€3.25, 30 minutes, 14 daily) and Mazara del Vallo (€4.40, 50 minutes, 14 daily).

# AROUND TRAPANI

· · · · · ·

There's not a lot in Trapani itself to keep tourists occupied, but the city has a good range of hotels and restaurants, making it an excellent base for those keen to explore the surrounding region. A trip to the medieval eyrie of Erice will often end up being a holiday highlight, as will an itinerary built around sampling Trapanese food and wine, which is some of the most impressive on the island.

## ☙ STRADA DEL VINO E DEI SAPORI ERICE DOC // EAT AND DRINK YOUR WAY AROUND THE REGION

This wine and food route celebrates the Erice DOC (*Denominazione di Origine Controllata*; Controlled Origin Denomination) wine that is produced in the province of Trapani. You can construct and follow your own itinerary of the region, or consider signing on for a four-day guided tour run by the Association Strada del Vino e dei Sapori Erice DOC ( ☎ 0923 81 17 00; www.stradadelvinoericedoc.it).

Erice DOC is an appellation that recognises indigenous grape varieties from the region, including Catarratto, Nero d'Avola, Grillo, Insolia, Frappato, Perricone and Zibibbo. The grapes in this region owe their distinctive flavour to the fact that they are grown in vineyards that lie at between 250m and 500m in height, but which are located close to the sea.

Along the route, there are also plenty of opportunities to sample regional food products. These include tuna and salt, which have been mainstays of western Sicily's diet and economy ever since Phoenician times, and the region's succulent strawberries and fragrant olive oil. Also of note are the marzipan sweets, pastries and almond biscuits that are made following ancient convent recipes in Erice.

## ERICE

pop 28,763 / elev 751m

Erice watches over the port of Trapani from the legendary mountain of Eryx, situated a giddy 750m above sea level. It's a mesmerising walled medieval town with stern-looking forts and churches, and its mountain charm is enhanced by the unpredictable weather that can take you from sunny afternoon to foggy evening in the space of a few minutes.

The town has sweeping views of the valley beneath it and the sea, and is home to Sicily's most famous cake shop, Maria Grammatico.

Erice has a notorious history as a centre for the cult of Venus (Astarte to the Phoenicians and Aphrodite to the Greeks). The mysterious Elymians claimed descent from Venus' famous Trojan son, Aeneas, who mentions the sanctuary as a holy landmark in the *Aeneid*. Inside the holy temple, acolytes practised the peculiar ritual of sacred prostitution, with the prostitutes accommodated in the temple itself. Despite countless invasions the sacred site long remained inviolate – there's no need to guess why!

### ESSENTIAL INFORMATION

**EMERGENCIES //** Police (Questura; ☎ 0923 55 50 00; Piazza Grammatico; ⊙ 24hr)

**TOURIST INFORMATION //** Tourist Office ( ☎ 0923 86 90 25; Via Tommaso Guarrasi 1; ⊙ 8am-2pm Mon-Sat)

WESTERN SICILY

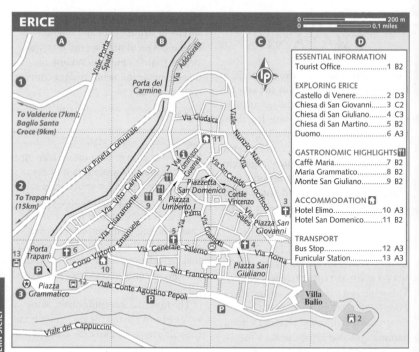

ERICE

| ESSENTIAL INFORMATION | |
|---|---|
| Tourist Office | 1 B2 |

| EXPLORING ERICE | |
|---|---|
| Castello di Venere | 2 D3 |
| Chiesa di San Giovanni | 3 C2 |
| Chiesa di San Giuliano | 4 C3 |
| Chiesa di San Martino | 5 B2 |
| Duomo | 6 A3 |

| GASTRONOMIC HIGHLIGHTS | |
|---|---|
| Caffè Maria | 7 B2 |
| Maria Grammatico | 8 B2 |
| Monte San Giuliano | 9 B2 |

| ACCOMMODATION | |
|---|---|
| Hotel Elimo | 10 A3 |
| Hotel San Domenico | 11 B2 |

| TRANSPORT | |
|---|---|
| Bus Stop | 12 A3 |
| Funicular Station | 13 A3 |

**WESTERN SICILY**

## ORIENTATION

All vehicles arrive in Piazza Grammatico, from where you enter the town through the Porta Trapani. The funicular station and the bus stop are also here. From the piazza, Corso Vittorio Emanuele, the town's steep main road, heads up to Piazza Umberto I, the central piazza. The other main road, which branches off Vittorio Emanuele, is Via Generale Salerno. This eventually brings you out at the castle.

## EXPLORING ERICE

Virgil once compared Eryx to Mt Athos for its altitude and spiritual pre-eminence. Not that the town resembles a sanctuary today – temples and convents have given way to carpet shops selling the town's famous *frazzate* (bright rugs

made from colourful rags) and innumerable souvenir stalls. Still, Erice is about wall-hugging alleys, votive niches and secret courtyards, all of which are best appreciated in the evenings and early mornings after the battalions of day-trippers leave.

## ♥ CASTELLO DI VENERE // PLAY AT BEING KING OF THE CASTLE

On the hilltop stands the ruins of the Norman **Castello di Venere** (Castle of Venus), built in the 12th and 13th centuries over an ancient temple of Venus that was destroyed by Roger I when he captured the town. In winter the ruins are often shrouded in mist that locals call '*il velo di Venere*' (the veil of Venus). When the mist clears, the terrace around the castle offers panoramic vistas northeast to San Vito lo Capo and Monte Cofano (659m), and southwest to Trapani.

### ♥ THE CHURCHES OF ERICE // SEEK OUT THE TOWN'S ECCLESIASTICAL TREASURES

The **Erice Monuments Ticket** (admission €5; ⊗ 10am-12.30pm Feb, 10am-4pm Mar, 10am-6pm Apr-Jun & Oct, 10am-8pm Jul & Aug, 10am-7pm Sep, 10am-1pm Nov-Dec) gives entrance to the town's five major ecclesiastical attractions: the Duomo's Campanile and Treasury, San Martino's wood sculptures, San Giuliano's *Gruppa Misteri* (Good Friday group sculptures) and San Giovanni's marble sculptures. Buy your ticket at any of the churches.

Of Erice's 60-odd churches, the **Duomo** (Via Vito Carvini; admission free; ⊗ 9.30am-1pm & 3-5.15pm) is the most interesting. It was built in 1312 by order of a grateful Frederick III, who had sheltered in Erice during the Sicilian Vespers uprising (1282–1314).

The church's interior was remodelled in the neo-Gothic style in 1865, but the 15th-century side chapels were conserved. Views from the top of the 28m-high **Campanile** (King Frederick's Tower; admission €2 or incl in the Erice Monuments Ticket), with its mullioned windows, are impressive.

## GASTRONOMIC HIGHLIGHTS

Caffè Maria (p82) offers a well-priced simple tourist menu comprising an antipasto, *primo* (first course), sweet, coffee and water for €13, which is worth considering as most of the town's restaurants serve mediocre food solely geared towards a tourist clientele.

### ♥ MONTE SAN GIULIANO €€

☎ 0923 86 95 95; www.montesangiuliano.it; Viccolo San Rocco 7; meals €32; ⊗ closed Mon

---

## ∼ WORTH A TRIP ∼

Segesta was the principal city of the Elymians, an ancient civilisation whose peoples claimed descent from the Trojans and who settled in Sicily in the Bronze Age. The Elymians were in constant conflict with Greek Selinunte, whose destruction (in 409 BC) the Elymians pursued with bloodthirsty determination. Such mutual antipathy was to have fatal consequences, and more than 100 years later the Greek tyrant Agathocles slaughtered over 10,000 Elymians and repopulated Segesta with Greeks.

Today, the remains of the city form one of the world's most magical **ancient sites** (☎ 0924 95 23 56; adult/over 65yr/concession €6/free/3; ⊗ 9am-4pm Nov-Mar, 9am-6pm Apr-Aug), which comprises a theatre high up on the mountain and a never-completed Doric temple. The latter dates from around 430 BC and is remarkably well preserved.

The site is set on the edge of a deep canyon in the midst of wild, desolate mountains and is accessed off the A29d autostrada running between Palermo and Trapani.

Autoservizi Tarantola operates a bus service between Segesta and Trapani's main bus station (€4.20, 50 minutes, four to five daily). Alternatively, you can catch a train from Trapani (€3.25, 25 minutes, three daily) or Palermo (€6.80, two to three hours, three daily) to Segesta Tempio; the site is about a 20-minute walk away. Note that you'll need to change trains at either Alcamo or Piraine if you're coming from Palermo.

Every 30 minutes a shuttle bus runs 1.5km uphill to the theatre and costs an additional €1.50. If you've got the energy, walk up instead – the views are spectacular.

WESTERN SICILY

## MARIA GRAMMATICO

This **pasticceria** (☎ 0923 86 93 90; www.mariagrammatico.it, in Italian; Via Vittorio Emanuele 14) is owned and run by the delightful Maria Grammatico, Sicily's most famous pastry chef and the subject of Mary Taylor Simeti's book *Bitter Almonds*.

In the early 1950s, Maria's father died suddenly of a heart attack. Her impoverished mother, pregnant with a sixth child, decided to send Maria, aged 11, and her younger sister to the cloistered San Carlo orphanage in Erice to learn the art of pastry making from the nuns. There, the children toiled in brutally hard conditions – beating sugar mixtures for six hours at a time, rising before dawn to prime the ovens, shelling kilos of almonds and surviving on an unrelenting diet of meatless pasta and vegetable gruel. At 22, Maria left the orphanage after having a nervous breakdown and started making sweets and pastries to survive. The rest, as they say, is history.

The world-famous *pasticceria* and associated **Caffè Maria** ( 8am-10pm summer, till 10pm in winter, closed Tue in winter), with its panoramic terrace, are good places to sample Sicilian treats such as *cannoli* filled with fresh ricotta; green *cassata* cakes made of almonds, sugar, vanilla, buttermilk curd and candied fruit; perfectly formed marzipan fruits; lemon-flavoured *cuscinetti* (small fried pastries); and *buccellati* (hard, baked cookies) twisted around fig, cinnamon and clove comfit. At Easter, the shop is filled with super-cute almond-citron baby lambs that are made to celebrate Erice's *I Misteri* celebration. Be warned that the produce here uses more sugar than is usual – your dentist would certainly not approve!

Tucked behind Corso Vittorio Emanuele, this restaurant is entered through a crumbling arch that leads onto a cool patio graced with drooping hydrangeas. In summer, you can eat on a terrace, which has a canopy of green vines; in winter, service is in three internal dining rooms. Classic Trapanese dishes such as *busiate* pasta and fish couscous feature on the menu.

### TRANSPORT

**BUS //** There is a regular AST bus service to/from Trapani (€2.10, 50 minutes, eight daily Monday to Saturday, four Sunday). All buses arrive and depart from Porta Trapani.

**FUNICULAR //** The best way to get to Erice is on this cable car (☎ 0923 56 93 06, 0923 86 97 20; www.funiviaerice.it, in Italian; Piazza Umberto I; one way/return €2.70/5;  noon-1am Mon, 7.45am-1am Tue-Fri, 8.45am-2am Sat & Sun, till 4am Thu Jul & Aug, from 9am Fri Jul & Aug, closed 1 Nov-10 Mar for annual maintenance). To get to the funicular from Trapani, catch bus 23 from Via GB Fardella down to the end of Via Alessandro Manzoni, which is the point where Trapani ends and Erice begins. You can walk to the funicular station, but it takes around 45 minutes from/to the centre of Trapani.

**PARKING //** Parking is available next to Porta Trapani and along Viale Conte Pepoli (free October to July, charged August and September).

# EGADI ISLANDS
· · · · · ·

pop 4383

For centuries, the Egadi Islanders have lived from the sea, as the prehistoric cave paintings on Levanzo illustrate. Later, when the islands were a key Carthaginian stronghold, one of the most critical battles of the Punic Wars was fought in 241 BC at Cala Rossa (Red Cove), which earned its name from the amount of Carthaginian blood spilt.

When the Arabs decided to take Sicily, they used the islands as a stepping-stone en route to their invasions, fortifying them heavily to prevent anyone else getting the same idea.

In the 17th century the islands were sold to Genovese bankers, who in turn sold them to the Florio family in 1874. The Florios established a branch of their lucrative tuna industry here, bringing great prosperity to the locals. The islands only became part of the Italian state in 1937.

Nowadays, the Egadi Islands (Isole Egadi) are popular destinations for swimming, diving, eating and general relaxation. Unfortunately, the waters around the islands have been terribly overfished, causing a dent in the local economy.

# FAVIGNANA

The largest of the islands is butterfly-shaped Favignana, which is dominated by Monte Santa Caterina (287m) to the west. You can easily explore it on a bicycle, as the eastern half of the island is almost completely flat. Around the coast, deep gouges in the cliffs are reminders of tufa quarrying that occurred in the past;

## GETTING TO THE EGADIS

Both Siremar and Ustica Lines run hydrofoils to the islands from Trapani; see p78 for details. Ustica also offers services between Marsala and Favignana (€9.80, 30 minutes, five daily in summer, three daily in winter) and Marsala and Marettimo (€17.30, 90 minutes, three daily in summer only). Both companies offer services between the islands. From Favignana you can connect easily to Levanzo (€5.80, 10 minutes) and Marettimo (€10.40, 30 minutes).

many of these have now been reclaimed by the crystal-clear waters and are atmospheric swimming spots, most notably around Cala Rossa and Cavallo.

## ESSENTIAL INFORMATION

**EMERGENCIES //** Ambulance ( ☎ 0923 92 12 83) Police (Carabinieri; ☎ 0923 92 12 02; Via Simone Corleo)

**TOURIST INFORMATION //** Tourist Office ( ☎ 0923 92 16 47; www.egadiweb.it; Piazza Madrice 3; ☺ 9am-12.30pm & 4.30-7pm Mon-Sat, 9.30am-12.30pm Sun Jun-Sep) Helpful office in Favignana town that can supply information on diving and boating operators, accommodation and excursions.

## EXPLORING FAVIGNANA

The first thing you'll see as you step off the boat is the Stabilimento Florio Tonnara, the town's historic tuna factory. Vincenzo Florio Sr (1799–1886), a brilliant Palermitan businessman who had built an empire in the sulphur, shipping and Marsala industries, also invented a way of steam-cooking and preserving canned tuna that revolutionised the fish-packing industry and cemented the success of his family's business empire. This *tonnara* was one of many the Florios ran around Sicily and it operated until 1977. Favignana town's other significant building, Palazzo Florio, was built in 1876 for Vincenzo's son Ignazio, who purchased the Egadis in 1874.

The best beaches are on the southern side of the island at Miramare and Lido Burrone; the bay at Cala Rossa is also a lovely swimming spot.

## GASTRONOMIC HIGHLIGHTS

Not surprisingly, tuna is the thing to eat on the islands, served in a multitude of ways. The food at Albergo Egadi (p306) is highly regarded, and there's a clutch of

WESTERN SICILY

popular eateries at the port; **Ristorante Amici del Mare** ( ☎ 0923 92 25 96; Piazza Marina 6) is probably the best of this bunch.

### 🌿 LA BETTOLA €€

☎ 0923 92 19 88; Via Nicotera 47; meals €34; ☽ closed Thu (except in summer) & 2 weeks in Dec

Family-run and Slow Food–recognised, La Bettola serves well-prepared seafood dishes such as *zuppa di cozze* (mussel soup), *linguine con sarde* (linguine with sardines) and *tonno in agrodolce* (tuna in a sweet and sour sauce). You can also order Trapanese specialities including couscous and *busiate*. There's a limited list of local and regional wines to accompany your meal.

## TRANSPORT

**BICYCLE & SCOOTER //** This is the best way to get around Favignana, giving you access to all the little coves and beaches dotting the island. There are plenty of places offering bikes, scooters and motorbikes for hire, including **SDB Motors** ( ☎ 347 9155376;

WESTERN SICILY

## LA MATTANZA

An ancient tradition, the Egadi Islands' *mattanza* (ritual tuna slaughter) survives despite the ever-decreasing number of tuna swimming into the local waters each year.

For centuries schools of bluefin tuna have used the waters around western Sicily as a mating ground. Locals can recall the golden days of the island's fishing industry, when it was not uncommon to catch giant breeding tuna of between 200kg and 300kg. Fish that size are rare these days and the annual catch is increasingly smaller due to the worldwide commercial overfishing of tuna.

Traditionally, tuna traps were set around the coast of Sicily once a year. The number of tuna caught by this method was relatively small and sustainable – the fact that the *mattanza* took place for around 900 years without overfishing is testament to this. Problems arose with the increase in commercial fishing in the 1960s: tuna was caught year-round, and deep waters were exploited using long-line fishing and indiscriminate means such as drift and gill nets. Anything that passed by was caught, and thus the oceans' fish resources were depleted.

According to some scientists, additional problems such as high legal fishing quotas and illegal fishing are causing 'irreversible' damage to bluefin tuna stock. Fishermen have largely lost their livelihoods, so some have reinvented La Mattanza as a tourist attraction.

From around 20 May to 10 June, tourists flock to the Egadi Islands to witness the event. For a fee you can join the fishermen in their boats and watch them catching the tuna at close hand, but keep in mind that nets have been known to come up empty in the last few years.

If you do decide to go, remember that this is no ordinary fishing expedition. The fishermen organise their boats and nets in a complex formation designed to channel the tuna into a series of enclosures, which culminate in the *camera della morte* (chamber of death). Once enough tuna are imprisoned, the fishermen close in and the *mattanza* begins. It is a bloody affair – up to eight or more fishermen at a time will sink huge hooks into a tuna and drag it aboard. Anyone who has seen Rossellini's classic film *Stromboli* will no doubt recall the *mattanza* scene, one of the most famous accounts of this ancient tradition.

www.sdbmotors.it; Piazza Madrice 16). Bicycle hire in the high season costs approximately €7 per day; scooter hire €30 to €35. Prices drop in the medium and low seasons.
**BUS //** Tarantola runs buses around the island from Piazza Marina in Favignana town. There is a coastal route and an inland route; both leave from near the main port.

# LEVANZO

There are two main reasons to visit Levanzo: to examine the prehistoric cave paintings at the Grotta del Genovese, and to spend some time swimming off the island's pebbly beaches.

## EXPLORING LEVANZO

### ♣ GROTTA DEL GENOVESE //
**MARVEL AT THE SURVIVAL OF THESE PREHISTORIC PAINTINGS**
The Upper Palaeolithic wall paintings and Neolithic incised drawings at the Genovese Cave were discovered in 1949 by Francesca Minellono, a painter from Florence who was holidaying on Levanzo and exploring its many caves. Between 6000 and 10,000 years old, the images mostly feature animals; the later ones also include men and tuna. The grotto can be visited on a **tour** ( ☎ 0923 92 40 32, 339 7418800; www.grottadelgenovese.it; adult/child under 5yr/child 5-10yr €20/free/10; ☑ 10.30am daily year-round, extra tour at 3pm Jul & Aug). The tour is by boat if weather conditions are favourable; otherwise, it's by 4WD. Advance bookings are essential. You can also visit the grotto by foot from the port. The walk takes 1½ hours and the entrance ticket costs €10/free/6 per adult/child under five years/child five to 10 years – you'll still need to book, though.

### ♣ SWIMMING SPOTS // **PLUNGE INTO THE ISLAND'S CRYSTAL-CLEAR WATERS**
There are three great spots on the island to go swimming, all a healthy walk from town. To get to Faraglione, take a left through town and walk about 1km west along the road until you see a couple of rocks sticking out of the water a few metres offshore. If you fancy something a little quieter, keep going until you get to Capo Grosso, on the northern side of the island, where there is also a lighthouse. Alternatively, take a right out of town and walk along the dirt road. The road forks 300m past the first bend; take the rocky path down towards the sea and keep going until you get to Cala Minnola, a small landing bay with crystal-clear water where, outside the month of August, you can swim in peace and tranquillity.

## GASTRONOMIC HIGHLIGHTS

### ♣ RISTORANTE PARADISO €€
☎ 0923 92 40 80; www.albergoparadiso.eu; Via Lungomare 8; meals €38; ☑ closed 10 Nov-10 Mar
A family-run Slow Food favourite, Paradiso offers a charming terrace overlooking the port and a menu filled with seafood delicacies such as *spaghetti con i ricci* (spaghetti with sea urchins), *lasagne di mare* (seafood lasagne) and *calamari fritti* (fried calamari). It also rents out simple rooms (see p307).

# MARETTIMO

The most westward of the Egadi Islands, Marettimo is a collection of green mountain peaks and white-washed houses dipping into a little harbour packed with bobbing fishermen's boats. It's also the wildest and least developed of the islands. However, with the overfishing of tuna affecting fishermen's incomes, the villagers are increasingly focusing on the economic potential of tourism. This doesn't mean that you'll find Marettimo packed at any time of the year – on the contrary, this tiny island is pretty much wilderness personified – but more accommodation options have cropped up in the last few years.

Note that the island virtually shuts down in the winter months.

## EXPLORING MARETTIMO

Marettimo is a perfect place for relaxation and swimming – there are good beaches at Cala Sarda, Cala Nera and stunning Cala Bianco. You can also go walking in unspoilt nature; there's only one road on the island and not that many cars – the main mode of transport is electric carts.

## GASTRONOMIC HIGHLIGHTS

### ☙ TRATTORIA IL VELIERO
☎ 0923 92 32 74; Via Umberto 22; meals €30

Il Veliero sports its Slow Food Movement badge with pride and deserves every bit of it. Owner and chef Peppe Bevilacqua goes to the market daily, picking out the freshest catches. Thanks to his labours, you might get to start with an octopus salad or marinated sardines, move onto fish couscous or a nice plate of spaghetti with *frutti di mare* (seafood), tuck into some grilled squid for a main, and have fruit or ice cream as your finale.

# SALINE DI TRAPANI

· · · · · ·

**If you follow the SP21 coastal highway (the Via del Sale or Salt Road) between Trapani and Marsala you will find yourself in a flat and featureless landscape of *saline* (shallow pools), softly shimmering heaps of salt and small decommissioned *mulini* (windmills). The salt from these marshes is considered the best in Italy and has been big business**

**since the 12th century; now, however, salt production has fallen off massively and only a cottage industry remains, providing for Italy's more discerning dinner tables. The best time to travel here is in summer, when the sun turns the saltpans rosy pink and makes the salt heaps glint. In winter, the heaps are covered with tiles and plastic tarpaulins to keep out the rain and are nowhere near as picturesque.**

# EXPLORING SALINE DI TRAPANI

The most attractive spot along the coast, where the saltpans glitter undisturbed by modern construction, is the Riserva Naturale di Stagnone (www.salineditrapani. it, in Italian), a noted wetlands area that takes in the Stagnone Islands (Isole delle Stagnone) – one of which is home to the noted archaeological site of Mozia – as well as the long arm of Isola Lunga, which protects the shallow waters of the lagoon.

### ☙ MOZIA // EVOKE PHOENICIAN LIFE AT THIS UNIQUE ARCHAEOLOGICAL SITE

The site of ancient Mozia (also known as Motya or Mothia) is located on the tiny island of San Pantaleo, bought by the ornithologist and amateur archaeologist Joseph Whitaker (1850–1936) in the early 20th century and bequeathed to the Joseph Whitaker Foundation by his daughter Delia on her death in 1971. Joseph, who was a member of an English family that gained great wealth from the Marsala trade, built a villa here and spent decades excavating the island and assembling a unique collection of Phoenician artefacts. What his weekend archaeology revealed was one of the most important Phoenician settlements in the Mediter-

**TOP FIVE**

**PASTICCERIE**

The west coast plays host to many of Sicily's best *pasticcerie* (cake and pastry shops), meaning that touring here can be a deliciously decadent exercise. Here's our thoroughly road-tested shortlist of the best:

* **Bar Pasticceria Scopello** (p71) – the fruit-based *granite* here are a revelation, particularly in a brioche for breakfast
* **Enzo & Nino (E&N)** (p90) – pause from the *passeggiata* for a sugar hit at Marsala's favourite cafe
* **La Rinascente, Trapani** (p77) – watch *cassata* being made the old-fashioned way
* **Maria Grammatico, Erice** (p82) – convent-trained Maria is the most famous pastry chef in Sicily and could well be the nicest, too
* **Tropical Bar** (p70) – the challenge here is to choose between the cakes and *gelato* – or then again, why not opt for both?

ranean, established in the 8th century BC and coveted for its strategic position. It is also the best-preserved Phoenician site in the world, as the Romans utterly destroyed Carthage, sowing the ground with salt so that no living thing could remain.

You can take a pleasant stroll around the island, following the path to excavations including the ancient port and dry dock, where you can see the start of a Phoenician road – now approximately 1m underwater – that once linked San Pantaleo with the mainland. Near the island's jetty is the recently refurbished **Whitaker Museum** (☎ 0923 71 25 98; adult/concession €9/5; ⏰ 9am-1pm Oct-Feb, 9am-1pm & 3-6.30pm Mar-Sep), which occupies Joseph's former villa and houses many objects excavated on the island. Nearby there is a bar/cafe serving drinks and snacks.

To access Mozia, you'll need to take one of the boats operated by **Arini e Pugliese** (☎ 347 7790218; return €5; ⏰ 9am-1.30pm & 2.30-7pm Mar-Oct, 9am-4pm Nov-Feb) from the landing point opposite the island. Nearby, in a beautifully restored *mulino* (mill), is the **Saline 'Etore e Infersa'**, home to a small **salt museum** (☎ 0923 71 25 98; adult/student €3/1; ⏰ 9.30am-1pm, 3pm-sunset, sometimes closed in winter).

# THE SOUTHWEST

**This is the least visited part of the province, but in many respects it's also the most interesting. The elegant town of Marsala, home to the island's famous fortified wine, is an ideal base for exploration. From here, destinations such as Saline di Trapani, the world-famous archaeological site at Selinunte and the multicultural fishing port of Mazara del Vallo are only a short trip away.**

## MARSALA

pop 82,337

Many know about its sweet dessert wines, but few people realise what a charmer the town of Marsala is. Though its streets are full of stately baroque buildings and graceful piazzas, pleasures here are simple – a friendly *passeggiata* most nights, plenty of aperitivo options and family-friendly restaurants aplenty.

Marsala was founded by the Phoenicians who escaped from Mozia after it was defeated in 397 BC by an army led by Dionysius I of Syracuse. They settled here on Capo Lilibeo, calling their city Lilybaeum and fortifying it with 7m-thick walls that ensured it was the last Punic settlement to fall to the Romans. In AD 830 it was conquered by the Arabs, who gave it its current name Marsa Allah (Port of God).

## ESSENTIAL INFORMATION

**EMERGENCIES //** Ambulance ( ☎ 0923 95 14 10) Police (Questura; ☎ 0923 92 43 71; Corso Antonio Gramsci; ☽ 24hr)

**TOURIST INFORMATION //** Tourist Office ( ☎ 0923 71 40 97; Via XI Maggio 100; ☽ 8.30am-1.30pm & 3-8pm Mon-Sat) Supplies good maps and brochures.

## ORIENTATION

The city of Marsala hugs a small promontory overlooking the Mediterranean Sea. The Old City is clustered around the tip, separated from the sea by Via Lungomare Boeo. Its main entrance is through the monumental Porta Nuova (New Gate) at Piazza della Vittoria, which feeds into the pedestrianised main street, Via XI Maggio. Porta Garibaldi on Piazza Mameli is an alternative entrance point. To access the centre of town from the train station, walk straight down Via Roma, which meets Via XI Maggio at Piazza Matteotti.

## EXPLORING MARSALA

### ❦ MUSEO ARCHAEOLOGICO BAGLIO ANSELMI // IMAGINE LIFE ON-BOARD A PUNIC WARSHIP

The partially reconstructed Carthaginian warship displayed in Marsala's Museo Archaeologico Baglio Anselmi ( ☎ 0923 95 25 35; Via Lungomare Boeo; admission €3; ☽ 9am-1.30pm Mon, Tue & Thu, 9am-6pm Wed & Fri-Sun) was sunk off the Egadi Islands during the First Punic War nearly 3000

years ago, and these delicate remnants are the only remaining physical evidence of Phoenician seafaring genius. Wood pieces from the wreck were discovered in 1969 by the captain of a dredger working in the Stagnone lagoon, and the hull was found in 1979; it's actually only a small part of the original ship, carefully reconstructed to give an impression of what it would have looked like. Manned by 68 oarsmen, the 35m-long warship is thought to have been part of the Carthaginian fleet attacked by the Romans in 241 BC at the Battle of Egadi. If you visit here after viewing the excavations on Mozia the ship resonates with history, providing a glimpse into a civilisation that was extinguished by the Romans.

The exhibition also includes objects found on-board: ropes, cooking pots, corks from amphorae, a brush, olive stones, a sailor's wooden button and even a stash of cannabis! In an adjacent room are a marble statue known as *La venere di lilybaeum* (The Venus of Lilybaeum) and two beautiful mosaics from the 3rd and 5th centuries AD, as well as other bits and bobs recovered from the nearby dig of the Insula Romana ( ☽ closed indefinitely), a 3rd-century Roman villa.

### ❦ PIAZZA DELLA REPUBBLICA // EXPLORE THE HEART OF THE OLD CITY

Marsala's most elegant piazza is dominated by the imposing Chiesa Madre (www.chiesamadremarsala.it; ☽ 7.30am-9pm). Although construction commenced in 1628, the church's facade wasn't completed until 1956 (courtesy of a cash donation by a returning emigrant). The cavernous interior, divided into three aisles highlighted by tall columns,

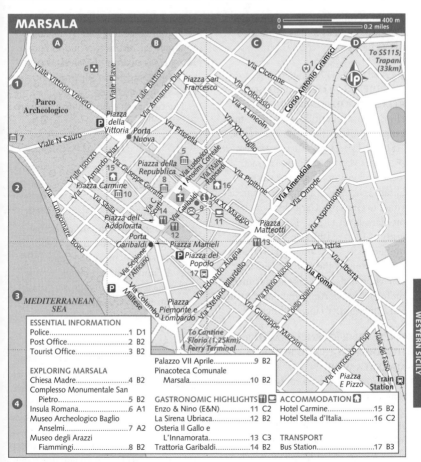

## MARSALA

contains a number of sculptures by the Gagini brothers but little else.

Located on the eastern side of the square is the arcaded **Palazzo VII Aprile**, formerly known as the Palazzo Senatorio (Senatorial Palace) and now the town hall.

Just behind the Chiesa Madre is the **Museo degli Arazzi Fiammingi** (☎ 0923 71 29 03; Via Giuseppe Garraffa 57; admission €2.50; 9.30am-1pm & 4.30-6pm Tue-Sat, 9.30am-12.30pm Sun), home to eight magnificent Flemish tapestries made in Brussels between 1530 and 1550.

## ♥ PINACOTECA COMUNALE MARSALA // SEE CONTEMPORARY ART IN A MEDIEVAL SETTING

Housed in a restored Carmelite convent that dates from 1155, when the Carmelites first came to Marsala with Roger I's widow Adelaide, this **contemporary art gallery** (☎ 0923 71 16 31; www.pinacotecamarsala.it; Piazza Carmine; admission free; 10am-1pm & 5-7pm) is primarily devoted to the municipality's relatively minor collection of paintings and sculptures by Italian artists of the 20th-century such as Mario Sironi, Giacomo Baragli,

Arnaldo Pomodoro, Fausto Pirandello, Corrado Cagli, as well as Domenico Maria Lazzaro.

### ❧ COMPLESSO MONUMENTALE SAN PIETRO // CHECK OUT SOME RELICS OF THE RISORGIMENTO

Housed in a beautifully restored 15th-century convent, this arts centre ( ☎ 0923 71 87 41; Via Ludovico Anselmi Correale; admission free; ⏲ 9.30am-1.30pm & 4-8pm Tue-Sun) attracts locals and visitors alike. The town's library is here, as is a small museum devoted to Giuseppe Garibaldi, who landed on Marsala on 11 May 1860 with his army of 1000 redshirts in the first stage of their successful campaign to conquer the kingdom of the Two Sicilies. The collection includes weapons, documents, uniforms and portraits but unfortunately lacks interpretive labels in English.

### ❧ CANTINE FLORIO // SAVOUR THE HISTORY, TASTE AND BOUQUET OF MARSALA WINE

Those keen to learn more about Marsala's famous fortified wine should sign up for a guided tour of this historic winery ( ☎ 0923 78 13 06; www.cantineflorio; Via Vincenzo Florio 1; English-language tours €5-10 depending on tasting; ⏲ tours at 11am & 4.30pm Mon-Fri, 10.30am Sat), which was established in 1833 by Vincenzo Florio Sr. The tours walk participants through the huge sweet-smelling cellars, which are home to giant vats made from Slovenian oak. Tour guides have fascinating facts aplenty to impart along the way: you'll learn, for instance, that Marsala comes in three classes (dry, medium-dry and sweet) and that 25% to 30% of Sicily's annual production is drunk in Italy, where the locals prefer it dry. The remaining 70% to 75% is exported overseas, where sweet Marsala is most popular. You'll finish in the tasting room, which is home to the

original document Lord Nelson signed in 1800 commissioning John Woodhouse to supply the British Navy with Marsala. Also here is an array of Marsala wines to taste, including Florio Superiore, the company's premium brand.

The cantine is a 30-minute walk from Piazza della Vittoria.

## GASTRONOMIC HIGHLIGHTS

### ❧ ENZO & NINO (E&N) €

☎ 0923 95 19 69; Via XI Maggio 130; ⏲ closed Wed (except in summer)

Strategically located on the main *passeggiata* route, this *pasticceria*/bar serves good coffee and an excellent range of cakes, *calzoni,* pizza slices and *arancine*. At lunch, you can sample simple dishes such as *timballi di pasta e di verdure* (oven-baked pasta and vegetables) and *torte salate* (savoury pies).

### ❧ LA SIRENA UBRIACA €

☎ 0923 02 05 00; www.lasirenaubriaca.it; Via Garibaldi 39; ⏲ closed Jan & Feb

A perfect choice for pre-dinner aperitivi and snacks, this classy *enoteca* stocks a great range of wine, olive oil, dips, olives and other local delicacies that you can try while sitting at the bar or at the outside tables. Just be careful you don't sample too many of the local tipples – the name means 'the drunken mermaid'!

### ❧ OSTERIA IL GALLO E L'INNAMORATA €€

☎ 0923 195 44 46; www.osteriailgalloelinnamorata. com; Via Stefano Bilardello 18; meals €25; ⏲ closed Tue

Marsala's only bearer of the Slow Food Movement badge has a simple but welcoming interior and a daily-changing menu of sensational dishes such as *arancinette* (small deep-fried rice balls stuffed with meat or fish), *calamari fritti e caponata* (fried calamari with slow-

## THE SWEET SMELL OF SUCCESS

Fresh out of sherry country in southern Spain, John Woodhouse's 'sweet nose' knew a business opportunity when he smelled it. The English soap merchant swiftly based himself in Marsala aiming to market its wine to the seemingly insatiable sweet palate of 18th-century England, but had to grapple with one problem: how was he to get the wine to England without it going bad? He added a dash of pure alcohol and, *voila,* Marsala's fortified wine was born.

The real success of the wine came when the British Navy used it as an alternative to port in order to supply the sailors' ration of one glass of wine per day. Lord Nelson placed a huge order in 1800, and soon other entrepreneurs wanted to get in on the action. Benjamin Ingham and his nephew, Joseph Whitaker, set up the first rival winery, exporting to the USA and Australia in 1806. The third big producer was canny Vincenzo Florio, who already owned the Egadi Islands and their lucrative tuna plants. All of the wineries were eventually bought by Cinzano in the 1920s, which merged them under the Florio label. In 1988, Cinzano sold the company to Illva Saronno, which now operates three labels: Florio, Duca di Salaparuta and Corvo.

For more information on Marsala and the companies that produce it today, see www.stradavinomarsala.it.

cooked tomatoes, aubergines, onion and courgettes (zucchini) in a sweet-and-sour sauce) and *pasta fresca gamberi, ricci e pistachio* (fresh pasta with small prawns, sea urchins and pistachios). All delicious, but in our opinion trumped by the best *scaloppine con marsala* (veal escalopes in a Marsala sauce) in Sicily, as is only appropriate in this Marsala-obsessed town.

### ❦ TRATTORIA GARIBALDI €€

☎ 0923 95 30 06; Piazza dell'Addolorata 35; meals €31; ✦ closed Sat lunch & Sun dinner

This traditional trattoria is often crowded with local family groups, who love its large vegetable and seafood antipasto buffet, predominantly seafood *secondi* and dessert array. Service can be harried and slightly begrudging as a result. It's best to order conservatively here, as the chefs don't seem as confident with specialist dishes such as *cuscus* or *involtini* (meat rolls) as they are with simply grilled fish or classic pasta dishes.

## TRANSPORT

**BOAT //** Ustica operates services between Marsala and Favignana (€9.80, 30 minutes, five daily in summer, three daily in winter).

**BUS //** AST travels to/from Trapani (€2.60, 40 minutes) and Mazara del Vallo (€2.60, 35 minutes, four daily) and Salemi runs regular daily services to/from Palermo (€8.80, 2½ hours). Buses arrive at Piazza del Popolo, off Via Mazzini in the centre of town.

**TRAIN //** The best way to travel along this part of the coast is by train. Regular services go to/from Trapani (€3.25, 30 minutes, 14 daily), Mazara del Vallo (€2.70, 15 to 30 minutes, 13 daily) and Palermo (€8, 3¼ to 3¾ hours, eight daily). You'll probably need to change at Alcamo, Trapani or Piraine for Palermo.

## MAZARA DEL VALLO

pop 51,369

Mazara's old quarter is vaguely redolent of a North African kasbah (in fact, it's known as La Casbah), full of narrow little streets that go around each other, and sprinkled with magnificent baroque and Norman-period buildings. It's small enough that you won't ever really get lost, and the dilapidated old buildings give it a rugged charm.

Mazara was one of the key cities of Saracen Sicily and the North African influence is still strongly felt here – the town is said to have one of the highest percentages of immigrants in Italy, with hundreds of people from Tunisia and Maghreb arriving annually to work on Mazara's fishing fleet. Most of the immigrants live within the labyrinth of the old town streets, giving the town a multicultural feel.

## ESSENTIAL INFORMATION

**EMERGENCIES //** Hospital (Ospedale Civico A Ajello; ☎ 0923 90 12 33; Via Salemi 175) Police ( ☎ 0923 93 27 66; Via Carlo Alberto della Chiesa 10) **TOURIST INFORMATION //** Tourist Information Point ( ☎ 0923 94 27 76; www.comune.mazara-del-vallo.tp.it/turismo, in Italian; Piazza Mokarta; ☙ 10am-12.30pm Tue, 10am-12.30pm & 4-6pm Wed, Fri & Sat, 4-6pm Sun) Just off the *lungomare* (seafront promenade), next to the castle.

## EXPLORING MAZARA DEL VALLO

### ♥ HISTORIC SITES // **EXPLORE THE ANCIENT HEART OF MAZARA**
The ragged remains of Count Roger's Norman castle have definitely seen better days, although their forlorn ruination is wonderfully atmospheric at night (when they are floodlit). The same goes for the twee little Chiesa di San Nicolò Regale (Porta Palermo; admission free), which overlooks the bustling fish market. A perfect cube, it has remained virtually unchanged since its construction in 1124.

Northwest of the church is La Casbah, a maze of tiny streets and alleyways that was once the heart of the Saracen city. Today, the area is run down but interest-

ing, if only because it retains a strong Arab connection through the Tunisians who now live here.

In summer, the town is inundated with holidaymakers who head straight to Tonnarella beach, on the western side of the city.

### ♥ MUSEO DEL SATIRO // **MARVEL AT A MASTERPIECE DREDGED FROM THE SEA**
The jewel in Mazara's crown is its Museum of the Satyr ( ☎ 0923 93 39 17; Piazza Plebiscito; admission €6; ☙ 9am-1.30pm & 3-9.30pm summer, 9am-6pm winter), located in the deconsecrated shell of the Chiesa di Sant'Egidio.

The museum tells the fascinating story of its central exhibit, a bronze statue known as *Il satiro danzante* (the Dancing Satyr). On entering, make sure you watch the 25-minute video before looking at anything else. In Italian, with English subtitles, it tells the story of a group of fishermen who were working their nets 40km off the shores of Tunisia in 1997 when they pulled up the bronze leg of a statue. Time elapsed and they continued to fish in the same area, wondering if they would ever find the rest of the statue. Extraordinarily, they did so the next year – a rare original casting from the Hellenistic era. Overcome by romanticism, the boat's captain tells the camera: 'Lying on the deck with its face turned to the sky, it looked like someone who'd clung on, waiting to be rescued'. What followed was a 4½-year period of painstaking restoration, during which time Mazara strenuously tussled with the powers in Rome to ensure the return of the satyr, which only came home in 2003.

And what a beauty. The sculpture depicts a bacchanalian satyr dancing wildly like a whirling dervish, arms outstretched, head flung back, the centrifugal force evident in his flowing hair. Originally, it would have been used in Dionysian processions – today it commands its own form of no-less-passionate worship here.

### 🌴 PIAZZA DELLA REPUBBLICA
### // ADMIRE A HANDSOME URBAN
### SPACE...WELL, MOST OF IT

Mazara's central piazza is an attractive space edged by elegant buildings, including the town's 11th-century **Cattedrale del San Salvatore** (Piazza della Repubblica; admission free; ⊙ irregular), which was completely rebuilt in the 17th century in the baroque style. Over the portal is a relief from the 16th century of Count Roger trampling a Saracen.

Other buildings on the piazza include the elegant, two-storey **Seminario dei Chierici** (dating from 1710), which houses the **Museo Diocesano** (Diocesan Museum; ☎ 0923 90 94 31; Via dell'Orologio; admission free; ⊙ 9am-1.30pm Mon-Sat), home to a library of 18th-century texts. On the opposite side of the square is the 18th-century **Seminario Vescovile**, with an impressive 11-arched portico.

Unfortunately, the 1970s office tower on the west side of the square is a visual affront of the highest order – how it managed to get a construction permit beggars belief.

## GASTRONOMIC HIGHLIGHTS

### 🌴 LA BETTOLA €€

☎ 0923 94 64 22; www.ristorantelabettola.it; Via Maccagnone 32; meals €38; ⊙ closed Wed

Mazara is Sicily's largest fishing centre, so it's not surprising that most restaurants here specialise in seafood. La Bettola is no exception, but is different to its competitors in one crucial respect – it's far, far better. Chef Pietro Sardo is

known as one of Sicily's best chefs and the dishes that emerge from his immaculate kitchen are simply sensational. Start with an antipasto plate – one hot and one cold if there are a few of you – and then be sure to try the day's fresh pasta dish, which will highlight whichever seafood was best at the market on that morning. Mains are equally tempting, with simply grilled fish and Sicilian classics such as *involtini di pesce spada* (swordfish roulade) featuring. Desserts are delicious, the wine list is impressive (including by the glass) and service is attentive. You'll find it opposite the old train station building.

### 🌴 RISTORANTE DEL PESCATORE €€€

☎ 0923 94 75 80; www.ristorantedelpescatore.com; Via Castelvetrano 191; meals €40; ⊙ closed Mon

The chef at this elegant restaurant lets his regionally sourced products speak for themselves, serving simple dishes such as prawns marinated in the juice of locally grown lemons, black peppercorns and olive oil from Castelvetrano. Desserts here are also good; try the *cassata*.

## TRANSPORT

**BOAT //** Ustica operates services between Mazara del Vallo and Pantelleria (€34, two hours, two daily six days per week) from June to September.

**BUS //** AST travels to/from Marsala (€2.60, 35 minutes, four daily) and Trapani (€5.40, 1¾ hours, one daily). Lumia runs services between Mazara and Agrigento (€8.50, two hours, three daily Monday to Saturday, one on Sunday) and Salemi runs regular services to/from Palermo (€8.30, 2½ hours). The bus station is next to the train station.

**TRAIN //** Regular services go to/from Trapani (€4.40, 50 minutes, 14 daily), Marsala (€2.70, 15 to 30 minutes, 13 daily) and Palermo (€8.30, three to 3½ hours, six daily). You'll need to change at Piraine or Alcamo for some Palermo services.

WESTERN SICILY

## AROUND MAZARA DEL VALLO

❦ **ROCCHE DI CUSA // PICNIC IN AN ANCIENT STONE QUARRY**

Most of the buttery yellow stone used to construct the great temples of Selinunte was hewn at these ancient Greek quarries. The setting is charming – overgrown and wild, it's dotted with olive trees and wildflowers. Huge column drums forever awaiting transport to Selinunte are scattered around, and if you look carefully you will come across two carved columns ready for extraction. When removed, the columns would have been transported to Selinunte across wooden logs by oxen or slaves.

To get here from Mazara del Vallo, take the SS115 to Campobello di Mazara, then follow the signs to the Rocche di Cusa (Cave di Tufo).

## SELINUNTE

The ruins of Selinunte are some of the most impressive of the ancient Greek world, and the site is one of the most captivating in Sicily. Unfortunately, the nearby village of Marinella di Selinunte hasn't retained any of its ancient predecessor's grandeur and beauty. Its smelly marina, shoddily constructed holiday accommodation and overcrowded beach should be avoided if at all possible.

There are a few tourist cafes around the site's car park and a clutch of restaurants along the waterfront, the best of which is probably **Al Ristorante Pierrot** ( ☎ 09244 62 05; www.ristorantepierrotselinunte.it; Via Marco Polo 108; meals €25-30; ☯ closed winter).

Also in the car park is a **tourist information office** ( ☯ 9am-6.30pm summer, 9am-4pm winter) that can supply a map of the site, brochures and bus timetables (Italian-language only).

**EXPLORING SELINUNTE**

Selinunte was once one of the richest and most powerful cities in the world, with over 100,000 inhabitants and an unrivalled temple-building program. The most westerly of the Greek colonies, it had been established by a group of settlers from nearby Megara Hyblaea in 628 BC who had been attracted by its wonderful location atop a promontory between two major rivers (now silted up), the Modione and Cottone, the latter forming a secure natural harbour. The plains surrounding the site were overgrown with celery (*selinon* in Greek), so the Greeks named their new colony Selinunte.

Originally allied with Carthage, it switched allegiance after the Carthaginian defeat by Gelon of Syracuse at Himera in 480 BC. Under Syracusan protection it grew in power and prestige. The city's growth resulted in a litany of territorial disputes with its northern neighbour, Segesta, which ended abruptly in 409 BC when the latter called for Carthaginian help. Selinunte's former ally happily obliged and arrived to take revenge.

Troops commanded by Hannibal utterly destroyed the city after a nine-day siege, leaving only those who had taken shelter in the temples as survivors; they were spared not out of a sense of humanity but because of the fear that they might set fire to the temples and prevent their looting. In a famous retort to the Agrigentan ambassadors who sought to negotiate for the survivors' lives, Hannibal replied that as they hadn't been able to defend their freedom, they deserved to be slaves. One year later, Hermocrates of Syracuse took over the city and initiated its recovery. In 250 BC, with the Romans about to conquer the city, its citizens were relocated to Lilybaeum (Marsala), the Carthaginian capital in Sicily, but not before they destroyed as much as they could. What they left standing, mainly temples, was finished off by an earthquake in the Middle Ages.

The city was forgotten until the middle of the 16th century, when a Dominican monk identified its location. Excavations began in 1823, courtesy of two English archaeologists, William Harris and Samuel Angell, who uncovered the first metopes.

### ❦ THE RUINS // WALK IN THE FOOTSTEPS OF THE GREEKS

The **archaeological site** (☎ 0924 46 251; www.selinunte.net; adult/concession €6/3; ☺ 9am-6.30pm summer, 9am-4pm winter) is divided into the acropolis, the ancient city, the eastern temples and the Sanctuary of Malophoros. It is spread out over a vast area dominated by the hill of Manuzza, the site of the ancient city proper, and deserves a visit of at least three hours to do it justice. The ticket office is near the eastern temples, on the western edge of Marinella di Selinunte. There are electric carts (€3 per 30 minutes) that can help mobility-impaired visitors get around the site.

### The Acropolis

The acropolis, the heart of Selinunte's political and social life, occupies a slanted plateau overlooking the now-silted-up Gorgo di Cottone. It is crossed by two thoroughfares – one running north–south, the other east–west, dividing the acropolis into four separate sections.

Huddled in the southeastern part are five temples (A, B, C, D and O). The northernmost is **Temple D**, built towards the end of the 6th century BC and dedicated to either Neptune or Venus. **Temple C**, under restoration and so covered in scaffolding when this book was being

WESTERN SICILY

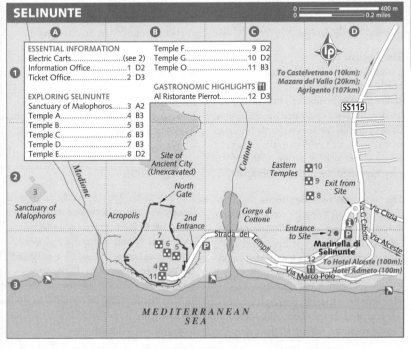

**SELINUNTE**

0 — 400 m
0 — 0.2 miles

**ESSENTIAL INFORMATION**
Electric Carts.........................(see 2)
Information Office.................1  D2
Ticket Office...........................2  D3

**EXPLORING SELINUNTE**
Sanctuary of Malophoros.......3  A2
Temple A................................4  B3
Temple B................................5  B3
Temple C................................6  B3
Temple D................................7  B3
Temple E................................8  D2
Temple F................................9  D2
Temple G..............................10  D2
Temple O..............................11  B3

**GASTRONOMIC HIGHLIGHTS** 🍴
Al Ristorante Pierrot............12  D3

To Castelvetrano (10km);
Mazara del Vallo (20km);
Agrigento (107km)

SS115

Site of Ancient City (Unexcavated)

Eastern Temples  🔟10  9  8  Exit from Site

North Gate

Modione

Sanctuary of Malophoros

Acropolis

2nd Entrance

Gorgo di Cottone

Cottone

Strada dei Templi

Entrance to Site  2  P

Via G. Caboto
Via Clizia
Via Alceste

**Marinella di Selinunte**

12  To Hotel Alceste (100m); Hotel Admeto (100m)

Via Marco Polo

7  6  5  P
4
11

*MEDITERRANEAN SEA*

researched, is the oldest temple on the site, built in the middle of the 6th century BC. The stunning metopes found by Harris and Angell were once a part of this formidable structure, as was the enormous Gorgon's mask that adorned the pediment; both of these can be viewed in the Museo Archeologico Regionale (p47) in Palermo. Experts believe that the temple was dedicated to Apollo. Adjacent is the smaller Temple B, which dates from the Hellenistic period and could have been dedicated to the Agrigentan physiologist and philosopher Empedocles, whose water-drainage scheme saved the city from the scourge of malaria (a bitter irony for William Harris, who contracted the disease during the initial excavations and died soon after). The two other temples, Temple A and Temple O, closest to the sea, are the most recent, built between 490 and 480 BC. They are virtually identical in both style and size, and it's been suggested that they might have been dedicated to the twins Castor and Pollux.

### The Ancient City
Occupying the hill of Manuzza, to the north of the acropolis, the ancient city, where most of Selinunte's inhabitants lived, is the least excavated of all the sites. Exploration of the area has only begun in recent years, and evidence suggests that survivors of the destruction of 409 BC may have used the city as a necropolis.

### The Sanctuary of Malophoros
If you walk west from the acropolis across the now-dry river Modione (formerly the Selinon) and up a dirt path, you'll reach the ravaged ruins of the temple dedicated to Demeter, the goddess of fertility, after 20 minutes or so. Amid the debris, two altars can be made out; the larger of the two was used for sacrifices. Although they're not much to look at, these are

some of the most important finds of the site as they provide an insight into the social history of Selinunte. Thousands of votive offerings to Demeter have been found in the area (nearly 12,000), including stelae crowned with real human heads.

### The Eastern Temples
North of the site entrance is the most stunning of all Selinunte's ruins, crowned by the majestic Temple E. Built in the 5th century BC and reconstructed in 1958, it stands out due to its completeness. It is the first of the three temples close to the ticket office. Next to it is Temple F, which dates from the middle of the 6th century BC and was originally decorated with metopes that are now in the collection of the Museo Archeologico Regionale in Palermo. Temple G, the northernmost temple, was built in the 6th century BC and, although never completed, was one of the largest temples in the Greek world. Today it is a massive pile of impressive rubble surrounded by an olive grove.

### View from the Beach
No visit to Selinunte is complete without a walk along the stunning stretch of beach below, from where there are marvellous views of the cliff-top temples. The path down is to the left of the acropolis parking area.

### TRANSPORT

**BUS //** Salemi (€1, 30 minutes, six daily) travels from Marinella di Selinunte to Castelvetrano's train station.
**CAR //** Take the Castelvetrano exit off the A29 and follow the brown signposts for about 6km. If you're driving from Agrigento, take the SS115 and follow the signposts.
**TRAIN //** There are services from Castelvetrano to Mazara del Vallo (€2.70, 20 minutes, 14 daily), Marsala (€3.80, 45 minutes, 14 daily) and Palermo (€7.40, 2½ hours, seven daily). If travelling to Palermo you may have to change at Cinisi, Alcamo or Piraine.

# THE BEST OF
# SICILIAN ART & ARCHITECTURE

Centuries of foreign domination have left Sicily with a lavish artistic and architectural legacy. Ancient Greek temples litter the long southern coast while blazing mosaics adorn Roman villas and Byzantine churches, and forbidding Norman castles guard remote hilltop towns. Arriving later, Sicily's baroque maestros took the style to new, mind-bending heights.

ABOVE The clocktower of Noto's splendid Cattedrale di San Nicolò (p217)

# THE BEST
# CLASSICAL CITIES

**1 VALLEY OF THE TEMPLES //
AGRIGENTO**

The model for Unesco's logo and one of
the world's best-preserved Greek temples,
the Tempio della Concordia (p254) is the
star turn of this stunning area. The ruins
are what's left of Akragas, once the fourth-
largest city in the known world.

**2 PARCO ARCHEOLOGICO DELLA
NEAPOLIS // SYRACUSE**

A major power in ancient times, Syracuse boasts one of Sicily's great classical
monuments – the Teatro Greco (p206), a
supremely well-preserved Greek amphitheatre. In the theatre's shadow, you can
explore caves where slaves once laboured.

OLIVIER CIRENDINI

### 3 SELINUNTE // THE SOUTHWEST
You don't have to be an archaeologist to be bowled over by the remarkable Greek temples at Selinunte (p95). Among Sicily's most impressive, they are beautifully set against a sunny seaside backdrop that looks particularly fabulous in spring, when wild-flowers set the scene ablaze with colour.

### 4 SEGESTA // AROUND TRAPANI
Standing in proud isolation in the midst of rugged, green hills, the ruins of ancient Segesta (p81) are an unforgettable sight. Pride of place goes to the stately 5th-century-BC temple but don't miss the amphitheatre, dramatically gouged out of the hillside.

### 5 SOLUNTO // AROUND PALERMO
Originally founded by Phoenicians in the 8th century BC, ancient Solunto (p62) underwent several incarnations, including a period as the Roman city of Soluntum. Its remaining ruins, sprawled attractively over a steep seafront hillside, mostly date to the Roman era.

TOP Springtime at the ruins of Selinunte (p95) BOTTOM LEFT Dramatic scenery surrounds the temple at Segesta (p81) BOTTOM RIGHT The magnificent Tempio della Concordia in the Valley of the Temples (p255)

# THE BEST
# BAROQUE CATHEDRALS

**1 DUOMO // SYRACUSE**

Syracuse's flamboyant cathedral (p202) lords it over the city's beautiful showpiece square. Its sumptuous facade is typically baroque but the columns that run down the side tell of a former life as a temple to the Greek goddess Athena.

**2 CATTEDRALE DI SAN NICOLÒ // NOTO**

In a town noted for its sublime baroque buildings, the spectacular Cattedrale di San Nicolò (p217) trumps the lot. Standing in monumental pomp at the top of a grandiose staircase, it stylishly fuses the best of baroque and neoclassical architecture.

RICCARDO LOMBARDO/CUBOIMAGES/PHOTOLIBRARY

### 3 CATTEDRALE DI SAN GIORGIO // RAGUSA

Fans of the TV series *Inspector Montalbano* might recognise this towering baroque cathedral (p223), often used as a backdrop. The work of Sicily's grand baroque maestro Rosario Gagliardi, it's a masterclass in overstated style and unrestrained passion.

### 4 CHIESA DI SAN GIORGIO // MODICA

A commanding presence, Modica's great cathedral (p220) looms over the town's serpentine streets and bustling medieval centre. Its stentorian facade is a stunning example of baroque on a grand scale while the echoing interior drips in silver and gold.

### 5 CATTEDRALE DI SANT'AGATA // CATANIA

The highlight of Catania's centre is its wedding-cake cathedral (p177). Dedicated to the city's patron saint Agata, it's unique among Sicily's baroque churches for its black and white tones, a reflection of the volcanic stone used in its construction.

TOP The flamboyant interior of Cattedrale di Sant'Agata, Catania (p177) BOTTOM LEFT Ragusa's stately Cattedrale di San Giorgio (p223) BOTTOM RIGHT Baroque grandeur in Chiesa di San Giorgio, Modica (p220)

# THE MOST
# MAGNIFICENT MOSAICS

**1 CAPPELLA PALATINA // PALERMO**
Sicily's greatest work of Arab Norman art
is this sparkling mosaic-encrusted chapel
in the Palazzo dei Normanni (p43). Every
inch of the arched interior is emblazoned
with golden mosaics and biblical figures.
Precious inlaid marble and an Arab-carved
wooden ceiling complete the picture.

**2 VILLA ROMANA DEL CASALE //**
**PIAZZA ARMERINA**
This villa (p238) is home to some of the
world's finest Roman mosaics. Buried
for centuries under a layer of mud, they
stand out for their scale, use of colour,
and scenes of mythological monsters and
bikini-clad girls working out with weights.

RUSSELL MOUNTFORD

### 3 CATTEDRALE DI MONREALE // MONREALE

An outstanding example of Norman architecture, Monreale's famous cathedral (p60) harbours a dazzling interior of Byzantine-influenced mosaics depicting stories from the Old Testament.

### 4 DUOMO // CEFALÙ

The robust, fortress-like exterior of this hulking Norman church (p110) guards one of Sicily's most celebrated mosaics – the depiction of Christ Pantocrator in the apse. Dating to the mid-12th century, it's a remarkably lifelike depiction of a severe man with drawn cheeks and a dark beard.

### 5 LA MARTORANA // PALERMO

A favourite venue for local weddings, Palermo's most popular medieval church (p42) is a treasure trove of Byzantine mosaics. Highlights include portraits of King Roger II, Sicily's great 12th-century Norman monarch, being crowned by Christ, and George of Antioch, the church's Syrian founder, lying at the feet of the Madonna.

TOP The stunning interior of Cappella Palatina, Palermo (p43) BOTTOM LEFT Vivid colours adorn Cattedrale di Monreale, Monreale (p60) BOTTOM RIGHT Ancient mosaics in Villa Romana del Casale, Piazza Armerina (p238)

TOP Caccamo's imposing castle (p114) RIGHT
Castello di Lombardia in Enna stands amid lush
greenery (p235)

# THE BEST MEDIEVAL FORTRESSES

**1 PALAZZO DEI NORMANNI //
PALERMO**

This palace (p43) has long been the nerve centre of island power. It once housed one of Europe's most glittering courts and it is now the seat of Sicily's regional government. Politics becomes religion which becomes art in the Cappella Palatina.

**2 CASTELLO DI LOMBARDIA // ENNA**

As impressive as this formidable 14th-century castle (p235) is, the real highlight is the sweeping panorama that unfolds from the top of Torre Pisana, the tallest of the castle's six remaining towers. As far as the eye can see, great swaths of rolling green countryside stretch off in all directions.

**3 CASTELLO // CACCAMO**

One of Italy's largest castles, Caccamo's impregnable fort (p114) served as a Norman stronghold and then a base for the powerful 14th-century Chiaramonte family. It's protected by a series of forbidding walls and ingenious fortifications, and commands magnificent views.

**4 CASTELLO VENTIMIGLIA //
CASTELBUONO**

An evocative sight, the enormous castle (p116) that gives Castelbuono its name is said to be haunted. Every month the ghost of a long-dead queen runs the lengths of its corridors, which now host a small museum and art gallery.

# TYRRHENIAN COAST

## 3 PERFECT DAYS

### ❦ DAY 1 // CEFALÙ & THE COAST

Spend the morning in Caccamo (p114), exploring its fine Norman castle. After enjoying a lunch fit for a foreign invader at A Castellana, head east along the autostrada to Cefalù (p110), a picturesque coastal town offering both historical attractions and a vibrant beach culture. Climb the steep steps up to La Rocca (p112) to enjoy a panoramic view from the ruined ramparts, and then make your way back down the hill to view the magnificent Byzantine mosaics inside the town's cathedral (p110). End your day by appreciating the backdrop of the cathedral and La Rocca over an aperitivo in Piazza del Duomo.

### ❦ DAY 2 // MADONIE GETAWAY

It's time to head for the hills. You can follow our driving tour (p120) or instead concentrate on one or two destinations – a day spent exploring the twin towns of Petralia Soprana (p118) and Petralia Sottana (p118) gives a wonderful taste of Madonie culture, as does an excursion to Castelbuono (p116) and Collesano (p120), traditional strongholds of the Dukes of Ventimiglia.

### ❦ DAY 3 // ANCIENT RUINS

If your holiday plans include a trip to the Aeolian Islands, consider allowing a day before your ferry departs from Milazzo to visit the nearby archaeological site at Tyndaris (p126). The site's spectacular clifftop setting and its evocative remnants of a basilica, theatre and agora (market place) make it well worth the effort. Afterwards, drop by the remains of a large 4th-century Roman villa at Marina di Patti (p126), where mosaic remnants are on show.

# TYRRHENIAN COAST

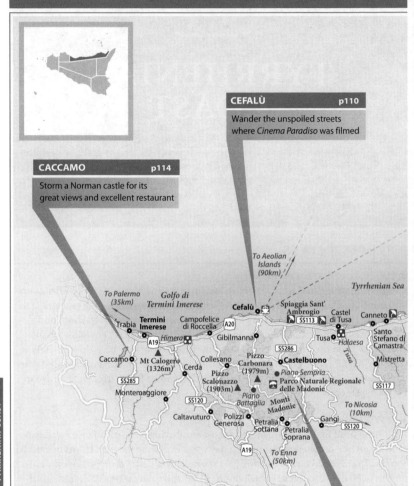

**CEFALÙ**   p110

Wander the unspoiled streets where *Cinema Paradiso* was filmed

**CACCAMO**   p114

Storm a Norman castle for its great views and excellent restaurant

To Aeolian Islands (90km)

*Tyrrhenian Sea*

To Palermo (35km)

*Golfo di Termini Imerese*

Trabia

**Termini Imerese**

Himera

Campofelice di Roccella

A20

Gibilmanna

**Cefalù**

Spiaggia Sant' Ambrogio

SS113

Castel di Tusa

Canneto

Tusa

*Halaesa*

Santo Stefano di Camastra

SS286

Caccamo

Mt Calogero (1326m)

Cerda

Collesano

Pizzo Carbonara (1979m)

**Castelbuono**

*Piano Sempria*

Mistretta

SS285

Pizzo Scalonazzo (1903m)

Parco Naturale Regionale delle Madonie

SS117

Montemaggiore

SS120

*Piano Battaglia*

Monti Madonie

To Nicosia (10km)

Caltavuturo

Polizzi Generosa

Petralia Sottana

Petralia Soprana

Gangi

SS120

A19

To Enna (50km)

**PARCO NATURALE REGIONALE DELLE MADONIE**   p115

Sample some of Sicily's best regional cuisine in this magnificent mountain landscape

## DISTANCE CHART (KM)

| | Termini Imerese | Castelbuono | Cefalù | Milazzo |
|---|---|---|---|---|
| Castelbuono | 48 | *Note: Distances are approximate* | | |
| Cefalù | 30 | 18 | | |
| Milazzo | 158 | 130 | 128 | |
| San Marco d'Alunzio | 92 | 65 | 64 | 69 |

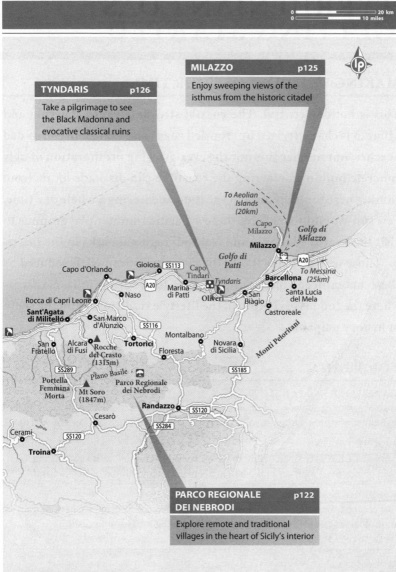

**MILAZZO**                    p125

Enjoy sweeping views of the isthmus from the historic citadel

**TYNDARIS**                   p126

Take a pilgrimage to see the Black Madonna and evocative classical ruins

**PARCO REGIONALE**            p122
**DEI NEBRODI**

Explore remote and traditional villages in the heart of Sicily's interior

0 — 20 km
0 — 10 miles

To Aeolian Islands (20km)

Capo Milazzo

*Golfo di Milazzo*

**Milazzo**

A20

To Messina (25km)

*Golfo di Patti*

**Barcellona**

Capo d'Orlando

Gioiosa   SS113

Capo Tindari

*Tyndaris*

Marina di Patti

Oliveri

San Biàgio

Santa Lucia del Mela

Rocca di Capri Leone

Naso

**Sant'Agata di Militello**

San Marco d'Alunzio

SS116

Montalbano

Novara di Sicilia

Castroreale

*Monti Peloritani*

San Fratello

Alcara di Fusi

**Rocche del Crasto** (1315m)

Floresta

**Tortorici**

SS289

Piano Basile

Parco Regionale dei Nebrodi

SS185

Portella Femmina Morta

Mt Soro (1847m)

**Randazzo**

SS120

Cesarò

SS284

Cerami

SS120

**Troina**

A20

*TYRRHENIAN COAST*

## GETTING AROUND

The A20-E90 tolled autostrada follows the coastline between Palermo and Milazzo, as does one of Sicily's busiest rail lines. Trains stop at Cefalù, Milazzo and nine other towns en route. To do justice to the Madonie and Nebrodi parks, it's a good idea to hire a car – only a few of the mountain towns are easily accessible by bus from the coast.

# TYRRHENIAN COAST
## GETTING STARTED

## MAKING THE MOST OF YOUR TIME

This is holiday central. The coastal stretch between Palermo and Milazzo is characterised by crowded roads and even-more-crowded beaches, but neither this nor the ever-growing proliferation of ugly concrete buildings marring the coastline can dissuade locals from coming here for their annual vacation and having a whale of a time. Few sun-worshippers leave these sybaritic summer playgrounds to visit the nearby Madonie and Nebrodi regional parks in the interior. Those who do make it into the mountains are swiftly seduced by these magnificent natural landscapes harbouring hilltop villages where the food is exceptional, the lifestyle traditional and the sense of history palpable.

## TOP TRAILS

### ❧ ARCHAEOLOGICAL SITES
Abandon your deck chair and umbrella for a few mornings to soak up history rather than the sun while visiting the ruins of ancient settlements such as Tyndaris (p126).

### ❧ CATHEDRALS
Every town, however small, seems to have a lavishly decorated cathedral gracing its main piazza. Start a survey of the best at the magnificent Duomo di Cefalù (p110).

### ❧ FABULOUS FORTRESSES
This coast has been fortified against possible invaders for millennia. Check out some of its sensationally sited strongholds, including the Norman castle at Caccamo (p114).

### ❧ MONTI MADONIE
Take our driving tour through the Madonie mountains, visiting historic hilltop villages and dining in acclaimed restaurants along the way (p120).

### ❧ SLOW FOOD
Discover the delights of local food products, dishes and traditions when eating your way through the Madonie (p115) and Nebrodi (p122) regional parks.

# GETTING AWAY FROM IT ALL

* **Explore Mistretta** Wander around this tranquil time capsule perched on the eastern border of the Parco Regionale dei Nebrodi (p123).

* **Savour the silence in Petralia Soprana** The cobbled streets of this charming eyrie in the Madonie mountains are often deserted (p118).

* **Soak in the thermal spa at Termini Imerese** There are plenty of therapies on offer at the historic Grand Hotel delle Terme (p114).

* **Hike the Piano Battaglia** Take an isolated walk across carpets of spring wildflowers after the ski bunnies have decamped for the beach (p119).

# BEST BEACHES

Stake a claim to a sandy patch of paradise at the following resorts and throw yourself into the swing of the Sicilian summer scene.

* **Cefalù** This wildly popular resort town balances magnificent cultural attractions with a beach scene that is as renowned as Taormina's (p110).

* **Oliveri** This sandy stretch of beach beneath the ancient settlement of Tyndaris hosts fewer holidaymakers than many of its neighbours (p126).

* **Sant'Agata di Militello** A garish funfair, *gelato* vendors, gentle waves and a seafront promenade just perfect for the *passeggiata* (evening stroll) make this boisterous resort a popular choice for families (p124).

# TOP EATING EXPERIENCES

**A CASTELLANA**
Delicious food served in the grain stores of Caccamo's Norman castle (p114).

**AL BAGATTO**
The most atmospheric *enoteca* (wine bar) on the coast (p126).

**CASALE DRINZI**
Rustic Madonie cuisine served in a welcoming Collesano chalet (p120).

**DA SALVATORE**
A family-run trattoria in the charming hilltop town of Petralia Soprana (p118).

**FIASCONARO**
Come here to sample manna cake, a heaven-sent Madonie delight (p117).

**NANGALARRUNI**
Forest-fresh mushrooms are the highlight at this Castelbuono restaurant (p117).

# RESOURCES

* **AAST Milazzo** (www.aastmilazzo.it) A map of Milazzo and other information.

* **Cefalù.it** (www.cefalu-sicily.it) A map of Cefalù and other information.

* **Parco dei Nebrodi** (www.parcodeinebrodi. it, in Italian) Official site of the Parco Regionale dei Nebrodi.

* **Parco delle Madonie** (www.parcodellema donie.it, in Italian) Official site of the Parco Naturale Regionale delle Madonie.

* **Parks.it** (www.parks.it) English-language information about the Madonie and Nebrodi parks.

TYRRHENIAN COAST

# CEFALÙ
· · · · · ·

pop 13,764

**The squares, streets and churches of this medieval town are so postcard-pretty that it's no wonder director Giuseppe Tornatore chose to set parts of his much-loved film *Cinema Paradiso* here. Unfortunately, you won't be alone in admiring the honey-hued stone buildings, mosaic-adorned cathedral and dramatic backdrop of La Rocca (the Rock) when you visit – during summer, holidaymakers from every corner of the country flock to Cefalù to relax in resort hotels, stroll the narrow cobbled streets and sun themselves on the long sandy beach.**

The town is perfectly suited to slow, pedestrianised exploration. The little port is lined with narrow fishing boats and populated with local fishermen who can often be observed maintaining their boats, mending their nets and discussing the day's catch. The *lungomare* (seafront promenade) is very popular for the *passeggiata*, as is the main street, Corso Ruggero.

Cefalù is only a one-hour rail trip from Palermo, and there is also convenient car parking next to the train station. From the front of the station building, turn right and walk down Via Gramsci to reach Via Matteotti, which heads directly into the old town centre. If you are heading for the beach, turn left from the station into Via Gramsci, then take a right down Via N Martoglio and Via Vazzano, which will bring you to the western end of the *lungomare*.

## ESSENTIAL INFORMATION

**EMERGENCIES //** Ambulance ( ☎ 118 or ☎ 0921 42 45 44) Hospital ( ☎ 0921 92 01 11;

Contrada da Pietra Pietrapollastra) Police Emergency ( ☎ 113); Questura ( ☎ 0921 92 60 11; Via Roma 15)

**TOURIST INFORMATION //** Presidio Parco delle Madonie ( ☎ 0921 92 33 27; www.parcodellemadonie.it, in Italian; Corso Ruggero 116; ☽ 7.30am-8pm) Knowledgeable and friendly staff supply information about the Madonie regional park. Tourist Office ( ☎ 0921 42 10 50; www.cefalu-sicily.it; Corso Ruggero 77; ☽ 8am-8pm Mon-Fri, 8am-2pm Sat, 9am-1.30pm Sun) Run by extremely helpful English-speaking staff.

## EXPLORING CEFALÙ

Most of Cefalù's sights are found in the historic town centre around Corso Ruggero and Piazza del Duomo. The only exception is La Rocca – to appreciate the magnificent views from this ancient eyrie you'll need to brave a steep one-hour walk up the town's famous Salita Saraceno (Saracen Staircase), which winds up through three tiers of the city walls. For fabulous sea views, make your way to the 17th-century Bastione Capo Marchiafava, off Via Bordenaro.

### ❦ DUOMO DI CEFALÙ // A MOSAIC-ADORNED OUTPOST OF NORMAN POWER

Cefalù's cathedral ( ☎ 0921 92 20 21; Piazza del Duomo; admission free; ☽ 8am-7pm Apr-Sep, 8am-5pm Oct-Mar) is one of the jewels in Sicily's Arab-Norman crown, only equalled in magnificence and beauty by the Cattedrale di Monreale and Palermo's Cappella Palatina. Legend tells us that it was built by Roger II in the 12th century to fulfil a vow to God after his fleet was saved during a violent storm off Cefalù. In fact, it was more likely the result of Roger's tempestuous relationship with the Palermitan archbishopric. Eager to curb the growing influence of the papacy in Sicily (with whom the Palermo archbishopric had close ties), Roger thought that building a mighty church so far from Palermo would prove an effective reminder of his power across the island and pose a disincentive to any potential usurpers. It's thus hardly surprising that the cathedral's architecture is distinctly fortress-like.

Inside, in the central apse, a towering figure of Christ All Powerful is the focal point of the elaborate Byzantine mosaics, which are the oldest and best preserved in Sicily (they predate those of Monreale by 20 or 30 years). In his hand, a compassionate-looking Christ holds an open Bible bearing a Latin and Greek inscription from John 8:12: 'I am the light of the world; he who follows me shall not walk in darkness.' Other mosaic groups include the Virgin with Four Archangels dressed as Byzantine officials.

The 16 interior columns with Roman capitals probably came from the Tempio di Diana on La Rocca (p112).

To the left of the main entrance are the cathedral's **cloisters** (adult/student €3/1; ⏲ 10am-1pm & 2-4pm or 6pm, depending on available light), which feature ancient columns supporting graceful Arab-Norman arches.

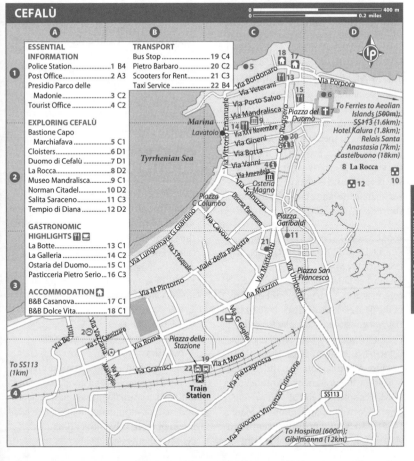

CEFALÙ

You can enjoy the view of the cathedral's soaring twin pyramid towers, framed by La Rocca, over a morning coffee or evening aperitif in the Piazza del Duomo.

### ☙ LA ROCCA // ASCEND TO THE REALM OF THE GIANTS

Looming 278m above the town, **La Rocca** (admission free; 9am-7pm May-Sep, 9am-5pm Oct-Apr) appears a suitable home for the giants that are said to have been the first inhabitants of Sicily. It was here that the Arabs had their citadel until 1063, when the Norman Conquest brought the people down from the mountain to the port below. From the summit there are wonderful views of the town below, and in the area itself are remnants of the **Norman citadel** as well as traces of the 4th- or 5th-century **Tempio di Diana** (Temple of Diana), part of an ancient acropolis that once occupied the area.

To access the site, look for the steps to the right of the Banco di Sicilia on Piazza Garibaldi. From here the path to the summit is clearly signposted. The site is gated, and is always closed in wet weather as the stairs can be dangerously slippery.

### ☙ MUSEO MANDRALISCA // SEE THE FAMOUS SMILE OF AN UNKNOWN MAN

The rather faded collection of Greek ceramics and Arab pottery on display in the **Museo Mandralisca** (☎ 0921 42 15 47; www.museomandralisca.it; Via Mandralisca 13; adult/child under 6yr/child 6-10yr/child 11-15yr €5/free/1/3; 9am-1pm & 3-7pm, till late Jul & Aug) is of marginal interest. Indeed, if it wasn't for the presence of Antonello da Messina's splendid *Ritratto di un uomo ignoto* (Portrait of an Unknown Man; 1465) there would be little incentive to visit this small, privately owned museum showcasing a collection amassed by parliamentarian, archaeologist and natural-history buff, Baron Mandralisca (1809–64).

Acquired by the Baron after he discovered it being used as a makeshift cupboard door in Lipari, da Messina's painting is considered to be one of the most distinctive portraits of the Italian Renaissance. The unnamed subject sports a smirk that is almost as enigmatic and thought provoking as the Mona Lisa's – albeit without the attendant hype.

### ☙ THE BEACH // CLAIM A PATCH OF THIS PEOPLE'S PARADISE

Cefalù's crescent-shaped beach is one of the most popular along the whole coast. In summer it is packed, so be sure to arrive early to get a good spot. Though some sections require a ticket, the area closest to the old town is public and you can hire a beach umbrella and deck chair for approximately €15 per day.

## GASTRONOMIC HIGHLIGHTS

Despite being packed with restaurants, Cefalù is one of the only major towns on the island to be totally ignored by both the Gambero Rosso and Osteria D'Italia (Slow Food Movement) restaurant guides – a damning but deserved indictment. There are only a few establishments worthy of recommendation:

### ☙ LA BOTTE €€

☎ 0921 42 43 15; Via Veterani 20; meals €29; closed Mon

This small, family-run restaurant just off Corso Ruggero serves a good choice of antipasti, seasonally driven pasta dishes and seafood-dominated mains. The fixed menu of three fish courses plus a side dish (€26) offers good value.

### ✽ LA GALLERIA €€

☎ 0921 42 02 11; www.lagalleriacefalu.it; Via XXV Novembre 22-24; meals €35; ✌ closed Thu all year & Mon in winter

This is about as hip as Cefalù gets. Functioning as a restaurant, cafe, internet point, bookshop and occasional gallery space, La Galleria has an informal vibe and an elegant internal garden where dishes such as fresh pasta with mushrooms and black truffles are served. The chef's aspiration towards culinary innovation is signalled by the popular four-course degustation menus on offer (fish €30 and meat €25).

### ✽ OSTARIA DEL DUOMO €€

☎ 0921 42 18 38; www.ostariadelduomo.it; Via Seminario 5; meals €30; ✌ closed Mon

Its outdoor tables facing the cathedral and reputation for serving fresh dishes utilising locally sourced produce make this a safe choice. Try the house speciality of *carpaccio de pesce* (raw, thinly sliced fish) accompanied by your selection from the extensive wine list.

### ✽ PASTICCERIA PIETRO SERIO €

☎ 0921 42 22 93; Via G Giglio 29; ✌ closed Wed & btwn 1-3.30pm Sep-Jul

The town's best coffee, *gelato* and cakes can be found at this popular *pasticceria* (pastry shop) near the train station.

## TRANSPORT

**BOAT //** Ustica Lines ( ☎ 0923 87 38 13; www.usticalines.it) runs a daily hydrofoil service between Cefalù and the Aeolian Islands between 1 June and 16 September (€20.25 to €43 one-way depending on Aeolian destination). During the same period, it also runs hydrofoils to/from Palermo (€17.95, one hour, one daily). Tickets are available at Pietro Barbaro ( ☎ 0921 42 15 95; Corso Ruggero 82).

**BUS //** Buses depart from outside the train station regularly from Monday to Saturday, with occasional Sunday services. AST ( ☎ 840 000323; www.aziendasicilianatrasporti.it, in Italian) and Lombardo & Glorioso ( ☎ 0921 92 11 79; www.lombardoeglorioso.it, in Italian) operate occasional services to Castelbuono. SAIS ( ☎ 091 704 12 11; www.saistrasporti.it, in Italian) travels to Palermo (€5.40, one hour, four daily), Castelbuono (€2.50, 90 minutes, six daily) and other destinations in the Madonie. Sommatinese ( ☎ 0921 42 43 01; www.sommatinese.it, in Italian) operates a local service to Gibilmanna.

**CAR & MOTORCYCLE //** Cefalù is situated just off the A20-E90 toll road that travels between Messina and Palermo. To hire a bike, Vespa or motorbike, try

## ACCOMMODATION

There are plenty of options along the coast, though most tend to be heavily booked in summer. In the mountains, a decent room can be harder to find, particularly in the Parco Regionale dei Nebrodi. Here are four of our favourites:

★ A luxury retreat set in a former Benedictine monastery, Relais Santa Anastasia (p308) is between Cefalù and Castelbuono.

★ Albergo Il Castello (p308) offers great value in Petralia Sottana.

★ One of Sicily's first art hotels, Atelier sul Mare (p309) is located right at the water's edge at Castel di Tusa.

★ The welcoming Green Manors Country Hotel (p309) is an *agriturismo* (farm stay) 9km outside the medieval town of Castroreale.

For detailed accommodation listings, see p308.

Scooters for Rent ( ☎ 0921 42 04 96; www.scootersforrent.it; Via Matteotti 13b; per day/week 50cc Vespas €35/175, city bikes €10/45).

**PARKING //** Finding a car park can be a nightmarish challenge in summer. Try the convenient car parking next to the train station (€2 for the first two hours and €1 every extra hour) or on the *lungomare*.

**TRAIN //** Regular services go to Palermo (from €4.90, 45 minutes to 1¼ hours, 13 daily) and virtually every other town on the coast.

# AROUND CEFALÙ

· · · · · ·

### ♥ TERMINI IMERESE // SIGN UP FOR A THERMAL SPA THERAPY

The Romans discovered the therapeutic value of Termini Imerese's mineral-laden waters way back in 252 BC, and the town has been a popular thermal spa centre ever since. These days, all of the spa action occurs at the Grand Hotel delle Terme ( ☎ 091 811 35 57; www.grandhoteldelleterme.it; Piazza delle Terme 2; per person with half-pension €120-820; P ✂ ⌘ ), a large Liberty-style building dating from 1890. Built on the site of the original Roman baths, the hotel's natural steam baths and bathing pools are popular with Italians seeking treatment for conditions including obesity, rheumatism, psoriasis and bronchial problems. The complex also includes a 'beauty farm' offering cosmetic and relaxation treatments.

From the Grand Hotel delle Terme, in the lower town, you can walk to the upper town to visit a clutch of churches, including the 17th-century cathedral and Chiesa di Santa Maria della Misericordia (Church of Our Lady of Mercy) and the 14th-century Chiesa di Santa Caterina (Church of Saint Catherine), which has lovely 15th-century frescoes illustrating the life of the saint by local artists Nicolo and Giacomo Graffeo. Unfortunately, the coast surrounding the town is blighted with an ugly commercial port.

Trains travel between Termini Imerese and Cefalù (€3.25, 30 minutes, 13 daily) and between Termini Imerese and Palermo (€3.25, 25 to 45 minutes, every 20 minutes). AST operates buses to/from Cefalù (€3.20, one hour, three daily) and Palermo (€3.20, one hour, four daily). The train station is southeast of the town centre along the coast; all buses arrive and depart just in front of the train station.

### ♥ CACCAMO // SPEND A DAY IN A NORMAN STRONGHOLD

Lorded over by its imposing castle ( ☎ 0918 14 92 52; admission €2; ⊙ 9.30am-1pm & 4-8.30pm Mon-Sat May-Sep, 9.30am-1pm & 3-7.30pm Mon-Sat Oct-Apr), the hilltop town of Caccamo is a popular day trip from both Cefalù and Palermo. Though the area was settled in ancient times, the town was officially founded in 1093, when the Normans began building their fortress on a rocky spur of Monte San Calogero. The castle was enlarged by the noble Chiaramonte family in the 14th century and is now one of Italy's largest and most impressive, with walls and fortifications that originally included ingenious traps for any intruder who might have breached the outer perimeter.

Beyond the castle's first gate, a ramp leads to a broad courtyard that gives access to the Torre Mastra, from where you can enjoy a magnificent 360-degree view of the surrounding countryside.

Nestled in the shadow of the castle, accessed downhill from Corso Umberto I, is the picturesque Piazza Duomo. It's home to an 11th-century cathedral known as the Chiesa Madre, which is dedicated to St George. Remodelled twice (in 1477 and 1614), the cathedral's sacristy has some lovely carvings of the *Madonna con bambino e angeli* (Madonna with Child and Angels) and *Santi*

TYRRHENIAN COAST

*Pietro e Paolo* (Sts Peter and Paul), both by Francesco Laurana.

For lunch, make your way to the Slow Food–celebrated **A Castellana** (☎ 091 814 86 67; www.castellana.it; Piazza dei Caduti 4; set menus €20-24; ☺ closed Mon), located in the grain stores of the castle. It has a panoramic terrace for summer dining and is renowned for its assured treatment of classic Sicilian dishes. You can order à la carte or opt for an excellent-value set menu comprising four courses plus coffee.

Caccamo is on the SS285 between Palermo and Agrigento. **Randazzo** (☎ 091 814 82 35; www.autobusrandazzo.altervista.org, in Italian) buses travel to/from Cefalù (€3.90, 70 minutes, one daily), Palermo (€3.90, 70 minutes, four daily) and Termini Imerese (€2.90, 30 minutes, eight daily). There are no Sunday services.

❦ **HIMERA // VISIT AN ANCIENT BATTLEGROUND WHERE GREEKS FOUGHT CARTHAGINIANS**
Founded in 648 BC by Greeks from Zankle (now Messina), this usually deserted **archaeological site** (admission €2; ☺ 9am-6pm Mon-Sat, 9am-1pm Sun) was named after the river Imera, which flows nearby. It was the first Greek settlement on this part of the island and was a strategic outpost on the border of the Carthaginian-controlled west. In 480 BC the town was the scene of a decisive battle, with the combined armies of Theron of Agrigento and Gelon of Syracuse defeating a sizable Carthaginian army led by Hamilcar, who threw himself on the funeral pyre of the Carthaginian dead in a heroic act of self-immolation. The Carthaginians had intended to take Himera and then wrest control of the island from Greek hands, but the Greek victory put an end to all that. In 409 BC, Himera paid the price for Carthage's defeat, when Hamilcar's nephew Hannibal destroyed the town in revenge for his uncle's death.

Unfortunately, the remains here are disappointing when compared with other Greek sites around the island. The only recognisable ruin is the **Tempio della Vittoria** (Temple of Victory), a Doric structure supposedly built to commemorate the defeat of the Carthaginians. Whatever its origin, Hannibal did a good job of destroying it.

Some artefacts recovered from the site are kept in a small **antiquarium** about 100m west of the site's entrance (it's up a small lane off the other side of the main road). Although the more impressive pieces are in Palermo's Museo Archeologico Regionale (p47), you can still see well-sculpted lion-head spouts that were used to drain water off the temple's roof.

**Nancini & Saso** (☎ 091 814 44 97; www.nancinisaso.com) buses travel between Termini Imerese and Villaura, stopping at Himera en route (€2.30, 15 minutes, three daily Monday to Saturday).

# PARCO NATURALE REGIONALE DELLE MADONIE
· · · · · ·

**Travellers making their way between Palermo and Cefalù have the option of visiting two very different destinations within the space of a few days. After spending time jostling with armies of sun-seeking holidaymakers on the over-developed coast, savvy visitors inevitably choose to abandon their deckchairs and head to the hills to savour the spectacular scenery and tranquil surrounds of the 400-sq-km Madonie regional park.**

The Monti Madonie (Madonie mountains) are crowned by Pizzo Carbonara –

at 1979m the highest mountain in Sicily after Mt Etna – and the regional park takes in farms, hilltop towns and ski resorts.

Here, the seasons are distinct: spring sees spectacular spreads of wildflowers carpeting the mountain slopes; autumn brings with it wild mushrooms and the rich hues of forest foliage; winter prompts downhill action on the ski slopes; and June and July offer blissfully cool temperatures and an escape from the coastal crowds.

This is an area where people live and work, not just a nature reserve, meaning that you can combine hiking with visits to historic hilltop towns and meals in some of Sicily's best restaurants. It's perfectly suited to slow, culturally rich travel.

The body responsible for the park is **Ente Parco delle Madonie** ( ☎ 0921 68 40 11; www.parcodellemadonie.it, in Italian; Corso Paolo Agliata 16, Petralia Sottana; ⏰ 9am-3.30pm Sun & Mon, 3.30-7.30pm Tue-Sat), which has its headquarters (the Presidio) in Petralia Sottana and a branch office, **Presidio Parco delle Madonie** ( ☎ 0921 92 33 27; Corso Ruggero 116; ⏰ 7.30am-8pm) in Cefalù. The offices have details about the park and several one-day walks, as well as information about transport and accommodation. They also stock the 1:50,000 *Madonie/Carta dei Sentieri e del Paesaggio* map, which highlights the region's walking trails.

# CASTELBUONO

**pop 9296 / elev 423m**
The charming capital of the Madonie is set amid ancient manna ash and chestnut forests. It owes much of its building stock and character to the Ventimiglias, a powerful noble family who ruled the town between the 14th and 16th centuries.

There is a **Park Information Office** ( ☎ 0921 67 11 24; www.comune.castelbuono.pa.it, in Italian; ⏰ 9am-1pm & 3-6pm Mon-Sat, 9am-1pm Sun) on the town's main street, Via Umberto 1.

## EXPLORING CASTELBUONO

**♥ CASTLE // BRAVE A GHOSTLY ENCOUNTER IN THIS MEDIEVAL FORTRESS**
Originally known as the *Castello del Buon Aere* (Castle of Good Air), the enormous castle ( ☎ 0921 67 12 11; Piazza Castello) that soars

---

**TYRRHENIAN COAST**

## GETTING TO THE MADONIE REGIONAL PARK

The best way to explore the park is by car, but it's also possible to access the major towns by bus from the coast.

### BY CAR

To access the park from Termini Imerese, head east for 22km along the coastal SS113 to Campofelice di Roccella and then turn off for Collesano, 13km inland. From Cefalù it is even easier: just follow the directions for the Santuario di Gibilmanna (Sanctuary of Gibilmanna), 14km to the south on the SP54bis.

### BY BUS

SAIS and AST operate services from Palermo to Castelbuono via Termini Imerese and Collesano (€5.40, 2½ hours, eight daily Monday to Saturday, one on Sunday). Both AST and Lombardo & Glorioso operate services from Cefalù to Castelbuono (€2.50, 90 minutes, four daily) via Collesano (€2.90, 45 minutes, five daily). SAIS also operates one service per day between Cefalù and the Madonie, stopping at Polizzi Generosa, Petralia Sottana and Petralia Soprana.

above Castelbuono's golden patchwork of houses gave the town its name and is its most distinctive landmark. Built by Francesco I Ventimiglia in 1316, it was closed for renovation at the time of research but will offer displays on local archaeology and Castelbuono's history when it reopens.

Popular legend has it that the castle is haunted by the 14th-century Queen Constance Chiaramonte, who is said to run along the corridors, regular as clockwork, on the first Tuesday of the month. At the heart of the fortress is the **Cappella di Sant'Anna** (Chapel of St Anne), which dates from 1683 and is decorated with marvellous stuccowork from the school of Serpotta. It houses the supposed skull of the saint in a silver urn.

### ☙ MUSEO NATURALISTICO FRANCESCO MINÀ PALUMBO // LEARN ABOUT THE NATURAL HISTORY OF THE MADONIE

Named after the naturalist Francesco Minà Palumbo (1837–99), this unassuming **museum** (☎ 0921 67 18 95; www.museominapalumbo.it; Via Roma 72; adult/concession €6/3; 🕙 9am-1pm & 3-7pm) is housed in the former convent of Santa Venera. It's home to a collection of artefacts that gives an exhaustive insight into the botany, natural history, minerals and archaeology of the Madonie mountains.

## GASTRONOMIC HIGHLIGHTS

Castelbuono's rustic regional cuisine showcases fruits of the Madonie such as *funghi di bosco* (forest mushrooms) and *cinghiale* (wild boar).

### ☙ A RUA FERA €

☎ 0921 67 67 23; Via Roma 71; 🕙 closed Tue (except in summer) & all of Oct

His use of gourmet local ingredients make Antonio Marannano's pizzas a cut above the competition. His pasta dishes are also delicious, with choices such as *pappardelle fresche con funghi di stagione* (fresh pappardelle noodles with seasonal mushrooms) featuring on a small but tempting menu.

### ☙ FIASCONARO €

☎ 0921 67 12 31; www.fiasconaro.com; Piazza Margherita 10; 🕙 closed Wed

Home of *mannetto* (manna cake), a local speciality, this much-loved *pasticceria* on the main road leading to the castle is packed with treats such as buttery *cornetti* (croissants), decadently sweet *cassata siciliana* and the unusual *testa di Turco* (Turk's head; blancmange with puff pastry in the middle). Its home-made *gelato* is also very good. The *pasticceria* is on one side of the road and the Fiasconaro cafe is opposite – it's perfectly acceptable to purchase your sweet treat at the *pasticceria* and take it to the cafe.

### ☙ NANGALARRUNI €€

☎ 0921 67 14 28; www.hostarianangalarruni.it; Via Alberghi delle Confraternite 10; meals €35; 🕙 closed Wed

Famous throughout Sicily for its delicious dishes featuring forest mushrooms and wild boar, Nangalarruni deserves equal renown for its wine list, which features a wide range of local vintages as well as selections from throughout Italy. To try a number of the house specialities, consider opting for the four-course set menu (€32). Slow Food–recommended.

### ☙ ROMITAGGIO €€

☎ 0921 67 13 23; www.romitaggio.it; Contrada da San Guglielmo; meals €30; 🕙 closed Wed

Make your way to this ancient Benedictine monastery, 4km from Castelbuono on the San Guglielmo road, to sample traditional Madonita dishes including antipasto with *salsicce secche* (dried sausage), *ricotta fresca* (fresh ricotta),

TYRRHENIAN COAST

*provola della madonie* (local provolone cheese) and home-preserved olives. Slow Food–acclaimed delights such as *capretto aggiassato* (stewed kid) and *coniglio alla menta* (rabbit with mint) are highlights of the menu. Note: no credit cards.

# PETRALIA SOPRANA

**pop 3562 / elev 1147m**
Beautifully positioned at the top of a hill above a tree line of pines, Petralia Soprana (from the Italian word *sopra*, meaning 'on' or 'above') is one of the best-preserved small towns in north-central Sicily, full of picturesque stone houses and curling wrought-iron balconies brimming with geraniums. It's also the highest village in the Madonie. There's not much for visitors to do except wander around the narrow cobbled lanes, visit a couple of churches and have lunch at Da Salvatore (p118).

## EXPLORING PETRALIA SOPRANA

### 😋 A WALK AROUND TOWN // VISIT A CLUTCH OF CHURCHES

For a small town, Petralia Soprana possesses a lot of churches. The most beautiful is the 18th-century **Chiesa di Santa Maria di Loreto**, at the end of Via Loreto, off the main square, Piazza del Popolo (follow the signs to Da Salvatore). Inside is an altarpiece by Gagini and a *Madonna* by Giacomo Mancini. To the right of the church through an arch is the town's belvedere, with views across the valley and to Etna on a clear day. The town's **cathedral**, located on the opposite side of Piazza del Popolo off Piazza dei Quattro Cannoli, was consecrated in 1497 and has an elegant 18th-century portico and a 15th-century *campanile* (bell tower). It is dedicated to Sts Peter and Paul.

## GASTRONOMIC HIGHLIGHTS

### 😋 DA SALVATORE €

☎ 0921 68 01 69; Piazza San Michele 3; meals €20; 🕐 closed Tue (except in summer), dinner in winter, 2 weeks in Jul & 2 weeks in Sep

Salvatore Ruvutuso, his wife Maria and their three children run this acclaimed trattoria near the Chiesa di Santa Maria di Loreto and have infused the place with a wonderfully welcoming, family-friendly atmosphere. Kick off with a selection of the delicious antipasti (be sure to include the pungent, Slow Food–acclaimed *provola delle madonie* and the frittata) and then choose from a daily menu that will probably feature a rustic pasta, vegetable soup or fragrant stew. Pizzas are only served in the evening. Note: no credit cards.

## TRANSPORT

**CAR & MOTORCYCLE //** To reach Petralia Soprana from Petralia Sottana, drive up Corso Paolo Agliata to Piazza Umberto and follow the winding narrow road leading uphill from the right-hand side of the Chiesa Madre, veering right at the first fork.

**PARKING //** There is limited free car parking in Piazza del Popolo. Alternatively, park on the side of the road leading uphill into town.

# PETRALIA SOTTANA

**pop 3143 / elev 1000m**
Below Petralia Soprana, the town of Petralia Sottana (from the Italian *sotto*, meaning 'under') is the gateway to the regional park and the headquarters of the **Ente Parco delle Madonie** (☎ 0921 68 40 11; www.parcodellemadonie.it, in Italian; Corso Paolo Agliata 16; 🕐 9am-3.30pm Sun & Mon, 3.30-7.30pm Tue-Sat), which is located in the foyer of the municipal building and supplies maps and walking itineraries for the Madonie. Staff at the Museo Civico Antonio Collisani (p119) supply brochures and information about both the town and the park.

## EXPLORING PETRALIA SOTTANA

**☙ A WALK AROUND TOWN // JOIN THE LOCALS FOR THE EVENING PASSEGGIATTA**

Petralia Sottana is dominated by its main street, Corso Paolo Agliata, which is a popular shopping strip during the day and hosts the town's surprisingly busy *passeggiata* in the early evening. Like Petralia Soprana, the town possesses a number of handsome churches, including the baroque Chiesa di San Francesco on the Corso and the 17th-century Chiesa Madre at the end of the Corso on Piazza Umberto. The *campanile* of the latter is the town's major landmark. On the road leading to Petralia Soprana is the Chiesa di Santissima Trinità alla Badia, which has a handsome marble altarpiece carved by Giandomenico Gagini.

**☙ MUSEO CIVICO ANTONIO COLLISANI // POP IN TO VISIT THE FOSSILS**

☎ 0921 64 18 11; www.petraliasottana.net, in Italian; Corso Paolo Agliata 100; adult/concession €2/1; ⏲ usually 9am-7pm but hr can vary

Focusing on the archaeology and geology of the Madonie, this small but interesting museum has an impressive display of fossils found in the area and is worth a short visit. There's also an excellent education centre for young children (resources in Italian only).

## GASTRONOMIC HIGHLIGHTS

**☙ PETRAE LEJUM €**

☎ 0921 04 19 47; Corso Paolo Agliata 113; meals €19; ⏲ closed Fri dinner (except in Aug)

The atmosphere at this place leaves something to be desired (garish murals, ugly knick-knacks along with a blaring TV), but the warm welcome, delicious food and bargain prices well and truly compensate. Menu highlights include a sophisticated range of salads, loads of wild-boar dishes and a lavish and delicious mixed antipasto plate. It's a Slow Food showcase.

## TRANSPORT

**PARKING //** There is a car park overlooking the valley right where the road takes a dog-leg turn into Corso Paolo Agliata.

# AROUND PETRALIA SOTTANA

**☙ PIANO BATTAGLIA // SKI, WALK OR BIKE THE MADONIE'S SLOPES**

More Swiss than Sicilian, the little ski resort at Piano Battaglia (www.piano battaglia.it, in Italian) is dotted with chalets that play host to an ever-growing number of Sicilian downhill skiers in winter.

The Mufara (northern slopes) skiing complex goes up to heights of 1840m and serves 3.5km of runs, while the Mufaretta (southwest slopes) reaches 1680m, with a run about 500m long. There are two ski lifts up to the ski runs. You can also do cross-country and alpine skiing.

With the advent of spring Piano Battaglia becomes an equally good walking and mountain-biking area, with plenty of signposted paths and a profusion of wildflowers. One popular walk starts at the Rifugio Ostella della Gioventù Piero Merlino in Piano Battaglia and heads north–northwest, taking in Pizzo Scalonazzo (1903m) and Pizzo Carbonara to end in an area of oak woodland at Piano Sempria (1300m). The hostel (p308) can help you with itineraries and guides.

# COLLESANO

**pop 4144 / elev 917m**

The upper reaches of this charming medieval town are dominated by the pink-and-cream Basilica San Pietro on Corso Vittorio Emanuele and the weathered remains of a nearby Norman castle. Like Castelbuono, the town was once governed by the Ventimiglias and retains an aristocratic air. There are a number of churches worthy of a visit, including the frescoed 15th-century Duomo (aka Santa Maria la Nuova), the 12th-century Chiesa di St Maria la Vecchia, the 17th-century Chiesa di St Maria del Gesù and the early-16th century Chiesa di St Giacomo.

## EXPLORING COLLESANO

☙ **MUSEO TARGA FLORIO // TAKE A SPIN THROUGH AUTOMOTIVE HISTORY**

After visiting the town's churches, consider making a pit stop at the Museo Targa Florio ( ☎ 0921 66 46 84; www.museo targaflorio.it; Corso Vittorio Emanuele 3; adult/over 65yr €2/1; ☼ 9.30am-12.30pm & 4-7.30pm Tue-Sun Apr-Oct, 9.30am-12.30pm & 3-6.30pm Nov-Mar, closed Thu afternoon Nov-Mar). The museum displays photographs and memorabilia documenting the Targa Florio, which is the oldest sports-car racing event in the world.

Established by wealthy automobile enthusiast Vincenzo Florio in 1906, the 72km-race along the treacherous narrow roads of the Monti Madonie had an extremely high degree of difficulty, with the circuit's hairpin bends testing both the driver's skill and the car's performance (Porsche won the most times, followed closely by Alfa Romeo). The race was discontinued in 1977 due to safety concerns.

## GASTRONOMIC HIGHLIGHTS

☙ **CASALE DRINZI €**

☎ 0921 66 40 27; www.casaledrinzi.it; Contrada Drinzi, SP9; pizzas €3.50-6.50, meals €17; ☼ closed most of Feb

This wooden chalet in the hills immediately above Collesano is a gem. Rustic dishes issue from the always-busy kitchen and feature Slow Food–recognised regional ingredients such as *Fagiolo Badda Nera* (beans grown in the area around Polizzi Generosa). Treats such as the *degustazione di antipasti* (a plate of stuffed zucchini flowers, deep-fried ricotta, *lardo*-topped bruschetta and chargrilled local onions) and *pappardelle al sugo di selvaggina* (home-made pasta ribbons with a game sauce) are only two of the universally pleasing dishes on offer. Pizzas are added to the menu at night – a good reason to book into the on-site B&B (singles/doubles €30/50).

# DRIVING TOUR: MONTI MADONIE

**Map p121**
**Distance: approximately 113km**
**Duration: one, two or three days**

This tour takes in the most picturesque towns in the Madonie mountains and rewards leisurely exploration if you can spare two or three days. To see everything in one day is possible, but will be tiring.

From Cefalù, follow the winding SP54bis for approximately 15km to reach the Santuario di Gibilmanna (1; ☎ 0921 42 18 35; ☼ 8.30am-1pm & 3.30-5pm, till 8pm in summer), spectacularly perched 800m above sea level on a slope of the Pizzo Sant'Angelo mountain peak. Here, in the 17th century, the Virgin Mary is supposed to have restored sight to two blind worshippers and speech to a mute. The miracle was later confirmed by the

Vatican, and consequently the church has become one of Sicily's most important shrines. The views over the Madonie from the belvedere in front of the church are quite spectacular.

From Gibilmanna, head southeast on the SP9 for approximately 18km towards **Castelbuono** (2; p116), presided over by its magnificent 14th-century castle, and then take the winding SS286 to the picturesque mountain town of **Petralia Soprana** (3; p118), 35km south in the heart of the regional park. The road is poorly maintained, with lots of potholes,

but is fringed by dense forest and offers wonderful views over the valleys.

After lunching in Petralia Soprana or its sister town of **Petralia Sottana** (4; p118), take the SS120 to the charming town of **Polizzi Generosa** (5), nestled at the entrance to the Imera Valley. The 19km drive will take approximately 30 minutes. Given the nomenclature *generosa* (generous) by Frederick II in the 1230s, the town is now primarily known as a trekking base for the Madonie, and is riddled with churches that are often shrouded in mist. While here, be sure

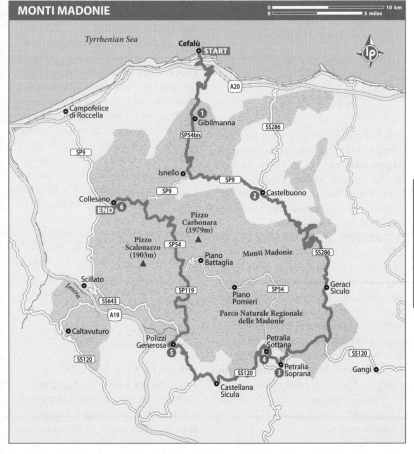

MONTI MADONIE

TYRRHENIAN COAST

to visit the Chiesa Madre, home to a Flemish depiction of the *Madonna and Child with Angels* from the early 16th century, and a *Madonna of the Rosary* by Giuseppe Salerno.

The last stop on your tour is the medieval town of Collesano (6; p120), approximately 26km northwest on the SP119 and SP54 (an alternative route is via the SS643 and SP54). After exploring the compact upper town, you can choose to overnight in the simple rooms at Casale Drinzi (p120) on the eastern outskirts of town, or take the picturesque one-hour drive along the SP9 back to Castelbuono and check into the Relais Santa Anastasia (p308) to spend a day or two relaxing amid idyllic surrounds.

# PARCO REGIONALE DEI NEBRODI
· · · · · ·

**The Nebrodi regional park was established in 1993 and constitutes the single largest forested area in Sicily. In fact, this is Sicilian author Gesualdo Bufalino's real 'island within an island', dotted with remote and traditional villages that host few visitors.**

The forest ranges in altitude from 1200m to 1500m, and is an undulating landscape of beech, oak, elm, ash, cork, maple and yew trees that shelter the remnants of Sicily's wildlife: porcupines, San Fratello horses and wildcats, as well as a healthy population of birds of prey such as golden eagles, lanner and peregrine falcons and griffon vultures. The high pastures have always been home to hardworking agricultural communities that harvest delicious mushrooms, churn out creamy ricotta, and graze cows, sheep, horses, goats and pigs.

The highest peak in the park is Monte Soro (1847m), and the Lago di Biviere is a lovely natural lake supporting herons and stilts.

Accessing information about the park can be difficult. There are several information offices (Alcara di Fusi ☎ 0941 79 39 04, Via Ugo Foscolo 1; Bronte ☎ 338 299 30 77, Castello di Nelson; Cesarò ☎ 095 773 20 61, Via Bellini 79; Mistretta Via T Aversa 26; Radazzo ☎ 095 799 16 11, Corso Umberto 197), but all keep irregular hours and most staff speak Italian only. For more information, see www.parks.it/parco.nebrodi or www.parcodeinebrodi.it.

# SAN MARCO D'ALUNZIO

**pop 2098 / elev 550m**
This spectacularly situated hilltop town, 9km from the coast, was founded by the Greeks in the 5th century BC and then occupied by the Romans, who named it Aluntium and built structures such as the Tempio di Ercole (Temple of Hercules) at the town's entrance. A Norman church, now roofless, was subsequently built on the temple's red marble base.

Southeast of the town is the trekking base, Longi, and southwest is Alcara di Fusi, a small village situated beneath the impressive Rocche del Crasto (1315m), a nesting site of the golden eagle.

The tourist information office (🕙 9am-1pm & 3-7pm) is opposite the Chiesa Madre on Via Aluntia. There are – sadly – no cafes or restaurants in the town worthy of recommendation.

## EXPLORING SAN MARCO D'ALUNZIO

❦ A WALK AROUND TOWN //
**EXPLORE AN ARRAY OF NORMAN AND BYZANTINE MONUMENTS**
Virtually all of San Marco d'Alunzio's older buildings and its 22 churches were

TYRRHENIAN COAST

## GETTING TO THE NEBRODI REGIONAL PARK

The best way to explore the park is by car, as bus services are few and far between.

### BY CAR

The SS116 starts at Capo d'Orlando on the coast, climbs to Floresta (1275m), the highest village in the park, and then makes a spectacular descent to Randazzo, with unforgettable views of Mt Etna.

Cutting through the heart of the park is the enchanting SS289, which links Sant'Agata di Militello with Cesarò in the interior. Along the route is San Fratello, a typical Nebrodi town originally founded by Roger I's third wife, Adelaide di Monferrato, for her Lombard cousins (hence the strange local dialect).

### BY BUS

Interbus ( ☎ 0935 22460; www.interbus.it, in Italian) operates services between Santo Stefano di Camastra and Mistretta (35 minutes, five daily Monday to Friday, fewer on weekends), Messina and Cesarò (three hours, one daily Monday to Saturday), Messina and Mistretta (two hours, one daily) and Messina and Randazzo (two hours, one daily).

made using locally quarried marble. The most impressive of the churches is the Chiesa di Santa Maria delle Grazie, where there's a Domenico Gagini statue of the *Madonna con bambino e San Giovanni* (Madonna with Child and St John) from 1481. Next to the 16th-century Chiesa di San Teodora is the Museum of Byzantine & Norman Culture & Figurative Art ( ☎ 0941 79 77 19; Badia Nica, Via Ferraloro; admission €1.60; �9am-1pm & 3.30-7pm), a lovely space showing fresco fragments from the town's churches and a somewhat motley collection of columns, capitals and other bits and pieces that have been excavated in the area surrounding the town. At the top of the hill are the scant remains of the first castle built by the Normans in Sicily.

## AROUND THE NEBRODI REGIONAL PARK

❤ MISTRETTA // TAKE A SCENIC DETOUR TO A NEBRODI TIME CAPSULE

Located on the western border of the park, accessed via the SS117 from Santo

Stefano di Camastra, is the charming hilltop time capsule of Mistretta. The streets here have hardly changed over the past 300 years, and most of the locals look as if they've been around for almost as long. Little disturbs the mountain quietude – the only action occurs at the Gran Bar (164 Via Libertà; ☉5.45am-1pm & 2.35-10pm Wed-Mon), an old-fashioned bar/*pasticceria* housed in a building dating from 1660. Its homemade biscuits are delicious; be sure to sample a few.

## COASTAL RESORT VILLAGES

The 83km stretch of coastline between Cefalù and Capo d'Orlando to the east is dotted with little coves, relatively clean beaches and family-friendly resort villages. Beyond Capo d'Orlando the coast becomes more developed and industrialised the closer you get to Milazzo, the main point of departure for the Aeolian Islands.

TYRRHENIAN COAST

## TOP FIVE

### PANORAMIC VIEWS

Whether it be across the Tyrrhenian Sea to the Aeolian Islands or over the spectacular forests of the Madonie and Nebrodi regional parks, you'll never be short of opportunities to appreciate great vistas when travelling through this part of the island.

★ **Ancient ruins, Tyndaris** (p126) Spectacular sea views from this clifftop archaeological site

★ **Belvedere, Petralia Soprana** (p118) A dramatic vista of the Monti Madonie

★ **Belvedere, Santuario di Gibilmanna** (p120) All the way to the peak of Pizzo Carbonara

★ **Ramparts, Caccamo Castle** (p114) You'll view sea on one side, mountains on the other

★ **Ruins of La Rocca, Cefalù** (p112) Appreciate a bird's-eye view of the town and sea

---

❦ CASTEL DI TUSA // SEE WHERE CLASSICAL RUINS AND CONTEMPORARY ART COEXIST

Named after the castle that now lies in ruins 600m above it, this small coastal resort about 25km east of Cefalù is best known for the controversial **Fiumara d'Arte**, an open-air sculpture park featuring a collection of contemporary artworks scattered along the *fiumara* (riverbed) of the Tusa River. From the beach, a small road leads 9km inland to the parent village of Tusa. Between the coastal resort and the village you'll see a signpost for **Halaesa** (admission €2; ☽ 9am-1hr before sunset), a Greek city founded in the 5th century BC. Beautifully positioned on a hill, it commands fine views of the surrounding countryside and – on a clear day – the Aeolian Islands. The most conspicuous remains are those of its agora and its massive, rusticated walls. Just down the hill are the barely recognisable remains of a small theatre.

The town is serviced by trains from Milazzo (€7, 1½ to 1¾ hours, 10 daily) and Palermo (€6.10, 1½ hours, nine daily). The station is at Tusa.

❦ SANT'AGATA DI MILITELLO // VISIT THE GATEWAY TO THE NEBRODI MOUNTAINS

This popular resort town grew up around the Torre della Marina, a coastal watchtower erected in the 13th century. In summer it's usually crammed with Italians eager to make the most of the long stretch of pebbled beach. There are few cultural sites other than the much-modified **Castello Gallego** (☽ 8.30am-12.30pm & 3.30-7.30pm Tue-Sat) in the town centre.

Sant'Agata is a gateway for the Parco Regionale dei Nebrodi, and if you are going to head into the park it may be worth starting your trip with a quick visit to the **Museo Etno-Antropologico dei Nebrodi** (☎ 0941 72 23 08; Via Cosenz 70; admission free; ☽ 8.30am-1.30pm Mon-Sat), which has displays on traditional mountain life.

There are frequent trains from Milazzo (€4.95, one hour, 18 daily) and Palermo (from €7.70, 1¾ to two hours, 15 daily).

❦ CAPO D'ORLANDO // JOIN THE SEASIDE SWIMMING SCENE

The busiest resort town on the coast after Cefalù, Capo d'Orlando was founded –

legend tells us – when one of Charlemagne's generals, a chap called Orlando, stood on the headland and declared it a fine place to build a castle. The ruins of this structure are still visible. In 1299 Frederick II of Aragon was defeated here by the rebellious baron Roger of Lauria, backed up by the joint forces of Catalonia and Anjou. More-recent rebels include the town's shopkeepers and traders, who made a name for themselves in the 1990s with their stand against the Mafia's demands for *pizzo* (protection money).

Visitors come here for the beaches, both sandy and rocky, that are on either side of town. The best swimming is to the east.

There is a tourist office ( ☎ 0941 90 33 29; www.aastcapodorlando.it, in Italian; Via A Volta 11; ☯ 9am-1pm & 4-7pm Mon-Fri, 9am-1pm Sat). The best restaurant in town is La Tartaruga ( ☎ 0941 95 50 12; www.hoteltartaruga.it; Via Lido San Gregorio 41; meals €35; ☯ closed Mon & Nov) in the seafront hotel of the same name.

The best way to get here is by train from Milazzo (€4.40, 40 to 50 minutes, 19 daily) or Palermo (from €7.95, 2¼ hours, 14 daily).

# MILAZZO

· · · · · ·

### pop 32,590

**Hardly Sicily's prettiest town, Milazzo is hemmed in on its eastern perimeter by industrial development that can make even the most open-minded visitor run for the nearest hydrofoil. Indeed, the prime reason for setting foot in this town is to get to the Aeolian Islands. But, away from the refineries and busy dock, Milazzo has a pretty *Borgo Antico* (Old Town), and the isthmus that juts out to the north is an area of great natural beauty dotted with rocky coves.**

The town's new archaeological museum was due to open in late 2010; for details, inquire at the tourist office in the attractive main square, Piazza Caio Duilio.

## ESSENTIAL INFORMATION

**EMERGENCIES //** Ambulance ( ☎ 118) Hospital ( ☎ 090 929 52 62; Contrada Grazia) Police Emergency ( ☎ 113); Questura ( ☎ 090 923 03 11)
**TOURIST INFORMATION //** Tourist Office ( ☎ 090 922 28 65; www.aastmilazzo.it; Piazza Caio Duilio 20; ☯ 8.30am-1.30pm Mon-Sat & 3-6pm Mon only) Located in a former Carmelite convent dating from the 16th century.

## EXPLORING MILAZZO

❦ IL CASTELLO // STAND WHERE GARIBALDI STORMED THE RAMPARTS
Milazzo's enormous castle was built by Frederick II in 1239 and added to by Charles V Aragon. It was originally the site of a Greek acropolis, then that of an Arab-Norman citadel. At one time the whole of Milazzo fitted within its huge walls, which command great views of the bay and the Aeolians. In 1860, Garibaldi's troops successfully stormed the castle, which was at that time manned by Bourbon soldiers.

To access the castle, climb the Salita Castello, which rises up through the atmospheric Old Town. The site was closed for restoration at the time of research, so opening hours and entry fees were unavailable.

❦ CAPO MILAZZO // TAKE A PANORAMIC DRIVE ALONG THE ISTHMUS
If you have a car, it's worth driving along the Strada Panoramica around Capo Milazzo; the rugged coastline is quite beautiful. Alternatively, you can arrange

a boat trip (ask at the tourist office) around the rocky cape to **Baia del Tonno** on the western side of the isthmus. Right at the end of the isthmus is the lighthouse, from where you can take a short walk down to the **Santuario Rupestre di San Antonio da Padova** (☙ Sun), situated beside the crystal-clear waters.

# GASTRONOMIC HIGHLIGHTS

### ❦ AL BAGATTO €€

☎ 090 922 42 12; Via Massimiliano Regis 11; meals €30; ☙ closed lunch, all day Sun & 2 weeks in Sep

Enter the frosted-glass doors of this bustling *enoteca* and it will be immediately apparent that you've made the right dining choice. It features mellow jazz and even-more-mellow lighting, there's a fabulous wine list and the genial host stops by every table to check that everything is just as it should be (which it inevitably is). The menu is strong on local, Slow Food–celebrated dishes such as *costolette di maialino nero in salsa di senape all'antica* (cutlet of black pork in a mustard-fruit sauce). There are only seven tables, so be sure to make a booking – if you don't score a table, you can join the local bohemian set and prop yourself at the bar to enjoy a delicious plate of antipasto and glass of wine.

### ❦ SALAMONE E MARE €€€

☎ 090 928 12 33; Strada Panoramica 36; meals €55; ☙ closed Mon, except in summer

North along the isthmus, this restaurant has a terrace that juts out over the water, endowing it with wonderful views that are perfectly complemented by a menu dominated by locally caught seafood,

---

## ∼ WORTH A TRIP ∼

To visit the beautiful ruins at Capo Tindari, turn off the autostrada at the sign for Oliveri, from where signs will direct you to the **Santuario della Madonna** (Sanctuary of the Madonna; ☎ 0941 36 90 03; www.santuariotindari.it; ☙ 6.45am-12.45pm & 2.30-6pm Mon-Sat, till 7pm Sun, closes 1hr later in Jul & Aug). If you're coming from the west, the site is 6km from Patti on the SS113.

The enormous church can be seen from miles around: it sits right on the cape, its dome glistening in the sun. A sanctuary was built here in the 16th century to house the icon of the *Bruna Madonnina del Tindari* (Black Madonna of Tindari), but the current garishly decorated building mainly dates from the 20th century. The inscription underneath the icon reads *Nigra sum, sed hermosa* (I am black, but I am beautiful).

From the sanctuary, a path leads to the entrance of a more ancient holy place, **Tyndaris** (☎ 0941 36 90 23; adult/EU student under 18yr or over 65yr/EU student €2/free/1; ☙ 9am-7pm), founded by Dionysis of Syracuse after his victory over the Carthaginians in 396 BC. The secluded ruins (a basilica, agora, Roman house and Greek theatre) are set on the cliff edge amid prickly pears, olives and cypress trees. In summer you can clearly see the Aeolian Islands and the lovely Oliveri lagoon in the bay below. There's also a small museum displaying artefacts excavated at the site.

If you're keen to view more Roman ruins after seeing these, purchase a combined ticket (€3/free/1.50) to Tyndaris and the remnants of the 4th-century **Villa Romana** (☎ 0941 36 15 93; ☙ 9am-1hr before sunset), located in Marina di Patti beneath the motorway viaduct. Walkways erected over the original floors of this large villa allow visitors to see what's left of ornate mosaics featuring hunting scenes and floral designs.

simply but expertly prepared. Dishes such as the *carpaccio di pescespada* (thinly sliced raw swordfish) and *spaghetti ai gamberi* (spaghetti with prawns) will please every palate.

# TRANSPORT

**BOAT //** The main ferry and hydrofoil operators (Ustica Lines, Siremar and NGI) all have ticket offices along Via dei Mille opposite the port. See p142 for details of ferry travel between Milazzo and the Aeolian Islands.

**CAR & MOTORCYCLE //** Milazzo is situated just off the A20-E90 toll road that travels between Messina and Palermo.

**INTERCITY BUS //** Buses depart from Piazza della Repubblica near the port. Giuntabus ( ☎ 090 67 57 49; www.giuntabustrasporti.com) runs an hourly service to/from Messina (€3.80, 50 minutes, 15 daily Monday to Saturday, three Sunday).

**LOCAL BUS //** AST buses 4 and 5 run between the train station and port every 35 minutes between 6.35am and 8.10pm (on Sundays there are fewer departures and the last service is at 4.35pm). Bus 6 goes to Capo Milazzo. Tickets (€0.90, valid for two hours) can be bought inside the train station or at the shop opposite the quayside bus stop with the AST sign.

**PARKING //** If you want to leave your car here while you island-hop, private garages charge approximately €12 per day. Street parking (within blue lines only) costs €0.35 per 30 minutes.

**TAXI //** A taxi from the station to the port will cost approximately €13.

**TRAIN //** Regular services travel to Palermo (from €10.10, 2¼ to 3½ hours, 14 daily) and Messina (€3.25, 20 to 40 minutes, 19 daily).

# AEOLIAN ISLANDS

## 3 PERFECT DAYS

### ☘ DAY 1 // EXPLORING LIPARI & VULCANO

Get off to a good start with a pastry and cappuccino at Pasticceria Subba (p138), before heading up to Lipari Town's citadel (p135) to explore the Museo Archeologico Eoliano (p136) and its extensive archaeological collection. Afterwards, grab a quick bite to eat and head down to Marina Corta for a boat tour (p138) of the island and neighbouring Vulcano (p143). Remember your swimsuit as you'll have the chance to swim and wallow in Vulcano's famous mud baths (p144). End the day with dinner back in Lipari Town.

### ☘ DAY 2 // STROMBOLI'S FIERY VOLCANO

Catch a hydrofoil to Stromboli (p153) at the far north of the archipelago. Spend the morning relaxing on the black sandy beaches (p157) and strolling the tiny white-washed streets. Lunch on seafood in preparation for the day's main event – the sunset trek up the volcano (p155). It's a five- to six-hour hike but you'll be rewarded (hopefully) with a spectacular fireworks display over the Sciara del Fuoco (p156).

### ☘ DAY 3 // LAID-BACK SALINA

Enjoy a day of relative tranquillity on Salina (p147), the second largest and most verdant of the islands. Have a quick look around Santa Marina Salina (p148), then pick up some wheels and head off to Malfa (p149) to taste the local Malvasia wine. Nearby, the beach at Pollara (p149) is famous for its role in the film *Il Postino*. Spend the evening in Lingua (p148), delighting over the *granite* (crushed-ice drinks) and delicious seafood.

## TRANSPORT

**AIR //** The only way to get to the Aeolian Islands by air is to take a helicopter. Between June and September **Air Panarea** ( ☎ 090 983 44 28; www.airpanarea. com) operates transfers from Reggio di Calabria airport to Lipari, Vulcano, Salina and Panarea (all €200); Filicudi (€240); Stromboli and Alicudi (both €300).

**BOAT //** The main point of departure for the Aeolians is Milazzo (p125), from where there are regular year-round car ferries and hydrofoils. There are also year-round services from Messina, Reggio di Calabria and Naples, and summer-only services from Cefalù and Palermo. Services are most frequent between June and September and much reduced in winter, when heavy seas can affect schedules. Ferries are cheaper, less frequent and much slower than hydrofoils, although they are less vulnerable to bad weather. The main operating companies are **Ustica Lines** ( ☎ 0923 87 38 13; www.usticalines.it), which operates hydrofoils only; **Siremar** ( ☎ 892123; www.siremar.it), which has hydrofoils and ferries; and **NGI** ( ☎ 800 250000; www.ngi-spa.it), which runs ferries only. Note that the information listed below refers to high-season crossings and is not comprehensive – check the respective company websites for more detailed information. From Milazzo, there are hydrofoils to Vulcano (€14.90, 45 minutes, 17 daily), Lipari (€15.80, one hour, 18 daily), Salina (€17.25, 1½ to two hours, 12 daily), Panarea (€17.80, 2¼ hours, eight daily), Stromboli (€21.45, three hours, eight daily), Filicudi (€22.75, 2½ hours, three daily) and Alicudi (€22.75, 3¼ hours, three daily). Get tickets from the sales offices on Via dei Mille. Year-round Ustica Lines hydrofoils also serve Lipari from Messina (€22.90, 1½ to 3¾ hours, five daily summer, one daily winter) and Reggio di Calabria (€23.90, two to three hours, four daily summer, one daily winter), with summer-only services from Cefalù (€29.90, 3½ hours, one daily) and Palermo (€38.70, four hours, two daily). Siremar runs ferries from Naples to Lipari (€59, 13½ hours, twice weekly) and the other islands. Lipari is the Aeolians' main transport hub, with connections to all the other islands – see p142 for further details.

**BUS //** Between April and September **Giuntabus** ( ☎ 090 67 37 82; www.giuntabustrasporti.com) runs a daily shuttle bus between Catania airport and Milazzo, leaving Milazzo at 8.45am and Catania at 5pm. The journey takes one hour and 50 minutes and tickets, available on the bus, cost €12. You can also book tickets for a private shuttle bus (€25 per person, minimum two people, up to five departures daily) covering the same route on www.eoliebooking.com.

**CAR & MOTORCYCLE //** If you are only visiting the islands for a couple of days, it'll probably be too expensive to take your own car – leave it in a garage in Milazzo (from €12 per day – see p127) – but for longer trips, it works out cheaper than hiring one. You can take cars onto Lipari, Vulcano and Salina, all of which also have scooter- and car-rental outlets. Note, however, that restrictions apply and between July and September you can only take a car if you have booked accommodation for at least seven days.

# LIPARI
· · · · · ·

### pop 11,240

**Lipari is the largest, busiest and most accessible of the Aeolian Islands. The main focus is Lipari Town, the archipelago's principal transport hub and the nearest thing that islanders have to a capital city. A busy little port with a pretty, pastel-coloured seafront and plenty of accommodation, it makes the best base for island hopping. Away from the town, Lipari reveals a rugged and typically Mediterranean landscape of low-lying *macchia* (dense shrubland), silent, windswept highlands, precipitous cliffs and dreamy blue waters.**

Named after Liparus, the father-in-law of Aeolus (the Greek god of the winds), Lipari was settled in the 4th millennium BC by the Stentillenians, Sicily's first known inhabitants. These early islanders developed a flourishing economy based on obsidian, a glassy volcanic rock used to make primitive tools. Commerce continued under the Greeks, but the arrival of the Romans in the 3rd century BC signalled the end of the islanders' good

*(Continued on page 134)*

AEOLIAN ISLANDS

# AEOLIAN ISLANDS

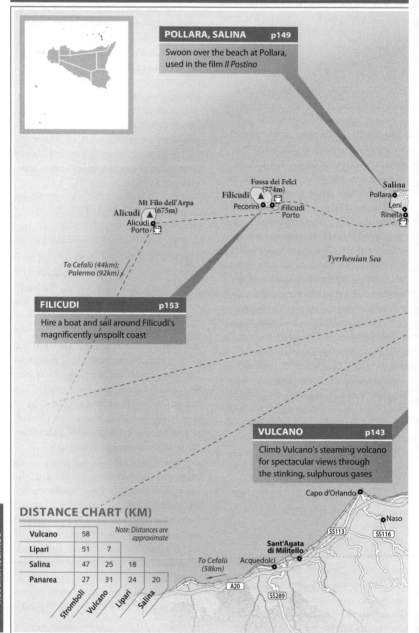

**POLLARA, SALINA** p149

Swoon over the beach at Pollara, used in the film *Il Postino*

Fossa dei Felci (774m)

**Filicudi**

Pecorini

Filicudi Porto

**Salina**

Pollara

Leni

Rinella

Mt Filo dell'Arpa (675m)

**Alicudi**

Alicudi Porto

*Tyrrhenian Sea*

To Cefalù (44km); Palermo (92km)

**FILICUDI** p153

Hire a boat and sail around Filicudi's magnificently unspoilt coast

**VULCANO** p143

Climb Vulcano's steaming volcano for spectacular views through the stinking, sulphurous gases

Capo d'Orlando

Naso

SS113

SS116

Sant'Agata di Militello

To Cefalù (58km)

Acquedolci

A20

SS289

## DISTANCE CHART (KM)

*Note: Distances are approximate*

| | Stromboli | Vulcano | Lipari | Salina |
|---|---|---|---|---|
| Vulcano | 58 | | | |
| Lipari | 51 | 7 | | |
| Salina | 47 | 25 | 18 | |
| Panarea | 27 | 31 | 24 | 20 |

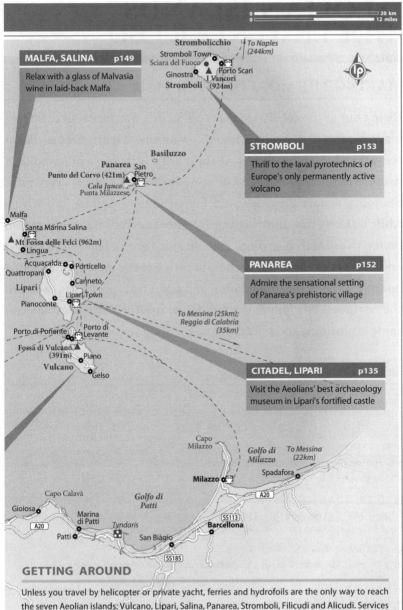

**MALFA, SALINA** p149

Relax with a glass of Malvasia wine in laid-back Malfa

**STROMBOLI** p153

Thrill to the laval pyrotechnics of Europe's only permanently active volcano

**PANAREA** p152

Admire the sensational setting of Panarea's prehistoric village

**CITADEL, LIPARI** p135

Visit the Aeolians' best archaeology museum in Lipari's fortified castle

## GETTING AROUND

Unless you travel by helicopter or private yacht, ferries and hydrofoils are the only way to reach the seven Aeolian islands: Vulcano, Lipari, Salina, Panarea, Stromboli, Filicudi and Alicudi. Services run year-round, with most passing through Lipari, the main transport hub. You can take cars onto Lipari, Vulcano and Salina, but you'll need to check for summer restrictions. Boats and scooters are available for hire on all the islands, and bikes and cars on some.

# AEOLIAN ISLANDS
## GETTING STARTED

## MAKING THE MOST OF YOUR TIME

Rising out of the cobalt-blue seas off Sicily's northeastern coast, the Unesco-protected Aeolian Islands (Vulcano, Lipari, Salina, Panarea, Stromboli, Filicudi and Alicudi) are a little piece of paradise, a magical outdoor playground offering thrills and spills at every turn. Stunning waters provide sport for swimmers, sailors and divers while trekkers can climb hissing volcanoes and gourmets can sup on honey-sweet Malvasia wine. The obvious base is Lipari, the largest and liveliest of the seven islands, but it's not the only option. Salina boasts excellent accommodation and good transport links, while to the northeast, Stromboli is a holiday in itself with its awesome volcanic explosions, great beaches and thrilling sense of isolation.

## TOP TOURS & COURSES

**❧ CULINARY SALINA**
A gourmet delight, Salina is famous for its sweet Malvasia wine. You can visit vineyards and take cooking lessons at the Capo Faro resort near Malfa (p149).

---

**❧ FILICUDI'S WATERS**
Sail around the gloriously unspoilt Filicudi coastline with I Delfini, taking in sea caves and jutting rock towers (p153).

---

**❧ LIPARI BOAT TOUR**
Explore Lipari's plunging cliffs and hidden coves on a boat trip. Make sure to bring your swimsuit so you can splash around in the inviting waters (p138).

---

**❧ STROMBOLI TREK**
Sign up with Magmatrek to hike Stromboli's volatile volcano and witness spouting fountains of red-hot lava lighting up the night sky (p155).

---

**❧ VULCANO'S VOLCANO**
It might not smell very nice, but it's a hair-raising experience to stand on the summit of Vulcano's Fossa di Vulcano and watch streams of sulphurous vapour emerging from the crater (p143).

---

# GETTING AWAY FROM IT ALL

For much of the year the Aeolians lie peacefully undisturbed, but once the summer season hits its stride the islands' population almost doubles. But if you know where to go you can always find a quiet backwater.

★ **Escape to Salina's hinterland** Away from the coast, Salina's rural interior is a green and tranquil haven (p149).

★ **Flee to Filicudi** This tiny speck of an island rarely gets very busy, even in the height of the season (p153).

★ **Sail out to Alicudi** If you really want to get away from it all, you can't get much further than Alicudi, one of the Mediterranean's most isolated spots (p153).

# ADVANCE PLANNING

Once you've booked your accommodation (p302), which is always worth doing, there's not a great deal you'll need to prepare, although you'd do well to consider the following:

★ **Taking a car** Work out if it's worth taking a car and check whether restrictions apply (p142).

★ **Check weather reports** The easiest way to get to the Aeolians is by *aliscafo* (hydrofoil), but services are sometimes suspended in bad weather.

★ **Trekking on Stromboli** You can only climb Stromboli with a guide. It's usually OK to book a day or so ahead, but in busy periods try for up to a week in advance (p155).

# TOP SWIMMING SPOTS

☙ **CAMPOBIANCO (LIPARI)**
Slide down natural pumice chutes into crystalline azure waters (p139).

☙ **FORGIA VECCHIA (STROMBOLI)**
The best of Stromboli's black volcanic beaches, sandwiched between limpid waters and green mountain slopes (p157).

☙ **PISCINA DI VENERE (VULCANO)**
Transparent turquoise waters in a natural rock amphitheatre (p145).

☙ **POLLARA (SALINA)**
A tiny, rocky beach backing onto a volcanic crater, made famous by the film *Il Postino* (p149).

☙ **SPIAGGIA VALLE I MURIA (LIPARI)**
Dwarfed by dark plunging cliffs, this pebbly beach is Lipari's best (p139).

# RESOURCES

★ **Eolie Booking** (www.eoliebooking.com) Book a shuttle bus from Catania Airport to Milazzo, plus accommodation.

★ **Estate Eolie** (www.estateeolie.net) News and practical tips on all seven islands.

★ **Lipari Comune** (www.comunelipari.it) Transport information, accommodation lists, links and island maps.

★ **Lipari Tourist Office** (www.aasteolie.191.it) Has a wealth of practical and inspirational info on all the islands.

*(Continued from page 129)*

fortunes. The Roman authorities were in a vengeful mood after the islanders had sided against them in the First Punic War, and reduced the island to a state of poverty through punitive taxation. Over the next thousand years or so, volcanic eruptions and pirate attacks – most famously in 1544, when Barbarossa burnt Lipari Town to the ground and took off with most of its female population – kept the islanders in a state of constant fear. Unremitting poverty ensured large-scale emigration, which continued until well into the 20th century, leaving the island remote and unwanted. During Italy's fascist period in the 1930s, Mussolini used Lipari Town's castle to imprison his political opponents. Things gradually started to improve with the onset of tourism in the 1950s, and now Lipari sits at the heart of one of Sicily's most revered holiday destinations.

## ESSENTIAL INFORMATION

**EMERGENCIES //** Ambulance ( ☎ 090 988 54 67) Farmacia Sparacino ( ☎ 090 981 13 92; Via Vittorio Emanuele 174; ☉ 10am-1pm & 5-9pm) Ospedale Civile ( ☎ 090 988 51 11; Via Sant'Anna) Operates a first-aid service. Police Station ( ☎ 090 981 13 33; Via Guglielmo Marconi)

**TOURIST INFORMATION //** Tourist Office ( ☎ 090 988 00 95; www.aasteolie.191.it; Via Vittorio Emanuele 202; ☉ 9am-1pm & 4.30-7.30pm Mon-Fri, 8.30am-1.30pm Sat & Sun Jul & Aug) The only tourist office in the Aeolians. Pick up a free copy of *Ospitalità in Blu*, which contains details of accommodation and services on all the islands.

## ORIENTATION

Hydrofoils and ferries dock at Marina Lunga, one of two ports at Lipari Town (the other is Marina Corta on the other side of the clifftop citadel). From the hydrofoil jetty, walk up to the small

## ACCOMMODATION

Aeolian accommodation is largely seasonal, with most places opening between Easter and October. Hotels (accommodation on the islands is mainly in hotels) tend to be three-star and above, with prices universally high. That said, standards are also high and you'll find some really lovely places to stay. Lipari, Stromboli and Salina offer the most choice.

★ A magnificent retreat, Salina's **Hotel Signum** (p311) has the lot: an infinity pool, tasteful rooms, a spa complex and a terrace restaurant.

★ With a range of rooms in the heart of Lipari Town, **Diana Brown** (p309) offers value for money, location and a portside welcome.

★ Modest, difficult to get to, and cut off from the world, Filicudi's **Pensione La Sirena** (p312) offers sunny rooms in a quiet corner of paradise.

★ Perfectly placed for the beach at Canneto (3km from Lipari Town), **Casajanca** (p309) oozes rustic charm.

★ Relax into the Stromboli beach scene at **La Sirenetta Park Hotel** (p311), a stylish waterfront complex.

For detailed accommodation listings, see p309.

roundabout near the Esso petrol station, and you'll see the main street, Via Vittorio Emanuele, running off southwards. All of Lipari Town's sights are within easy walking distance of this central strip. Marina Corta is south of the town centre, at the end of Via Garibaldi. For the nearest beach, follow the seafront road north out of town and continue through the tunnel to Canneto, about 3km away. This road continues around the island, a journey of about 30km.

# EXPLORING LIPARI

Lipari's main sights, such as they are, are in Lipari Town. However, to find the best swimming spots and enjoy some sensational views you'll need to head into the island's rugged hinterland.

## LIPARI TOWN

Although it's the main tourist centre in the Aeolians, Lipari Town hasn't yet sold its soul, and it retains a charming, laid-back island vibe. There are few sights beyond the soaring clifftop citadel and archaeological museum, but it's lovely to stroll the labyrinthine alleyways with the sun on your face and nothing to do but enjoy the relaxed atmosphere.

### ☙ CITADEL // EXPLORE ARCHAEOLOGICAL TREASURES IN LIPARI'S HILLTOP CASTLE

After the pirate Barbarossa rampaged through Lipari in 1544, murdering most of the men and enslaving the women, the island's Spanish overlords fortified Lipari by constructing a citadel (also known as the castle) around the main town centre. The town has since moved downhill but much of the citadel's impregnable wall structure survives.

LIPARI ISLAND

To Salina (10km); Filicudi (33km); Alicudi (50km); Cefalù (94km); Palermo (142km)

La Parete dei Gabbiani
Punta Castagna
Acquacalda
Porticello — Spiaggia della Papesca
Rocche Rosse
Quattropani
Mt Pilato (476m)
Campobianco
Old Kaolin Mine
Mt Chirica (602m)
Spiaggia Bianca
Pietra del Bagno
Canneto
Mt San Angelo (594m)
San Calogero
Pianoconte
To Panarea (20km); Stromboli (40km); Naples (284km)
Secca del Bagno
Lipari Town
Quattrocchi
To Messina (65km); Reggio di Calabria (75km)
Spiaggia Valle i Muria
Tyrrhenian Sea
To Vulcano (6km)
To Milazzo (40km)
Pietra Menalda
Bocche di Vulcano

### Cattedrale di San Bartolomeo

The best approach to the citadel is Via Concordato, a stairway that leads up from Via Garibaldi to the Cattedrale di San Bartolomeo. A fine example of 17th-century baroque architecture, the church was built to replace the original Norman cathedral, which was destroyed by Barbarossa. Despite his Arab name (Khair-ed-din Barbarossa), Barbarossa was born on a Greek island under Ottoman control, and eventually became an Ottoman admiral. Little remains of the 12th-century original except for a section of Benedictine cloister to the right of the main entrance. The interior is hung with chandeliers and features a silver statue of St Bartholomew (1728), Lipari's patron saint, with his flayed skin tucked under his arm.

There are a few other baroque churches up here, but more interesting are the

AEOLIAN ISLANDS

archaeological ruins. In the sunken area opposite the cathedral, you can see the remains of a series of circular huts, the oldest of which date to the 17th century BC. Nearby, at the southern end of the citadel, you'll find some Greek sarcophagi displayed at the Parco Archeologico, and an open-air amphitheatre that was built in 1978.

### Museo Archeologico Eoliano

If you're at all interested in early Mediterranean history, the collection of prehistoric and ancient finds at the Museo Archeologico Eoliano ( ☎ 090 988 01 74; Via del Castello; admission adult/under 18yr & over 65yr/18-25yr €6/free/3; ⏰ 9am-1.30pm & 3-7pm Mon-Sat, 9am-1.30pm Sun) is considered one of the most complete in Europe. The museum is divided into several sections, each housed in a separate building, but the two most important are the Sezione Preistorica (Prehistoric Section) in the Palazzo Vescovile (Bishop's Palace) next to the Cattedrale, and the Sezione Classica (Classical Section) over on the other side of the church. At the time of writing, the Sezione Classica was the only section open in the afternoon.

The Sezione Preistorica is devoted to artefacts found on Lipari, beginning with the Neolithic and Bronze Ages upstairs and continuing in chronological order to the Greek era downstairs. It provides a fascinating insight into the development of the island's earliest cultures. Amid the plethora of artefacts is some finely sculpted obsidian, telling evidence of the relative sophistication of the island's prehistoric civilisation. Prehistoric finds from the other islands are housed in a small pavilion directly in front of the Palazzo Vescovile.

On the other side of the cathedral is the Sezione Classica and its collection of finds from Lipari's 11th-century BC necropolis. These include a sizable collection of burial urns as well as models of a Bronze Age burial ground and Lipari's necropolis. Upstairs is an impressive array of decorated vases and the museum's most treasured items: the world's largest collection of Greek theatrical masks.

There are also a number of statuettes – the one of *Andromeda con bambino* (Andromeda with Child) is particularly beautiful – and some elegant jewellery. The next room contains polychromatic vases decorated by an artist simply known as Il Pittore Liparoto (the Lipari Painter; 300-270 BC).

Other sections worth a quick look are the Sezione Epigrafica (Epigraphic Section), over the road from the Sezione Preistorica, which has a small garden littered with engraved stones and a room of Greek and Roman tombs; and the Sezione Vulcanologica (Vulcanology Section), which illustrates the Aeolians' vulcanological geology.

### ♥ TOWN CENTRE // EXPERIENCE THE EXUBERANT STREET LIFE

One of the great pleasures of Lipari Town is simply wandering its streets, browsing the souvenirs, planning your next meal, enjoying the bright colours – in short, lapping up the laid-back island atmosphere. Lipari's liveliest street is Via Vittorio Emanuele, a cheerful thoroughfare lined with bars, cafes, restaurants and delis. About two-thirds of the way down, you'll see a lush, technicolour fruit display announcing the presence of Fratelli Laise ( ☎ 090 981 27 31; Via Vittorio Emanuele 118), a traditional greengrocer's piled high with wines, sweets, *anis* (aniseed) biscuits, pâtés, capers and olive oils – an excellent place to stock up on picnic

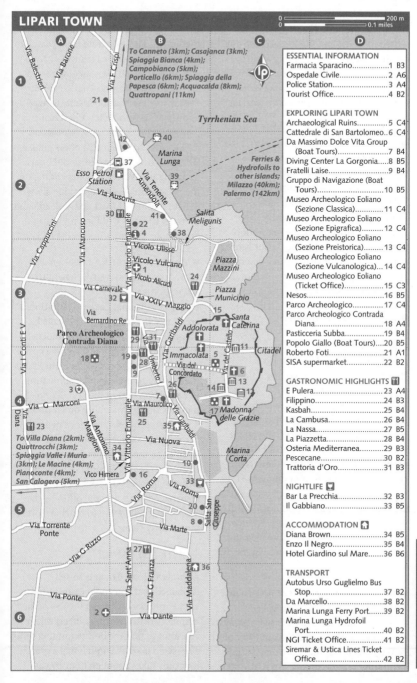

# LIPARI TOWN

0 — 200 m
0 — 0.1 miles

To Canneto (3km); Casajanca (3km);
Spiaggia Bianca (4km);
Campobianco (5km);
Porticello (6km); Spiaggia della
Papesca (6km); Acquacalda (8km);
Quattropani (11km)

*Tyrrhenian Sea*

Ferries &
Hydrofoils to
other islands;
Milazzo (40km);
Palermo (142km)

*Marina
Lunga*

Esso Petrol
Station

*Salita
Meligunis*

*Piazza
Mazzini*

*Piazza
Municipio*

*Santa
Caterina*

**Parco Archeologico
Contrada Diana**

*Citadel*

Addolorata

Immacolata

*Via del
Concordato*

*Madonna
delle Grazie*

To Villa Diana (2km);
Quattrocchi (3km);
Spiaggia Valle i Muria
(3km); Le Macine (4km);
Pianoconte (4km);
San Calogero (5km)

*Marina
Corta*

## ESSENTIAL INFORMATION
Farmacia Sparacino.................1 B3
Ospedale Civile......................2 A6
Police Station.........................3 A4
Tourist Office.........................4 B2

## EXPLORING LIPARI TOWN
Archaeological Ruins..............5 C4
Cattedrale di San Bartolomeo..6 C4
Da Massimo Dolce Vita Group
 (Boat Tours)........................7 B4
Diving Center La Gorgonia.....8 B5
Fratelli Laise...........................9 B4
Gruppo di Navigazione (Boat
 Tours)................................10 B5
Museo Archeologico Eoliano
 (Sezione Classica).............11 C4
Museo Archeologico Eoliano
 (Sezione Epigrafica)..........12 C4
Museo Archeologico Eoliano
 (Sezione Preistorica).........13 C4
Museo Archeologico Eoliano
 (Sezione Vulcanologica)...14 C4
Museo Archeologico Eoliano
 (Ticket Office)...................15 C3
Nesos...................................16 B5
Parco Archeologico..............17 C4
Parco Archeologico Contrada
 Diana................................18 A4
Pasticceria Subba.................19 B4
Popolo Giallo (Boat Tours)...20 B5
Roberto Foti.........................21 A1
SISA supermarket.................22 B2

## GASTRONOMIC HIGHLIGHTS
E Pulera...............................23 A4
Filippino..............................24 B3
Kasbah.................................25 B4
La Cambusa.........................26 B4
La Nassa..............................27 B5
La Piazzetta.........................28 B4
Osteria Mediterranea...........29 B3
Pescecane...........................30 B2
Trattoria d'Oro....................31 B3

## NIGHTLIFE
Bar La Precchia....................32 B3
Il Gabbiano.........................33 B5

## ACCOMMODATION
Diana Brown.......................34 B5
Enzo Il Negro......................35 B4
Hotel Giardino sul Mare.......36 B6

## TRANSPORT
Autobus Urso Guglielmo Bus
 Stop..................................37 B2
Da Marcello.........................38 B2
Marina Lunga Ferry Port.......39 B2
Marina Lunga Hydrofoil
 Port..................................40 B2
NGI Ticket Office.................41 B2
Siremar & Ustica Lines Ticket
 Office................................42 B2

AEOLIAN ISLANDS

provisions. The street really comes into its own in the early evening, when it's closed to traffic and the locals come out for their *passeggiata* (evening stroll).

Another atmospheric area is Marina Corta, down at the end of Via Garibaldi, a pretty little marina ringed by popular bars and restaurants.

### ❦ PASTICCERIA SUBBA // BITE INTO HEAVENLY CAKES

One of Lipari's great indulgences is a cake from Pasticceria Subba ( ☎ 090 981 13 52; Via Vittorio Emanuele 92; ❧ 7am-10pm), Lipari's most famous *pasticceria* (pastry shop). In business since 1930, the main shop fronts Via Vittorio Emanuele but behind is a lovely outdoor seating area where you can linger over a coffee and mouth-wateringly wicked pastries and cakes.

### ❦ PARCO ARCHEOLOGICO CONTRADA DIANA // EXPLORE LIPARI'S RUINS

A block back from Via Vittorio Emanuele is the Parco Archeologico Contrada Diana (admission free; ❧ 9am-1pm & 3-6.30pm). This grandly titled archaeological park is effectively a field full of confusing classical ruins. What you are looking at are the remnants of Lipari's original Greek walls (5th and 4th centuries BC) and a few Roman houses. At the southwestern end of the park is the necropolis, where the tombstones are still visible in the overgrown grass. Parents with toddlers might take more pleasure in letting their loved ones loose in the adjacent park.

### ❦ BOAT TOURS // WEIGH ANCHOR AND SAIL THE ARCHIPELAGO

A boat tour around Lipari is a good way of seeing the island, and the only way of getting to some of the more inaccessible swimming points (unless you rent your own boat). There are numerous agencies in town offering tours of Lipari and further afield. These operate from March to October, and include Gruppo di Navigazione ( ☎ 338 2931986; www.navigazioniregina.com; Via Garibaldi), Popolo Giallo ( ☎ 338 7208988; www.popologiallo.it; Salita San Giuseppe) and Da Massimo Dolce Vita Group ( ☎ 090 981 30 86, 333 2986624; www.damassimo.it; Via Maurolico 2), which also offers guided treks of Stromboli and hires out boats and dinghies. Prices vary depending on the season, but as a rough guide allow €15 for a tour of Lipari and Vulcano and between €35 and €40 for a night trip to Stromboli.

### ❦ EASTER CELEBRATIONS // WITNESS THE ISLAND'S SOULFUL PROCESSIONS

Lipari's traditional Easter celebrations are heartfelt and theatrical. Events kick off on Palm Sunday, when islanders gather to follow the Via Crucis, a costumed candle-lit procession from Piazza Mazzini up to the citadel, culminating in a re-enactment of the crucifixion. The mood is similarly sombre on Good Friday, when groups of barefoot penitents accompany statues of Christ around town in an atmosphere of funereal silence. Easter Day is more light-hearted, with two processions, one headed by the resurrected Jesus and the other by the Virgin Mary, meeting in Marina Corta to much noisy rejoicing.

## AROUND LIPARI

Although Lipari Town is so self-contained that you could easily spend your entire holiday there, the rest of the island is worth checking out, especially if you want to find the best swimming spots. The island is small enough that a grand tour only takes about an hour by car.

## ❦ BEACHES & SWIMMING // DIVE INTO TURQUOISE WATERS

### East Coast

The nearest beach to Lipari Town is the long, pebbly strip at Canneto, 3km away on the other side of a jutting headland. About 1km further north, Spiaggia Bianca (White Beach) is the most popular beach on the island, its name a reference to the layers of pumice dust that once covered it. These have been slowly washed away by the rough winter seas, leaving it a dark shade of grey.

From Canneto the road rises as it follows the coast northwards. After a few kilometres you'll pass Campobianco, where huge gashes of white rock streak down the green hillside. These are the result of extensive pumice quarrying which, until quite recently, was an important local industry. This unlikely place is one of the better spots for a swim, as you can slide down the pumice chutes directly into the water. However, the chutes are only accessible by sea so you'll either have to rent a boat or sign up for a tour to get to them.

Above Campobianco, Monte Pilato (476m) is a mountain of pumice and obsidian that was formed by a volcanic explosion in AD 700. Around its crater, which is accessible by a path from the northern end of Campobianco, lie fields of solidified obsidian known as Rocche Rosse (Red Rocks). Beyond Campobianco at Porticello there's another pebble beach, Spiaggia della Papesca, dusted white by the fine pumice that gives the sea its limpid turquoise colour.

### West Coast

One of Lipari's best beaches is Spiaggia Valle i Muria, almost directly west of Lipari Town on the other side of the island. A dark, pebbly beach lapped by

## SEASICKNESS

A trip to the Aeolians inevitably involves time at sea, either on hydrofoils, ferries or tour boats. Seasickness can make this difficult and at times quite nauseating (as we can vouch for!). If you do suffer from seasickness, locals recommend you sit at the back of the hydrofoil/boat and eat something dry and salty. If that doesn't work, ask a pharmacist for *qualcosa per mal di mare* (something for seasickness).

wonderful clean waters and surrounded by dramatic cliffs, it's not the easiest to get to, so if you're thinking of coming, come prepared for the day. From Lipari Town take the road towards Pianoconte until you see signs. You'll then have to leave your car/scooter and walk down for about 10 or 15 minutes through an idyllic landscape of long grass, flowers and cacti. Alternatively, get a boat to drop you off (and pick you up). There's a little hut that serves food and drinks, or bring your own picnic – pick up provisions at the SISA supermarket ( ☎ 090 981 15 87; Via Vittorio Emanuele) in Lipari Town.

## ❦ QUATTROCCHI // SWOON OVER FABULOUS COASTAL VIEWS

The best views in Lipari are from a celebrated viewing point known as Quattrocchi (Four Eyes), 3km west of Lipari Town. To get there, follow the road for Pianoconte – it's about 300m beyond the turn off for Spiaggia Valle i Muria. You'll know you're in the right place when you see a sensational coastal panorama unfold in front of you. Stretching off to the south, great, grey cliffs plunge into the sea, while in the distance plumes of sinister smoke rise from the dark heights of neighbouring Vulcano.

AEOLIAN ISLANDS

## TOP **FIVE**

### DIVING SPOTS AROUND LIPARI

★ **Punta Castagna** (difficult; depth 10m to 40m) – a spectacular dive with a 10m white pumice platform interrupted by multicoloured channels

★ **Secca del Bagno** (difficult; depth 40m to 45m) – a breathtaking collection of colourful walls that are swathed with schools of technicolour fish

★ **Pietra Menalda** (medium; depth 18m to 40m) – see the homes of octopuses, eel, groupers and other sea critters on the southern side of the island

★ **Pietra del Bagno** (all levels; 20m to 40m) – circumnavigate the Bagno rock, while witnessing colourful rock surfaces and sea life

★ **La Parete dei Gabbiani** (medium; 20m to 45m) – a black-and-white dive: black lava rock streaked with white pumice stone, hiding cracks that are home to lobsters

☻ HIKING // **EXPLORE THE HILLY HINTERLAND**

Away from the more obvious coastal pleasures, there's some lovely hiking on Lipari. Most walks involve fairly steep slopes, although the summer heat is as likely to wear you down as the terrain. Take all the usual precautions: a hat, sunblock, plenty of water, and try to avoid the midday sun. One popular hike is the hour-long walk between Quattropani and Acquacalda on the north coast, which affords spectacular views of Salina and distant Stromboli. Another leads down from the abandoned Old Kaolin Mine be-

tween Pianoconte and Quattropani to the Roman baths of San Calogero, famous in antiquity for the thermal spring that flowed at a constant temperature of 60°C.

In Lipari Town, you can organise guided walks through Nesos ( ☎ 338 4793064; www.nesos.org; Via Vittorio Emanuele 24).

☻ DIVING // **PLUNGE INTO AN UNDERWATER WORLD**

Lipari's crystalline waters provide plenty of sport for snorkellers and scuba divers. For information on courses or to rent equipment, contact Diving Center La Gorgonia ( ☎ 090 981 26 16; www.lagorgonia diving.it; Salita San Giuseppe, Marina Corta) in Lipari Town. A single dive costs €32 if you have your own kit or €50 if you have to hire; courses cost between €55 and €200.

# GASTRONOMIC HIGHLIGHTS

The waters of the archipelago abound with fish, including tuna, mullet, cuttlefish and sole, all of which end up on restaurant tables. Swordfish is a particular favourite although you'll only find fresh swordfish between May and July; outside of that period it will almost certainly be frozen. Another island staple is *pasta all'eoliana*, a simple blend of capers, olive oil and basil. The local wine is Malvasia, which has a DOC *(Denominazione di Origine Controllata)* accreditation and a sweet taste of honey.

Many restaurants close at the end of October for the winter season. All the eateries listed here are in Lipari Town unless otherwise indicated.

☻ E PULERA €€€

☎ 090 981 11 58; www.pulera.it; Via Diana; meals €35-50; ☽ dinner only Apr-Sep

With ceramic-inlaid tables set out in a delightful open-air courtyard and the air thick with the scent of orange and lemon trees, this is one of Lipari's most romantic restaurants. It's a memorable place to dine on crowd-pleasers such as pecorino cheese with balsamic vinegar and fresh mint, and swordfish caked in ground almonds. Service is also first class, as is the thoughtful wine list. Reservations are required.

### ☙ FILIPPINO €€€

☎ 090 981 10 02; www.filippino.it; Piazza Municipio; meals €35-50; ☯ closed Mon Oct-Mar

Celebrating its 100th anniversary in 2010, Filippino is a mainstay of Lipari's culinary scene, considered by many the island's finest restaurant. It's a smart place with seating in an elegant glass pavilion and a small army of white waist-coated waiters serving the international clientele. The accent is on innovative Sicilian cooking, so expect original tanta-lisers such as ricotta soufflé and mousse *al gelsomino* (jasmine mousse). Dress appropriately and book ahead.

### ☙ KASBAH €€

☎ 090 981 10 75; Via Maurolico 25; pizzas from €6, meals €35; ☯ 7pm-3am mid-Mar–Oct

Choose the ambience that suits you best: the sleek white contemporary banquettes in the interior dining room or the vine-draped candlelit garden out the back. The food is excellent, including superb pizzas and delicacies such as *orecchiette con carciofi* (ear-shaped pasta with artichokes) and *involtini di tonno* (tuna rolls). For meat eaters, the *agnello stracotto in umiodo alla siciliana* (stewed lamb with almonds and dates) is a definite hit.

### ☙ LA CAMBUSA €

☎ 349 4766061; Via Garibaldi 72; meals €20-25; ☯ closed Nov-Easter

If a retired fisherman was to open a trattoria, this is how it would be – cosy, with old seafaring prints and a menu of traditional fish staples. And true to form, the food at La Cambusa is wholesome, unpretentious and popular. Locals and visitors squeeze into the tiny interior for classics such as spaghetti *con gamberetti* (with prawns) and *sarde a beccaficco* (fresh sardines stuffed with breadcrumbs, raisins, pine nuts and parsley, then lightly fried).

### ☙ LA NASSA €€

☎ 090 981 13 19; Via G Franza 41; meals €35-40; ☯ closed Nov-Easter

Housed in a lovely family villa back from the bustle on Via Vittorio Emanuele, this is a charming restaurant specialising in authentic island cuisine. The onus is on fresh fish such as *cernia*, *sarago* and *dentice*, but there are some great meat and veg dishes too, including Aeolian sausages flavoured with island herbs; and *caponata*, Sicily's celebrated sweet-and-sour aubergine ratatouille. Reservations recommended.

### ☙ LA PIAZZETTA €€

☎ 090 981 25 22; off Via Vittorio Emanuele; pizzas €4.50-7, meals €25; ☯ closed Tue Sep-Jun

A lively pizzeria/restaurant with out-door seating on a pretty piazza, located behind Pasticceria Subba. Inside, jolly yellow walls are adorned with colourful tiles, and happy diners crunch into large, tasty pizzas at tightly packed tables. For something richer go for the house speciality *risotto alla piazzetta* (risotto with prawns, cream, parsley, apple, saffron and garlic).

### ☙ LE MACINE €€

☎ 090 982 23 87; www.lemacine.org; Via Stradale 9, Pianoconte; meals €35-40; ☯ closed Tue

A country restaurant in the village of Pianoconte about 4.5km from Lipari Town. Decorated with terracotta pots and old farm tools, it comes into its own in summer, when meals are served on the terrace. Despite the country setting, seafood is the main attraction, starring in dishes such as fish in *ghiotta* sauce (a blend of olive oil, capers, tomatoes, garlic and basil) and lobster-filled ravioli. Reservations are advised, as is the free shuttle service. Slow Food recommended.

### ❤ OSTERIA MEDITERRANEA €€
☎ 090 981 25 11; Via Vittorio Emanuele 148; meals €25; ⏳ Easter-Oct

Offering excellent value for money, prompt, friendly service and delicious food, this is an excellent choice. Large juicy olives arrive with the wine, whetting your appetite for wonderful seafood dishes, such as *bistecca di tonno con cipolatta in agrodolce* (tuna steak with sweet-and-sour onions). The location is also a plus, affording grandstand views of the *passeggiata* on Via Vittorio Emanuele.

### ❤ PESCECANE €
☎ 090 981 27 06; Via Vittorio Emanuele 223; pizzas from €4.50, meals €20-25

One of a number of pizzerias and trattorias on the main strip, Pescecane is a local favourite, a laid-back trattoria-cum-pizzeria that serves excellent wood-fired pizzas and typical island food. There's a great antipasto buffet with a selection of delicious marinated vegetables and some wonderful pasta dishes, including a fiery spaghetti *al fuoco* (with garlic, chilli, cherry tomatoes and baked ricotta).

### ❤ TRATTORIA D'ORO €€
☎ 090 981 13 04; Via Umberto I 28-32; meals €25-30; ⏳ closed Sun Nov-Mar

Looking all the world like an obvious tourist trap, this old-school trattoria is where Lipari's ferry sailors often come for their dinner. Inside, the look is typically Sicilian with ceramic plates, displays of wine bottles and maritime paraphernalia,

and the menu is heavily biased towards seafood, with plenty of cuttlefish, anchovies and tuna. Service is gruffly efficient, although they're not going to win any awards for their warm welcome.

## NIGHTLIFE

### ❤ BAR LA PRECCHIA
☎ 090 981 13 03; Via Vittorio Emanuele 191

If you fancy a late-night drink or want a prime people-watching perch during *passeggiata*, pull up a chair at this hugely popular bar. It has an enormous menu of drinks, from *cafe frappe* and fruit milkshakes to cocktails and wine, and stays open until the small hours. Occasional live music adds to the party atmosphere.

### ❤ IL GABBIANO
☎ 090 981 14 71; Marina Corta

One of a number of bars and cafes on Marina Corta, Il Gabbiano is a typical Lipari outfit with a tiny, nondescript interior and tables laid out on a pretty piazza. Like everywhere on the island, it's touristy but it does a wonderful *spremuta d'arancia* (fresh squeezed orange juice, €4) and it's a great spot for whiling away the hours over a cool drink. Ice cream and snacks are also available.

## TRANSPORT

**BOAT //** The main port is Marina Lunga, where you'll find a joint Siremar ( ☎ 090 981 12 20; www.siremar.it) and Ustica Lines ( ☎ 090 981 24 48; www.usticalines.it) ticket office at the head of the hydrofoil jetty. Timetable information is displayed here and is also available at the tourist office. From Lipari you can catch ferries and hydrofoils to all the other islands: Vulcano (ferry/hydrofoil €4.40/5.80, 25/10 minutes), Santa Marina Salina (ferry/hydrofoil €6.70/8.80, 45/25 minutes), Panarea (ferry/hydrofoil €7.50/10.40, two/one hours), Stromboli (ferry/hydrofoil €12.40/17.80, four/1¾ hours), Filicudi (ferry/hydrofoil €11.10/15.80, 2¾/1¼ hours) and Alicudi (ferry/hydrofoil €13.95/18.85, four/two hours). Services also run to Milazzo and ports on the Sicilian and Italian mainland.

**BUS //** Island bus services are run by Autobus Urso Guglielmo ( ☎ 090 981 12 62; Via Cappuccini 9; tickets €1.50-1.90) from the bus stop near the Esso petrol station. One main route serves the island's eastern shore, from Canneto to Acquacalda, while another runs to the western highland settlements of Quattrocchi, Pianoconte and Quattropani. If you plan on using the bus a lot, you'll save money by buying a ticket booklet (six/10 for €7/10).

**CAR & MOTORCYCLE //** Lipari is not big – only 38 sq km – but to explore it you'll need your own wheels. There are various outfits around the port where you can hire bikes, scooters and cars, including Da Marcello ( ☎ 090 981 12 34; www.noleggiodamarcello.com; Via Tenente Amendola) and Roberto Foti ( ☎ 090 981 23 52; www.robertofoti.it; Via F Crispi 31). Allow about €10 per day for a bike, between €15 and €25 per day for a scooter, and from €30 to €50 per day for a small car.

# VULCANO
· · · · · ·

**pop 720**

Approaching Vulcano, it's difficult not to feel a slight shiver down your spine as you spot the white trails of smoke rising from the island's ominous peaks. However, any sense of disquiet is quickly supplanted by a more earthy reaction as you get your first whiff of the vile sulphurous gases that infuse the air. Vulcano's volcanic nature has long been impressing visitors – the ancient Romans believed it to be the chimney of the fire god Vulcan's workshop – and the island is today celebrated for its therapeutic mud baths and hot springs. The main drawcard, however, remains the Fossa di Vulcano, or Gran Cratere (Large Crater), the steaming volcano that towers over the island's northeastern shores.

There's no sightseeing as such on Vulcano, but it's a great place to spend

a day or two, swimming off the dark volcanic beaches, sailing the wild coast or climbing the sleeping crater. Most of the action is centred on touristy Porto di Levante and the black beaches at Porto di Ponente, but once you get away from these places, the landscape takes on a quiet, rural aspect with allotments, birdsong and a surprising amount of greenery.

## ESSENTIAL INFORMATION

**EMERGENCIES //** Emergency Doctor ( ☎ 090 985 22 20; Via Favaloro) Farmacia Bonarrigo ( ☎ 090 985 22 44; Via Favaloro 1) Police ( ☎ 090 985 21 10)

## ORIENTATION

Boats dock at the Porto di Levante. From here it's a short walk – bear right as you exit the harbour area – to the *fanghi* (mud baths), hidden behind a small hillock of rocks. Continuing beyond the mud pools, the road leads to Porto di Ponente, where you'll find a number of hotels and Spiaggia Sabbia Nera (Black Sand Beach), a long stretch of black sand. For the Fossa di Vulcano, bear left as you disembark and continue until you see a yellow sign saying '*escursioni cratere*' indicating the way.

## EXPLORING VULCANO

♥ FOSSA DI VULCANO // CLIMB THE STEAMING VOLCANO
The reason most people come to Vulcano is to climb its main volcano, the dormant 391m-high Fossa di Vulcano (admission to the path €3). This is one of three volcanic systems on the island and the only one that is still active. It hasn't erupted since 1890 and despite the foul fumes that emanate from its crater, is

extremely unlikely to do so again. The summit path is a well-trodden trail that you can easily do on your own – it takes about an hour up to the lowest point of the crater's edge.

To get to the start point follow the yellow sign saying '*escursioni cratere*', which sends you down Via Provinciale for about 500m until a gravel track leads up to the left. You might find the going a bit tough at first thanks to the black sandy soil, but this soon gives way to clay-like rock that is much easier underfoot. There are no special risks but you'll need to wear strong, closed shoes and protect yourself against the sun: there's no shade on the path, so make sure you bring a hat and sunscreen, as well as plenty of water.

The summit is a desolate expanse of browny-red rubble set around the

main crater, which falls to a depth of around 50m and is accessible by way of a steep trail. For stunning 360-degree views of all the islands lined up to the north, walk clockwise around the crest of the crater. Along the path you'll pass fumaroles that constantly vent gases. Don't walk too closely to these as the temperature of the escaping gas can be searing.

More sedentary volcano-watchers can visit the small museum, **Vulcano Informa** ( ☎ 090 985 25 28; Via Porto di Ponente; admission free; ☺ 9.30am-12.30pm & 5-8pm Jun-Sep), which has displays about Vulcano and a video (in English, French and Italian) about Stromboli's last big eruption.

### ☙ THE FANGHI // LUXURIATE IN GLOOPY GEOTHERMAL MUD

If you didn't know that it's good for you (and apparently it is), basking in Vulcano's celebrated **fanghi** (admission €2, incl visit to the faraglione €2.50; shower €1; ☺ 7am-11pm summer, 8am-5pm winter) wouldn't be a particularly appealing prospect. A small circular pool of thick, coffee-coloured mud lying at the bottom of a *faraglione* (which is a long stone tower jutting up into the sky) and stinking of rotten eggs, it's not exactly what you'd call a five-star beauty farm. But the warm sulphurous mud has long been considered an excellent treatment for rheumatic pains and skin diseases, and if you don't mind smelling funny for a few days, rolling around in the mud can be a tantalising experience.

Once you have had time to relax in the muddy water, get some soft clay from the bottom of the pool and apply it to your body and face. Don't let any of the mud get in your eyes as the sulphur is acidic and can damage the retina (keep your hair mud-free too). Wait for the clay

## MUD-BATH TIPS

★ Don't stay in longer than 10 or 15 minutes – the water/mud is slightly radioactive. Pregnant women should avoid it altogether.

★ Don't use your favourite fluffy towel or one you've 'borrowed' from a hotel – most hotels will provide a special *fanghi* towel on request.

★ If you have a sulphite allergy, stay away.

★ Remember to remove watches and jewellery.

★ Take flip-flops or sandals – there are hot air vents that can scald your feet.

★ Wear a swimsuit you don't mind destroying: once the smell gets in, it's easier to buy a new one than to get rid of the pong.

mask to dry, wash it off in the pool, then run to the natural spa around the corner, where there are hot, bubbling springs in a small natural sea-water pool. You're advised to spend another five to 10 minutes lolling about.

❦ **PORTO DI PONENTE** // **BASK ON VULCANO'S FAMOUS BLACK SANDS**
Vulcano's beach scene is centred on the **Spiaggia Sabbia Nera** (Black Sand Beach), a smooth strip of black sand at **Porto di Ponente**, about 10 minutes' walk beyond the mud pools on the far side of the peninsula. This is one of the few sandy beaches in the Aeolians, and it's a scenic spot, curving around a bay of limpid, glassy waters out of which rise jutting *faraglioni*. From the beach, a road traverses a small isthmus to Vulcanello (123m), a bulb of land that was spewed out by a volcanic eruption in 183 BC. Here you'll find the

famous **Valle dei Mostri** (Valley of the Monsters), a group of wind-eroded dark rocks that have formed grotesque shapes.

❦ **GELSO & THE INTERIOR** //
**ESCAPE THE CROWDS TO GELSO'S TRANQUIL BEACHES**
On the island's southern coast, **Gelso** is a gorgeous little port with a couple of black-sand beaches that rarely get very crowded. There is a bus service to get there but you'll be much better off hiring a car or scooter (see the Vulcano transport section, p147), as services are limited and it's a 15km walk back if you get stranded.

There's not much to Gelso itself, but before you get to the village, a steep dirt track (pedestrians only) branches off to **Spiaggia dell'Asina** (Donkey Beach), a crescent sweep of black sand giving onto inviting waters. The second beach, **Spiaggia Cannitello**, is surrounded by lush, almost tropical greenery. Both beaches have a rudimentary bar/cafe, where you can hire sun lounges and umbrellas.

En route to Gelso, take time for a detour to **Capo Grillo**, accessible from the island's main settlement of Piano, which commands breathtaking views of Lipari and Salina.

❦ **BOAT TOURS & DIVES** // **SAIL ROUND THE ISLAND AND SWIM ITS WATERS**
In summer you can take **boat tours** of the island from the port – local operators set up in kiosks – for about €15 per person. Highlights to look out for include the **Grotta del Cavallo**, a sea cave known for its light effects, and the **Piscina di Venere**, a natural swimming pool set in its own rocky amphitheatre.

This mythical spot owes its name to a legend in which Venus, the goddess of love, swam here in an attempt to recover her lost virginity (although quite how she hoped to do it is not recorded). If you prefer to go it alone, you can rent boats from **Noleggio da Tonino** ( ☎ 335 5859790; www.noleggiodatonino.it, in Italian; Via Porticciolo di Ponente) at Porto di Ponente or the **Centro Nautica Baia di Levante** ( ☎ 339 3372795; www.baialevante.it; ✆ Apr-Oct) to the left of the hydrofoil dock. As a rough guide, allow for anything between €60 and €120 per day for a four-person boat.

To head under the wet stuff, the **Diving Centre Saracen** ( ☎ 090 985 21 89; www.divingcentersaracen.com; Via Porto di Ponente; ✆ Easter-Oct) offers a range of dives costing from €45 (equipment included), plus snorkelling excursions from €35.

## GASTRONOMIC HIGHLIGHTS

Vulcano's restaurants tend to be overpriced tourist traps but there are some welcome exceptions. All the eateries listed here are in Porto di Levante unless otherwise indicated.

### ❦ DA VINCENZINO €€

☎ 090 985 20 16; Via Porto di Levante 125; meals €30-35; ✆ closed Nov-Apr

This bustling restaurant on the main strip is one of Vulcano's few year-round options. Go through the plant-lined entrance and you emerge into a large, light-filled hall with rows of tables laid out between white columns. It's set up to cater to large groups but this doesn't detract from the food, which is excellent and abundant. The menu caters to most tastes, with everything from grilled steak to seafood salad to a selection of local cheeses.

### ❦ LA FORGIA MAURIZIO €€

☎ 090 985 24 26; Via Porto di Levante; meals €30; ✆ closed Nov-Easter

The owner of this devilishly good restaurant spent 20 winters in India, and this is one of the few places in Sicily (let alone the Aeolian Islands) where you can order *riso al curry* (curried rice). On the whole, though, the food is regional in inspiration, with crowd pleasers such as *maccheroni alla norma* (macaroni with aubergines) and *involtini di pesce spada* (stuffed swordfish rolls). The tasting menu is an excellent deal at €30 including wine and dessert.

### ❦ RITROVO REMIGIO €

☎ 090 985 20 85; Porto di Levante; cannoli €2

Forget the volcanoes, the beaches, the spectacular views. The single most compelling reason to visit Vulcano is to eat a *cannolo* (tube of biscuity pastry filled with sweetened ricotta) from this otherwise undistinguished bar/*gelateria* (ice-cream shop) near the port. They are some of the best in Sicily. They might look no different to other *cannoli* but somehow the biscuity tube is, well, more biscuity, and the creamy ricotta cheese is, in some indescribable way, more creamy. There's also a selection of ice cream.

### ❦ TRATTORIA MANIACI PINA €

☎ 368 668555; Gelso; meals €20-25; ✆ May-Oct

On the south side of the island beside Gelso's black-sand beach, this atmospheric, down-to-earth trattoria is as traditional as they get, with blue-chequered tablecloths and wooden tables. It's a great place to eat fresh fish accompanied by a chilled carafe of local white wine. What exactly is on the menu depends on what fish is good that day, but if it's on, the *totani ripieni* (stuffed squid) is highly recommended.

## TOP **FIVE**

### EATING & DRINKING EXPERIENCES

★ **A cannolo at Ritrovo Remigio, Vulcano** (p146) – *cannoli* (biscuity pastry tubes filled with sweetened ricotta) are served across Sicily: those served at this Vulcano bar are some of the best

★ **An almond granita at da Alfredo, Salina** (p151) – people come from far and wide for Alfredo's historic *granite* (ice drinks flavoured with ground almonds or fresh fruit)

★ **Dinner at Filippino, Lipari** (p141) – dine on modern Sicilian cuisine at Lipari's finest restaurant

★ **Tasting Malvasia wine, Salina** (p149) – grapes cultivated on Salina's volcanic slopes are used to make the Aeolians' acclaimed Malvasia wine

★ **A pizza at L'Osservatorio, Stromboli** (p158) – the pizzas are fine, but the main event here is the view up to Stromboli's smoking flanks

## TRANSPORT

**BIKE //** Bikes, scooters and quads can be hired from Noleggio Sprint da Luigi ( ☎ 090 985 22 08, cnr Via Provinciale & Via Porto di Levante) and Noleggio Paolo ( ☎ 090 985 21 12; Via Porto di Levante), both of whom can also organise island tours. Budget on €15 for a bike for the day, and between €15 and €35 for a scooter.

**BOAT //** Vulcano is an intermediate stop between Milazzo (ferry/hydrofoil €10.80/15, two hours/45 minutes) and Lipari (ferry/hydrofoil €4.40/5.80, 25/10 minutes), with regular services in both directions. Ticket offices are near the dock at Porto di Levante.

**BUS //** Bus Vulcania Tour di Scaffidi ( ☎ 090 985 30 73) runs buses across the island, to Porto di Ponente (€1.55), Piano and Capo Grillo (€2, approximately seven daily Monday to Saturday, two Sunday) and, between mid-June and mid-September, to Gelso (€2.30, 20 minutes, approximately three daily). There's a timetable posted at the beginning of Via Provinciale, near Ritrovo Remigio. Buy tickets on the bus. If you're going to the beaches at Gelso ask the driver to let you off at the dirt track.

**CAR & MOTORCYCLE //** Noleggio Paolo ( ☎ 090 985 21 12; Via Porto di Levante) has hire cars starting at €25 per day.

**TAXI //** Call Santi ( ☎ 366 3028712).

## SALINA

· · · · · ·

pop 2200

**In stark contrast to the exposed volcanic terrain of the other Aeolian Islands, Salina boasts a lush, verdant landscape. Woodlands, wildflowers, thick yellow gorse bushes and serried ranks of grape vines carpet its hillsides in vibrant colours and cool greens, while high coastal cliffs plunge into the breaking waters below. The island – the second largest in the archipelago – is the only one to enjoy natural freshwater springs and it's these, combined with the volcanic soil, that make it so fertile. The Aeolians' famous Malvasia wine is produced here, and Salina's fat, juicy capers flavour many local dishes.**

Although named after the *saline* (salt works) of Lingua, Salina is shaped by two extinct volcanoes, Monte dei Porri (850m) and Monte Fossa delle Felci (962m), the Aeolians' two highest peaks. These rise in the centre of the island forming a natural barrier between the main settlements and ensuring that the

**AEOLIAN ISLANDS**

sleepy villages retain their own individual atmosphere. Tourism has encroached on island life, particularly in Santa Marina Salina and nearby Lingua, but away from these, there's a distinct feeling of remoteness – a sense that the rest of the world really is a very long way away. If that sounds good, you'll love Salina.

## ESSENTIAL INFORMATION

**EMERGENCIES //** Emergency Doctor ( ☎ 090 984 40 05) Farmacia Comunale ( ☎ 090 984 30 89; Via Risorgimento, Santa Marina Salina) Police ( ☎ 090 984 30 19; Via Lungomare, Santa Marina Salina)

## ORIENTATION

Most boats dock at Santa Marina Salina, the island's main settlement. The town's main road, Via Risorgimento, runs parallel to the seafront one block back from the port. Salina's other main settlements are: Lingua, 3km south of Santa Marina Salina; Malfa, on the northern coast; inland Leni; and Rinella, a tiny fishing hamlet on the southern coast. Note that hydrofoils dock at Rinella as well as Santa Marina Salina.

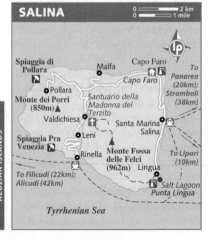

## EXPLORING SALINA

☙ SANTA MARINA SALINA // **WALK THE WHITEWASHED STREETS**
Salina's main port, Santa Marina Salina is a typical island settlement with a lively main drag and steeply stacked houses rising up the hillside. It's not a big place and there are no specific sights, but it's attractive enough and it makes an ideal base for exploring the rest of the island. The principal street is Via Risorgimento, a pretty pedestrian-only strip lined by gorgeous island houses (varicoloured cubes with round windows), design shops, some cafes and a few *alimentari* (grocery shops). If the hunger pangs strike, follow your nose to Il Fornaio (Via Risorgimento 150), a fabulous bakery that serves delicious *cornetti* (Italian croissants), biscuits and *sfincione palermitana* (Palermitan spongy pizza topped by onion and tomato).

☙ LINGUA // **GRAB A GRANITA ON THE LINGUA SEAFRONT**
Three kilometres south of Santa Marina Salina, the tiny village of Lingua is a popular summer hangout, with a number of hotels (one notably luxurious), a few trattorias and a small beach. Its main feature is the salt lagoon, which sits under an old lighthouse at the end of the village. Until quite recently the salt works were an important local employer, but nowadays the lagoon only provides sustenance for the migrating birds that pass through in spring and autumn en route to and from Africa.

The centre of the summer scene is seafront Piazza Marina Garibaldi. The place to head for here is da Alfredo ( ☎ 090 984 30 75; Piazza Marina Grande), a bar/*gelateria* famous across Sicily for its *granite* – see p151.

## ❤ MONTE FOSSA DELLE FELCI // SUMMIT THE AEOLIANS' HIGHEST PEAK

For jaw-dropping views, climb to Salina's (and indeed the Aeolians') highest point, Monte Fossa delle Felci (962m). The two-hour ascent starts from the Santuario della Madonna del Terzito (Sanctuary of the Madonna of Terzito), at Valdichiesa in the valley separating the island's two volcanoes. An imposing 19th-century church, the sanctuary is an important place of pilgrimage for islanders, particularly around the Feast of the Assumption on 15 August. From the church you can follow a signposted track up through pine and chestnut woodlands and fields of ferns, all the way to the top. Along the way you'll see plenty of colourful flora, including wild violets, asparagus and a plant known locally as *cipudazza* (Latin *Urginea marittima*), which was sold to the Calabrians to make soap but is used locally as mouse poison!

Once you've reached the summit (the last 100m are particularly tough), the views are breathtaking, particularly from the southeast ridge where you can look down over the Lingua salt lagoon and over to Lipari and Vulcano. To get to the sanctuary by public transport take the bus from Santa Marina Salina to Malfa, then change for a Rinella-bound bus and ask the driver to let you off at the sanctuary.

## ❤ MALFA // SOAK UP THE RELAXED ATMOSPHERE

On the island's north coast, Malfa is the largest settlement on Salina. As you enter from Santa Marina Salina, the town tumbles down the hillside to a small shingle beach, backed by the ruins of some old fisherfolk's houses. On first sight, it's not an especially attractive town but it

has a tranquil laid-back atmosphere and in amongst the sloping lanes are a few hidden gems. Chief among these is the Hotel Signum (see p311 for a full review), whose fabulous Wellness Center ( ☎ 090 984 42 22; www.hotelsignum.it; Via Scalo 15; admission €40, treatments extra; ☯ Oct-Mar) is the perfect place for a revitalising soak in hot spring water or a cleansing sweat in a stone steam house. For a more sobering experience, the Museo dell'Emigrazione Eoliana (Emigration Museum; ☎ 090 34 42 93; Palazzo Marchetti, Via Conti; admission free; ☯ 9am-1pm & 4-7.30pm Mon-Sat summer, 9am-1pm Mon-Sat winter) chronicles the sad story of emigration from the Aeolian Islands.

## ❤ WINE & COOKING // TASTE MALVASIA AND LEARN TO COOK ISLAND-STYLE

Around Malfa there are a number of wineries where you can try the local Malvasia wine (see the boxed text, p150). Signposted off the main road near the entrance to town, Fenech ( ☎ 090 984 40 41; www.fenech.it; Via Fratelli Mirabilo 41) is a prize-winning local producer whose 2003 Malvasia was voted one of Italy's top 100 wines. To organise a tasting, contact the winery in advance.

Another important Malvasia is produced at the luxurious resort of Capo Faro ( ☎ 090 984 43 30; www.capofaro.it; Via Faro 3) on the 13-acre Tasca d'Almerita estate just outside town. Here you can visit the vineyards and take cooking lessons in the Anna Tasca Lanza cookery school. Options include two- or four-day courses costing from €800 to €1300 per person including accommodation.

## ❤ SWIMMING & SAILING // FIND SALINA'S TOP SWIMMING SPOTS

Salina's most famous beach is at Pollara, sandwiched dramatically between

## MALVASIA

Salina's good fortune is its freshwater springs. It is the only island of the Aeolians with natural water sources, the result of which is the startling greenery. The islanders have put this to good use, producing their own style of wine, Malvasia. It is thought that the Greeks brought the grapes to the islands in 588 BC, and the name is derived from Monenvasìa, a Greek city.

The wine is still produced according to traditional techniques using the Malvasia grape and the now-rare red Corinthian grape. The harvest generally occurs in the second week of September when the grapes are picked and laid out to dry on woven cane mats. The drying process is crucial: the grapes must dry out enough to concentrate the sweet flavour but not too much, which would caramelise them.

The result is a dark-golden or light-amber wine that tastes, some say, of honey. It is usually drunk in very small glasses and goes well with cheese, sweet biscuits and almond pastries.

the sea and the steep slopes of an extinct volcanic crater. Although land access to the beach (which was used as a setting for the film *Il Postino*) has been closed due to the danger of landslides, you can still descend the steep steps at the northwest edge of the village and admire the spectacular view with its backdrop of volcanic cliffs.

Over on the island's south coast, there are a couple of decent swimming spots near Rinella, a tiny hamlet whose pastel-coloured houses huddle around a small port. There's a sandy beach down by the village centre, but if that gets too cramped follow the path to Punta Megna, from where you can access the pebbly Spiaggia Pra Venezia.

Some of the best swimming spots in the area are only accessible by sea, so you'll need to sign up for a boat tour or hire a boat for yourself. Salina Relax Boats ( ☎ 338 6609640; Via Roma 86, Santa Marina Salina) offers various tours of Salina and the other islands, costing between €50 and €80 per person (which includes food and snorkel hire), as well as hiring out boats and running a water-taxi service.

## GASTRONOMIC HIGHLIGHTS

The majority of restaurants are located in hotels, although it is possible to eat in them if you are not a guest by making a reservation. All the eateries listed here are in Santa Marina Salina unless otherwise indicated.

### 🌱 A' CANNATA €€
☎ 090 984 31 61; Via Umberto I 13, Lingua; meals €35

At the entrance to Lingua, this is an unassuming restaurant run by a family of local fishermen. Diners sit down in a sun-filled seafront pavilion to spectacular seafood meals, often combined with juicy local vegetables and Salina's showpiece Malvasia wine. Start with the house speciality, *maccheroni* (macaroni), before moving onto a *secondo* (second course) of *calamaretti* (baby squid) cooked with Malvasia. Slow Food recommended.

### 🌱 ALFREDO IN CUCINA €€
☎ 090 984 33 07; Via Pantano; meals €35-40

Run by the son of the legendary Alfredo (see da Alfredo, p151), and just around the corner from his dad's bar, this elegant little restaurant specialises in modern island cuisine. Traditional combinations are deconstructed and reinterpreted with considerable panache, resulting in dishes such as tuna with orange-infused caramelised onion. The intimate interior is a tight fit but there's a welcoming atmosphere and a large summer terrace for dining under the stars.

### ♥ DA ALFREDO €

☎ 090 984 30 75; Piazza Marina Grande; granite €2.50, sandwiches from €5

Perhaps the most famous person on Salina, Alfredo has been wowing the summer crowds with his *granite* for decades. They're all sublime, but the *pièce de résistance* is his *granita alla mandorla*, made with locally grown almonds. Another house speciality is *pane cunzato*, a kind of open sandwich with toppings – usually a combination of tuna, ricotta, aubergines, tomatoes, capers and olives – piled high on a base of crispy bread.

### ♥ 'NNI LAUSTA €€

☎ 090 984 34 86; Via Risorgimento; pizzas from €5, meals €35-40

Chic wine bar downstairs, acclaimed restaurant upstairs, this is one of Salina's 'in' addresses. Stop by for an early evening aperitif before adjourning upstairs to dine on contemporary seafood such as tuna tartare or a mussel and farro salad. It's a smart place but like most island restaurants it's not overly formal. The look is light and summery with high ceilings, white lacquered tables and an outdoor terrace. Reservations advised.

### ♥ TRATTORIA CUCINOTTA €€

☎ 090 984 35 23; Via Risorgimento 6; meals €25-30

With its sunny alfresco seating and friendly, unpretentious vibe, this delightful family-run trattoria is an excellent choice for authentic island cooking. For a real taste of Salina, opt for spaghetti *all'eoliana* (with tuna, capers, olives and cherry tomatoes) – the very best of the island's bountiful garden table. It's located at the far end of Via Risorgimento, and while it's open year-round it's best to phone ahead during winter.

## TRANSPORT

**BIKE //** Hire mountain bikes and scooters from Antonio Bongiorno ( ☎ 090 984 34 09; www.noleggiobongiorno.it; Via Risorgimento 240, Santa Marina Salina; hire per hr/day bikes €3.50/10.50, scooters €8.50/31).

**BOAT //** Siremar (www.siremar.it) and Ustica Lines (www.usticalines.it) run hydrofoils to Santa Marina Salina from Lipari (€8.80, 25 minutes, 12 to 16 daily) and Milazzo (€17.25, 1½ to two hours, 12 to 16 daily). There are also less frequent services to/from Stromboli and Panarea, and two daily sailings to/from Messina and Reggio di Calabria. Most services call at Rinella en route. Siremar and Ustica share a ticket office ( ☎ 090 984 30 03; Piazza Santa Marina Salina 2, Santa Marina Salina).

**BUS //** Citis ( ☎ 090 984 41 50; www.trasportisalina.it) buses run from Santa Marina Salina to Lingua (€1.70, five minutes, nine daily Monday to Saturday, six Sunday), Malfa (€1.70, 35 minutes, nine daily Monday to Saturday, six Sunday), Rinella (€2.40, 45 minutes to one hour, nine daily Monday to Saturday, six Sunday), Pollara (€2.10, 50 minutes, seven daily Monday to Saturday, five Sunday), Valdichiesa (€2.10, 35 to 50 minutes, nine daily Monday to Saturday, six Sunday) and Leni (€2.40, 40 to 55 minutes, nine daily Monday to Saturday, six Sunday). Timetables are posted around the island. If you're going to Rinella or Pollara from Santa Marina Salina, you'll have to change at Malfa.

**CAR & MOTORCYCLE //** Antonio Bongiorno ( ☎ 090 984 34 09; www.noleggiobongiorno.it; Via Risorgimento 240, Santa Marina Salina) hires cars for €60 per day.

# PANAREA
· · · · · ·

**pop 320**

**Exclusive and expensive, Panarea is the smallest and most fashionable of the Aeolians, attracting the international jet-setters and Milanese fashionistas for a taste of *dolce far niente* (sweet nothing). In summer, luxury yachts fill the tiny harbour and flocks of day-trippers traipse around the car-free whitewashed streets of San Pietro, the port and principal settlement. Panarea is a strictly summer-only destination with very little going on outside of the tourist season – in fact, arrive between November and Easter and you'll probably find nothing open at all.**

## EXPLORING PANAREA

### ☙ VILLAGGIO PREISTORICO //
### EXPLORE PREHISTORIC RUINS AND BLISSFUL COVES

Once you've pottered around San Pietro for a while, head off southwards towards Cala Junco and Panarea's **Villaggio Preistorico** (Prehistoric Village) – signs point the way. En route you'll pass **Spiagetta Zimmari**, a small stretch of brown sand backed by a steep sand dune. From the beach, steps lead up to **Punta Milazzese**, where the ruins of the Villaggio Preistorico lie on an elevated natural platform surrounded on all sides by the sea. Some 23 huts have been unearthed and it's reckoned that the headland was inhabited as far back as the 14th century BC. Pottery found here shows distinctly Minoan influences, lending credence to the theory that there were ties between the islanders and the Cretans.

Just before you reach the ruins a set of steps leads down to **Cala Junco**, a beautiful little cove with a pebble beach and dreamy aquamarine waters. For something more energy-sapping take the signposted trail up to **Punta del Corvo** (421m), Panarea's highest point, about two hours' walk away.

### ☙ OFFSHORE //
### BOAT AROUND PANAREA'S PRIVATE ARCHIPELAGO

To explore the five islets that lie off Panarea's eastern shore you'll need to hire a boat – ask at the seafront kiosks at San Pietro or try **Nautilus** ( ☎ 333 4233161; Baia di Drautto) at Drautta, south of San Pietro; prices start at about €65 per day.

Nearest to Panarea is **Dattilo**, which has a pretty little beach called Le Guglie. There's also good swimming at **Lisca Bianca**, on a small white beach on the isle's southern side. On the seabed beneath the narrow channel between Lisca Bianca and **Bottaro** (actually nothing more than a protruding rock), lies the wreck of a 19th-century English ship. Divers can hire scuba equipment and organise dives at **Amphibia** ( ☎ 335 1245332; www.amphibia.it, in Italian; Via Comunale) in San Pietro. South of Dattilo is **Lisca Nera**, while to the north, **Basiluzzo**, the largest of the five islets, is given over to the cultivation of capers. At the back of the island, visible from land, is the impressive wreck of a Roman ship.

### ☙ SPIAGGIA FUMAROLA //
### SUNBATHE ON A STONE BEACH

To the north of San Pietro, and again signposted, is **Spiaggia Fumarola**, a stone beach at the bottom of a treacherous, overgrown descent. Outside of peak months this is an isolated spot ideal for a quiet swim, but in July and August, the sun-seekers move in en masse and the ringing of mobile phones becomes incessant.

AEOLIAN ISLANDS

## ♥ DA FRANCESCO // DINE DOWN BY THE PORT

Up a short flight of stairs from the port (follow the signs), **Da Francesco** ( ☎ 090 98 30 23; Via San Pietro; meals €30; ⌚ Mar-Nov) is as close as you'll get to a value-for-money eatery on Panarea. It's a laid-back trattoria with an outdoor terrace, fine sea views over to Stromboli, and a straightforward menu of pastas and fish dishes. Try the speciality spaghetti *alla disgraziata* (with tomatoes, aubergines, chilli, capers and olives).

## TRANSPORT

**BOAT //** In summer **Siremar** ( ☎ 090 98 30 07; www.siremar.it) and **Ustica Lines** ( ☎ 090 98 33 44; www.usticalines.it) run up to eight hydrofoils daily to/from Lipari (€10.40, one hour) and Milazzo (€17.80, 2¼ hours). In winter, there are only two daily services. From Panarea, you can also sail to/from Stromboli (€11, 30 to 40 minutes by hydrofoil, 1¼ hours by ferry, one to four departures daily). The ticket office is at the port at San Pietro.

**CAR & MOTORCYCLE //** Cars are not allowed on Panarea but you won't need one as the island is small enough to get around on foot. The preferred mode of transport is golf carts. To arrange a taxi contact **Pantaxi** ( ☎ 333 3138610).

# STROMBOLI
· · · · · ·

**pop 400**

**Emerging out of the blue haze like a menacing maritime pyramid, Stromboli's smoking silhouette conforms perfectly to one's childhood idea of a volcano. In fact, the island of Stromboli is a volcano, or rather it's the tip of a vast underwater volcano that rises from the seabed 1476m below. The most isolated and captivating of the Aeolian Islands, it's a hugely popular day-trip destination as well as the summer favourite**

---

## ∼ WORTH A TRIP ∼

**Filicudi** and **Alicudi** are the least visited and least developed of the Aeolian Islands. They're also the oldest, dating back to tectonic activity 700,000 years ago. Of the two, Filicudi is the more enticing, its wild, beautiful coastline lapped by crystal clear waters and pitted by deep grottoes. Offshore, the wrecks of ancient Greek and Roman ships provide fabulous diving opportunities. The place to head for is **Pecorini**, a tiny fishing hamlet clustered around a small pebble beach, where you can stay at super-friendly **La Sirena** (see p312) and eat superb seafood at its acclaimed **restaurant** ( ☎ 090 988 99 97; meals €30-35).

For messing around on the water, see Nino Terrano from **I Delfini** ( ☎ 090 148 46 45; www.idelfinifilicudi.it; Pecorini), who can usually be found at Pecorini's small marina. He hires out boats (€100 per day including petrol) or sails you around the island (€40 to €80, about one hour), taking you into the **Grotta del Bue Marino** sea cave and pointing out the 71m-high rock tower, **Scoglio della Canna**. He also organises dives to the **Museo Sottomarino** area, where you can explore the sunken relics of nine crumbling ships. On shore 1km southwest of the port is **Capo Graziano**, the remains of a prehistoric village. Hydrofoils run to Filicudi from Lipari (€15.80, 1¼ hours, at least two daily).

Alicudi is as isolated a place as you'll find in the entire Mediterranean basin, with minimal facilities and no marked roads. About the only thing to do here is climb **Monte Filo dell'Arpa** (675m) and admire the views.

AEOLIAN ISLANDS

of designers Dolce and Gabbana, who have a holiday home here. But to best appreciate its primordial beauty and the romance that lured Roberto Rossellini and his lover Ingrid Bergman here in 1949, you'll need to give it a few days.

Volcanic activity has scarred and blackened much of the island but the northeastern corner is inhabited and it's here that you'll find the island's famous black beaches (some very good, with excellent sand), and the main settlement sprawled attractively along the volcano's lower slopes. But despite the picture-postcard appearance, life here is tough: food and drinking water have to be ferried in, there are no roads across the island, and until relatively recently there was no electricity in Ginostra on the southwest coast. If the weather turns rough and the sea goes wild, ferries and hydrofoils are cancelled and the island is completely cut off. And if all that isn't enough, there's still the constant possibility of the volcano blowing its top, as it did in February 2007, although fortunately without any harmful consequences.

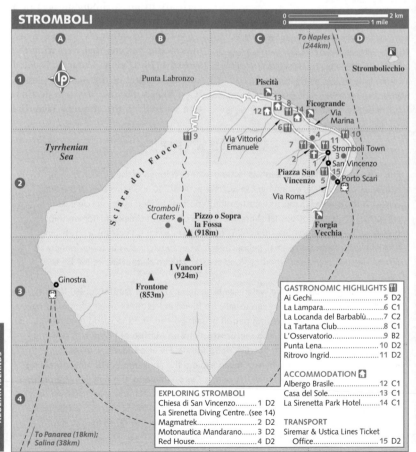

**STROMBOLI**

GASTRONOMIC HIGHLIGHTS 🍴
Ai Gechi.................................5 D2
La Lampara............................6 C1
La Locanda del Barbablù........7 C2
La Tartana Club.....................8 C1
L'Osservatorio......................9 B2
Punta Lena.........................10 D2
Ritrovo Ingrid.....................11 D2

ACCOMMODATION 🏠
Albergo Brasile....................12 C1
Casa del Sole......................13 C1
La Sirenetta Park Hotel........14 C1

EXPLORING STROMBOLI
Chiesa di San Vincenzo..........1 D2
La Sirenetta Diving Centre..(see 14)
Magmatrek............................2 D2
Motonautica Mandarano.......3 D2
Red House............................4 D2

TRANSPORT
Siremar & Ustica Lines Ticket
    Office.............................15 D2

# ESSENTIAL INFORMATION

**EMERGENCIES //** Emergency Doctor
(☎ 090 98 60 97; Via Vittorio Emanuele) Police
(☎ 090 98 60 21; Via Roma) On the left as you walk up
Via Roma.

# ORIENTATION

Boats arrive at Porto Scari, downhill
from the main town. Most accommodation, as well as the meeting point
for guided hikes, is a short walk up the
Scalo Scari on Via Roma. At the top of
Via Roma is the central square, Piazza
San Vincenzo, from where Via Vittorio Emanuele continues westwards.
To hit the crater path, follow Via Vittorio Emanuele until you see signs for
L'Osservatorio off to the left. Note that
there is no street lighting on Stromboli
except in a couple of main streets and
on Piazza San Vincenzo, so bring a
torch.

# EXPLORING STROMBOLI

❦ THE VOLCANO // SCALE EUROPE'S
MOST ACTIVE VOLCANO
The youngest of the Aeolian volcanoes,
Stromboli was formed only 40,000 years
ago and its gases continue to send up an
almost constant spray of liquid magma,
a process defined by vulcanologists as
*attività Stromboliana* (Strombolian
activity).

The most recent major eruptions took
place on 27 February 2007. Two new
summit craters were formed and lava
flowed down the mountain's western
flank but little real harm was done.
Previously, an eruption in April 2003
showered the village of Ginostra with
rocks, and activity in December 2002
produced a tsunami, causing damage to

## VOLCANO GUIDES

To climb to the top of Stromboli you'll
need to hire a guide or go on an organised trek. To avoid disappointment
always sort this out in advance.
Magmatrek (☎ 090 986 57 68; www.
magmatrek.it; Via Vittorio Emanuele; excursion
per person €28, ☉ Easter-Nov) Has experienced,
multilingual (English-, German- and French-
speaking) guides that lead daily treks up the volcano
(maximum group size of 20 people). It can also put
together tailor-made treks for individuals or groups.
Book early, if possible up to a week before you want
to climb.
Stromboli Guide (☎ 090 98 61 44; www.
stromboliguide.it; c/o Agenzia Il Vulcano a Piede,
Via Roma; ☉ 10am-12.30pm, 4-7.30pm) Another
reputable outfit led by a guide affiliated with the
Associazione Guide Alpine Italiane.

Stromboli town, injuring six people and
closing the island to visitors for a few
months.

Since 2005 access to the summit has
been strictly regulated. You can walk
freely to 400m, but to continue on to the
summit (924m) you are legally required
to go with a guide (see the boxed text
above). It's a demanding five- to six-hour
trek up to the top and back and you'll
need to have the following equipment:
proper walking shoes, a backpack that
allows free movement of both arms,
clothing for cold and wet weather, a
change of T-shirt, a handkerchief to
protect against dust (wear glasses not
contact lenses), a torch, one to two litres
of water and some food. If you haven't
got any of these, Totem Trekking (☎ 090
986 57 52; www.totemtrekking.stromboli.com; Piazza
San Vincenzo 4; ☉ 10am-1pm & 4-7.30pm) hires
out all the necessary equipment: boots
(€6), backpacks (€5), torches (€3) and
windbreakers (€5).

## STROMBOLI FACTS

* Stromboli is Europe's only permanently active volcano and the youngest in the Aeolian archipelago.

* There are usually two major explosions every year.

* The island has been inhabited since Neolithic times but the volcano has never destroyed Stromboli town.

* Stromboli was used to control important trade routes in the Tyrrhenian Sea, as it overlooks the other Aeolian Islands, the Italian mainland and the Straits of Messina. Because of this and its exploding crater, it was known as the 'Lighthouse of the Mediterranean'.

* The pinnacle of rock known as Strombolicchio, which can be seen just off the coast near Ficogrande, is the remnants of the original volcano that collapsed into the sea. Strombolicchio is what is left of the central cylinder (the neck) of the volcano, in which the lava solidified.

* The word 'sciara' comes from the Arabic sharia (meaning 'street'), thus the Sciara del Fuoco is a 'Street of Fire'.

* On 30 December 2002 landslides caused by volcanic activity provoked two tidal waves between 5m and 10m high. Stromboli town and Ginostra were both hit.

* The 2002–2003 eruptions increased the crater size from 35m to 125m.

* The 2007 eruption opened two new craters on the summit.

Departure times for organised treks vary from 3.30pm to 6pm, depending on the season, but are always timed so that you can observe sunset from the mountain top and watch the crater's fireworks for about 45 minutes as night falls. The descent to Piazza San Vincenzo takes about two hours, normally arriving around 10.30pm.

If you don't fancy going all the way, you can take a walk up to L'Osservatorio (see p158), from where there are fabulous views up to the Sciara del Fuoco (the blackened laval scar that runs down the mountain's flank) and the crater explosions. These usually take place every 20 minutes or so and are preceded by a loud belly-roar as gases force the magma into the air. It is incredibly exciting! On a still night the livid red Sciara and exploding cone are dramatically visible.

♥ BOAT TOURS // WATCH THE VOLCANIC FIREWORKS FROM A BOAT

One of the most popular ways of viewing Stromboli's nocturnal fireworks is to take a boat tour of the island. Società Navigazione Pippo ( ☎ 090 98 61 35) and Antonio Cacetta ( ☎ 339 5818200) are among the numerous outfits running boat tours out of Porto Scari. There are two tours to choose from: a three-hour daytime cruise of the island, with swimming breaks at Strombolicchio (the rock islet jutting out of the water off the north coast) and a quick visit to Ginostra, and a 2½-hour sunset excursion to watch the Sciara del Fuoco explosions from the sea. Both cost €20 per person.

🌱 SWIMMING & DIVING // **TOP UP YOUR TAN ON STROMBOLI'S BLACK BEACHES**

Stromboli's black sandy beaches are the best in the Aeolian archipelago. Particularly beautiful is Forgia Vecchia, about 300m south of the port, a tranquil stretch of black pebbles curving around a tranquil bay and backed by the volcano's green slopes. The most popular beach is Ficogrande, a strip of rocks and black volcanic sand about 10 minutes' walk from the hydrofoil dock: turn right out of the harbour and follow the shore as it curves around to the northwest. Opposite the beach at La Sirenetta Park Hotel, La Sirenetta Diving Center (☎ 338 8919675; www.lasirenettadiving.it; La Sirenetta Hotel, Via Marina 33; ☽ late May–mid-Sep) offers diving courses as well as accompanied dives. Further west there's another decent beach at Piscità.

🌱 RED HOUSE // **SEE WHERE ROSSELLINI ROMANCED INGRID BERGMAN**

Stromboli doesn't really have any sights as such apart from the Chiesa di San Vincenzo (Piazza San Vincenzo) on the main square. What it does have, though, is the rusty-red house where Ingrid Bergman and Roberto Rossellini lived together whilst filming *Stromboli, Terra di Dio* in 1949. Film buffs will remember the scandal provoked by their liaison – both Rossellini and Bergman were married to other people at the time – which was the talk of the film world for a long time afterwards. You can't actually go into the house, which is just down from Piazza San Vincenzo on the right, but it's interesting to see the scene of such a famous romance.

# GASTRONOMIC HIGHLIGHTS

Eating out in Stromboli is an expensive business as most food items have to be shipped in. Seafood is ubiquitous but pizza provides a good alternative.

🌱 AI GECHI €€

☎ 090 98 62 13; Vico Salina 12, Porto Scari; meals €35; ☽ dinner only Tue-Sun

Follow the arrows to this great hideaway, at the end of an alley off Via Roma. A local favourite, it's a tastefully outfitted Aeolian house whose shaded veranda serves as the dining area. A towering cactus and the whitewashed look gives it a vaguely South American feel, but the ship lamps, friendly barefoot waitstaff and gorgeous seafood are pure Mediterranean. Expect traditional food with a slightly modern twist.

🌱 LA LAMPARA €

☎ 090 98 60 19; Via Vittorio Emanuele 27; pizzas €8-10; ☽ 6pm-late

A pizza on La Lampara's noisy, vine-draped terrace is an excellent value-for-money alternative to the pricier seafood. There are all the usual toppings plus one or two Strombolian specialities, including pizza with juicy local prawns. The laid-back outdoor atmosphere is particularly suited to families with young kids.

🌱 LA LOCANDA DEL BARBABLÙ €€€

☎ 090 98 61 18; www.barbablu.it; Via Vittorio Emanuele 17; set menus €38 or €50; ☽ mid-Apr–mid-Oct

This is one of Stromboli's top restaurants. Housed in a Pompeian red-and-yellow house near Piazza San Vincenzo, it's a fashionable port of call for the August aperitif set, with a lively bar and a rustic-chic restaurant. There's no à la carte – instead you have to choose

AEOLIAN ISLANDS

between one of two fish-only set menus (although you can book a vegetarian menu), based on the day's catch and the chef's inspiration. Bookings essential. It also has five elegant B&B rooms (doubles €140 to €240).

### ♥ LA TARTANA CLUB €€€
☎ 090 98 60 25; Via Marina; meals from €35; ☀ late May-Oct

Break bread with the president of Italy and Dolce and Gabbana at this chic restaurant-bar, a long-standing favourite of Stromboli's beautiful people. Lunch is a casual buffet on the seafront terrace, but the evening scene is more refined, with aperitivi and cocktails at the piano bar and diners romancing over candlelit tables. The menu is traditional in inspiration, with classics such as linguine and anchovies and veal cutlets with Malvasia wine.

### ♥ L'OSSERVATORIO €€
☎ 090 98 63 60; pizzas from €7, meals €25-30

You'll remember a meal here. Not for the big-barn ambience, nor even for the food, which is fine if nothing exceptional. No, the real reason to make the 1km slog up here (bring a torch if walking at night) is to marvel at the amazing views of the Sciara del Fuoco and its evening pyrotechnics display. The menu is standard pasta and seafood, but the pizzas are excellent and it does delicious doorstop *panini* (filled bread roll; €3.50) at lunch.

### ♥ PUNTA LENA €€
☎ 090 98 62 04; Via Marina; meals €35; ☀ Apr-Oct

With its waterfront terrace and magnificent seafood, Punta Lena is a model

family-run restaurant. There's nothing flash about the place – decoration is limited to fresh flowers and soothing seascapes over Strombolicchio – but the food is as good as you'll get anywhere on the island. Signature dishes include *gamberetti marinati* (marinated prawns) and spaghetti *alla stromboliana* (with wild fennel, cherry tomatoes and breadcrumbs).

### ♥ RITROVO INGRID €
☎ 090 98 63 85; Piazza San Vincenzo; pizza from €6.50; ☀ 8am-midnight, to 3am Jul & Aug

There can be few better spots to breakfast than the panoramic terrace of this Stromboli institution. An all-purpose cafe/*gelateria*/pizzeria, it's busy throughout the day as islanders come for their morning cappuccino, tourists pop in for an ice cream and trekkers compare notes over an evening pizza.

## TRANSPORT

**BOAT //** Stromboli is the most remote of all the Aeolians. Boats connect the island with Lipari (ferry/hydrofoil €12.40/17.80, four/1¾ hours) and Milazzo (hydrofoil €21.45, three hours). There are up to eight daily services in high season, but this falls to two a day in winter. In bad weather the service is often disrupted or cancelled altogether. Ticket offices for Ustica Lines ( ☎ 090 98 60 03; www.usticalines.it) and Siremar ( ☎ 090 98 60 16; www.siremar.it) are at the port.

**CAR & MOTORCYCLE //** There are no cars on Stromboli, just scooters, electric karts and three-wheeler vehicles known locally as *ape*. You can hire scooters from Motonautica Mandarano ( ☎ 090 98 62 12; Via Marina; per day about €20). From the port follow the road to your left; you'll find it after about 300m.

**TAXI //** Call Sabbia Nera Taxi ( ☎ 090 98 63 90).

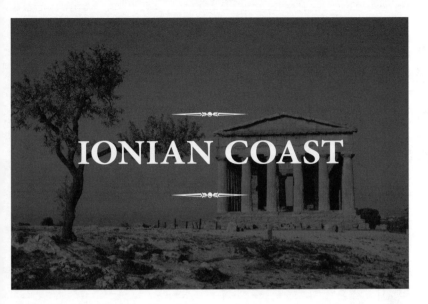

# IONIAN COAST

## 3 PERFECT DAYS

❦ DAY 1 // **TAORMINA'S GREEK RUINS & GREAT VIEWS**
Wake up in Taormina (p168), the king of Sicily's Ionian resorts. After admiring the stunning setting of the Teatro Greco (p169) and its memorable views to Mt Etna, spend the rest of the morning exploring the town's medieval streets, browsing among the delis on Corso Umberto I (p169) and thrilling to the verdant delights of Villa Comunale (p171). After lunch head down to Isola Bella (p171) for some seaside fun.

❦ DAY 2 // **ETNA'S FUMING HEIGHTS**
You'll have seen it looming in the distance and now is the time to explore Mt Etna (p189). You can take a tour from Taormina (p172) or Catania, or, better still, pick up a car and go it alone. The easiest approach is the southern ascent via Rifugio Sapienza (p191) and a cable car, which takes you up to 2500m. From there you can follow with a guide or venture into the black wilderness on your own. Once back safely, decamp to Nicolosi (p314) for a comfortable and convenient overnight stay.

❦ DAY 3 // **CATANIA'S VIVACIOUS STREET LIFE**
Head to Catania (p176) for a shot of urban energy and gastronomic exercise. Start off by admiring the baroque churches on Via Crociferi (p179) and the grand palazzi (palaces or mansions) of Piazza del Duomo (p176) before ducking down to La Pescheria fish market (p177) and an unforgettable seafood lunch at Osteria Antica Marina (p182). Set the rest of the day aside for strolling along Via Etnea (p177) followed by a night out around Piazza Bellini (p184).

# IONIAN COAST

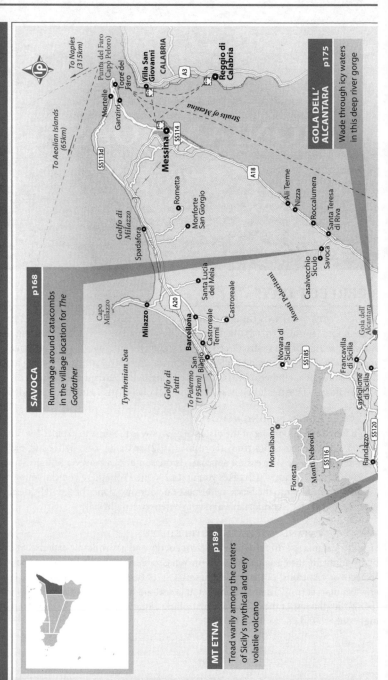

**SAVOCA** p168

Rummage around catacombs in the village location for *The Godfather*

**GOLA DELL' ALCANTARA** p175

Wade through icy waters in this deep river gorge

**MT ETNA** p189

Tread warily among the craters of Sicily's mythical and very volatile volcano

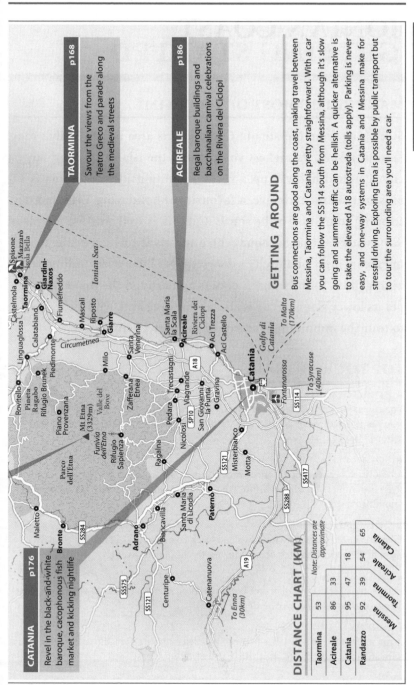

**IONIAN COAST**

**TAORMINA**   p168

Savour the views from the Teatro Greco and parade along the medieval streets

**ACIREALE**   p186

Regal baroque buildings and bacchanalian carnival celebrations on the Riviera dei Ciclopi

**CATANIA**   p176

Revel in the black-and-white baroque, cacophonous fish market and kicking nightlife

## GETTING AROUND

Bus connections are good along the coast, making travel between Messina, Taormina and Catania pretty straightforward. With a car you can follow the SS114 south from Messina, although it's slow going and summer traffic can be hellish. A quicker alternative is to take the elevated A18 autostrada (tolls apply). Parking is never easy, and one-way systems in Catania and Messina make for stressful driving. Exploring Etna is possible by public transport but to tour the surrounding area you'll need a car.

## DISTANCE CHART (KM)

Note: Distances are approximate

| | Messina | Taormina | Acireale | Catania |
|---|---|---|---|---|
| Taormina | 53 | | | |
| Acireale | 86 | 33 | | |
| Catania | 95 | 47 | 18 | |
| Randazzo | 92 | 39 | 54 | 65 |

# IONIAN COAST
## GETTING STARTED

## MAKING THE MOST OF YOUR TIME

Stretching from Messina to Catania, this area boasts Sicily's most famous resort, its highest volcano and the island's second-largest city. Perched halfway up a rocky mountainside, Taormina is sophisticated and exclusive, a favourite of holidaying VIPs and day-tripping tourists. To the south, Catania is well worth a couple of days, with its regal baroque centre and vivacious street life. Brooding menacingly on the city's doorstep, Mt Etna offers unforgettable hiking, both to the summit craters and around the woods that carpet its lower slopes. Etna is also a wine area and, with a car, it's fun to tour the mountain in search of the perfect vintage.

## TOP TOURS & TRAILS

**❦ ETNA TOURING**
You can explore Mt Etna on your own, but going with a guide ensures that you won't miss anything or accidentally stumble into a fuming crater (see the boxed text, p193).

- - - - - - - - - - - - - - - - - - - - - - - - - - - - - - - - - - - - - - - - - - - - - - - - - - - - - - - - -

**❦ GOLA DELL'ALCANTARA**
A renowned beauty spot, this deep rocky canyon is bisected by the freezing Alcantara river. In summer you can wade through the waters, sunbathe or walk along the surrounding nature trails (p162).

- - - - - - - - - - - - - - - - - - - - - - - - - - - - - - - - - - - - - - - - - - - - - - - - - - - - - - - - -

**❦ SAIL AHOY**
Take a boat tour to explore the caves and black volcanic rocks of the Riviera dei Ciclopi, the popular stretch of coastline north of Catania (p188).

- - - - - - - - - - - - - - - - - - - - - - - - - - - - - - - - - - - - - - - - - - - - - - - - - - - - - - - - -

**❦ ISOLA BELLA**
This picture-perfect bay offers the best swimming near Taormina, as well as excellent diving courtesy of Nike Diving Centre (p171).

- - - - - - - - - - - - - - - - - - - - - - - - - - - - - - - - - - - - - - - - - - - - - - - - - - - - - - - - -

**❦ FERROVIA CIRCUMETNEA**
If you prefer to keep a distance between yourself and Etna's volatile craters, jump on a train and tour the small towns that circle the volcano's base (p193).

- - - - - - - - - - - - - - - - - - - - - - - - - - - - - - - - - - - - - - - - - - - - - - - - - - - - - - - - -

# GETTING AWAY FROM IT ALL

This part of Sicily heaves in summer as tourists flock to the coastal resorts and the main trails up Mt Etna. But there are quiet pockets of peace in the mayhem.

* **Follow in the Godfather's footsteps** Hidden away in the hills north of Taormina, atmospheric Savoca was used as a film location for *The Godfather* (p168).

* **Seafood in a quiet marina** Turn your back on the crowds and head to the tiny fishing hamlet of Santa Maria la Scala for a seafood lunch (p187).

* **Picnic in Pineta Ragabo** On Mt Etna's quieter northern slopes, this huge wood is a lovely place for a picnic under the pines (p192).

# ADVANCE PLANNING

To experience the best of the coast's festivals, check timings, book accommodation and, if necessary, buy tickets.

* **Festa di Sant'Agata** Catania grinds to a halt between 3 and 5 February as millions take to the streets to celebrate the city's patron saint. Accommodation must be booked well in advance (p181).

* **Carnevale** Plan ahead to be in Acireale in February. The town's spectacular carnival celebrations are among the most popular in Sicily, with great parades of huge papier mâché figures (p187).

* **Taormina Arte** Get in early with reservations and ticket requests for Taormina's film, music and theatre festival held over July and August (p172).

# TOP TRATTORIAS

**♥ TRATTORIA DI DE FIORE**
This charming Catania eatery is the place for *pasta alla Norma*, a Sicilian classic (p183).

----------------------------------------

**♥ TRATTORIA LA GROTTA**
It doesn't get any more authentic than this seafood trattoria at Santa Maria la Scala (p187).

----------------------------------------

**♥ ANTICO ORTO DEI LIMONO**
Feast on filling country fare in a converted oil press in Nicolosi (p194).

----------------------------------------

**♥ OSTERIA ANTICA MARINA**
Superb seafood in the shadow of Catania's raucous fish market (p182).

----------------------------------------

**♥ LA PIAZZETTA**
Locals recommend this family-run Taormina trattoria (p173).

----------------------------------------

# RESOURCES

* **Parks.it** (www.parks.it/parco.etna/) A good introduction to the Parco dell'Etna and environs.

* **Taormina Tourist Office** (www.gate2 taormina.com) A comprehensive website with historical background and practical details.

* **Trasporti sullo Stretto** (www.trasporti sullostretto.it, in Italian) Has up-to-date timetables of ferry crossings to/from Messina.

* **Comune di Catania** (www.comune.catania. it) Extensive listings, as well as suggested itineraries and transport info.

# MESSINA
. . . . . .

pop 243,380

Just a few kilometres from the Italian mainland, Messina sits on a curved harbour at the northernmost point of Sicily's Ionian Coast. For centuries, it has been a major transport hub and today it's an important gateway to and from the island. A big, busy, traffic-clogged city, it is unlikely to waylay you long, but if you do find yourself passing through, it has an impressive centre with wide boulevards and elegant turn-of-the-century buildings, its cathedral is one of Sicily's finest, and the local swordfish is celebrated by gourmets across the island. Historical monuments are thin on the ground, though, as the city was virtually razed to the ground by an earthquake in 1908 and then devastated by mass bombing in WWII.

Messina is, and always has been, about the strait, the impossibly narrow stretch of water that divides Sicily from the Italian peninsula. The Greeks mythologised the strait's clashing currents as the twin monsters of Charbydis (the whirlpool) and Scylla (the six-headed monster), and strong currents still make swimming a danger. They are not the only danger, though. Beneath the choppy sea is a geological fault line that poses a constant threat. In 1908 it provoked a devastating earthquake – Europe's deadliest ever – which sank the shore by half a metre and killed between 84,000 and 200,000 people.

Modern seismologists worry about what effect it could have on a bridge built across the channel. Plans to construct the world's largest suspension bridge over the strait – already on the drawing board for years – are still a bone of contention with successive national governments regularly giving them the go-ahead, then cancelling them, then resurrecting them. At the time of research the bridge was on again.

## ESSENTIAL INFORMATION

**EMERGENCIES //** Ospedale Piemonte ( ☎ 090 22 21; Viale Europa) Police Station ( ☎ 090 3 66 11; Via Placida 2)

**TOURIST INFORMATION //** Tourist Office ( ☎ 090 67 29 44; infotur@comune.messina.it; Piazza Repubblica 44; ☒ 9am-1.30pm Mon-Fri, 3-5pm Tue & Thu) To the left as you face the train station.

## ORIENTATION

Driving in Messina is not an especially pleasant experience, although once you've made it through to the city centre, the grid system makes navigation a bit easier. The main things to know are that the principal streets, Via Garibaldi and Via Vittorio Emanuele II, run parallel to the sea, and that the main transport hub is Piazza della Repubblica, at the southern end of the waterfront. Here you'll find the train station and intercity bus stops; Bluvia ferries also dock near here. To get to the city centre from Piazza della Repubblica, turn left into Via Giuseppe La Farina and take the first right into Via Tommaso Cannizzaro to reach Piazza Cairoli.

## EXPLORING MESSINA

❦ PIAZZA DEL DUOMO // CATCH A PERFORMANCE AT THE DUOMO'S ASTRONOMICAL CLOCK

Messina's one great sight is the Norman Duomo (Piazza del Duomo; ☒ 7am-7pm Mon-Sat, 7.30am-1pm & 4-7.30pm Sun), one of Sicily's finest cathedrals, or at least a faithful replica of one of Sicily's finest cathedrals. The original, which was built in the 12th century, was accidentally burnt to the ground in 1254. It was subsequently rebuilt several times, after earthquakes in 1783 and 1908, and, again, after a WWII incendiary bomb reduced it to rubble in 1943. Very little remains of the original structure, except for the stripy marble inlay, the tracery of the facade and the fantastic Catalan Gothic portal. Inside there's an impressive carved altar and a huge inlaid organ, the third largest in Europe. Other treasures, such as the famous **Manta d'Oro** (Golden Mantle) used to 'cloak' holy pictures during reli-

gious celebrations, are kept in the **Museo della Cattedrale** ( ☎ 090 67 51 75; admission €3; ⏱ 10am-1pm Mon-Sat).

Outside, you can't miss the 60m **campanile** (admission €3.50; ⏱ 10am-1pm Mon-Sat) and its incongruous **astronomical clock**, said to be the world's largest. Built in Strasbourg in 1733, it strikes at noon, setting in motion a procession of bronze automata that sets off a comical roaring lion and crowing cockerel. Climb the tower to see the enormous figures up close.

Facing the tower, the marble **Fontana di Orione** (1553) commemorates

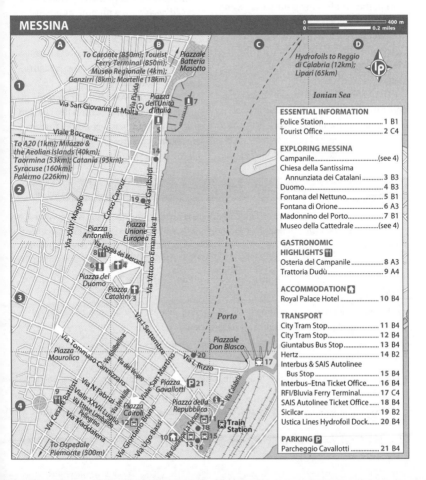

Orion, the mythical founder of Messina, while nearby on Piazza Catalani, the 12th-century **Chiesa della Santissima Annunziata dei Catalani** (☺ special services only) is a fine example of Arab-Norman construction.

**☙ MUSEO REGIONALE // PONDER MESSINA'S ART COLLECTION AT THE CITY MUSEUM**

Pick up a tram at Piazza Cairoli and take a ride up the sickle-shaped harbour. Halfway along, you'll see the 16th-century **Fontana del Nettuno** (Neptune's Fountain) in the middle of two busy roads, and the colossal golden statue, the **Madonnino del Porto**, towering over the port. Carry on to the end of the line for the **Museo Regionale** ( ☎ 090 36 12 92; Viale della Libertà 465; adult/concession €5/3; ☺ 9am-1.30pm Mon-Fri & 4.30-7pm Tue, Thu & Sat, 9am-12.30pm Sun), home to Messina's considerable art collection. The most famous work is the *San Gregorio* (St Gregory) polyptych by local boy Antonello da Messina (1430–79).

Although in pretty shabby condition, its five panels are wonderfully figurative. Other highlights include *Madonna con bambino e santi* (Virgin with Child and Saints) by the same artist, and two splendid works by Caravaggio (1571–1610): *L'Adorazione dei pastori* (Adoration of the Shepherds) and *Risurrezione di Lazzaro* (Resurrection of Lazarus).

# GASTRONOMIC HIGHLIGHTS

Messina is famous for its quality *pesce spada* (swordfish), which is typically served *agghiotta*, with pine nuts, sultanas, garlic, basil and tomatoes.

**☙ OSTERIA DEL CAMPANILE €€**
☎ 090 71 14 18; Via Loggia dei Mercanti 9; pizzas €6, meals €25; ☺ closed Sun

With its warm wooden interior and prime location – just behind the Duomo – this cosy hostelry is a good bet for classic coastal cuisine. The menu features all the usual suspects – pizza, pasta with

## ACCOMMODATION

There's no shortage of accommodation in this busy holiday area. Taormina is expensive but has some delightful midrange to top-end hotels, while Catania specialises in excellent-value B&Bs. Elsewhere, there are hotels and *agriturismi* (farm stays) dotted around the Etna area.

★ Contemporary design goes head to head with retro styling at **BAD** (p313), a sexy B&B in Catania.

★ Housed in a classy turn-of-the-century Taormina villa, **Hotel Villa Belvedere** (p312) offers refined accommodation and superb views.

★ Soak away your stresses with an outdoor jacuzzi at Taormina's laid-back **Isoco Guest House** (p312).

★ Nicolosi's **Hotel Alle Pendici** is a warm, welcoming retreat after a day hiking on Etna (p314).

★ Kick back in style on one of Catania's 'in' streets with a room at **Il Principe** (p313).

For detailed accommodation listings, see p312.

## TOP **FIVE**

### LOCAL SPECIALITIES

* ★ **Swordfish, Messina** (p166) – you'll find *pesce spada* (swordfish) on menus across Sicily, but the best are caught in the Strait of Messina between May and July

* ★ **Pasta alla Norma, Catania** (p181) – named after a Bellini opera, this is a classic Catania dish of fried aubergine (eggplant), tomato and salted ricotta

* ★ **Honey, Zafferana Etnea** (p192) – this small town on Etna's eastern slopes is celebrated for its honey, made with a range of local fruits

* ★ **Wine, Mt Etna** (p192) – grapes grown on Etna go to make Etna DOC, one of Sicily's best-known wines

* ★ **Mussels, Ganzirri** (p168) – diners head up here from Messina to dine on *cozze* (mussels) cultivated in a salt lake

seafood, grilled meat and fish – as well as a few novelties such as *risotto gamberi e curry* (prawn and curry risotto). In summer, tables flood the outside area, creating a buzzing streetside atmosphere.

### 🍴 TRATTORIA DUDÙ €

☎ 090 67 43 93; Via Cesare Battisti 122-124; meals €20; 🕙 closed Sun

This is a homey, family-run trattoria, ideal for a hearty lunch. It's not a smart place, its interior a cheerful jumble of fading family photos, *presepi* (Nativity scene) figures, puppets and assorted bric-a-brac, but the food is tasty and excellent value. Of the pastas, the spaghetti *con vongole e cozze* (with clams and mussels) is absolutely spot on and the delicious swordfish more than lives up to its reputation.

## TRANSPORT

**BOAT //** Messina is the main point of arrival for ferries and hydrofoils from the Italian mainland. Detailed time-table information is available online at www.trasportisullostretto.it, in Italian. Caronte & Tourist ( ☎ 800 627414; www.carontetourist.it) serves Villa San Giovanni (passenger/car €1.50/31, 25 minutes). RFI/Bluvia (www.rfi.it; Porto di Messina, Piazzale Don Blasco) oper-ates frequent passenger-only ferries to/from Reggio di Calabria (€3.30, 35 minutes) and car ferries to/from Villa San Giovanni (passenger/car €1.50/28, 35 minutes). Ustica Lines ( ☎ 090 36 40 44; www.usticalines.it; Via Vittorio Emanuele II) runs hydrofoils to/from Reggio di Calabria (€4.30, 15 minutes, two daily) and Lipari (€23.90, 1½ hours, five daily summer, once daily winter).

**BUS //** Giuntabus ( ☎ 090 67 57 49; Piazza della Repubblica) runs a service to Milazzo (€3.80, 50 minutes, 15 daily Monday to Saturday, three Sunday) for connections to the Aeolian Islands. Interbus ( ☎ 090 66 17 54; www.interbus.it; Piazza della Repubblica 6) runs a regular service to Taormina (€3.90, 1½ hours, hourly Monday to Saturday, twice Sunday), while SAIS Au-tolinee ( ☎ 090 77 19 14; www.saisautolinee.it, in Italian; Piazza della Repubblica 6) serves Palermo (€5.10, two hours, at least four daily Monday to Saturday, three Sunday), Catania (€7.70, 1½ hours, half-hourly Monday to Saturday, eight Sunday) and Catania airport (€8.50, two hours, at least nine daily Monday to Saturday, six Sunday). In town, an electric tram runs from Piazza Cairoli via the train station up to the Museo Regionale. Buy tickets (single €1.20) from *tabacchi* (tobacco shops).

**CAR & MOTORCYCLE //** For Palermo, Milazzo (connections to the Aeolian Islands), Taormina, Catania and Syracuse, turn right from the docks and follow Via Vittorio Emanuele II along the waterfront up to Piazza dell'Unità d'Italia. Here, double back on Corso Cavour and turn right into Viale Boccetta, following the green

A20 autostrada (motorway) signs. Car hire is available at **Hertz** ( ☎ 090 34 44 24; www.hertz.it; Via Vittorio Emanuele II 113) and **Sicilcar** ( ☎ 090 4 69 42; www. sicilcar.net; Via Garibaldi 187).

**PARKING //** If you have no luck parking on the street (blue lines denote pay-and-display meter parking), there's a useful multistorey car park, **Parcheggio Cavallotti** (Via I Settembre; ⌚ 5am-11.30pm Mon-Sat), near Piazza Cairoli.

**TRAIN //** As a rule buses are a better bet than trains, particularly to Milazzo and Taormina, but there are several daily trains to Catania (€6.70, 1½ to two hours), Syracuse (€9.35 to €20.50, 2½ to three hours) and Palermo (€11.45, 3½ hours).

# AROUND MESSINA
· · · · · ·

🌱 **GANZIRRI //** DINE ON MUSSELS IN A LAKESIDE RESTAURANT
From Messina the coast curves around to Sicily's most northeasterly point, **Punta del Faro** (also called Capo Peloro), just 3km across the water from the Italian mainland. South of the cape is the lakeside town of **Ganzirri**, a popular summer hangout and pretty setting for a fish dinner. Mussels are the local speciality – they're cultivated in the salty lake waters – and **La Napoletana** ( ☎ 090 39 10 32; Via Lago Grande 29; meals €30-35; ⌚ closed Wed) is a good place to try them. A family-run restaurant housed in a neoclassical villa, it specialises in local seafood, so expect plenty of mussels, clams, swordfish and *stoccafisso* (stockfish).

On the other side of the cape, **Mortelle** is the area's most popular summer resort, where the Messinese go to sunbathe and hang out.

🌱 **SAVOCA //** EXPLORE THE VILLAGE USED TO FILM 'THE GODFATHER'
Sandwiched between the Peloritani mountains and the sea, the SS114 hugs the coast as it heads south towards Taormina. It's a slow drive, past never-ending towns that merge one into another, but with the sparkling blue sea to keep you company it's not unpleasant. (You can cover the same ground much more quickly on the elevated A18 autostrada.) For a change of scene take a detour to the tiny, trapped-in-time village of **Savoca**, high in the hills 4km inland from Santa Teresa di Riva.

Surrounded by encroaching green peaks, the village seems unchanged since medieval times with its gated walls, rustic stone cottages and haunting churches. It even has its own **catacombs** (admission by donation; ⌚ 9am-noon & 3-7pm Tue-Sat, 3-7pm Sun), beneath a Cappucini monastery, where the macabre bodies of a few mummified bigwigs stand in a series of wall niches.

However, the village's main claim to fame is its association with *The Godfather* film – Michael Corleone's marriage to Apollonia was filmed here. One of the locations used was the **Bar Vitelli**, a rustic bar located by the village entrance and a lovely spot for a cool lemon *granita* (crushed-ice drink). For more information about the village, ask at the small **tourist office** ( ☎ 0942 76 11 25; http://turismo. comune.savoca.me.it; Via San Michele; ⌚ 9.40am-1pm & 3-6.20pm Tue-Sun).

# TAORMINA
· · · · · ·

pop 11,095 / elev 204m
**Spectacularly perched on the side of a mountain, Taormina is Sicily's most sophisticated summer destination, a chic resort town beloved of holidaying high-rollers and visiting celebs. And while the town is unashamedly touristy, it remains an achingly beautiful spot with gorgeous medieval churches,**

a stunning Greek theatre and sweeping views over the Gulf of Naxos and Mt Etna.

Founded in the 4th century BC, it enjoyed great prosperity under the Greek ruler Gelon II and later under the Romans, but fell into quiet obscurity after being conquered by the Normans in 1087. Its modern reincarnation as a tourist destination dates to the 18th century, when it was discovered by northern Europeans on the Grand Tour. Goethe was an early fan, as was DH Lawrence, who lived here between 1920 and 1923, and over the years it has seduced a whole army of writers, artists, aristocrats and royals.

Note that it gets extremely busy in July and August and virtually shuts down between November and Easter. The best time to visit is either side of high season, April to May or September to October.

## ESSENTIAL INFORMATION

**EMERGENCIES //** Ospedale San Vincenzo ( ☎ 0942 57 92 97; Contrada Sirina) Two kilometres downhill from the town centre. Police Station ( ☎ 0942 61 11 11; Corso Umberto I 219)
**TOURIST INFORMATION //** Tourist Office ( ☎ 0942 2 32 43; www.gate2taormina.com; Palazzo Corvaja, Corso Umberto I; ☺ 8.30am-2pm Mon-Fri, 4-7pm Mon-Thu) Has helpful multilingual staff and plenty of practical information.

## ORIENTATION

Unless your hotel has parking facilities you'll need to leave your car at one of the signposted car parks (Porta Catania or Lumbi) just outside the historic centre and walk into town from there. All the sights and most of the hotels and restaurants are within easy walking distance of the main drag, Corso Umberto I, which traverses the pedestrianised medieval centre.

## EXPLORING TAORMINA

❦ TEATRO GRECO // **THRILL TO THE SPECTACULAR SETTING OF AN ANCIENT GREEK THEATRE**
Taormina's Teatro Greco (Greek Theatre; ☎ 0942 2 32 20; Via Teatro Greco 40; adult/concession €6/3, audioguide €5; ☺ 9am-7pm May-Aug, 9am-6.30pm Apr & Sep, 9am-5pm Oct & Mar, 9am-4pm Nov-Feb) is one of Sicily's great sights – a near-perfect ancient amphitheatre with dramatic views over snowcapped Etna. Originally built in the 3rd century BC, it's the second-largest Greek theatre in Sicily (only Syracuse is bigger) and arguably the world's most dramatically sited.

Despite its name, much of what you see today is Roman in origin, resulting from a radical 1st-century AD overhaul. The Greeks had originally incorporated the breathtaking panorama into their design but in AD 1 the Romans obscured it by adding a tall *scaenae frons* (colonnaded backdrop) and converting the stage and orchestra pit into a semicircular gladiatorial arena. Further additions were made in the 12th century when a noble Spanish family built a villa over part of the theatre (to the right as you face the stage). Fortunately, time has swept many of these alterations away, and the crumbling backdrop once again reveals the stunning panorama.

In summer the theatre is used to stage events during the Taormina Film Fest and Taormina Arte (for details, see p172). In the high season the site is best explored early in the morning to avoid the crowds.

❦ CORSO UMBERTO I // **JOIN THE DAILY PARADE ON THE MAIN DRAG**
One of the chief delights of Taormina is simply strolling the main street, Corso

# TAORMINA

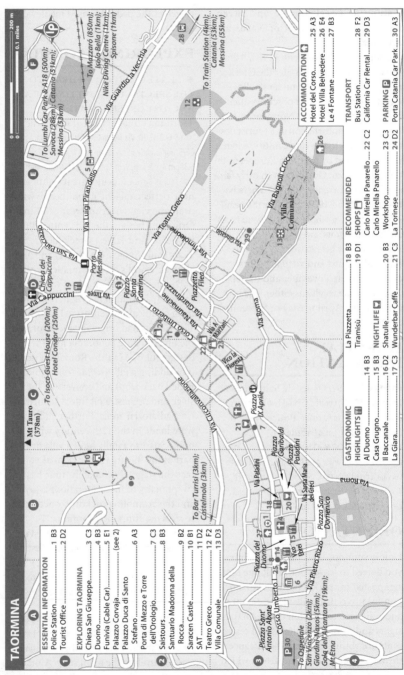

**ESSENTIAL INFORMATION**

| | |
|---|---|
| Police Station..................... | 1 B3 |
| Tourist Office..................... | 2 D2 |

**EXPLORING TAORMINA**

| | |
|---|---|
| Chiesa San Giuseppe........... | 3 C3 |
| Duomo.................................. | 4 B3 |
| Funivia (Cable Car)............. | 5 E1 |
| Palazzo Corvaja................... | (see 2) |
| Palazzo Duca di Santo | |
| Stefano............................. | 6 A3 |
| Porta di Mezzo e Torre | |
| dell'Orologio.................... | 7 C3 |
| Saistours............................. | 8 B3 |
| Santuario Madonna della | |
| Rocca................................ | 9 B2 |
| Saracen Castle.................... | 10 B1 |
| SAT..................................... | 11 D2 |
| Teatro Greco....................... | 12 F2 |
| Villa Comunale.................... | 13 D3 |

**GASTRONOMIC HIGHLIGHTS** 🍴

| | |
|---|---|
| Al Duomo............................ | 14 B3 |
| Casa Grugno....................... | 15 B3 |
| Il Baccanale........................ | 16 D2 |
| La Giara.............................. | 17 C3 |
| La Piazzetta....................... | 18 B3 |
| Tiramisù.............................. | 19 D1 |

**NIGHTLIFE** 🍷

| | |
|---|---|
| Shatulle.............................. | 20 B3 |
| Wunderbar Caffè................ | 21 C3 |

**RECOMMENDED SHOPS** 🛍

| | |
|---|---|
| Carlo Mirella Panarello....... | 22 C2 |
| Carlo Mirella Panarello | |
| Workshop.......................... | 23 C3 |
| La Torinese........................ | 24 D2 |

**ACCOMMODATION** 🏠

| | |
|---|---|
| Hotel del Corso.................. | 25 A3 |
| Hotel Villa Belvedere.......... | 26 E4 |
| Le 4 Fontane..................... | 27 B3 |

**TRANSPORT** 🚍

| | |
|---|---|
| Bus Station........................ | 28 F2 |
| California Car Rental.......... | 29 D3 |

**PARKING** 🅿

| | |
|---|---|
| Porta Catania Car Park....... | 30 A3 |

Umberto I, browsing among the designer delis, admiring the medieval churches and eyeing up fellow holidaymakers. The street's northern end is marked by Palazzo Corvaja, a robust 14th-century building where the Sicilian parliament first sat in 1411 and where visitors now go to seek information at the tourist office.

Halfway down, and flanked by the rococo Chiesa San Giuseppe ( 9am-noon & 4-8pm), Piazza IX Aprile is a favourite hangout, a wonderful viewing balcony with huge coastal views and expensive cocktails at the Wunderbar Caffè (see p173). By the cafe, a 12th-century clock tower, Porta di Mezzo e Torre dell'Orologio, leads through to the Borgo Medievale, Taormina's oldest quarter, and Piazza del Duomo, a pretty little square set around an ornate baroque fountain. On the square's eastern flank, the Duomo ( 9am-noon & 4.30-8pm) is one of Taormina's finest buildings, a beautifully understated 13th-century church with an austere crenellated facade. Nearby, Palazzo Duca di Santo Stefano sports some elegant Norman Gothic windows.

### ❧ VILLA COMUNALE // LUXURIATE IN THE LUSH GREENERY OF THESE PANORAMIC GARDENS

Commanding superb views, Taormina's public gardens, the Villa Comunale (Via Bagnoli Croce; 9am-midnight summer, 9am-10pm winter) are an absolute joy. The brainchild of Lady Florence Trevelyan Cacciola, a 19th-century Scottish aristocrat who escaped to Taormina after an affair with the heir to the English throne, they provide the perfect antidote to the crowded streets above. Tranquil paths lead through banks of perfectly manicured magnolia, hibiscus and bougainvillea bushes while overhead towering cypress trees provide welcome shade.

### ❧ BEACHES // SUNBATHE AND SPLASH AROUND CRYSTALLINE WATERS

The nearest beach to Taormina is at Mazzarò, accessible by funivia (cable car one way/return €2/3; 8am-1.30am Tue-Sun & 9am-1.30am Mon summer, 8am-8.15pm Tue-Sun & 9am-8.15pm Mon winter) from Via Luigi Pirandello. It's a popular pebbly beach well serviced with umbrellas and deck chairs to hire (from about €6 per day). To the south of the beach, and an easy walk past the Sant'Andrea hotel, is Isola Bella, a tiny island set in a stunning cove. This was once home to Florence Trevelyan and it is her house that sits in silent solitude on top of the rocky islet.

There's wonderful snorkelling in the crystalline waters or you can hire a boat and pootle around the rocky bays. If you prefer your adventures underwater, Nike Diving Centre ( 339 1961559; www.divenike taormina.com; Contrada Isola Bell) offers a range of packages from its base at the northern end of the beach, costing from €40 (kite hire included) for a single dive.

For a real sandy beach you will have to go to Spisone, just beneath the autostrada exit – turn left from the cable-car station and it's about a 10-minute walk.

### ❧ MONTE TAURO // HIKE TO THE SUMMIT FOR UNFORGETTABLE VIEWS

The short 20-minute climb to the top of Monte Tauro (378m) is not exactly Himalayan but it is steep and the final steps are quite hard work. Your reward is a massive panoramic view over Taormina's rooftops, the Teatro Greco and, beyond, to the coast. From Via Circonvallazione, a signposted path leads up past the Santuario Madonna della Rocca, and beyond towards the windswept ruins of a Saracen castello (castle).

You can't actually get to the castle – a locked gate blocks the path – but it's the views rather than the sights that are the real appeal here.

🌱 **CASTELMOLA // HEAD UP THE HILL FOR DELICIOUS ALMOND WINE**
Some 5km up the hill from Taormina, Castelmola is a small hilltop village capped by a ruined medieval castle. It makes an easy and pleasant detour from Taormina, particularly if you stop at Bar Turrisi ( ☎ 0942 2 81 81; Via Pio IX 16) to savour a glass of delicious almond wine. This whimsical bar, built on four levels overlooking the church square, is decorated with an eclectic collection of Sicilian memorabilia, including painted carts and an alarming stone *minchia* (you'll know what this is when you see it). You can walk up to Castelmola from Taormina in about an hour, otherwise there are regular buses.

🌱 **TOURS // TAKE A DAY TRIP TO ETNA**
If you're based in Taormina and want to explore further afield without having to hire a car or deal with public transport, a day trip is well worth considering. SAT ( ☎ 0942 2 46 53; www.satgroup.it; Corso Umberto I 73) is one of a number of agencies that organises day trips to Mt Etna and the nearby beauty spot, Gola dell'Alcantara (€40), as well as to Syracuse (€45), Palermo and Cefalù (€55), and Agrigento (€50). Saistours ( ☎ 0942 62 06 71; www.saistours.com; Corso Umberto I 222) offers a range of more sporty tours, such as quad-bike (€89) and mountain-bike (€89) tours of Etna.

## FESTIVALS & EVENTS

Taormina Arte (www.taormina-arte.com) Between July and August, opera, dance and theatre performances are staged at the Teatro Greco.

Taormina Film Fest (www.taorminafilmfest. it) Hollywood big shots arrive in mid-June for six days of film screenings, premieres and press conferences at the Teatro Greco. Tickets, available online at www.ticketone. it, start at €5.

Giuseppe Sinopoli Festival (www.sinopoli festival.it) First held in 2005, this classical-music festival attracts important Italian orchestras and enthusiastic audiences. Concerts, held over four days in early October, are held in Palazzo Corvaja and the Teatro Greco.

## GASTRONOMIC HIGHLIGHTS

There's no getting around it – eating in Taormina is expensive. Prices are universally higher here than in the rest of Sicily and service is not always what it should be. That said, there are some excellent restaurants and as long as you avoid the obvious tourist traps you can eat well. Note that reservations are essential at the more exclusive places.

🌱 **AL DUOMO** €€
☎ 094 262 56 56; Vico Ebrei 11; meals €35-40, tasting menu €60; ☾ closed Mon
Right in the heart of the action, this highly acclaimed restaurant specialises in traditional, even historic, regional cuisine – one of its specialities, *fava a maccu* (fava bean purée), is supposedly mentioned in Aristophenes' 5th-century-BC comedy *The Frogs*. History apart, Al Duomo is an atmospheric spot with a romantic terrace and a pleasant brick interior. Try the stewed lamb or fresh fish with olives and capers.

🌱 **CASA GRUGNO** €€€
☎ 094 22 12 08; Via Santa Maria dei Greci; meals €60-80
Contemporary Mediterranean food in suggestive medieval surroundings – that's the recipe that has put Casa Grugno on Sicily's gastronomic map.

Housed in a 16th-century Catalan Gothic palazzo, complete with a romantic internal garden, this is the domain of Austrian chef Andreas Zangerl, who specialises in modern deconstructions of island classics. Signature dishes include sushi-style raw seafood starters and a lovely, light ricotta mousse. Bookings essential.

### ❧ IL BACCANALE €€

☎ 0942 62 53 90; Piazzetta Filea 1; meals €25-30

Resembling a Sicilian theme park with old black-and-white photos, gaudy paintings and a kitsch Caltagirone ceramic panel depicting a Bacchanalian banquet scene, this colourful trattoria knows how to impress. Thankfully, the food is less ostentatious. There's classic *insalata caprese* (tomato and mozzarella salad) and *pasta alla Norma* (pasta with aubergine, tomato and ricotta), a long list of fishy mains and a complimentary almond liqueur to round things off.

### ❧ LA GIARA €€€

☎ 094 22 33 60; Vico la Floresta 1; meals €60

A meal on the rooftop terrace at La Giara is a Taormina classic. This is one of the best-looking restaurants in town, with a smooth ivory-white art deco interior and a piano bar worthy of Bogart in *Casablanca* mood. The food is modern but grounded in island tradition, with dishes such as risotto with wild herbs, and squid served in a Marsala reduction. Bookings essential.

### ❧ LA PIAZZETTA €€

☎ 094 262 63 17; Via Paladini 5; meals €25-30; ⟲ closed Mon winter

Ask locals for a recommendation and many will reply *'si mangia bene a Piazzetta'* (you eat well at La Piazzetta). A welcoming family-run outfit with tables on a picturesque square, it serves authentic Sicilian food at honest prices. Start with *risotto con cozze e finochietto selvatico* (risotto with mussels and wild fennel) before tucking into fish baked in sea salt or filleted and served with almonds.

### ❧ TIRAMISÙ €€

☎ 0942 2 48 03; Via Cappuccini 1; pizzas from €7, meals €30-40; ⟲ closed Tue

This stylish but unpretentious place near Porta Messina is a definite hit. Whether you're in the mood for a simple pizza and beer or something more elaborate, say *linguine cozze, menta e zucchine* (thin ribbons of pasta with mussels, mint and courgettes) followed by succulent chargrilled steak, you'll leave a happy bunny, especially if you complete your meal with one of its trademark tiramisus.

## NIGHTLIFE

Taormina's nightlife revolves around the town's numerous bars and cafes, most of which have outdoor seating.

### ❧ SHATULLE

☎ 0942 2 30 56; Piazza Paladini 4; ⟲ closed Mon

An intimate square just off Corso Umberto I, Piazza Paladini is a perennial favourite with Taormina's young, well-dressed night owls. One of the best, and most popular, of the square-side bars is this hip, gay-friendly spot that has outdoor seating, an inviting vibe and a fine selection of cocktails (starting from about €5.50).

### ❧ WUNDERBAR CAFFÈ

☎ 0942 62 50 32; Piazza IX Aprile 7

A Taormina landmark since the *dolce vita* 1960s, this glamorous and achingly expensive cafe has served them all – Tennessee Williams, who liked to watch

IONIAN COAST

'the squares go by', Greta Garbo, Richard Burton and Elizabeth Taylor. With tables spread over the vibrant piazza and white-jacketed waiters taking the orders, it is still very much the quintessential Taormina watering hole.

## RECOMMENDED SHOPS

Shopping is a popular pastime in Taormina, particularly on Corso Umberto I. Here you'll find inviting delis and attractive boutiques selling high-quality ceramic goods, lace and linen tableware, antique furniture and jewellery.

### ❤ CARLO MIRELLA PANARELLO
Corso Umberto I 122 & Via A Marzani

Sicily has a long tradition of ceramic production and this is a good bet for original ceramic designs. The workshop is on Via A Marzani (ring the bell for admission), while around the corner on Corso Umberto I, the shop sells more traditional jewellery, bags and hats.

### ❤ LA TORINESE
☎ 094 22 33 21; Corso Umberto I 59

One of a number of delis on the main drag, La Torinese is a treasure trove of gastronomic delights. Bottles of wine, local liqueurs and olive oil are lined up in dispensary cabinets, while shelves groan under the weight of jarred capers, conserves and honeys.

## TRANSPORT

**BUS //** The bus is the best way to reach Taormina. The bus station is on Via Luigi Pirandello, a 400m walk from Porta Messina, the northeastern entrance to the old town. Etna Trasporti ( ☎ 0942 62 53 01; www.etnatrasporti.it) runs direct to/from Catania airport (€5.60, 1½ hours, six daily Monday to Saturday, four Sunday). Interbus ( ☎ 0942 62 53 01; www. interbus.it) services run to/from Messina (€3.90, 1½ hours, hourly Monday to Saturday, twice Sunday), Catania (€4.60, 1½ hours, 14 daily Monday to Saturday, eight Sunday) and Castelmola (15 minutes, at least seven daily).

**CAR & MOTORCYCLE //** Taormina is on the A18 autostrada and the SS114. The historic centre is closed to nonresident traffic and Corso Umberto I is closed to all traffic. You can hire cars and scooters at California Car Rental ( ☎ 0942 2 37 69; Via Bagnoli Croce 86) near Villa Comunale. Reckon on €30/60 per day for a Fiat Panda/Vespa.

**PARKING //** Some top-end hotels offer limited parking, otherwise you'll have to leave your car in one of the two car parks outside the historic centre: Porta Catania or Lumbi. Both are within walking distance of Corso Umberto I.

**TRAIN //** Taormina's train station is some 2km downhill from the main town, making the train a last resort. If you do arrive this way, and there are direct trains to/from Catania and Messina, catch the Interbus service (one way €1.50) up to town. It runs roughly every 30 to 90 minutes, less often on Sunday.

# AROUND TAORMINA
· · · · · ·

## GIARDINI-NAXOS

pop 9560

The unpretentious resort of Giardini-Naxos is a popular alternative to more expensive Taormina. Action is centred on the seafront, a long parade of hotels, bars, pizzerias and souvenir shops strung along the beach. It heaves in summer but outside of the high season (Easter to October) there's nothing going on and you won't miss much if you pass it by.

### ESSENTIAL INFORMATION

**TOURIST INFORMATION //** Tourist Office ( ☎ 0942 25 10 10; Via Tysandros 54; ⊕ 9am-1pm Mon-Fri, 3.30-6.30pm Mon-Thu) Can provide accommodation lists and handy maps.

# EXPLORING GIARDINI-NAXOS

**♥ THE BEACH //** **SUN YOURSELF ON GIARDINI'S LONG SANDY STRIP**
Giardini's long beach (mainly sand and coarse grey pebbles) curves around the crescent-shaped bay between Capo Taormina and Capo Schisò, a lick of pre-historic lava at the southern end. There is a small *spiaggia libera* (free beach), but most of it is given over to lidos (private beach clubs), where you pay around €2 for entry, €4 for a sun lounge and €2 for an umbrella. If you fancy a bit of exercise, canoes can be hired for about €6 per hour.

**♥ GREEK RUINS //** **INVESTIGATE THE REMAINS OF SICILY'S OLDEST GREEK SETTLEMENT**
You'd never know it to look at it, but Giardini-Naxos is the oldest Greek settlement in Sicily, its origins dating back to 735 BC. You can visit the rather scant remains of the original settlement – a 300m stretch of wall, a small temple and a couple of other structures – at the southern end of the seafront road.

There's also a small **museum** ( ☎ 0942 5 10 01; Via Schisò; adult/concession €2/1; ☺ 9am-7pm), with bits and bobs uncovered during the excavation.

**♥ RISTORANTE PIZZERIA ROYALE //** **EAT PIZZA ON THE SEAFRONT**
Of the restaurants that line the seafront, Ristorante Pizzeria Royale ( ☎ 0942 36 68; Lungomare Schisò 34; pizzas from €5, meals €25; ☺ closed Wed) is an excellent midrange option. Like everywhere in Giardini it's touristy but that shouldn't detract from the decent food and friendly family atmosphere. The menu is typical of these parts, with a range of seafood pastas and grilled meat and fish, but it's the pizzas that really stand out – served bubbling hot straight from the wood-fired oven.

## TRANSPORT

**BUS //** Regular Interbus ( ☎ 0942 62 53 01; www.interbus.it) buses run between Giardini-Naxos and Taormina's bus station, stopping off at the train station en route.
**TRAIN //** Giardini shares its train station with Taormina. It's situated at the northern end of the seafront, about 10 minutes' walk from the town centre.

## ∼ WORTH A TRIP ∼

Located some 15km inland from Giardini-Naxos, the **Gola dell'Alcantara** is a vertiginous 25m-high natural gorge bisected by the freezing waters of the Alcantara river (the name is derived from the Arabic *al qantara,* meaning bridge). Characterised by its weirdly symmetrical rock formations – created when a red-hot lava flow hit the water and splintered the basalt into lava prisms – it's a spectacular sight well worth searching out.

The gorge is now part of the Parco Botanico e Geologico Terralcantara, which is within the Parco Fluviale dell'Alcantara regional park. It's out of bounds between November and March due to the risk of flash flooding, but is open during the rest of the year. To get down to the bottom there's a lift (€5) near the car park or a 224-step staircase some 200m or so uphill from the lift. Once down by the river, you can hire waders to splash around in the icy waters or simply sunbathe on the surrounding banks. There are also 3.5km of nature trails in the area. For further details contact the **park office** ( ☎ 0942 98 50 10) or check out its useful website at www.terralcantara.it.

# CATANIA
· · · · · ·

**pop 296,470**

Sicily's second-largest city, Catania rarely gets glowing press. And while it's true that the city is surrounded by an ugly urban sprawl and is noisy, chaotic and unkempt, it's equally true that it's a vibrant, enthralling place with energy to sell and a beautiful, Unesco-listed historic centre. Grandiose black-and-white palazzi tower over baroque piazzas and seething markets, while hundreds of bars, clubs and eateries cater to the city's fun-loving population. All the while, Mt Etna broods darkly in the near distance, her uncomfortable presence adding a thrilling edge to life in the city.

Catania, or Katane as it was called, was originally founded by the Chalcidians in 729 BC, growing to become a major regional power in the 4th and 5th centuries BC. In subsequent centuries it was ruled by a succession of foreign powers, first the Romans, then the Byzantines, Saracens and Normans, but by the mid-17th century it had once again become a prosperous commercial centre. Then, in the late 1600s, disaster struck. Twice. First, Mt Etna erupted in 1669, engulfing the city in boiling lava and killing 12,000 people. Then, in 1693, a huge earthquake hit leaving a further 20,000 people dead. But out of the ashes arose the city that stands today. Under the supervision of architects Giovanni Vaccarini and Stefano Ittar, a new street grid was created incorporating spacious squares and streets of differing widths, all designed to provide escape routes and greater shelter in case of another eruption. Grandiose palazzi and churches were built in baroque style out of the black volcanic rock that Etna had rained down on the city.

In modern times, years of neglect left many of the city's great buildings on the verge of decay but renovations in the early 2000s restored many of them to their former glory.

## ESSENTIAL INFORMATION

**EMERGENCIES //** Ospedale Vittorio Emanuele ( ☎ 095 743 54 52; Via Plebiscito 628) Has a 24-hour emergency doctor. Police Station ( ☎ 095 736 71 11; Piazza Santa Nicolella)

**TOURIST INFORMATION //** Airport Tourist Office ( ☎ 095 093 70 23; ☺ 9am-9pm) Municipal Tourist Office ( ☎ 095 742 55 73; www.comune.catania.it; Via Vittorio Emanuele II 172; ☺ 8.15am-7.15pm Mon-Fri, 8.15am-12.15pm Sat)

## ORIENTATION

Catania's main train station and intercity bus terminal are a 15-minute walk east of the city centre, near the port on Piazza Giovanni XXIII. Southwest of the square is Via Vittorio Emanuele II, which runs east–west through the heart of the city, while Via Etnea runs north–south from Piazza del Duomo. Most sights are concentrated around and west of Piazza del Duomo.

## EXPLORING CATANIA

❦ PIAZZA DEL DUOMO // FEAST ON MAGNIFICENT BAROQUE ARCHITECTURE

Catania's sumptuous showpiece square, Piazza del Duomo, is a magnificent sight. The centrepiece of Giovanni Vaccarini's 18th-century city makeover, it is surrounded by a number of grandiose palazzi – Palazzo degli Elefanti, seat of Catania's Town Hall, Palazzo Chierici, an ex-seminary, and the city's great baroque cathedral – all built in the city's trademark grey-black volcanic stone. In the centre of the piazza is the city's most memorable monument, the smiling **Fontana dell'Elefante** (Fountain of the Elephant). This comical statue is composed of a naive elephant, known locally as Liotru and now the symbol of the city, surmounted by an improbable Egyptian obelisk. Legend has it that the statue originally belonged to the 8th-century magician Eliodorus and that it has magical powers to ward off dangers from Mt Etna.

Facing the statue is Catania's other defence against the volcano, the **Cattedrale di Sant'Agata** ( ☎ 095 32 00 44;  7am-noon & 4-7pm Mon-Sat, 7.30am-noon & 4.30-7pm Sun), with its impressive marble facade sporting two orders of columns taken from the Roman amphitheatre (see p181). Inside the huge vaulted interior lie the relics of the city's patron saint, the young virgin Agata, who resisted the advances of the nefarious Quintian (AD 250) and was horribly mutilated (her breasts were hacked off and her body was rolled in hot coals). You can actually visit the dungeons where these atrocities were committed under the **Chiesa di Sant'Agata al Carcere** (Piazza San Carcere;  8.30am-1pm & 3-8pm Tue-Sat) behind the Roman amphitheatre on Piazza Stesicoro. The saint's jewel-drenched effigy is ecstatically venerated on 5 February in one of Sicily's largest festivals – see p181.

 **STREET MARKETS // DIVE INTO CATANIA'S TEEMING MARKETS**
Catania's great markets are street theatre at its most thrilling. The best show in town is the raucous fish market, **La Pescheria** (Via Pardo;  7am-2pm Mon-Sat), which takes over the streets behind Piazza del Duomo every workday morning. Tables groan under the weight of decapitated swordfish, ruby-pink prawns and polystyrene trays full of clams, mussels, sea

urchins and all manner of mysterious sea life, while all around fishmongers gut silvery fish and high-heeled housewives step daintily over pools of blood-stained water. It's absolutely riveting. If you fancy a taste of the exotic ware on display, there are a number of excellent fish restaurants down here.

The show continues at the **food market** in the adjoining streets, where carcasses of meat, skinned sheep's heads, strings of sausages, huge wheels of cheese and mountains of luscious fruit and veg are all rolled together in a few jam-packed alleyways.

To get to these markets, go down the steps at the south of Piazza del Duomo near the **Fontana dell'Amenano**, a commemoration of the Amenano river on whose banks the Greeks founded the city of Katane. Alternatively, duck under the adjacent **Porta Uzeda**, an impressive 17th-century gate built to connect Via Etnea with the port.

Catania's third great market is on Piazza Carlo Alberto, off Via Etnea. **La Fiera** (  8am-1pm Mon-Fri, 8am-7pm Sat), as it's known locally, is a chaotic kasbah selling everything from fruit and veg to bootleg CDs and knock-off designer bags.

 **VIA ETNEA // WINDOW SHOP AND PEOPLE WATCH ON CATANIA'S MAIN DRAG**
It's not difficult to see how Catania's main shopping street got its name – on a clear day you can see Mt Etna rising menacingly at the end of it. **Via Etnea** runs straight from Piazza del Duomo up to the foothills below Etna. Lined with modern department stores, bars and pavement cafes, it's busy at most times but positively heaves on Saturday afternoons when shoppers pile in from the suburbs to hang out and update their

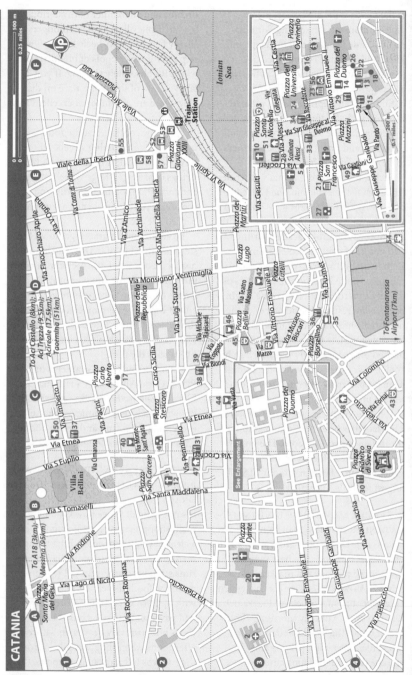

CATANIA

wardrobes. At its southern end, **Piazza dell'Università** is a great place to take stock over a coffee and cake. There are a number of cafes, but pride of place goes to the **Grand Café Tabbacco** ( ☎ 095 31 04 29; Via Etnea 28), an elegant old-school *pasticceria* (pastry shop) with outdoor seating and a devilish selection of *dolci* (sweets), fresh-fruit tarts and cakes. On the other side of the square is **Palazzo dell'Università**, the Vaccarini-designed building that houses the city university. On the eastern flank is another Vaccarini edifice, **Palazzo Sangiuliano**.

To escape the madding crowds, continue up to the lovely **Villa Bellini** ( ⏱ 6am-10pm) gardens where you can relax on a shady bench and admire views up to Etna.

❧ **MUSEO BELLINIANO // PAY HOMAGE TO CATANIA'S OPERA MAESTRO VINCENZO BELLINI**
One of Italy's great opera composers, Vincenzo Bellini was born in Catania in 1801, in a house on Piazza San Francesco.

The house has since been converted into a small museum, the **Museo Belliniano** ( ☎ 095 715 05 35; admission free; Piazza San Francesco 3; ⏱ 9am-1pm Mon-Sat), which boasts an interesting collection of Bellini memorabilia, including original scores, photographs and his death mask. In his short life (he died aged 34), Bellini composed 10 operas, including the famous trio: *La sonnambula* (The Sleepwalker), *I puritani* (The Puritans) and *Norma*, which has since been immortalised as the name of Sicily's most famous pasta dish – *pasta alla Norma*.

The place to see a Bellini opera is the **Teatro Massimo Bellini** ( ☎ 095 715 09 21; www.teatromassimobellini.it; Piazza Bellini), Catania's sumptuous gilt-encrusted theatre. See p185 for further details.

❧ **BAROQUE CHURCHES // STROLL ALONG VIA CROCIFERI FOR A LESSON IN BAROQUE BEAUTY**
A lovely, tranquil spot for a morning stroll, **Via Crociferi** is one of Catania's

most attractive streets, famous for its exuberant baroque churches and imposing 18th-century palazzi. At the bottom, Piazza San Francesco is lorded over by the Chiesa di San Francesco (☾ 8.30am-noon & 4-7.30pm), which houses six of the 11 giant candelabras that are paraded around town during the Festa di Sant'Agata (see p181). Nearby, the Arco di San Benedetto, an arch built by the Benedictines in 1704, marks the beginning of Via Crociferi. According to legend, the arch was built in a single night to defy a city ordinance against its construction on the grounds that it was a seismic liability.

On the left past the arch is the Chiesa di San Benedetto (☾ 7am-noon & 3.30-6pm Thu, 10am-noon Sun), built between 1704 and 1713. Inside, there is some splendid stucco and marble work, as well as a

rather graphic fresco of a woman being tortured in front of a curious sultan.

About halfway up on the right-hand side, the Chiesa di San Giuliano is famous for its convex facade designed by Vaccarini between 1738 and 1751. Opposite, Via Gesuiti leads up to Piazza Dante and Sicily's largest church, the monumentally ugly Chiesa di San Nicolò all'Arena (☾ 9am-1pm). The church was commissioned in 1687 but building was interrupted by the earthquake of 1693 and then by problems with its size – it measures 105m long, 48m wide and 62m high – and it was never actually finished. Much more impressive than the church is the adjoining Monastero di San Nicolò all'Arena, Europe's second-largest monastery. Built in 1703 and now part of the city university, it boasts a grand internal cloister and one of Sicily's

## 48 HOURS IN CATANIA

### GOURMET TRAVELLER
Catania provides plenty of opportunities for enthusiastic gourmets. Whet your appetite at La Pescheria (p177) fish market before adjourning for a languid seafood lunch at a market-side restaurant. After a well-deserved pause pick yourself up with a late afternoon coffee and dolci (sweets) at Grand Café Tabbacco (p177). On your second day, nose around La Fiera (p177) market and snack on arancini (fried rice balls) at nearby Spinella (p183). Dinner is the time to try pasta alla Norma, the city's signature dish, at Trattoria di De Fiore (p177).

### TRACE THE CITY'S HISTORY
Already a major power when the Romans barged in during the 3rd century BC, Catania retains little of its classical past, but you can sniff around the sunken ruins of what was once a vast Roman amphitheatre, the Anfiteatro Romano (p181), and visit a 2nd-century Roman theatre, the Teatro Romano (p181). More evident are Catania's baroque treasures – the soaring Cattedrale di Sant'Agata (p176) takes pride of place, but also impressive are the palazzi around Piazza del Duomo (p176) and the churches of Via Crociferi (p179).

### A VOLCANIC EXCURSION
Leaning menacingly over the city, Mt Etna (p189) is a thrilling sight, a far-from-extinct volcano that could go off at any time. Just hope it doesn't erupt as you head up on a day trip from Catania. Recover on day two, exploring the vineyards and woods that carpet the mountain's lower slopes (p192).

most important libraries. You can't actually enter the cloisters but you see them from the surrounding corridors.

🌱 ROMAN RUINS // GET UNDER THE CITY'S SKIN AT HER ROMAN RUINS

Little remains of the prosperous Roman city that Catania once was, but on Piazza Stesicoro you can walk among the sunken ruins of the Anfiteatro Romano (Roman Amphitheatre; admission free; 🕙 9am-1.30pm & 2.30-6pm). It doesn't look like much today, but in its 2nd-century-BC heyday it was vast, extending as far south as Via Penninello and seating up to 16,000 spectators. Go down to the vaults and you'll get an inkling of just how complex a structure it must have been.

There are more theatrical ruins on Via Vittorio Emanuele II, where you can visit the 2nd-century remains of a Teatro Romano (Roman Theatre) and its small rehearsal theatre, the Odeon (Via Vittorio Emanuele II 266; theatre & odeon €3; 🕙 9am-1pm & 2.30-6pm Mon-Sat, 9am-1.30pm Sun).

🌱 CASTELLO URSINO // SWOON OVER SCULPTURE AT THE CITY CASTLE

Catania's foreboding castle, the 13th-century Castello Ursino, once guarded the city from atop a seafront cliff. However, the 1693 earthquake changed the landscape and the whole area to the south was reclaimed by the lava, leaving the castle completely landlocked. The castle now houses the Museo Civico ( 🕿 095 34 58 30; Piazza Federico di Svevia; admission free; 🕙 9am-1pm & 3-7pm Mon-Sat) and its valuable archaeological collection. Put together by Catania's most important aristocratic family, the Biscaris, the collection features some colossal classical sculpture, as well as a number of Greek vases and fine mosaics.

🌱 LE CIMINIERE // BROWSE THROUGH MUSEUMS AT THIS EYE-CATCHING CULTURAL COMPLEX

Catania's answer to London's Tate Modern, Le Ciminiere is a modern museum complex housed in a converted sulphur refinery. There are two museums and two permanent exhibitions, one dedicated to old radios and the other displaying a fascinating collection of historic maps, as well as a cafe-restaurant and performance spaces.

Of the museums, the most interesting is the Museo Storico dello Sbarco in Sicilia ( 🕿 095 53 35 40; admission €4; 🕙 9am-12.30pm Tue-Sun, 3-5pm Tue & Thu), which illustrates the history of the WWII Allied landings in Sicily. The other museum, the Museo del Cinema, takes a specialist look at Catania's early-20th-century film industry. Check with the municipal tourist office for details of temporary exhibitions.

## FESTIVALS & EVENTS

Festa di Sant'Agata Hysterical celebrations accompany a million Catanians as they follow the Fercolo (a silver reliquary bust of the saint) as it's carried along the main street of the city with spectacular fireworks exploding all around. Held 3 to 5 February.

Estate Catanese Classical music, jazz, dance and outdoor theatre are staged in venues across town between the end of June and September.

Etnafest Exhibitions, film screenings, concerts and science shows are held between June and September at Le Ciminiere and venues in the Etna area.

Sicily Jazz and More Italian and international jazz stars perform at Le Ciminiere in November.

## GASTRONOMIC HIGHLIGHTS

Eating out in Catania is a real pleasure. There's a huge choice of snack bars, trattorias and restaurants, and the city's street food is superb. Be sure not to miss the savoury *arancini* (fried rice balls), *cartocciate* (bread stuffed with ham, mozzarella, olives and tomato) and *pasta alla Norma*, which originated here.

### ☙ AL CORTILE ALESSI €€

☎ 095 31 54 44; Via Alessi 34-36; pizzas from €6, meals €30; ☺ closed Mon

On a back lane just off Via Crociferi, this laid-back pizzeria-cum-restaurant is popular with weekend diners of all ages. There is a full menu but the real draw are the delicious pizzas that are cooked in a wood-fired oven. In winter the exposed-brick interior makes for cosy dining, while in summer the outdoor courtyard is fun with its creeping banana plants and overhanging silk tapestries.

### ☙ AMBASCIATA DEL MARE €€

☎ 095 34 10 03; www.ambasciatadelmare.it; Piazza Duomo 6; meals €35-40; ☺ closed Mon

Overlooking the fish market, La Pescheria, this refined restaurant has built a strong local reputation serving creative seafood. And while the standard is undeniably high – the oysters and stylish antipasti are superb – the pastas don't always hit the mark. Ditto the wine-red dining hall, which looks good but gets very cramped when full. Bookings recommended.

### ☙ IL BORGO DI FEDERICO €

☎ 095 67 98 19; Piazza Federico di Svevia 100; pizzas from €5, meals €18

The restaurants around Castello Ursino are known for their meat, particularly barbecued meat, and Il Borgo di Federico is no exception. A modest, unpretentious outfit with a bustling, TV-on-in-the-corner atmosphere, it's a good place for a filling antipasto buffet – olives, fried

croquettes, frittata, cured meats, octopus salad – followed by a no-nonsense plate of *polpette* (meat balls).

### ☙ METRÓ €€

☎ 095 32 20 98; www.ristorantemetro.it; Via Crociferi 76; meals €30-35; ☺ closed Sat lunch & Sun

A delightful restaurant with outdoor seating on Via Crociferi, Metró ticks all the right boxes. The look is simple with bright lighting and wine bottles on the walls but the menu is altogether more ambitious, featuring a fabulous carpaccio starter and a wonderful *lasagnette con ricotta infornata e pinoli* (lasagne with baked ricotta and pine nuts). The wine list is imaginative, although it's heavily biased towards regional producers. Slow Food Movement recommended.

### ☙ OSTERIA ANTICA MARINA €€

☎ 095 34 81 97; www.anticamarina.it; Via Pardo 29; meals €30-35; ☺ closed Wed

Given its location on the fish market, this could not be anything but one of Catania's most popular fish restaurants, the place locals take out-of-towners to impress them over lunch. It might look like a rustic mountain retreat with its heavy wood tables and rough stone walls but the food is pure ocean heaven. Try the raw anchovy salad starters and *strozza pretti* (rough pasta fingers) with red tuna and you'll get the idea. Bookings essential.

### ☙ OSTERIA I TRE BICCHIERI €€€

☎ 095 715 35 40; Via S Giuseppe al Duomo 31; meals €60; ☺ 8pm-midnight Tue-Sun

Don't be fooled by the name, this is a formal top-end restaurant. Housed in an imposing 18th-century townhouse, its three vaulted dining rooms set an elegant stage for innovative regional cuisine and an impressive 600-strong wine list. Signature dishes include *tartare di pesce* (fish tartare of swordfish, red tuna and prawns) and *risotto al pesto e cozze* (risotto with pesto and mussels). Booking essential.

### ♥ OSTERIA PIZZERIA ANTICA SICILIA €€

☎ 095 715 10 75; Via Roccaforte 15; pizzas €6, meals €30

With its gaudy frescoes, stark white lights and busy workaday atmosphere, this bustling trattoria is no place for a romantic tête-à-tête. But if you're after a decent, value-for-money dinner, it will do very nicely, thank you. Seafood is the star, with staples such as *linguine ai ricci* (thin pasta ribbons with sea urchins) and *calamari arrosto* (roast squid).

### ♥ SICILIA IN BOCCA ALLA MARINARA €€

☎ 095 250 02 08; Via Dusmet 35; meals €30-35; ☾ closed Mon lunch

Catania's 14th-century sea walls provide the suggestive setting for this popular restaurant. With the smell of the sea wafting in on the breeze, seafood is the obvious choice – it does a delicious swordfish carpaccio with citrus fruit dressing – but there are also excellent pizzas. Sit in the lively brick-arched dining hall or enjoy views of the Duomo from the upstairs terrace.

### ♥ SPINELLA €

☎ 095 32 72 47; Via Etnea 300; snacks from €1.80

If you don't fancy a sit-down lunch but want something tasty on the hoof, this innocuous-looking bar serves the best *arancini* in town. These difficult to eat balls, or rather cones, of rice, *ragù* and peas are large enough to keep the hunger pangs at bay for a few hours, especially if followed by one of the bar's famous *dolci*.

## HAVE A SELTZ

Heaven on a hot day, or at any other time for that matter, is a €1 *seltz* from one of the kiosks on Via Dusmet down by the fish market, La Pescheria. A *seltz* is a nonalcoholic mix of fizzy water (on draft at the kiosks), freshly squeezed lemon juice and natural fruit syrup. There are various flavours but the *seltz mandarino* (with mandarin orange) is our favourite.

### ♥ TRATTORIA CASALINGA €€

☎ 095 31 13 19; Via Biondi 19; meals €25-30; ☾ Mon-Sat

This is one of Catania's best-known and best-loved trattorias. A homey, family-run eatery presided over by patron Nino, it does a thriving business feeding lunching office workers and hungry theatre-goers – Teatro Massimo Bellini is not far away. The onus is on earthy regional food, so roll up for salami and cheese starters, pastas with seasonal vegies and juicy grilled meats/fish. Creamy *cannoli* (pastry shells stuffed with sweet ricotta) will leave you smiling as you leave.

### ♥ TRATTORIA DI DE FIORE €

☎ 095 31 62 83; Via Coppola 24-26; meals €20; ☾ closed Mon

Named after Bellini's famous opera, *pasta alla Norma* is a Catanian classic, a delicious mix of creamy aubergines, tomatoes and salted ricotta. Variations are served across Sicily but none compare to the masterpiece that Mamma Rosanna dishes up at this, her charming, old-school trattoria. Follow it with a mixed meat grill and you might just have trattoria perfection. What's more, service comes with a smile, there's no *coperto* (bread and cover charge) and the decor is pleasantly unassuming.

# NIGHTLIFE

Not surprisingly for a busy university town, Catania has a great nightlife. There are dozens of cafes, bars and live music venues across town but hubs include Piazza Bellini, a student favourite, Via Montesano and Via Penninello. Opening hours are generally from around 9pm to 2am, although things often don't hot up until around midnight.

To see what's going on pick up a copy of *Lapis* at the tourist office.

## BARS & ENOTECHE

### ❤ ENERGIE CAFÉ
☎ 331 4054510; www.myspace.com/energiecafe; Via Monte Sant'Agata 10

A favourite with Catania's stylish aperitivo set, Energie Café is a slick urban bar with kaleidoscopic '70s-inspired decor, streetside seating and laid-back jazz-infused tunes. If you're at a loose end on a Sunday afternoon, Fashion Aperitif is a mellow happy hour with a rich buffet and live DJ set.

### ❤ HEAVEN
Via Teatro Massimo 39; ☯ 9pm-2am

Pedestrianised Via Teatro Massimo heaves late at night as crowds swill outside the many bars. One of the best-known addresses is Heaven, a trendy lounge bar sporting kooky black and white designs and a 12m-long LED-lit bar. Outside, where most people end up, there's seating on massive black leather sofas. DJs up the ante on Wednesday, Friday and Saturday nights.

### ❤ PERBACCO WINE BAR
☎ 095 250 34 78; Via Vasta 12-14; ☯ 8am-late

This is one of Catania's most popular wine bars. Locals of all ages crowd the sofas and wicker chairs under the burgundy canopies to chat, sip and snack until the wee hours. There's a warm, laid-back buzz and a good selection of cocktails, wines (mainly Sicilian and Italian) and rum.

### ❤ TERTULIA
☎ 095 715 26 03; Via Michele Rapisardi 1-3; ☯ 10am-1am Mon-Fri, 5pm-1am Sat & Sun

A fully paid-up member of the city's cultural scene, Tertulia is a cool bookshop cafe. It's a relaxed spot where you can catch up on your email (there's free wi-fi) over a cappuccino or glass of wine, attend a book presentation or watch an arthouse film with like-minded aficionados. There are also exhibitions and the occasional jazz concert.

## LIVE MUSIC & THEATRE

### ❤ ENOLA JAZZ CLUB
☎ 095 32 62 47; Via Mazza 14

The godfather of Catania's jazz scene, the Enola Jazz Club attracts big-name Italian and international artists to its pocket-sized stage, while also trumpeting new and emerging local talent. Like all self-respecting jazz clubs it's a tight squeeze with a fairly nondescript decor, but that in no way diminishes the hot, steamy atmosphere.

### ❤ LA LOMAX
☎ 095 286 28 12; http://alanlomaxct.blogspot.com; Via Fornai 44

This multipurpose cultural centre hosts all sorts of events – club nights, folk-music festivals, modern art exhibitions – as well as housing a song and dance school and running a range of courses. A relative newcomer to the scene, it's up near Castello Urbino, hidden away in a small street off Via Plebiscito. Check *Lapis* or the centre's website for upcoming events.

### ♥ TEATRO MASSIMO BELLINI

☎ 095 715 09 21; www.teatromassimobellini.it; Piazza Bellini

Catania's premier theatre is named after the city's most famous son, composer Vincenzo Bellini. Sporting the full red-and-gold-gilt look, it stages a year-round season of opera and an eight-month program of classical music from November to June. Tickets, which are available online, start at around €13 and rise to €84 for a first night front-row seat.

### ♥ ZÒ

☎ 095 53 38 71; www.zoculture.it; Piazzale Asia 6

Part of Le Ciminiere complex (see p181), Zò is dedicated to promoting contemporary art and performance. It hosts an eclectic program of events that ranges from club nights, concerts and film screenings to art exhibitions, dance performances, installations and theatre workshops. Check out its website for upcoming events, many of which are free of charge.

# TRANSPORT

**AIR //** Catania's **Fontanarossa airport** (CTA; ☎ 095 723 91 11; www.aeroporto.catania.it) is 7km southwest of the city centre. **AMT Alibus 457** (€1, 30 minutes, every 20 minutes) runs to the airport from the train station. A taxi for four people plus luggage costs about €28.

**BOAT //** From the ferry terminal on the southeastern edge of the historic centre, there are ferries to/from Naples and Civitavecchia. **Grimaldi** ( ☎ 081 49 64 44; www.grimaldi-ferries.com) boats sail to/from Civitavecchia. Fares per person for a *poltrona* (airline-type armchair) in low/high season cost €54/84 (car €90). **TTT Lines** ( ☎ 800 915365; www.tttlines.it) operates the daily Naples ferry (per person for a *poltrona* low/high season €38/60).

**BUS //** There are two main bus terminuses in Catania: Interbus, Etna and SAIS Autolinee run to/from the Terminal Bus on Via Archimede; AST buses go to/from Piazza Giovanni XXIII in front of the train station. As a rule buses are quicker than trains for most destinations. **AST** ( ☎ 095 746 10 96; www.aziendasicilianatrasporti.it) runs to many provincial towns around Catania, including Nicolosi (€2.40, one hour, half-hourly). Tickets are available at the Terminal Bar over the road from the bus stops. **Interbus – Etna Trasporti** ( ☎ 095 53 03 96; www.interbus.it) has buses to Syracuse (€5.70, 1¼ hours, hourly Monday to Saturday, six Sunday) and Taormina (€4.60, 1½ hours, 14 daily Monday to Saturday, eight Sunday), while **SAIS Autolinee** ( ☎ 095 53 61 68; www.saisautolinee.it) serves Palermo (€14.20, 2½ hours, 13 daily Monday to Saturday, nine Sunday) and Messina (€7.70, 1½ hours, half-hourly Monday to Saturday, eight Sunday). Get tickets from the ticket office at Via d'Amico 181. In town, local buses 1 to 4 run from the train station to Via Etnea, and buses 4 to 7 to Piazza del Duomo. Tickets, from *tabacchi,* cost €1 and last 90 minutes.

**CAR & MOTORCYCLE //** Catania is easily reached from Messina on the A18 autostrada as well as from Palermo on the A19. From the autostrada, signs for the city centre direct you to Via Etnea. Choosing to drive in town means you will have to deal with the city's complicated one-way system – for example, you can only drive along Via Vittorio Emanuele II from west to east, while the parallel Via Giuseppe Garibaldi runs from east to west.

**PARKING //** Parking is extremely difficult in the city centre. If you're bringing your own car, consider staying at a hotel/B&B with parking facilities; if you're hiring a car, the advice is to pick up the car as you leave town and return it when you re-enter.

**TAXI //** For a taxi, call **CST** ( ☎ 095 33 09 66). There are taxi ranks at the train station and on Piazza del Duomo.

**TRAIN //** Frequent, but very slow, trains connect Catania with Messina (€6.70, 1½ to two hours) and Syracuse (€6, 1¼ hours), while there are one or two direct services to Palermo (€12) and Agrigento (€11.10). The private Circumetnea train line circles Mt Etna, stopping at the towns and villages on the volcano's slopes. For more information, see p193.

# RIVIERA DEI CICLOPI

· · · · · ·

**Extending north of Catania, the Riviera dei Ciclopi is an attractive stretch of coastline that makes a good, value-for-money alternative to Taormina. Until quite recently it was a desperately poor area of isolated fishing villages, but tourism has given it a much needed impetus and it is now a lively summer stomping ground. There are few sandy beaches but the swimming is excellent, and there are plenty of hotels, restaurants and bars. The coast owes its name to a Homeric legend according to which the towering black rocks that rise out of the sea – actually great hunks of solidified lava – were thrown by the blinded Cyclops, Polyphemus, in a desperate attempt to stop Odysseus escaping.**

## ACIREALE

**pop 52,855**

The main town on the Riviera, Acireale is set on a series of lava terraces that drop down to the sea about 17km north of Catania. Although it's not exactly undiscovered, it remains largely tourist free, which is a mystery because it's a great-looking town with a stately baroque centre and a number of imposing public buildings. Two kilometres downhill, the small fishing village of Santa Maria la Scala is a perfect port of call for a seafood lunch.

Acireale has long been known for its thermal waters but its modern claim to fame is its spectacular Carnevale festivities.

### ESSENTIAL INFORMATION

**TOURIST INFORMATION //** Tourist Office ( ☎ 095 89 52 49; Via Romeo 2; ◷ 8am-2pm & 3-9pm)

### ORIENTATION

Piazza Duomo is the heart of the city, with Corso Umberto I, Acireale's main street, running north, and Via Ruggero Settimo trickling south and out of town. Via Cavour leads to Piazza San Domenico and the market area.

### EXPLORING ACIREALE

❧ **HISTORIC CENTRE // DISCOVER ACIREALE'S REGAL BAROQUE HEART** To see Acireale's stunning architecture, start at Piazza Duomo, a grandiose piazza surrounded on three sides by monumental buildings. On the western flank is the cathedral ( ◷ 8am-12.30pm & 3.30-8pm), built in the early 1600s and topped by towering conical-capped spires. Inside, the echoing vaults and chapels are richly frescoed. Next to the cathedral, the Basilica dei Santi Pietro e Paolo ( ◷ 8am-12.30pm & 3.30-8pm) displays a typically elaborate 18th-century facade, while over the road Palazzo Municipale (Town Hall) impresses with its wrought-iron balconies and imposing central portal.

From the piazza, Via Ruggero Settimo leads south to Piazza Lionardo Vigo and the gorgeous Basilica di San Sebastiano ( ◷ 8am-12.30pm & 3.30-8pm), one of the town's finest baroque buildings. Behind the majestic facade, itself preceded by a grand balustrade and statues of Old Testament characters, the interior features some fine, if rather faded, frescoes recounting episodes from the life of St Sebastian.

Nearby, the streets around Piazza Marconi host Acireale's noisy *pescheria* (fish market).

❧ **PUPPET THEATRES // CATCH A SHOW AND LEARN ABOUT ACIREALE'S PUPPET TRADITIONS** Acireale has a long tradition of puppet theatre and there are a couple of places where you can learn all about it: **L'Antico Teatro dei Pupi** (www.teatropu pimacri.it; Via Alessi 5; admission free; ☺ 9.30am-12.30pm & 4.30-7.30pm), which has a collection of puppets and theatrical paraphernalia, and the **Teatro-Museo dell'Opera dei Pupi** ( ☎ 095 764 80 35; www.operadeipupi. com; Via Nazionale 195; admission free; ☺ 9am-noon & 6-9pm Wed, Sat & Sun summer, 9am-noon & 3-6pm winter), which stages evening performances every Thursday and Sunday in July and August.

### ❧ CARNEVALE // LET YOUR HAIR DOWN AT THE ANNUAL STREET PARTY

The best time to visit Acireale is during February's **Carnevale** (www.carnevaleacireale. com) when the town puts on one of the best spectacles in Sicily. The stars of the show are the elaborately decorated floats, some bedecked in technicolour flower displays, others carrying huge papier mâché caricatures of local celebrities. All around bands play, costumed dancers leap about and confetti rains down. The exact dates vary each year but you can get details on the event's comprehensive website. And if you miss it first time round, don't worry, there's a rerun, albeit on a smaller scale, in early August.

### ❧ SANTA MARIA LA SCALA // BUILD YOUR APPETITE WALKING TO THIS FISHING VILLAGE

There are two reasons to make the 2km downhill walk to the minute fishing village of Santa Maria la Scala. One is the walk itself which, once you've crossed the main road, is a lovely country stroll with gorgeous coastal views. The other is to eat seafood at one of the delightful trattorias. To get to the village, which consists of little more than a tiny harbour, a church, some houses and a black beach, follow Via Romeo down from Piazza Duomo, cross the main road and keep going.

## GASTRONOMIC HIGHLIGHTS

### ❧ LA TAVERNA €€

☎ 095 60 12 61; Via Ercole 4, Acireale; pizzas from €5, meals €25-30

La Taverna is a straight-up trattoria, serving traditional Sicilian food at honest prices. Given its location in the midst of the fish market, it's at its best at lunch when hungry locals pop in for a grilled catch of the day or *calamari arrosto* (roast squid). Seafood is the obvious choice, but it also does some fine nonfish dishes, such as *pasta con funghi porcini* (pasta with porcini mushrooms), and all the usual pizzas.

### ❧ L'OSTE SCURO €€

☎ 095 763 40 01; Piazza Lionardo Vigo 5-6, Acireale; meals €30-35

With the shouts of the nearby fish market ringing in the air and views over to the Basilica di San Sebastiano, this is a fine setting for a filling fish meal. Tuck into the seafood classic *pasta con gamberi, zucchini e zafferano* (pasta with prawns, courgettes and saffron) followed by a towering sauté of mussels and clams or a catch of the day cooked in sea water.

### ❧ TRATTORIA LA GROTTA €€

☎ 095 764 81 53; Via Scalo Grande 46, Santa Maria la Scala; meals €30; ☺ closed Tue

Eating at La Grotta, the best of the Santa Maria la Scala restaurants, is a memorable experience. As you enter you pass the fish counter where your order is picked out and unceremoniously weighed before going straight in the pot. You then go through to your table in the dining area, atmospherically set in the body of a cave. When it comes, the food is superb. The house speciality is *insalata di mare* (seafood salad), a mouth-watering mix of prawns, calamari and octopus, and the grilled fish is quite sensational.

# ACI TREZZA

A few kilometres south of Acireale, Aci Trezza is a small fishing village with a lively seafront and a number of good restaurants. Offshore, a series of surreal, jagged basalt rocks, the Scogli dei Ciclopi, rise out of the sea. These are the mythical missiles that the blinded Cyclops, Polyphemus (who lived in Etna), is supposed to have thrown at the fleeing Odysseus. Aci Trezza is also celebrated as the setting of *I Malavoglia,* Giovanni Verga's 19th-century literary masterpiece of life in a poor, isolated fishing community.

## EXPLORING ACI TREZZA

### ❤ THE SEAFRONT // SWIM, SIP AND TOP UP YOUR TAN

The principal activity in Aci Trezza is hanging out on the seafront, sunbathing in the day – wooden platforms are set up over the black volcanic rocks – and waltzing up and down after dark. You can enjoy the spectacle from one of the *lungomare* (seafront promenade) bars, such as **Café de Mar** (Lungomare Ciclopi; ☽ 8pm-late), next to Grand Hotel i Faraglioni, where white sofas and armchairs are scattered across a palm-shaded garden.

To explore the coast's caves, coves and bays, there are a number of operators at the port offering boat tours. One such, **Vaporetto Polifemo** ( ☎ 095 27 73 70; www.vaporettopolifemo.it), runs daily excursions along the coast from €10.

### ❤ LA CASA DEL NESPOLO // PEEP INTO THE WORLD OF GIOVANNI VERGA

A typical 19th-century house, **La Casa del Nespolo** ( ☎ 095 711 66 38; www.museocasadelnespolo.info; Via Arciprete De Maria 15; admission €1.55; ☽ 9.30am-1pm & 5-9pm Jul-Aug, shorter hr rest of year) is a small museum celebrating Giovanni Verga's great novel *I Malavoglia* and Luchino Visconti's 1948 film adaptation of it, *La Terra Trema.* The collection includes a selection of 19th-century household objects and work tools but the most interesting exhibits are the photos that Verga himself took of Aci Trezza.

### ❤ TRATTORIA VERGA DA GAETANO // DINE ON ACI TREZZA'S FINEST FISH

One of many restaurants in the port area, **Trattoria Verga da Gaetano** ( ☎ 095 27 63 42; Via Provinciale 119; meals €30-35) has an excellent local reputation. It's situated right in the heart of town – overlooking a terrace above ranks of moored fishing boats – and decorated with hundreds of framed pictures, photos and posters. The menu is typical, proposing, among other fishy dishes, marinated anchovies, linguine with scampi and delicious prawn kebabs.

# ACI CASTELLO

pop 18,195

Marking the beginning, or end, of the Riviera dei Ciclopi, Aci Castello is only 9km from Catania's city centre, making it an easy day trip from the city, even by public transport (take bus 534 from Piazza Borsellino). There's swimming and sunbathing off the black volcanic rocks, otherwise the main attraction is the **castello** (adult/under 7yr & over 60yr/7-10yr €1.50/free/0.50; ☽ 9am-1pm & 3-8pm May-Sep, 9am-1pm & 3-5pm Oct-Apr) set atop a vast black rock. La Rocca di Acicastello, as the rock is known, is apparently something of a vulcanological rarity having emerged from an underwater fissure. Grafted onto its top, the dark, brooding Norman castle was built in the 13th century on top of an earlier Arab fortification. It's in surprisingly good shape considering its age and now hosts a small museum with a collection of geological rock samples and bizarre prehistoric skulls.

# MT ETNA
· · · · · ·

## elev 3329m

**Dominating the landscape of eastern Sicily, Mt Etna is a massive brooding presence. At 3329m it is Italy's highest mountain south of the Alps and the largest active volcano in Europe. It's in an almost constant state of activity and eruptions occur frequently, most spectacularly from the four summit craters, but more often, and more dangerously, from the fissures and old craters on the mountain's flanks. This activity, which is closely monitored by 120 seismic activity stations and satellites, means that it is occasionally closed to visitors.**

The volcano, known locally as Mongibello (derived from the Latin word *mons*, meaning mountain, and *gibel*, meaning mountain in Arabic), emerged out of volcanic activity about 35,000 years ago. Not surprisingly, the ancients viewed it with awe. The Greeks believed that Vulcan, god of fire and metalwork, had his workshop here, and that Polyphemus, the one-eyed Cyclops, lived in a cave on its slopes. Another legend held that Typhon, a 100-headed monster, was trapped under the mountain by Zeus and has been spitting out flames ever since.

The first recorded eruption took place in about 1500 BC, since when it has erupted more than 200 times. The most devastating eruption was in 1669 when a massive river of lava poured down the southern slope, destroying 16 towns, engulfing a good part of Catania and killing up to 12,000 people. More recently, spectacular eruptions in 2002 caused immense damage to the infrastructure on the southern side of the mountain and a violent eruption in September 2007 threw up a 400m-high cloud of ash causing the temporary closure of Catania airport.

Since 1987 the volcano and its slopes have been part of a national park, the Parco dell'Etna. Encompassing 590 sq km and some 21 towns, the park's varied landscape ranges from the severe, snow-capped mountain top to lunar deserts of barren black lava, beech woods and lush vineyards where the area's highly rated DOC wine is produced.

## ESSENTIAL INFORMATION

**EMERGENCIES //** Soccorso Alpino della Guardia di Finanza ( ☎ 095 53 17 77) Mountain rescue.

**TOURIST INFORMATION //** Linguaglossa Tourist Office ( ☎ 095 64 30 94; www.prolocolin guaglossa.it, in Italian; Piazza Annunziata 5; ⊙ 9am-1pm & 4-8pm Mon-Sat summer, 9am-1pm & 3-7pm Mon-Sat winter, 9am-noon Sun year-round) On Etna's north side. Nicolosi Tourist Office ( ☎ 095 91 44 88; www.aast-nicolosi.it; Piazza Vittorio Emanuele, Nicolosi; ⊙ 9am-1pm Mon-Fri, 4-6pm Mon, Tue & Thu) Parco dell'Etna Office ( ☎ 095 82 11 11; www. parcoetna.ct.it, in Italian; Via del Convento 45, Nicolosi; ⊙ 9am-2pm & 4-7.30pm) About 1km from the centre of Nicolosi.

## ORIENTATION

The two main approaches to Etna are from the north and south. The southern route, signposted as Etna Sud, is via

Nicolosi and Rifugio Sapienza, 18km further up the mountain. The northern approach, Etna Nord, is through Piano Provenzano, 16km southwest of Linguaglossa.

## DRIVING TOUR: ETNA'S WESTERN FLANK

**Distance: 78km**
**Duration: one day**
The five small towns on the western side of the Parco dell'Etna offer a wonderful escape from the crowds that flock to Etna's better-known trails. Tourism has

not affected these towns like it has many others in the area and although none has any absolute must-see sights, they all have their own unique character.

Heading west out of **Catania** (**1**; p176) on the SS121 brings you to **Paternò** (**2**), a scruffy workaday town built around a huge 11th-century Norman **castello**. Originally built in 1072 as a defence against the Saracens, the castle has been much rebuilt over the centuries and now all that remains is the castle keep. But more than the building, what impresses are the sweeping views up to Etna.

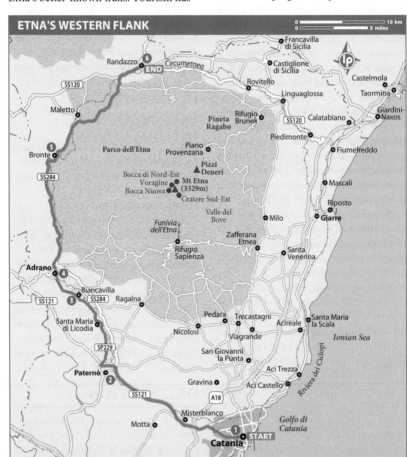

ETNA'S WESTERN FLANK

Continuing northwards on the SP229 you'll pass huge *fichi d'india* (prickly pears) and orange groves (and piles of litter) on the way to Biancavilla (3), a small town founded by Albanian refugees in 1480 but now typically Sicilian with its many baroque churches. Some 3km further on, the market town of Adrano (4) boasts one of the area's most striking sights, a robust Norman castello rising from a huge fortified base. Commissioned by the Norman Count Roger II in the late 11th century, it now houses a small museum (☎ 095 769 26 61; Piazza Umberto; admission €2; 9am-1pm & 4-7pm Tue-Sat, 9am-1pm Sun) displaying local archaeological finds. Nearby, on Via Catania, you can see the remains of Adranon, the 4th-century-BC Greek settlement over which the modern town was built.

From Adrano, the SS284 heads directly north through acres of nut groves to Bronte (5), famous throughout Italy for its pistachio nuts. Before pushing on make sure to try a pistachio ice cream from one of the bars on the main strip, Corso Umberto. Beyond Bronte, the road leads through an increasingly rugged landscape, interspersed with chunks of lava flow, as it heads up to Randazzo (6), the most interesting of the Etna towns.

Although the closest to the summit, the town has consistently escaped destruction, at least at the hands of Etna. It wasn't so lucky in WWII and heavy bombing meant that much of its grey medieval centre had to be reconstructed. The main sights are the three crenellated churches – the Cattedrale di Santa Maria, the Chiesa di San Nicolò and the Chiesa di San Martino – which in the 16th century used to take turns to act as the town cathedral. Round off the day with dinner at San Giorgio e Il Drago (☎ 095 92 39 72; Piazza San Giorgio; meals €30; closed Tue), a Slow Food Movement recommended trattoria with outdoor seating in the historic centre.

# EXPLORING MT ETNA

### ❧ RIFUGIO SAPIENZA // HEAD UP THE WELL-TRODDEN SOUTHERN ROUTE

Whether driving yourself or coming by public transport (for details, see p194), the starting point for the southern ascent is Rifugio Sapienza (1923m), a small cluster of souvenir shops and bars based around a mountain refuge. From here there are various options for getting up to the crater area. The easiest is to take the Funivia dell'Etna (☎ 095 91 41 41; www.funiviaetna.com; cable car €28.50, cable car, bus & guide €53; 9am-4.30pm) up to 2500m and then a minibus up to the Torre del Filosfo at 2920m.

Alternatively, you can forego the minibus and walk from the upper cable-car station. It's quite a steep 2km walk and you should allow yourself up to four hours to get back in time for the return cable car. Another option is to walk all the way from Rifugio Sapienza, but this is a strenuous climb that will take about four hours (less on the way down). Note that in windy weather the cable-car service is suspended and replaced by a minibus.

There are four craters at the top: Bocca di Nord-Est (Northeast crater), Voragine, Bocca Nuova and Cratere Sud-Est (Southeast crater). The two you're most likely to see are Cratere Sud-Est, a perfect black cone and one of the most active, and Bocca Nuova, the youngest of the four. How close you can get will depend on the level of volcanic activity. If you're hiking without a guide, always err on the side of caution as the dangers around the craters are very real. To the east of the crater area, the Valle del Bove, a massive depression formed after a cone collapsed several thousand years ago, falls away in a precipitous 1000m drop, smoke billowing up from its blackened depths.

### ♥ PIANO PROVENZANO //
#### APPROACH THE MOUNTAIN FROM THE NORTH

The gateway to Etna's quieter and more picturesque northern slopes is **Piano Provenzano** (1800m), a small ski station about 16km up from Linguaglossa. From here, **STAR** ( ☎ 347 4957091) runs jeep tours up the slopes between May and October. You can do one of two tours: a two-hour trip up to Pizzi Deneri and the Volcanic Observatory at 2800m, or a longer, three-hour excursion up to the main crater at 3200m. Both involve some walking and afford spectacular views of the Peloritani, Nebrodi and Madonie mountain ranges and the Valle del Bove. Further down, there's lovely summer walking in the pine, birch and larch trees of the **Pineta Ragabo**, a vast wood accessible from the Mareneve road between Linguaglossa and Milo.

Note that you'll need your own car to get to Piano Provenzano and the Pineta Ragabo, as no public transport passes this way.

### ♥ WINE & HONEY TASTING //
#### FEAST ON ETNA'S GORGEOUS FOOD AND WINE

Mt Etna is an important wine area, producing Etna DOC, one of 22 Sicilian wines to carry the *Denominazione di Origine Controllata* denomination. There are numerous wineries in the area where you can taste the local vino, including **Gambino** ( ☎ 095 227 26 78; www.vinigambino.it; contrada Petto Dragone; ☺ 8.30am-5.30pm, reservations preferred) near Linguaglossa. The Linguaglossa tourist office (p189) can provide further names and addresses.

Another gastronomic treat is the honey produced in **Zafferana Etnea**. This small town on Etna's eastern slopes has a long tradition of apiculture and apparently produces up to 35% of Italy's honey. To see what's so special about it visit **Oro d'Etna** ( ☎ 095 708 14 11; www.orodetna.it; Via San Giacomo 135), where you can try honey made from orange blossom, chestnuts and lemons.

## TOP TIPS

**Time your visit** The best time for walking is between April and May, and September and October. It gets very busy, and very hot, in high summer.

**Bring the right kit** Even when it's boiling hot at lower altitudes, it's windy up top and temperatures can fall below freezing. You'll need proper walking boots/shoes, a wind jacket, warm headgear and gloves. If you don't have your own, you can hire a kit at Rifugio Sapienza. In summer pack sunscreen, sunglasses and a hat, and make sure you have enough bottled water. If you usually wear contact lenses, bring glasses as there's usually a lot of dust swirling around.

**Get a decent map** The best is Selca's 1:25,000 *Mt Etna*, otherwise pick up the free *Mt Etna and Mother Nature* map from tourist offices.

**Bring a mobile phone and a compass** If walking independently, a mobile phone is an excellent safety precaution, though it may not work in certain locations. Also take a compass as fog is not uncommon.

**Cash or credit card** The funivia ticket office accepts both.

## GUIDED TOURS

There are many operators offering guided tours up to the craters and elsewhere on the mountain, and even if your natural inclination is to avoid them, they are well worth considering. The guides know the mountain inside out, and are able to direct you to the most spectacular points, as well as explain what you're looking at. They also offer a valuable safety precaution. Tours typically involve some walking and 4WD transport. Recommended reliable operators:

**Acquaterra** ( ☎ 095 50 30 20; www.acquaterra.com) Also offers snow-shoe excursions and canoeing on the Alcantara river.

**Etna Experience** ( ☎ 095 723 29 24; www.etnaexperience.com)

**Etna Sicily Touring** ( ☎ 392 5090298; www.etnasicilytouring.com)

**Gruppo Guide Alpine Etna Nord** ( ☎ 095 64 78 33; www.guidetnanord.com; Piazza Santa Caterina 24, Linguaglossa)

**Gruppo Guide Alpine Etna Sud** ( ☎ 095 791 47 55; www.etnaguide.com; Via Etnea 49, Nicolosi)

Prices vary depending on the tour you take but you should bank on from €45 per person for a half-day tour (usually morning or sunset) and about €60 for a full day.

❦ SKIING & CYCLING // **TAKE TO ETNA'S PISTES AND TRAILS**

Sicily is an unlikely skiing destination but you can ski on Etna (both downhill and cross-country) between December and March. The state of the slopes and how many lifts are working depends on the latest volcanic activity – check the current situation at www.etnasci.it, in Italian – but in decent conditions there are five pistes on the southern side of the mountain and three on the northern side. A daily ski pass costs €23 in Nicolosi (south) and €15 in Linguaglossa (north).

If cycling is your thing, there are some fine (albeit tough) trails around the mountain; you can hire bikes from Etna Touring ( ☎ 095 791 80 00; www.etnatouring.com; Via Roma 1) in Nicolosi for €12 per day. It can also organise guided rides on request.

❦ FERROVIA CIRCUMETNEA // **TAKE A TRAIN TRIP AROUND ETNA'S BASE**

A good way to enjoy armchair views of Etna is to jump on the Ferrovia Etnea (FCE; ☎ 095 54 12 50; www.circumetnea.it) train. Operating out of Catania, this slow train follows a 114km trail around the base of the volcano, stopping off at a number of small towns on the way (see p190) and affording great views. From Catania it takes two hours to reach Randazzo (one way/return €4.85/7.80) in the mountain's northern reaches. To get to the FCE station in Catania catch the metro from the main train station to the FCE station at Via Caronda (metro stop: Borgo) or take bus 429 or 432 up Via Etnea and ask to be let off at the 'Borgo' metro stop.

## GASTRONOMIC HIGHLIGHTS

❦ AGRITURISMO SAN MARCO €€
☎ 389 4237294; www.agriturismosanmarco.com; meals €23

Find your way to this welcoming *agriturismo* (farm stay) near Rovitello for authentic farmhouse food in a lovely bucolic setting. Kick off with a selection of cured meats and local cheeses,

IONIAN COAST

before tucking into a bowl of fresh pasta with meaty *ragú* and a *secondo* (second course) of succulent grilled meat. Bookings are required, but you'll need to call for directions anyway.

❦ **ANTICO ORTO DEI LIMONO** €€

☎ 095 91 08 08; Via Grotte 4; pizzas from €5, set menu €26; ☾ closed Tue

There can be few better ways of rounding off a day in the mountains than a meal at this delightful Nicolosi restaurant. Tastefully housed in a converted wine and oil press, it specialises in delicious tried-and-tested country fare. It's all good but standouts include the abundant house antipasto (a mix of creamy ricotta, salami and marinated vegetables) and an excellent pasta with *ragù*, peas and

mushrooms. If you're really hungry, go for the pharaonic set menu, which at €26 is excellent value.

# TRANSPORT

**BUS //** AST ( ☎ 095 746 10 96; www.aziendasicili anatrasporti.it) runs a daily bus from Catania to Rifugio Sapienza (return €5.60) via Nicolosi, departing at 8.15am and returning at 4.30pm. Between 15 June and 15 September there's a second departure, leaving Catania at 11.20pm. Ferrovia Etnea (FCE; ☎ 095 54 12 50; www.circumetnea.it) operates infrequent weekday buses between Catania and Linguaglossa (€4.20, 1¼ hours).

**CAR & MOTORCYCLE //** Nicolosi is about 17km northwest of Catania on the SP10. From Nicolosi it's a further 18km up to Rifugio Sapienza. For Linguaglossa take the A18 autostrada from Catania, exit at Fiume-freddo and follow the SS120 towards Randazzo.

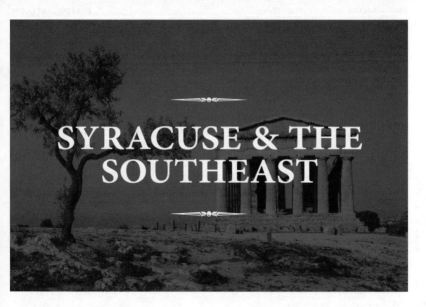

# SYRACUSE & THE SOUTHEAST

## 3 PERFECT DAYS

### ❧ DAY 1 // SAVOUR STUNNING SYRACUSE
Before the sun gets too hot head up to the Parco Archeologico della Neapolis (p205) to explore Syracuse's superb classical ruins. Afterwards, visit the Museo Archeologico Paolo Orsi (p206), one of Sicily's top archaeological museums, and then lunch in Ortygia (p208). Spend the afternoon strolling Ortygia's baroque lanes, before winding down with a drink on Piazza del Duomo (p202) and a late seafood dinner.

### ❧ DAY 2 // TOUR SICILY'S UNESCO-LISTED BAROQUE TOWNS
Pick up a car and head south to search out Sicily's great baroque towns. First stop is Noto (p216) and its unforgettable main street, Corso Vittorio Emanuele. Whilst here make sure to get an ice cream from Corrado Costanzo (p218), arguably Sicily's best *gelateria* (ice-cream shop). From Noto push on to Modica (p220), where you can lunch with the locals at the Osteria dei Sapori Perduti (p222). The last leg leads on to Ragusa (p223), or more specifically Ragusa Ibla (p223). The stunning cathedral here is a masterclass in baroque architecture.

### ❧ DAY 3 // COASTAL PLEASURES
Take the time to explore the area's lovely, low-key coastline. You could spend a very pleasant day bird-watching, walking and sunbathing at the Riserva Naturale Oasi Faunistica di Vendicari (p219), but if you want to see a bit more continue south to the Cape Area's Marzamemi (p220), a good spot for a seafood lunch and a drop of local wine. The end of the road, quite literally, is Portopalo di Capo Passero (p220), a summer resort with beautifully transparent waters.

# SYRACUSE & THE SOUTHEAST

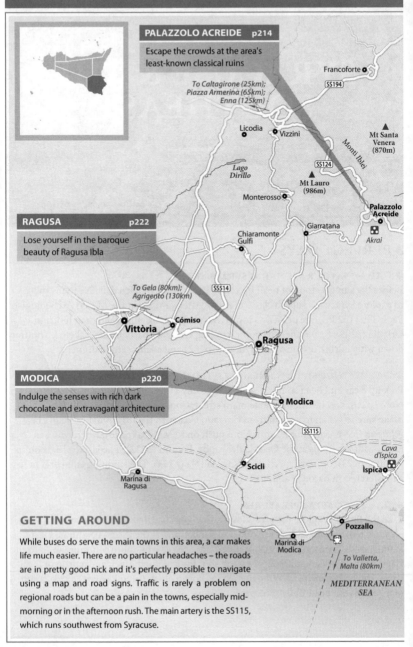

SYRACUSE & THE SOUTHEAST

**PALAZZOLO ACREIDE**  p214

Escape the crowds at the area's least-known classical ruins

Francoforte

SS194

To Caltagirone (25km);
Piazza Armerina (65km);
Enna (125km)

Licodia     Vizzini

Mt Santa
Venera
(870m)

Monti Iblei

SS124

Lago
Dirillo

Mt Lauro
(986m)

Monterosso

Palazzolo
Acreide

Akrai

**RAGUSA**  p222

Lose yourself in the baroque beauty of Ragusa Ibla

Chiaramonte
Gulfi

Giarratana

To Gela (80km);
Agrigento (130km)

SS514

Vittòria     Cómiso

Ragusa

**MODICA**  p220

Indulge the senses with rich dark chocolate and extravagant architecture

Modica

SS115

Cava
d'Ispica

Scicli

Ispica

Marina di
Ragusa

## GETTING AROUND

While buses do serve the main towns in this area, a car makes life much easier. There are no particular headaches – the roads are in pretty good nick and it's perfectly possible to navigate using a map and road signs. Traffic is rarely a problem on regional roads but can be a pain in the towns, especially mid-morning or in the afternoon rush. The main artery is the SS115, which runs southwest from Syracuse.

Marina di
Modica

Pozzallo

To Valletta,
Malta (80km)

MEDITERRANEAN
SEA

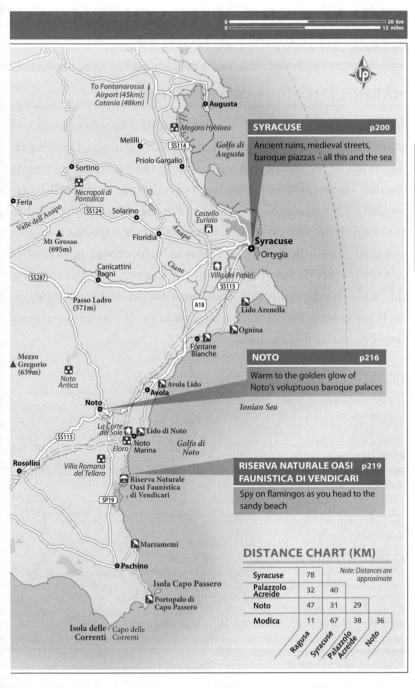

0 — 20 km
0 — 12 miles

To Fontanarossa
Airport (45km);
Catania (48km)

Augusta

Megara Hyblaea

Melilli

SS114

Golfo di
Augusta

Priolo Gargallo

Sortino

Necropoli di
Pantalica

Ferla

Valle dell'Anapo

SS124   Solarino

Castello
Eurialo

Mt Grosso
(695m)

Floridia

Anapo

Syracuse

Ortygia

Canicattini
Bagni

Ciane

Villa dei Papiri

SS287

SS115

Passo Ladro
(571m)

A18

Lido Arenella

Mezzo
Gregorio
(639m)

Noto
Antica

Ognina

Fontane
Bianche

Avola Lido

Avola

Noto

La Corte
del Sole

Lido di Noto

SS115

Eloro   Noto
Marina

Golfo di
Noto

Ionian Sea

Rosolini

Villa Romana
del Tellaro

Riserva Naturale
Oasi Faunistica
di Vendicari

SP19

Marzamemi

Pachino

Isola Capo Passero

Portopalo di
Capo Passero

Isola delle   Capo delle
Correnti   Correnti

**SYRACUSE**   p200

Ancient ruins, medieval streets,
baroque piazzas – all this and the sea

**NOTO**   p216

Warm to the golden glow of
Noto's voluptuous baroque palaces

**RISERVA NATURALE OASI**   p219
**FAUNISTICA DI VENDICARI**

Spy on flamingos as you head to the
sandy beach

## DISTANCE CHART (KM)

| | Ragusa | Syracuse | Palazzolo Acreide | Noto |
|---|---|---|---|---|
| Syracuse | 78 | | Note: Distances are approximate | |
| Palazzolo Acreide | 32 | 40 | | |
| Noto | 47 | 31 | 29 | |
| Modica | 11 | 67 | 38 | 36 |

# SYRACUSE & THE SOUTHEAST
## GETTING STARTED

SYRACUSE & THE SOUTHEAST

## MAKING THE MOST OF YOUR TIME

With its outstanding classical ruins, beautiful baroque towns and sandy beaches, this is the Sicily that many come to see. The temptation is to stay in Syracuse, hanging out in the piazzas and sunning yourself on the seafront, but drag yourself away and you'll be rewarded with some of Sicily's most charming towns. Noto, Modica and Ragusa are the star performers with their baroque treasures and gastronomic delights – ice cream in Noto, chocolate in Modica and one of Sicily's finest restaurants in Ragusa – but the countryside is also worth exploring. Prehistoric tombs stud huge rocky ravines while birds and beach bunnies make for the Riserva Naturale Oasi Faunistica di Vendicari.

## TOP TOURS & COURSES

**❦ ART COURSES**
Stay at I Tetti Siciliando hotel in Modica and sign up for a one- or two-week course in mosaic work, painting or wood restoration (p316).

**❦ GUIDED NATURE WALKS**
Join the locals on a guided walk in the Syracuse countryside courtesy of the Natura Sicula association (p208).

**❦ ITALIAN COOKERY CLASSES**
Brush up your cooking skills with a three-hour lesson at La Corte del Sole hotel near Lido di Noto (p219).

**❦ LEARN THE LANGUAGE**
In Syracuse, Biblios Cafe runs language courses enlivened by shopping trips to the local market, cooking lessons and visits to local wine producers (p205).

**❦ MONTALBANO TOUR**
Follow in the footsteps of TV detective Salvo Montalbano on an Allakatalla (p218) or Echoes Events (p282) tour of the series' locations: Palazzolo Acreide, Noto, Pantalica, Modica, Scicli, Donnafugata and Ragusa.

# GETTING AWAY FROM IT ALL

Syracuse and the main baroque towns can get busy in peak months but you don't have to go far to escape the crowds.

* **Walk solo among classical ruins** Little known and little publicised, the remains of ancient Akrai sit in grassy solitude overlooking Palazzolo Acreide (p215).

* **Descend into Ispica's Grand Canyon** Explore the rocky catacombs and cave dwellings of Cava d'Ispica (p223).

* **Visit the Land of the Dead** You're sure to find peace walking among the Bronze Age tombs at the Necropoli di Pantalica (p214).

# BAROQUE TREASURES

Sicily's southwest contains some of the island's finest baroque architecture.

* **Chiesa di San Giorgio, Modica** In a town of more than 25 churches, Modica's cathedral towers head-and-shoulders above the rest (p221).

* **Corso Vittorio Emanuele, Noto** Few streets in Sicily can match the beauty of this magnificent strip in Noto's historic centre (p217).

* **Duomo, Syracuse** Lording it over the city's showpiece square, this majestic cathedral incorporates a stunning facade and columns from an ancient Greek temple (p202).

* **Piazza Duomo, Ragusa** A fabulous film-set of a square overlooked by the city's remarkable cathedral (p223).

# TOP FOODIE ADDRESSES

**❦ ANTICA DOLCERIA BONAJUTO**
Modica's oldest chocolate maker produces some strange and wonderful concoctions (p221).

**❦ CAFFÈ SICILIA**
This Noto cafe is *the* place to cool down with a *granita* (crushed-ice drink; p218).

**❦ CANTINA RUDINÌ**
Stop off at this established wine producer to taste some of the local tipple (p220).

**❦ JONICO-A RUTTA 'E CIAULI**
Seafood in the sun and great views over Syracuse's historic centre (p209).

**❦ RISTORANTE DUOMO**
One for a special occasion, Ragusa's top restaurant is considered one of Sicily's best (p226).

# RESOURCES

* **Istituto Nazionale Dramma Antico** (www.indafondazione.org) For details of Syracuse's classical-drama season.

* **Modica Comune** (www.comune.modica.rg.it) Accommodation and restaurant listings.

* **Noto Comune** (www.comune.noto.sr.it) Info about monuments, events and transport.

* **Ragusa Comune** (www.comune.ragusa.it) Comprehensive information on Ragusa and its environs.

* **Syracuse Comune** (www.comune.siracusa.it/essereturista/turismo/home.htm, in Italian) Listings, transport information and details of the main sights.

# SYRACUSE

· · · · · ·

**pop 124,085**

**More than any other city, Syracuse encapsulates Sicily's timeless beauty. Ancient Greek ruins rise out of lush citrus orchards, cafe tables spill out onto dazzling baroque piazzas, and medieval lanes lead down to the sparkling blue sea. But handsome as it is, the city is no museum piece – life goes on here much as it has done for 3000 years, as you'll soon see from the snarling mid-morning traffic and noisy markets.**

It's difficult to imagine now but in its heyday Syracuse was the largest city in the ancient world, bigger even than Athens and Corinth. It was founded by Corinthian colonists, who landed on the island of Ortygia in 734 BC and set up the mainland city four years later. It quickly flourished, growing to become a rich commercial town and major regional powerhouse. Victory over the Carthaginians at the Battle of Himera in 480 BC paved the way for a golden age, during which art and culture thrived and the city's cruel tyrannical kings commissioned an impressive program of public building. The finest intellectuals of the age flocked to Syracuse, cultivating the sophisticated urban culture that was to see the birth of comic Greek theatre.

Syracuse's independence abruptly came to an end in 211 BC when invading Romans breached the city's defences, ingeniously devised by Archimedes, and took control. Under Roman rule Syracuse remained Sicily's capital but the city's glory days were behind it and decline set in. It was briefly the capital of the Byzantine empire but was sacked by the Saracens in 878 and reduced to little more than a fortified provincial town. The population fell drastically, and famine, plague and earthquakes marked the next 800 years. The Val di Noto earthquake in 1693, however, was the catalyst for energetic urban renewal as planners took advantage of the damaged city to undertake a massive program of baroque reconstruction.

Following the unification of Italy in 1865, Syracuse was made a provincial capital and the city began to expand once more, a trend that continued with the ugly urban development of the postwar years.

## ESSENTIAL INFORMATION

**EMERGENCIES //** Ospedale Umberto I (Map p201; ☎ 0935 72 42 36; Via Testaferrata); Police Station (Map p203; ☎ 0931 46 35 66; Piazza San Giuseppe 6)

**TOURIST INFORMATION //** Municipal Tourist Office (Map p203; ☎ 800 055500; Via Roma 31; ☷ 9am-1pm & 2-5.30pm Mon-Fri, 9am-noon Sat); Ortygia Tourist Office (Map p203; ☎ 0931 46 42 55; Via Maestranza 33; ☷ 8am-2pm & 2.30-5.30pm Mon-Fri, 8am-2pm Sat)

## ORIENTATION

Syracuse's main sights are concentrated in two areas: Ortygia, and 2km across town, the Parco Archeologico della Neapolis. Ortygia, Syracuse's historic centre and most atmospheric neighbourhood, is an island joined to the mainland by a couple of bridges. It is well signposted and has a useful car park (Parcheggio Talete). If coming by bus, you'll be dropped off at the bus terminal in front of the train station. From here it's about a 1km walk to Ortygia – head straight down Corso Umberto. Alternatively, a free shuttle bus connects the station with Piazza Archimede in Ortygia. Via Roma is Ortygia's main thoroughfare.

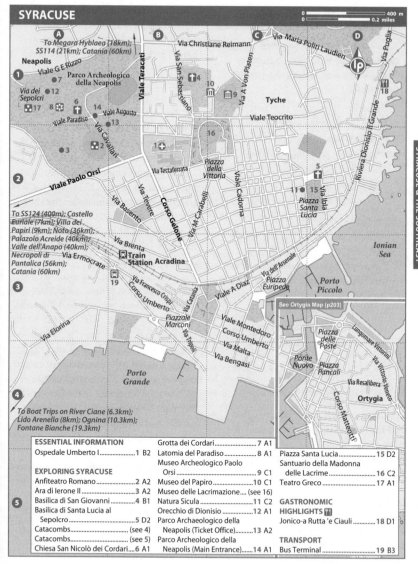

**SYRACUSE**

SYRACUSE & THE SOUTHEAST

| ESSENTIAL INFORMATION | | Grotta dei Cordari...................7 A1 | | Piazza Santa Lucia..................15 D2 |
|---|---|---|---|---|
| Ospedale Umberto I..................1 B2 | | Latomia del Paradiso..............8 A1 | | Santuario della Madonna |
| | | Museo Archeologico Paolo | | delle Lacrime................16 C2 |
| **EXPLORING SYRACUSE** | | Orsi.......................9 C1 | | Teatro Greco........................17 A1 |
| Anfiteatro Romano..................2 A2 | | Museo del Papiro...................10 C1 | | |
| Ara di Ierone II......................3 A2 | | Museo delle Lacrimazione....(see 16) | | **GASTRONOMIC** |
| Basilica di San Giovanni.........4 B1 | | Natura Sicula.......................11 C2 | | **HIGHLIGHTS** |
| Basilica di Santa Lucia al | | Orecchio di Dionisio..............12 A1 | | Jonico-a Rutta 'e Ciauli..........18 D1 |
| Sepolcro..................5 D2 | | Parco Archeologico della | | |
| Catacombs........................(see 4) | | Neapolis (Ticket Office)........13 A2 | | **TRANSPORT** |
| Catacombs........................(see 5) | | Parco Archeologico della | | Bus Terminal.........................19 B3 |
| Chiesa San Nicolò dei Cordari....6 A1 | | Neapolis (Main Entrance)......14 A1 | | |

Syracuse's most important ancient ruins are in the Parco Archeologico della Neapolis near the northern entrance to town. There's parking here and it is signposted from around town. Bus 12 links the archaeological park with Ortygia.

# EXPLORING SYRACUSE

## ORTYGIA

A tangled maze of atmospheric alleyways and refined piazzas, Ortygia is a joy to wander. Its skinny lanes are lined with

## ACCOMMODATION

Accommodation in the area runs the gamut from small, family-run B&Bs to stylish hotels and luxurious *agriturismi* (farm stays).

★ Lie back and luxuriate at **Villa dei Papiri** (p315), a ravishing rural retreat near Syracuse.

★ A laid-back B&B in Syracuse's baroque centre, **Viaggiatori, Viandanti e Sognatori** (p315) is a friendly, bohemian bolt-hole.

★ Overlooking a nature reserve near Noto, **La Corte del Sole** (p316) oozes farmhouse chic.

★ Exuding old-world charm, Ragusa's **Risveglio Ibleo** (p317) sets the B&B standard.

★ Read up on Sicilian literature at refined **Hotel DeMohàc** (p316) in Modica's medieval centre.

For detailed accommodation listings, see p314.

attractive palazzi, trattorias and cafes and the central square, Piazza del Duomo, is one of Sicily's most spectacular piazzas. The area, accessed by way of Ponte Nuovo, is best explored on foot.

### ❦ PIAZZA DEL DUOMO // HANG OUT IN BAROQUE STYLE

Syracuse's showpiece square is a masterpiece in baroque town planning. A long, rectangular piazza flanked by flamboyant palazzi, it sits on what was once Syracuse's ancient acropolis (fortified citadel). Little remains of the original Greek building but if you look along the side of the Duomo (Cathedral; Map p203; ⏱ 8am-6pm), you'll see a number of thick Doric columns incorporated into the cathedral's

structure. These date to the 5th-century BC and are all that survive from the mighty Greek temple that once stood here. The temple, dedicated to Athena, was renowned throughout the Mediterranean, in no small part thanks to Cicero, who visited Ortygia in the 1st century BC. Its roof was crowned by a golden statue of Athena that served as a beacon to sailors at sea; nowadays a statue of the Virgin Mary stands in the same spot.

The Duomo's most striking feature is the columned facade (1728–53) that was added by Andrea Palma after the church was damaged in the 1693 earthquake. Inside, look out for a 13th-century Norman font in the baptistry, adorned by seven bronze lions.

To the north of the Duomo, over Via Minerva, **Palazzo Municipale** (Map p203), or Palazzo Senatoriale, is home to Syracuse city council. Built in 1629 by the Spaniard Juan Vermexio, it is nicknamed 'Il Lucertolone' (The Lizard) after the architect's signature – a small lizard carved into a stone on the left corner of the cornice. On the other side of the Duomo, the elegant, 17th-century **Palazzo Arcivescovile** (Archbishop's Palace; Map p203) is home to the Biblioteca Alagoniana and some rare 13th-century manuscripts.

Over the square, in the northwestern corner, is the **Palazzo Beneventano del Bosco** (Map p203), which has a pretty 18th-century facade, while at its southern end is the **Chiesa di Santa Lucia alla Badia** (Map p203), dedicated to St Lucy, the city's patron saint.

The best vantage point on the square is the **Gran Caffè del Duomo** (Map p203; ☎ 0931 215 44; Piazza del Duomo 18), a popular cafe opposite the Duomo. This is the perfect people-watching perch and a great place to enjoy a languid glass of wine.

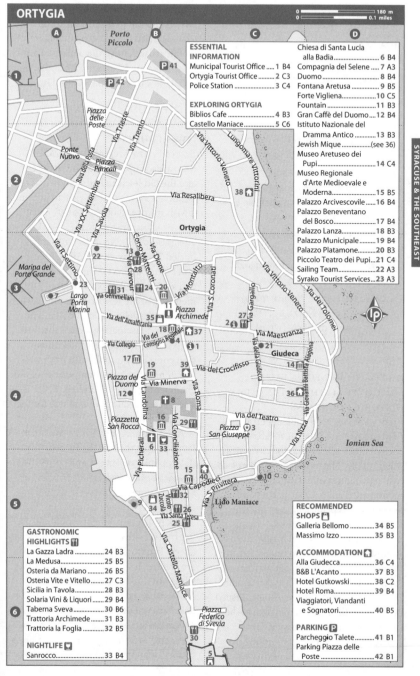

# ORTYGIA

0 — 180 m
0 — 0.1 miles

**ESSENTIAL INFORMATION**
Municipal Tourist Office ..... 1 B4
Ortygia Tourist Office ......... 2 C3
Police Station ...................... 3 C4

**EXPLORING ORTYGIA**
Biblios Cafe ......................... 4 B3
Castello Maniace................. 5 C6
Chiesa di Santa Lucia
  alla Badia ......................... 6 B4
Compagnia del Selene ..... 7 A3
Duomo................................. 8 B4
Fontana Aretusa ................. 9 B5
Forte Vigliena....................10 C5
Fountain .............................11 B3
Gran Caffè del Duomo ....12 B4
Istituto Nazionale del
  Dramma Antico ............13 B3
Jewish Mique .................(see 36)
Museo Aretuseo dei
  Pupi ................................14 C4
Museo Regionale
  d'Arte Medioevale e
  Moderna..........................15 B5
Palazzo Arcivescovile .....16 B4
Palazzo Beneventano
  del Bosco.........................17 B4
Palazzo Lanza...................18 B3
Palazzo Municipale .........19 B4
Palazzo Platamone...........20 B3
Piccolo Teatro dei Pupi ...21 C4
Sailing Team.....................22 A3
Syrako Tourist Services...23 A3

**GASTRONOMIC HIGHLIGHTS**
La Gazza Ladra ..................24 B3
La Medusa..........................25 B5
Osteria da Mariano ..........26 B5
Osteria Vite e Vitello........27 C3
Sicilia in Tavola.................28 B3
Solaria Vini & Liquori .......29 B4
Taberna Sveva...................30 B6
Trattoria Archimede ........31 B3
Trattoria la Foglia ............32 B5

**NIGHTLIFE**
Sanrocco.............................33 B4

**RECOMMENDED SHOPS**
Galleria Bellomo ...............34 B5
Massimo Izzo ....................35 B3

**ACCOMMODATION**
Alla Giudecca....................36 C4
B&B L'Acanto ....................37 B3
Hotel Gutkowski...............38 C2
Hotel Roma........................39 B4
Viaggiatori, Viandanti
  e Sognatori......................40 B5

**PARKING**
Parcheggio Talete............41 B1
Parking Piazza delle
  Poste ...............................42 B1

Porto
Piccolo

Piazza
delle
Poste

Ponte
Nuovo

Piazza
Pancali

Marina del
Porto Grande

Largo
Porta
Marina

Ortygia

Piazza
Archimede

Giudeca

Piazza del
Duomo

Piazzetta
San Rocco

Piazza
San Giuseppe

Ionian Sea

Lido Maniace

Piazza
Federico
di Svevia

**SYRACUSE & THE SOUTHEAST**

## TOP **FIVE**

### PIAZZAS

★ **Piazza del Duomo, Syracuse** (p202) – Syracuse's refined outdoor drawing room is set around the city's triumphal Duomo

★ **Piazza Municipio, Noto** (p217) – Noto's golden baroque architecture surrounds this graceful square

★ **Piazza Duomo, Ragusa** (p223) – sloping down from Ragusa's fairy-tale cathedral, this is an open-air masterpiece

★ **Piazza del Popolo, Palazzolo Acreide** (p214) – an impressive baroque square in a charming and oft-overlooked country town

★ **Corso Umberto I, Modica** (p221) – OK, so it's not a piazza, but Modica's lively central street cuts a dashing swath

❧ **LEGENDARY FOUNTAINS // MULL OVER MYTHS AT THE CITY'S HISTORIC FOUNTAINS**
Fresh water has been bubbling up at the **Fontana Aretusa** (Map p203; Via Picherali) since ancient times when it was the city's main water supply. The fountain, now *the* place to hang out on summer evenings, is a monumental affair set around a pond full of papyrus plants and grey mullets. Legend has it that the goddess Artemis transformed her beautiful handmaiden Aretusa into the spring to protect her from the unwelcome attention of the river god Alpheus. In her watery guise, Aretusa fled from Arcadia under the sea, hotly pursued by Alpheus, their waters mingling as she came to the surface in Ortygia.

The mythical goddess of hunting, Artemis, is the star turn of the 19th-century

fountain that's the highlight of **Piazza Archimede** (Map p203), a handsome square circled by imposing Catalan Gothic palazzi, including **Palazzo Lanza** (Map p203) and **Palazzo Platamone** (Map p203), now home to the Banca d'Italia.

❧ **THE GIUDECCA // EXPLORE HIDDEN CORNERS OF THE OLD JEWISH GHETTO**
East of Piazza Archimede, Via Maestranza leads up to Via della Giudecca and the old Jewish ghetto, known as the Giudecca. Here you can visit an ancient Jewish miqwe (ritual bath; Map p203; ☎ 0931 2 22 55; Via GB Alagona 52; admission €5; ☿ guided tours 11am, noon, 4pm, 5pm & 6pm Mar-Oct) that lies buried 20m beneath the Alla Giudecca hotel. The baths were once connected to a synagogue, but were blocked by members of the Jewish community when they were expelled from the island in 1492. It's a fascinating sight – the three deep pools intended for total immersion constantly bubble with fresh water, which now has to be pumped out of the chamber to prevent flooding. There is a separate, private pool that was for the sole use of the rabbi.

A short walk away, Syracuse's much-loved puppet theatre, the **Piccolo Teatro dei Pupi** (Puppet Theatre; Map p203; ☎ 0931 46 55 40; www.pupari.it; Via della Giudecca 17; tickets from €7) stages puppet shows re-enacting traditional tales involving magicians, love-struck princesses, knights and dragons. See the website for a calendar of performances. The workshop, where the puppets are created, is at Via della Giudecca 19, while just down the road, the small **Museo Aretuseo dei Pupi** (Map p203; ☎ 0931 46 55 40; Piazza San Giuseppe; admission €2; ☿ 11am-1pm & 4-6pm Mon-Sat Mar-May, Sep & Oct, 10.30am-1pm & 4-6.30pm Mon-Sat Jun-Aug) chronicles Sicily's history of puppet theatre.

❦ **MUSEO REGIONALE D'ARTE
MEDIOEVALE E MODERNA //** BRUSH
UP ON MEDIEVAL AND MODERN ART
Housed in the 13th-century Palazzo Bellomo, the **Museo Regionale d'Arte Medioevale e Moderna** (Map p203; ☎ 0931
6 95 11; Via Capodieci 14; adult/concession €8/4;
🕙 9am-7pm Tue-Sat, 9am-1pm Sun) has an
eclectic collection of sculpture, painting,
ceramic work, jewellery and clothing.
Many of the collection's best pieces are
in Sala V, which is dedicated to works
from the 14th century. Highlights include a *Madonna col bambino* (Madonna
with Child) attributed to the Sicilian
artist Domenico Gagini, and the gallery's
undisputed masterpiece, Antonello da
Messina's *L'Annunciazione* (Annunciation, 1474), only recently returned
to Syracuse after a long restoration in
Rome.

❦ LANGUAGE COURSES // LEARN
TO SPEAK LIKE A NATIVE
Right in the heart of the Ortygia action,
**Biblios Cafe** (Map p203; ☎ 0931 2 14 91; www.
biblios-cafe.it; Via del Consiglio Reginale 11) is a well-
known cafe-cum-bookshop that organ-
ises a whole range of cultural activities,
including visits to local vineyards, art
classes and language courses. Italian lessons, which emphasise everyday conver-
sational language, can be organised on
an individual basis (€25 per hour) or as
part of a course lasting from a week to a
month (per one/four weeks €220/700).

## THE MAINLAND

Although not as picturesque as Ortygia,
the mainland city boasts a number of fascinating archaeological sights. The most
compelling is the Parco Archeologico
della Neapolis to the north of the city
centre, but you'll also find plenty of interest at the city's renowned archaeological museum, the Museo Archeologico
Paolo Orsi. Underground, an extensive
network of catacombs dates from the
Roman era.

❦ **PARCO ARCHEOLOGICO DELLA
NEAPOLIS //** RELIVE ANCIENT
DRAMAS AMONG HAUNTING RUINS
To the northwest of the city centre, the
**Parco Archeologico della Neapolis** (Map
p201; ☎ 0931 6 62 06; adult/concession €8/4, incl Museo Archeologico Paolo Orsi €9/4.50; 🕙 9am-6pm daily
Mar-Sep, 9am-3pm Mon-Sat, 9am-1pm Sun Oct-Feb)
is where you'll find Syracuse's greatest
classical ruins. Neapolis (New City) was
one of the five quarters of the ancient
city (the others were Ortygia, Akradina,
Tyche and Epipoli), and it was here that
many of the city's great civic and religious buildings were situated. The star
of the show was, and is, the stunning
5th-century-BC theatre, but there is also
a crumbling Roman amphitheatre and a
series of dank caves once used as prisons.

The park's ticket office is on the corner of Via Cavallari and Viale Augusto,
over the road from the main entrance.
Near the ticket office you'll find toilets
(€0.30), a cafe and a series of souvenir
stalls. There's also a bar with a pizzeria
just inside the main entrance, next to the
small **Chiesa San Nicolò dei Cordari**
(Map p201).

On the left after the church is the first
ancient monument, the 3rd-century-AD
**Anfiteatro Romano** (Roman Amphitheatre; Map p201). Although it's not in
great nick, enough remains to give an idea
of its original size – it was the largest in
southern Italy, only slightly smaller than
the Arena in Verona. Used by the Romans
to stage gladiator fights and horse races, it
was all but destroyed in the 16th century,
as the city's Spanish rulers stripped it of
stone to build Ortygia's walls.

SYRACUSE & THE SOUTHEAST

Immediately west of the amphitheatre, the giant rectangular area that you see is the 3rd-century-BC **Ara di Ierone II** (Altar of Hieron II; Map p201). Only the foundations remain of what was once a vast altar used for public sacrifices. According to the Greek historian Diodorus Siculus, up to 450 oxen were slaughtered here at the city's annual feast.

### Latomia del Paradiso

Further down Via Paradiso, on the right-hand side, is the entrance to the **Latomia del Paradiso** (Garden of Paradise; Map p201), an ancient limestone quarry pitted with caves and full of orange and olive trees. The Greeks ran the quarries along the lines of a concentration camp, putting prisoners to work cutting blocks of limestone out of the subterranean caves and imprisoning them in the impregnable grottoes. The garden's most famous sight is the ear-shaped grotto known as the **Orecchio di Dionisio** (Ear of Dionysius; Map p201). Named by Caravaggio on a visit in 1608, the cave has remarkable acoustic qualities which, according to legend, Syracuse's tyrannical king Dionysius used to eavesdrop on his prisoners' conversations. In reality, the grotto – 23m high and 65m deep – was probably used as a rock quarry.

Beyond, but blocked off to visitors, is the **Grotta dei Cordari** (Rope-makers' Cave; Map p201), where the ancient city's rope-makers would toil away in the humid air.

### Teatro Greco

From the Latomia it's a quick hop up to the lustrous white **Teatro Greco** (Greek Theatre; Map p201), the park's principal sight and one of the best-preserved Greek theatres in existence. Built in the 5th century BC, and later added to in the 3rd and 2nd centuries BC, the great auditorium

could seat up to 16,000 people. From the 5th century onwards, the theatre was the focal point of Syracuse's buzzing cultural scene, staging works by Sophocles, Euripides and Aeschylus, whose *The Persians*, *Prometheus Bound* and *Prometheus Unbound* were premiered here in his presence.

When the Romans took Syracuse in the 3rd century they made alterations to the theatre, mostly so that they could stage gladiatorial combats and *naumachiae* (mock naval battles) in the flooded arena. Some of the seats bear inscriptions to Syracuse's notables, namely Hieron II's family, and the gods. For the best views climb up to the tomb-riddled Via dei Sepolcri.

If you're a fan of classical drama, try to time your visit to coincide with the Cycle of Classical Plays, held annually in May and June. For more details see p208.

### ✤ MUSEO ARCHEOLOGICO PAOLO ORSI // BROWSE SICILY'S GREATEST ARCHAEOLOGICAL COLLECTION

Housed in the grounds of Villa Landolina, the **Museo Archeologico Paolo Orsi** (Map p201; ☎ 0931 46 40 22; Viale Teocrito; adult/concession €8/4, incl Parco Archeologico della Neapolis €9/4.50; ☒ 9am-6pm Tue-Sat, 9am-1pm Sun) boasts Sicily's largest archaeological collection. More than 18,000 artefacts are on display, ranging from prehistoric fossils and earthenware pottery to classical Greek and Roman statuary.

The star of the show is undoubtedly the sculpture, the development of which can be traced from rudimentary Greek work to the more sophisticated style of the later Roman period. Good examples of both styles include the 6th-century-BC carving of *Dea Madre* suckling twins, which was unearthed in the Greek colony of Megara Hyblaea; and the celebrated *Venere Anadiomene*, a 1st-century-AD Roman copy of an earlier Greek work, depicting a voluptuous Venus rising from the sea. Other treats are the lovely terracotta votive offerings to Demeter, and more famously the grimacing terracotta face of the Gorgon with Pegasus.

### ❦ MUSEO DEL PAPIRO // FOLLOW THE PAPER TRAIL AT THE PAPYRUS MUSEUM

In a residential block next to the Museo Archeologico Paolo Orsi, the small Museo del Papiro (Map p201; ☎ 0931 6 16 16; www.museodelpapiro.it; Viale Teocrito 66; admission free; ❧ 9am-1pm Tue-Sun) is dedicated to the papyrus plant, with exhibits including model boats, papyrus documents and various papyrus products. The papyrus plant grows in abundance around the River Ciane, near Syracuse, and was used to make paper in the 18th century. The museum also features some interesting papyrus canoes and a copy of the Rosetta Stone.

### ❦ MAINLAND CHURCHES // APPRECIATE A CARAVAGGIO AND INVESTIGATE ANCIENT CATACOMBS

Built over the spot where Syracuse's patron saint Lucia is said to have been martyred in AD 304, the Basilica di Santa Lucia al Sepolcro (Map p201; ❧ currently closed for restoration) looms large over Piazza Santa Lucia. It's an impressive sight with its columned portico, Norman tower and 18th-century octagonal chapel known as the Sepolcro. But the main drawcard is Caravaggio's *Seppellimento di Santa Lucia* (The Burial of Saint Lucy, 1609), which after a lengthy restoration at Palazzo Bellomo (see p205) has finally been restored to its rightful place over the basilica's main altar. Beneath the church

is an impressive network of catacombs, used by the early Christians to bury their dead.

According to Roman law, Christians were not allowed to bury their dead within the city limits (which during the Roman occupation did not extend beyond Ortygia), so the early Christians used the outlying district of Tyche for burials, accessing underground aqueducts unused since Greek times. New tunnels were carved out, and the result was a labyrinthine network of burial chambers.

The city's most extensive catacombs lie beneath the Basilica di San Giovanni (Map p201; Via San Sebastiano; ❧ 9.30am-12.30pm & 2.30-5.30pm Tue-Sun), itself a pretty, truncated church that was once the city's main cathedral. The catacombs (Map p201; ☎ 0931 6 46 94; www.kairos-web.com; adult/concession €6/4; ❧ 9.30am-12.30pm & 2.30-5.30pm Tue-Sun), visitable by guided tour only, are for the most part dank and a little spooky. Thousands of little niches line the walls, and tunnels lead off from the main chamber *(decumanus maximus)* into *rotonde*, round chambers used by the faithful for praying.

### ❦ SANTUARIO DELLA MADONNA DELLE LACRIME // LOOK UP AT THIS MODERN LANDMARK

Supposedly modelled on the shape of a tear drop, the 102m-high spire of the Santuario della Madonna delle Lacrime (Sanctuary of Our Lady of the Tears; Map p201; www.madonnadellelacrime.it; Viale Teocrito; admission free; ❧ 8am-noon & 4-7pm) dominates Syracuse's skyline. The (dare we say ugly?) modern church beneath it houses a statue of the Virgin Mary that allegedly wept for five days in 1953 and bestowed over 300 miraculous cures. To learn more, head to the Museo delle Lacrimazione (Museum of the Lacrymation; admission €1.55; ❧ 9am-12.30pm & 4-6pm) on the sanctuary's lower floor.

## 🌱 BOATS & BEACHES // TAKE TO THE AZURE WATERS

When the heat of the summer kicks in, the sparkling blue waters that surround Ortygia's sea walls look very tempting. The best swimming in town is off the rocks at Forte Vigliena (Map p203), although beach bunnies would do better to make the short trip south to the sandy blue-flag beaches at Lido Arenella (off Map p201). Be warned, though, that it gets very busy here, particularly on summer weekends. Further south, there's good swimming at rocky Ognina (off Map p201) and the popular Fontane Bianche (off Map p201) beach.

To get out onto the water, there are a number of outfits offering cruises along the coast. Between March and October, Compagnia del Selene (Map p203; ☎ 340 0558769; www.compagniadelselene.it; Via Malta 63) runs boat tours around Ortygia (50-minute tour costs €10 per person), offering great views of the historic centre and Castello Maniace (Map p203), a robust 13th-century castle that is otherwise off-limits to the public.

For something more romantic, book a berth on one of the four yachts run by Sailing Team (Map p203; ☎ 0931 6 08 08; www.sailingteam.biz; Via Savoia 14; day trip for up to 12 people €350) and set off down the southern coast to explore beaches and uncontaminated nature reserves. It also runs trips to the Aeolian Islands and sailing courses – see its website for details. Both outfits operate out of the Marina del Porto Grande on Ortygia, near the Grand Hotel.

## 🌱 GUIDED TOURS // EXPLORE THE CITY WITH A LOCAL EXPERT

Syracuse has a host of professional guides offering tours of the city and environs. They generally escort groups so prices are steep, ranging from €150 for half a day to €225 for a whole day (groups of up to 18 people). The tourist office can put you in touch with authorised operators, otherwise contact Syrako Tourist Services (Map p203; ☎ 0931 2 41 33; www.syrako.it; Largo Porta Marina), which can arrange guides on your behalf. To explore the local countryside, Natura Sicula (Map p201; ☎ 328 8857092; www.naturasicula.it; Piazza Santa Lucia 24/C) is a local association that runs excursions and guided nature walks (about €6 per person).

## FESTIVALS & EVENTS

Cycle of Classical Plays (Map p203; ☎ 0931 48 72 48 or 800 542644; www.indafondazione.org; Corso Matteotti 29; tickets from €15) Classical Greek drama returns to Syracuse's ancient Teatro Greco. Two plays are produced each year with performances (in Italian) held in May and June. Programs and ticket information are available on the website.

Festa di Santa Lucia Held between 13 and 20 December and repeated on the first Sunday in May, this festival commemorates Syracuse's patron saint. The highlight is a procession during which an enormous silver statue of the saint is carried from the cathedral to Piazza Santa Lucia accompanied by exploding fireworks.

## GASTRONOMIC HIGHLIGHTS

Ortygia is the best place to eat. Its narrow lanes are chock-full of trattorias, restaurants, cafes and bars, and while some are obvious tourist traps, many are not, and you'll have no trouble finding somewhere to suit your style. Most places specialise in seafood so expect plenty of fishy pastas and grilled catch-of-the-days.

## 🌱 JONICO-A RUTTA 'E CIAULI €€

Map p201; ☎ 0931 6 55 40; Riviera Dioisio il Grande 194; pizzas from €5, meals €30; 🕒 closed Tue

It's a long and not particularly enticing hike to this seafront restaurant, but once you're there you'll appreciate the effort. Inside it's all exposed brickwork and rusty farm tools; outside on the terrace it's pure bliss, with the sun in your face, a cooling sea breeze and dreamy views. Not surprisingly, fish features heavily on the menu, appearing in dishes such as spaghetti *alla palermitana* (with sardines and fennel) and *orata c'aranci* (sea bream cooked in orange juice). Alternatives include grilled steaks and evening pizzas.

### ❦ LA GAZZA LADRA €
Map p203; ☎ 340 0602428; Via Cavour 8; meals €20; ☾ closed Mon

Great food served in welcoming surroundings at honest prizes: the recipe for success sounds simple but few manage it as well as this friendly, pocket-sized osteria. Run by a husband-and-wife team, it's a bright, laid-back place with colourful photos on white walls, iron-and-glass tables and an open kitchen. The food? Hearty, filling fare made with ripe local ingredients – try the *pasta alla Norma* (with creamy aubergines), fresh seafood and homemade puddings. Slow Food recommended.

### ❦ LA MEDUSA €€
Map p203; ☎ 0931 6 14 03; Via S Teresa 21-23; meals €25-30; ☾ closed Mon

This is one of the best-known and most popular restaurants in Ortygia. It made its name serving delicious couscous, but chef-owner Kamel also knows his way around a fish – the *antipasto del mare* (seafood starter) and *fritto misto* (mixed fish fry) come highly recommended. But beware, helpings are enormous so be careful not to over-order. Service is friendly and accommodating, although you will need to book ahead.

### ❦ OSTERIA DA MARIANO €
Map p203; ☎ 0931 6 74 44; Vicolo Zuccolà 9; meals €20; ☾ closed Mon

Any restaurant that is full on a Monday night in February is doing something right...and Da Mariano was heaving! Old-timer waiters squeezed past tightly-packed tables dishing out earthy country food to legions of boisterous diners. Antipasti of bruschette, ricotta, salami and marinated vegetables were followed by simple pastas of *penne* (pasta tubes) in meaty sausage sauce and *dolci* (sweets) of sesame biscuits and candied ginger.

### ❦ OSTERIA VITE E VITELLO €€
Map p203; ☎ 0931 46 42 69; Piazza Francesco Corpaci 1; meals €33; ☾ closed Sun

Bucking the trend for seafood, this cheerful Ortygia trattoria flies the flag for meat-eaters (and how). Delicious *involtini* (meat rolls) are stuffed with prosciutto, cheese and onion; pork steaks are cased in crusts of green Sicilian pistachios; ricotta ravioli is served in a rich pork *ragù* (meat sauce). It's all delightfully decadent, especially as portions are encyclopaedic in size and the wine list is long enough to satisfy most amateur aficionados. Slow Food recommended.

### ❦ SICILIA IN TAVOLA €€
Map p203; ☎ 392 4610889; Via Cavour 28; meals €23; ☾ closed Mon

One of a number of popular eateries on Via Cavour, this snug hole-in-the-wall trattoria has built a strong local reputation on the back of its homemade pasta and fresh seafood. To taste for yourself try the prawn ravioli, which is served with small cherry tomatoes and chopped mint, or the delicious fettuccine *allo scoglio* (with seafood sauce). Adding to the fun is a bustling atmosphere and the

SYRACUSE & THE SOUTHEAST

cheerful clutter that adorns the wooden walls. Reservations are recommended here.

### ☘ SOLARIA VINI & LIQUORI €

Map p203; ☎ 0931 46 30 07; www.enotecasolaria. com; Via Roma 86; snacks from €5; ☺ closed Sun

This small, rustic *enoteca* (wine shop) is wonderfully old-school, with rows of rough wooden tables and dark bottles lined up on floor-to-ceiling shelves. But it's not just a shop, and you can stop by for a glass of wine and a bite to eat – think platters of cheese, olives, prosciutto, anchovies and sardines. The wine list is extensive (see the website) and, although biased towards Italian and Sicilian labels, includes a number of French vintages and some champagnes.

### ☘ TABERNA SVEVA €€

Map p203; ☎ 0931 2 46 63; Piazza Federico di Svevia 1-2; meals €30; ☺ closed Wed

Away from the main tourist maelstrom, the charming Taberna Sveva is tucked away in a quiet corner of Ortygia. On warm summer evenings the outdoor terrace is the place to sit, with alfresco tables set out on a tranquil cobbled square in front of Syracuse's 13th-century castle. The food is traditional Sicilian, so expect plenty of tuna and swordfish and some wonderful pastas. Particularly good are the gnocchi *al pistacchio* (with olive oil, parmesan, pepper, garlic and grated pistachio nuts).

### ☘ TRATTORIA ARCHIMEDE €€

Map p203; ☎ 0931 6 97 01; Via Gemmellaro 8; set menus €13-18, meals €28; ☺ closed Sun

Although this Ortygia eatery serves its fair share of tourists, there's no denying its historic credentials – it has been in business since 1938. But while times change, the restaurant's loyalty to

local seafood remains entrenched and the menu is distinctly fishy, with such crowd-pleasers as *tagliolini al nero di seppie* (string-like pasta with cuttlefish ink) and *pesce all'acqua pazza* (fish cooked with garlic, tomatoes, capers and olives).

### ☘ TRATTORIA LA FOGLIA €€

Map p203; ☎ 0931 6 62 33; www.lafoglia.it; Via Capodieci 21; meals €30-35; ☺ closed Tue Nov-Mar

Sporting a bizarre look that's half Edwardian country house, half boho chic, this is one Syracuse restaurant where the decor is as memorable as the food. Classical music is piped into the brocaded dining room as diners sit down to a menu that matches heart-warming starters (leek-and-potato soup anyone?) with homemade pastas and seafood staples such as grilled *pesce spada* (swordfish) and *polpette di tonno* (tuna meatballs).

## NIGHTLIFE

A vibrant university town, Syracuse has a lively cafe culture, with many bars and cafes spilling over Ortygia's pretty streets. Piazzetta San Rocco is a popular spot, as is the seafront around Fontana Aretusa.

### ☘ SANROCCO

Map p203; ☎ 333 9854177; Piazzetta San Rocco

Hip about-towners head to Sanrocco, the smoothest of the bars on Piazzetta San Rocco, for early evening *aperitivi* (complete with bountiful bar snacks) and cocktails late into the night. Inside, it's a narrow, stone-vaulted affair, but the main action is outside on the vivacious piazzetta where summer crowds gather until the early hours. Occasional live music and DJ sets fuel the laid-back vibe.

# RECOMMENDED SHOPS

Browsing Ortygia's quirky boutiques is great fun. Good buys include papyrus paper, ceramics and handmade jewellery.

### ❧ GALLERIA BELLOMO

Map p203; ☎ 0931 6 13 40; www.bellomogallery. com; Via Capodieci 15

Papyrus paper is the reason to come to this Ortygia gallery near Fontana Aretusa. Here you'll find a range of papery products, including greeting cards, bookmarks and writing paper, as well as a series of watercolour landscapes. Prices start at around €3 for a postcard, rising to hundreds of euros for original works of art.

### ❧ MASSIMO IZZO

Map p203; ☎ 0931 2 23 01; Piazza Archimede 25

The flamboyant jewellery of Messina-born Massimo Izzo is not for the faint-hearted. Featuring bold idiosyncratic designs and made with Sciacca coral, gold and precious stones, his handmade pieces are often inspired by themes close to the Sicilian heart: the sea, theatre and classical antiquity.

# TRANSPORT

**BUS //** Buses are generally faster and more convenient than trains. From the bus terminal (Map p201) on Corso Umberto near the train station, Interbus ( ☎ 0935 2 24 60; www.interbus.it) runs buses to Noto (€3, one hour, six daily Monday to Saturday, two Sunday), Catania (€5.70, 1¼ hours, hourly Monday to Saturday, six Sunday) and its airport, and Palermo (€13, 3¼ hours, two daily Monday to Saturday, three Sunday). You can buy tickets at the kiosk by the bus stops. AST ( ☎ 840 000323; www.aziendasicilianatrasporti.it) runs services to Piazza Armerina (€8.80, four hours, one daily) and Ragusa (€6.90, 2¼ hours, four daily Monday to Saturday, two Sunday). Tickets are available at the train station bar.

Free (white) shuttle buses connect the train station with Ortygia and the main car parks, while local bus 12 runs between Ortygia and Parco Archeologico della Neapolis. A two-hour city bus ticket costs €1.

**CAR //** The dual-carriageway SS114 heads north from Syracuse to Catania, while the SS115 runs south to Noto and Modica. While the approach roads to Syracuse are rarely very busy, traffic gets increasingly heavy as you enter town and can be pretty bad in the city centre.

**PARKING //** If you're staying in Ortygia, the best place to park is Parcheggio Talete (Map p203; free 5am-9pm, €1 9pm-5am) on Via V Veneto. Nearby, there's also parking on Piazza delle Poste but here you'll pay €0.60 per hour. Note that most of Ortygia is a limited traffic zone, restricted to residents and those with special permission. On-street parking is hard to find during the week, but less so on Sunday when it's often free.

**TRAIN //** Up to 10 trains depart daily for Messina (€9.35, 2½ to three hours) and Catania (€6, 1¼ hours). Some go on to Rome, Turin, Milan and other long-distance destinations. There are also slow trains to Noto (€3.25, 35 minutes, eight Monday to Saturday, one Sunday) and Ragusa (€7.35, 2¼ hours, three daily).

SYRACUSE & THE SOUTHEAST

# AROUND SYRACUSE
· · · · · ·

The area around Syracuse is not always especially attractive, especially north of town where the coast is blighted by ugly oil refineries and heavy industry, but there are a few sights that reward exploration.

# EXPLORING AROUND SYRACUSE

### ❧ CASTELLO EURIALO //
### INVESTIGATE SYRACUSE'S CASTLE DEFENCES

Seven kilometres west of town in the outlying quarter of Epipolae is the Castello Eurialo (off Map p201; ☎ 0931 71 17 73; adult/concession €4/2; ⏰ 9am-6pm daily summer, 9am-3pm Mon-Sat & 9am-1pm Sun winter), the stronghold of Syracuse's Greek defensive works. Built during the reign of Hieron II, it was adapted and fortified by Archimedes and was considered impregnable. Unfortunately for Syracuse, the castle was taken by the Romans without a fight. The views back to Syracuse make it worth the trip.

### ❦ MEGARA HYBLAEA // LOSE YOURSELF AMONG ANCIENT GREEK RUINS

If you can find them in the midst of the surrounding industrial sprawl, the ruins of ancient Megara Hyblaea (off Map p201; adult/concession €4/2; ☺ 9am-1hr before sunset) are well worth a detour. The city, founded in 728 BC by Greeks from Megara, prospered until 483 BC when it was razed to the ground by the Syracuse dictator Gelon. It was then rebuilt in 340 BC only to be destroyed a second time by the Romans in 213 BC. Most of the ruins you see today date to the 4th-century city. You'll need your own car to get there – it's 20km north of Syracuse, signposted off the SS114.

### ❦ THE RIVER CIANE & THE OLYMPEION // TAKE A BOAT TRIP UP A MYTHICAL RIVER

A popular diversion between May and September is a boat trip (off Map p201; per person €10) up the Ciane, a mythical river dedicated to the nymph Ciane, who tried to thwart the abduction of Persephone by Hades. A spring, 2km upriver, is said to have been formed by her tears. The river habitat – a tangle of lush papyrus – is the only place outside North Africa where papyrus grows wild. Along the way, you can check out the ruins of the Olympeion, a temple from the 6th century BC.

The embarkation point for the boats is 5km outside Syracuse on the SS115 – from town follow signs to Palazzolo Acreide.

# THE SOUTHEAST
· · · · · ·

**Dominated by the Monti Iblei hills, Sicily's southeast harbours some of the island's most beautiful towns. In particular, Unesco-listed Noto, Modica and Ragusa stand out for their sumptuous baroque architecture and stunning historic centres. And while these places are not exactly undiscovered they are not yet on the main tourist radar, and outside of peak periods are largely free of visitors. Elsewhere, the region is quietly rural, its gently rugged landscape characterised by weathered limestone cliffs and deep rocky gorges.**

## DRIVING TOUR: BAROQUE TOWNS

Distance: 71km
Duration: two days

A land of remote rocky gorges, sweeping views and silent valleys, Sicily's southeastern corner is home to the 'baroque triangle', an area of Unesco-listed hilltop towns famous for their lavish baroque architecture. This tour takes in some of the finest baroque towns in Sicily, all within easy driving distance of each other.

Just over 35km south of Syracuse, Noto (1; p216) is home to what is arguably Sicily's most beautiful street – Corso Vittorio Emanuele (p217), a pedestrianised boulevard lined with golden baroque palazzi. From Noto, push on along the SS115 to Ispica, a hilltop town overlooking a huge canyon, the Cava d'Ispica (p223), riddled with prehistoric tombs. Continuing up the SS115 for a further 18km brings you to Modica (3; p220), a bustling town set in a deep rocky gorge. There's excellent accommodation here and a wealth of great restaurants, so this makes a good place to overnight. The best of the baroque sights are up in **Modica Alta** (p221), the high part of town, but make sure you have energy left for the *passeggiata* (evening stroll) on **Corso Umberto I** (p221) and dinner at **Osteria dei Sapori Perduti** (p222).

Next morning, a short, winding, up-and-down drive through rock-littered hilltops leads to **Ragusa** (4; p223), one of Sicily's nine provincial capitals. The town is divided in two – it's **Ragusa Ibla** (p223) that you want, a claustrophobic warren of grey stone houses and elegant *palazzi* that opens up onto **Piazza Duomo** (p223), a superb example of 18th-

century town planning. Although you can eat well in Ragusa, consider lunching in **Chiaramonte Gulfi** (5; p225), a tranquil hilltop town some 20km to the north along the SP10, famous for its olive oil and delicious pork.

# VALLE DELL'ANAPO & AROUND

### ♥ VALLE DELL'ANAPO // WALK AMIDST WILDFLOWERS IN THIS UNSPOILT VALLEY

For some beautifully wild and unspoilt countryside, take the SS124 northwest

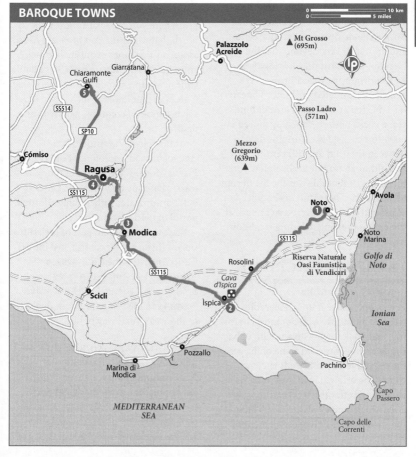

from Syracuse towards Palazzolo Acreide. After about 36km, turn off right towards Ferla. The signposted road plunges steeply down to the floor of the **Valle dell'Anapo** (Anapo Valley), a deep limestone gorge. Once at the bottom you can leave your car by the Forestry Commission hut and walk through the woodlands on foot. It's pretty gentle walking, although paths marked 'B' are slightly more challenging.

### 👻 NECROPOLI DI PANTALICA // PEER INTO REMOTE PREHISTORIC TOMBS

Continuing about 5km up from the valley floor you come to Ferla, a small town with an attractive baroque centre, and another 11km beyond that the **Necropoli di Pantalica** (admission free), an important Iron- and Bronze-Age necropolis. Situated on a huge plateau, it's an extensive, isolated area of limestone rocks honeycombed by more than 5000 tombs. The site's origins date to between the 13th and 8th century BC, and although no one is absolutely sure, it is thought that this was the Siculi capital of Hybla. There's no ticket office or main entrance, but there's a car park at the end of the long, winding road down from Ferla.

# PALAZZOLO ACREIDE

**pop 9085 / elev 670m**

Few people make it up to Palazzolo Acreide, but those who do find a charming, laid-back town with a wealth of baroque architecture and some of the area's finest (and least publicised) ancient ruins. The original medieval town was abandoned after the 1693 earthquake, after which a new Palazzolo was built in the shadow of the Greek settlement of Akrai.

## ESSENTIAL INFORMATION

**TOURIST INFORMATION //** Tourist Office ( ☎ 0931 47 21 81; www.comune.palazzolo.acreide.sr.it; Piazza del Popolo 7;  ⊙ 9am-1pm & 3-7pm)

## EXPLORING PALAZZOLO ACREIDE

### 👻 THE HISTORIC CENTRE // STROLL PALAZZOLO'S PRETTY BAROQUE STREETS

The town's central focus is **Piazza del Popolo**, which is a striking square dominated by the ornate bulk of the **Chiesa di San Sebastiano** and **Palazzo Municipale**, Palazzolo's impressive town hall. From here you can take a short walk north that will bring you to Piazza Moro as well as two other exquisite baroque churches: on the square's northern flank **Chiesa Madre**, and on the southern side, **Chiesa di San Paolo**, which is a theatrical ensemble of columns, gargoyles and fleur-de-lis.

At the top of Via Annunziata (the main road leading right out of Piazza Moro) is the fourth of the town's baroque treasures, the **Chiesa dell'Annunziata**, with a richly adorned portal of twirling columns.

Back up in the main part of the *centro storico* (historic city centre), just off Via Carlo Alberto is the **Casa-Museo di Antonino Uccello** ( ☎ 0931 88 14 99; www.antoninouccello.it; Via Machiavelli 19; admission free;  ⊙ 9am-1pm & 2.30-7pm), a museum dedicated to the area's rural way of life.

### 👻 AKRAI // TAKE YOUR SEAT IN AN ANCIENT GREEK THEATRE

A 20-minute uphill walk from Piazza del Popolo, the **archaeological park** ( ☎ 0931 88 14 99; Colle dell'Acromonte; admission €4;  ⊙ 9am-7pm Mon-Sat, 9am-5pm Sun Apr-Oct, 9am-4pm Mon-Sat Nov-Mar) of Akrai is one of

## TOP **FIVE**

### ANCIENT SITES

★ **Teatro Greco, Parco Archeologico della Neapolis, Syracuse** (p205) – the highlight of Syracuse's ancient ruins is this dramatic Greek amphitheatre

★ **Akrai, Palazzolo Acreide** (p215) – walk among the grassy ruins of what was once a thriving Greek colony

★ **Villa Romana del Tellaro, the Noto Coast** (p219) – expressive mosaics depict mythical scenes at this ancient Roman villa

★ **Megara Hyblaea, near Syracuse** (p212) – the remnants of a 4th-century-BC city resist the encroaching onslaught of modern industry

★ **Eloro, the Noto Coast** (p219) – as much as the ruins, it's the dreamy coastal setting that's the main draw here

the area's best-kept secrets. The city of Akrai, Syracuse's first inland colony, was established to defend the overland trading route to other Greek settlements. Nowadays, its ruins are an evocative sight, even if the lack of explanatory signs means that you're often not sure what you're looking at.

The most impressive (and obvious) ruin is the **Greek theatre**, built at the end of the 3rd century BC but later altered by the Romans. A perfect semicircle, it once had a capacity of 600. Behind the theatre are two *latomie* (quarries), which were later converted into Christian burial chambers. The larger of the two, the **Intagliata**, has catacombs and altars cut into its sides, while the narrower one, the **Intagliatella**, has a

wonderful relief of a large banquet cut into the rock face.

South of the archaeological zone are a series of 3rd-century-BC stone sculptures known as the **Santoni** (Holy Men). It's a 15-minute walk down to the statues, but you'll need to go with a guide as the area around the statues is closed to the general public.

## GASTRONOMIC HIGHLIGHTS

### ❦ IL PORTICO €€

☎ 0931 88 15 32; Via Orologio 6; pizzas from €4, meals €25, tasting menus €35-45; ☒ closed Tue

Just back from Via Carlo Alberto, this formal little restaurant has swagged rose curtains, high-backed chairs and florid painted ceilings. The food focuses on local Iblean mountain dishes, so expect plenty of grilled meats, mushrooms and cheeses. Typical of the house style is the *ravioli casarecci di ricotta al sugo di maiale* (homemade ricotta ravioli with pork *ragù*) and cheese platter.

### ❦ PASTICCERIA CAPRICE €

☎ 0931 88 28 46; Corso Vittorio Emanuele 21; snacks from €1.50; ☒ daily

This popular cafe-cum-cake-shop is a great spot for a quick bite of lunch or a mid-afternoon pick-me-up. There's a daily selection of pastas and simple meat dishes, which you can follow up with something from the tempting display of cakes, biscuits and ice cream. Seating is in a grand back room with vaulted ceiling and chandeliers or on a thin streetside terrace.

## TRANSPORT

**BUS //** Regular AST buses connect with Syracuse (€4, 1¼ hours).

**CAR //** Palazzolo is 40km west of Syracuse via the scenic SS124.

# NOTO

**pop 23,765 / elev 160m**

Located less than 40km south of Syracuse, Noto boasts one of Sicily's most beautiful historic centres. The *pièce de résistance* is Corso Vittorio Emanuele, an elegantly manicured walkway flanked by thrilling baroque palazzi and churches. Stunning at any time of the day, it is especially fabulous in the early evening when the lovely red-gold buildings seem to glow with a soft inner light.

Although a town called Noto or Netum has existed here for many centuries, the Noto that you see today dates to the early 18th century, when it was almost entirely rebuilt in the wake of the devastating 1693 earthquake. Author of many of the finest buildings was Rosario Gagliardi, a local architect whose extroverted style also graces churches in Modica and Ragusa.

## ESSENTIAL INFORMATION

**EMERGENCIES //** Police Station ( ☎ 0931 83 52 02; Via Brindisi 1)

**TOURIST INFORMATION //** Tourist Office ( ☎ 0931 57 37 79; www.comune.noto.sr.it; Piazza XVI Maggio; ☺ 9am-1pm & 3-7pm winter, 9am-1pm & 4-8pm summer)

## ORIENTATION

Noto's historic centre is set out on a grid system. Most sights are on Corso Vittorio Emanuele, a pedestrian-only street that runs westwards from Porta Reale and the Giardini Pubblici (Public Gardens). Running parallel to Corso Vittorio Emanuele are Via Cavour to the north and Via Silvio Spaventato to the south, below which is Via Ducezio.

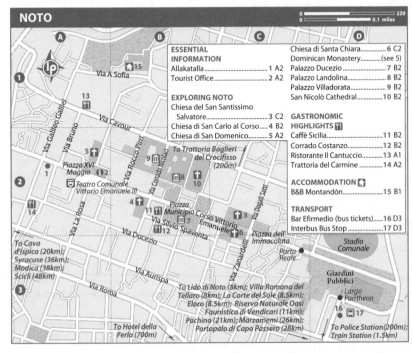

NOTO

| | |
|---|---|
| **ESSENTIAL INFORMATION** | Chiesa di Santa Chiara..............6 C2 |
| Allakatalla.....................................1 A2 | Dominican Monastery...........(see 5) |
| Tourist Office...............................2 A2 | Palazzo Ducezio........................7 B2 |
| | Palazzo Landolina.....................8 B2 |
| **EXPLORING NOTO** | Palazzo Villadorata...................9 B2 |
| Chiesa del San Santissimo | San Nicolò Cathedral.............10 B2 |
| Salvatore..................................3 C2 | |
| Chiesa di San Carlo al Corso....4 B2 | **GASTRONOMIC HIGHLIGHTS** |
| Chiesa di San Domenico...........5 A2 | Caffè Sicilia...............................11 B2 |
| | Corrado Costanzo.....................12 B2 |
| | Ristorante Il Cantuccio...........13 A1 |
| | Trattoria del Carmine .............14 A2 |
| | |
| | **ACCOMMODATION** |
| | B&B Montandòn.......................15 B1 |
| | |
| | **TRANSPORT** |
| | Bar Efirmedio (bus tickets)......16 D3 |
| | Interbus Bus Stop ...................17 D3 |

## EXPLORING NOTO

### ❦ CATTEDRALE & PIAZZA MUNICIPIO // SWOON BEFORE THE BEAUTY OF NOTO'S BAROQUE CENTRE

About halfway along Corso Vittorio Emanuele, the graceful **Piazza Municipio** is flanked by Noto's most dramatic buildings. To the north, sitting in stately pomp at the head of Paolo Labisi's monumental staircase is the **Cattedrale di San Nicolò** (www.cattedralenoto.it, in Italian; Piazza Municipio; 🕒 9am-1pm & 3-8pm), a fusion of neoclassical and baroque architectural styles. Dedicated to San Nicolò and originally built in 1776, it owes its current form to a decade-long makeover that was only completed in June 2007. Inside, the relics of Noto's patron saint, St Corrado Confalonieri, are kept in a silver urn.

The cathedral is surrounded by a series of elegant palaces. To the left (west) is **Palazzo Landolina**, once home to the powerful Sant'Alfano family, while over the road **Palazzo Ducezio** has a lovely columned facade interspersed with round arches. Designed in 1746 by Vincenzo Sinatra, it now houses Noto's Town Hall.

### ❦ PALAZZO VILLADORATA // SEE HOW THE SICILIAN ARISTOCRACY LIKED TO LIVE

The only one of Noto's palazzi that is open to the public, **Palazzo Villadorata** (Palazzo Nicolaci; ☎ 338 7427022; Via Corrado Nicolaci; admission €4; 🕒 10am-1pm & 3.30-6.30pm mid-Oct–mid-Mar, 10am-1pm & 3.30-8pm mid-Mar–mid-Oct), also known as Palazzo Nicolaci, reveals the luxury to which the local nobility were accustomed. The flamboyant tone is established by a series of wrought-iron balconies supported by a swirling pantomime of grotesque figures: mythical monsters, griffins, cherubs and sirens. Inside, the decor is equally opulent, with heavy glass chandeliers, frescoed ceilings and crafty wall paintings designed to look like brocaded wallpaper.

### ❦ CHURCHES // CLOCK THE PANORAMAS FROM NOTO'S BELLTOWERS

Offering great views of the cathedral, the **Chiesa di Santa Chiara** (Corso Vittorio Emanuele; admission to roof €1.50; 🕒 10am-noon Mon-Fri, 10am-noon & 3-5pm Sat & Sun) was built by the baroque maestro Rosario Gagliardi between 1745 and 1758. The oval-plan interior is typically lavish, although the main drawcard is the panoramic view from the rooftop terrace. For an alternative viewing platform, head down the road to the **Chiesa di San Carlo al Corso** (Corso Vittorio Emanuele; bell tower admission €1.50; 🕒 9am-12.30pm & 4-7pm) where you can climb to the top of the *campanile* (belltower). If you suffer from vertigo, stick to admiring the handsome concave facade with its three orders of rising columns.

Towering over the tourist office on Piazza XVI Maggio are the **Chiesa di San Domenico** and the extraordinary **Dominican Monastery**, both designed by Rosario Gagliardi.

Back towards **Porta Reale** is the **Chiesa del Santissimo Salvatore** with its adjoining nunnery, which was reserved for the daughters of local nobility. The interior is the most impressive in Noto, but unfortunately it is closed to the public.

### ❦ TOURS & EXCURSIONS // TOUR SOUTHERN SICILY'S BEAUTY SPOTS

If you want to join an organised tour, **Allakatalla** ( ☎ 0931 57 40 80; www.allakatalla.it; Corso Vittorio Emanuele 47) offers a wide range of packages, ranging from guided excursions to Syracuse to week-long jaunts around Mt Etna's vineyards and the locations used in the *Inspector Montalbano* TV series.

## FESTIVALS & EVENTS

Noto's big annual jamboree is the **Infiorata**, held around the third Sunday in May. The highlight of the festival is the decoration of Via Corrada Nicolaci, with works of art made entirely from flower petals.

## GASTRONOMIC HIGHLIGHTS

There are a number of restaurants in the historical centre, but pride of place goes to a cafe, famous for its *granite* (crushed-ice drinks), and a *gelateria* that churns out fabulous ice cream.

### 🍴 RISTORANTE IL CANTUCCIO €€
☎ 0931 83 74 64; Via Cavour 12; meals €35; 🕑 dinner Tue-Sun, lunch Sun

Housed in what was once a storeroom of the noble Palazzo Marchese del Cantuccio, this welcoming, intimate restaurant is a lovely place to dine on innovative regional cooking. Chef Valentina takes classic Sicilian ingredients and arranges them in exciting new ways: try the gnocchi *al pesto del cantuccio* (with basil, parsley, mint, capers, almonds and cherry tomatoes).

### 🍴 TRATTORIA DEL CARMINE €
☎ 0931 83 87 05; Via Ducezio 1; meals €18; 🕑 closed Mon

Much loved by locals and visiting celebs – look for the photo of Maria Grazia Cucinotta (the sexy one in the film *Il Postino*) on the wall – this is a modest family-run trattoria that serves honest, down-to-earth Sicilian food. Expect antipasti of ricotta, olives and sliced salamis, pastas with meat *ragùs*, *involtini* and straightforward roast meats.

### 🍴 TRATTORIA DEL CROCIFISSO €€
☎ 0931 57 11 51; www.ilcrocifisso.it; Via Umberto 48; meals €30; 🕑 closed Wed

This smart eatery is one of Noto's top restaurants. It's up in the high part of town, a steep 10-minute walk from Corso Vittorio Emanuele, and offers a carefully constructed menu built around seasonal, local produce. Fish and meat feature in equal measure in dishes such as spaghetti *con gamberi e cuori di carciofi* (with prawns and artichokes) and *maiale al nero d'avola* (pork in a wine reduction), while the select wine list showcases local Sicilian labels. Slow Food recommended.

## TRANSPORT

**BUS //** Regular AST (☎ 840 000323; www.azienda sicilianatrasporti.it) and **Interbus** (☎ 0935 2 24 60; www.interbus.it) services run to/from Syracuse (€3, one hour) and Catania (€6.70, 2½ hours). Buy tickets at Bar Efirmedio (Via di Piemonte 6) near the bus station on Largo Pantheon. Local year-round buses also connect with Noto Marina.

---

## ICE CREAM & GRANITE

It's a heady claim, but some say Noto has the two best *gelaterie* (ice-cream shops) in the world! Facing off for the honours are the **Caffè Sicilia** (☎ 0931 83 50 13; Corso Vittorio Emanuele 125) and, just round the corner, **Corrado Costanzo** (☎ 0931 83 52 43; Via Silvio Spaventa 9). Of the two, Corrado has the better ice cream – try a lick of pistachio or *amaro* (dark liqueur) flavour – but Caffè Sicilia is famous for its *granite* (drinks made of crushed ice with fruit juice). Depending on the season, you could go for *fragolini* (tiny wild strawberries) or *gelsi* (mulberry) flavours, or stick to the classic *caffè* (coffee) or *mandorla* (almond).

Both places make superb *cassata* (made with ricotta cheese, chocolate and candied fruit), *dolci di mandorle* (almond cakes and sweets) and *torrone* (nougat).

**CAR //** The SS115 connects Noto with Syracuse, about 36km to the northeast.

**TRAIN //** Regular trains run from Syracuse (€3.25, 35 minutes, eight Monday to Saturday, one Sunday), but the station is located about 1.5km south of the historic centre.

# THE NOTO COAST

☙ **ELORO // EXPLORE GREEK RUINS IN A LUSH SEASIDE SETTING**

Noto's coastal satellite is **Lido di Noto**, a typical beach town of holiday villas and resort hotels that's practically deserted for 10 months of the year. Just south of here is the archaeological site of **Eloro** (admission free; ☉ 9am-1pm), where the sparse ruins of the 7th-century-BC Syracusan colony of Helorus lie in lush green grass. It's an attractive setting, even if it's quite hard to make out what you're looking at. In fact, excavations have so far unearthed a portion of the city walls, a small temple dedicated to Demeter and a theatre. On either side of the hill are long, sandy beaches.

☙ **LA CORTE DEL SOLE // STUDY COOKERY AT A CHIC COUNTRY HOTEL**

Overlooking the green fields of Eloro is **La Corte del Sole** (☎ 0931 82 02 10; www.lacortedelsole.it; Contrada Bucachemi, Lido di Noto), a stylish hotel housed in a traditional Sicilian *masseria* (fortified farmhouse). A delightful place to stay, it also offers a range of activities including **cooking lessons** (per 3hr €50), run by the hotel chef and, in winter, tours to study the 80 or so types of wild orchids found in the area.

☙ **RISERVA NATURALE OASI FAUNISTICA DI VENDICARI // GET BACK TO NATURE AT THIS PROTECTED OASIS**

Butting onto the ruins of Eloro is the **Riserva Naturale Oasi Faunistica di Vendicari** (☎ 0931 6 74 50; admission free; ☉ 7am-8pm Apr-Oct, 7am-5pm Nov-Mar), a wonderful stretch of wild coastline, encompassing three separate marshes and a number of sandy beaches. From the main entrance (signposted off the Noto–Pachino road), it's about a 10-minute walk to the nearest beach, where you can pick up a path along the coast.

The reserve, which boasts its own Swabian tower and an abandoned tuna-processing plant, is an important marine environment, providing sanctuary to resident and migratory birds, including the black-winged stilt, the stork, wild goose and flamingo. Observation posts enable you to watch in relative comfort.

☙ **VILLA ROMANA DEL TELLARO // MARVEL AT ANCIENT ROMAN MOSAICS**

Continuing south towards Pachino on the main SP19 brings you to the **Villa Romana del Tellaro** (☎ 338 9733084; www.villaromanadeltellaro.com; adult/concession €6/3; ☉ 9am-7pm), a Roman villa harbouring some fascinating mosaics. The villa was largely destroyed by fire in the 4th century AD, but painstaking excavation has brought to light fragments of the original floor mosaics that depict hunting scenes and episodes from Greek mythology.

☙ **THE CAPE AREA // EAT, DRINK AND ENJOY THE COLOURS**

Although Sicily's southeastern cape offers little in the way of excitement, its electric colours, laid-back atmosphere and relative lack of development make it a relaxing stopoff. The main centre is **Pachino**, a busy market town surrounded by fertile vineyards, while **Marzamemi**, 5km away, is a quiet fishing town that doubles as a low-key summer resort. On the road

SYRACUSE & THE SOUTHEAST

between the two, **Cantina Rudinì** (☎ 0931 59 53 33; www.vinirudini.it; Contrada Camporeale) is a good place to stock up on the local Nero d'Avola wine. Once in Marzamemi, a fish meal at **Ristorante Giramapao** (☎ 0931 84 11 49; Via Marzamemi 77; meals €38; ☺ closed Mon) does wonders for the soul, especially if it's grilled catch-of-the-day accompanied by a carafe of local wine.

From Marzamemi the road follows the coast south to **Portopalo di Capo Passero**, a popular summer hangout. The small island off the coast is **Isola Capo Passero**, with a castle and nature reserve.

# MODICA

**pop 54,720 / elev 296m**
With its steeply stacked medieval centre and spectacular baroque cathedral, Modica is one of southern Sicily's most atmospheric towns. But unlike some of the other Unesco-listed cities in the area, it doesn't package its treasures into a single easy-to-see street or central piazza: rather, they are spread around the town and take some discovering. It can take a little while to orientate yourself in Modica but once you've got the measure of the bustling streets and steep staircases you'll find a warm, genuine town with a welcoming vibe and a strong sense of pride.

An important Greek and Roman city, Modica's heyday came in the 14th century when, as the personal fiefdom of the Chiaramonte family, it was one of the most powerful cities in Sicily.

## ESSENTIAL INFORMATION

**EMERGENCIES //** Police Station (☎ 0932 76 92 11; Via del Campo Sportivo 48)
**TOURIST INFORMATION //** Tourist Office (☎ 0932 75 96 34; www.comune.modica.rg.it; Corso Umberto I 141; ☺ 9am-1pm & 3.30-7.30pm Mon-Sat, 10am-1pm Sun)

## ORIENTATION

Modica is divided into two parts: Modica Alta (High Modica) and Modica Bassa (Low Modica). Whether driving or coming by public transport you'll arrive in Modica Bassa. The main street here, Corso Umberto I, forms the bottom of the V-shaped wedge on which the historic centre sits. Most hotels and restaurants are in Modica Bassa, within easy walking distance of Corso Umberto, although the cathedral and a number of churches are up in the high town. It's a fairly tough climb to get to the top.

## EXPLORING MODICA

❦ **CHIESA DI SAN GIORGIO & MODICA ALTA //** **LORD IT OVER TOWN AT MODICA'S LOOMING CATHEDRAL**
The highlight of a trip to Modica – quite literally as it's up in Modica Alta – is the **Chiesa di San Giorgio** (Corso San Giorgio; ☺ 8am-1pm & 3.30-7.30pm), one of Sicily's most extraordinary baroque churches. Considered Rosario Gagliardi's great masterpiece, it stands in isolated splendour at the top of a majestic 250-step staircase, its sumptuous three-tiered facade towering above the medieval alleyways of the historic centre. The glitzy interior, a sun-lit kaleidoscope of silvers, golds and egg-shell blues, displays all the hallmarks of early-18th-century Sicilian baroque.

Marking the highpoint of Modica Alta, the **Chiesa di San Giovanni Evangelista** (off Piazza San Giovanni) is another grand baroque church that is prefaced by a sweeping staircase. Nearby, located at the end of Via Pizzo, a viewing balcony offers great panoramas over the old town.

❦ **CORSO UMBERTO I** // **JOIN THE CROWDS ON MODICA'S LIVELY THOROUGHFARE**
Bisecting Modica Bassa, Corso Umberto I is the place to lap up the lively local atmosphere. A wide avenue flanked by graceful palaces, churches, restaurants, bars and boutiques, it is where the locals come to parade during the evening *passeggiata*. Originally a raging river ran through town, but after major flood damage in 1902 it was dammed and Corso Umberto was built over it. Obvious landmarks include the **Cattedrale di San Pietro** (Corso Umberto I; 9am-1pm & 4-7.30pm), an impressive church atop a rippling staircase lined with life-sized statues of the apostles; and the **Chiesa Santa Maria del Carmine** (Piazza Matteoti; 9am-1pm & 4-7.30pm), also known as Santa Maria dell'Annunziata.

For a break from baroque, head off the corso to Via Grimaldi where the **Chiesa Rupestre di San Nicolò Inferiore** (Piazzetta Grimaldi; admission €2; 10am-1pm & 4-7pm Mon-Sat, 4-7pm Sun) boasts some rich Byzantine frescoes. Ring the bell for admission.

Back on the main street, next to the tourist office in Palazzo della Cultura, the **Museo Civico** (Corso Umberto I 149; admission €3; 10am-1pm & 4-7pm Tue-Sun) houses Modica's collection of archaeological finds from Modica and Cava d'Ispica, dating back to the Neolithic period.

❦ **ANTICA DOLCERIA BONAJUTO** // **DROOL OVER THE CHOCOLATES AT THIS FAMOUS CONFECTIONERY STORE**
Modica has long been celebrated for its chocolate, and *the* place for the best is the **Antica Dolceria Bonajuto** ( 0932 94 12 25; www.bonajuto.it; Corso Umberto I 159; 9am-1.30pm & 4-8.30pm). Here, in the kitchen behind the shop counter, everything is made by hand according to traditional recipes. The results – which include chocolate flavoured with salt, chilli, cinnamon, vanilla and orange peel – are displayed in antique glass-fronted cases. Two house specialities to look out for are *mpanatigghi* (a biscuit-like chocolate ravioli) and *aranciata e cedrata* (balls of orange peel cooked in honey).

## GASTRONOMIC HIGHLIGHTS

❦ **FATTORIA DELLE TORRI** €€
 0932 75 12 86; Vico Napolitano 14, Modica Alta; meals from €35; closed Sun evening & Mon
This is one of Modica's smartest restaurants. Housed in an elegant 18th-century palazzo, it has a beautiful dining area with tables set under stone arches and bay windows looking onto a small internal garden. The seafood is particularly gorgeous, especially when combined with a crisp, dry white wine such as Cerasuolo di Vittoria.

❦ **I BACCANTI** €
 0932 94 65 94; Via Grimaldi 72; meals €20; closed Mon
Hidden away in a small *centro storico* alley, this is a small, intimate restaurant with a vaulted stone ceiling and racks of wine bottles on the bare walls. In keeping with the understated look, the food is local but creative. *Ravioli di ricotta*, for example, is not served in the usual meat-based tomato sauce but with mushrooms, cherry tomatoes and basil – a much lighter mix. The wine list is also well thought out, with a number of interesting Sicilian labels.

❦ **OSTERIA DEI SAPORI PERDUTI** €
 0932 94 42 47; Corso Umberto I 228-30; meals €20; closed Tue
This local favourite offers superb value for money and delicious, no-nonsense

farmhouse food. Minestrones, bean soups, pasta with sausage, boiled meats and seasonal veggies are mainstays of the earthy menu, which is written in dialect but also has helpful photos to aid your selection (and, no, this isn't your typical tourist menu with crappy polaroids of wilting spaghetti). In fact, everything about the place is right, from the rustic decor to the efficient service to the huge helpings served in earthenware bowls.

### ♥ TAVERNA NICASTRO €
☎ 0932 94 58 84; Via S Antonino 28; meals €15-20; ☽ dinner only Tue-Sat

With more than 60 years of history, this is one of Modica Alta's most authentic and atmospheric restaurants. It's only open in the evenings, which gives the kitchen time to prepare the daily batch of *sugo di maiale* (pork *ragù*) and the house speciality – *coniglio allo Nicastro* (a sort of rabbit casserole). The emphasis is very much on meat, although you'll also find beans and plenty of grilled vegetables. Desserts are good, though a glass of sweet wine is even better.

## TRANSPORT

**BUS //** Modica's bus station is at Piazzale Falcone-Borsellino at the top end of Corso Umberto I. From here buses run to/from Syracuse (€6, 2½ hours, nine daily Monday to Saturday, four Sunday), Noto (€3.90, 1½ hours, three daily Monday to Saturday, one Sunday) and Ragusa (€2.40, 25 minutes, hourly Monday to Saturday, four Sunday).

**CAR //** From Noto to Modica it's about 40km along the SS115.

**PARKING //** Parking can be a problem in Modica, particularly if you arrive here mid-morning. A good place to try is Corso Garibaldi (turn right at the Cattedrale di San Pietro), where you can often find a free space.

# SOUTH OF MODICA

### ♥ SCICLI // ENJOY VIEWS OF A FINE BAROQUE TOWN
About 10km southwest of Modica, Scicli is a pleasant country town with a charming baroque centre and a pretty, palm-fringed central piazza. Overlooking everything is a rocky peak topped by an abandoned church, the **Chiesa di San Matteo**. It's not too hard a walk up to the church to admire the views over town – simply follow the yellow sign up from Palazzo Beneventano and keep going for about 10 minutes.

### ♥ CAVA D'ISPICA // EXPLORE TROGLODYTE CAVES IN THIS LUSH CANYON
Stretching for some 13km between Modica and Ispica, the **Cava d'Ispica** (admission €2; ☽ 9am-1.30pm Mon-Sat) is a verdant gorge studded with thousands of natural caves and grottoes. Evidence of human habitation dates back to about 2000 BC, and over the millennia the caves have served as Neolithic tombs, early Christian catacombs and medieval dwellings. A number of rock churches also survive from the Byzantine period. The canyon, accessible from the Noto side of Ispica (it's signposted off the main Noto–Ispica SS115), is not always open so check ahead with the Modica tourist office.

# RAGUSA

**pop 72,755  /  elev 502m**
Set amidst the rocky peaks northwest of Modica, Ragusa is a town of two faces. Sitting on the top of the hill is Ragusa Superiore, a busy workaday town with sensible grid-pattern streets and all the trappings of a modern provincial capital, while etched into the hillside further down is Ragusa Ibla. This sloping area of

tangled alleyways, grey stone houses and baroque palazzi is effectively Ragusa's historic centre and it's quite magnificent.

Like every other town in the region, Ragusa Ibla (the old town) collapsed after the 1693 earthquake and a new town, Ragusa Superiore, was built on a high plateau above the original settlement. But the old aristocracy was loathe to leave the tottering palazzi and rebuilt Ragusa Ibla on exactly the same spot. The two towns were subsequently merged in 1927.

## ESSENTIAL INFORMATION

**EMERGENCIES //** Police Station ( ☎ 0932 62 49 22; Via Mario Raspardi)
**TOURIST INFORMATION //** Tourist Office ( ☎ 0932 68 47 80; www.comune.ragusa.it; Piazza San Giovanni; ☼ 9am-1pm & 3-7pm Mon-Fri, 9am-1pm Sat) Up in Ragusa Superiore.

## ORIENTATION

If you're driving, follow signs to Ragusa Ibla, where the main sights, hotels and restaurants are. Leave your car in one of the signposted car parks and walk into town. From the car park under Piazza della Repubblica it's a 10-minute walk or so to the central Piazza Duomo – follow Via Del Mercato, then Via XI Febbraio; go left up Via Ten Di Stefano then along its continuation, Via Capitano Bocchieri. If taking public transport you will arrive in Ragusa Superiore, whose main streets are Via Roma and Corso Italia. From the upper town a local bus runs down to Giardino Ibleo in Ragusa Ibla.

## EXPLORING RAGUSA

❦ RAGUSA IBLA // LAP UP THE SIGHTS IN RAGUSA'S BAROQUE CENTRE
Ragusa Ibla is a joy to wander, its labyrinthine lanes weaving through

rock-grey palazzi to open onto beautiful, sun-drenched piazzas. It's easy to get lost but you can never go too far wrong, and sooner or later you'll end up at Piazza Duomo, Ragusa's sublime central square. At the top end of the sloping square is the town's pride and joy, the 1744 Cattedrale di San Giorgio ( ☎ 0932 22 00 85; Piazza Duomo; ☼ 10am-12.30pm & 4-6.30pm Wed-Mon, 10am-12.30pm Tue), set high above a grand staircase behind a palatial iron gate (the entrance is up the stairs to the left of the church). One of Rosario Gagliardi's finest accomplishments, the extravagant convex facade rises like a three-tiered wedding cake, supported by gradually narrowing Corinthian columns and punctuated by jutting cornices. The interior is not quite as sumptuous, although there are two paintings by Dario Guerci here and a statue of St George on horseback.

The piazza is a lovely place to hang out, particularly if armed with a delicious wine-flavoured ice cream from Gelati Di Vini ( ☎ 0932 22 89 89; Piazza del Duomo 20; ice cream from €1.80), a popular bar-cum-*gelateria* near the cathedral.

East of the piazza, Corso XXV Aprile leads down to a second eye-catching Gagliardi church, Chiesa di San Giuseppe (Piazza Pola), with an elliptical interior topped by a cupola decorated with a fresco of the *Gloria di San Benedetto* (Glory of St Benedict, 1793) by Sebastiano Lo Monaco. Continuing downhill brings you to the Giardino Ibleo, a pleasant public garden on the edge of the old town. To the right of the park's entrance, you can see the Catalan Gothic portal of what was once the large Chiesa di San Giorgio Vecchio, but is now mostly ruined. In the lunette there is an interesting bas-relief of St George killing the dragon.

SYRACUSE & THE SOUTHEAST

SYRACUSE & THE SOUTHEAST

# RAGUSA

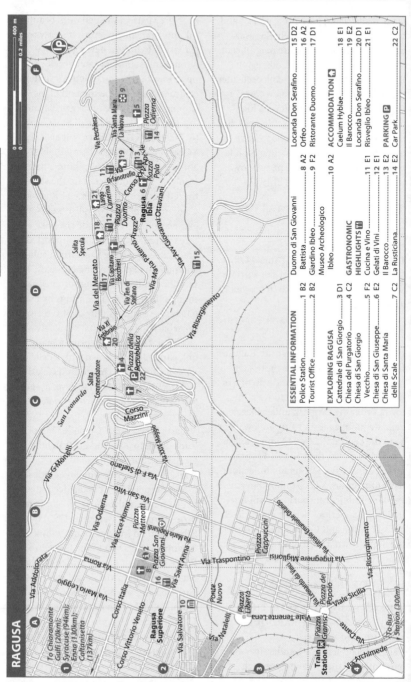

At the other end of Ragusa Ibla, the **Chiesa del Purgatorio** (Piazza della Repubblica) is one of the few churches in town to have survived the great 1693 earthquake.

### ♥ RAGUSA SUPERIORE // WALK DOWN FROM RAGUSA'S NEW TOWN ON THE HILLTOP

One of the best reasons for heading up to Ragusa Superiore, Ragusa's modern and less-attractive half, is to walk down again. It takes about half an hour to descend the *Salita Commendatore*, a winding pass of stairs and narrow archways that leads down to Ragusa Ibla past the **Chiesa di Santa Maria delle Scale**, a 15th-century church with great views. To reach the *Salita*, follow Corso Italia eastwards and then pick up Via XXIV Maggio.

The main attraction up top is the **Duomo di San Giovanni Battista** (☎ 0932 62 16 58; www.cattedralesangiovanni.it, in Italian; Piazza San Giovanni), a vast 19th-century church whose highly ornate facade is set off by Mario Spada's pretty *campanile*. Nearby, below Ponte Nuovo, the **Museo Archeologico Ibleo** (☎ 0932 62 29 63; Via Natalelli; admission €3; ⏰ 9am-1.30pm & 4-7.30pm) houses finds from the 6th-century-BC Greek settlement of Kamarina on the coast.

## GASTRONOMIC HIGHLIGHTS

Ragusa has a good selection of eateries ranging from luxury fine-dining restaurants to cheerful neighbourhood trattorias. All but one of the following listings are in Ragusa Ibla.

### ♥ CUCINA E VINO €€

☎ 0932 68 64 47; Via Orfanotrofio 91; meals €33; ⏰ closed Wed

Whether sat outside in the shadow of the 18th-century Palazzo Battaglia or inside in the white barrel-vaulted interior, this is a lovely place to eat. The menu – in fact there are two, one for fish and one for meat – is more ambitious than most in this price bracket, with adventurous

SYRACUSE & THE SOUTHEAST

## ∼ WORTH A TRIP ∼

Some 20km north of Ragusa, **Chiaramonte Gulfi** is a delightful hilltop town with a gastronomic reputation. It produces a highly-rated olive oil accredited with the *Denominazione d'Origine Protetta* (DOP) quality rating and is famed for its pork products.

The place to buy ham, and indeed to lunch on superb pork, is **Ristorante Majore** (☎ 0932 92 80 19; www.majore.it; Via dei Martiri Ungheresi 12; meals €20-25; ⏰ closed Mon), a much-acclaimed trattoria just off central Piazza Duomo. It's unpretentious and old-school, and the menu is unapologetically meaty, with signature dishes risotto *alla majore* (with pork *ragù* and local cheese) and *falsomagro alla siciliana* (pork meatballs stuffed with salami, cheese, eggs and carrot).

To build up an appetite, wander the knot of old medieval streets in the historic centre and crow over the vast views. There are also eight museums in town, the most interesting of which is the **Museo dell'Olio** (Olive Oil Museum; ☎ 0932 71 11 11; www.comune.chiaramonte.rg.it; admission €1; ⏰ 8.30am-1.30pm Mon-Fri, 9.30am-1pm & 3-6pm Sat & Sun) in Palazzo Montesanto. The highlight is an old olive press from 1614, but there's also a collection of old farming tools and other curios relating to rural life.

To get to Chiaramonte Gulfi from Ragusa, the shortest and most scenic drive is via the SP10.

SYRACUSE & THE SOUTHEAST

antipasti and unusual mains such as *cernia* (grouper) served with onion marmalade. Friendly service and a decent wine list round off the evening. Slow Food recommended.

### 😋 IL BAROCCO €

☎ 0932 65 23 97; Via Orfanotrofio 29; pizzas from €4.50, meals €20-25; 🕙 closed Wed

This bright, welcoming trattoria is no place to escape the crowds, but the food is tasty and excellent value for money. Fish lovers can opt for that great Sicilian staple pasta *con le sarde* (with sardines), while meat-eaters will be spoilt for choice among the grilled meats and local sausage dishes. Wood-fired pizzas provide a tempting evening alternative.

### 😋 LA RUSTICANA €€

☎ 0932 22 79 81; Corso XXV Aprile 68; meals €20-25; 🕙 closed Tue

Fans of the *Montalbano* TV series will want to eat here, as this is where scenes set in the fictional Trattoria San Calogero were filmed. In reality, it's a cheerful, boisterous trattoria whose generous portions and relaxed vine-covered terrace ensure a loyal clientele. The food is defiantly *casareccia* (home-style), so expect no-frills pastas and uncomplicated cuts of grilled meat.

### 😋 LOCANDA DON SERAFINO €€€

☎ 0932 24 87 78; Via Giovanni Ottaviano; tasting menu €78; 🕙 closed Tue

This memorable restaurant might be housed in a series of rocky caves, but there's nothing remotely primitive about it. Its look is elegant yet understated, with warm lighting, starched-white tables and bare rock walls, while the food is traditional with a modern twist: try the lasagnette with cocoa and ricotta cheese, or rabbit with bacon and Sicilian pistachio nuts. Reservations recommended.

### 😋 ORFEO €€

☎ 0932 62 10 35; Via Sant'Anna 117, Ragusa Superiore; meals €25-30; 🕙 closed Sun

Up in Ragusa Superiore, this is a long-standing Ragusa address. The setting is not the most beautiful in town, but the traditional cuisine continues to find favour with locals and visiting business people who come for classics like *polpette con piselli* (meatballs with peas) or gnocchi *radiccio e provola al fumo* (with red chicory and smoked cheese).

### 😋 RISTORANTE DUOMO €€€

☎ 0932 65 12 65; www.ristoranteduomo.it; Via Capitano Bocchieri 31; meals €90, tasting menu €120; 🕙 closed Sun lunch & Mon

This is generally regarded as one of Sicily's best restaurants. Behind the stained-glass door, a quintet of small rooms are outfitted like private parlours, ensuring a suitably romantic ambience for Chef Ciccio Sultano's refined creations. These combine ingredients in an imaginative and unconventional way while making constant use of classic Sicilian ingredients such as pistachios, fennel, almonds and Nero d'Avola wine. Booking is essential.

## TRANSPORT

**BUS //** AST (www.aziendasicilianatrasporti.it) and Interbus-Etna Trasporti (www.etnatrasporti. it) buses serve the bus station at Via Zama in Ragusa Superiore. There are regular connections to Catania (€7.50, one hour and 50 minutes), Syracuse (€6.90, 2¼ hours) and Modica (€2.40, 25 minutes). City buses 1 and 3 run from Piazza del Popolo in the upper town to Piazza Pola and the Giardino Ibleo in Ragusa Ibla.

**CAR //** If coming from Modica 15km away, or Syracuse some 90km to the northeast, take the SS115.

**PARKING //** Unless your hotel has parking or can advise you on where to park, your best bet is to leave your car at the car park below Piazza della Repubblica in Ragusa Ibla, much of which is closed to non-residential traffic.

**TAXI //** Call ☎ 0932 24 41 09.

# CENTRAL SICILY

## 3 PERFECT DAYS

### ❦ DAY 1 // ANCIENT RELICS

Make an early start in Piazza Armerina (p238) and beat the coach parties to Villa Romana del Casale (p238). Once you've applauded the villa's extraordinary Roman mosaics, head out to Morgantina (p243) to investigate the ruins of an ancient Greek city. Spend the late afternoon exploring Piazza Armerina's historic centre (p241), making sure to head up the hill to the landmark cathedral (p241). Round the day off with a relaxed trattoria meal at Amici Miei (p242) or a more formal dinner at Al Fogher (p242).

### ❦ DAY 2 // CERAMICS IN CALTAGIRONE

Make your way to Caltagirone (p243), a delightful hilltop town known for its ceramics. Get into the swing of things by climbing the Scalinata di Santa Maria del Monte (p244) and inspecting the Museo della Ceramica (p245). Afterwards clear your head with a wander around the Giardino Pubblico (p245), a pretty shaded park with views over to Mt Etna. While away the rest of the day strolling through the attractive old town and admiring the fancy baroque churches.

### ❦ DAY 3 // ENNA AND THE HILLTOP TRAIL

Lording it over the hills and valleys of central Sicily, Enna (p232) is the king of the area's hilltop towns. Visit its impregnable Castello di Lombardia (p235) and the impressive Duomo (p235) before heading over the valley to Calascibetta (p232). Afterwards push on to Nicosia (p232), another handsome hilltop town, with a grand central square and 14th-century cathedral.

# CENTRAL SICILY

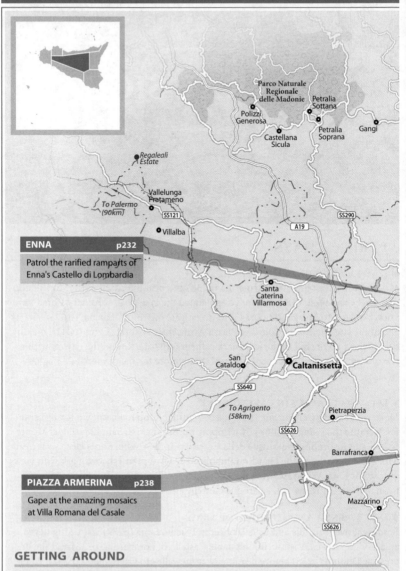

CENTRAL SICILY

Parco Naturale
Regionale
delle Madonie

Polizzi
Generosa

Petralia
Sottana

Petralia
Soprana

Gangi

Castellana
Sicula

Regaleali
Estate

Vallelunga
Pratameno

To Palermo
(90km)

SS121

A19

SS290

Villalba

**ENNA**            **p232**

Patrol the rarified ramparts of
Enna's Castello di Lombardia

Santa
Caterina
Villarmosa

San
Cataldo

**Caltanissetta**

SS640

To Agrigento
(58km)

Pietraperzia

SS626

Barrafranca

**PIAZZA ARMERINA**    **p238**

Gape at the amazing mosaics
at Villa Romana del Casale

Mazzarino

SS626

## GETTING AROUND

Getting around this part of Sicily by public transport is a trying, time-consuming experience. Buses
are better than trains but your own wheels will make life a whole lot easier. The main towns are well
signposted and easy to find, but if you head into the hills, be prepared for potholes in the roads, long,
winding ascents and sporadic signposting. If possible, satnav is a good idea.

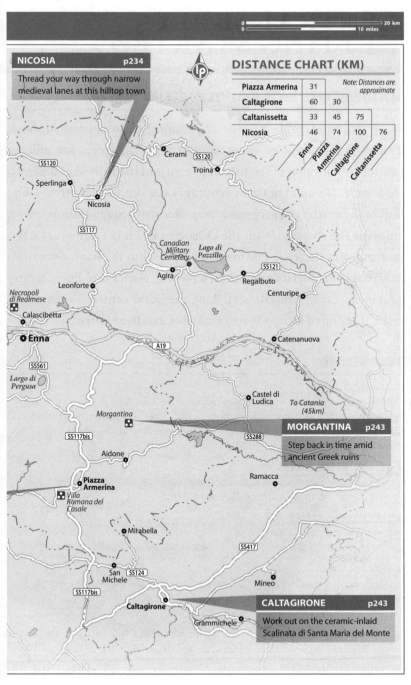

**NICOSIA**  p234

Thread your way through narrow medieval lanes at this hilltop town

**DISTANCE CHART (KM)**

Note: Distances are approximate

| | Enna | Piazza Armerina | Caltagirone | Caltanissetta |
|---|---|---|---|---|
| Piazza Armerina | 31 | | | |
| Caltagirone | 60 | 30 | | |
| Caltanissetta | 33 | 45 | 75 | |
| Nicosia | 46 | 74 | 100 | 76 |

**MORGANTINA**  p243

Step back in time amid ancient Greek ruins

**CALTAGIRONE**  p243

Work out on the ceramic-inlaid Scalinata di Santa Maria del Monte

CENTRAL SICILY

# CENTRAL SICILY GETTING STARTED

## MAKING THE MOST OF YOUR TIME

Sicily's wild and empty interior is a beautiful, uncompromising land, a timeless landscape of silent, sunburnt peaks, grey stone villages and forgotten valleys. Traditions live on and life is lived at a gentle, rural pace. It's an area that encourages the simple pleasures – long lunches of earthy country food, meandering through hilltop towns, enjoying the scenery. With the exception of Piazza Armerina's Roman mosaics there are few must-see sights, but the handsome town of Caltagirone merits more than a passing glance and Enna, a busy provincial capital, boasts a striking medieval centre. Northeast of Enna, a string of hilltop towns make for excellent touring.

## TOP TRAILS

### ❦ ANCIENT ROMANS
Ogle bikini-clad girls and mythical macho men at the Villa Romana del Casale, near Piazza Armerina. The villa's thrilling mosaics are a superb sight, depicting episodes from ancient mythology, hunting scenes and groups of lasses working out with weights (p238).

### ❦ STAIRWAY TO HEAVEN
Climb Caltagirone's celebrated Scalinata di Santa Maria del Monte, a 142-step staircase topped by the town's former cathedral (p244).

### ❦ MYTHS & ANCIENT CULTS
Follow in the footsteps of the gods in Enna, centre of an ancient cult to Demeter, and nearby Lago di Pergusa where Persephone was famously abducted by Hades (p235).

### ❦ FOOD & WINE
Hidden away in the wilds west of Caltanissetta, the beautiful Regaleali wine estate is a foodie oasis, running vineyard tours, tastings and cooking classes (p247).

### ❦ HILLTOP TOWNS
Dating to ancient times, fortified by the Normans and thick with baroque churches, central Sicily's hilltop towns bear all the scars and strains of their long histories. With a car they make fascinating exploring (p232).

# GETTING AWAY FROM IT ALL

It's not difficult to find peace and quiet in this sparsely populated part of central Sicily.

★ **Walk in the shadow of the ancients** Escape the crowds by heading out to the ruins of ancient Morgantina, spread over two windswept hills (p243).

★ **Sup on fine wine in Regaleali** One of Sicily's most important wine estates, Regaleali is about as remote as it gets (p247).

★ **Picnic at Lago di Pozzillo** Stock up on picnic provisions and head out to this picturesque lake in the hills between Agira and Regalbuto (p232).

# ADVANCE PLANNING

Traditional celebrations are heartfelt in these parts and watching them is an unforgettable experience. You won't need to book tickets but it pays to think ahead about accommodation.

★ **Holy Week** Plan to be in Enna for one of the town's sinister Holy Week processions, the best of which is on Good Friday (p236).

★ **Festa di San Giacomo** Book ahead for Caltagirone's annual shindig on 24 and 25 July. The highlight is the spectacular illumination of the town's famous staircase (p244).

★ **Palio dei Normanni** Accommodation is at a premium in Piazza Armerina on 13 and 14 August as crowds gather for the annual medieval pageant (p242).

# TOP LOOKOUTS

❦ **CASTELLO DI LOMBARDIA, ENNA** Survey sweeping swaths of sunbaked hills from Enna's great Norman castle (p235).

❦ **CENTURIPE** Known as the Balcone di Sicilia (Balcony of Sicily), Centuripe provides grandstand views of Mt Etna (p232).

❦ **SCALINATA DI SANTA MARIA DEL MONTE, CALTAGIRONE** Sit at the top of Caltagirone's towering staircase and take inspiration from the views beneath you (p244).

❦ **PIAZZA DUOMO, PIAZZA AMERINA** Admire landscape views from in front of Piazza Armerina's cathedral (p241).

❦ **AIDONE** A sleepy hilltop village with sweeping views over forgotten valleys (p243).

# RESOURCES

★ **Turismo Enna** (www.turismoenna.it, in Italian) Info on sights, monuments and transport in Enna and its environs.

★ **Piazza Net** (www.piazzanet.it) Inspirational rather than practical infor on Piazza Armerina, its history, monuments and events.

★ **Villa Romana del Casale** (www.romana delcasale.it) Comprehensive website with up-to-date information and useful FAQS.

★ **Comune di Caltagirone** (www.comune. caltagirone.ct.it, in Italian) Difficult to navigate but has listings, transport and historical background.

# ENNA

pop 28,075 / elev 931m

**Italy's highest provincial capital, Enna stands head and shoulders above the hills and valleys of central Sicily. From below it's a dramatic sight, a seemingly impregnable town perched on a precipitous hilltop, but make it to the top and you'll discover an unpretentious working town with a handsome medieval centre and, cloud cover permitting, some fabulous views. There's not enough to warrant an extended stay but it is a great place to escape the tourist pack and enjoy some cool mountain air, particularly in summer when the sun bakes everything around to a yellowing crisp.**

The city has a long and chequered history. In ancient times it was famous as the centre of a cult of Demeter, but its strategic position meant that it was often fought over and successive waves of colonising forces conquered it, including the Carthaginians, Romans, Byzantines and Arabs. In 1087 the Normans wrested it from the Arabs and turned it into an important fortified town. Throughout much of its history, it remained an important agricultural centre, supplying far-flung places with grain, wheat, cotton and cane, a tradition that continues today, albeit on a far smaller scale.

## ESSENTIAL INFORMATION

**EMERGENCIES //** Ospedale Umberto I ( ☎ 0935 51 61 11; Contrada Ferrante, Enna Bassa) Police ( ☎ 0935 52 21 11; Via San Giovanni 2)
**TOURIST INFORMATION //** Tourist Information Point ( ☎ 0935 56 15 34; in car park next to Castello di Lombardia; ⊙ 10am-6pm daily Mar-Oct)

## ORIENTATION

The town of Enna is split in two: the hilltop historic centre, Enna Alta, and the modern town, Enna Bassa, below. Everything of interest is up in Enna Alta. The bus station is on Viale Diaz. To get to the town centre from there, turn right and follow Viale Diaz to Corso Sicilia, turn right again and follow it to Via Sant'Agata, which leads to Via Roma, Enna Alta's main street. The train station is about 4km out of the town centre.

## DRIVING TOUR: ENNA TO ETNA

Distance: 115km
Duration: one or two days

Stand on the top of Enna's Castello di Lombardia and you'll see a vast panorama of undulating sunbaked hills, seemingly deserted and stretching away as far as the eye can see. It's through this enticing landscape that the following route leads, taking in a number of hilltop towns and moving ever closer to the brooding bulk of Mt Etna.

From Enna (1; p232) cross over the valley and climb the 2km or so up to Calascibetta (2). A densely packed maze of narrow streets set above a sheer precipice, the town was originally built by the Saracens during their siege of Enna in 951 and was later strengthened by the Norman king Roger I. The most impressive sight is the 14th-century Chiesa Madre ( ⊙ 9am-1pm & 3-7pm), Calascibetta's landmark cathedral, although 3km to the northwest, the Necropoli di Realmese (3; admission free) is worth investigating with some 300 rock tombs dating from 850 BC.

Continuing on the SS121 from Calascibetta, the road winds and weaves

# ENNA

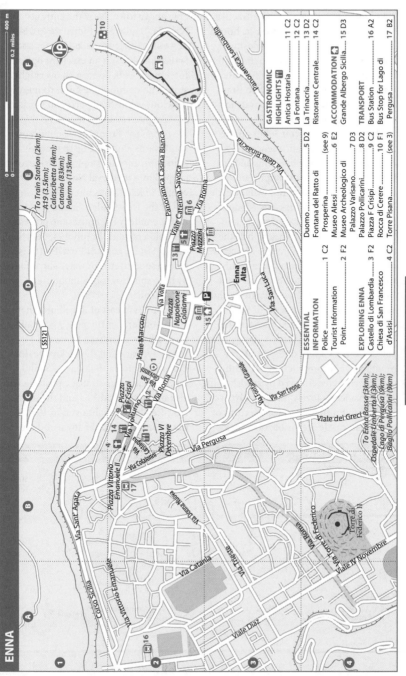

To Train Station (2km);
A19 (3.5km);
Calascibetta (4km);
Catania (83km);
Palermo (135km)

To Enna Bassa (3km);
Ospedale Umberto I (3km);
Lago di Pergusa (9km);
Baglio Pollicarini (9km)

CENTRAL SICILY

## ESSENTIAL INFORMATION
| | |
|---|---|
| Police | 1 C2 |
| Tourist Information Point | 2 F2 |

## EXPLORING ENNA
| | |
|---|---|
| Castello di Lombardia | 3 F2 |
| Chiesa di San Francesco d'Assisi | 4 C2 |
| Duomo | 5 D2 |
| Fontana del Ratto di Prosperina | (see 9) |
| Museo Alessi | 6 E2 |
| Museo Archeologico di Palazzo Varisano | 7 D3 |
| Palazzo Pollicarini | 8 D2 |
| Piazza F Crispi | 9 C2 |
| Rocca di Cerere | 10 F1 |
| Torre Pisana | (see 3) |

## GASTRONOMIC HIGHLIGHTS
| | |
|---|---|
| Antica Hostaria | 11 C2 |
| La Fontana | 12 C2 |
| La Trinacria | 13 D2 |
| Ristorante Centrale | 14 C2 |

## ACCOMMODATION
| | |
|---|---|
| Grande Albergo Sicilia | 15 D3 |

## TRANSPORT
| | |
|---|---|
| Bus Station | 16 A2 |
| Bus Stop for Lago di Pergusa | 17 B2 |

20km up to **Leonforte (4)**, an attractive baroque town once famous for its horse breeding. The town's most imposing building is the **Palazzo Baronale** but the star attraction is the lavish **Granfonte** fountain. Built in 1651 by Nicolò Branciforte, it is made up of 24 separate jets against a sculpted facade.

The next leg takes you 30km up the SS117 through dramatic scenery to **Nicosia (5)**. Set on four hills, this ancient town was once the most important of a chain of fortified Norman towns stretching from Palermo to Messina. Modern times have been tougher, though, and between 1950 and 1970 nearly half the town's population emigrated. The centre of action is **Piazza Garibaldi**, a handsome square dominated by the elegant 14th-century facade and Catalan-Gothic campanile of the **Cattedrale di San Nicolò**. From the piazza, Via Salamone leads past crumbling Franco-Lombard palazzi to the **Chiesa di Santa Maria Maggiore**, a reconstruction of a 13th-century church destroyed by landslide in 1757. Inside is a lovely marble polyptych by Gagini. From the terrace the ruins of a Norman **castle** are visible on a rocky

crag above town. Near the entrance to Nicosia, **Baglio San Pietro** ( ☎ 0935 64 05 29; www.bagliosanpietro.com, in Italian; Contrada San Pietro; meals €25) is an excellent option for a meal break or even an overnight stop, with comfortable guest rooms and delicious wood-fired *porchetta* (suckling pig) on the restaurant menu; bookings are necessary. From Nicosia, push on southwards along the SP18 towards **Agira (6)**, another sloping hillside town capped by a medieval Norman castle. A couple of kilometres out of Agira on the SS121 the well-tended **Canadian Military Cemetery (7)** houses the graves of 490 soldiers killed in July 1943. Further on the SS121, **Lago di Pozzillo (8)** is a picturesque stretch of water surrounded by hills and groves of almond trees, ideal for a picnic.

Some 13km east of Regalbuto, there's a turn-off for **Centuripe (9)**, a small town whose grandstand views of Mt Etna have earned it the nickname, the Balcone di Sicilia (Balcony of Sicily). Unfortunately, its strategic position has also brought bloodshed and the town has often been fought over. In 1943 the Allies captured the town and the

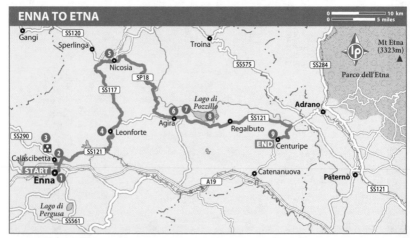

## ACCOMMODATION

This is not Sicily's most visited region and hotel accommodation is limited. In the towns, you'll often be better off in a B&B, while the countryside boasts a number of lovely *agriturismi* (farm stays).

★ Bed down on Caltagirone's *scalinata* (staircase) at **B&B Tre Metri Sopra il Cielo** (p318), a wonderful, friendly B&B.

★ As much contemporary art gallery as hotel, **Suite d'Autore** (p318) cuts a dashing figure in Piazza Armerina's historic centre.

★ Relax into rural life at **Azienda Agriturismo Gigliotto** (p317), a slick *agriturismo* set on its own wine estate.

★ Still a working farm, **Baglio San Pietro** (p317) offers rustic accommodation and filling farmhouse cooking.

★ Sleep in a monk's cell and dream of mythical maidens at **Baglio Pollicarini** (p317), an historic *agriturismo* near Lago di Pergusa.

For detailed accommodation listings, see p317.

Germans, realising that their foothold in Sicily had slipped, retreated to the Italian mainland.

# EXPLORING ENNA

### ☙ CASTELLO DI LOMBARDIA // STORM ENNA'S LANDMARK NORMAN CASTLE

One of Sicily's most formidable castles, the **Castello di Lombardia** (admission free; ☯ 9am-8pm summer, 9am-4pm winter) guards Enna's highest point, at the easternmost edge of the historic centre. The original castle was built by the Saracens and later reinforced by the Normans; Frederick II of Hohenstaufen ordered that a powerful curtain wall be built with towers on every side. The wall is still intact but only six of the original 20 towers remain, of which the tallest is the **Torre Pisana**, which you can climb from the Cortile dei Cavalieri, one of the castle's well-preserved inner courtyards. From the top, there are fabulous views over the valley to the town of Calascibetta and to the northeast to Mt Etna.

### ☙ ROCCA DI CERERE // WATCH THE SUNSET FROM ATOP AN ANCIENT TEMPLE

Just below the entrance to the castle is a huge rock, the **Rocca di Cerere**, which was once home to Enna's Temple of Demeter (Ceres to the Romans), goddess of fertility and agriculture. The temple, built in 480 BC by the tyrant Gelon, is supposed to have featured a statue of King Triptolemus, the only mortal to witness the rape of Demeter's daughter Persephone (see the boxed text on p237).

There's not much left of the temple now, but the rocky platform, accessible by a series of steep steps, is a great place for a picnic or to take in the sunset.

### ☙ DUOMO // ADMIRE THE INTERIOR DECORATION OF ENNA'S SHOWY CATHEDRAL

The **Duomo** (Via Roma; ☯ 9am-1pm & 4-7pm) is the most impressive of the historic buildings that line Via Roma, Enna's showpiece street. Built over 200 years after the original Gothic cathedral burnt down in 1446, it boasts an imposing facade, complete with a square 17th-century belltower, and a truly sumptuous interior. Traces remain of the original church, including the transept and polygonal apses, but the rest is pure baroque, including an ornamental coffered wood ceiling, hanging chandeliers and a dramatic, scene-stealing altar. Other points of interest include the bases of the grey basalt columns, decorated with grotesque carvings of snakes with human heads; the pulpit and stoup, both set on Graeco-Roman remains from the Temple of Demeter; 17th-century presbytery paintings by Filippo Paladino; and the altarpieces by Guglielmo Borremans.

### ❦ MUSEUMS // BROWSE RELIGIOUS JEWELS AND ARCHEOLOGICAL ARTEFACTS

Next to the cathedral, the Museo Alessi (Via Roma 465; ❧ currently closed), houses the cathedral's valuable treasury, including a 17th-century jewel-encrusted golden crown by Leonardo and Giuseppe Montalbano.

Over on the other side of Piazza Mazzini is the Museo Archeologico di Palazzo Varisano ( ☎ 0935 50 7611; ❧ currently closed for renovation), which has a small collection of archaeological artefacts excavated from around the region.

About 100m further down Via Roma, opposite the Grande Albergo Sicilia, is the Catalan-Gothic Palazzo Pollicarini, one of Enna's most handsome buildings.

### ❦ PIAZZA F CRISPI // CLOCK THE VIEWS FROM THIS PANORAMIC PIAZZA

As you continue down Via Roma, you eventually come to Piazza Vittorio Emanuele II, Enna's main square. Forming much of the piazza's northern flank is the sombre bulk of the Chiesa di San Francesco d'Assisi and its 15th-century belltower. Just off the piazza is another small square, Piazza F Crispi, which commands sweeping views over the valley to Calascibetta. In the centre of the piazza, graffiti emblazons the Fontana del Ratto di Prosperina, a monumental fountain commemorating Enna's most enduring legend (see the boxed text, opposite).

### ❦ LAGO DI PERGUSA // SEE WHERE HADES ABDUCTED PERSEPHONE

Surrounded by woodland about 9km south of town, Lago di Pergusa is one of Sicily's few natural lakes. It's a popular summer hangout with some sandy beaches, a number of big resort-style hotels and an unlikely motor-racing circuit, but out of season it's a rather forlorn place offering little reason to linger. Certainly, there is nothing to connect it to the mythical tale of Persephone, for which it's so famous – see the boxed text, opposite.

To get to the lake, take local bus 5 from the bus stop on Via Pergusa. By car it's signposted along the SS561.

## FESTIVALS & EVENTS

Holy Week The week building up to Easter is marked by solemn religious celebrations, during which the city's religious confraternities parade around in creepy capes and white hoods. The main events are on Palm Sunday, Good Friday and Easter Sunday.

Festa di Maria Santissima della Visitazione Fireworks and scantily clad farmers mark the town's patron saint's day on 2 July. The farmers, dressed in white sheets, drag an effigy of the Madonna of the Visitation through town on a cart called La Nave d'Oro (Golden Ship).

## THE MYTH OF PERSEPHONE

The tale of Hades' capture of Demeter's daughter Persephone (also known as Proserpina) is one of the most famous Greek myths. According to Homeric legend, Hades (god of the underworld) emerged from his lair and abducted Persephone while she was gathering flowers around Lago di Pergusa. Not knowing where her daughter had disappeared to, Demeter (goddess of the harvest) forbade the earth to bear fruit as she wandered the world looking for her. Eventually, she turned to Zeus, threatening that if he didn't return her daughter she would inflict eternal famine on the world. Zeus submitted to her threat and ordered Hades to release Persephone, although stipulating that every year she should spend six months in the underworld with Hades and six months in Sicily with her mother. Demeter still mourns during Persephone's time in the underworld, bringing winter to the world; her joy at her daughter's return is heralded by the blossoms of springtime.

# GASTRONOMIC HIGHLIGHTS

Unlike the coast, the staple here is meat, and local dishes usually involve lamb or beef and a tasty array of mushrooms and grilled vegetables. Specialities include *castrato* (charcoal-grilled castrated ram) and *polpettone* (stuffed lamb or meatballs). Soups and sausages are also a feature.

### 🌶 ANTICA HOSTARIA €€

☎ 0935 2 25 21; Via Castagna 9; meals €33; 🕑 closed Tue

Housed in the stable block of an 18th-century palazzo, this is one of Enna's best restaurants. There's nothing especially memorable about the rustic decor but the food is another matter. The menu is seasonal, and past successes have included wild-asparagus risotto, fava-bean purée and roast pork with almonds. The wine list is also a cut above average with some fine Sicilian labels.

### 🌶 LA FONTANA €

☎ 0935 2 54 65; Via Volturno 6; meals €20; 🕑 closed Mon

A long-standing trattoria opposite Piazza F Crispi, this is a relaxed spot for some filling Sicilian country fare, like *minestrone di verdura* (vegetable minestrone)

followed by grilled chicken or *fegato arrosto* (roast liver). There's seating in the cheerful interior or, in summer, on the panoramic piazza.

### 🌶 LA TRINACRIA €€

☎ 0935 50 20 22; Viale Caterina Savoca 20; meals €30; 🕑 closed Sun

A great new restaurant on the scenic road down from the castle. Diners are met with a big welcoming smile and then plied with huge helpings of fabulous country food. Antipasti of hams, salami, fried croquettes, cheese, olives and marinated vegetables are followed by pharaonic pasta dishes and juicy cuts of roast meat. It's a popular spot, which ensures a warm boisterous atmosphere, and the central location means you can waddle back to your hotel without too much trouble.

### 🌶 RISTORANTE CENTRALE €€

☎ 0935 50 09 63; www.ristorantecentrale.net; Piazza VI Dicembre 9; meals €25; 🕑 closed Sat

This historic family-run restaurant has hosted a roll call of famous diners, including Italy's last king, Vittorio Emanuele III, and opera maestro Placido Domingo. Yet there's nothing fancy about the place, neither in look nor culinary style, with the onus on tried-and-tested dishes based on delicious local ingredients such as sausages, mushrooms and seasonal veggies.

## TRANSPORT

**BUS //** The bus is the best way to reach Enna by public transport. Enna's **bus station** (Viale Diaz) is in the upper town, but service is more frequent from the stop in Enna Bassa, 3km downhill. **SAIS** ( ☎ 0935 50 09 02; www.saisautolinee.it) runs services to Catania (€7.30, 1¼ hours, 10 daily Monday to Friday, seven Saturday) and Palermo (€9.40, 1¾ hours, up to seven daily Monday to Friday, four Saturday). For Agrigento change at Caltanissetta (€3.90, one hour, six daily Monday to Friday, four Saturday). Regular buses also run to Piazza Armerina (€3.20, 30 minutes, nine daily Monday to Friday, five Saturday). Services to all destinations are drastically reduced on Sundays. Hourly local buses connect Enna Bassa with the upper town, except on Sundays when it's every two hours.

**CAR //** Enna is on the main Catania–Palermo A19 autostrada, about 83km from Catania, 135km from Palermo.

# SOUTH OF ENNA
· · · · · ·

**South of Enna, the landscape becomes less dramatic, flattening out and taking on a more rural aspect as rugged mountain scenery gives way to gentle cultivated fields dotted with busy agricultural towns. The two main attractions are Piazza Armerina, celebrated for its Roman mosaics, and Caltagirone, a centre of traditional ceramic production. Both towns have decent accommodation and interesting historic centres. The remains of the Greek city of Morgantina, northeast of Aidone, are considerable and worth more than the trickle of visitors they receive.**

## PIAZZA ARMERINA

pop 20,840 / elev 697m
Set amid fertile farming country, this charming market town takes its name

from the Colle Armerino, one of the three hills on which it is built. It is actually two towns in one: the original Piazza was founded by the Saracens in the 10th century on the slope of the Colle Armerino, while a 15th-century expansion to the southeast was redefined by an urban grid established in the 17th century.

You can easily spend a day or two pottering about its labyrinthine streets and visiting the extraordinary mosaics at Villa Romana del Casale. With the addition of some pleasant accommodation and tasty restaurants, Piazza Armerina becomes an unexpected treat.

### ESSENTIAL INFORMATION

**TOURIST OFFICES //** Municipal Tourist Office ( ☎ 0935 68 30 49; www.comune.piazzaarmerina.en.it; Piazza Santa Rosalia; ⏰ 9am-1pm & 3.30-7pm Mon-Fri)

### ORIENTATION

Orientate yourself from the large area comprising Piazza Generale A Cascino and Piazza Falcone e Borsellino, just off the main road through town. From here Via Mazzini leads down to Piazza Garibaldi, the old town's focal square. Most of the town's sites are an easy walk from here, including the cathedral at the top of Via Cavour. For the Roman mosaics, 5km out of town at Villa Romana del Casale, follow the signs from Piazza A De Gaspari.

### EXPLORING PIAZZA ARMERINA

❤ VILLA ROMANA DEL CASALE //
MARVELLOUS MOSAICS AT SICILY'S FINEST ROMAN SITE
In a wooded valley 5km southwest of the town centre, the Unesco-listed Villa Romana del Casale ( ☎ 0935 68 00 36;

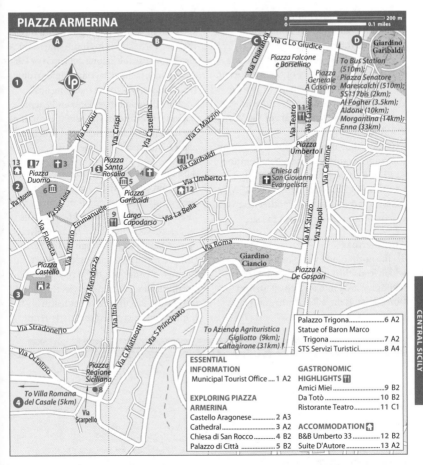

**PIAZZA ARMERINA**

| | |
|---|---|
| Palazzo Trigona | 6 A2 |
| Statue of Baron Marco Trigona | 7 A2 |
| STS Servizi Turistici | 8 A4 |

**ESSENTIAL INFORMATION**
Municipal Tourist Office .... 1 A2

**EXPLORING PIAZZA ARMERINA**
Castello Aragonese ............. 2 A3
Cathedral ........................... 3 A2
Chiesa di San Rocco ........... 4 B2
Palazzo di Città .................. 5 B2

**GASTRONOMIC HIGHLIGHTS**
Amici Miei ........................ 9 B2
Da Totò ........................... 10 B2
Ristorante Teatro ............. 11 C1

**ACCOMMODATION**
B&B Umberto 33 ............. 12 B2
Suite D'Autore ................ 13 A2

CENTRAL SICILY

www.villaromanadelcasale.it; ☺ closed for restoration) is central Sicily's biggest attraction, a lavish ancient villa decorated with the finest Roman floor mosaics in existence. Unfortunately, the villa closed for restoration from October 2010. No reopening date had been set, although you can check the latest news on the website.

The villa, sumptuous even by decadent Roman standards, is thought to have been the country retreat of Marcus Aurelius Maximianus, Rome's co-emperor during the reign of Diocletian (AD 286–305). Certainly, the size of the complex – four

interconnected groups of buildings spread over the hillside – and the 3535 sq metres of multicoloured floor mosaics suggests a palace of imperial standing.

Following a landslide in the 12th century, the villa lay under 10m of mud for some 700 years, and was thus protected from the damaging effects of air, wind and rain. It was only when serious excavation work began in the 1950s that the mosaics were brought back to light. Since then much of the complex has been unearthed but work continues and outbuildings remain to be investigated.

The mosaics cover almost the entire floor of the villa and are considered unique for their natural, narrative style, the range of their subject matter and variety of colour. Many of them were laid by craftsmen from Carthage in North Africa, which at the time was the most culturally sophisticated part of the Western Roman Empire.

If the villa has reopened and you want to arrange a guide, contact the **Comune di Piazza Armerina** ( ☎ 0935 98 22 46) or **STS Servizi Turistici** ( ☎ 0935 68 70 27; www. guardalasicilia.it; Via Scarpello 2-4); otherwise you can organise one directly at the site.

### The Thermae

To the north of the villa's **main entrance**, which leads through the remnants of a triumphal arch into an elegant **atrium** (forecourt), is the villa's baths complex, the **thermae** (baths). Accessible via the **palaestra** (gymnasium), which has a splendid mosaic depicting a chariot race at the Circus Maximus in Rome (the room is also known as the Salone del Circo or Circus Room), is the octagonal **frigidarium** (cold room), where the radiating apses contained cold plunge pools and a **tepidarium** (warm room), where you can now see the exposed brickwork and vents that allowed hot steam into the room.

### The Peristyle & Great Hunt

The main part of the villa is centred on the **peristyle**, a vast open-air courtyard lined with amusing animal heads. This is where guests would have been received before being taken through to the **basilica** (throne room), which you can view through a window. Of the rooms on the northern side of the peristyle, the most interesting is a dining room featuring a hunting mosaic called the **Little Hunt**.

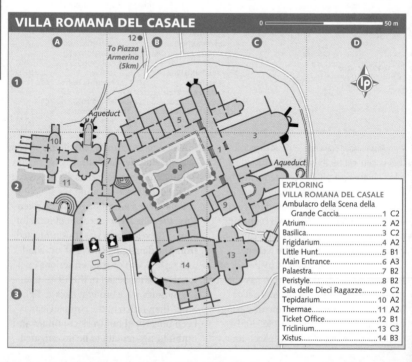

**VILLA ROMANA DEL CASALE**

0 — 50 m

To Piazza Armerina (5km)

Aqueduct

Aqueduct

CENTRAL SICILY

Little because the big hunt is over on the eastern flank of the peristyle in the **Ambulacro della Scena della Grande Caccia** (Corridor of the Great Hunt). This 64m-long corridor is emblazoned with dramatic hunting scenes of tigers, leopards, elephants, antelopes, ostriches and a rhino – animals that the Romans eventually hunted to extinction in North Africa. The first figure is resplendent in a Byzantine cape and is flanked by two soldiers, most likely Maximianus himself and two members of his personal guard.

### The Bikini Girls

Just off the southern end of the Ambulacro della Scena della Grande Caccia, in the **Sala delle Dieci Ragazze** (Room of the 10 Girls), the villa's most famous mosaic depicts nine (originally there were 10) bikini-clad girls working out with weights and dinky dumbbells.

### Mythical Trials

Over on the other side of the Ambulacro is a series of apartments, whose floor illustrations reproduce scenes from Homer and other mythical episodes. Of particular interest is the **triclinium** (banquet hall), with a splendid depiction of the labours of Hercules, where the tortured monsters are ensnared by a smirking Odysseus.

To view the **xystus** (elliptical courtyard), which you can see from the triclinium, you have to exit the building and walk around the apse. As it's uncovered, the mosaic work is in pretty poor nick.

❤ **THE HISTORIC CENTRE //**
**INVESTIGATE MEDIEVAL LANES,**
**BAROQUE CHURCHES AND**
**TUMBLEDOWN PALAZZI**
Often overlooked by people rushing to the Villa Romana del Casale, Piazza's hilltop medieval centre is worth more than the passing glance that many people

---

## GETTING TO THE SITE

If driving, follow signs along the SP15 from Piazza Amerina's town centre. By public transport it's harder but not impossible. Between May and September CTS Autolinee runs seven daily buses to the site, departing from Piazza Senatore Marescalchi on the hour (9am to noon and 4pm to 7pm) and returning from the villa on the half-hour.

Outside summer you will have to walk – it's downhill, not too strenuous, and takes about an hour. The walk back is only steep for the last part. Taxis will take you there, wait for an hour, and drive you back to town for about €25; to book a taxi, call ☎ 0935 68 05 01.

---

give it. The highpoint, quite literally, is the hilltop **cathedral** (Piazza Duomo; ⊙ 8am-noon & 3.30-7pm). A landmark for miles around – the towering dome rises to a height of 66m – it's a huge, bulky affair with a severe 18th-century facade and an airy blue-and-white interior. Of note is the altar painting, a copy of a Byzantine painting *Madonna delle Vittorie* (Virgin of the Victories), which was supposedly presented to Count Roger I by Pope Nicholas II. To the side of the main church, the 44m-high belltower is a leftover from an earlier 14th-century church.

The handsome square in front of the cathedral affords splendid views of the surrounding countryside and is flanked by **Palazzo Trigona**, a baronial palace that has been earmarked for a new archaeological museum. In the centre of the square, the statue is of **Baron Marco Trigona**, the aristocrat who financed the cathedral's construction.

Off Piazza Duomo is **Via Monte**, the arterial road of the 13th-century city, with its warren of tiny alleys fanning

**CENTRAL SICILY**

out like the ribs of a fishbone. This is the town's most picturesque quarter. Alternatively, take Via Floresta, beside Palazzo Trigona, to arrive at the ruins of the 14th-century Castello Aragonese.

From the cathedral, Via Cavour hairpins down to Piazza Garibaldi, the elegant heart of the old town. Overlooking the square is Palazzo di Città, Piazza's refined Town Hall, and the Chiesa di San Rocco (known as the Fundrò), next to which there's a pretty internal courtyard.

### ❧ PALIO DEI NORMANNI // CHEER THE MEDIEVAL SHENANIGANS AT PIAZZA'S ANNUAL PAGEANT

Piazza Armerina bursts into life on 13 and 14 August for its great annual event – a medieval pageant celebrating Count Roger's capture of the town from the Moors in 1087. Events kick off on the 13th with costumed parades and a re-enactment of Count Roger being presented with the city keys. The highlight on the 14th is the great joust, known as the *quintana,* between the four districts of the city – Monte, Canali, Castellina and Casalotto. At the end of the day the winning district is presented with a standard depicting Our Lady of the Victories.

## GASTRONOMIC HIGHLIGHTS

### ❧ AL FOGHER €€€

☎ 0935 68 41 23; www.alfogher.net; Contrada Bellia SS117bis; meals €50; ☉ closed Sun evening & Mon
This is one of central Sicily's top restaurants, serving sophisticated modern cuisine to a demanding and appreciative clientele. It's about 3km out of town, but your journey is rewarded with dishes such as suckling pig with tuna egg sauce and asparagus, or mullet served with yellow capsicum (pepper), wild rice and

pistachio. Equal attention is given to the wine list, which contains up to 400 labels. Reservations required.

### ❧ AMICI MIEI €€

☎ 0935 68 35 41; Largo Capodarso 5; meals €25-30, pizzas from €4.50; ☉ closed Thu
With its exposed stone walls, low wooden ceiling, wine racks and wood-fired pizza oven; this friendly trattoria looks the part perfectly. It's not just looks, though, and the food is spot on. The pizzas are great – locals come here for takeaway – and the pastas hale and hearty. Special mention should also go to the *antipasto della casa,* a fabulous platter of frittata, sliced pancetta, cheese, caponata, and ricotta with balsamic vinegar.

### ❧ DA TOTÒ €€

☎ 0935 68 01 53; Via G Mazzini 27; meals €23; ☉ closed Mon
Don't let the stark white lights and bland decor put you off, this popular trattoria serves excellent value-for-money food. Antipasti are of the ham, cheese and grilled veg variety, while pastas are paired with earthy sauces of porcini mushrooms or ripe local vegetables. Main courses are similarly unpretentious with peppered grilled steak a menu mainstay. Service is friendly and the laidback atmosphere conducive to a nice, relaxed meal.

### ❧ RISTORANTE TEATRO €€

☎ 0935 8 56 62; Via Teatro 1; meals €25; ☉ closed Wed
Dine in the shadow of Piazza Armerina's local theatre at this welcoming family-run trattoria. The theatre theme translates to framed theatre bills on the white walls and a showy roof fresco – better the outside terrace – but the food is far from stagey. There are excellent pizzas, filling pastas and a huge range of meat dishes.

## TRANSPORT

**BUS //** **AST** ( ☎ 840 000323; www.aziendasicili anatrasporti.it) runs a daily service to Syracuse (€8.80, four hours, one daily). **SAIS** ( ☎ 0935 50 09 02; www. saisautolinee.it) buses connect Piazza Armerina with Enna (€3.20, 30 minutes, nine daily Monday to Friday, five Saturday).

**CAR //** The SS117bis links Piazza Armerina with Enna 33km to the north.

# AROUND PIAZZA ARMERINA

### ♣ AIDONE // PIECE TOGETHER ANCIENT HISTORY AT AIDONE'S ARCHAEOLOGY MUSEUM

Heading northwest from Piazza Armerina, the road leads past attractive woodland and rocky grass banks to the sleepy hilltop village of Aidone. Although a nice enough place – check out the grandstand views over the surrounding valley – the one reason to stop off is to visit the **Museo Archeologico** ( ☎ 0935 8 73 07; Convento dei Cappuccini; admission incl Morgantina €3; ⏰ 8am-6pm Mon-Sat, 8am-2pm Sun). This small museum whets the appetite for the Greek ruins at Morgantina with a small collection of artefacts from the site and displays chronicling life in ancient times and the recent excavation work.

### ♣ MORGANTINA // WANDER THROUGH THE REMAINS OF AN ANCIENT GREEK COLONY

At the end of a paved track, 4km downhill from Aidone, are the noteworthy remains of **Morgantina** (admission incl Museo Archeologico at Aidone €3; ⏰ 9am-1hr before sunset), an ancient Greek settlement spread across two hills and the connecting valley. Morgeti, an early Sicilian settlement, was founded in 850 BC on Cittadella hill, but this town was destroyed in 459 BC and a new one was built on a second hill, Serra Orlando. It was an important trading post during the reign of the Syracusan tyrant Hieron II (269–215 BC) but slipped into decline after defeat by the Romans in 211 BC and was eventually abandoned. In 1955 archaeologists identified the site and began its excavation, which continues to this day.

The centre of town is the two-storey **agora** (marketplace), whose trapezoidal stairway was used as seating during public meetings. The upper level had a **market** and you can still see the walls that divided one shop from the next. The lower level was the site of the 1000-capacity **theatre**, which was originally built in the 3rd century BC but later altered by the Romans. It remains in excellent condition.

To the northeast are the city's **residential quarters**, where the town's well-off lived, as testified by the ornate wall decorations and handsome mosaics in the inner rooms. Another residential quarter has been found behind the theatre and its considerable ruins are well worth checking out.

To get to the site you'll need your own transport as no buses stop near by.

# CALTAGIRONE

**pop 39,505** / **elev 608m**

Caltagirone, an attractive hilltop town, is renowned throughout Sicily for its ceramics. The area's high-quality clay has supported production for more than a 1000 years and still today the industry is an important money-spinner. The town's earliest settlers worked with terracotta but it was the Arabs, arriving in the 10th century, who kick-started the industry by introducing glazed polychromatic colours, particularly the yellows and blues that have distinguished the local ceramics ever since. Everywhere you go

## TOP FIVE

### HILLTOP TOWNS

★ **Caltagirone** (p243) Rebuilt after an earthquake in 1693, Caltagirone boasts a charming baroque townscape and a lively, welcoming atmosphere.

★ **Enna** (p232) Rising to a height of 931m, Italy's highest provincial capital has a handsome medieval core.

★ **Calascibetta** (p232) This is the town you see over the valley from Enna, crawling up the hillside to culminate in a robust 14th-century cathedral.

★ **Nicosia** (p232) Spread over four hills, this once-powerful town retains reminders of its Norman golden age.

★ **Leonforte** (p232) Pride of place at this baroque town goes to an elaborate 17th-century fountain.

in Caltagirone you're reminded of its ceramic traditions, most emphatically at the Scalinata di Santa Maria del Monte, the town's celebrated ceramic-inlaid staircase.

Caltagirone's history dates to pre-Greek times but the town's name is Arabic in origin, a derivation of the words *kalat* and *gerun,* meaning 'castle' and 'cave'. Little remains of the town's early incarnations as it was almost entirely destroyed by earthquake in 1693 and subsequently rebuilt in the baroque style so typical of Sicily's southeast.

## ESSENTIAL INFORMATION

**TOURIST INFORMATION //** Tourist Information Desk ( ☎ 0933 4 13 65; www.comune. caltagirone.ct.it; Galleria Luigi Sforzo, Piazza Municipio; ⏱ 9am-7pm Mon-Sat) Near the bottom of the Scalinata di Santa Maria del Monte.

## ORIENTATION

Caltagirone is divided into an upper and lower town, with everything of interest in the upper town. Orientate yourself around Piazza Municipio, the upper town's focal square. From here, the Scalinata di Santa Maria del Monte rises to the northeast, while shop-lined Via Vittorio Emanuele heads off west and Via Luigi Sturzo runs northeast to Viale Regina Elena, a ring road with useful parking. Just south of Piazza Municipio, Piazza Umberto connects with Via Roma,which runs down to the Giardino Pubblico. Buses stop off in Piazza Umberto.

## EXPLORING CALTAGIRONE

❦ **SCALINATA DI SANTA MARIA DEL MONTE //** CLIMB CALTAGIRONE'S PHOTOGENIC, AND VERY STEEP, STAIRCASE

Caltagirone's most evocative sight is this monumental staircase, known locally as the Scalinata di Santa Maria del Monte, which rises from Piazza Municipio to the Chiesa di Santa Maria del Monte, at the top of the town. Built in the early 17th century to connect the old hilltop centre with newer developments around Piazza Municipio, it was originally divided into several flights of steps separated by small squares. These were eventually unified in the 1880s to create the 142-step flight that stands today. The hand-painted majolica tiles were a relatively recent addition, only being added in 1956. It's all very impressive, although by the time you get to the top, you'll probably be more interested in having a sit-down than admiring the tilework. Fortunately, the huge views will quickly restore your will to move. The steps, lined with colourful ceramic shops, are at their finest during Caltagirone's annual celebration, the Festa di San Giacomo (Feast of St James) on 24 and 25 July, when the entire staircase is lit by more than 4000 oil lamps.

At the bottom of the staircase, Piazza Municipio is overshadowed by a number of grand buildings, including the Galleria Luigi Sturzo. Named after a revered former mayor, Luigi Sturzo (1871–1959), and housed in Palazzo Senatorio, where once the town senate sat, the gallery hosts temporary exhibitions and the tourist information desk.

### ☘ CERAMIC CALTAGIRONE // TOUR THE TOWN'S CERAMIC HOT SPOTS

Down from the main historic centre, the Museo della Ceramica (Regional Ceramics Museum; ☎ 0933 5 84 18; Via Roma; adult/concession €3/2; ☺ 9am-6pm) is the place to learn about the Sicilian ceramics industry. Exhibits, which include Greek terracotta works, medieval kitchenware and some excessively elaborate 18th-century majolica statuettes, chronicle developments from prehistoric times to the 19th century.

For a more contemporary take, head up to the Museo d'Arte Contemporanea Caltagirone (☎ 0933 2 10 83; Viale Regina Elena 10; admission free; ☺ 9.30am-1.30pm Mon, Tue, Thu-Sat, 9am-12.30pm Sun, 4-7pm Tue & Fri-Sun), whose collection includes works by the renowned local artist Gianni Ballarò.

If you're in the market for a souvenir, there are about 120 ceramics shops in town. Two recommended stores are Le Maioliche (☎ 0933 5 31 39; www.varsallona.it; Discesa Collegio 1), where local artist Ricardo Varsallona exhibits his traditional and modern works, and Ceramiche Failla (☎ 0933 3 40 00; Scalinata di Santa Maria del Monte 45) on the main scalinata (staircase).

### ☘ GIARDINO PUBBLICO // TAKE TIME OUT IN CALTAGIRONE'S LANDSCAPED PARK

Next to the Museo della Ceramica, the Giardino Pubblico is a lovely place to see out the late afternoon, perhaps with an ice cream or a glass of something cool at the park bar. Manicured avenues lead down to a central space where ceramic-tiled benches look onto an art nouveau pavilion. Look the other way for views stretching into the distance – on a clear day, as far as Mt Etna.

### ☘ CHURCHES // ADMIRE BAROQUE WORKMANSHIP AND AN ILLUMINATING NATIVITY SCENE

Caltagirone has an extraordinary number of churches, almost 30 in the historic centre alone. Most are baroque, dating to the building boom of the early 18th century, although some have earlier origins. One such, the Chiesa di San Francesco d'Assisi (Piazza San Francesco d'Assisi) dates to the 13th century but now displays an extraordinarily flamboyant baroque facade. Near the church, the 17th-century Ponte San Francesco (San Francesco Bridge) is worth a close look for its ceramic floral embellishments.

Higher up in the old town, down a side street off the scalinata, the Chiesa del Carmine (Piazza del Carmine; ☺ 10.30am-1pm & 3.30-6.30pm) is worth a quick look for its huge terracotta presepe (nativity scene) – presepi are another Caltagirone tradition – covering 72 sq metres.

## GASTRONOMIC HIGHLIGHTS

### ☘ CORIA €€€

☎ 0933 2 65 96; www.ristorantecoria.it; Via Infermeria 24; meals from €40; ☺ closed Mon winter, Wed summer

Sicily's gourmets have been watching Caltagirone's top restaurant for some

CENTRAL SICILY

time and it is now an established address on the island's fine-dining circuit. Its reputation rides on innovative regional cuisine, as exemplified in reworked classics such as *spaghetti con sarde in crema di finocchietto* (spaghetti with sardines in a fennel sauce) and *biscotto con crema di arance e gelatino di cioccolato e menta* (biscuit with orange cream and chocolate and mint jelly). Reservations required.

### ❤ IL LOCANDIERE €€

☎ 0933 5 82 92; Via Luigi Sturzo 55-59; meals €30; ⊗ closed Mon

Those in the know head to this smart little restaurant for top-quality seafood and impeccable service. What exactly you'll eat depends on the day's catch, but the fish couscous is superb and the *casarecce con ragù di tonno* (pasta fingers with tuna sauce) a surefire hit. *Dolci* show-stoppers include delicious *connoli a cucchiao* (cannoli made with fig cream), and the wine list is long enough to please most palates.

### ❤ IL PALAZZO DEI MARCHESI DI SANTA BARBARA €€

☎ 0933 2 24 06; Via San Bonaventura 22; pizzas from €4, meals €30; ⊗ closed Mon

As you head up the baronial staircase to the 1st floor of the aristocratic palace, you might wonder where exactly you're heading. The answer is a smart, friendly restaurant, highly regarded for its excellent seasonal cuisine. The onus is on meat – the *straccetti di manzo con cuori di carciofo in crema di asparagi selvatici* (pork with artichoke hearts in a wild asparagus sauce) is a standout – but fish and pizzas are also available.

### ❤ LA PIAZZETTA €€

☎ 0933 2 41 78; Via Vespri 20; pizzas from €4.50, meals €25; ⊗ closed Thu

For many locals Saturday night means a slap-up meal at La Piazzetta, a much-loved

*centro storico* (historic city centre) restaurant. That might mean a pizza and beer or something more substantial like fresh pasta with pistachio pesto followed by a mountainous mixed grill. It's not haute cuisine but the food is tasty, the atmosphere is convivial and prices are honest.

## TRANSPORT

**BUS //** There are AST ( ☎ 840 000323; www.azien dasicilianatrasporti.it) buses to/from Piazza Armerina (€3.90, 1½ hours, seven daily Monday to Saturday) and Syracuse (€9.80, three hours, one daily Monday to Saturday) and an SAIS ( ☎ 0935 50 09 02; www.saisauto linee.it) service to/from Enna (€5.20, 1¼ hours, daily).

**CAR //** Caltagirone is just off the SS417, the road that connects Gela on the south coast with Catania in the east. From Piazza Armerina, follow the SS117bis south and then cut across country on the SS124.

**PARKING //** If you're staying in the upper town, there's useful parking on Viale Regina Elena.

# THE WESTERN INTERIOR

· · · · · ·

**Bearing the scars of a history of neglect and poverty, Sicily's western interior is a bleached landscape of rolling hills and small, isolated towns. For centuries the area was divided into large *latifondi* (landed estates) owned by absentee landlords, and still today the area seems remote and largely cut off from the rest of the world. It's a tough area to travel without your own car, although interest is mainly limited to the main city Caltanissetta and the large Regaleali wine estate.**

## CALTANISSETTA

pop 60,245 / elev 568m

One of Sicily's nine provincial capitals, Caltanissetta is the largest city in the area, a scruffy, workaday place with little

## WINE TASTING & COOKING COURSES

The area west of Caltanissetta is wild and remote, a kind of Sicilian Timbuktu. But if you want to get away from everything, head to the beautiful Regaleali estate ( ☎ 092 154 40 11; www.tascadalmerita.it) near the village of Vallelunga. One of five wine-producing estates owned by the Tasca d'Almerita family, it has some 400 hectares of vineyards, a high-tech winery and a residential cooking school ( ☎ 0934 81 46 54; www.annatascalanza.com) run by Anna Tasca Lanza. Visits to the winery are limited to guided tours (with optional tastings) for between eight and 25 people, which must be booked ahead. Cooking courses range from five-day packages (€2500 per person including accommodation) to a day-long lesson and lunch (€150). Further details are available on the website.

obvious appeal. But if you do find yourself passing through, there's a fine central piazza and, in the suburbs, a mildly interesting archaeological museum.

The city, originally founded by the Greeks, enjoyed prosperity in the first half of the 20th century as capital of the Sicilian sulphur-mining industry and is today an important agricultural centre.

### ESSENTIAL INFORMATION

**TOURIST INFORMATION //** Tourist Office ( ☎ 0934 53 98 26; Corso Vittorio Emanuele II 109; ☺ 9am-1pm Mon-Fri, 4-6pm Wed)

### EXPLORING CALTANISSETTA

☙ PIAZZA GARIBALDI // DINE IN THE SHADOW OF THE DUOMO
Caltanissetta's historic centre converges on Piazza Garibaldi, which is a handsome pedestrian-only piazza flanked by the Duomo, the town hall and the baroque Chiesa di San Sebastiano. The Duomo has a late-Renaissance appearance, but substantial alterations made in the 19th century have ruined the overall effect. Inside, if you find the church open, are frescoes by the 18th-century Flemish artist Guglielmo Borremans.

Hidden away in a tiny alleyway just off the piazza, Vicolo Duomo ( ☎ 0934 58 23 31; Vicolo Neviera 1; meals €30; ☺ closed Sun & lunch

Mon) is the place to eat in town. A colourful, Slow Food recommended trattoria, it specialises in earthy country fare such as pasta with spring peas and fava beans, and pork shin in Nero d'Avola wine.

☙ MUSEO ARCHEOLOGICO // DIG INTO CALTANISSETTA'S PREHISTORIC PAST
In the suburbs, sporadically signposted from the city centre, the Museo Archeologico ( ☎ 0934 56 70 62; Contrada Santo Spirito; adult/concession €2/1; ☺ 9am-1pm & 3.30-7pm, closed last Mon of month) displays a collection of prehistoric finds from all over Sicily, including vases, tools, early Sicilian ceramics and rare terracotta figurines from the Bronze Age.

The church you'll see near the museum car park is the 12th-century Abbazia di Santo Spirito, one of the few surviving relics from the city's Norman period.

### TRANSPORT

**BUS //** From the bus station on Via Colaianni, SAIS Autolinee ( ☎ 800 211020; www.saisautolinee.it) runs to Enna (€3.90, one hour) at least four times daily, while SAIS Trasporti ( ☎ 0934 56 40 72; www.saistrasporti.it) operates up to 10 daily buses to/from Agrigento (€5.80, 1¼ hours).

**CAR //** Coming from Enna or the north take the A19 autostrada to join with the SS640, which passes through Caltanissetta en route to Agrigento.

CENTRAL SICILY

# MEDITERRANEAN COAST

## 3 PERFECT DAYS

### ❦ DAY 1 // TEMPLES IN AGRIGENTO
Sicily's most popular archaeological site, Agrigento's Valley of the Temples (p254) is well worth an entire day. Start in the eastern zone (p255) where you'll find the two most famous temples, the Tempio di Hera and the outstanding Tempio della Concordia, before crossing to the western side (p256) and a picnic lunch in the Giardino della Kolymbetra (p256). Afterwards, and if you have any strength left, head up to the Museo Archeologico (p257).

### ❦ DAY 2 // PAMPER YOURSELF IN SCIACCA
From Agrigento it's 60km to Sciacca (p263), a spa town famous for its Rio-like carnival celebrations (p266). Treat yourself to a massage and mudpack at the Nuovo Stabilimento Termale (p265) and a fish feast at the port (p265). After a lazy lunch, head out to the Castello Incantato (p265) to pore over its collection of weird sculpted heads. Spend the rest of the day strolling through the attractive historic centre (p263) and perusing the characteristic ceramic shops (p265).

### ❦ DAY 3 // SWIMMING, SUNBATHING & THE ODD ANCIENT RUIN
The coastal stretch between Agrigento and Sciacca offers great swimming and pockets of unspoilt nature. Join the local sunseekers at the Scala dei Turchi (p261), a celebrated beauty spot near Realmonte, or push on to the lovely sandy beach at the Riserva Naturale Torre Salsa (p261), where there's also some fine coastal walking. Further west, you can explore the ruins of Eraclea Minoa (p262) before heading down to the beach, one of the best on this stretch of the coast.

# AGRIGENTO

· · · · · ·

**pop 59,135**

**At one time the fourth-largest city in the known world, Agrigento, or Akragas as it was then known, is home to Sicily's most impressive Greek ruins. Situated about 3km below the ugly modern city, the Unesco-listed Valley of the Temples is one of the most mesmerising sites in the Mediterranean, boasting the best-preserved Doric temples outside Greece. On the travel radar since Goethe sang their praises in the 18th century, they are now Sicily's single biggest tourist site, with more than 600,000 visitors a year.**

Up the hill, modern Agrigento is not an immediately appealing prospect. Huge motorway elevations converge on a ragged hilltop centre scarred by brutish tower blocks and riddled with choking traffic. However, hidden behind this depressing outer ring is an attractive medieval kernel with some fine accommodation and a lively evening buzz.

Ancient Akragas was founded by settlers from Gela and Rhodes in 581 BC. The presence of a ready water supply ensured its rapid growth and by the 5th century BC it had become one of the Mediterranean's great cities, with a population of 200,000 and a reputation as a party hot spot. The Greek poet Pindar described it as 'the most beautiful (city) of those inhabited by mortals' and wrote that its citizens 'feasted as if there were no tomorrow'.

Its good fortunes began to waver in the 4th and 3rd centuries BC as it passed successively between Greek, Carthaginian and Roman hands. The Romans, who took the city in 210 BC, renamed it Agrigentum and encouraged farming and trade, thus laying the foundations for its future as an important Byzantine commercial centre.

In the 7th century the bulk of the city's inhabitants moved up the hill to the site of the present-day city, virtually abandoning the old town. Experts still don't know exactly why, but the most credible theories suggest it was to escape the threat of the North African Saracens. As a defence policy it worked well for close on 200 years until the city fell to the Saracens at the start of the 9th century.

Agrigento didn't change much until the 19th century, when the western half of the city was built. Allied bombing in WWII forced a second wave of development in the post-war years, culminating in a bout of construction in the '60s and '70s. Many of the tower blocks that overshadow the Valley of the Temples date to this period.

## ESSENTIAL INFORMATION

**EMERGENCIES //** Ospedale Civile San Giovanni di Dio (Map p254; ☎ 0922 40 13 44; Contrada da Consolida) Police Station (Map p254; ☎ 0922 48 31 11; Piazza Vittorio Emanuele 2)
**TOURIST INFORMATION //** Main Tourist Office (Map p254; ☎ 800 236837; www.comune. agrigento.it; Piazzale Aldo Moro 1; ✹ 8am-2pm Mon-Fri, 8am-1pm Sat) Inside the Provincia building, offers information on the city and province. Tourist Information Point (Map p254; train station; ✹ 8am-8pm Mon-Fri, 8am-2pm Sat)

## ORIENTATION

There are two centres of interest in Agrigento: the historic centre and the Valley of the Temples. The historic centre's main street is Via Atenea, which runs westwards from Piazzale Aldo Moro to Piazza Pirandello. The intercity bus station is on Piazza Rosselli, just north of Piazzale Aldo Moro, while the train station is to the south, on Piazza Marconi.

*(Continued on page 254)*

# MEDITERRANEAN COAST

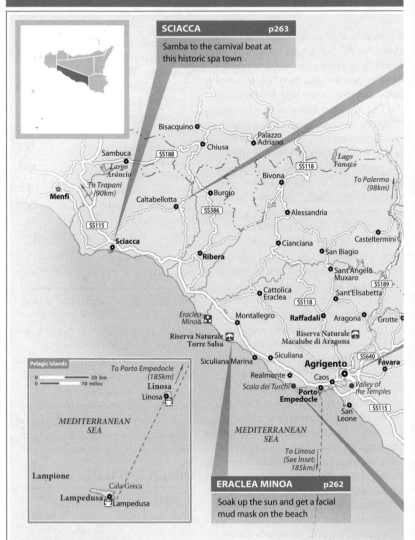

**SCIACCA** p263

Samba to the carnival beat at this historic spa town

Bisacquino

Palazzo Adriano

Chiusa

Sambuca

SS188

Largo Aràncio

*Lago Fanacò*

SS118

Bivona

**Menfi**

To Trapani (90km)

Caltabellotta

Burgio

To Palermo (98km)

SS386

Alessandria

SS115

**Sciacca**

Cianciana

Casteltermini

San Biagio

**Ribera**

Sant'Angelo Muxaro

SS189

Cattolica Eraclea

Sant'Elisabetta

SS118

*Eraclea Minoa*

Montallegro

**Raffadali**

Aragona

Grotte

**Riserva Naturale Torre Salsa**

**Riserva Naturale Macalube di Aragona**

Siculiana

SS640

Siculiana Marina

**Agrigento**

Favara

Realmonte

Caos

*Scala dei Turchi*

Valley of the Temples

**Porto Empedocle**

SS115

San Leone

*MEDITERRANEAN SEA*

To Linosa (See Inset; 185km)

**Pelagic Islands**

0 —— 20 km
0 —— 10 miles

To Porto Empedocle (185km)

**Linosa**

Linosa

*MEDITERRANEAN SEA*

Lampione

Cala Greca

**Lampedusa**

Lampedusa

**ERACLEA MINOA** p262

Soak up the sun and get a facial mud mask on the beach

## GETTING AROUND

Agrigento is served by buses and trains from across the island and is well connected by road. Getting to the town is no problem, but once there parking most definitely is difficult. The main coastal road is the SS115, an excellent, well-maintained road that runs westwards to Sciacca and eastwards to Gela and on up to Syracuse. Inland, the country roads that link the small towns rarely get busy but can be confusing unless you know exactly where you're going.

MEDITERRANEAN COAST

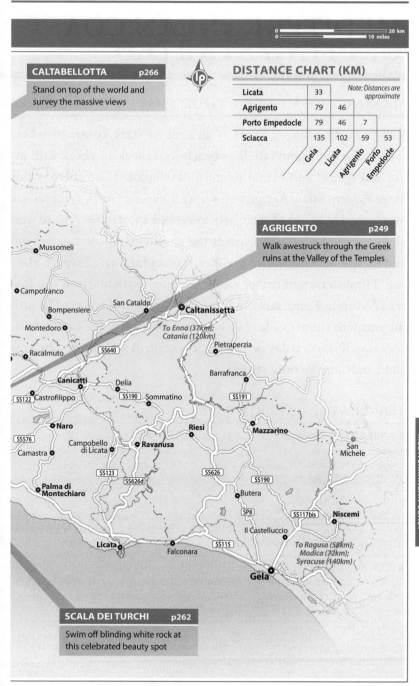

0 ———— 20 km
0 ———— 10 miles

**CALTABELLOTTA**   p266

Stand on top of the world and survey the massive views

## DISTANCE CHART (KM)

| | Gela | Licata | Agrigento | Porto Empedocle |
|---|---|---|---|---|
| Licata | 33 | | | |
| Agrigento | 79 | 46 | | |
| Porto Empedocle | 79 | 46 | 7 | |
| Sciacca | 135 | 102 | 59 | 53 |

Note: Distances are approximate

**AGRIGENTO**   p249

Walk awestruck through the Greek ruins at the Valley of the Temples

Mussomeli

Campofranco

Bompensiere          San Cataldo          **Caltanissetta**

Montedoro                         To Enna (37km);
                                  Catania (120km)

Racalmuto          SS640                    Pietraperzia

**Canicatti**       Delia                   Barrafranca

SS122  Castrofilippo   SS190  Sommatino        SS191

**Naro**                              **Riesi**         **Mazzarino**

SS576   Campobello                                        San
Camastra  di Licata   **Ravanusa**                       Michele

        SS123    SS626d          SS626        SS190

**Palma di**                                Butera
**Montechiaro**
                                      SP8        SS117bis    **Niscemi**

                                    Il Castelluccio

**Licata**                    SS115          To Ragusa (58km);
        Falconara                            Modica (72km);
                                             Syracuse (140km)

                                    **Gela**

**SCALA DEI TURCHI**   p262

Swim off blinding white rock at this celebrated beauty spot

MEDITERRANEAN COAST

# MEDITERRANEAN COAST
## GETTING STARTED

## MAKING THE MOST OF YOUR TIME

Sicily's Mediterranean coast is an area of stark contrasts where spectacular ruins and fabulous beaches sit cheek-to-cheek with industrial sprawl and brutal modern development. Nowhere is this more evident than Agrigento, whose amazing Greek temples are overlooked by ranks of unsightly tower blocks. However, head west of Agrigento and you'll discover the development soon peters out and the landscape takes on a wilder, less contaminated aspect. Here you'll find some wonderful sandy beaches, particularly at the Riserva Naturale Torre Salsa and Eraclea Minoa, and tracts of beautiful, unspoilt countryside. Further west, the pretty spa town of Sciacca is well worth a day or two for its excellent seafood restaurants and handsome historic streets.

## TOP TRAVEL EXPERIENCES

**❦ GREEK TEMPLES**
Retrace the glories of Sicily's Greek past at Agrigento's Valley of the Temples. The temples, the best outside Greece, are what's left of ancient Akragas, once the Western world's fourth-largest city (p254).

**❦ SUN & SWIMMING**
For memorable swimming search out the Scala dei Turchi, a chalk-white natural staircase that leads down to beautiful crystalline waters. Further west, the beach at Eraclea Minoa is one of the coast's finest (p261).

**❦ CARNIVAL**
Known since ancient times for its thermal waters, Sciacca puts on one of the best carnival parties in Sicily, with parades of towering papier mâché caricatures and much eating and drinking (p266).

**❦ SEAFOOD**
Discover the delights of Sicily's spectacular seafood at the busy, workaday port of Licata, home to one of Sicily's top restaurants (p268).

MEDITERRANEAN COAST

# GETTING AWAY FROM IT ALL

The crowds generally stick to the coast, with attention concentrated on the main towns of Agrigento and Sciacca. Outside of high summer it never gets unbearably busy, but you can always find peace by heading inland.

* **Walk among mini-volcanoes** Just 15km north of Agrigento, the Riserva Naturale Macalube di Aragona is famous for its pint-size mud volcanoes (p260).

* **Clock the views from Caltabellotta** This towering hilltop town commands huge panoramic views (p266).

* **Admire artwork in Mazzarino** Visit the baroque churches in sleepy Mazzarino, many of which are decorated by the Tuscan artist Filippino Paladino (p269).

# ADVANCE PLANNING

There are several top experiences that you'd do well to book in advance.

* **A guide at the Valley of the Temples** You don't need a guide for the temples but if you want one, you can organise it before arriving (see the boxed text, p257).

* **Spa treatment at Sciacca** Sciacca's thermal waters are big business, so it pays to arrange an appointment if you want to pamper yourself (p265).

* **Sciacca's carnival** One of Sicily's top events, Sciacca's carnival celebrations attract huge crowds, putting pressure on the town's limited accommodation. Get in early to avoid disappointment (p266).

* **Ristorante La Madia** Licata's acclaimed restaurant is one of Sicily's finest, so make reservations (p268).

# TOP RESTAURANTS

**🍴 RISTORANTE LA MADIA**
Dine on creative regional cuisine at Licata's gastronomic hot spot (p268).

----

**🍴 LEON D'ORO**
Locals love this Agrigento restaurant for its seafood and fine wine (p260).

----

**🍴 LA LAMPARA**
A smart modern restaurant serving seafood in Sciacca (p265).

----

**🍴 IL DÉHORS**
Diners are treated to sophisticated cuisine and views of the Valley of the Temples (p259).

----

**🍴 TRATTORIA AL FARO**
Fresh fish portside in Sciacca together with a laid-back trattoria vibe (p266).

----

# RESOURCES

* **Grand Hotel delle Terme** (www.grand hoteldelleterme.com, in Italian) Details on the spa treatments (plus costs) available in Sciacca.

* **Parco Valle dei Templi** (www.parcovalle deitempli.it) Official website of the Valley of the Temples.

* **Servizio Turistico Regionale Sciacca** (www.servizioturisticoregionalesciacca.it) Sciacca carnival programs, accommodation listings, histories and itineraries.

* **Valle dei Templi** (www.lavalledeitempli. it) Up-to-date information on the Valley of the Temples, its guides, opening hours etc.

*(Continued from page 249)*

The Valley of the Temples is about 3km below the modern town: from Piazza Marconi take Via Francesco Crispi and Via Panoramica Valle dei Templi for the Valley's eastern entrance and car park.

# EXPLORING AGRIGENTO

### ❦ VALLEY OF THE TEMPLES (VALLE DEI TEMPLI) // APPLAUD THE EXTRAORDINARY BEAUTY OF AGRIGENTO'S GREEK TEMPLES

One of southern Europe's most compelling archaeological sites, the 1300-hectare

**Parco Valle dei Templi** (Map p256; ☎ 0922 62 16 11; adult/EU under 18yr & over 65yr/EU 18-25yr incl Quartiere Ellenistico-Romano €10/free/5; ⏰ eastern zone 8.30am-7pm, western zone 9am-7pm summer, 9am-5pm winter, eastern zone night visits 7.30-9.30pm Mon-Fri, 7.30-11.30pm Sat & Sun Jul-early Sep) encompasses the ruins of the ancient city of Akragas. The highlight is the stunning Tempio della Concordia, one of the best-preserved Greek temples in existence and one of a series built on a ridge to act as beacons for homecoming sailors.

The park is divided into two distinct areas – the eastern zone, where the most

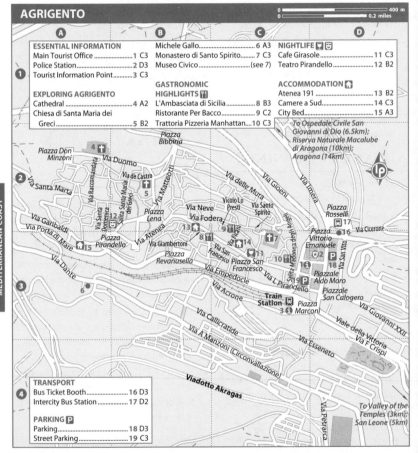

**AGRIGENTO**

0 — 400 m
0 — 0.2 miles

**ESSENTIAL INFORMATION**
Main Tourist Office ..................... 1 C3
Police Station ............................... 2 D3
Tourist Information Point .......... 3 C3

**EXPLORING AGRIGENTO**
Cathedral ...................................... 4 A2
Chiesa di Santa Maria dei
  Greci ........................................... 5 B2

Michele Gallo ............................... 6 A3
Monastero di Santo Spirito ...... 7 C3
Museo Civico .......................... (see 7)

**GASTRONOMIC HIGHLIGHTS** 🍴
L'Ambasciata di Sicilia ............... 8 B3
Ristorante Per Bacco .................. 9 C2
Trattoria Pizzeria Manhattan ...10 C3

**NIGHTLIFE** 🍷 🎭
Cafe Girasole ............................... 11 C3
Teatro Pirandello ....................... 12 B2

**ACCOMMODATION** 🏠
Atenea 191 ................................... 13 B2
Camere a Sud ............................... 14 C3
City Bed ........................................ 15 A3

**TRANSPORT**
Bus Ticket Booth ........................ 16 D3
Intercity Bus Station ................. 17 D2

**PARKING** 🅿
Parking ......................................... 18 D3
Street Parking ............................ 19 C3

## ACCOMMODATION

Agrigento is one of Sicily's major tourist destinations and the city reflects this with a wide range of accommodation. Elsewhere the choice is more limited, but there are some excellent B&Bs and *agriturismi* (farm stays).

★ An unexpected blast of contemporary art and style awaits at **FARM** (p319), a slick *agriturismo* near Butera.

★ Run by a friendly young couple, **Camere a Sud** (p318) offers fab B&B accommodation in Agrigento's historic centre.

★ Lie in the lap of luxury and look up to the Valley of the Temples from the refined **Hotel Villa Athena** (p319).

★ The pick of Sciacca's accommodation, **Al Moro** (p319) offers contemporary decor and a cracking location in the town's historic centre.

★ Housed in a tastefully converted stone farmstead, **Vecchia Masseria** (p319) is an elegant *agriturismo* in the heart of the countryside.

For detailed accommodation listings, see p318.

spectacular temples are, and, over the road, the western zone. There are two ticket offices, one at the park's eastern edge by the Tempio di Hera and another at Piazza Alexander Hardcastle on the main SS118 road between the two zones. The car park is by the eastern entrance.

### The Eastern Zone

If you only have time to explore part of the park, make it the eastern zone, where you'll find the park's three best-preserved temples. Overlooking the eastern ticket office, the 5th-century-BC **Tempio di Hera** (Temple of Hera), also known as the Tempio di Giunone (Temple of Juno), is perched on the edge of a ridge. Though partly destroyed by an earthquake in the Middle Ages, much of the colonnade remains intact as does a long altar, originally used for sacrifices. The traces of red are the result of fire damage, most likely during the Carthaginian invasion of 406 BC.

From here, the path continues westwards, past a gnarled 800-year-old olive tree and a series of Byzantine tombs built into the city walls, to the **Tempio della Concordia** (Temple of Concord). This remarkable edifice, the model for Unesco's logo, has survived almost entirely intact since it was constructed in 430 BC. There are several reasons why it has survived while other temples have not, one being that it was converted into a Christian basilica in the 6th century and the main structure was reinforced. The principle reason, however, is more down to earth. Beneath the hard rock on which the temple stands is a layer of soft clay that acts as a kind of natural shock absorber, protecting it from earthquake tremors. Whether the Greek engineers knew this when they built the temple is the subject of debate but modern scholars tend to think that they did. In 1748 the temple was restored to its original form and given the name it's now known by.

The last of the zone's temples, the **Tempio di Ercole** (Temple of Hercules), is the oldest, dating from the end of 6 BC.

MEDITERRANEAN COAST

Eight of its 38 columns have been raised and you can wander around the remains of the rest.

Down from the main temples, you can see a little temple set on a high base. This is known as the **Tomba di Terone** (Tomb of Theron), although it dates to 75 BC, about 500 years after the death of Theron, Agrigento's Greek tyrant.

### The Western Zone

The main feature of the western zone is the crumbled ruin of the **Tempio di Giove** (Temple of Olympian Zeus). Covering an area of 112m by 56m with columns 20m high, this would have been the largest Doric temple ever built had its construction not been interrupted by the Carthaginians sacking Akragas. The incomplete temple was later destroyed by an earthquake. Lying flat on his back amid the rubble is an 8m-tall telamon (a sculpted figure of a man with arms raised), originally intended to support the temple's weight. It's actually a copy of the original, which is in the Museo Archeologico.

A short hop away, four columns mark the **Tempio dei Dioscuri** (Temple of

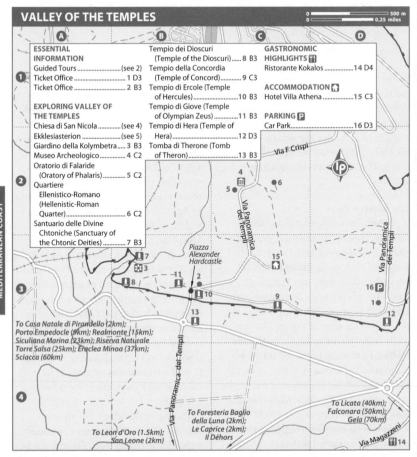

**VALLEY OF THE TEMPLES**

0 — 500 m
0 — 0.25 miles

**ESSENTIAL INFORMATION**
Guided Tours .............................(see 2)
Ticket Office ................................. 1 D3
Ticket Office ................................. 2 B3

**EXPLORING VALLEY OF THE TEMPLES**
Chiesa di San Nicola ..............(see 4)
Ekklesiasterion ........................(see 5)
Giardino della Kolymbetra..... 3 B3
Museo Archeologico...............4 C2
Oratorio di Falaride
   (Oratory of Phalaris) .............5 C2
Quartiere Ellenistico-Romano
   (Hellenistic-Roman Quarter)....................6 C2
Santuario delle Divine Chtoniche (Sanctuary of the Chtonic Deities) .............7 B3

Tempio dei Dioscuri
   (Temple of the Dioscuri)......8 B3
Tempio della Concordia
   (Temple of Concord)............9 C3
Tempio di Ercole (Temple of Hercules)..........................10 B3
Tempio di Giove (Temple of Olympian Zeus) ...............11 B3
Tempio di Hera (Temple of Hera)................................12 D3
Tomba di Therone (Tomb of Theron)..........................13 B3

**GASTRONOMIC HIGHLIGHTS**
Ristorante Kokalos .................14 D4

**ACCOMMODATION**
Hotel Villa Athena .................15 C3

**PARKING**
Car Park....................................16 D3

Via F. Crispi

Piazza Alexander Hardcastle

Via Panoramica dei Templi

Via Panoramica dei Templi

To Casa Natale di Pirandello (2km);
Porto Empedocle (9km); Realmonte (15km);
Siculiana Marina (23km); Riserva Naturale
Torre Salsa (25km); Eraclea Minoa (37km);
Sciacca (60km)

Via Panoramica dei Templi

To Foresteria Baglio della Luna (2km);
Le Caprice (2km);
Il Déhors

To Leon d'Oro (1.5km);
San Leone (2km)

To Licata (40km);
Falconara (50km);
Gela (70km)

Via Magazzeni
14

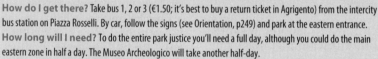

## VALLEY OF THE TEMPLES FAQS

**How do I get there?** Take bus 1, 2 or 3 (€1.50; it's best to buy a return ticket in Agrigento) from the intercity bus station on Piazza Rosselli. By car, follow the signs (see Orientation, p249) and park at the eastern entrance.

**How long will I need?** To do the entire park justice you'll need a full day, although you could do the main eastern zone in half a day. The Museo Archeologico will take another half-day.

**When's the best time of day to visit?** In summer it gets very busy, so try to arrive early. Alternatively, early evening is another good time as it's cooler and the temples take on a lovely golden hue. Note also that between July and early September the eastern zone of the park is open for night visits from 7.30pm to 9.30pm Monday to Friday, and 7.30pm to 11.30pm Saturday and Sunday.

**What will I need to bring?** It gets extremely hot in June, July and August, so make sure you have a hat, sunscreen and plenty of water. A torch (flashlight) is useful for night visits, and remember that if you want to claim a ticket discount you'll need a passport or ID card as proof of age.

**Is it worth getting a guide?** Your call, but a good guide can make the difference between an interesting visit and a memorable one. For more details, see p258.

**Where can I get good online information?** You'll find up-to-date practical information at www.parcovalledeitempli.it and www.lavalledeitempli.it.

the Dioscuri, or Temple of Castor and Pollux), a 5th-century-BC temple that was destroyed by earthquake and partially rebuilt in the 19th century. Just behind is a complex of altars and small buildings believed to be part of the 6th-century-BC **Santuario delle Divine Chtoniche** (Sanctuary of the Chthonic Deities).

In a natural cleft near the sanctuary is the **Giardino della Kolymbetra** (Kolymbethra Garden; adult/child €2/1; 🕙 10am-5pm Oct-Mar, 10am-6pm Apr-Jun, 10am-7pm Jul-Sep), a lush garden with more than 300 (labelled) species of plants and some welcome picnic tables. Note, however, that it's a steep climb down to the garden, best avoided if you've got dicky knees.

### 🌿 MUSEO ARCHEOLOGICO // POUR OVER ARTEFACTS UNEARTHED IN THE VALLEY

About halfway between Agrigento's town centre and the Valley of the Temples, the **Museo Archeologico** (Map p256; ☎ 0922 40 15 65; Contrada San Nicola 12; adult/EU under 18yr & over 65yr/EU 18-25yr €8/free/4; 🕙 9.30am-7pm Tue-Sat, 9am-1pm Sun & Mon) houses a comprehensive collection of artefacts from ancient Akragas and sites in the Agrigento area. In *sala* (room) 3 there are some wonderful ceramics in black and red dating from the 6th to the 3rd centuries BC, including an outstanding *krater*, a red ceramic chalice from 490 BC. Further highlights include the 7.75m-tall telamon in *sala* 6, originally part of the Tempio di Giove, and, in *sala* 9, a fine marble *ephebus* (a statue of a young boy), sculpted in 470 BC.

In the museum's grounds is the 13th-century **Chiesa di San Nicola**, which has a fine Gothic doorway, and, on the church's esplanade, a 3rd-century-BC open-air meeting space called the **Ekklesiasterion**. Alongside this is the **Oratorio di Falaride** (Oratory of Phalaris), a temple dating from the 1st century BC, which was later converted into an oratory.

Located over the road from the museum, the **Quartiere Ellenistico-Romano** (Hellenistic-Roman Quarter; admission with ticket to Parco Valle dei Templi; 🕙 8.30am-7pm) is a residential quarter from ancient Akragas where about 20 houses have been unearthed.

❧ THE TOWN CENTRE // WANDER ALONG THE WINDING LANES OF AGRIGENTO'S MEDIEVAL CORE

Agrigento's lively, medieval centre is centred on Via Atenea, an attractive strip lined with smart shops, trattorias and bars. From the street, claustrophobic alleyways wind upwards through tightly packed palazzi to the city's magnificent cathedral (Map p254; Via Duomo; ⊗ 9.30am-12.30pm & 4-6pm). A striking 11th-century church much altered over the centuries – the unfinished bell tower was added in the 1400s – it boasts a wonderful Norman ceiling and a mysterious letter from the Devil. Old Nick is reputed to have tried to lure the Virgin of Agrigento into temptation by writing to her promising her all the treasure in the world. The Virgin was having none of it, though, and she dobbed him in to the priest, who still holds this mysterious missive.

Downhill from the cathedral, the small Chiesa di Santa Maria dei Greci (Map p254; ⊗ 9am-1pm & 4-7pm Mon-Sat) stands on the site of a 5th-century Doric temple dedicated to Athena. Inside are some badly damaged Byzantine frescoes and the remains of the original Norman ceiling.

Back towards Piazzale Aldo Moro, at the top of a set of steps off Via Atenea, the Monastero di Santo Spirito (Monastery of the Holy Spirit; Map p254; Via Santo Spirito) was founded by Cistercian nuns around 1290. A handsome Gothic portal leads inside, where the nuns are still in residence, praying, meditating and baking heavenly pastries, including *dolci di mandorla* (almond pastries), pistachio *cuscusu* and *bucellati* (rolled sweet dough with figs). To buy some, press the doorbell, say 'Vorrei comprare qualche dolci' (I'd like to buy a few cakes) and see how you go.

Upstairs, the small Museo Civico (Map p254; ☎ 0922 40 14 50; admission €2.50; ⊗ 9am-1pm & 3-6pm Mon-Fri, 9am-1pm Sat) is worth a quick visit as much for the views over the Valley of the Temples as its poorly labelled miscellany of objects.

## FESTIVALS & EVENTS

Sagra del Mandorlo in Fiore (Festival of the Almond Blossom; www.mandorloinfiore.net) The city's big annual shindig is a folk festival, celebrated on the first Sunday of February, when the Valley of the Temples is cloaked in almond blossoms.

Festa di San Calogero (Feast of St Calogero) A week-long festival during which the statue of St Calogero, who saved Agrigento from the plague, is carried through the town while spectators throw loaves of spiced bread at the saint. Begins on the first Sunday in July.

## GUIDES

You don't need to be an archaeologist to appreciate the Valley's temples, but a guide can really bring its drama to life. Agrigento's main tourist office can provide you with a list of multilingual guides, otherwise you can arrange one at the main entrance to the archaeological park. The official rate is €140 for half a day. Two excellent English-speaking guides are Michele Gallo ( ☎ 0922 40 22 57, 360 397930; www.sicilytravel.net) and Luigi Napoli ( ☎ 0922 2 91 41, 333 5498963; www.luiginapoli.tk), a native-born Agrigentan whose knowledge of the temples is only surpassed by his enthusiasm and mastery of idiomatic English. Both offer individual and group tours of the temples, and can organise visits to areas of interest further afield.

## SHH! WE'RE IN A CHURCH!

By virtue of a remarkable acoustic phenomenon known as *il portavoce* (the carrying voice), even the faintest sound carries in Agrigento's cathedral, but the system only seems to work in the favour of the priest standing in the apse. Should any parishioner whisper in the back row near the cathedral door, the priest can hear their every word even though he's standing some 85m away!

# GASTRONOMIC HIGHLIGHTS

There are a few excellent trattorias up in Agrigento's historic centre but many of the smarter restaurants are dotted around the area between the Valley of the Temples and San Leone on the sea. Agrigento itself is famous for the unctuous Arab sweet *cuscusu* (looks like semolina couscous but is made of almonds and pistachio).

## TOWN CENTRE

### 🍽 L'AMBASCIATA DI SICILIA €

Map p254; ☎ 0922 2 05 26; Via Giambertoni 2; meals €20-25; 🕑 closed Sun

For memorable floodlit views of the Valley of the Temples, pull up a chair on the terrace of this trattoria just off central Via Atenea. The 'Sicilian Embassy' is one of Agrigento's longest-standing trattorias, a modest eatery with a small, twee interior, a few outdoor tables – the better option – and a traditional menu offering the likes of rustic antipasto, spaghetti with pistachio nuts and *involtini* (meat rolls).

### 🍽 RISTORANTE PER BACCO €€

Map p254; ☎ 0922 55 33 69; Vicolo Lo Presti 2; meals €30; 🕑 closed Mon

This is one of the better restaurants signposted off Via Atenea. Behind the wooden door is a barnlike dining hall with wood beams, brick arches and an incongruous picture of a half-naked girl behind the long bar. The onus is on seafood – *spaghetti ai frutti di mare* (seafood spaghetti) is a good bet – but there are some excellent nonfish options, including a filling *fusilli* (corkscrews of pasta) with bacon, tomato, courgette (zucchini) and chilli.

### 🍽 TRATTORIA PIZZERIA MANHATTAN €

Map p254; ☎ 0922 2 09 11; Salita Madonna degli Angeli; set menu meat/fish €15/18; 🕑 closed Sun

On first appearance, this trattoria looks no different from others in these parts – menu posted outside, simple interior, no frills. Yet, come lunch time there are queues to get in. The reason is the excellent value-for-money food. There are two set menus (fish or meat), or you can order from the regular menu. And it's good, too, as you'll discover if you order *spaghetti alla siciliana* (spaghetti with tomato, aubergine/eggplant, basil and ricotta).

## VALLEY OF THE TEMPLES

### 🍽 IL DÉHORS €€€

off Map p256; ☎ 0922 51 10 61; Contrada Maddalusa; meals €40; 🕑 closed Mon

The restaurant of the Foresteria Baglio della Luna (see p319) is an elegant fine-dining establishment offering innovative Sicilian cuisine and views over the Valley of the Temples. Fresh local seafood features heavily, appearing in sophisticated creations such as sea bream with pecorino cheese and aubergine tartare or grilled tuna with mint couscous and pepper sauce. Reservations required.

### 🍽 LE CAPRICE €€

off Map p256; ☎ 0922 41 13 64; Via Cavaleri Magazzeni; meals €30-35; 🕑 closed Mon

Long considered one of Agrigento's better restaurants, Le Caprice is set in its own park complete with pool and swans. It's a big place – it can cater to around 500 people – renowned for its swimmingly fresh seafood. Start with a plate from the lush antipasto buffet before diving into the restaurant's signature dish, mixed seafood grill. A glass of cool local white is the perfect accompaniment.

### ♣ LEON D'ORO €€

off Map p256; ☎ 0922 41 44 00; Viale Emporium 102; meals €35; ⦿ closed Mon

Everyone in Agrigento knows Leon d'Oro. A much-lauded local favourite, it specialises in the fish and fowl that typify Agrigento's cuisine. The menu is in local dialect, in keeping with the rustic ambience, but dishes to look out for include *baccalà* (salted cod) with potatoes and *calamari su agrumi* (cuttlefish served with local citrus fruits). Owner Totò also keeps an exceptional cellar and is more than happy to advise on wine choices.

### ♣ RISORANTE KOKALOS €€

Map p256; ☎ 0922 60 64 27; Viale Magazzeni 3; pizzas from €6, meals €25-30

Looking all the world like a Wild West ranch, this restaurant-cum-pizzeria enjoys an excellent local reputation for its value-for-money food and delicious wood-fired pizzas. You'll need a car to get here – it's up a dusty track off the road to San Leone – but once ensconced on the summer terrace you can sit back and enjoy a *margherita* (pizza with tomato, mozzarella and basil) followed by *semifreddo alle mandorle* (an almond ice-cream dessert).

## NIGHTLIFE

### ♣ CAFÉ GIRASOLE

Map p254; Via Atenea 68-70; ⦿ closed Sun

By day this popular cafe-cum-wine-bar does brisk business serving coffee and *panini* to working locals, but in the evening it morphs into a trendy hangout for the 30-something aperitif set who stop by for cocktails and table snacks. It has a good atmosphere and outdoor seating on central Via Atenea.

### ♣ TEATRO PIRANDELLO

Map p254; ☎ 0922 59 03 60; Piazza Pirandello; tickets €7-20

Run by the Comune di Agrigento, this is the third-largest theatre in Sicily after the Teatro Massimo in Palermo and Catania's Teatro Massimo Bellini. The program, which runs from November to April, is largely given over to works

---

### ∼ WORTH A TRIP ∼

Some 15km north of Agrigento, near the town of Aragona, the **Vulcanelli di Macalube** are a bizarre and fascinating sight. A series of metre-high mud volcanoes rising out of a barren expanse of cracked mud, they are the result of a rare geological phenomenon known as sedimentary volcanism. This is a process by which pressurised natural gas, in this case methane, forces underground soils to explode through the earth's surface. Once on the surface, the bubbling mud dries in the sun, thus creating the pint-sized volcanoes.

The *vulcanelli* are now part of the **Riserva Naturale Macalube di Aragona** (☎ 0922 69 92 10; www.macalife.it; admission free; ⦿ 9am-7pm), managed by Legambiente, Italy's main environmental organisation. To get to the site you will need your own transport – there are buses from Agrigento to Aragona but that still leaves you 4km short of the reserve.

by local hero Luigi Pirandello, but you'll also find the odd musical thrown in. Ask at the main tourist office for program details and information about ticket purchase.

## TRANSPORT

**BUS //** For most destinations, the bus is the easiest way to get to Agrigento. The intercity bus station (Map p254) and ticket booths are on Piazza Rosselli, just off Piazza Vittorio Emanuele. **Cuffaro** ( ☎ 0922 91 63 44; www. cuffaro.info) runs services to Palermo (€8.10, two hours, nine daily Monday to Saturday, three Sunday). **SAIS Trasporti** ( ☎ 0922 2 93 24; www.saistrasporti.it) runs buses to Catania and Catania airport (€12.20, three hours, at least 10 daily) and Caltanissetta (€5.80, 1¼ hours, at least 10 daily). **SAL** ( ☎ 0922 40 13 60; www. autolineesal.it) serves Palermo's Falcone-Borsellino airport (€11.50, 2½ hours).

**CAR //** Agrigento is easily accessible by road from all of Sicily's main towns. The SS189 and SS121 connect with Palermo, while the SS115 runs along the coast. For Enna, take the SS640 via Caltanissetta. In town, Via Atenea, the main street in the historic centre, is closed to traffic from 9am to 8pm.

**PARKING //** Parking is a nightmare in Agrigento. There's metered parking at Piazza Vittorio Emanuele and on the streets around Piazzale Aldo Moro, although you'll have to arrive early to find a space.

**TRAIN //** Trains run regularly to/from Palermo (€7.90, 2½ hours, 11 daily). There are also two daily direct trains to/from Catania (€11.10, four hours). The train station has left-luggage lockers (per 12 hours €2.50).

# WEST OF AGRIGENTO

· · · · ·

The main SS115 road follows the coast westwards from Agrigento, passing through some fine countryside as it runs on to the historic spa town of Sciacca. En route you'll pass a number of excellent sandy beaches, a nature reserve and what is left of an ancient Greek town that was supposedly founded by the Cretan king Minos, the man behind the Minotaur myth.

## AGRIGENTO TO SCIACCA

❤ CASA NATALE DI PIRANDELLO //
PAY HOMAGE TO LITERARY GENIUS
AT PIRANDELLO'S BIRTHPLACE
Southwest of Agrigento in the suburb of Caos, about 2km along the SS115 to Porto Empedocle, is the Casa Natale di Pirandello ( ☎ 0922 51 18 26; admission €2; ⊙ 9am-1pm & 3-7pm), birthplace of Luigi Pirandello (1867–1936). One of the giants of modern Italian literature, and winner of the 1934 Nobel Prize for Literature, Pirandello started his career writing short stories and novels, but is best known as a playwright, author of masterpieces such as *Sei personaggi in ricerca di un autore* (Six Characters in Search of an Author) and *Enrico IV* (Henry IV).

He left Agrigento as a young man but returned most summers to spend time at the family villa, which is now a small museum, stacked full of first editions, photographs, reviews and theatre bills. Pirandello's ashes are kept in an urn buried at the foot of a pine tree in the garden.

Just a few kilometres down the road, Porto Empedocle, the main port for ferries to the Pelagic Islands, has its own literary claim to fame. Andrea Camilleri, Italy's most popular living author and creator of Inspector Montalbano, was born here in 1925.

❤ BEACHES & BEAUTY SPOTS //
SEARCH OUT SANDY BEACHES AND
PANORAMIC PATHS
The nearest beach to Agrigento is at San Leone, the town's vivacious seafront satellite. However, with your own wheels you'll find some stunning spots further west along the SS115.

MEDITERRANEAN COAST

One of the most beautiful, and least publicised, sights in the Agrigento area is the Scala dei Turchi. This is a blindingly white rock shaped like a giant staircase that juts out into the sea near the small town of Realmonte, 15km west of Agrigento. Named after the Arab and Turkish pirates who used to hide out from stormy weather here, it's a popular spot with local sunseekers who come to sunbathe on the milky-smooth rock and swim in the indigo sea. Take a picnic to make a full day of it, otherwise you can lunch at the Lido Scala dei Turchi at the top of the steps down to the beach.

A further 5km or so west of Realmonte, there's a great sandy beach at Siciliana Marina and lovely walking at the WWF-administered Riserva Naturale Torre Salsa (www.wwftorresalsa.it), where well-marked trails offer sweeping panoramic views of the surrounding mountains and coast. A good place to cool off is the beautiful Torre Salsa beach, accessed from the reserve's northern entrance.

🌱 ERACLEA MINOA // EXPLORE THE SCENIC RUINS OF A MYTHICAL GREEK CITY

Nowadays a small summer resort – empty for most of the year, packed in July and August – Eraclea Minoa was an important Greek settlement in ancient times. According to legend it was originally founded by the Cretan king Minos who came to Sicily in pursuit of Daedalus, a former favourite who had fallen out of grace and escaped from Crete. Historical evidence suggests the city was established by Greek colonists in the 6th century BC and went on to flourish in the 4th and 5th centuries. The scant remains of the city can now be seen at the archaeological park (admission €4; 🕙 9am-1hr before sunset Mon-Sat) on a headland back from the main seafront village. The ruins are relatively scarce – the crumbling remains of the soft sandstone theatre are covered with protective plastic – but the views and singing scrub are gorgeous.

## LAMPEDUSA

Lampedusa, the largest of the three Pelagic Islands (the other two are Linosa and Lampione), lies 205km south of Sicily, closer to Tunisia than Italy. Surrounded by stunning aquamarine waters, it's a popular summer holiday destination whose year-round population of 6100 more than trebles in July and August. In winter transport connections are cut back to a bare minimum and almost every hotel and restaurant shuts up shop.

The island's single main attraction is its beaches, which are strung along the 11km south coast. The most famous, and one of the Mediterranean's most beautiful, is Spiaggia dei Conigli (aka Rabbit Beach) at Isola dei Conigli, a dreamy secluded bay lapped by shallow, turquoise waters. The beach is part of a unique nature reserve, the only place in Italy where *Caretta caretta* (loggerhead sea turtles) lay their eggs (between July and August). Other beaches include Cala Francese, Cala Galera and Cala Greca.

Siremar ( ☎ 892123; www.siremar.it) runs year-round ferries to Lampedusa (€50.60, 8¼ hours) from Porto Empedocle. Then, between May and October, Ustica Lines ( ☎ 0923 87 38 13; www.usticalines.it) runs five weekly hydrofoils (€56.70, 4¼ hours). You can also fly directly to Lampedusa from Palermo and, in summer, from Rome, Milan, Verona and Bologna.

## TOP FIVE

### BEACHES

* ★ **Spiaggia dei Conigli** (p262) – a heavenly Lampedusa bay, one of the Med's finest swimming spots
* ★ **Torre Salsa** (p262) – six kilometres of sand, dunes and rocks in a protected nature reserve
* ★ **Scala dei Turchi** (p262) – a lick of ghostly wind-whipped white rock lapped by crystalline waters
* ★ **Eraclea Minoa** (p262) – popular sand beach backed by trees and chalk-white cliffs
* ★ **Falconara** (p268) – a lovely strip of sand overlooked by a 14th-century castle

Once you've done the history, head down to the beach, a wonderful, photogenic strip of golden sand backed by willowy eucalyptus trees, cypress groves and chalk cliffs. Here you can indulge in a refreshing facial massage. There's a natural mud rock at the western end of the beach, where you can scrape the mud off the rock and rub it onto your skin – you'll see all the locals doing the same. Dry off in the sun then rinse in the sea and you'll have removed 10 years in 10 minutes.

# SCIACCA

**pop 40,930**

Famous for its historic spas and flamboyant carnival celebrations, Sciacca is the main town on this stretch of the coast. It was founded in the 5th century BC as a thermal resort for nearby Selinunte and later flourished under the Saracens, who arrived in the 9th century and named it *Xacca* (meaning 'water' in Arabic), and

the Normans. Its healing waters continue to be the big drawcard, attracting coach-loads of Italian tourists who come to treat their assorted ailments in the sulphurous vapours and mineral-rich mud. Spas and thermal cures apart, it's a laid-back town with an attractive medieval core and some excellent seafood restaurants.

## ESSENTIAL INFORMATION

**EMERGENCIES //** Hospital ( ☎ 0925 96 21 11; Via Pompei) Police Station ( ☎ 0925 96 50 11; Via Jacopo Ruffini 12)

**TOURIST INFORMATION //** Tourist Office ( ☎ 0925 2 27 44; www.servizioturisticoregionale sciacca.it; Corso Vittorio Emanuele 84; ☽ 9am-2pm Mon-Fri, 3.30-6.30pm Wed) On the main strip, with helpful English-speaking staff.

## ORIENTATION

Sciacca still retains much of its medieval layout, which divided the town into quarters, each laid out on a strip of rock descending towards the sea. Today interest is mainly focused on the main artery, Corso Vittorio Emanuele, and the historic centre rising above it. About halfway along the street, Piazza Scandaliato is a popular hangout, with views (and stairs) down to the fishing harbour below.

## EXPLORING SCIACCA

♥ HISTORIC CENTRE // STROLL ALONG THE MEDIEVAL STREETS, ADMIRING ELEGANT PALAZZI

The place to start is Sciacca's main street, Corso Vittorio Emanuele, an attractive strip lined with impressive palazzi, ceramic shops and some interesting churches. At the western end, Palazzo Steripinto is an imposing example of 16th-century Catalan Gothic architecture, recognisable by its ashlar rustication and twin-mullioned windows. Just to the south, near Porta San Salvatore, are two interesting churches: the 14th-century **Chiesa di Santa Margherita**, which features a superb Renaissance portal and a rather chipped baroque interior; and the **Chiesa del Carmine**, whose odd-looking 13th-century rose window predates the majolica-tiled dome by some 600 years.

Continuing east along Corso Vittorio Emanuele brings you to **Piazza Scandaliato**, the sloping piazza opposite the tourist office. Here you can hang out with the locals, perhaps over a coffee or lemon *granita* (crushed-ice drink) at the **Gran Caffè Scandaglia** ( ☎ 0925 2 10 82; Piazza Scandaliato 5-6), watching the world go by and discussing the events of the day. The square's western end is formed by the **Chiesa di San Domenico**, an 18th-century reconstruction of a 16th-century church.

Further east, **Piazza Duomo** is home to Sciacca's handsome **Chiesa Madre** (Piazza Duomo; ☺ 8am-noon & 4.30-7.30pm). First erected in 1108, it was rebuilt in 1656, incorporating three apses from the original Norman structure and adding a never-completed facade.

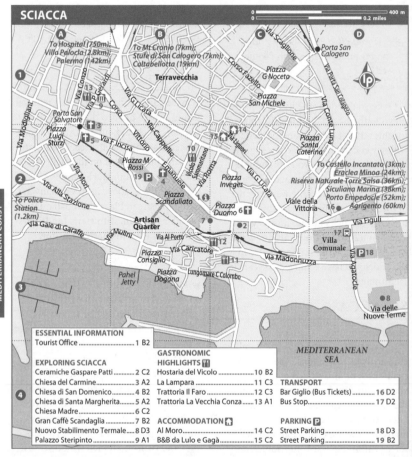

## SCIACCA

**ESSENTIAL INFORMATION**

Tourist Office ......................................... 1 B2

**EXPLORING SCIACCA**

| | | |
|---|---|---|
| Ceramiche Gaspare Patti | 2 | C2 |
| Chiesa del Carmine | 3 | A2 |
| Chiesa di San Domenico | 4 | B2 |
| Chiesa di Santa Margherita | 5 | A2 |
| Chiesa Madre | 6 | C2 |
| Gran Caffè Scandaglia | 7 | B2 |
| Nuovo Stabilimento Termale | 8 | D3 |
| Palazzo Steripinto | 9 | A1 |

**GASTRONOMIC HIGHLIGHTS** 🍴

| | | |
|---|---|---|
| Hostaria del Vicolo | 10 | B2 |
| La Lampara | 11 | C3 |
| Trattoria Il Faro | 12 | C3 |
| Trattoria La Vecchia Conza | 13 | A1 |

**ACCOMMODATION** 🏠

| | | |
|---|---|---|
| Al Moro | 14 | C2 |
| B&B da Lulo e Gagà | 15 | C2 |

*MEDITERRANEAN SEA*

**TRANSPORT**

| | | |
|---|---|---|
| Bar Giglio (Bus Tickets) | 16 | D2 |
| Bus Stop | 17 | D2 |

**PARKING** 🅿

| | | |
|---|---|---|
| Street Parking | 18 | D3 |
| Street Parking | 19 | B2 |

### ❤ CERAMICHE GASPARE PATTI //
**PICK OUT A CERAMIC KEEPSAKE**

Sciacca has a long-standing tradition of ceramic production and there are numerous shops selling brightly coloured crockery. For something more original look up **Ceramiche Gaspare Patti** ( ☎ 0925 99 32 98; Corso Vittorio Emanuele 95), an Aladdin's cave of a shop in front of the Chiesa Madre. Gaspare Patti prides himself on his idiosyncratic style and his shop is packed with strange and original creations, well worth a look even if you're not going to buy.

### ❤ SPA TREATMENTS // **PAMPER YOURSELF WITH A MASSAGE AND MUDPACK**

The place to take the waters in town is the **Nuovo Stabilimento Termale** ( ☎ 0925 96 11 11; www.grandhoteldelleterme.com, in Italian; Via Agatocle 2), a thermal-baths complex next door to the Grand Hotel delle Terme. Here you can indulge in a vast range of treatments, including shiatsu massages, mudpacks and hydrotherapy in a 32°C pool. Prices range from €32 for a straightforward facial to €197 for an uplifting 50-minute breast-toning treatment. With your own car you could also head up to Monte Cronio, 7km out of town, to breathe the natural cave vapours of the **Stufe di San Calogero** ( ☎ 0925 2 61 53).

### ❤ CASTELLO INCANTATO //
**PONDER THE BIZARRE WORKS OF A MADCAP LOCAL ARTIST**

About 3km east of town, the **Castello Incanato** (Enchanted Castle; ☎ 0925 99 30 44; www.castelloincantato.net; admission €3; ☽ 9am-1pm & 4-8pm Tue-Sat summer, 9am-1pm & 3-5pm Tue-Sun winter) is actually a large park festooned with thousands of sculpted heads. The man behind this bizarre collection was Filippo Bentivegna (1888–1967), a local artist who used sculpture to exorcise the memories of an unhappy sojourn in the USA – each head is supposed to represent one of his memories. His eccentricities were legion and still today people enjoy recalling them. Apparently, he regarded his work as a sexual act and demanded to be addressed as '*Eccellenza*' (Your Excellency).

## GASTRONOMIC HIGHLIGHTS

Seafood is the big thing here, with a number of excellent restaurants down by the port.

### ❤ HOSTARIA DEL VICOLO €€€
☎ 0925 2 30 71; www.hostariadelvicolo.it; Vicolo Sammaritano 10; meals €45; ☽ closed Sun evening & Mon
Tucked away in a tiny alley in the old town, this formal restaurant is a culinary *tour de force*: heavy tablecloths, noiseless service and an ample wine list. The menu is traditional Sicilian with modern twists, and the fresh pasta is great. For a *primo* (first course) try the *taglioni al nero di seppia e ricotta salata* (flat strings of pasta with cuttlefish ink and salted ricotta), while *merluzzo ai fichi secchi* (cod with dried figs) makes for a superb main course.

### ❤ LA LAMPARA €€
☎ 0925 8 50 85; Via Caricatore 33; meals €35; ☽ closed Mon
In contrast with the scruffy portside streets, La Lampara is a modish, contemporary restaurant serving a modern, creative fish menu. Not all the dishes work – for €10 you'd expect more from the prawn salad starter – but those that do (and that's most of them) are excellent. Highly recommended is the tuna steak, cooked in

MEDITERRANEAN COAST

## SCIACCA CARNIVAL

Sciacca's carnival is famed throughout Sicily for its flamboyance and fabulous party atmosphere. Held between the last Thursday before Lent and Shrove Tuesday, and repeated in mid-May, it features an amazing parade of huge papier mâché figures mounted on floats.

The festival opens with carnival king Peppi Nappa receiving the city's keys. The technicolour floats are then released into the streets with their bizarre cast of grotesque caricatures – the figures are handmade each year according to traditional methods and modelled on political and social personalities. The floats go around the winding streets of the old town, while masked men and women dance to locally composed music and satirical poetry is read aloud.

sesame seeds and served with balsamic vinegar, and the chocolate cake with pistachio ice cream.

#### ♥ TRATTORIA AL FARO €
☎ 0925 2 53 49; Via Al Porto 25; set menus €17.50-25; ✢ closed Sun

If the idea of budget seafood usually sets alarm bells ringing, think again. This welcoming portside trattoria is one of the few places where you can feast on delicious fresh fish and still get change from €20. You won't get much variety – what's served depends on what the boats have brought in – but tasty staples to look out for include *pasta con le sarde* (with sardines, fennel, breadcrumbs and raisins) and grilled *calamari* (cuttlefish). Slow Food Movement recommended.

#### ♥ TRATTORIA LA VECCHIA CONZA €€
☎ 0925 2 53 85; Via Gerardi 39; meals €25-30; ✢ closed Mon

Near the medieval Porta San Salvatore, this laid-back eatery is popular with lunching locals. It's decked out in typical trattoria style with brick arches and hanging ceramics and serves a predominantly fish-based menu. Follow an antipasto of *polpettine di acciughe* (anchovy balls) with delicious *risotto alla marinara in salsa zafferano* (risotto with seafood in a saffron sauce).

### TRANSPORT

**BUS //** Lumia (☎ 0922 2 04 14; www.autolinee lumia.it) serves Agrigento (€6, 1¾ hours, 11 daily Monday to Saturday, two Sunday) and Trapani (€8.30, four hours, three daily Monday to Saturday, one Sunday). All buses arrive at the Villa Comunale on Via Figuli and leave from Via Agatocle. Buy your tickets at Bar Giglio at Viale della Vittoria 22.

**CAR //** Sciacca is about 60km from Agrigento along the SS115.

**PARKING //** There's parking on Via Agatocle near the Nuovo Stabilimento Termale and on the unnamed piazza beneath Piazza Scandaliato.

## AROUND SCIACCA

#### ♥ CALTABELLOTTA // FEAST ON PANORAMIC VIEWS FROM THIS HILLTOP VILLAGE

It's quite a drive up to Caltabellotta. Not so much because of the distances involved – it's only 19km northeast of Sciacca – but because the road rises almost vertically as it winds its way up to the hilltop village at 949m above sea level. But make it to the top and you're rewarded with some amazing panoramic views of 21 (apparently) surrounding villages. The highest vantage point is the ruined Norman castle at the top of the village, where a peace treaty was signed in 1302 ending the Sicilian Vespers. Viewed from here, the town's terracotta roofs and

MEDITERRANEAN COAST

grey houses appear to cling to the cliffside like a perfect mosaic. Below the castle, the restored Chiesa Madre retains an original Gothic portal and pointed arches. On the edge of the village lies the derelict monastery of San Pellegrino, from where you can see caves that were used as tombs as far back as prehistoric times.

If you're without a car, Lumia buses serve Caltabellotta from Sciacca (€2.60, 50 minutes, four daily Monday to Friday).

# EAST OF AGRIGENTO

· · · · · ·

**The area east of Agrigento is one of marked contrasts. Located only a few kilometres inland from the industrial horror show that surrounds Gela and you're in another world, a silent, rural world of green fields, hills and sleepy medieval towns. The coast is surprisingly free of tourist development and with your own transport you'll find some wild, unspoilt beaches.**

## GELA

pop 77,115

Despite a distinguished past as one of Sicily's great ancient cities, modern Gela is a disappointment, a chaotic industrial city with a reputation as a mafia hot spot. Little remains of its heyday as the economic engine room of the great Greek colony that eventually founded Akragas, Eraclea Minoa and Selinunte. The city was sacked by Carthage in 405 BC and then razed to the ground by forces from Agrigento in 282 BC. More recently it was the first Italian town to be liberated by the Allies in WWII (in July 1943), but not before it had been bombed to rubble in the build-up to the invasion. Post-war development

saw the construction of the vast petrochemical refineries that still blight the city and swathes of cheap housing blocks. Other than a fascinating archaeology museum and remains of the city's ancient fortifications, there are no real sights and no compelling reasons to stop by.

### ORIENTATION

If driving, follow signs for the town centre and museum, which is at the eastern end of Corso Vittorio Emanuele, the town's principal east–west street. A few blocks below the corso, the never-ending seafront is lined with bars, pizzerias and restaurants.

### EXPLORING GELA

❦ **MUSEO ARCHEOLOGICO // LOSE YOURSELF AMONG RELICS OF GELA'S ARTISTIC PAST**

The Museo Archeologico ( ☎ 0933 91 26 26; Corso Vittorio Emanuele; adult/concession incl acropoli & Capo Soprano €3/1.50; ◷ 9am-6pm, closed last Mon of month) is the only place offering an insight into Gela's great artistic past. It contains artefacts from the city's ancient acropolis and is rightly famed for its staggering collection of red-and-black *kraters* (vases used to mix wine and water), the largest such collection in the world. These terracotta vases were a local speciality between the 7th and 4th centuries BC, admired throughout the Greek world for the delicacy of their designs and superb figurative work. Other treasures include Italy's most important collection of ancient vases dating from the 8th to the 6th centuries, and some 600 silver coins minted in Agrigento, Gela, Syracuse, Messina and Athens. At one time the collection numbered over 1000 coins, but it was stolen in 1976 and only about half of it was ever recovered. More recently,

MEDITERRANEAN COAST

the city has acquired three unusual terra-cotta altars. These were found in 2003 in a 5th-century-BC warehouse, which had been buried under 6m of sand.

Outside the museum a gate leads through to a small **acropoli** (acropolis; adult/concession incl Museo Archeologico & Capo Soprano €3/1.50; ☉ 9am-1hr before sunset), where you can see the scant remains of the ancient Greek acropolis. Adding little to the atmosphere (at least little of any good) are the belching chimneys of a nearby petrochemical plant.

### ☙ CAPO SOPRANO // DIG AROUND GELA'S ANCIENT GREEK FORTIFICATIONS

At the western edge of town, some 4km west of the museum, you will find the remains of Gela's ancient **Greek fortifications** (adult/concession incl Museo Archeologico & acropoli €3/1.50; ☉ 9am-1hr before sunset) at Capo Soprano. Built by the tyrant of Syracuse, Timoleon, in 333 BC, they are in a remarkable state of preservation, most likely the result of being covered by sand dunes for thousands of years until they were discovered in 1948.

The 8m-high walls were built to prevent sand being blown into the city by the blustery sea wind. Today many of the walls are in ruins and the authorities have planted trees to act as a buffer against the encroaching sand. It makes for a pretty site, planted with mimosa and eucalyptus trees, perfect for a picnic. Some 500m from the walls, next to the hospital, are the ruins of Sicily's only surviving **Greek baths** (Via Europa; ☉ daily), which date to the 4th century BC.

### TRANSPORT

**BUS //** From Piazza Stazione, in front of the train station, there are regular buses to Agrigento and nearby towns, as well as Syracuse and Caltanissetta.

**CAR //** Gela is well connected by road: the SS115 leads westwards to Agrigento and east to Ragusa and Modica, while the SS117bis connects with Caltagirone (via the SS417) and Piazza Armerina.

# AROUND GELA

### ☙ FALCONARA // ESCAPE TO THE BEACH

In WWII Sicily's southern coast was heavily defended against the threat of an Allied invasion and still today abandoned pillbox defences litter the area around Gela. The best beaches are to the west of town beyond the so-called Gela Riviera, and are wild and unspoilt. At **Falconara**, 20km west of Gela, you can lay your towel out at a superb sandy beach overlooked by an impressive 14th-century castle, the **Castello di Falconara**. This is not open to the public as it's privately owned by an aristocratic family, but you can stay by booking through **I Castelli** ( ☎ 095 779 30 97; www.icastelli.net).

### ☙ LICATA // JOIN THE BUSTLE AND EAT IN STYLE

Some 10km or so down the SS115 is the workaday port of **Licata**. This doesn't look like much as you approach, but hidden behind the dreary suburbs is a charming, if rather worn, historic centre. The centre of action is **Piazza Progresso**, which divides the two main streets, Corso Roma, flanked by elegant baroque palazzi, and Corso Vittorio Emanuele.

At the top of town, a 16th-century **castle** affords views down to the harbour. Pleasant as it is wandering along Licata's bustling streets, the main reason to stop off here is to eat. For a memorable fine-dining experience, **Ristorante La Madia** ( ☎ 0922 77 14 43; www.ristorantelamadia.it; Via Filippo Re Capriata 22; meals €60; ☉ closed Tue) is a Michelin-starred restaurant considered one of Sicily's finest. A labour of love for local-born chef Pino Cuttaia, it serves modern Sicilian dishes based on authentic Mediterranean ingredients, such as *merluzzo* (code) smoked over pine cones or cuttlefish served with fennel cream. For something simpler, head to the **Hostaria L'Oste e il Sacrestano** ( ☎ 0922 77 47 36; Via Sant'Andrea 19; meals €30; ☺ closed Sun dinner & Mon), a Slow Food Movement recommended eatery just off Corso Vittorio Emanuele, where you can feast on local meats and freshly fished seafood.

Beyond Licata, the unexceptional town of **Palma di Montechiaro** is the ancestral seat of the princes of Lampedusa, made famous by Giuseppe Tomasi di Lampedusa, author of *Il Gattopardo* (The Leopard). The family's 17th-century ancestral palace has not been occupied for some time, although the **Chiesa Matrice** still stands and can be visited.

## ❧ HILLTOP TOWNS // TOUR THE SILENT INTERIOR, STOPPING OFF TO ADMIRE THE VIEWS

From Gela, it's an easy 20km drive along the SP8 up to the lovely hilltop village of **Butera**. Prosperous and content under the Spanish rule of the Branciforte family, Butera lacks the down-at-heel atmosphere of many rural towns in the interior, even if its location ensures an air of self-sufficient isolation. It has a lovely town church, the **Chiesa Madre**, with some modest treasures, a Renaissance triptych and a painting of the Madonna by Filippino Paladino, but the main sight is the panorama that unfolds beneath you from the hilltop **Norman castle**.

Continuing northwards, winding through kilometres of deserted farmland, passing the occasional tractor, the SS191 leads up to **Mazzarino**, the historic seat of the Branciforte clan. Now a small, sleepy town, it's definitely worth a quick look for its clutch of baroque churches, many of which boast works of art by the Tuscan 16th-century artist Filippino Paladino, and the ostentatious funerary monuments of the Branciforte princes. Unfortunately, many of the churches are closed to the public, but you can get into them by asking at the super-helpful **tourist office** ( ☎ 0934 38 49 84; Corso Vittorio Emanuele 410; ☺ 9am-1pm & 4-8pm summer, 9am-1pm & 3-7pm winter) on the main street.

About halfway between Butera and Mazzarino (as the crow flies, not as you'd drive it), **FARM** ( ☎ 934 34 66 00; www.farm-ospitalitadicampagna.it; Contrada Strada Butera) is a great *agriturismo* (farm stay) that not only offers top-notch accommodation (see p319) but also stages contemporary art exhibitions by young international artists.

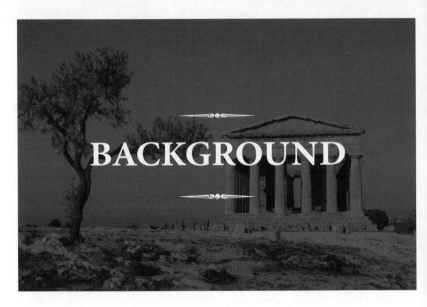

# BACKGROUND

### ❧ HISTORY
Sicily's history is as epic as they come – full of invasions, intrigues and internecine battles. Our summary will help you to understand the island's complex multicultural heritage and ongoing social and political challenges (p271).

### ❧ THE SICILIANS
The locals are characterised by their devotion to family, tradition, the Church and minding their own business. And like it or not, most of them will have some sort of tie with the Mafia (p280).

### ❧ SICILY ON PAGE & SCREEN
Settle into some serious pretrip research by immersing yourself in the darkly dramatic body of literature and films that has been produced here. And when you arrive, use our guide to customise your individual film- or book-inspired itinerary (p287).

### ❧ FOOD & WINE
Sample the street snacks, seafood and sweet treats that are the hallmarks of the local cuisine, and we guarantee you'll be in seventh heaven – particularly if you accompany them with a glass or two of our recommended local wines (p292).

### ❧ FOOD & DRINK GLOSSARY
Our handy guide to the local culinary lingo will have you ordering *caffè*, *carciofi*, *coniglio* and the *carta dei vini* like a local as you eat your way around the island (p299).

# HISTORY
· · · · · · ·

The first evidence of an organised settlement on Sicily belongs to the Stentillenians, who came from the Middle East and settled on the island's eastern shores sometime between 4000 and 3000 BC. But it was the settlers from the middle of the second millennium BC who radically defined the island's character and whose early presence helps us understand Sicily's complexities. Thucydides (c 460–404 BC) records three major tribes: the Sicanians, who originated either in Spain or North Africa and settled in the north and west (giving these areas their Eastern flavour); the Elymians from Greece, who settled in the south; and the Siculians (or Sikels), who came from the Calabrian peninsula and spread out along the Ionian Coast.

## GREEKS & PHOENICIANS

The acquisition of Sicily was an obvious step for the ever-expanding Greek city-states. Following the earlier lead of the Elymians, the Chalcidians landed on Sicily's Ionian Coast in 735 BC and founded a small settlement at Naxos. They were followed a year later by the Corinthians, who built their colony on the southeastern island of Ortygia, calling it Syracoussai (Syracuse). The Chalcidians went further south from their own fort and founded a second town called Katane (Catania) in 729 BC, and the two carried on stitching towns and settlements together until three-quarters of the island was in Hellenic hands.

The growing Greek power in the south and east created uncomfortable tensions with the Phoenicians, who had settled on the western side of the island around 850 BC; in turn, the Phoenicians' alliance with the powerful city-state of Carthage (in modern-day Tunisia) was of serious concern to the Greeks. By 480 BC the Carthaginians were mustering a huge invading force of some 300,000 mercenaries. Commanded by one of their great generals, Hamilcar, the force landed on Sicily and besieged Himera (near Termini Imerese), but the vast army was defeated by the crafty Greek tyrant Gelon, whose troops breached Hamilcar's lines by pretending to be Carthaginian reinforcements.

A much-needed period of peace followed in Sicily. The Greek colonies had lucrative trade deals thanks to the island's rich resources, and the remains of their cities testify to the extent of their wealth and sophistication.

With the advent of the Peloponnesian Wars, Syracuse decided to challenge the hegemony of mainland Greece. Athens, infuriated by the Sicilian 'upstart', decided to

| » 1250–850 BC | » 735–580 BC | » 241 BC |
|---|---|---|
| Settlers found small colonies at Stentinello, Megara Hyblaea and Lipari. They begin the lucrative business of trading obsidian. | Greek cities are founded at Naxos in 735, Syracuse in 734, Megara Hyblaea in 728, Gela in 689, and Selinunte and Messina in 628. Agrigento is established in 581. | Sandwiched between the superpowers of Carthage and Rome, Sicily becomes the battleground for a war whose outcome is to place it firmly within the Roman Empire. |

BACKGROUND

attack Syracuse in 415 BC, mounting upon it the 'Great Expedition' – the largest fleet ever assembled. Despite the fleet's size and Athens' confidence, Syracuse fought back and the mainland Greek army suffered a humiliating defeat.

Though Syracuse was celebrating its victory, the rest of Sicily was in a constant state of civil war. This provided the perfect opportunity for Carthage to seek its revenge for Himera, and in 409 BC a new army led by Hamilcar's bitter but brilliant nephew Hannibal wreaked havoc in the Sicilian countryside, completely destroying Selinunte, Himera, Agrigento and Gela. The Syracusans were eventually forced to surrender everything except the city of Syracuse itself to Carthage.

## THE ROMANS

The First Punic War (264–241 BC) saw Rome challenge Carthage for possession of Sicily, and at the end of the war the victorious Romans claimed the island as their first province outside the Italian mainland. Under the Romans, the majority of Sicilians lived in horrifyingly reduced circumstances; native inhabitants were refused the right to citizenship and forced into indentured slavery on *latifondi* – huge landed estates that were to cause so many of the island's woes in later years. Not surprisingly, Rome's less-than-enlightened rule led to a revolt by slaves in 135 BC and the Second Servile War in 104–101 BC.

## A BYZANTINE INTERLUDE

After Rome fell to the Visigoths in AD 470, Sicily was occupied by Vandals from North Africa, but their tenure was relatively brief. In 535 the Byzantine general Belisarius landed an army and was welcomed by a population that, despite over 700 years of Roman occupation, was still largely Greek, both in language and custom. The Byzantines were eager to use Sicily as a launching pad for the retaking of Saracen lands (those lands owned by the combined forces of Arabs, Berbers and Spanish Muslims, collectively known as the Saracens), but their dreams were not to be realised.

## ENTER ISLAM

In AD 827, the Saracen army landed at Mazara del Vallo. Palermo fell in 831, followed by Syracuse in 878. Under the Arabs, churches were converted to mosques and Arabic was implemented as the common language. At the same time, much-needed land reforms were introduced and trade, agriculture and mining were fostered. New crops

| » 241 BC–AD 470 | » 535 | » 827–965 |
|---|---|---|
| As the superpower's first colony, Sicily suffers the worst of Roman rule: native inhabitants are refused the right of citizenship and forced into indentured slavery. | Keen to use the island as a launching pad for retaking Saracen lands, the Byzantines conquer Sicily; Syracuse temporarily becomes the empire's capital in 663. | The Saracens land at Mazara del Vallo. Sicily is united under Arab rule and Palermo is the second-largest city in the world after Constantinople. |

were introduced, including citrus trees, date palms and sugar cane, and a system of water supply and irrigation was developed.

Palermo was chosen as the capital of the new emirate and, over the next 200 years, it became one of the most splendid cities in the Arab world, a haven of culture and commerce rivalled only by Córdoba in Spain.

# THE KINGDOM OF THE SUN

The Arabs called the Normans 'wolves' because of their barbarous ferocity and the terrifying speed with which they were mopping up territory on the mainland. By 1053, after six years of mercenary activity, Robert Guiscard (c 1015–85), the Norman conquistador, had comprehensively defeated the combined forces of the Calabrian Byzantines, the Lombards and the papal forces at the Battle of Civitate.

Having established his supremacy, Robert turned his attentions to expanding the territories under his control. To achieve this, he had to deal with the Vatican. In return for being invested with the titles of duke of Puglia and Calabria in 1059, Robert agreed to chase the Saracens out of Sicily and restore Christianity to the island. He delegated this task – and promised the island – to his younger brother Roger I (1031–1101), who landed his troops at Messina in 1061, capturing the port by surprise. In 1064 Roger tried to take Palermo but was repulsed by a well-organised Saracen army; it wasn't until Robert arrived in 1072 with substantial reinforcements that the city fell into Norman hands.

Impressed by the island's cultured Arab lifestyle, Roger shamelessly borrowed and improved on it, spending vast amounts of money on palaces and churches and encouraging a cosmopolitan atmosphere in his court. He also wisely opted for a policy of reconciliation with the indigenous people; Arabic and Greek continued to be spoken along with French, and Arab engineers, bureaucrats and architects continued to be employed by the court. He was succeeded by his widow, Adelasia (Adelaide), who ruled until 1130 when Roger II (1095–1154) was crowned king.

### THE ENLIGHTENED LEADER

Roger II was a keen intellectual whose court was unrivalled for its exotic splendour and learning. His rule was remarkable not only for his patronage of the arts, but also for his achievement in building an efficient and multicultural civil service that was the envy of Europe. He also enlarged the kingdom to include Malta, most of southern Italy and even parts of North Africa.

| » 1059–72 | » 1072–1101 | » 1130–1154 |
|---|---|---|
| The Norman conquistador Robert Guiscard vows to expel the Saracens from Sicily. With the help of his younger brother, Roger I, he seizes Palermo in 1072. | Sicily's brightest period in history ensues under Roger I, with a cosmopolitan and multicultural court. Many significant palaces and churches are built during this time. | Roger II builds one of the most efficient civil services in Europe. His court is responsible for the creation of the first written legal code in Sicilian history. |

## THE SETTING SUN

Roger's son and successor, William I (1108–66), inherited the kingdom upon his father's death in 1154. Nicknamed 'William the Bad', he was a vain and corrupt ruler.

The appointment of Walter of the Mill (Gualtiero Offamiglia) as archbishop of Palermo at the connivance of the pope was to create a dangerous power struggle between church and throne for the next 20 years – a challenge that was taken up by William II (1152–89) when he ordered the creation of a second archbishopric at Monreale.

William II's premature death at the age of 36 led to a power tussle, and an assembly of barons elected Roger II's illegitimate grandson Tancred (c 1130–94) to the throne. His accession was immediately contested by the German (or Swabian) king Henry VI (1165–97), head of the House of Hohenstaufen, who laid claim to the throne by virtue of his marriage to Roger II's daughter, Constance.

Tancred died in 1194, and no sooner had his young son, William III, been installed as king than the Hohenstaufen fleet docked in Messina. On Christmas Day of that year Henry VI declared himself king and young William was imprisoned in the castle at Caltabellotta in southern Sicily, where he eventually died (in 1198).

## WONDER OF THE WORLD

Henry paid scant attention to his Sicilian kingdom, and died prematurely of malaria in 1197. He was succeeded by his young heir Frederick (1194–1250), known as both Frederick I of Sicily and Frederick II of Hohenstaufen.

Frederick was a keen intellectual with a penchant for political manoeuvring, but he was also a totalitarian despot who fortified the eastern seaboard from Messina to Syracuse and sacked rebellious Catania in 1232. Under his rule, Sicily became a centralised state playing a key commercial and cultural role in European affairs, and Palermo gained a reputation as the continent's most important city. In the latter years of his reign Frederick became known as Stupor Mundi, 'Wonder of the World', in recognition of his successful rule.

When Frederick died in 1250, he was succeeded by his son Conrad IV of Germany (1228–54), but the island was initially ruled by his younger and illegitimate son, Manfred (1232–66). Conrad arrived in Sicily in 1252 to take control but died of malaria after only two years. Manfred again took the reigns, first as regent to Conrad's infant son Conradin and then, after forging an alliance with the Saracens, in his own right in 1258.

BACKGROUND

| » 1145 | » 1154 | » 1198–1250 |
|---|---|---|
| El Idrisi's planisphere (a large, silver global map) – an important medieval geographical work that accurately maps Europe, North Africa and western Asia – is completed. | William I inherits the kingdom, triggering a power struggle between church and throne. Walter of the Mill is appointed archbishop of Palermo. | Under Frederick I, Palermo is considered Europe's most important city and Sicily is a key player in Europe. But Frederick imposes heavy taxes and restrictions on free trade. |

# THE SICILIAN VESPERS

In 1266 the Angevin army, led by Charles of Anjou, brother of the French King Louis IX, defeated and killed Manfred at Benevento on the Italian mainland. Two years later, another battle took the life of Manfred's 15-year-old nephew and heir, Conradin, who was publicly beheaded in Naples.

After such a bloody start, the Angevins were hated and feared. Sicily was weighed down by onerous taxes, religious persecution was the order of the day and Norman fiefdoms were removed and awarded to French aristocrats.

On Easter Monday, 1282, the city of Palermo exploded in rebellion. Incited by the alleged rape of a local girl by a gang of French troops, peasants lynched every French soldier they could get their hands on. The revolt spread to the countryside and was supported by the barons, who had formed an alliance with Peter of Aragon, who landed at Trapani with a large army and was proclaimed king. For the next 20 years, the Aragonese and the Angevins were engaged in the War of the Sicilian Vespers – a war that was eventually won by the Spanish.

# FIVE HUNDRED YEARS OF SOLITUDE

By the end of the 14th century Sicily had been thoroughly marginalised. The eastern Mediterranean was sealed off by the Ottoman Turks, while the Italian mainland was off-limits on account of Sicily's political ties with Spain. As a result the Renaissance passed the island by, reinforcing the oppressive effects of poverty and ignorance. Even Spain lost interest in its colony, choosing to rule through viceroys.

By the end of the 15th century, the viceroy's court was a den of corruption, and the most influential body on the island became the Catholic Church (whose archbishops and bishops were mostly Spaniards). The church exercised draconian powers through a network of Holy Office tribunals, otherwise known as the Inquisition.

Reeling under the weight of state oppression, ordinary Sicilians demanded reform. But Spanish monarchs were preoccupied by the wars of the Spanish succession and Sicily was subsequently passed around from European power to European power like an unwanted Christmas present. Eventually the Spanish reclaimed the island in 1734, this time under the Bourbon king Charles I of Sicily (1734–59).

Under the reign of Charles I's successor, Ferdinand IV, the landed gentry vetoed any attempts at liberalisation. Large exports of grain continued to line the pockets of the aristocracy while normal Sicilians died of starvation.

| » 1266–82 | » 1487 | » 1669 |
|---|---|---|
| Charles of Anjou is crowned king in 1266 but is ousted in a violent uprising. Peter of Aragon takes power, and the Spanish commence 500 years in power. | The end of religious tolerance is cemented by the expulsion of Jews from all Spanish territories. The Spanish Inquisition starts terrorising Sicily. | The worst eruption in Etna's history levels Catania and the east-coast towns. It's preceded by a three-day earthquake. The eruption lasts four months. |

## EXIT FEUDALISM

Although Napoleon never occupied Sicily, his capture of Naples in 1799 forced Ferdinand to move to Sicily. The Bourbon king's ridiculous tax demands were soon met with open revolt by the peasantry and the more far-sighted nobles, who believed that the only way to maintain the status quo was to usher in limited reforms. After strong pressure, Ferdinand reluctantly agreed in 1812 to the drawing up of a constitution whereby a two-chamber parliament was formed and feudal privileges were abolished.

## THE RISORGIMENTO

With the final defeat of Napoleon in 1815, Ferdinand once again united Naples and Sicily as the 'Kingdom of the Two Sicilies', taking the title Ferdinand I. For the next 12 years the island was divided between a minority who sought an independent Sicily, and a majority who believed that the island's survival could only be assured as part of a unified Italy, an ideal being promoted on the mainland as part of the political and social movement known as the Risorgimento (reunification period).

On 4 April 1860 the revolutionary committees of Palermo gave orders for a revolt against the tottering Bourbon state. The news reached Giuseppe Garibaldi, who decided that this was the perfect moment to begin his campaign for the unification of Italy. He landed in Marsala on 11 May 1860 with about 1000 soldiers – the famous *mille* – and defeated a Bourbon army of 15,000 at Calatafimi on 15 May, taking Palermo two weeks later.

Despite his revolutionary fervour, Garibaldi was not a reformer in the social sense, and his soldiers blocked every attempt at a land grab on the part of the ordinary worker. On 21 October a referendum was held that saw a staggering 99% of eligible Sicilian voters opt for unification with the Piedmontese House of Savoy, which controlled most of Northern and Central Italy. Its head, King Victor Emmanuel II, aspired to rule a united Italy and had supported Garibaldi's expedition to Sicily. He was to become the first king of a unified Italy on 17 March 1861.

# FASCISM, CONSERVATISM & WWII

Sicily struggled to adapt to the Savoys. The old aristocracy by and large maintained all of their privileges, and hopes of social reform soon dwindled.

What the island really needed was a far-reaching policy of agrarian reform, including a redistribution of land. The partial break-up of large estates after the aboli-

| » 1820–60 | » 1860 | » 1861 |
|---|---|---|
| The first uprising against the Bourbons occurs in Palermo. It is followed by others in Syracuse in 1837 and Palermo in 1848. | Garibaldi lands in Marsala and defeats the Bourbon army, taking Palermo two weeks later. The island is free of the Spanish for the first time since 1282. | King Victor Emmanuel II becomes the first king of a unified Italy on 17 March. |

tion of feudalism still only benefited the *gabellotti* (agricultural middlemen who policed the peasants on behalf of the aristocracy), who leased the land from the owners only to then charge prohibitive ground rents to the peasants who lived and worked on it.

To assist them with their rent collections the bailiffs enlisted the help of local gangs, who then took on the role of intermediary between the tenant and the owner, sorting out disputes and regulating affairs in the absence of an effective judicial system. These individuals were called *mafiosi* and were organised into small territorial gangs drawn up along family lines. They effectively filled the vacuum that existed between the people and the state, comfortably slotting in to the role of local power brokers.

In 1922, Benito Mussolini took power in Rome. With the growing influence of the Mafia dons threatening to jeopardise his dominance in Sicily, Mussolini dispatched Cesare Mori to Palermo with orders to crush lawlessness and insurrection on Sicily. Mori did this by ordering the round-up of individuals suspected of involvement in 'illegal organisations'.

By the 1930s, Mussolini had bigger fish to fry – his sights were set on the colonisation of Libya as Italy's Fourth Shore, ultimately dragging Sicily into WWII. Chosen as the springboard for the recapture of mainland Italy, Sicily suffered greatly from heavy Allied bombing. Ironically, the war presented the Mafia with the perfect opportunity to get back at Mussolini and it collaborated with the Allied forces, assisting the capture of the island in 1943.

## POSTWAR WOES & MANI PULITE

The most powerful force in Sicilian politics in the latter half of the 20th century was the Democrazia Cristiana (DC; Christian Democrats), a centre-right Catholic party that appealed to the island's traditional conservatism. Allied closely with the Church, the DC promised wide-ranging reforms while at the same time demanding vigilance against godless communism. It was greatly aided in its efforts by the Mafia, which ensured that the local DC mayor would always top the poll. The Mafia's reward was *clientelismo* (political patronage) that ensured it was granted favourable contracts.

This constant interference by the Mafia in the island's economy did much to nullify the efforts of Rome to reduce the gap between the prosperous north and the poor south. The well-intentioned Cassa del Mezzogiorno (Southern Italy Development

| » 1860–94 | » 1922–43 | » 1943–44 |
|---|---|---|
| The emergence of the *mafiosi* fills the vacuum between the people and the state. The need for social reform strengthens the growing trade union, the *fasci*. | Benito Mussolini brings Fascism and almost succeeds in stamping out the Mafia. He drags Sicily into WWII by colonising Libya. Sicily suffers greatly from Allied bombing. | The Mafia collaborates with the Allied forces, assisting the capture of the island. Sicily is taken in 39 days. Mafia Don Calogero Vizzini is appointed as the island's administrator. |

BACKGROUND

Fund), set up in 1950, was aimed at kick-starting the pitiful economy of the south, and Sicily was one of its main beneficiaries, receiving state and European Communities (EC) money for all kinds of projects. However, the disappearance of large amounts of cash eventually led the central government to scrap the fund in 1992, leaving the island to fend for itself.

In the same year, the huge Tangentopoli (Bribesville) scandal (the institutional-isation of kickbacks and bribes, which had been the country's modus operandi since WWII) made headline news. Although it was largely focused on the industrial north of Italy, the repercussions of the widespread investigation into graft (known as *Mani Pulite*, or Clean Hands) were inevitably felt in Sicily, a region where politics, business and the Mafia were long-time bedfellows. The scandal eventually brought about the demise of the DC party.

In the meantime, things were changing in regard to how the Sicilians viewed the Mafia, thanks to the investigating magistrates Paolo Borsellino and Giovanni Falcone. They contributed greatly to change the climate of opinion against the Mafia on both sides of the Atlantic, and made it possible for ordinary Sicilians to speak about and against the Mafia more freely. When they were tragically murdered in the summer of 1992, it was a great loss for Italy and Sicily, but it was these deaths that finally broke the Mafia's code of *omertà* (silence) that had ruled the island for so long.

## 21ST-CENTURY SICILY

Even though today's Sicily is better off than at any other time in its history, it still has enormous economic, social and political hurdles to overcome. Chief among these is unemployment, with levels on the island generally agreed to be much higher than those elsewhere in Italy. Considering that official national rates in June 2010 put overall employment at 8.5% and youth unemployment at 27.7%, this is a frightening day-to-day reality for Sicilians, particularly those aged between 16 and 25.

Another huge issue that Sicilians are grappling with is the impact of illegal immi-gration. Being so close to North Africa, the island has always been a crossroads, but competition for jobs combined with huge strains on already-inadequate housing and infrastructure means that many Sicilians are unhappy with the island's status as an unofficial gateway into Europe.

The situation has become so fraught that in early 2009, demonstrations were held on the island of Lampedusa – where large numbers of the illegal immigrants arrive – protesting against construction of a second detention centre to house arrivals and

| » 1951–75 | » 1992 | » 1995–99 |
|---|---|---|
| Sicily's petrochemical, citrus and fishing industries collapse, leading to widespread unemployment. One million Sicilians emigrate to northern Europe. | The Tangentopoli scandal makes headlines, and it eventually brings about the demise of the DC party. | Giulio Andreotti, the Italian prime minister, is charged with Mafia association, and goes on trial. He is acquitted due to lack of evidence in 1999. |

calling for the Italian government to introduce a 'push back' policy at sea. A few months later, the Berlusconi government passed a regulation on public security that criminalised 'irregular entry and stay' in Italy and authorised local authorities to ask associations of unnamed citizens to patrol the territory of a municipality and report illegal immigrants to the authorities. Amnesty International described the regulation as 'excessively severe immigration control measures that do not meet Italy's obligations under international human rights law' and warned that they 'may result in discrimination and vigilantism'.

## » 2006

The Sicilian Godfather, Bernardo Provenzano, is arrested after 40 years on the run. His arrest marks an important milestone in the fight against the Mafia.

## » 2009

Prime Minister Silvio Berlusconi announces that his government will cover €1.3 billion of the estimated €6.1 billion to construct a bridge over the Strait of Messina.

## » 2010

Sicily continues to grapple economically, with June figures presenting a harsh reality: overall employment at 8.5% and youth unemployment at 27.7%.

BACKGROUND

# THE SICILIANS
· · · · · · ·

When asked to nominate their nationality, most locals will say 'Sicilian' rather than 'Italian', reinforcing a generally held Italian belief that the Sicilian culture and character are markedly different to those of the rest of the country. Though sharing many traits with fellow residents of the Mezzogiorno (the part of southern Italy comprising Sicily, Abruzzo, Basilica, Campania, Calabria, Apulia, Molise and Sardinia), Sicilians have a dialect and civil society that are as distinctive as they are fascinating.

The reason for this difference is perhaps summed up best by author Giuseppe di Lampedusa in *Il Gattopardo* (*The Leopard*), when his protagonist the Prince of Salina tries to explain the Sicilian character to a Piedmontese representative of the new Kingdom of Italy: 'This violence of landscape, this cruelty of climate, this continual tension in everything, and even these monuments of the past, magnificent yet incomprehensible because not built by us and yet standing round us like lovely mute ghosts… All these things have formed our character, which is thus conditioned by events outside our control as well as by a terrifying insularity of mind.'

## IDENTITY

The local stereotype is that Palermo and Catania stand at opposite ends of the island's character. 'In Palermo, we're more traditional, more conservative', says Massimo, a Palermo shopkeeper. 'The Catanians are more outward looking, and better at commerce.' Some ascribe the Palermitans' conservative character to their Arab predecessors, while the Greeks get all the credit for the Catanians' democratic outlook, their sense of commerce and their alleged cunning. Beyond this divide, Sicilians are generally thought of as conservative and suspicious (usually by mainland Italians), stoical and spiritual, confident and gregarious, and as the possessors of a rich and dark sense of humour.

> '*Sicilians have a dialect and civil society that are as distinctive as they are fascinating*'

Colonised for centuries, Sicilians have absorbed myriad traits – indeed, writer Gesualdo Bufalino believed Sicilians suffered from an 'excess of identity', at the core of which was the islanders' conviction that Sicilian culture stands at the centre of the world. This can feel terribly exclusive to the visitor, and there is still an awful lot of Sicily that is beyond the prying eyes of the tourist.

That said, it is difficult to make blanket assertions about Sicilian culture, if only because there are huge differences between the more modern-minded city dwellers and those from the traditionally conservative countryside. It is certain, however, that modern attitudes are changing conservative traditions. In the larger university cities such as Palermo, Catania, Syracuse and Messina, you will find a vibrant youth culture and a liberal lifestyle.

## PUBLIC VS PRIVATE

Family is the bedrock of Sicilian life, and loyalty to family and friends is one of the most important qualities you can possess. As Luigi Barzini (1908–84), author of *The Italians,* noted, 'A happy private life helps tolerate an appalling public life.' This chasm between the private arena and public forum is a noticeable aspect of Sicilian life, and has evolved over years of intrusive foreign domination.

Maintaining a *bella figura* (beautiful image) is very important to the average Sicilian, and striving to appear better off than you really are (known as *spagnolismo*) is a regional pastime. Though not confined to Sicily, *spagnolismo* on the island has its roots in the excesses of the Spanish-ruled 18th century, when the race for status was so competitive that the king considered outlawing extravagance. In this climate, how you and your family appeared to the outside world was (and still is) a matter of honour, respectability and pride. In a social context, keeping up appearances extends to dressing well, behaving modestly, performing religious and social duties and fulfilling all essential family obligations; in the context of the extended family, where gossip is rife, a good image protects one's privacy.

In this heavily patriarchal society, 'manliness' is a man's prime concern. The main role of the 'head of the family' is to take care of his family, oil the wheels of personal influence and facilitate the upward mobility of family members through a system of influence known as *clientelismo,* which basically allows people to secure jobs, contracts and opportunities through association with the Mafia. Women, on the other hand, are traditionally the repository of the family's honour, and even though unmarried couples commonly live together nowadays, there are still young couples who undertake lengthy engagements for the appearance of respectability.

Traditionally, personal wealth is closely and jealously guarded. Family money can support many individuals, while emigrant remittances have vastly improved the lot of many villagers.

## A WOMAN'S PLACE

'In Sicily, women are more dangerous than shotguns', said Fabrizio (Angelo Infanti) in *The Godfather.* 'A woman at the window is a woman to be shunned', proclaimed the writer Giovanni Verga in the 19th century. And 'Women are too stupid to be involved in the complex world of finance', decided a judge when faced with a female Mafia suspect in the 1990s. As in many places in the Mediterranean, a woman's position in Sicily has always been a difficult one.

A Sicilian mother and wife commands the utmost respect within the home, and is expected to act as the moral and emotional compass for her family. Although – or perhaps because – male sexuality holds an almost mythical status, women's modesty – which includes being quiet and feminine, staying indoors and remaining a virgin until married – has had to be ferociously guarded. To this day the worst insult that can be directed to a Sicilian man is *cornuto,* meaning that his wife has been unfaithful.

But things are changing for Sicilian women. More and more unmarried women live with their partners, especially in the cities, and enjoy the liberal lifestyle of many other Western countries. Improvements in educational opportunities and changing attitudes mean that the number of women with successful careers is growing, although a 2008 Global Gender Gap Index published by the World Economic Forum still placed Italy near the bottom of the list of European nations when it comes to closing the gap between the sexes in terms of political, professional and economic parity. Sicily and Italy also have some of the lowest percentages in Europe of women in government. In 2009, only four ministers out of 21 and only 193 of 952 parliamentarians were female, and a number of those women are alleged to have attained their positions because prime minister Silvio Berlusconi found them attractive. It's a situation that feminist organisations such as Sicily's Arcidonna (www.arcidonna.org, in Italian) are working to change.

## SAINTS & SINNERS

Religion is a big deal in Sicily. With the exception of the small Muslim communities of Palermo and the larger Tunisian Muslim community in Mazara del Vallo, the overwhelming majority of Sicilians consider themselves practising Roman Catholics. Even before the 1929 Lateran Treaty between the Vatican and Italy, when Roman Catholicism became the official religion of the country, Sicily was incontrovertibly Catholic, mostly due to 500 years of Spanish domination. In 1985 the treaty was renegotiated, so that Catholicism was no longer the state religion and religious education was no longer compulsory, but this only reflected the reality of mainland Italy north of Rome; in Sicily, the Catholic Church remains strong and extremely popular.

Pilgrimages remain a central part of the religious ritual, with thousands of Sicilians travelling to places such as the Santuario della Madonna at Tyndaris or the Santuario di Gibilmanna in the Madonie mountains.

In the small communities of the interior you will find that the mix of faith and superstition that for centuries dictated Sicilian behaviour is still strong. The younger, more cosmopolitan sections of society living in the cities tend to dismiss their elders' deepest expressions of religious devotion, but most people still maintain an air of respect.

## IMMIGRATION & EMIGRATION

Immigration and emigration are among the most pressing contemporary issues, and Sicily is no stranger to the subject. Since the end of the 19th century the island has suffered an enormous drain of human resources through emigration. Between 1880 and

### BRIDGING THE CULTURAL DIVIDE

Maria Sanciolo-Bell was born in Sicily, lives in Australia and spends much of her time forging cultural links between the island and the rest of the world. A director of Echoes Events (www.echoesevents.com), a cultural tourism and events company with offices in Melbourne and Catania, she and her Sicilian business associate Gaetano Failla are passionate about Sicilian culture and run a huge range of programs celebrating it. Whether it be running opera masterclasses with Sicilian maestros, conducting regional cookery courses, sponsoring international art exchanges or taking international visitors on tours of the locations used in the *Inspector Montalbano* TV series and *Godfather* films, Echoes plays an important role in raising the cultural profile of Sicily and profiling its attractions on the world stage. As she says: 'Many people only know of Sicily in relation to the Mafia. We are committed to raising awareness of its incredibly rich and diverse heritage and to making people aware of the cultural interrelationships – rather than the cultural divides – between Sicily and the rest of the world.'

1910, over 1.5 million Sicilians left for the US, and in 1900 the island was the world's main area of emigration. In the 20th century, tens of thousands of Sicilians moved away in search of a better life in Northern Italy, North America, Australia and other countries. Today, huge numbers of young Sicilians – often the most educated – continue to leave the island.

> 'Immigration and emigration are among the most pressing contemporary issues'

This brain-drain epidemic is the result of the grim unemployment rate (see p278) and the entrenched system of patronage and nepotism, which makes it difficult for young people to get well-paid jobs without having the right connections. Also, the fact that Sicily is one of the favoured ports of call for the thousands of *extracomunitari* (immigrants from outside the EU) who have flooded into Italy, some of them illegally (see p278), has led to extra strain being placed on housing and infrastructure as well as increased competition for jobs.

## THE MAFIA

### ORIGINS

The word 'Mafia' took more than 110 years of common usage before it was officially acknowledged as referring to an actual organisation. Although formally recorded by the Palermitan prefecture in 1865, the term was not included in the Italian penal code until 1982.

The origins of the word have been much debated. The author Norman Lewis has suggested that it derives from the Arabic *mu'afah* or 'place of refuge'. Nineteenth-century etymologists proposed *mahjas,* the Arabic word for 'boasting'. Whatever the origin, the term *mafioso* existed long before the organisation known as the Mafia, and was used to describe a character that was elegant and proud, with an independent vitality and spirit.

The concept of the *mafioso* goes all the way back to the late 15th century when the restricted commercial opportunities were so stifling that even the overprivileged feudal nobles were forced to make changes in order to survive. They introduced a policy of resettlement that forced thousands of farmers off the land and into new towns; the idea was to streamline crop growth, but it also destroyed the lives of the peasants in the process. Many of the aristocrats moved to big cities such as Palermo and Messina, leaving their estates in the hands of *gabellotti* (bailiffs), who were charged with collecting ground rents. They, in turn, employed the early *mafiosi* – who were small gangs of armed peasants – to help them solve any 'problems' that came up on the way. The *mafiosi* were soon robbing large estates and generally causing mayhem, but the local authorities were inept at dealing with them as they would quickly disappear into the brush.

The bandits struck a mixture of fear and admiration into the peasantry, who were happy to support any efforts to destabilise the feudal system. They became willing accomplices in protecting the outlaws, and although it would be another 400 years before crime became 'organised', the 16th and 17th centuries witnessed a substantial increase in the activities of brigand bands. The bands were referred to as Mafia, while

BACKGROUND

the peasants' loyalty to their own people resulted in the name Cosa Nostra (Our Thing). The early-day Mafia's way of protecting itself from prosecution was to become the modern Mafia's most important weapon: the code of silence, or *omertà*.

## THE 'NEW' MAFIA

Up until WWII the Mafia had operated almost exclusively in the countryside, but with the end of the conflict Cosa Nostra began its expansion into the cities. It took over the construction industry, channelling funds into its bank accounts and creating a network of kickbacks that were factored into every project undertaken. In 1953, a one-off meeting between representatives of the US and Sicilian Mafias resulted in the creation of the first Sicilian Commission, which had representatives of the six main Mafia families (or *cosche,* literally meaning 'artichoke') to efficiently run its next expansion into the extremely lucrative world of narcotics. At the head of the commission was Luciano Liggio from Corleone, whose 'family' had played a vital role in developing US–Sicilian relations.

Throughout the 1960s and '70s the Mafia earned billions of dollars from the drug trade. Inevitably, the raised stakes made the different Mafia families greedy for a greater share and from the late 1960s onwards Sicily was awash with vicious feuds that left hundreds dead.

The most sensational assassination was that of the chief prefect of police, General Carlo Alberto Dalla Chiesa, whom the national government had sent to Sicily to direct anti-Mafia activities. Dalla Chiesa was ambushed in the heart of Palermo in 1982, and his brutal murder led to prosecutors and magistrates being granted wider powers of investigation.

The first real insight into the 'New Mafia' came with the arrest of *mafioso* Tommaso Buscetta, also in 1982. After nearly four years of interrogation, headed by the courageous Palermitan investigating magistrate Giovanni Falcone, Buscetta broke the code of silence. His revelations shocked and fascinated the Italian nation, as he revealed the innermost work-

---

**DON'T MISS...**

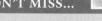

### THE MAFIA ON SCREEN

★ **Il Capo dei Capi (The Boss of all Bosses)** // 2007 Italian TV miniseries about Totò Riina (see p284)

★ **Dimenticare Palermo (To Forget Palermo)** // 1989 Italian political thriller directed by Francesco Rosi and co-written by Gore Vidal

★ **Excellent Cadavers** // Alexander Stille's 1995 book about Giovanni Falcone (see p284) was made into a TV movie directed by Ricky Tognazzi in 1999 and a documentary directed by Marco Turco in 2005

★ **Il Giorno della Civetta (The Day of the Owl)** // Damiano Damiani's 1968 film was based on Leonardo Sciascia's novel (see p287)

★ **The Godfather Trilogy** // Francis Ford Coppola's 1972–90 masterwork

★ **In Nome della Legge (In the Name of the Law)** // Pietro Germi's 1949 Italian Neorealist film was co-written by Federico Fellini

★ **La Piovra (The Octopus)** // Hugely popular 1984–2001 Italian TV miniseries

★ **Salvatore Giuliano** // Francesco Rosi's 1962 Neorealist film

ings of La Società Onorata (the Honoured Society; the Mafia's chosen name for itself). Tragically, Falcone was assassinated in 1992, as was another courageous anti-Mafia magistrate, Paolo Borsellino.

In 1986, 500 top *mafiosi* were put on trial in the first *maxiprocesso* (supertrial) in a specially constructed bunker near Palermo's Ucciardone prison. The trial resulted in 347 convictions, of which 19 were life imprisonments and the others jail terms totalling a staggering 2665 years.

In January 1993, the authorities arrested the infamous *capo di tutti capi* (boss of bosses), Salvatore (Totò) Riina, the most wanted man in Europe. He was charged with a host of murders, including those of magistrates Falcone and Borsellino, and sentenced to life imprisonment.

## THE ANTI-MAFIA MOVEMENT

The anti-Mafia movement is alive and kicking in Sicily, tracing its roots back to the beginning of today's Mafia. According to historians, the movement first appeared in the late 19th century, and lasted in its first incarnation until the 1950s. The movement strove for agrarian reform, targeting the Mafia, conservative political elites and the *latifondisti* (big landowners), but its efforts were shattered when the lack of economic prospects in the postwar era drove thousands of young Sicilians to emigrate in search of work and a better life.

During the 1960s and 1970s, the anti-Mafia movement was headed by political radicals, mainly members of the left-wing groups disenchanted with the Socialist and Communist parties. Giuseppe 'Peppino' Impastato became famous during this period; the son of a *mafioso,* Impastato mocked individual *mafiosi* on his popular underground radio show. He was assassinated in 1978. Things were at their worst for the anti-Mafia movement in the 1980s, when the Mafia was particularly intolerant of anyone perceived as a potential threat. The assassination in 1982 of General Dalla Chiesa is now seen as one of the major elements in sparking a new wave in the anti-Mafia movement, with Sicilians from all sections of society – from educators and students to political activists and parish priests – becoming involved.

> '*The anti-Mafia movement is alive and kicking in Sicily*'

The reformist Christian Democrat Leoluca Orlando, who was elected mayor of Palermo during the 1980s, also helped to increase anti-Mafia sentiment. He led an alliance of left-wing movements and parties to create Palermo Spring, which invalidated the public-sector contracts previously given to Mafia families, restored and reopened public buildings, and aided in the arrests of leading *mafiosi*. During the 1990s, Orlando left the Christian Democrats and set up the anticorruption movement La Rete (the Network), bringing together a broad collection of anti-Mafia individuals and reform organisations. (The party was eventually absorbed by Romano Prodi's Democrat Party in 1999.)

Civilian efforts saw housewives hanging sheets daubed with anti-Mafia slogans from their windows, shopkeepers and small entrepreneurs forming associations to oppose extortion, and the formation of groups such as Libera (www.libera.it), cofounded in 1994 by Rita Borsellino, the sister of the murdered judge Paolo Borsellino. Libera managed

BACKGROUND

to get the Italian parliament to permit its member organisations to legally acquire properties that had been seized from the Mafia by the government, establishing agricultural cooperatives, *agriturismi* and other legitimate enterprises on these lands (see www.liberaterra.it). Even the Catholic Church, long silent on the Mafia's crimes, finally began to have outspoken anti-Mafia members. The best known was Giuseppe Puglisi, who organised local residents to oppose the Mafia, and who was murdered in 1993.

## THE MAFIA TODAY

Since Salvatore Riina's conviction, other top *mafiosi* have followed him behind bars, most notably his successor Leoluca Bagarella, arrested in 1995; the Sicilian 'Godfather', Bernardo Provenzano, caught in 2006 after 20 years on the run; Salvatore lo Piccolo, Provenzano's successor, arrested in 2007; and Domenico Raccuglia (aka 'the Veterinarian'), number two in the organisation, arrested in 2009 after 15 years on the run. No-one would be so foolish to suggest that the power of the Mafia is a thing of the past, but these arrests have meant that the powerful core of the organisation is being weakened.

Today's Mafia has infiltrated daily life, becoming intertwined with legal society: its collaborators and their children are now 'respectable' and influential citizens. Whatever the business activity, the Mafia will often have a hand in it; for example, a legitimate business might secure a building contract, but the Mafia will then tell it where to buy cement or where to hire machinery. Critics call this 'the Invisible Mafia', and point out that a large number of Sicilian business owners still pay some kind of *pizzo* (protection money).

Providing a bright note amidst all this is the organisation Addiopizzo (www.addiopizzo.org), which campaigns against these iniquitous payments, urging consumers to support businesses that have said 'no' to paying *pizzo*. Its motto, 'A people who pay the *pizzo* are a people without dignity', seems to have struck a chord across the island and a number of tourism businesses – among others – are actively supporting the campaign, devising tours that support restaurants, shops and hotels that have said no to this Mafia extortion (see www.addiopizzotravel.it).

# SICILY ON PAGE & SCREEN
· · · · · · ·

Writers and filmmakers have long been inspired by Sicily's harsh landscape, rich history and complex society. They haven't often seen the island through rose-tinted glasses – endemic poverty and corruption are hard to romanticise or whitewash – but their words, images and narratives offer an invaluable insight into the local culture and society.

## SICILY IN PRINT

Dogged by centuries of isolation, and divided into an illiterate peasantry and a decadent aristocracy, it is hardly surprising that prior to the 19th century Sicily suffered from a complete absence of notable literature.

With such a context it is interesting to learn that the first official literature in Italian was written in Palermo in the 13th century at the School of Poetry patronised by Frederick II. But such high-minded works were irrelevant to the illiterate peasantry whose main pleasure was the regular celebration of saint's days and religious occasions and, later, the popular theatre of the *opera dei pupi* (puppet theatre; see p52 for details).

### LOCAL VOICES

The political upheaval of the 19th and 20th centuries finally broke the silence of the Sicilian pen when the literary colossus Giovanni Verga (1840–1922) emerged onto the scene. Living through some of the most intense historical vicissitudes of modern Italy – the unification of Italy, WWI and the rise of Fascism – his work was to have a major impact on Italian literature. His greatest novel, *I Malavoglia* (The Malavoglia Family; 1881), essentially a story about a family's struggle for survival through desperate times in Sicily, is still a permanent fixture on every Sicilian schoolchild's reading list.

Since then Sicilian writers have produced fiction to rival the best contemporary European works. Playwright and novelist Luigi Pirandello (1867–1936) was awarded the Nobel Prize for Literature in 1934 for a substantial body of work that included the play *Sei Personaggi in Ricerca di un Autore* (Six Characters in Search of an Author; 1921). Poet Salvatore Quasimodo (1901–68) won the award in 1959 for his exquisite lyric verse, which included delightful translations of works by Shakespeare and Pablo

---

**DON'T MISS...**

**LITERARY SETTINGS**

★ **Aci Trezza** // Giovanni Verga's *I Malavoglia* is set in this fishing village on the Ionian Coast (p188)

★ **Palazzo dei Normanni, Palermo** // Much of Barry Unsworth's *The Ruby in her Navel* is set in this Norman fortress (p43)

★ **Palma di Montechiaro, near Agrigento** // Thought to be Giuseppe di Lampedusa's inspiration for the town of Donnafugata in his novel *Il Gattopardo* (The Leopard)

★ **Porto Empedocle** // Features in Luigi Pirandello's early novels and is the inspiration for Andrea Camilleri's fictional town of Vigàta (p261)

★ **Syracuse** // The setting for Elio Vittorini's *Conversazione in Sicilia* (p200)

BACKGROUND

Neruda. Elio Vittorini (1908–66) captured the essence of the Sicilian migration north in his masterpiece *Conversazione in Sicilia* (1941), the story of a man's return to the roots of his personal, historical and cultural identity.

Sicily's most famous novel was a one-off by an aristocrat whose intent was to chronicle the social upheaval caused by the end of the old regime and the unification of Italy. Giuseppe Tomasi di Lampedusa (1896–1957) published *Il Gattopardo* (The Leopard) in 1958 to immediate critical acclaim. Though strictly a period novel, its enduring relevance lies in the minutely accurate observations of what it means to be Sicilian. See p12 for more information.

> '*The political upheaval of the 19th and 20th centuries finally broke the silence of the Sicilian pen*'

Much of Sicily's 20th-century literature is more political than literary. None is more so than the work of Danilo Dolci (1924–97), a social activist commonly known as the 'Sicilian Gandhi'. His *Report from Palermo* (1959) and subsequent *Sicilian Lives* (1981), both detailing the squalid living conditions of many of Sicily's poorest inhabitants, earned him the enduring animosity of the authorities and the Church. (Cardinal Ernesto Ruffini publicly denounced him for 'defaming' all Sicilians.) He, too, was nominated for the Nobel Prize and was awarded the Lenin Peace Prize in 1958.

The other great subject for modern Sicilian writers is, of course, the Mafia. For a masterful insight into the island's destructive relationship with organised crime, search out the work of Leonardo Sciascia (1921–89), whose novel *Il Giorno della Civetta* (The Day of the Owl; 1961) was the first Italian novel to take the Mafia as its subject. Throughout his career, Sciascia probed the topic, practically inventing a genre of his own. His protégé Gesualdo Bufalino (1920–96) won the prestigious Strega Prize in 1988 for his novel *Le Menzogne della Notte* (Night's Lies), the tale of four condemned men who spend the eve of their execution recounting the most memorable moments of their lives. Bufalino went on to become one of Italy's finest writers, mastering a style akin to literary baroque – intense, tortured and surreal. His haunting novel *La Diceria dell'Untore* (The Plague Sower; 1981), which won Italy's Campiello Prize, is the story of a tuberculosis patient at a Palermo sanatorium in the late 1940s. Guiding the reader through a landscape of doom, Bufalino invokes the horrors of wartime and the hopelessness of the patients who come to know each other 'before our lead-sealed freight car arrives at the depot of its destination'.

Well-known feminist novelist and playwright Dacia Maraini (born 1936) has written a number of novels set in Sicily, including the award-winning historical romance *La Lunga Vita di Marianna Ucrìa* (The Silent Duchess; 1990), which was made into the film *Marianna Ucrìa* by Italian director Roberto Faenze in 1997.

## THROUGH FOREIGN EYES

A number of foreigners or expats have also written about Sicily. Enjoyable but lightweight titles include Peter Moore's humorous travelogue *Vroom by the Sea* (2007), which recounts the adventures he has exploring the island on a Vespa named Donatella (so named because it's the same shade of lurid orange as Donatella Versace);

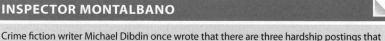

## INSPECTOR MONTALBANO

Crime fiction writer Michael Dibdin once wrote that there are three hardship postings that no Italian cop wants: Sicily, Sardinia and the Alto Adige. We're pretty sure that Inspector Salvo Montalbano, the much-loved protagonist in Andrea Camilleri's Montalbano books (www.andreacamilleri.net, in Italian), would indignantly deny that this was the case. When not using his boundless stores of intuition and charm to solve crimes in the fictional town of Vigàta (based on Camilleri's birthplace of Porto Empedocle near Agrigento), this proudly Sicilian sleuth divides his time between gastronomy (only local dishes) and his long-suffering girlfriend, Livia. Our favourite excerpt of dialogue in his books would have to be the following: Waiter: 'What can I get for you, Inspector?' Montalbano: 'Everything'.

There are 17 novels and four short-story collections in the Montalbano series, all of them set in Sicily. Start with the inspector's first outing in *La Forma dell'Acqua* (The Shape of Water; 1994) and you're unlikely to want to stop until you've read them all.

Devotees of the acclaimed Montalbano TV series starring Luca Zingaretti can book an Inspector Montalbano tour with Echoes Events (see p282) or Allakatalla (see p218). Both of these tours visit Ragusa, where the series is filmed, and Echoes can organise for you to eat at Don Calogero's trattoria or stay overnight in the Inspector's beachside house in Scicli.

Brian P Johnston's *Sicilian Summer: A Story of Honour, Religion and the Perfect Cassata* (2007), which is full of village politics and eccentric personalities; and Marlena de Blasi's *That Summer in Sicily* (2008), a Mills and Boon–ish story about a Sicilian woman's relationship with a much-older member of the Sicilian aristocracy.

Mary Taylor Simeti's *On Persephone's Island* and Peter Robb's *Midnight in Sicily* are much more substantial. Simeti, an American who has been living on the island since 1962, offers fascinating insights into its history, culture and cuisine; and Robb's portrait of the Mezzogiorno is notable for its impeccable research and compelling narrative, especially the sections dealing with the Mafia.

Historical novels of note include Barry Unsworth's *The Ruby in Her Navel* (2006) and Tariq Ali's *A Sultan in Palermo* (2005). Both are set against the backdrop of the Norman court of Roger II (known to his Arabic subjects as Sultan Rujeri).

And finally, mention should be made of three eminently readable histories: *The Day of Battle: The War in Sicily and Italy 1943–1944* (2008) by Rick Atkinson; *The Normans in Sicily* (2004) by John Julius Norwich; and *The Sicilian Vespers: A History of the Mediterranean World in the Later Thirteenth Century* (1992) by Steven Runciman.

## SICILY ON FILM

The rich emotional, psychological and physical landscape of Sicily has inspired some of the world's best filmmakers, and has provided the setting for innumerable works on film.

Visconti's two classics, *La Terra Trema* (The Earth Shook; 1948) and *Il Gattopardo* (The Leopard; 1963), illustrate the breadth of Sicilian tales – the former a story of grinding poverty and misfortune in a benighted fishing family, while the latter oozes

## ON LOCATION

Why not devise a tour of scenic film locations around the island?

★ **Aci Trezza** // *La Terra Trema* (p188)

★ **Bagheria, near Palermo** // *Il Gatopardo, The Godfather III, Baaria – La Porta del Vento*

★ **Catania** // *Divorzio all'Italiana* (p176)

★ **Cefalù** // *Nuovo Cinema Paradiso* (p110)

★ **Ciminna and Mondello, near Palermo** // *Il Gattopardo*

★ **Lampedusa** // *Respiro*

★ **Palermo** // *The Godfather III, Palermo Shooting, Johnny Stecchino, Il Gattopardo* (p33)

★ **Punta Secca, Ragusa, Donnalucata, Modica, Donnafugata, Ragusa Ibla, Scicli** // *Inspector Montalbano* TV series (p212)

★ **Ragusa & Ispica** // *Kaos* (p212)

★ **Salina** // *Il Postino* (p147)

★ **Savoca** // *The Godfather I* (p168)

★ **Stromboli** // *Stromboli: Terra di Dio* (p153)

★ **Taormina** // *Il Piccolo Diavolo* (p168)

the kind of grand decadence that one imagines preceded the French Revolution.

Antonioni's enigmatic mystery *L'Avventura* (The Adventure; 1960) focuses on the disappearance of one member of a group of bored and spoiled Roman socialites on a cruise around the Aeolian Islands, and though its existentialist plot has been described by many critics as impenetrable and pretentious, its stunning visuals are universally admired.

In Rossellini's *Stromboli: Terra di Dio* (Stromboli: Land of God; 1950), the explosive love affair between a Lithuanian refugee and a local fisherman is aptly viewed against the backdrop of the erupting volcano, while the hypnotic beauty of Michael Radford's *Il Postino* (The Postman; 1994) seduces viewers into a false sense of security, which is shattered by the film's tragic denouement.

However, it is Francis Ford Coppola's modern masterpiece, *The Godfather* trilogy (Part I, 1972; Part II, 1974; Part III, 1990) that really succeeds in marrying the psychological landscape of the characters with their physical environment. The varying intensities of light and dark superbly mirror the constant undercurrent of quivering emotion and black betrayal. The *coup de grâce* is the final scene of Part III, where Mascagni's opera, *Cavalleria Rusticana,* a foreboding story of love and betrayal, is interspersed with scenes of Michael Corleone's final acts of murder that ultimately lead to the death of the person he loves most, his daughter. For a list of other films about the Sicilian Mafia, see p284.

Other directors who have worked here include the Taviani brothers, who filmed *Kaos* in 1984, seeking to reproduce the mad logic of Sicilian-born author Luigi Pirandello's universe. The aptly named film is a series of tales about loss, lust, love, emigration and death played out through fantastical story lines. The film's title comes from the village near Agrigento where Pirandello was born (although it is spelled with a 'C').

Sicilians enjoy a good guffaw, and Pietor Germi's *Divorzio all'Italiana* (Divorce, Italian Style), set on the island, was a big hit here when it was released in 1961. More recent comedies include Roberto Benigni's *Il Piccolo Diavolo* (The Little Devil; 1988) and *Johnny Stecchino* (Johnny Toothpick; 1991).

BACKGROUND

Other films set in Sicily include Wim Wender's *Palermo Shooting* (2008), lambasted by most critics as pretentious and boring; and *Sicilia!* (1999), a film version of Elio Vittorini's acclaimed novel *Conversazione in Sicilia* directed by Danièle Huillet and Jean-Marie Straub.

Sicily itself has produced few directors of note, with the best-known exception being Giuseppe Tornatore (born 1956). Tornatore followed up on the incredible success of his semi-autobiographical film *Nuovo Cinema Paradiso* (Cinema Paradiso; 1988) with films including *Malèna* (2000), starring Monica Bellucci in a coming-of-age story set in Sicily in the 1940s; *L'Uomo delle Stele* (The Star Maker; 1995), also set in rural Sicily in the 1940s; and *Baarìa – La Porta del Vento* (Baarìa – Door of the Wind; 2009), the story of three generations of a local family between 1920 and 1980. Two versions of *Baarìa* were made: the first in the local Sicilian dialect of Baari-otu and the second dubbed in Italian.

> *'The rich emotional, psychological and physical landscape of Sicily has inspired some of the world's best filmmakers'*

Like Tornatore, Roman-born Emanuele Crialese has made Sicily his muse. Two of his films, *Respiro* (2002) and *Nuovomondo* (The Golden Door; 2006), are set here. *Respiro* is about a woman whose unorthodox behaviour challenges her family and islander neighbours, while *Nuovomondo* is a dreamy record of a Sicilian family's emigration to New York at the turn of the 20th century.

# FOOD & WINE

· · · · · · ·

'Leave the gun. Take the *cannoli*.' Sicily's food is so good that even the mobsters in *The Godfather* turned to it for comfort. And indeed, in this nation where food is at the centre of existence and where there are many delicious regional variations, the cuisine of Sicily is considered one of the country's best. A huge part of anyone's visit here will be taken up with eating, and with learning the many unwritten (and written) rules of eating the Sicilian way – understanding the strict order of the dining ritual, matching tastes and preparation methods, choosing the right dessert, having the right coffee. Fortunately, this will be immensely enjoyable, as Sicily's kitchen is packed with fresh ingredients, shiny fish straight out of the Mediterranean, unusual additions such as almonds and pistachios, and delectable combinations such as pasta with sardines, saffron and sultanas.

Traditional recipes have survived here for centuries, and Sicily's rich pantry was filled over a long period. The abundance of fruit and vegetables has been evident since the times of the ancient Greeks – Homer famously said of the island, 'Here luxuriant trees are always in their prime, pomegranates and pears, and apples glowing red, succulent figs and olives swelling sleek and dark', and wrote about wild fennel and caper bushes growing on the hills. But it wasn't until the Arabs came to the island that the cuisine really took shape. The Saracens brought the ever-present aubergine (eggplant), as well as citrus fruits, and they are believed to have introduced pasta to the island. They also spiced up the dishes with saffron and sultanas, and contrasted the dishes' delicate flavours with the crunch of almonds and pistachios. In fact, the Arabs were so influential that couscous is present on every menu in western Sicily.

> '*Sicily's food is so good that even the mobsters in* The Godfather *turned to it for comfort*'

And, on top of this, the Saracens brought sugar cane to Sicily, helping it develop all those fantastic sweets. The classic *cassata* comes from the Arabic word *qas'ah,* referring to the terracotta bowl used to shape the cake; *cannolo* comes from *canna* – cane (as in sugar cane).

What's really impressive about Sicily's cuisine is that most of these amazing tastes came out of poverty and depredation. The extravagant recipes of the *monsù* (chefs; from the French *monsieur le chef*) employed by the island's aristocrats were adapted to fit the budget and means of the less fortunate. Ordinary Sicilians applied the principle of preserving the freshness of the ingredients, and most importantly, never letting one taste overpower another. And that's the crunch of it, so to speak, the key to all of Sicily's dishes: simplicity. Prepare to have your taste buds educated, converted and pampered.

## THREE COLOURS

Sicily's favourite ingredients can be grouped according to the *tricolore* – the three colours of the Italian flag. The following are the basics that will be found in the pantry of any Sicilian; through these you can get to the core of the island's cuisine.

## RED

You may think red is the colour of passion, but when it comes to Sicilian cooking, it's also the colour of the most important ingredient of all: the tomato. *Il pomodoro* or *il pomodorino* (cherry tomato) is at the foundation of most sauces, whether it's cooked, blanched or simply scattered fresh over a heap of pasta. Sicilian tomatoes are renowned throughout Italy for their sweet flavour and you'll often see tomatoes hanging in bunches outside the houses (especially on the island of Salina, where the locals claim it's the best way to keep them fresh). Sun-dried tomatoes are another way of preserving tomatoes, and many Sicilians use this version in the winter months, when fresh tomatoes aren't easy to find.

Peppers are another must-have vegetable for Sicilians, and you'll find both the bell-shaped version and the long, pointy type in many starters and antipasti. A favourite dish involving red, green and yellow peppers is *peperonata in agridolce,* where peppers are stewed with onions, pine nuts, raisins and capers.

---

### DON'T MISS...

#### SLOW FOOD SENSATIONS

* ★ **Gelato al pistachio** // made with Bronte pistachios
* ★ **Insalata con arance e cipolla** // made with fresh oranges and Giarratana onions
* ★ **Caponata** // made with Pantelleria capers
* ★ **Granita di limone** // made with Interdonato or Verdello lemons
* ★ **Latte di mandorla** // made with Noto almonds
* ★ **Canestrato cheese** // accompanied by a glass of Nero d'Avola wine
* ★ **Madonie or Nebrodi provola cheese** // with Iblei Mountains thyme honey

## WHITE

Garlic is, of course, a major ingredient in Sicilian cooking. It is added to around 80% of savoury recipes, and it sometimes forms the main component of a sauce, as in *spaghetti aglio olio* (spaghetti with garlic and oil) – simple and delicious. Sicilians use crushed fresh cloves, most commonly on grilled or baked fish, or fry it thinly sliced to flavour the oil.

'White' is also for cheese. Sicilians like to sprinkle liberal helpings of a strong cheese called *caciocavallo* on their pasta dishes (despite the word *cavallo,* which means 'horse', the cheese is actually made from cows milk). Parmesan has only recently found its way onto the menu, and Sicilians will shriek with horror if you sprinkle it on the wrong sauce. Ricotta cheese, both dried and fresh, often features on Sicilian menus. Eaten really fresh (as in 24 hours old), it tastes like heaven. *Pecorino* cheese is another favourite. Made of sheeps milk, it has a strong aroma and is often added to sauces; the most distinctive *pecorini* come from the Madonie and Nebrodi Mountains, and are highlighted as important but endangered by the Slow Food Foundation for Biodiversity.

*Mandorle* (almonds) usually come blanched. They are widely cultivated throughout Sicily and they add a wonderful crunch to many a dish. Almonds are also used to

BACKGROUND

make one of the most common *granite* (flavoured crushed ice), as well as wonderful biscuits. The Sicilians have invented *latte di mandorla,* a delicious cold drink that is basically almond pulp and water; it is drunk mostly in the west, where you can also buy it in supermarkets, and it's freshly made in many bars.

### GREEN

Good olive oil is one of the prime delicacies of Sicilian cuisine, and several traditional olive varieties have been grown on the island for centuries. The main types are *biancolilla* (southwestern Sicily), *nocellara* and *ogliarola messinese* (northeast), *cerasuola* (between Sciacca and Paceco) and *nocellara del Belice* (Trapani province).

> '*Aside from Dolce & Gabbana, pasta is Italy's (and Sicily's) most famous export*'

You'll detect the smell of *basilico* (basil) wafting from most Sicilian kitchens. While the herb is used in northern Italy mainly for making pesto, the Sicilians have taken this a step further, making *pesto alla Trapanese* with its fragrant leaves. In this dish, basil is combined with blanched and peeled tomatoes, grated *pecorino* cheese, a healthy clove or two of garlic and some crushed almonds. The ingredients are bashed together with a pestle and mortar, some good olive oil is added, and the sauce is mixed with short pasta.

Pistachios are hugely popular in Sicily. Brought to Sicily by the Arabs and cultivated on the fertile volcanic-soil plains of the island, the nut is used in both savoury and sweet recipes – some of the best ice cream is made from pistachios. And the good news is that, if eaten regularly, the pistachio can significantly reduce cholesterol (although that unfortunately does not apply when eaten in ice-cream form!).

## STAPLES

Bread, pasta, antipasti, fish, meat…with so many delicious staples in Sicilian cuisine, you'll be spoilt for choice. You'll also find loads of traditional regional specialities to sample, many made with products showcased by the **Fondazione Slow Food** (www.fondazioneslowfood.com) organisation (see p19).

### BREAD

Bread has always been a staple food for the Sicilian peasant. Made from durum wheat, Sicilian bread is coarse and golden, fashioned into myriad ritualistic and regional shapes, from braids to rings to flowers. Baked bread is treated with the greatest respect and in the past only the head of the family had the privilege of slicing the loaf.

Periods of dire poverty and starvation no doubt gave rise to the common use of breadcrumbs, which served to stretch meagre ingredients and fill up hungry stomachs. Such economy lives on in famous dishes such as *involtini,* in which slices of meat or fish are wrapped around a sometimes-spicy breadcrumb stuffing and then pan-fried or grilled. Some other popular dishes made with a bread-dough base include *sfincione* (local form of pizza made with tomatoes, onions and sometimes anchovies), *impanata* (bread-dough snacks stuffed with meat, vegetables or cheese) and *scaccie* (discs of bread dough spread with a filling and rolled up into a pancake).

## PASTA

Aside from Dolce & Gabbana, pasta is Italy's (and Sicily's) most famous export. While fresh pasta *(pasta fresca)* is now common on most Sicilian restaurant menus, it is dry pasta that has always been the staple of Sicily and southern Italy – mainly because dry pasta is more economical.

The most famous of all Sicilian pasta dishes is *pasta con le sarde* (pasta with sardines). It is a heavy dish, but the liberal use of wild mountain fennel (unique to Sicily), onions, pine nuts and raisins gives the sardines a wonderfully exotic flavour. Other famous dishes include Catania's *pasta alla Norma,* with its rich combination of tomatoes, aubergines and salted ricotta. In the interior you will often find sauces made from meat and game (including wild boar, rabbit and beef) or cheese. Baroque Modica is where the island's best lasagne *(lasagne cacate)* is made; in this version, two kinds of cheese – ricotta and pecorino – are added to minced beef and sausage, and spread between layers of homemade pasta squares.

## ANTIPASTI

Sicilians aren't big on antipasti (literally 'before pasta'), but their love of strong flavours and unusual combinations lends itself well to the antipasto platter. It is a great way to explore some of the wonderful Sicilian flavours, ranging from marinated sardines and slivers of raw herring to fruity cheeses and a whole range of marinated, baked and fresh vegetables, the most famous of which is *caponata* (cooked vegetable salad made with tomatoes, aubergines, celery, capers, olives and onions).

## FISH

The extensive development of fishing and – until recent years – the widespread presence of fish such as sardines, tuna and mackerel off the island's shores have ensured that fish is a staple food.

A Palermitan favourite is *sarde a beccafico alla Palermitana* (sardines stuffed with anchovies, pine nuts, currants and parsley). However, the filet mignon of the marine world is the *pesce spada* (swordfish), served either grilled with lemon, olive oil and oregano, or as *involtini* (slices of swordfish rolled around a spicy filling of onions, currants, pine nuts and breadcrumbs).

The best swordfish is caught in Messina, where they serve the classic *agghiotta di pesce spada* (also called *pesce spada alla Messinese*), a mouthwatering dish flavoured with pine nuts, sultanas, garlic, basil and tomatoes. The Egadi Islands are home to two splendid fish dishes: *tonno 'nfurnatu* (oven-baked tuna with tomatoes, capers and green olives) and *alalunga di Favignana al ragù* (fried albacore served in a spicy sauce of tomatoes, red chilli peppers and garlic). It is not uncommon to see the sauce of the latter dish appear as part of your pasta dish. Finally, a popular food throughout the island is calamari or *calamaretti* (baby squid), which is prepared in a variety of ways, including stuffed, fried, or cooked in a tomato sauce.

BACKGROUND

## MEAT

Although you can find a limited number of meat dishes along the coast, you won't taste the best until you move further inland. The province of Ragusa is renowned for its imaginative and varied uses of meat, particularly mutton, beef, pork and rabbit. Its most famous dish is *falsomagro,* a stuffed roll of minced beef, sausages, bacon, egg and *pecorino* cheese. Another local speciality is *coniglio all'agrodolce* (sweet-and-sour rabbit), which is marinated in a sauce of red wine flavoured with onions, olive oil, bay leaves and rosemary. In the Madonie mountains, the town of Castelbuono is the home of *capretto in umido* (stewed kid) and *agnello al forno alla Madonita* (Madonie-style roast lamb). Locally caught *cinghiale* (wild boar) is served in stews, sauces and sausages. Don't be put off if goat or kid dishes are described on the menu as *castrato* – it means the goat was castrated, giving the meat a tender quality. Thankfully, it doesn't refer to what's on your plate.

## SAGRE

The sharing of food is a central feature of all the most important social occasions, and the Sicilian calendar is dotted with *sagre* (festivals dedicated to a culinary item or theme). The classic way to celebrate a feast day is to precede it with a day of eating *magro* (lean), because the feast day is usually a day of overindulgence. Here's a list of some of the best-known food festivals:

★ **Sagra del Mandorlo in Fiore (Festival of the Almond Blossom)** – held in Agrigento on the first Sunday in February (p258)

★ **Sagra della Ricotta (Festival of Ricotta)** – held in Vizzini, near Caltagirone, in April (www.sagradellaricotta.it, in Italian)

★ **Sagra del Carciofo (Festival of the Artichoke)** – held in Cerda, near Palermo, on 25 April (www.comune.cerda.pa.it, in Italian)

★ **Sagra del Cappero (Festival of the Caper)** – held on the island of Salina on the first Sunday in June

★ **StraGusto (Festival of Mediterranean Street Food)** – held in Trapani over three days in July (www.stragusto.it)

★ **Sagra della Cipolla (Festival of the Onion)** – held in Giarratana near Ragusa on 14 August

★ **Festival Internazionale del Cuscus (International Couscous Festival)** – held in San Vito Lo Capo every September (p72)

★ **Sagra del Miele (Honey Festival)** – held in Sortino, located between Catania and Syracuse, in late September or early October (www.sagradelmiele.it, in Italian)

★ **Sagra del Pistachio (Festival of the Pistachio Nut)** – held in Bronte in late September or early October (www.comune.bronte.ct.it, in Italian, or www.bronteinsieme.it)

★ **Festa dei Sapori Madoniti d'Autunno (Festival of Autumn Flavours)** – held in Petralia Sottana in October (www.petraliasottana.net, in Italian)

## SWEETS

Sicily's extraordinary pastries are rich in colour and elaborately designed. The queen of Sicilian desserts, the *cassata,* is made with ricotta, sugar, vanilla, diced chocolate and candied fruits; in Palermo, they describe a woman as 'lovely as a *cassata*'. In the west you can find *cuccia,* an Arab cake made with grain, honey and ricotta. The famous *cannoli,* pastry tubes filled with sweetened ricotta and sometimes candied fruit or chocolate pieces, are found pretty much everywhere. Also look out for *pasta di mandorle* (almond cookies) and *pasta paradiso* (melting moments).

Other Sicilian sweets worth sampling are *gelso di melone* (watermelon jelly), *buccellati* (little pies filled with minced fruit), *pupe* (sugar dolls made to celebrate Ognissanti on 1 November), *ucchiuzzi* (biscuits shaped like eyes, made for the Festa di Santa Lucia on 13 December) and *biscotti regina* (sesame-coated biscuits).

> *'in Palermo, they describe a woman as "lovely as a cassata"'*

If you are in Palermo around late October, before the festival of Ognissanti (All Souls' Day), you will see plenty of stalls selling the famous *frutti della Martorana,* named after the church that first began producing them. These marzipan biscuits, shaped to resemble fruits (or whatever takes the creator's fancy), are part of a Sicilian tradition that dates back to the Middle Ages.

Any decent *pasticceria* (pastry shop) will have an enormous spread of freshly made cakes and pastries. It is very common for Sicilians to have their meal in a restaurant and then go to a pastry shop, where they have a coffee and cake while standing at the bar.

## GELATI & GRANITE

Despite Etna's belly of fire, its peak is a natural freezer, and snow that falls on Etna lasts well into the searing summer, insulated by a fine blanket of volcanic ash. The Romans and Greeks treasured the snow, using it to chill their wine, but it was the Arabs who first started the Sicilian mania for all things icy – *granita* (flavoured crushed ice), *cassata* ice cream, *gelato* (ice cream) and *semifreddo* (literally 'semi-frozen'; a cold, creamy dessert).

The origins of ice cream lie in the Arab *sarbat* (sherbet), a concoction of sweet fruit syrups chilled with iced water, which was then developed into *granita* (where crushed ice was mixed with fruit juice, coffee, almond milk and so on) and *cremolata* (fruit syrups chilled with iced milk), the forerunner to *gelato.*

Home-made *gelato (gelato artiginale)* is sold at cafes and bars across the island, and is truly delicious. You should try it like a Sicilian – first thing in the morning in a brioche!

*Granite* are sometimes topped with fresh whipped cream, and are often eaten with a brioche. Favourite flavours include coffee and almond, though lemon is great in summer. During July, August and September, try a *granita di gelsi* (mulberry), a delicious seasonal offering.

# WINE

Sicily's vineyards cover nearly 120,000 hectares, making it the second-largest wine-producing region in Italy. But while grapes have always been grown here, Sicilian wine is not well known outside the island.

The most common varietal is Nero d'Avola, a robust red similar to Syrah or Shiraz. Vintages are produced by numerous Sicilian wineries, including Planeta (www.planeta.it), which has four estates around the island; Donnafugata (www.donnafugata.it) in Western Sicily; Azienda Agricola COS (www.cosvittoria.it) near Mount Etna; and Azienda Agricola G Milazzo (www.milazzovini.com) near Agrigento. Try Planeta's Plumbago and Santa Cecilia labels, Donnafugata's Mille e una Notte, COS' Nero di Lupo and Milazzo's Maria Costanza and Terre della Baronia Rosso.

Local Cabernet Sauvignons are less common but worth sampling; the version produced by Tasca d'Almerita (www.tascadalmerita.it) at its Regaleali estate in Caltanissetta province is particularly highly regarded (the estate also produces an excellent Nero d'Avola under its Rosso del Conte label).

The Sangiovese-like Nerello Mascalese and Nerello Cappuccio are used in the popular Etna Rosso DOC; try the Contrada Porcaria and Contrada Sciaranuova vintages produced by the Passopisciaro (www.passopisciaro.com) estate or the Serra della Contessa, Rovittello and Pietramarina produced by Vinicola Benanti (www.vinicolabenanti.it).

There is only one Sicilian DOCG *(denominazione d'origine controllata e garantita)*, Cerasuolo di Vittoria (see p18), a blend of Nero d'Avola and Frappato grapes. Look for Planeta's vintages, which are produced at its estate in Dorilli, and those by COS.

Though the local reds are good, the region is probably best known for its white wines, including those produced at Abbazia Santa Anastasia (www.abbaziasantanastasia.it) near Castelbuono, and Fazio Wines (www.faziowines.it) near Erice, Tasca d'Almerita and Passopisciaro.

Common white varietals include Carricante, Chardonnay, Grillo, Inzolia, Cataratto, Inzolia, Cataratto, Grecanico and Corinto. Look out for Tasca d'Almerita's Nozze d'Oro Inzolia blend, Fazio's Catarratto Chardonnay, Abbazia Santa Anastasia's chardonnay blends, and Passopisciaro's Guardiola Chardonnay.

Most wines are fairly cheap, though (as for any wine) prices vary according to the vintage. In a restaurant a bottle of decent wine should cost you around €15 to €25, with a table wine *(vino da tavola)* at around €10.

Sicilian dessert wines are excellent, and are well worth buying to take home. Top of the list is Marsala's sweet wine; the best (and most widely known) labels are Florio and Pellegrino. Sweet Malvasia (from the Aeolian island of Salina) is a fruity wine whose best producer is Carlo Hauser – just look for his name on the bottle and you know you have a good drop. Italy's most famous Moscato (Muscat) is the Passito di Pantelleria from the island of the same name; it has a deep-amber colour and an extraordinary taste of apricots and vanilla.

The subscription-based Gambero Rosso Wine Guide (www.gamberorosso.it) is generally considered to be the bible of Italian wines and offers plenty of information about Sicilian wines and wineries.

# FOOD & DRINK GLOSSARY

· · · · · · ·

## THE BASICS

**bicchiere** bee-*kye*-re glass
**cameriere/a** ka-mer-*ye*-re/a waiter (m/f)
**carta dei vini** *kar*-ta dey-*vee*-nee wine list
**cena** *che*-na dinner
**coltello** kol-*te*-lo knife
**conto** *kon*-to bill/cheque
**cucchiaio** koo-*kya*-yo spoon
**enoteca** e-no-*te*-ka wine bar
**forchetta** for-*ke*-ta fork
**friggitoria** free-jee-to-*ree*-a fried-food stand
**osteria** os-te-*ree*-a informal restaurant
**pasticceria** pas-tee-che-*ree*-a patisserie/pastry shop
**pranzo** *pran*-dzo lunch
**prima colazione** *pree*-ma ko-la-*tsyo*-ne breakfast
**ristorante** ree-sto-*ran*-te restaurant
**spuntino** spoon-*tee*-no snack
**tovagliolo** to-va-*lyo*-lo napkin/serviette
**trattoria** tra-to-*ree*-a informal restaurant
**vegetaliano/a** ve-je-ta-*lya*-no/a vegan (m/f)
**vegetariano/a** ve-je-ta-*rya*-no/a vegetarian (m/f)

## STAPLES

**aceto** a-*che*-to vinegar
**aglio** *a*-lyo garlic
**burro** *boo*-ro butter
**formaggio** for-*ma*-jo cheese
**insalata** een-sa-*la*-ta salad
**latte** *la*-te milk
**miele** *mye*-le honey
**olio** *o*-lyo oil
**oliva** o-*lee*-va olive
**pane** *pa*-ne bread
**panna** *pa*-na cream
**peperoncino** pe-pe-ron-*chee*-no chilli
**riso** *ree*-so rice
**sale** *sa*-le salt
**uovo/uova** *wo*-vo/*wo*-va egg/eggs
**zucchero** *tsoo*-ke-ro sugar

## MEAL PREPARATION

**arrosto/a** a-*ros*-to/a roasted
**bollito/a** bo-*lee*-to/a boiled

**cotto/a** *ko*·to/a cooked
**crudo/a** *kroo*·do/a raw
**fritto/a** *free*·to/a fried
**griglia** *gree*·lya grilled

## FISH & SEAFOOD (PESCE E FRUTTI DI MARE)

**acciughe** a·*choo*·ge anchovies
**aragosta** a·ra·*go*·sta lobster
**calamari** ka·la·*ma*·ree squid
**cozze** *ko*·tse mussels
**frutti di mare** *froo*·tee dee *ma*·re seafood
**gamberoni** gam·be·*ro*·nee prawns
**granchio** *gran*·kyo crab
**merluzzo** mer·*loo*·tso cod
**ostriche** os·*tree*·ke oysters
**pesce spada** *pe*·she *spa*·da swordfish
**polpi** *pol*·pee octopus
**sarde** *sar*·de sardines
**seppia** *se*·pya cuttlefish
**sgombro** *sgom*·bro mackerel
**tonno** *to*·no tuna
**vongole** *von*·go·le clams

## MEAT (CARNE)

**agnello** a·*nye*·lo lamb
**bistecca** bi·*ste*·ka steak
**capretto** kap·*re*·to kid (goat)
**coniglio** ko·*nee*·lyo rabbit
**fegato** fe·*ga*·to liver
**manzo** *man*·dzo beef
**pollo** *po*·lo chicken
**salsiccia** sal·*see*·cha sausage
**trippa** *tree*·pa tripe
**vitello** vee·*te*·lo veal

## FRUIT & VEGETABLES

**arancia** a·*ran*·cha orange
**asparagi** as·*pa*·ra·jee asparagus
**carciofi** kar·*chyo*·fee artichokes
**carota** ka·*ro*·ta carrot
**cavolo** *ka*·vo·lo cabbage
**ciliegia** chee·*lye*·ja cherry
**cipolle** chee·*po*·le onions
**fagiolini** fa·jo·*lee*·nee green beans
**fico** *fee*·ko fig
**finocchio** fee·*no*·kyo fennel

**fragole** *fra*·go·le strawberries
**funghi** *foon*·gee mushrooms
**lampone** lam·*po*·ne raspberry
**limone** lee·*mo*·ne lemon
**mela** *me*·la apple
**melanzane** me·lan·*dza*·ne aubergine
**melone** me·*lo*·ne cantaloupe; rock melon
**patate** pa·*ta*·te potatoes
**pepe** *pe*·pe pepper
**peperoni** pe·pe·*ro*·nee capsicum
**pera** *pe*·re pear
**pesca** *pes*·ka peach
**piselli** pee·*se*·lee peas
**pomodori** po·mo·*do*·ree tomatoes
**rucola** *roo*·ko·la rocket
**spinaci** spee·*na*·chee spinach
**tartufo** tar·*too*·fo truffle
**uva** *oo*·va grapes

## GELATO

**amarena** a·ma·*re*·na wild cherry
**bacio** *ba*·cho chocolate and hazlenuts
**cioccolato** cho·ko·*la*·to chocolate
**cioccolato fondente** cho·ko·*la*·to fon·*den*·te dark chocolate
**cocco** *ko*·ko coconut
**cono** *ko*·no cone
**coppa** *ko*·pa cup
**crema** *kre*·ma egg·custard flavour
**fior di latte** fyor dee *la*·te 'flower of milk'; sweet cream
**frutta di bosco** *froo*·ta dee *bos*·ko wild berries
**grande** *gran*·de large
**mandorla** *man*·dor·la almond
**media** *me*·dya medium
**nocciola** no·*cho*·la hazelnut
**piccolo** *pee*·ko·lo small
**pistachio** pee·*sta*·cho pistachio
**stracciatella** stra·cha·*te*·la chocolate·chip
**vaniglia** va·*nee*·lya vanilla
**zuppa inglese** *tsoo*·pa een·*gle*·ze trifle

## DRINKS

**acqua** *a*·kwa water
**birra** *bee*·ra beer
**caffè** ka·*fe* coffee
**tè** te tea
**vino rosso** *vee*·no *ro*·so red wine
**vino bianco** *vee*·no *byan*·ko white wine

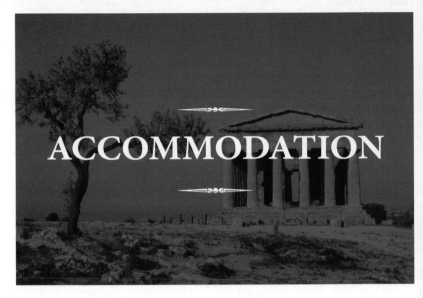

# ACCOMMODATION

## FINDING ACCOMMODATION

There's no shortage of alluring accommodation options in Sicily. At the budget end of the price spectrum you can opt for a *pensione* (guesthouse) or a B&B, both of which will generally be of one- to three-star standard. *Alberghi* (hotels), which may range from one star to five stars, are more expensive. *Locande* (inns) and *affittacamere* (rooms for rent) are not included in the star classification system; they are usually the cheapest options on offer although in some areas (such as the Aeolian Islands) the standard can be very high and prices are adjusted accordingly.

Around Etna and Piano Battaglia in the Madonie Park there's a number of *rifugi* (mountain chalets), most of which are open all year. Many are operated by Club Alpino Siciliano (www.clubalpinosiciliano.it).

*Agriturismi* (working farms and country houses that offer rooms to visitors on holiday) are becoming more common and are well worth considering, as is the small but slowly growing number of boutique hotels on the island.

## PRICES & BOOKING

In our reviews, we have cited the price range from low season to high season. Low-season rates usually apply from October to Easter (with the exception of the Christmas period). In the high season (particularly in August), it is absolutely imperative to book well ahead for any accommodation on the coast or islands.

Be warned that prices in the high season can climb into the stratosphere. You may also have to commit to a multiday stay and/or half board during this time.

### BOOK YOUR STAY ONLINE

For more accommodation reviews and recommendations by Lonely Planet authors, check out the online booking service at www.lonelyplanet.com/hotels. You'll find the true, insider low-down on the best places to stay. Reviews are thorough and independent. Best of all, you can book online.

## PRICE GUIDE

The following is a guide to the pricing information used in this chapter. Unless otherwise stated, prices quoted are for a double room with private bathroom.

| € | up to €80 |
|---|---|
| €€ | €80 to €200 |
| €€€ | €200-plus |

Most accommodation on the coast is open year-round; resorts on the islands tend to open only from Easter to the end of October.

Many options do not have *camera singola* (single rooms); instead, you'll pay a slightly lower price for use of a double room with *camera doppia* (twin beds) or *camera matrimoniale* (double bed).

In reviews, the Parking icon indicates that the hotel has on-site parking (usually around €10 to €15 per day). This can be useful in busy resorts such as Taormina and Cefalù, where it can be all-but-impossible to find a car park. The internet icon indicates that guests have access to use of a computer terminal with internet access. Most hotels reviewed also offer wi-fi access.

# PALERMO

For a major city, Palermo has relatively few accommodation options worthy of recommendation. And that's not the only problem – the fact that this is a busy city means that most hotel rooms come complete with street noise. It's also worth noting that many options occupy floors in historic palazzi, where stairs rather than lifts provide the only access.

### 🌱 AL GIARDINO DELL'ALLORO €
Map p48; ☎ 091 617 69 04; www.giardinodellalloro.it; Vicolo San Carlo 8 (cnr with Via Alloro 78); s €35-50, d €75-85; 🅿 💻

Overlooking a tranquil garden in the heart of the Kalsa district, this arty B&B is clean and well maintained. There's a comfortable family suite sleeping four, and five simple doubles, most of which overlook the courtyard. The winter breakfast room features racy art that could be a bit hard to digest early in the morning; in summer, breakfast is in the courtyard.

### 🌱 ALLA KALA €€
Map p48; ☎ 091 743 47 63; www.allakala.it, in Italian; Corso Vittoria Emanuele 71; s €70-80, d €100-120; 🅿 💻

Near the old part of the port, this B&B has spacious rooms with a muted colour scheme and very nice bathrooms. Service levels are high – staff will happily deliver breakfast to your room, for instance – but some travellers have noted that street noise can make sleeping difficult.

### 🌱 B&B PANORMUS €
Map p48; ☎ 091 617 58 26; www.bbpanormus.com; Via Roma 72; s €25-65, d €40-100; 🅿

Keen prices, a charming host and attractive rooms decorated in the Liberty style make this one of the city's most popular B&Bs. It's on the top floor of a palazzo on Via Roma, accessed via a lift. Each of the five impeccably clean rooms has its own private bathroom down the passageway and there's a convivial breakfast room where all guests share a long table.

### 🌱 BB22 €€
Map p48; ☎ 335 790 87 33; www.bb22.it; Largo Cavalieri di Malta 22; s €80-100, d €110-160; 🅿

Owner Patty hails from Milan, and has endowed this wonderfully located B&B with a generous allocation of that city's sleek designer style. The rooms are comfortable and staff go out of their way to be helpful, supplying restaurant recommendations, making bookings and advising on sightseeing itineraries.

## ONLINE RESOURCES

★ www.agriturismo-sicilia.it

★ www.bed-and-breakfast-sicily.it

★ www.sicilylocation.com

★ www.thinksicily.co.uk

### ♥ GRAND HOTEL ET DES PALMES €€

Map p54; ☎ 091 602 81 11; www.grandhotelet
despalmes.it; Via Roma 398; r €115-185, ste €270-
335; 🖭 💻

This hotel has been the scene of Palermitan intrigues, double-dealings and liaisons
ever since it was built in the late 19th century. The grand Liberty-style salons still
impress with their huge chandeliers and
gigantic mirrors, and the recently renovated rooms offer a high level of comfort
and amenity, featuring marble bathrooms
(with tub) and elegant furnishings. Make
sure you check the website for specials;
prices can plunge in the low season.

### ♥ HOTEL GARIBALDI €€

Map p54; ☎ 091 601 70 11; http://hotel-garibaldi
-palermo.h-rez.com/; Via Emerico Amari 146; s €69-
87, d €88-129; 🅿 🖭 💻

A smart new four-star hotel near the
Teatro Politeama, the Garibaldi has been
receiving rave reviews from guests, and
what's not to like? Its rooms are clean
and comfortable, there's a business
centre and parking is free.

### ♥ HOTEL LETIZIA €€

Map p48; ☎ 091 58 91 10; www.hotelletizia.com;
Via dei Bottai 30; s €50-100, d €60-160; 🖭

This small hotel in the heart of the Kalsa
district has faux-aristo decor that some
guests will love and others may find a tad
tacky. It also runs the cheaper **B&B Ai
Bottai** (s/d/apt €65/85/180) upstairs, which
has a similar decor and the same contact
information. Both offer comfortable,
reasonably priced rooms.

### ♥ HOTEL UCCIARDHOME €€

Map p54; ☎ 091 34 84 26; www.hotelucciard
home.com; Via Enrico Albanese, 34-6; s €89-135, d
€94-169; 🖭

This hotel's marketing spiel urges guests
to become a 'prisoner of relaxation' at
this boutique hotel opposite Palermo's
main prison. The large rooms come
complete with ultracomfortable beds and
are decorated in an elegant minimalist
style. There's also a wine bar for relaxing
after a day spent exploring the city.

### ♥ QUINTOCANTO HOTEL & SPA €€

Map p44; ☎ 091 58 49 13; www.quintocantohotel.
com; Corso Vittorio Emanuele 310; s €70-100, d
€95-180; 🖭

Housed in a 16th-century palazzo next to
the Quattro Canti that has undergone a
modern transformation, the Quintocanto is known for its chic decor, wellness
centre and excellent restaurant, which is
operated by the team from Mondello's
acclaimed Bye Bye Blues (p60). The buffet breakfast is served in the outdoor
courtyard in summer and in an attractive
dining hall in winter.

### ♥ SAN FRANCESCO €€

Map p48; ☎ 091 888 83 91; www.sanfrancescopal
ermo.it; Via Merlo 30; s €60, d €80-90; 🖭

Run by a friendly young couple, the San
Francesco has only three rooms but each
is atmospheric – one has a vaulted roof
and the other two have traditional wood-
beamed ceilings. The quiet but central
location is hard to beat and the breakfast
gets rave reviews from guests.

## AROUND PALERMO

### ♥ ANTICA STAZIONE FERROVIA DI FICUZZA // FICUZZA €

Map p61; ☎ 091 846 00 00; www.anticastazione.
it; off the SS118, between Palermo & Corleone; per
person €35

Occupying a decommissioned 19th-century train station in the middle of thick woods where Bourbon princes once hunted game, this restaurant and hotel offers a truly unique accommodation option. Rooms are simple but comfortable, and the restaurant is a real highlight (Slow Food aficionados rave about it). Staff can assist you with outdoor activities in the nearby national park, including horse-riding, hiking and mountain-bike riding.

☙ **HOTEL CLELIA // USTICA** €€

☎ 091 844 90 39; www.hotelclelia.it, in Italian; Via Sindaco 1; s €29-95, d €48-158; 🖭 🖳

This neat three-star hotel has a good restaurant (p64) and welcoming management. It also rents out holiday houses sleeping two to four people. Staff can help organise scooter and boat hire, diving and snorkelling tours and guided walks.

# WESTERN SICILY

## CASTELLAMMARE DEL GOLFO

☙ **HOTEL CALA MARINA** €

☎ 0924 53 18 41; www.hotelcalamarina.it; Via Don L Zangara 1; s €40-60, d €50-120; 🅿 🖳

Only a 20-minute drive from Falcone-Borsolino airport, this small hotel overlooking the harbour is known for its helpful staff and clean, comfortable rooms. It's worth paying a bit extra for an executive room as these come with balconies overlooking the sea. The good continental breakfast costs an extra €3 and on-site parking costs €5.

## SCOPELLO

☙ **PENSIONE TRANCHINA** €

☎ 092 454 10 99; www.pensionetranchina.com; Via A Diaz 7; per person B&B €36-46, half board €55-72; 🖭

This *pensione* in a fully renovated old building gets rave reviews from guests, all of whom wax lyrical about friendly and helpful owners Marisin and Salvatore and the wonderful home-cooked dinners on offer. Rooms are clean and comfortable; some have balconies overlooking the sea.

☙ **TONNARA DI SCOPELLO** €€

☎ 339 307 19 70 (9am-1pm), 338 641 91 33 (1-9pm); www.tonnaradiscopello.com; Largo Tonnara Scopello; 🅿

The accommodation is basic, prices are high and there's no TV or telephone, but all this will be forgiven the minute you set eyes on this historic *tonnara* (former tuna processing plant) set in a small cove on the water's edge. Groups of between two and six can be accommodated in each of the 10 apartments, and a minimum seven-day stay is required in summer. The *tonnara* has its own pebbled swimming beach and a seafront terrace. Pricing varies wildly according to availability, the season and the number of guests.

## TRAPANI

☙ **AL RESIDENCE SAN DOMENICO** €

Map p75; ☎ 0923 59 33 14; Via Badia Grande 9; s €38-60, d €60-90; 🌣 Mar-Sep; 🖭

This excellent apartment hotel is located on one of Trapani's most charming squares, directly opposite La Rinascente Pasticceria (p77) and a small street market selling fresh fruit and vegetables. There are 21 apartments (one of which is set up for mobility-impaired guests) sleeping between two and five. Amenities include free wi-fi and a small kitchenette with fridge and microwave. There's even an upstairs terrace with BBQ that guests can use. The friendly management team operates another residence, the **Alle Due Badie** (Map p75; ☎ 0923 2 40 54; Via Badia Nuova 33; www.duebadie.it; s €45-65, d €75-95; 🖭), which is open year-round and offers similar rooms. Neither residence serves breakfast.

### ❤ ALBERGO MACCOTTA €

Map p75; ☎ 0923 2 84 18; www.albergomaccotta.it, in Italian; Via degli Argentieri 4; s €30-40, d €60-75; 🗙 🖳

This unassuming hotel in the centre of the Old Town offers clean and neat rooms. There's no atmosphere to speak of, staff don't speak English and you'll have to go elsewhere for breakfast, but prices are extremely reasonable, the location is quiet and there are features including satellite TV in every room.

### ❤ LE CHIAVI DI SAN FRANCESCO €€

Map p75; ☎ 0923 43 80 13; www.lechiavidisan franceso-tp.com; Via Tartaglia 18-24; s €65-85, d €80-105; 🗙

Located opposite the Chiesa di San Francesco (the name means 'the Keys to San Francesco'), this popular hotel has 16 rooms featuring cheerful colour schemes and small but clean bathrooms; some come complete with kitchenette. Wi-fi is available on the 4th-floor terrace where breakfast is served. It's worth opting for a superior room, as these are larger and lighter.

## ERICE

Note that temperatures in Erice can plummet in winter, and hotels tend to skimp on heating when there aren't many guests.

### ❤ BAGLIO SANTA CROCE €€

Off Map p80; ☎ 0923 89 11 11; www.bagliosantac roce.it; Contrada Ragosia da Santa Croce, Valderice; per person B&B €54-65, half board €70-82; 🅿 🖳

This converted 17th-century *baglio* is located 9km east of Erice in Valderice. Set amid citrus groves and lush gardens, the hotel (which also has a modern extension) has 67 rooms, some with exposed stone walls and wooden ceiling beams. There's a restaurant and the swimming pool is a great addition in summer.

### ❤ HOTEL ELIMO €€

Map p80; ☎ 0923 86 93 77; www.hotelelimo.it; Corso Vittorio Emanuele 75; s €85, d €110; 🅿

Rooms at the Elimo offer enchanting views of the windswept coastal plain and shimmering sea below. The communal spaces are intimate and full of shady alcoves, beamed ceilings and marble fireplaces, while the plant-filled and terracotta-tiled terrace is sunny and looks onto the sea. The rooms are neat and light, with comfortable beds.

### ❤ HOTEL SAN DOMENICO €€

Map p80; ☎ 0923 86 01 28; www.hotel-sandomenico. it; Via Tommaso Guarrasi 26; €65-100, d €80-140; 🗙

The most comfortable rooms in town are on offer at this immaculately kept, family-run hotel. The best of the bunch has its own terrace and all have modern bathrooms. Breakfast features fresh pastries and is quite delicious.

## EGADI ISLANDS

### FAVIGNANA

Be sure to book well in advance if you plan to visit during La Mattanza.

### ❤ ALBERGO EGADI €€

☎ 0923 92 12 32; www.albergoegadi.it; Via Colombo 17, Favignana town; s €65-115, d €100-200; 🗙

Staying here is a real treat. The stylish rooms feature attractive colour schemes and excellent bathrooms; the two on the top floor share a panoramic terrace. The hotel also has a restaurant, which offers a seafood-dominated tasting menu that changes each night.

### ❤ CAS AL'MARE €€€

☎ 0923 921576; www.casalmarefavignana.com; Strada Comunale Frascia; s €130-190, d €160-280; 🅿 🗙

A resort right at the water's edge, chic Cas al'Mare has only five rooms, all converted from old fishermen's houses. It and its sister resort Casa Favonio (www.casafavonio.it) share a beach club and are two of the island's most stylish getaways.

### ☙ HOTEL IL PORTICO €€

☎ 0923 92 17 01; www.hotelilportico.it; Via Meucci, 3; s €55-150, d €80-200; 🖳 🖵

This modern hotel next to the main town's church is known for its high levels of service. Guests enthuse about the delicious breakfasts, which are served in the garden in summer, and about the rooftop terrace, which offers sun lounges and a small spa pool.

### ☙ VILLAGGIO ALBERGO L'OASI €€

☎ 0923 92 16 35; www.loasifavignana.it; Contrada Camaro 32; s €60-110, d €80-160; 🅿 🖳

Set in a lush garden, these affordably priced rooms and apartments are perfect for families. Rooms are simple but comfortable; apartments come with a private terrace (complete with outdoor dining setting) and some have balconies with sea views.

## LEVANZO

### ☙ ALBERGO PARADISO €€

☎ 0923 92 40 80; www.albergoparadiso.eu; Via Lungomare; per person €60-85; 🕑 closed mid-Dec–early Mar; 🖳

Levanzo's most attractive accommodation option has 15 rooms and a pretty geranium-clad terrace where you can eat well (meals €38). Rooms are simply furnished, but have sea views.

## MARETTIMO

### ☙ MARETTIMO RESIDENCE €€

☎ 0923 92 32 02; www.marettimoresidence.it; Via Telegrafo 3; s €50-130, d €75-165, plus cleaning charge of €35-55; 🖵 🛁

This small apartment complex shaded by bougainvillea and palm trees caters mostly to families. Each of the 42 apartments comes with a kitchen and a small porch,

and there's pricey internet (€5 per 15 minutes). There's a small swimming pool, a kids playground, a coffee shop and a barbecue area. It's open year-round.

## MARSALA

### ☙ HOTEL CARMINE €€

Map p89; ☎ 0923 71 19 07; www.hotelcarmine.it; Piazza Carmine 16; s €70-90, d €100-125; 🖳 🖵

The Carmine has atmosphere and amenities in spades – something that can't be said for too many hotels in this price bracket. The building it occupies started life as a 12th-century Carmelite monastery and has been restored with great sensitivity and style. All 28 rooms are extremely comfortable and public areas include a gorgeous bar-lounge, a walled garden and an elegant salon where a lavish breakfast buffet is served.

### ☙ HOTEL STELLA D'ITALIA €€

Map p89; ☎ 0923 76 18 89; www.bestwestern.it/stel laditalia_tp; Via Mario Rapisardi 7; s/d €80/120; 🖳 🖵

Opened in 2006, this Best Western hotel is close to the Chiesa Madre and is a good back-up if the Carmine is full. Rooms are comfortable but characterless, with features such as satellite TV and minibar.

## SELINUNTE

The hotels in Marinella di Selinunte are sorely lacking in charm. Be warned that the smell from the marina can be a bit whiffy.

### ☙ HOTEL ALCESTE €€

Off Map p95; ☎ 0924 4 61 84; www.hotelalceste.it; Via Alceste 3, Marinella di Selinunte; s €50-65, d €70-90; 🕑 closed Oct-Mar; 🅿 🖳

This small hotel one street back from the water has a well-regarded restaurant and tidy rooms decked out with pine furnishings. It is within walking distance of the archaeological park, and the rooms on the upper floors have sea views. **Hotel Admeto** (off Map p95; s €62-103, d €50-110) – the high-rise around the corner – is owned by the same people and offers comfortable rooms with sea views and year-round operation.

# TYRRHENIAN COAST

## CEFALÙ

### ♥ B&B CASANOVA €

Map p111; ☎ 0921 92 30 65; Via R Porpora 3; www.casanovabb.it; s €35-60, d €50-90, without bathroom s €30-55, d €40-80; 🖳

Climb up the three floors of steep steps in this old building at the end of Corso Ruggero and you'll find a simple B&B with five rooms and a small roof terrace. We probably wouldn't have listed it if it weren't for its simply splendid 'Ruggero' room, which is huge (it can sleep four) and has a beautiful titled floor and painted ceiling. The single room, on the other hand, is so small and boxy that it feels akin to a prison cell.

### ♥ B&B DOLCE VITA €

Map p111; ☎ 0921 92 31 51; www.dolcevitabb.it; Via C O Bordonaro 8; s €35-70, d €45-110; 🖳 🖵

Cefalù's most popular B&B is close to the Duomo and overlooks the sea – a winning combination. Its six rooms feature bright paint schemes, terracotta tiles and simple furnishings; there are also two newly renovated apartments with kitchens (tall guests may have problems with the low ceilings). You can have your breakfast on the panoramic roof terrace and use the communal kitchen to prepare other meals.

### ♥ HOTEL KALURA €€

Off Map p111; ☎ 0921 42 13 54; www.hotel-kalura.com; Via Vincenzo Cavallaro 13, Località Caldura; s €70-140, d €80-270; 🅿 🖳 🖵

This small resort-style hotel has been managed by the same family for decades.

Situated on a rocky outcrop outside town (a five-minute drive or 2km walk along a coastal path), it has its own private beach and most rooms have good views. It is a good choice for families, with tons of activities – mountain bikes, canoes, pedalos, scuba diving, rock climbing and tennis – and two pools (one large and another for small children).

## CASTELBUONO

### ♥ RELAIS SANTA ANASTASIA €€€

☎ 0921 67 22 33; www.santa-anastasia-relais.it, in Italian; Contrada Santa Anastasia; s €90-190, d €180-245; 🅿 🖳 🖵

Set amid the picturesque vineyards of a highly regarded wine estate, this converted 12th-century abbey boasts extremely comfortable rooms, a sensational pool terrace with views of the Aeolian Islands and two restaurants serving food and wine from the estate. You'll find it 9km from Castelbuono in the direction of Cefalù.

## PIANO BATTAGLIA

### ♥ RIFUGIO CAS PIERO MERLINO €

☎ 0921 64 99 95; www.rifugiopieromerlino.it; Località Piano Battaglia-Mandria Marcate; r per person €35, incl full board €55

Run by the Club Alpino Siciliano, this simple chalet sports wood-panelled rooms sleeping two or four and is open year-round. There are eating and drinking areas, and staff can provide information on skiing, cycling and walking.

## PETRALIA SOTTANA

### ♥ ALBERGO IL CASTELLO €

☎ 0921 64 12 50; www.il-castello.net, in Italian; Via Generale di Maria 27; s €40, d €65; 🖳

This pretty-as-a-picture mountain inn has immaculate rooms and serves a delicious homemade breakfast buffet. It also runs a popular pizzeria in an adjoining building. Be warned, though: driving up the narrow winding streets to the hotel calls for Schumacher-standard driving skills.

## CASTEL DI TUSA

### ❤ ATELIER SUL MARE €€

☎ 0921 33 42 95; www.ateliersulmare.it; Via C Battisti 4; s €85-95, d €120-140, art rooms s €105-115, d €160-180; 🔀

Set up by Antonio Presti, the entrepreneur and art collector behind the town's Fiumara d'Arte project (p124), this hotel right at the water's edge has 17 'art rooms' conceptualised and realised by Italian and international artists between 1990 and 2007. There are also 20 standard rooms, all with original artworks and many with sea views. Check the website for special offers.

## MILAZZO

### ❤ CASSISI HOTEL €€

☎ 090 922 90 99; www.cassisihotel.com; Via Cassisi 5; s €60-90, d €90-120; 🔀 🖵

This recently opened hotel has an excellent location in a small street between the town's main square and the port. Its 14 rooms are attractively decorated, with double-glazed windows, good-quality linen and nice bathrooms. The ground floor has a lounge with big-screen TV and a small bar/breakfast area.

### ❤ PETIT HOTEL €€

☎ 090 928 67 84; www.petithotel.it; Via dei Mille; s €59-89, d €89-149; 🔀

Right opposite the hydrofoil dock, the Petit Hotel makes much of its ecofriendly credentials, using renewable energy sources, featuring latex mattresses and serving organic products as part of its delicious homemade breakfast. The extremely clean rooms are somewhat overpriced considering their spartan fittings.

## AROUND MILAZZO

### ❤ GREEN MANORS COUNTRY HOTEL €€

☎ 090 9746515; Via Porticato, near Castroreale; d incl breakfast & dinner €140-200; 🅿 🔀 🖵 🖭

Family-run and absolutely gorgeous, Green Manors is set in 7 acres of garden and offers everything guests look for a good *agriturismo*: attentive and friendly service, large pool, tranquil rural atmosphere and excellent food. There are nine individually decorated rooms, two of which have private terraces. Rates vary significantly according to time of year and length of stay – those cited above are a rough guide. It's a 40-minute drive from Milazzo and 90 minutes from Taormina.

# AEOLIAN ISLANDS

## LIPARI

### ❤ CASAJANCA €€

Off Map p137; ☎ 090 988 02 22; www.casajanca.it; Marina Garibaldi 115, Località Canneto; d €60-200; 🕙 May-Oct; 🔀

A stone's throw from the beach at Canneto, this is a charming little hotel with 10 rooms, all decorated with polished antique furniture and impeccable taste. The dappled courtyard, a relaxing place to enjoy breakfast, boasts a natural thermal water pool that's perfect for winter stays.

### ❤ DIANA BROWN €

Map p137; ☎ 090 981 25 84; www.dianabrown.it; Vico Himera 3; s €30-90, d €40-100, tr €50-130; 🕙 year-round; 🔀

In a narrow alleyway just off Lipari's main strip, Diana has delightful rooms decorated in island style with cool tiled floors, bright colours and welcome extras such as kettles and fridges. Some rooms also have fully-equipped kitchenettes. There's a sunny breakfast terrace and solarium with deck chairs, plus a book exchange and laundry service. Optional breakfast costs €5.

### ☙ ENZO IL NEGRO €€

Map p137; ☎ 090 981 31 63; www.enzoilnegro. com; Via Garibaldi 29; s €40-60, d €60-130; ☀ year-round; ⌗

This welcoming *pensione* is one of Lipari's few year-round options. In a private home near Marina Corta, it has large, clean rooms with tiled floors, fridges and basic, functional furniture. There are two panoramic terraces and a rooftop solarium overlooking the castle walls.

### ☙ HOTEL GIARDINO SUL MARE €€€

Map p137; ☎ 090 981 10 04; www.giardinosulmare. it; Via Maddalena 65; d €80-230; ☀ Mar-Nov; ⌗ ⌗ ⌗

Friendly and family-run, this hotel has chichi decor – cane furniture, ceramic tiles, summery colours – and a superb cliff-top location. The pool terrace, situated on the cliff edge, is fabulous, although if you prefer to swim in the sea there's direct access to a rocky platform below.

### ☙ VILLA DIANA €€

Off Map p137; ☎ 090 981 14 03; www.villadiana. com; Via Tufo 1; s €43-80, d €76-145; ☀ Apr-Oct; ℗ ⌗

This is a typical Aeolian villa, all sunshine, white walls and bright flowers. Just outside Lipari Town, it's a lovely place with coolly elegant rooms, great terrace views and a leafy garden of orange and lemon trees. Inside, paintings by the villa's original owner, the Swiss artist Edwin Hunziker, add a bohemian flavour.

## VULCANO

### ☙ HOTEL LES SABLES NOIRS €€€

Map p144; ☎ 090 98 50; www.framonhotels.com; Porto di Ponente; s €95-170, d €150-250; ☀ Apr-Oct; ⌗ ⌗

Vulcano's premier hotel sits beachside on the Spiaggia Sabbia Nera. Its large pool is surrounded by gardens and palms, while rooms are decorated in typical Mediterranean style, and many have flower-bedecked balconies. The restaurant's panoramic terrace offers sublime sunset views.

### ☙ PENSIONE GIARA €€

Map p144; ☎ 090 985 22 29; www.pensionelagiara. it; Via Provinciale 18; d €46-144; ☀ Apr-Oct; ⌗

Fronted by lemon trees, this is a cheerful, old-school *pensione* on the road from the port to the volcano. It's a modest affair with sunny white rooms and a rooftop terrace offering impressive volcano views (and an antique Sicilian carriage). A buffet breakfast is served on the terrace from May to October.

## SALINA

### ☙ CAPO FARO €€€

Map p148; ☎ 090 984 43 30; www.capofaro.it; Via Faro 3, Malfa; d €240-380; ⌗ ⌗ ⌗

Immerse yourself in luxury at this five-star boutique resort. A vision of island chic, it's surrounded by lush malvasia vineyards and has 20 rooms, all with sea-facing terraces and sharp white decor. Wine tastings and vineyard visits are available on request and budding cooks can sign up for a cooking course.

### ☙ HOTEL I CINQUE BALCONI €€

☎ 090 984 35 08; www.icinquebalconi.it, in Italian; Via Risorgimento 38; d €100-180, 4-person apt €90-100, ste €170-250; ⌗

Located behind a dusky-yellow facade on Santa Marina Salina's main drag, this is a charming, sun-filled boutique hotel that is set around a sweet central courtyard. Rooms are all slightly different but the over-riding look here is classic Mediterranean with white walls, majolica-tiled floors and polished period furniture.

### ❦ HOTEL MAMMA SANTINA €€€

☎ 090 984 30 54; www.mammasantina.it; Via Sanità 40; d €110-230; ☺Apr-Oct; ❄ ☒

A labour of love for its architect owner, this boutique hotel has inviting rooms decorated with original artwork and pretty tiles in traditional Aeolian designs. Many of the sea-view terraces come with hammocks, and on warm evenings, the attached restaurant has outdoor seating overlooking the softly lit pool and landscaped gardens.

### ❦ HOTEL SIGNUM €€€

☎ 090 984 42 22; www.hotelsignum.it; Via Scalo 15; d €130-280; ☺end Mar-Oct; ❄ ☒

Hidden in the tiny hillside lanes of Malfa, this is Salina's best hotel. Everything about the place is perfect, from the antique-clad rooms to the terrace restaurant, from the fabulous wellness centre – complete with natural spa baths – to the stunning infinity pool looking straight out to smoking Stromboli. Check the website for offers.

## PANAREA

### ❦ HOTEL LA PIAZZA €€€

☎ 090 98 31 54; www.hotelpiazza.it; Via San Pietro; s €100-290, d €140-350; ☺Apr-mid-Oct; ❄ ☒

Draped in bougainvillea, La Piazza offers exclusive and tranquil accommodation in cool, elegant rooms, all with spectacular views of Caletta Bay. There's also a gorgeous swimming-pool terrace, with direct access to the sea, and an excellent restaurant.

### ❦ HOTEL RAYA €€€

☎ 090 98 30 13; www.hotelraya.it; Via San Pietro; d €180-540; ☺Apr-mid-Oct; ❄ ☐ ☒

This is *the* hotel on Panarea – a honeycomb of exquisite white adobe-walled rooms tucked up against a flower-bedecked volcanic hillside. Each room is different but seductive details abound – batik bedspreads, picture-perfect terraces, private gardens, sea views at every turn. There's also a popular restaurant and summer disco.

## STROMBOLI

### ❦ ALBERGO BRASILE €

Map p154; ☎ 090 98 60 08; www.strombolialbergo brasile.it; Via Soldato Cincotta; d €70-80, half-board per person €65-85; ☺Apr-Oct

This laid-back *pensione* is a great budget option with cool, white rooms, no decor to speak of, and a pretty entrance courtyard with lemon and olive trees. Up top, the roof terrace commands views of the sea one side and the volcano the other. Half-board is compulsory in August.

### ❦ CASA DEL SOLE €

Map p154; ☎ 090 98 63 00; www.casadelsolestrom boli.it; Via Domenico Cincotta; dm €25-35, d €60-100, d without bathroom €50-80; ☺Mar-Oct

This wonderful guesthouse is near Ficograndе beach. A hacienda-style set-up centred on a picturesque courtyard overhung with vines and lemon blossom, it has dorms sleeping up to five people and private double rooms, as well as a lovely farmhouse kitchen. Note that it's a dark walk here from the centre at night.

### ❦ LA SIRENETTA PARK HOTEL €€€

Map p154; ☎ 090 98 60 25; www.lasirenetta.it, in Italian; Via Marina 33; s €95-150, d €130-310; ☺Apr-Oct; ❄ ☒

A lovely terraced complex on the beach at Ficogrande, this was Stromboli's first-ever hotel – the current owner's father counted Ingrid Bergman as an early guest. It's a laid-back place with white, summery rooms, a first-class restaurant and its own amphitheatre used to screen films and stage theatrical performances.

## FILICUDI

### ❦ PENSIONE LA SIRENA €€

☎ 090 988 99 97; www.pensionelasirena.it; Via Pecorini Mare; d €120-140, half-board per person €90-120; ⏰ Mar–Nov; ✂

La Sirena is the ideal place to relax into the laid-back Aeolian lifestyle. A wonderful *pensione* in the tiny fishing village of Pecorini, it has traditional, high-ceilinged rooms with French doors opening onto beach views and a superb seafood restaurant. There are also several houses spread across the village, sleeping between two and 12 people.

# IONIAN COAST

## MESSINA

### ❦ ROYAL PALACE HOTEL €€

Map p165; ☎ 090 65 03; www.nh-hotels.it; Via Tommaso Cannizzaro 3; s €60-125, d €95-165; P ✂

An unfortunate city-centre landmark, this grey concrete monster is easy to find, has parking (€11 per night; a definite plus) and offers comfortable, corporate-style rooms. The decor is a throwback to the dark days of the 1970s with dated, dizzying patterned carpets, low sofas and plenty of brown and orange.

## TAORMINA

### ❦ HOTEL CONDOR €€

Off Map p170; ☎ 0942 2 31 24; www.condorhotel.com; Via Cappuccini 25; d €70-120; ⏰ Mar–mid-Nov; P ✂

Just outside the pedestrianised centre is this cordial, family-run hotel. Rooms are bright and airy with minimal decor and plain, functional furniture. The best have small sea-view terraces (for which you pay slightly more). Breakfast is served on the panoramic rooftop terrace and parking is available (€10).

### ❦ HOTEL DEL CORSO €€

Map p170; ☎ 0942 62 86 98; www.hoteldelcorso taormina.com; Corso Umberto I 238; s €49-89, d €79-140; ✂

Boasting a prime position on the main drag, this welcoming hotel is one of the few located in the Borgo Medioevale and one of the few to remain open year-round. It's a modest affair with bright, unfussy rooms and a small breakfast terrace overlooking the crenellated Palazzo Duca di Santo Stefano.

### ❦ HOTEL VILLA BELVEDERE €€

Map p170; ☎ 0942 2 37 91; www.villabelvedere.it; Via Bagnoli Croce 79; s €98-130, d €98-200; ⏰ mid-Mar–mid-Nov; P ✂ ♨

Built in 1902, the jaw-droppingly pretty Villa Belvedere oozes class. Rooms are simple but refined with cream linens and terracotta floors, and the luxurious garden commands majestic sea views. There's even a swimming pool with a 100-year-old palm tree rising from a small island in the middle.

### ❦ ISOCO GUEST HOUSE €€

Off Map p170; ☎ 094 22 36 79; www.isoco.it; Via Salita Branco 2; s €65-120, d €85-120; ⏰ end Mar–Nov; P ✂ 🖥 💻

Every room in this welcoming, gay-friendly guesthouse is dedicated to an artist, so you have the pink Botticelli room, the black-and-white Herb Ritts room, and the Keith Haring room decorated with the artist's trademark graffiti figurines. There's also a stylish terrace, a sundeck and, best of all, an outdoor jacuzzi.

### ☙ LE 4 FONTANE €

Map p170; ☎ 347 075 06 24; www.le4fontane.it;
Corso Umberto I 231; s €40-50, d €60-90; ❄
Run by a friendly couple, this excellent
B&B has three spacious, colourful rooms
on the top floor of an old palazzo (no lift,
though). There's a convenient kitchen
and it's perfectly located on Taormina's
main drag, within easy walking distance
of the Lumbi car park.

## GIARDINI-NAXOS

### ☙ HOTEL LA RIVA €€

☎ 0942 5 13 29; www.hotellariva.com; Via Tysandros 52; s €55-77, d €70-110; P ❄
Right on the seafront, next to the tourist office, this is a lovely family-run
hotel with 40 rooms, all individually
decorated with traditional Sicilian furnishings and marvellous inlaid wood
bedsteads. There's nothing flash about
the place but it's got character and
the graceful owners extend a warm
welcome.

## CATANIA

### ☙ B&B CROCIFERI €

Map p178; ☎ 095 715 22 66; www.bbcrociferi.it; Via
Crociferì 81; s €50-65, d €70-85, tr/q €110/120; ❄
Beautifully located and with three
delightfully decorated rooms, this is a
great choice. Rooms are spacious with
tall ceilings and artistic accoutrements
from the owners' travels in India. Mario
offers tours of the coast in his private
boat and Teresa serves a memorable
breakfast in the gorgeous, plant-filled
kitchen.

### ☙ BAD €

Map p178; ☎ 095 34 69 03; www.badcatania.com;
Via Colombo 24; s/d €50/70, with external bathroom
€40/60, mini-apt €90-100; ❄
Housed in a nondescript palazzo within
a crab's claw of the fish market, this

funky boutique B&B is an explosion of
psychedelic patterns, kooky furniture,
contemporary art and loud, brash colours. And if you like the style you can
even buy T-shirts, bags and badges created by the young graphic designers who
own the place.

### ☙ CITY LOUNGE B&B €

Map p178; ☎ 095 286 17 03; www.city-lounge
-bed-and-breakfast.com; Via Gagliani 13; s €35,
d €45-65; P ▯
A home away from home, City Lounge
makes a great city-centre bolthole. Just
five minutes' walk from Piazza del Duomo, it has four thoughtfully decorated
guestrooms, a bright communal area
and, miracle of miracles, private parking
(which costs €5 per night). Breakfast,
which is served by the super-hospitable
Claudia, is a feast of delicious *dolci*
(sweets).

### ☙ HOTEL ETNEA 316 €

Map p178; ☎ 095 250 30 76; www.hoteletnea316.it;
Via Etnea 316; s/d/tr/q €60/80/105/140; ❄ ▯
Opposite the Villa Bellini gardens, the
charming Hotel Etnea has 10 tastefully
decorated rooms with comfy wrought-
iron beds, tall windows, traditional tiles
or wooden floors, and mustard-yellow
walls. There's also a sunny lounge and
breakfast room.

### ☙ IL PRINCIPE €€

Map p178; ☎ 095 250 03 45; www.ilprincipehotel.
com; Via Alessi 24; s €99-169, d €109-179; ❄ ▯
This refined hotel offers stylish rooms
on one of Catania's liveliest nightlife
streets. Double-glazed windows allow
you to enjoy the chic cream-coloured
rooms, kitted out with crisp modern
furniture, dark parquet floors and fluffy
bathrobes to wear on the way to the
Turkish bath. Check the website for
special offers.

# RIVIERA DEI CICLOPI

## ACIREALE

### ☙ AL DUOMO €€

☎ 347 907 83 23; www.alduomo.org; Via Calì 5; s/d/tr/q €60/80/110/140; ✵

The pick of Acireale's accommodation is this four-room apartment in a restored 19th-century palazzo. Just off Piazza Duomo, it's colourful and stylish, each room individually coloured with attractive vaulted ceilings and balcony views towards the town's baroque centre.

## ACI TREZZA

### ☙ EPOS B&B €

☎ 392 484 81 13; www.bbepos.it; Via Provinciale 262; s €35-50, d €50-80; ✵

About five minutes' walk from the seafront, this charming B&B is in an early-1900s house. Its five rooms, each named after a character from Homer's Odyssey, sport bold orange, red and yellow, and antique-style furniture. Guests have use of a kitchen, complete with a barbecue, and access to a small terrace.

### ☙ GRAND HOTEL I FARAGLIONI €€

☎ 095 093 04 64; www.grandhotelfaraglioni.com; Lungomare Ciclopi 115; s €95-110, d €105-130; ✵ 🖳 🖵

This drumlike four-star is a landmark on the Aci Trezza seafront. Inside, rooms are gleaming white with mod-cons and views over the Faraglioni (sea rock towers). There's sunbathing on a seaside sundeck and a popular restaurant, La Terrazza, where locals and visitors head for pizza and aperitivi.

## MT ETNA

### SOUTH

### ☙ HOTEL ALLE PENDICI €€

☎ 095 791 43 10; www.hotelallependici.com; Viale della Regione 18, Nicolosi; s €50-65, d €75-95

In Nicolosi, just off the main route up to the cable-car station, this country-style

hotel offers excellent value for money. Its rooms are tasteful, combining exposed brickwork with rustic wood furniture and the occasional hanging chandelier. Some have views up Etna's southern slopes.

### ☙ RIFUGIO SAPIENZA €€

☎ 095 91 63 56; www.rifugiosapienza.com; Piazzale Funivia; per person B&B/half-board/full board €55/75/90

As close to the summit as you can get, this Alpine-style chalet adjacent to the cable-car station offers cosy accommodation in 24 modern rooms decked out with functional furniture and warm, wooden floors. Downstairs, the bar-restaurant serves healthy helpings of honest, unpretentious mountain food.

### NORTH

### ☙ AGRITURISMO SAN MARCO €

☎ 389 423 72 94; www.agriturismosanmarco.com; per person B&B/half-board/full board €35/50/63; 🖳

Get back to basics at this delightful *agriturismo* near Rovitello. Run by a jovial elderly couple, it's a bit off the beaten track but the bucolic setting, rustic rooms and superb country cooking more than compensate. There's also a swimming pool and kids' play area complete with swing and slides. Call ahead for directions.

# SYRACUSE & THE SOUTHEAST

## SYRACUSE

### ORTYGIA

### ☙ ALLA GIUDECCA €€

Map p203; ☎ 0931 2 22 55; www.allagiudecca.it; Via GB Alagona 52; s €60-75, d €80-120; ✵

Located in Ortygia's old Jewish quarter, this gorgeous hotel boasts 23 suites of various sizes. They all differ slightly but the overall look is rustic chic with brick-tiled floors, exposed wood beams and period antiques, and they all have cooking facilities. Under the hotel you can visit an ancient Jewish *miqwe* (see p204).

### ☙ HOTEL GUTKOWSKI €€

Map p203; ☎ 0931 46 58 61; www.guthotel.it; Lungomare Vittorini 26, Ortygia; s/d €80/110; ✄ ☐

This modish boutique hotel is spread over two fishermens houses on the Ortygia waterfront. Rooms in the main structure have pretty tiled floors, colourful walls and retain a historical character, while those down the road exhibit a sharper, more modern look.

### ☙ HOTEL ROMA €€

Map p203; ☎ 0931 46 56 26; www.hotelroma.sr.it; Via Roma 66; s €75-85, d €105-150; ℗ ✄

A welcoming four-star, Hotel Roma has individually decorated rooms with polished parquet floors, wood-beamed ceilings and original works of art. Staff are attentive and friendly and if it all gets too much there's a sauna on the 1st floor. Parking costs €10.

### ☙ VIAGGIATORI, VIANDANTI E SOGNATORI €

Map p203; ☎ 0931 2 47 81; www.bedandbreakfastsicily.it; Via Roma 156; s €35-50, d €55-65, tr/q €75/100; ✄

Decorated with verve and boasting a prime location in Ortygia, this is Syracuse's best B&B. There's a lovely bohemian feel with books and pieces of antique furniture juxtaposed against silver and purple walls. The same family also runs the more modest **B&B L'Acanto** (Map p203; ☎ 0931 46 11 29; www.bebsicilia.it; Via Roma 15), which has the same prices.

### AROUND SYRACUSE

### ☙ VILLA DEI PAPIRI €€

Off Map p201; ☎ 0931 72 13 21; www.villadeipapiri.it; Contrada Cozzo Pantano; d €70-170, 4-person ste €140-269; ℗ ✄ ☐

This is pure *agriturismo* heaven. Immersed in an Eden of orange groves and papyrus reeds, eight family suites are housed in a beautifully converted 19th-century farmhouse, while double rooms are dotted around the lush grounds. Breakfast is served in a baronial stone-walled hall drenched in flowers and furnished in masterly style.

## PALAZZOLA ACREIDE

### ☙ B&B ATTIKO €

☎ 0931 87 53 94; www.attiko.it; Ronco Corridore 10; s €35-40, d €60-70; ✄

This unpretentious B&B makes for a lovely overnight stay. The convivial owner extends a hearty welcome to his family home, which has five guest rooms, some decorated in traditional style, others with more colourful ethnic furnishings. Topping everything is a panoramic rooftop terrace.

## NOTO

### ☙ B&B MONTANDÒN €

Map p216; ☎ 0931 83 63 89; www.b-bmontandon.it; Via A Sofia 50; s €40-50, d €60-80; ✄

Accessed via an imposing vaulted hallway, this snug B&B is in a crumbling palazzo near the top of town. A cheerfully cluttered hall leads onto three light-filled rooms, each with its own small balcony, wrought-iron bed and elegant furnishings.

### ☙ HOTEL DELLA FERLA €€

Off Map p216; ☎ 0931 57 60 07; www.hotelferla.it; Via A Gramsci; s €48-78, d €84-120; ℗ ✄

This small, family-run hotel is located in a residential area about 10 minutes' walk downhill from the historic centre. Rooms are large and bright with pine furnishings and small balconies, and the family that runs the place is extremely helpful. The free parking is another major plus.

# THE NOTO COAST

### ❤ LA CORTE DEL SOLE €€

Off Map p216; ☎ 0931 82 02 10; www.lacortedel sole.it; Contrada Bucachemi, Lido di Noto; d €80-196, half-board per person €79-125; ⓟ ⓧ ⓛ

This gorgeous rural retreat sits in isolated splendour near the Riserva Naturale Oasi Faunistica di Vendicari. A typical Sicilian farmstead of low-lying sandstone buildings set around a central courtyard, it has 34 ceramic-clad, wood-beamed rooms, an in-house restaurant and a long list of services (bike hire, cooking courses, shuttle bus to the sea).

## MODICA

### ❤ ALBERGO I TETTI DI SICILIANDO €

☎ 0932 94 28 43; www.siciliando.it; Via Cannata 24; r €60-70, without bathroom €50-60; ⓧ

This is a wonderful guesthouse in the old town, just off central Corso Umberto. The rooms are simple, spacious and airy, and many have views of Modica's steeply stacked houses. Extras include bike hire (per day/week €15/80), and art courses (minimum of six people) that last one to two weeks and cost €500 to €600, including accommodation.

### ❤ B & B IL CAVALIERE €

☎ 0932 94 72 19; www.bbilcavalieremodica.it; Corso Umberto I 259; r €70-80, ste €110-120; ⓧ

Stay in aristocratic style at this classy B&B on Modica's main strip. It's housed in a 19th-century palazzo that has been restored with a masterly hand and the large, high-ceilinged rooms retain original features such as tiled floors and frescoed ceilings. Patches of exposed stone and coloured wall panels add a modern touch.

### ❤ HOTEL DEMOHÀC €€

☎ 0932 75 41 30; www.hoteldemohac.it; Via T Campailla 15; s €55-65, d €85-110; ⓧ

Taking inspiration from Modica's literary legacy – poet and Nobel prize–winner Salvatore Quasimodo was born here in 1901 – the 10 rooms in this dapper hotel are each named after a writer. And in keeping with the bookish theme, they are decked out with good-looking antiques, chaise longues and writing tables.

### ❤ HOTEL RELAIS €€

☎ 0932 75 44 51; www.hotelrelaismodica.it; Via T Campanella; d €85-110; ⓧ ⓛ

Guests are assured a warm welcome at this inviting old-school hotel. Housed in a converted palazzo just off Corso Umberto I, it's an attractive hostelry with 10 bright, cheery rooms, each slightly different but all spacious and quietly elegant. There's free internet in reception and satellite TV in the rooms.

## RAGUSA

### ❤ CAELUM HYBLAE €€

☎ 0932 22 04 02; www.bbcaelumhyblae.it; Salita Specula 11, Ragusa Ibla; d €100-120

With its book-lined reception and crisp white decor, this stylish, family-run B&B exudes quiet sophistication. Each of the seven rooms has views over the cathedral and while they're not the biggest, they're immaculately turned out with unadorned walls, pristine beds and functional modern furniture.

### ❤ IL BAROCCO €€

☎ 0932 66 31 05; www.ilbarocco.it; Via Santa Maria La Nuova; s €55-80, d €90-125; ⓧ

An easy five-minute walk from central Piazza Duomo, this is a friendly three-star. Its distinctive salmon-pink facade complements a traditional interior of antique-style furniture, polished wood and baked floor tiles while rooms, accessible via a twisting iron staircase, are comfortable and decent-sized.

### ☙ LOCANDA DON SERAFINO €€
☎ 0932 22 00 65; www.locandadonserafino.it; Via XI Febbraio 15; r €148-196; 🖳 🖵

A tastefully converted townhouse provides the setting for this plush four-star near the entrance to Ragusa Ibla. Bare stone walls, vaulted ceilings and understated decor produce a sophisticated, low-key look that is just right for Ragusa's rocky centre. The eponymous restaurant (see p226) is one of the best in town.

### ☙ RISVEGLIO IBLEO €
☎ 0932 24 78 11; www.risveglioibleo.com; Largo Camerina 3, Ragusa Ibla; r per person €35-45; 🅿 🖳

This fab B&B, housed in an 18th-century Liberty-style villa, has spacious, high-ceilinged rooms, walls hung with family portraits, a piano, hundreds of books and a flower-flanked terrace overlooking the rooftops. On the ground floor there's also a kitchen available for guest use.

# CENTRAL SICILY

## ENNA
- - - - - - - - - - - - - - - - - - - - - - - - - - - - - -

Accommodation is in short supply in Enna but there are plenty of hotels and *agriturismi* around Lago di Pergusa, 9km south of town.

### ☙ BAGLIO POLLICARINI €€
Off Map p233; ☎ 0935 54 19 82; www.bagliopol licarini.it; Contrada Pollicarini; s €45-60, d €75-100, camping per person/tent €7/9; 🅿

This splendid *agriturismo* is housed in a 17th-century convent near the Lago di Pergusa. The monk's cells have long since been converted into comfortable guest rooms, but the thick stone walls, vaulted ceilings and fading frescoes

leave a historical imprint. There's also a dedicated camping area and an in-house restaurant (meals from €25).

### ☙ GRANDE ALBERGO SICILIA €€
Map p233; ☎ 0935 50 08 50; www.hotelsiciliaenna. it; Piazza Napoleone Colaianni 7; s €62-72, d €102-120; 🅿 🖳

Up in the historic centre, Enna's best hotel hides its lights behind a crude concrete facade. Once inside, you'll find a panoramic breakfast terrace and cheery, comfortable rooms with kitsch gold-framed Botticelli prints and wrought-iron bedsteads.

## NICOSIA
- - - - - - - - - - - - - - - - - - - - - - - - - - - - - -

### ☙ BAGLIO SAN PIETRO €€
☎ 0935 64 05 29; www.bagliosanpietro.com, in Italian; Contrada San Pietro; per person B&B €45, half/full board €62/75; 🅿 🖳

Near the entrance to Nicosia (on the SS117 to Agira), this is an *agriturismo* in the true sense of the word, a working farm with 10 comfortable, rustic-style rooms and a restaurant specialising in earthy country food. You can go horse-riding (one hour/half-day €18/50), organise an excursion or simply relax by the pool.

## PIAZZA ARMERINA
- - - - - - - - - - - - - - - - - - - - - - - - - - - - - -

### ☙ AZIENDA AGRITURISTICA GIGLIOTTO €€
Off Map p239; ☎ 0933 97 08 98; www.gigliotto.com; Contrada Gigliotto, SS117; s €60-80, d €80-100; 🅿 🖳

An ancient *masseria* (manor farm) dating from the 14th century, Gigliotto is set in rolling Tuscan-style countryside 9km south of Piazza Armerina. The homestead has 14 rural-styled rooms and a farmhouse restaurant with a picturesque outdoor terrace. Visits to the in-house winery and wine tastings can be arranged.

### ❦ B&B UMBERTO 33 €

Map p239; ☎ 0935 68 33 44; www.umberto33.com;
Via Umberto 33; s €35-50, d €60-80; ⊠

Run by superfriendly Giovanni, this
modest B&B is a real home away from
home. It has few frills but the three
guest rooms are clean as a pin, there's a
kitchen for guest use, and the location,
right in the heart of the historic centre, is
ideal. Guests are also treated to a complimentary bottle of wine from Giovanni's
*enoteca*.

### ❦ SUITE D'AUTORE €€

Map p239; ☎ 0935 68 85 53; www.suitedautore.
com; Via Monte 1; d €100-140; ⊠

With lime-green polystyrene furniture,
19th-century frescoes and a giant circular bed floating in a floor of liquid tiles,
this unique design hotel is one of Piazza
Armerina's great sights. Each of its seven
rooms is themed after a period in design, and everything you see – and that
includes works of contemporary art – is
for sale.

## CALTAGIRONE
--------------------------------------------------

### ❦ B&B TRE METRI SOPRA IL CIELO €

☎ 0933 193 51 06; www.bbtremetrisoprailcielo.it;
d €60-80; ⊠

Just off Caltagirone's famous staircase,
this is a fantastic B&B run by a friendly
and enthusiastic young couple. The
decor varies between the six rooms but
is universally tasteful and there can be
few finer places to breakfast than on the
spectacular balcony overlooking Caltagirone's rooftops and the hills beyond.

### ❦ LA PILOZZA INFIORATA €€

☎ 0933 2 21 62; www.lapilozzainfiorata.com; Via SS
Salvatore 97; s €45-60, d €60-90; ⊠

Graceful rooms await at this smart B&B
in the historic centre. Against a white
and sky-blue colour scheme, sloping

wood-beamed ceilings, antique furniture
and displays of backlit ceramics combine
to give the interior a low-key, elegant
look. Breakfast is served on the sweet
terrace in the warmer months.

# MEDITERRANEAN COAST

## AGRIGENTO
--------------------------------------------------

### TOWN CENTRE

### ❦ ATENEA 191 €

Map p254; ☎ 0922 59 55 94; www.atenea191.com,
in Italian; Via Atenea 191; s €45-60, d €65-85; ⊠

A labour of love for the multilingual
owner Sonia, rooms at this welcoming
B&B feature exuberant floral stencils,
traditional floor tiles and, in some,
18th-century frescoed ceilings. The
breakfast terrace has sweeping views
over the valley below, as do four of the
six rooms.

### ❦ CAMERE A SUD €€

Map p254; ☎ 349 638 44 24; www.camereasud.it;
Via Ficani 6; d €60-70, tr €80-90; ⊠

A lovely B&B in the centre of Agrigento,
Camere a Sud has three guest rooms
decorated with style and taste – traditional decor and contemporary textiles
are matched with bright colours and
modern art. The sumptuous breakfast
is served on the terrace in the warmer
months. Cash only.

### ❦ CITY BED €

☎ 0922 40 30 91; www.citybed.it; Via Garibaldi 61; s
€40-60, d €49-69; ⊠

An urbane pied-à-terre, City Bed offers
great value for money, a warm welcome
and classy rooms. Cool white tones and a
black-and-white chessboard floor set the
tone for the spacious entrance halls while
frescoed ceilings cap the cool, modern
rooms. Breakfast is served in a bar on
nearby Piazza Pirandello.

## VALLEY OF THE TEMPLES

### ❦ FORESTERIA BAGLIO DELLA LUNA €€€

Off Map p256; ☎ 0922 51 10 61; www.bagliodel
laluna.com; Contrada Maddalusa; s €140-210, d
€170-250; ⓟ ⚡

Dating back to the 13th century, the watchtower that guards over this romantic four-star houses the hotel's showpiece rooms – all wood-panelling, parquet and antique furniture. In the main structure, rooms are less showy and diners flock to the hotel restaurant, Il Déhors (p259), reckoned to be one of Agrigento's best.

### ❦ HOTEL VILLA ATHENA €€€

Map p256; ☎ 0922 59 62 88; www.hotelvillaathena.
it; Via Passeggiata Archeologica 33; s €150-240,
d €190-330; ⓟ ⚡ ⚡

With the Tempio della Concordia lit up in the near distance and palm trees lending an exotic Arabian-nights feel, the views from this historic five-star are magnificent. Housed in an aristocratic 18th-century villa, the hotel's interior, gleaming after a recent makeover, is a picture of white, ceramic cool.

## SCIACCA

### ❦ AL MORO €€

Map p264; ☎ 0925 8 67 56; www.almoro.com; Via
Liguori 44; s €55-65, d €80-100, ste €100-160; ⚡

Cool 21st-century decor combines with 13th-century architecture in Sciacca's historic centre. Al Moro is a slick, good-looking boutique B&B, with rooms revealing a clean, white colour scheme, exposed girders and jazzy mosaic-tiled bathrooms. The abundant breakfast is served downstairs in a vaulted stone hall just off a small courtyard.

### ❦ B&B DA LULO E GAGÀ €

Map p264; ☎ 349 614 08 80; www.bedandbreak
fastlulogaga.com; Vicolo Muscarnera 9; d €60; ⚡

Kooky, fun and original, Lulo's works of art are what sets this great B&B apart. Owls made of multicoloured pebbles, mosaic-framed mirrors and painted ceramics adorn the sunny little apartment while cacti and Egyptian hieroglyphics brighten the pint-sized terrace.

### ❦ VILLA PALOCLA €€

Off Map p264; ☎ 0925 90 28 12; www.villapalo
cla.it; Contrada Raganella; d/tr/q €115/140/180;
ⓟ ⚡ ⚡ ⚡

This charming hotel is an oasis of tranquillity just outside Sciacca. Housed in an 18th-century villa, and surrounded by orange groves, it retains a baronial feel with a cobbled courtyard and wrought-iron balconies. The interior is pure country house with lots of floral fabrics, ceramic tiles and dark wood.

## EAST OF AGRIGENTO

### ❦ FARM €€

☎ 0934 34 66 00; www.farm-ospitalitadicampagna.
it; Contrada Strada Butera; r €70-110; ⓟ ⚡ ⚡

Immersed in greenery, FARM looks all the world like a traditional Sicilian *agriturismo*. But behind the stone walls, it reveals a cutting-edge contemporary interior – works of modern art hang on violet walls, bare brick tiles are matched with ethnic drapes. There's even a small cinema and, outside, a red swimming pool.

### ❦ VECCHIA MASSERIA €€

☎ 0935 68 40 03; www.vecchiamasseria.com;
Contrada Cutuminello, SS117; s €50-90, d €70-160;
ⓟ ⚡ ⚡

It takes some getting to but once you've found this *agriturismo* about 20km northeast of Gela, you won't want to leave. With elegant, soothing rooms, a highly reputed restaurant, a swimming pool and a long list of services, it's ideally set up as a rural hideaway. No credit cards.

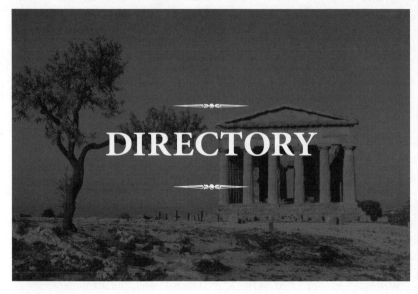

# DIRECTORY

## BUSINESS HOURS

Shops in Sicily generally open from around 9.30am to 1.30pm and then from around 4pm to 7.30pm Monday to Saturday. Many are closed on Monday morning and some smaller stores also close on Saturday afternoon. Some city department stores and many supermarkets have continuous opening hours from 9am to 8pm Monday to Saturday, with some also opening on Sunday morning, typically until 1pm.

Banks open from 8.30am to 1.30pm and 2.45pm to 3.45pm Monday to Friday. They are closed on weekends, but it is always possible to find an exchange office open in the larger cities and in major tourist areas.

Major post offices open from 8am to 6.30pm Monday to Friday and also 8am to 12.30pm on Saturday. Smaller post offices generally open from 8am to 1.30pm Monday to Friday and to 12.30pm on Saturday.

*Farmacie* (pharmacies) are usually open 9am to 1pm and 3.30pm to 7.30pm.

Most shut on Saturday afternoon, Sunday and holidays but a handful remain open on a rotation basis *(farmacie di turno)*. Closed pharmacies display a list of the nearest ones open.

Bars and cafes generally open 7am to 8pm, although some stay open later and turn into pub-style watering holes. Restaurants typically open from noon to 3pm and 7.30pm to 11pm (later in summer).

Opening hours for museums, galleries and archaeological sites vary enormously, although many are closed on Monday.

Note also that Sicilian opening hours are not always observed with rigid precision, especially in small towns and outside of the busy summer months.

Throughout this book, business hours are listed only if they differ from these standards.

## CHILDREN

Sicilians love children, but there are few special amenities for them, other than discounts on public transport and admission to sights. Many hotels/*pensioni* offer reduced rates for children or will add an extra bed or cot on request (usually for an extra 30% or so). Restaurants rarely have a kids' menu but most will happily serve a *mezzo porzione* (half portion).

You can stock up on nappies, baby formula and sterilising solutions at pharmacies and supermarkets. Fresh cow's milk is sold in bars that have a 'Latteria' sign and in supermarkets.

Car seats for infants and children are available from most car-rental firms, but you should always book them in advance.

For more information see Lonely Planet's *Travel with Children* or look up the websites www.travelwithyourkids.com and www.familytravelnetwork.com.

# CUSTOMS REGULATIONS

Duty-free sales within the EU no longer exist. Goods bought in and exported within the EU incur no additional taxes,

provided duty has been paid somewhere within the EU and the goods are for personal use.

Travellers entering Italy from outside the EU are allowed to import the following duty free: 200 cigarettes, 1L of spirits, 2L of wine, 60mL of perfume, 250mL of *eau de toilette,* and other goods up to the value of €175. Anything over this limit must be declared on arrival and the appropriate duty paid.

On leaving the EU, non-EU citizens can reclaim any Imposta di Valore Aggiunto (IVA) value-added tax on purchases equal to or over €155. The refund, which is typically around 12%, only applies to purchases made in affiliated outlets that display a 'Tax Free for Tourists' or similar sign. You have to complete a form at the point of sale, then get it stamped by Italian customs as you leave.

# DANGERS & ANNOYANCES

Despite Mafia notoriety, Sicily is not a dangerous place and the biggest threat you face is not from the local *capo* but from faceless pickpockets and bag-snatchers.

### SCAMS

Many scams play on visitors' insecurity with foreign banknotes. One simple con to watch out for is short-changing. A typical scene runs as follows: you pay for a €3 *panino* with a €20 note. The cashier then distractedly gives you a €2 coin and a €5 note before turning away. The trick here is just to wait and chances are that the €10 you're waiting for will appear without a word being said.

### THEFT

There's no need for paranoia but be on your guard against pickpockets and

DIRECTORY

---

## PRACTICALITIES

★ Sicily uses the metric system for weights and measures.

★ Plugs have two or three round pins, so bring an adapter.

★ The current is 220V, 50Hz.

★ Sicily's major regional newspapers are Palermo's *Il Giornale di Sicilia,* Catania's *La Sicilia* and Messina's *La Gazzetta del Sud.* Rome-based *La Repubblica* also has a section dedicated to Sicilian news.

★ English-language newspapers are available, usually one or two days late, in the big cities and major resorts.

bag-snatchers, particularly in crowded markets (Palermo and Catania especially) and when travelling to or from the airports.

A money belt for essentials is a good idea, but avoid delving into it in public by carrying a wallet with a day's worth of cash in it. Don't flaunt watches, cameras and other valuables. If you're carrying a bag or camera, wear the strap across the body and away from the road – moped thieves can swipe a bag and be gone in seconds.

Be careful when you sit down at a street-side cafe or restaurant – never drape your bag over an empty chair by the road or where you can't see it.

Cars, particularly those with foreign number plates or rental-company stickers, are also vulnerable. Never leave valuables in your car and if possible park in a secure parking lot.

Always report theft or loss to the police within 24 hours, and ask for a statement; otherwise, your travel insurance company won't pay out.

### TRAFFIC

Sicilian traffic can be a daunting prospect, particularly in Palermo where the only rule seems to be survival of the fastest. However, outside the main urban areas, the situation calms down and the main concern becomes the potholes on the roads and the iffy signposting. As a general rule, traffic is at its quietest between 2pm and 4pm and at lunchtime on Sunday, when few people are out and about.

Drivers are not keen to stop for pedestrians, even at pedestrian crossings. Sicilians simply step off the pavement and walk through the swerving traffic. In the major cities, roads that appear to be for one-way traffic often have special lanes

for buses travelling in the opposite direction, so always look both ways before stepping out.

## DISCOUNT CARDS

At many state museums and archaeological sites, EU citizens under 18 and over 65 enter free, and those aged between 18 and 25 get a 50% discount. To claim these discounts you'll need a passport, driving licence or ID card as proof of age. For travellers under 26, the Euro<26 (www.euro26.org) card is universally accepted.

## EMBASSIES & CONSULATES

For foreign embassies and consulates not listed here, look under 'Ambasciate' or 'Consolati' in the telephone directory. Alternatively, tourist offices might have a list.

**France** ( ☎ 091 58 34 05; www.ambafrance-it. org, in French & Italian; Via Principe di Belmonte 101, Palermo)

**Germany** ( ☎ 090 67 17 80; www.rom.diplo.de, in German & Italian; Via San Sebastiano 73, Messina)

**Netherlands** ( ☎ 091 58 15 21; www.olanda.it, in Italian; Via Emerico Amari 8, Palermo)

**UK** ( ☎ 091 32 64 12; http://ukinitaly.fco.gov.uk/it; Via Cavour 117, Palermo)

**US** ( ☎ 091 30 58 57; http://italy.usembassy.gov; Via Vaccarini 1, Palermo)

## FOOD & DRINK

Throughout this book, prices are quoted for meals, which includes a *primo* (first course), *secondo* (second course) and *contorno* (side dish) or *dolce* (dessert). As a price guide, expect to pay less than €20 in restaurants marked with a single euro symbol, between €20 and €40 at places with two euro symbols and upwards of €40 in restaurants marked with three euro symbols. Within each section, restaurants are listed in alphabetical order.

## WHERE TO EAT & DRINK

Sicilian eateries are divided into several categories. At the most basic level a *tavola calda* serves pre-prepared pasta, meat and vegetable dishes canteen-style, as well as snacks and *panini* (bread rolls with simple fillings). Cafes are also a good bet for a quick bite. Alongside coffee and *cornetti* (Italian croissants eaten for breakfast) many serve sweet and savoury snacks, and some have ice cream. For the sweet of tooth, you'll find more ice cream at a *gelateria* and cakes galore at a *pasticceria*.

Wine bars *(enoteche)* are popular and usually offer a limited menu of deli-style snacks or hot meals to accompany a selection of wines.

For a sit-down meal of pasta and meat or fish you'll want a trattoria or *ristorante* (restaurant). The difference between the two is fairly blurred, but as a rule trattorias are less formal and serve traditional, local food. *Ristoranti* generally have a wider selection of dishes and are more expensive. Menus are usually posted by the door.

Most eating establishments have a *coperto* (cover charge) of usually €1 to €3 per person; some also include a *servizio* (service charge) of 10% to 15%.

### WATER

While tap water is reliable and safe throughout the country, most Sicilians prefer to drink *acqua minerale* (bottled mineral water). It will be either *frizzante* (sparkling) or *naturale* (still) and you will be asked in restaurants and bars which you prefer. If you want a glass of tap water, ask for *acqua dal rubinetto*.

## VEGETARIANS & VEGANS

Vegetarianism is not specifically catered to in Sicily but the abundance of excellent fruit and veg means that many *antipasti,* pastas and *contorni* feature veg in some form or other. Salads are common and tasty, though you'll need to watch out for the odd anchovy or slice of ham. Similarly, check that your tomato sauce has not been cooked with meat in it. Vegans will be in for a tough time, with many dishes featuring some sort of animal product (butter, eggs or animal stock).

# GAY & LESBIAN TRAVELLERS

Although homosexuality is legal in Sicily, attitudes remain largely conservative and overt displays of affection could attract hostility. The legal age of consent is 16.

The gay scene is largely centred on Catania and Taormina, and to a lesser extent Palermo. For further information, Italy's largest gay organisation, the Bologna-based **Arcigay** (www.arcigay. it, in Italian), has branches in both Catania (www.arcigaycatania.it) and Palermo (http://arcigaypalermo.wordpress.com, in Italian). You can also pick up a copy of the free magazine *Clubbing,* which has club and event listings.

The international gay guide, *Spartacus International Gay Guide,* lists male-only venues all over Italy, while online you could try **GuidaGay.it** (www.gay.it/guida, in Italian), which has details of gay-friendly bars, clubs, beaches and hotels.

# HEALTH

Italy's public-health system is legally bound to provide emergency care to everyone. EU nationals are entitled to reduced-cost, sometimes free, medical

**DIRECTORY**

care with a European Health Insurance Card (EHIC), available from your home health authority. Non-EU citizens should take out health insurance.

For emergency treatment go to the *pronto soccorso* (casualty) section of an *ospedale* (public hospital), where it's also possible to receive emergency dental treatment. For less serious ailments call the local *guardia medica* (duty doctor) – ask at your hotel or nearest tourist office for the number. Pharmacists will fill prescriptions and can provide basic medical advice.

# HOLIDAYS

Most Sicilians take their annual holiday in August, deserting the cities for the cooler seaside or mountains. This means that many businesses and shops close for at least part of the month, usually around the Feast of the Assumption (Ferragosto) on 15 August. Easter is another busy period, with many resort hotels opening for the season the week before Easter.

Italian schools close for three months in summer, from mid-June to mid-September, for two weeks at Christmas and for a week at Easter.

## PUBLIC HOLIDAYS

Individual towns have public holidays to celebrate the feasts of their patron saints. National public holidays in Sicily include the following:

Capodanno (New Year's Day) 1 January
Epifania (Epiphany) 6 January
Pasquetta (Easter Monday) March/April
Giorno della Liberazione (Liberation Day) 25 April
Festa del Lavoro (Labour Day) 1 May
Festa della Repubblica (Republic Day) 2 June
Ferragosto (Feast of the Assumption) 15 August
Festa di Ognisanti (All Saints' Day) 1 November

Festa della Immacolata Concezione (Feast of the Immaculate Conception) 8 December
Natale (Christmas Day) 25 December
Festa di Santo Stefano (Boxing Day) 26 December

# INSURANCE

## MEDICAL INSURANCE

If you're an EU citizen, an EHIC (European Health Insurance Card) covers you for free or reduced-cost public medical care but not for emergency repatriation. It is available from health centres in your home country. Citizens from countries outside the EU should find out if there is a reciprocal arrangement for free medical care between their country and Italy (Australia, for example, has such an agreement; carry your Medicare card with you).

US citizens should check whether their health-insurance plan offers coverage for hospital or medical costs abroad – many don't. The US Medicare service provides no coverage outside the US. If you do need health insurance, make sure you get a policy that covers you for the worst possible scenario, such as an accident requiring an emergency flight home. Find out in advance if your insurance plan will make payments directly to providers or reimburse you later for overseas health expenditures abroad.

## TRAVEL INSURANCE

A travel-insurance policy to cover theft, loss and medical problems is highly recommended. It may also cover you for cancellation of and delays in your travel arrangements. Paying for your ticket with a credit card can often provide limited travel accident insurance and you may be able to reclaim the payment if the operator doesn't deliver.

Note that some policies specifically exclude 'dangerous activities', which can include scuba diving, motorcycling and even trekking.

# INTERNET ACCESS

Public wi-fi hotspots are fairly thin on the ground but many hotels and B&Bs now offer free wi-fi. In accommodation listings the internet icon is used only when there is a computer available for guest use; in reviews, wi-fi access is only mentioned when charges apply.

If you're bringing your own kit you shouldn't have too many problems hooking up in your room, or at least in the hotel reception or other communal areas. You might need a power transformer (to convert from 110V to 220V if your notebook isn't set up for dual voltage), an RJ-11 phone jack that works with your modem and a plug adapter.

# LEGAL MATTERS

The most likely reason for a brush with the law is if you have to report a theft. If you do have something stolen and you want to claim it on insurance you must make a statement to the police; insurance companies won't pay up without proof of a crime.

The Italian police is divided into three main bodies: the black-clad *carabinieri;* the *polizia,* who wear navy blue jackets; and the *guardia di finanza,* who fight tax evasion and drug smuggling. If you run into trouble in Italy, you're likely to end up dealing with either the *polizia* or the *carabinieri.* If, however, you land a parking ticket, you'll need to speak to the *vigili urbani* (traffic wardens).

The legal blood-alcohol limit is 0.05% and random breath tests do occur. Penal-ties for driving under the influence of alcohol can be severe.

In general, your embassy should be able to provide a list of local lawyers, interpreters and translators. See the front of destination chapters for emergency contact details.

# MAPS

## CITY MAPS

The city maps in this book, combined with tourist-office maps, are generally adequate for getting around. More-detailed maps are also available in city bookshops. Litografia Artistica Cartografica (LAC; www.globalmap.it) produces detailed maps of a number of Sicilian cities, including Agrigento, Catania, Palermo, Syracuse and Trapani, costing €6.50. Michelin (www.michelin.it) and Touring Club Italiano (TCI; www.touringclubstore.com) also produce decent city maps.

## DRIVING MAPS

The best road map is the TCI's *Sicilia* (1:200,000), available at bookshops, airports and motorway cafes in Sicily. The AA's *Road Atlas Italy* (1:250,000), available in the UK, includes Sicily. In Italy, the Istituto Geografico de Agostini (www.deagostini.it, in Italian) publishes the *Carta Stradale Sicilia* (1:200,000; €6.90). Michelin also has a reliable map, *Sicilia,* at a scale of 1:200,000.

## WALKING MAPS

For walking in the Mt Etna area, the 1:25,000 *Mt Etna* map produced by Selca is a good bet. The TCI produces a map of the Parco Regionale dei Nebrodi, at 1:50,000. For exploring the Parco Naturale Regionale delle Madonie, pick up the 1:50,000 *Madonie Carta dei Sentieri*

DIRECTORY

*e del Paesaggio* from the Palermo tourist office. Alternatively, the tourist offices in the Madonie and Cefalù sell the *Carta dei Sentieri del Paesaggio Cefalù* (1:50000) for €1.50.

# MONEY

Italy's currency is the euro (€). The euro is divided into 100 cents. Coin denominations are one, two, five, 10, 20 and 50 cents, €1 and €2. The notes are €5, €10, €20, €50, €100, €200 and €500.

Exchange rates are given on the inside front flap of this book. For the latest rates check out www.xe.com.

Money can be exchanged in banks, post offices and exchange offices. Banks generally offer the best rates, but shop around as rates fluctuate considerably.

## ATMS

Credit and debit cards can be used in ATMs (which are widespread and known locally as *bancomat*), displaying the appropriate sign. Visa and MasterCard are widely recognised, as are Cirrus and Maestro. Remember that every time you withdraw cash there will be fees. Typically you'll be charged a withdrawal fee as well as a conversion charge; if you're using a credit card you'll also be hit by interest on the cash withdrawn.

If an ATM rejects your card, don't despair. Try a few more ATMs displaying your credit card's logo before assuming the problem lies with your card.

## CREDIT & DEBIT CARDS

Though widely accepted, credit cards are not as ubiquitous in Sicily as they are in the UK or the States, and it's always a good idea to have some cash to hand. Many small guesthouses, trattorias and shops don't take credit cards and you can't always use them at petrol stations or at autostrada ticket barriers.

Major cards such as Visa, MasterCard, Eurocard, Cirrus and Eurocheques are accepted throughout Sicily. Amex is also recognised but it's less common.

Before leaving home, make sure to advise your credit-card holder of your travel plans. Otherwise, you risk having your card blocked – as a security measure, banks block cards when they notice out-of-the-ordinary transactions. Check also any charges you'll incur and what the procedure is if you experience problems or have your card stolen. Most card suppliers will give you an emergency number you can call free of charge for help and advice.

## TIPPING

You're not expected to tip on top of restaurant service charges but if you feel the service warrants it, you can leave a little extra, say €1 per person. If there is no service charge, you should consider leaving a 10% tip or rounding the bill up, although it is by no means obligatory. In bars, locals often place a €0.10 or €0.20 coin on the bar when ordering coffee. Tipping taxi drivers is not common practice, but you should tip porters at top-end hotels (€3 to €5).

# POST

Sicily's postal system, **Poste** (☎ 803 160; www.poste.it), is never going to win any awards for efficiency but sooner or later letters generally arrive. Delivery is guaranteed to Europe within three days and to the rest of the world within four to eight days.

Stamps *(francobolli)* are available at post offices and authorised tobacconists (look for the official *tabacchi* sign, a big

'T', often white on black), which you'll find in every town and village.

For more important items, use registered mail *(raccomandato)* or insured mail *(assicurato);* the cost depends on the value of the object being sent.

## SHOPPING

Shopping at Sicily's great markets is an experience to remember. Palermo's Mercato del Capo (p57) and Catania's La Pescheria fish market (p177) are more than just places to shop, they're extraordinary sights in themselves. These are Sicily's two best-known markets but every town worth its salt has at least one.

Sicily's food and wine provide rich shopping opportunities, with any number of local delicacies to choose from. The Aeolian Islands, along with Syracuse, Taormina and Cefalù, have a good number of gourmet delis.

Souvenir hunters are also spoiled for choice. Sicily has a rich tradition of ceramics, with production centred on Caltagirone, Santo Stefano di Camastra and Sciacca. Handmade jewellery is another local tradition, particularly on the west coast, in Trapani and Cefalù. Old-fashioned lace and embroidery can be found in Palermo and Taormina, or rural towns like Erice and Caltanissetta.

For the ultimate memento you could always purchase one of Sicily's paladin puppets or a miniature model of the traditional Sicilian cart, the originals of which are now collectors' items.

## TELEPHONE

Phone services are provided by a host of companies, including Telecom Italia (www.telecomitalia.it, in Italian), Italy's biggest telecommunications company.

Italian mobile phones operate on the GSM 900/1800 network, which is compatible with the rest of Europe and Australia but not with North American GSM 1900 or the Japanese system (although some GSM 1900/900 phones do work in Italy). If you have a GSM phone that you can unlock (check with your service provider), it can cost as little as €10 to activate a *pre-pagato* (pre-paid) SIM card. TIM (www.tim.it), Wind (www.wind.it) and Vodafone (www.vodafone.it) all offer SIM cards and all have retail outlets in Sicily. You'll need your passport to open an account. To recharge your card, simply pop into the nearest outlet or buy a *ricarica* (charge card) from a tobacconist.

Mobile call rates range from €0.09 to €0.30 per minute for domestic calls.

### USEFUL NUMBERS & CODES

Italian area codes all begin with '0' and consist of up to four digits. The area code is followed by a telephone number of anything from four to eight digits. Area codes are an integral part of all telephone numbers in Italy, even if you are calling within a single zone. For example, any number you ring in Palermo will start with ☎ 091, even if it's next door. When making domestic and international calls you must always dial the full number including the initial zero. Mobile-phone numbers begin with a three-digit prefix such as ☎ 333, ☎ 347, ☎ 390 etc.

To make an international call from Sicily, dial ☎ 00, then the relevant country and area codes followed by the telephone number.

| | |
|---|---|
| International access code | ☎ 00 |
| International direct-dial code | ☎ 39 |
| International operator | ☎ 170 |
| Directory enquiries (local and international) | ☎ 1254 or ☎ 89 24 12 |

# TIME

Sicily is one hour ahead of GMT. Daylight-saving time starts on the last Sunday in March, when clocks are put forward one hour. Clocks go back an hour on the last Sunday in October. Italy operates on the 24-hour clock, so rather than 6.30pm, you'll see 18.30 on transport timetables.

# TOILETS

Public toilets are rare in Sicily except at major tourist sites and archaeological parks. Most people use the facilities in bars and cafes – although you might need to buy a coffee first. In many places public loos are pretty grim; try to go armed with some tissues.

# TOURIST INFORMATION

You'll find tourist offices located throughout Sicily. Some are more helpful than others but most are able to provide accommodation lists, rudimentary maps and information on local tourist attractions. Most will also respond to written and telephone requests for information.

Opening hours vary but as a general rule they open from 8.30am to 12.30pm or 1pm and from 3pm to 7pm Monday to Friday. Hours are usually extended in summer, when some offices also open on Saturday or Sunday. Information booths at major train stations tend to keep similar hours, but in some cases operate only in summer.

Offices in popular destinations such as Palermo, Catania, Taormina, Syracuse and the Aeolian Islands are usually well stocked and staffed by employees with a working knowledge of at least one other language, usually English but also French or German.

Officially, Sicilian tourist offices are known as *Servizi Turistici Regionali* (Regional Tourist Services) but for the sake of simplicity we refer to them as 'tourist offices' in this guide. For a full list and other regionwide information, contact Sicily's **Regional Tourist Board** (☎ 091 707 82 01; www.regione.sicilia.it/turismo; Via Notarbartolo 9, Palermo).

# TRAVELLERS WITH DISABILITIES

Sicily is not an easy island for disabled travellers. Narrow cobbled streets, hair-raising traffic, blocked pavements and tiny lifts make life very difficult for wheelchair users, and those with sight or hearing difficulties.

Under European law, airports are obliged to provide assistance to passengers with reduced mobility, so if you need help en route to Sicily, or on arrival/departure, tell your airline when you book your ticket and they should inform the airport. Facilities are available at both Palermo and Catania airports.

If you are travelling by train, Trenitalia operates a **telephone helpline** (☎ 199 30 30 60) that has information on the services provided in stations, including provision of wheelchairs, guides and getting on and off trains. Further information is available online at www.trenitalia.com/trenitalia.html under the Other Services link.

If you are driving, the UK blue badge is recognised in Italy, giving you the same parking rights that local disabled drivers have. For more information, go to the **Institute of Advanced Drivers** (www.iam.org.uk) and search for Blue Badge Users.

Two organisations that might be helpful:

**Accessible Italy** (☎ +378 94 11 11; www.accessibleitaly.com) A San Marino–based company that

specialises in holiday services for the disabled, ranging from tours to the hiring of adapted transport.
**Tourism For All** ( ☎ in UK 0845 124 99 71; www.tourismforall.org.uk) A British charity that can provide general travelling information – check out the website's useful FAQ section.

## VISAS

For up-to-date information on visa requirements, see www.esteri.it/visti.

EU citizens do not need a visa to enter Italy. Nationals of some other countries, including Australia, Canada, Israel, Japan, New Zealand and the USA, do not need visas for stays of up to 90 days in Italy.

Other people wishing to visit Italy have to apply for a Schengen visa, which allows unlimited travel in Italy and 24 other European countries for a 90-day period. You must apply for a Schengen visa in your country of residence and you can not apply for more than two in any 12-month period. They are not renewable inside Italy.

Technically, all foreign visitors to Italy are supposed to register with the local police within eight days of arrival. However, if you're staying in a hotel or hostel you don't need to bother as the hotel will do it for you – this is why they always take your passport details.

## WOMEN TRAVELLERS

The most common form of discomfort for women travellers is harassment. Local men are not shy about staring and this can be disconcerting, especially if you're on your own. If you feel nervous about travelling solo, dressing smartly and wearing a wedding ring nearly always deters unwanted interest. If you do get hassled, the best response is usually just to ignore it, but if that doesn't work, politely say that you're waiting for your husband *(marito)* or fiancé *(fidanzato)* and, if necessary, walk away. Avoid becoming aggressive as this may result in unpleasant confrontation.

Avoid walking alone on deserted and dark streets, and look for centrally located hotels within easy walking distance of places where you can eat at night. Women should not hitchhike alone.

# TRANSPORT

## ARRIVAL & DEPARTURE

### AIR

Fares to Sicily fluctuate enormously: tickets are cheapest between November and March and most expensive between June and September. Holidays such as Christmas, New Year and Easter see huge price hikes. Flight schedules are also subject to seasonal variations with the number of flights increasing considerably in summer.

Several low-cost airlines serve Sicily from European destinations, including Ryanair, easyJet, Vueling and TUIFly.

**AIRPORTS**

Sicily's two main airports serve the island's two biggest cities: Palermo and Catania.

Named after two assassinated anti-Mafia judges, Palermo's **Falcone-Borsellino airport** (PMO; ☎ 091 702 01 11; www.gesap.it) is at Punto Raisi, 30km west of the city. Alitalia, blu-express.com, Wind Jet and Meridiana operate regular flights to/from most mainland Italian

cities; Ryanair, Vueling and Air Berlin are among the low-cost carriers serving London, Barcelona and Berlin. For information on transport to/from the airport, see p59.

Just 7km outside Catania, **Fontanarossa airport** (CTA; ☎ 095 723 91 11; www.aeroporto.catania.it) is served by up to 31 national and international airlines with connections to 13 Italian cities and destinations across Europe. For information on transport to/from the airport, see p185.

### THINGS CHANGE...

The information in this chapter is particularly vulnerable to change. Check directly with the airline or a travel agent to make sure you understand how a fare (and ticket you may buy) works and be aware of the security requirements for international travel. Shop carefully. The details given in this chapter should be regarded as pointers and are not a substitute for your own careful, up-to-date research.

## ONLINE TICKETS

Cheap Flights (www.cheapflights.com)
Ebookers.com (www.ebookers.com)
Expedia (www.expedia.com)
Kayak (www.kayak.com)
Orbitz (www.orbitz.com)
Priceline (www.priceline.com)
Travelocity (www.travelocity.com)

## CAR & MOTORCYCLE

Driving to Sicily is an arduous and expensive task. In terms of budget, you'll need to account for the cost of toll roads and the fact that Italian fuel prices are among the highest in Europe. Your journey time will depend on where you catch the ferry from – Genoa, Livorno, Civitavecchia, Naples or Villa San Giovanni.

The shortest ferry crossing is between Villa San Giovanni on the toe of the Italian mainland and Messina, but to get to Villa San Giovanni you will need to drive Italy's most notorious road, the tortuous toll-free A3 autostrada from Salerno.

From the French or Swiss borders you should allow for about 17 hours' driving but only if you keep to the motorways, go flat out (remember that the speed limit in Italy is 130km/h) and avoid traffic, which is something of a vain hope in the summer holiday period (July and August).

Once on Sicily a car or motorbike is a major plus but it is probably easier to hire one than take your own.

### BRINGING YOUR OWN VEHICLE

If you want to bring your own vehicle to Sicily you will need to have a valid driving licence, proof of ownership of the vehicle, and evidence of third-party insurance. If your vehicle is registered and insured in an EU country, your home-country insurance is sufficient. Theoretically, the International Insurance Certificate, also known as the Carta Verde (Green Card), is no longer required for EU-registered cars, but in case of an accident the police may still ask for it, so you might consider getting one – your car-insurance company can issue it.

Every vehicle travelling across an international border should display a nationality plate of its country of registration. A warning triangle (to be used in the event of a breakdown) is compulsory throughout Europe.

### DRIVING LICENCES & DOCUMENTATION

When driving in Sicily you should always carry your driving licence, the vehicle's registration papers and proof of third-party (liability) insurance. All EU member states' driving licences are recognised in Sicily. If you have a non-EU licence, you'll need to get an International Driving Permit (IDP) to go with your licence. Your national automobile association can issue this and it is valid for 12 months.

## TRAIN

If you have the time, getting to Sicily by train is worth considering: it's more environmentally friendly than flying, it's more relaxed, and perhaps best of all, it allows you to break up your journey. Most trains traversing Italy will make a stop off at Rome and Naples, for example.

Italy's national rail company, Trenitalia (☎ 89 20 21; www.trenitalia.com), operates direct trains to Sicily from a number of Italian cities, including Milan, Rome and Naples. If you're travelling from

TRANSPORT

## CLIMATE CHANGE & TRAVEL

Every form of transport that relies on carbon-based fuel generates CO2, the main cause of human-induced climate change. Modern travel is dependent on aeroplanes, which might use less fuel per kilometre per person than most cars but travel much greater distances. The altitude at which aircraft emit gases (including CO2) and particles also contributes to their climate change impact. Many websites offer 'carbon calculators' that allow people to estimate the carbon emissions generated by their journey and, for those who wish to do so, to offset the impact of the greenhouse gases emitted with contributions to portfolios of climate-friendly initiatives throughout the world. Lonely Planet offsets the carbon footprint of all staff and author travel.

anywhere outside of Italy you are going to have to change trains somewhere along the line in Italy, and it will most probably be in Rome. For detailed information on getting to Sicily from London, check out the relevant section on www.seat61.com.

If you're looking for Europe-wide train schedules, get hold of the *Thomas Cook European Timetable,* which is available from Thomas Cook offices worldwide as well as online at www.thomascookpublishing.com.

It is always advisable, but sometimes compulsory, to book seats on international trains. Some of the main international services include transport for private cars – an option worth examining to save wear and tear on your vehicle before it arrives in Sicily. On overnight hauls you can book a *cuccetta* (couchette) for about €20.

### SEA

Unless you're flying, arriving in Sicily involves a ferry crossing. Regular car/passenger ferries cross the Strait of Messina (the 3km stretch of water that separates Sicily from the Italian mainland) between Villa San Giovanni and Messina, or Reggio di Calabria and Messina (see p167 for details). Ferries also sail to Sicily from Genoa, Livorno,

Civitavecchia, Naples and Cagliari, and from Malta and Tunisia.

### ACROSS THE STRAIT OF MESSINA

RFI/Bluvia (www.rfi.it) Car ferries and passenger-only boats to Messina from Villa San Giovanni and Reggio di Calabria.

Caronte & Tourist ( ☎ 800 62 74 14; www.carontetourist.it) Car ferries to Messina from Villa San Giovanni.

### FROM ITALY, TUNISIA & MALTA

Grandi Navi Veloci ( ☎ 010 209 45 91; www.gnv.it) To Palermo from Genoa, Civitavecchia, Livorno, Tunis and Malta.

Grimaldi ( ☎ 081 49 64 44; www.grimaldi-ferries.com) To Palermo from Tunis and Salerno; to Catania from Genoa, Civitavecchia and Malta; to Trapani from Civitavecchia and Tunis.

SNAV ( ☎ 091 601 42 11; www.snav.it) To Palermo from Civitavecchia and Naples.

Tirrenia Navigazione ( ☎ 892 123; www.tirrenia.it) To Palermo from Naples and Cagliari; to Trapani from Cagliari. At the time of writing, Tirrenia was undergoing serious financial problems, but service was continuing as normal.

TTT Lines ( ☎ 800 915 365; www.tttlines.it) To Catania from Naples.

Ustica Lines ( ☎ 0923 87 38 13; www.usticalines.it) Summer services to Trapani, Ustica and Egadi Islands from Naples.

Virtu Ferries ( ☎ 095 53 57 11; www.virtuferries.com) This company runs ferries to Catania and Pozzallo from Malta.

TRANSPORT

During the high season, all routes are busy and you'll need to book several weeks in advance. The helpful search engine **Traghetti online** ( ☎ 892 112; www.traghettionline.net) provides comprehensive route details and an online booking service.

For Palermo, high-season fares (for an adult and car) start at approximately €120 from Genoa, €81 from Civitavecchia, and €35 from Naples. For Catania, you should bank on about €130 from Naples and €154 from Civitavecchia. Crossing the Strait of Messina costs €28 with a small car.

Note that while you do not need to show your passport on internal routes you should always keep some photo ID handy.

# GETTING AROUND

If at all possible, it's preferable to have your own car (or motorbike) in Sicily. Getting around the island on public transport is difficult and time-consuming although not impossible. Connections between the major cities and coastal resorts are fine, but if you want to venture off the beaten track you could find yourself up against it.

In most cases buses are better than trains, which tend to be very slow. That said, public transport is cheap and it does save you the hassle of dealing with incomprehensible one-way systems, narrow medieval streets, and nightmarish parking.

To get to the offshore islands there's an extensive system of hydrofoils and ferries. The frequency of services slows considerably in winter, when many of the islands virtually shut down until the next tourist season.

For Pantelleria and the Pelagic Islands, planes are probably a better way to go –

they are now cheaper than the ferries and also a lot faster.

## BICYCLE

There's no great cycling tradition in Sicily, but away from the main cities it can be a great way to see the countryside, particularly during spring (March to May) when it's not too hot and the wildflowers are out in bloom. Cycling is also an excellent way of getting round the smaller offshore islands. Note that much of Sicily is hilly so you'll need to be in pretty good shape to enjoy the scenery.

There are no special road rules for cyclists, but you would be wise to carry a helmet and lights. If cycling during the summer, make sure you have plenty of water and sunblock as the heat can be exhausting.

Bike hire is not exactly widespread but it's usually available at coastal resorts and on the smaller islands. Some small *pensioni* and *agriturismi* also offer use of bikes to guests. Bank on about €15 per day to hire a bike.

## BOAT

Sicily's offshore islands are served by *traghetti* (ferries) and *aliscafi* (hydrofoils). Services for the Aeolian Islands run from Milazzo; for the Egadi Islands from Trapani; for the Pelagic Islands from Porto Empedocle near Agrigento; and Ustica is served from Palermo and Trapani.

Services run year-round although they are pared back considerably in winter and can be affected by adverse sea conditions. See the Transport sections in the relevant destination chapters for details.

On overnight services (for example, to the Pelagic Islands or Pantelleria)

TRANSPORT

## DISTANCE CHART (KM)

Note: Distances are approximate

| | Agrigento | Caltanissetta | Catania | Cefalù | Enna | Marsala | Mazara del Vallo | Messina | Milazzo | Palermo | Ragusa | Sciacca | Syracuse | Taormina |
|---|---|---|---|---|---|---|---|---|---|---|---|---|---|---|
| Caltanissetta | 58 | | | | | | | | | | | | | |
| Catania | 165 | 112 | | | | | | | | | | | | |
| Cefalù | 133 | 100 | 180 | | | | | | | | | | | |
| Enna | 91 | 33 | 83 | 109 | | | | | | | | | | |
| Marsala | 132 | 195 | 305 | 181 | 228 | | | | | | | | | |
| Mazara del Vallo | 91 | 190 | 324 | 211 | 223 | 19 | | | | | | | | |
| Messina | 258 | 204 | 95 | 159 | 180 | 337 | 387 | | | | | | | |
| Milazzo | 291 | 237 | 128 | 136 | 213 | 317 | 347 | 33 | | | | | | |
| Palermo | 126 | 133 | 208 | 73 | 135 | 121 | 126 | 226 | 209 | | | | | |
| Ragusa | 131 | 126 | 101 | 218 | 130 | 256 | 215 | 201 | 234 | 250 | | | | |
| Sciacca | 57 | 115 | 240 | 215 | 148 | 109 | 64 | 340 | 348 | 183 | 181 | | | |
| Syracuse | 218 | 159 | 60 | 231 | 131 | 350 | 309 | 160 | 193 | 260 | 78 | 275 | | |
| Taormina | 214 | 162 | 47 | 206 | 135 | 355 | 321 | 53 | 86 | 255 | 157 | 287 | 115 | |
| Trapani | 157 | 225 | 312 | 168 | 234 | 31 | 69 | 324 | 301 | 104 | 284 | 127 | 355 | 359 |

travellers can choose between cabin accommodation or a *poltrona,* which is an airline-type armchair. Deck class is available only during the summer and only on some ferries, so ask when making your booking. All ferries carry vehicles.

The following companies serve Sicily's offshore islands:

**Navigazione Generale Italiana** (NGI; ☎ 800 250 000; www.ngi-spa.it) This company offers a ferry-only service operating out of Milazzo for the Aeolian Islands.

**Siremar** ( ☎ 892 123; www.siremar.it, in Italian) Ferries and hydrofoils to the Aeolian Islands from Milazzo. Also services to the Egadi Islands and Pantelleria from Trapani; to the Pelagic Islands from Porto Empedocle; and to Ustica from Palermo.

**Ustica Lines** ( ☎ 0923 87 38 13; www.usticalines. it) This company runs hydrofoils to Ustica, Pantelleria and the Egadi Islands from Trapani; to the Aeolian Islands from Milazzo and Messina; to the Pelagic Islands from Porto Empedocle; and to Pantelleria from Mazara del Vallo.

## BUS

Buses are generally the best way of getting around Sicily. They tend to be faster and more convenient than trains, if a little more expensive, and have the added advantage of dropping you off in town centres (many Sicilian train stations are situated a kilometre or so outside of the town they serve). Buses serve just about everywhere on the island, although in rural areas, services are often linked to school hours and market opening times which can mean leaving incredibly early or finding yourself stranded after 2pm. Also watch out for Sundays when services are cut back to the bone.

In larger cities, the main intercity bus companies have ticket offices or operate through agencies. In smaller towns and villages, bus tickets are often sold in bars or on the bus.

Sicily's four main bus companies – AST ( ☎ 840 000 323; www.aziendasicilianatrasporti.it),

Interbus ( ☎ 0935 224 60; www.interbus.it), **SAIS Autolinee** ( ☎ 800 21 10 20; www.saisauto linee.it) and **SAIS Trasporti** (www.saistras porti.it) – cover most island destinations as well as cities on the Italian mainland. Although it is not usually necessary to make reservations on buses, it's best to do so in the high season for overnight or long-haul trips.

## CAR & MOTORCYCLE

There's no escaping the fact that a car makes getting around Sicily much easier. That said, driving on the island is not exactly stress free, particularly in the big cities where traffic congestion, one-way systems and impossible parking can stretch nerves to the limit. But once on the open road, things calm down considerably and the going is generally pretty good.

Roads vary in quality. Some, like the main autostrade (motorways), are in pretty good nick, but small rural roads can sometimes be quite dodgy, especially after heavy rain when axle-breaking potholes appear and landslides lead to road closures.

Sicily has a limited network of motorways, which you'll see prefixed by an A on maps and signs on the island. The main east–west link is the A19, which runs from Catania to Palermo. The A18 runs along the Ionian Coast between Messina and Catania, while the A29 goes from Palermo to the western coast, linking the capital with Trapani and (through the western interior) Mazara del Vallo. The A20 runs from Palermo to Messina. Both the A18 and A20 are toll roads.

After autostrade, the best roads are the *strade statali* (state roads), represented on maps as 'S' or 'SS'. *Strade provinciali* (provincial roads) are sometimes little more than country lanes, but provide access to some of the more beautiful scenery and the small towns and villages. They are represented as 'P' or 'SP' on maps.

### AUTOMOBILE ASSOCIATIONS

The Italian automobile association is called the **Automobile Club Italiano** (www.aci.it in Italian) or ACI for short. It offers 24-hour roadside assistance ( ☎ 803 116 or ☎ 800 116 800 if calling from a non-Italian mobile phone). You do not have to join but will have to pay a fee of at least €100 if you require roadside help.

### FUEL & SPARE PARTS

Petrol stations are located on the main autostrade and state roads, as well as in cities and towns. The bigger ones are often open 24 hours but smaller stations generally open 7am to 7pm Monday to Saturday with a lunchtime break. Many stations also offer self-service. To use the self-service pumps you'll need to insert a bill (in denominations of €5, €10, €20 or €50) into a machine and then press the number of the pump you're using.

The cost of fuel in Sicily is high – at the time of research €1.40 for a litre of unleaded petrol *(benzina senza piombo)* and €1.22 for diesel *(gasolio)*.

If you run into mechanical problems the nearest petrol station should be able to advise a local mechanic, although few have workshops on-site.

### HIRE

The major car-rental firms are all represented at Palermo and Catania airports and in major cities. Agencies in seaside resorts also rent out scooters and motorcycles.

**Avis** ( ☎ 06 452 10 83 91; www.avisautonoleggio.it)
**Europcar** ( ☎ 199 30 70 30; www.europcar.it)

TRANSPORT

TRANSPORT

Hertz ( ☎ 02 694 30 019; www.hertz.it)
Maggiore ( ☎ 199 15 11 20; www.maggiore.it)
Sicily by Car ( ☎ 800 33 44 40; www.sicilybycar.it)
Sixt ( ☎ 06 65 21 11; www.sixt.it)

A small car, for example a Fiat Panda, will cost approximately €60/295 per day/week; for a scooter bank on about €25 to €30 per day. If possible, try to arrange your rental in advance as you'll get much better rates. Similarly, airport agencies charge more than city-centre branches.

To hire a car you'll need to be over 21 or more (23 or more for some companies) and have a credit card; for a scooter the minimum age is generally 18. When hiring, always make sure you understand what's covered in the rental agreement (unlimited mileage, tax, insurance, collision-damage waiver and so on) and what your liabilities are. It is also a good idea to get fully comprehensive insurance to cover any untoward bumps or scrapes that are quite likely to happen.

If you are hiring from a reputable company, it will usually give you an emergency number to call in the case of breakdown.

Note also that most hire cars have manual gear transmission.

### PARKING

Parking in Sicilian towns and cities can be difficult. Blue lines by the side of the road denote pay-and-display parking – buy tickets at the meters or from tobacconists – with rates ranging from €0.50 to €1 per hour. Typically, charges are applied between 8.30am and 1.30pm and then from 3pm and 8pm – outside these hours you can leave your car free. You'll also find car parks in the main cities and ports, charging anything from €6 per day. As a general rule, the easiest time to find street parking is the early afternoon between 2pm and 4pm.

Fines for parking violations are applied and you are not safe in a hire car as the rental agency will use your credit card to settle any fines incurred.

### ROAD RULES

Contrary to appearances there are road rules in Sicily.

★ Drive on the right and overtake on the left.

★ Wear seat belts in the front and back.

★ Wear a helmet when riding all two-wheeled vehicles.

★ Carry a warning triangle and fluorescent vest to be worn in the event of an emergency.

★ Keep your blood-alcohol limit under 0.05% while driving.

## ROAD SIGNS

Most Sicilian road signs are pretty self-explanatory, although it does help to know that *uscita* means exit and that town centres are indicated by the word *centro* and a symbol resembling a circular target. Autostrada signs are in green, main roads in blue, and tourist attractions such as archaeological sites (often referred to as *scavi,* meaning ruins) are in brown or yellow.

One recurring problem is that of the disappearing sign. The big towns are well signposted but off the main roads the situation is not always so clear cut. A typical scenario is that you're heading for a small town X, and spot a sign off to the left; you follow it only to discover that it's the last sign you'll ever see for X. In these situations you'll have to resort to trial and error or satnav.

## SPEED LIMITS

Speed limits are 130km/h on autostrade, 110km/h on nonurban highways and 50km/h in built-up areas.

* Keep your blood-alcohol limit at zero while driving if a new licence holder (those with a licence for less than three years).
* Do not use hand-held mobile phones while driving.
* Turn on your headlights while driving on roads outside municipalities.

### TOLL ROADS

Sicily's toll roads are the Messina–Palermo A20 autostrada and the Messina–Catania A18. Messina to Palermo costs €10.40; Messina to Catania €3.30. The process is simple: pick up a ticket at the automatic machine as you get on the autostrada and pay a cashier as you exit. Make sure you get into the right lane when you exit – follow the white signs illustrated with a black hand holding bank notes. Credit cards are not always accepted so have cash on hand.

## TAXI

Official taxis are white, metered and expensive. If you need a taxi, you can usually find one in taxi ranks at train and bus stations or by telephoning for one. However, if you book a taxi by phone, you will be charged for the trip the driver makes to reach you.

Rates vary from city to city, but as a rule the minimum charge is about €5. There's also a baffling array of supplementary charges for night-time/Sunday rides, to/from the airport, extra luggage etc. Reckon on about €10 to €15 for most urban routes.

## TRAIN

Travelling by train is an option between Sicily's major towns. Services are limited and slow although cheap and generally reliable. Trains are all operated by **Trenitalia** ( ☎ 89 20 21; www.trenitalia.com/trenitalia.html) except for those that trundle around the base of Etna, which are run by the private **Ferrovia Circumetnea** ( ☎ 095 54 12 50; www.circumetnea.it).

There are several types of train: Intercity (IC) or Intercity Night (ICN) trains are the fastest, stopping only at major stations; *espresso* trains stop at all but the most minor stations, while *regionale* trains are the slowest of all, halting at every stop on the line.

Note that all tickets must be validated *before* you board your train. Simply insert them in the yellow machines installed at the entrance to all train platforms. If you don't validate them you risk a fine. This rule does not apply to tickets purchased outside Italy.

### CLASSES & COSTS

There are 1st- and 2nd-class seats on Intercity trains but not on the slower *espresso* and *regionale* trains. Travel on Intercity trains means paying a supplement, included in the ticket, determined by the distance you are travelling. If you have a *regionale* ticket and end up hopping on an Intercity train you'll have to pay the difference on board.

Sample prices for one-way train fares are as follows (return fares are generally double).

| From | To | Fare |
| --- | --- | --- |
| Catania | Agrigento | €10.05 |
| Catania | Syracuse | €6.05 |
| Catania | Messina | €6.70 |
| Palermo | Agrigento | €7.90 |
| Palermo | Catania | €14.95 |
| Palermo | Messina | €11.45 |

TRANSPORT

## LEFT LUGGAGE

There are left-luggage facilities or lockers at most of the bigger train stations on the island. They are usually open 24 hours or close only for a few hours after midnight. Charges are typically about €4 per day per piece of luggage, although at Palermo it costs €13.40 for 24 hours.

## RESERVATIONS

There's no need to reserve tickets for travel within Sicily but if you're heading up to the Italian mainland on weekends or during holiday periods it's probably a good idea. A booking fee of about €3 is generally applied. Tickets can be booked at station ticket booths or at most travel agencies.

# LANGUAGE

Italian is a Romance language related to French, Spanish, Portuguese and Romanian, all of which are directly descended from Latin. The Romance languages belong to the Indo-European group of languages, which includes English, so you might spot some similarities between English and Italian.

English speakers can be hard to find beyond the more popular tourist resorts, where staff at hotels, restaurants and tourist offices usually have a basic grasp of the language, so it can be worthwhile learning a few basics Italian phrases.

Although standard Italian may be Sicily's official language and is spoken almost universally on the island, most locals speak Sicilian among themselves. Sicilian is referred to as an Italian dialect, but is sufficiently different for some to consider it a language in its own right.

Sicilians will readily revert to standard Italian when speaking to anyone from the mainland or abroad, although with the occasional Sicilian word thrown in.

Sicily has interesting relationship with the Italian language. Although it is com-monly accepted that modern standard Italian developed from the Tuscan dialect, Sicilians rightly assert that the first literature in the 'common vernacular' (Italian, as opposed to Latin or Greek) was produced in Sicily (at the court of Frederick I in the 13th century).

The Italian of today is something of a composite. What you hear on the radio and TV, in educated discourse and indeed in the everyday language of many people is the result of centuries of cross-fertilisation between the dialects, greatly accelerated in the postwar decades by the modern media.

If you'd like to learn more Italian than we've included here, get hold of a copy of Lonely Planet's comprehensive and user-friendly *Italian* phrasebook. Lonely Planet iPhone phrasebooks are available through the Apple App store.

## GRAMMAR

Italian has polite versus informal forms for 'you'. Many Sicilians, especially older people, expect to be addressed in the third-person polite for 'you'. That is *Lei* instead of *tu*. Also, it is not considered polite to use the informal greeting *ciao* when addressing strangers unless they use it first; it's better to say *buongiorno* (or *buona sera,* as the case may be) and *arrivederci* (or the more polite form, *arrivederla*). We have used the polite address for most of the phrases in this guide. Use of the informal address is indicated by 'inf' in brackets.

Italian has masculine and feminine forms of nouns and accompanying adjectives (usually ending in '-o' and '-a' respectively). Where both gender forms are given, they're marked with 'm' and 'f'.

# PRONUNCIATION

Italian pronunciation isn't very hard to master once you learn a few easy rules. Although some vowels and the stress on double letters require practice by English speakers, it's easy enough to make yourself understood.

Sicilian speakers tend to pronounce vowels more openly than in mainland Italy, and there's a tendency to emphasise consonants, so that a word like *buongiorno* (good day) sounds something like 'bawn·jaw·rrno'. The French influence also means that in certain parts of Sicily, particularly the west, the 'r' is not as rolled as it is in standard Italian.

## VOWELS

| | |
|---|---|
| a | as in 'art', eg *caro* (dear); sometimes short, eg *amico/a* (friend) |
| e | short, as in 'let', eg *mettere* (to put); long, as in 'there', eg *mela* (apple) |
| i | short, as in 'it', eg *inizio* (start); long, as in 'marine', eg *vino* (wine) |
| o | short, as in 'dot', eg *donna* (woman); long, as in 'port', eg *ora* (hour) |
| u | as the 'oo' in 'book', eg *puro* (pure) |

## CONSONANTS

The pronunciation of most Italian consonants is similar to that of their English counterparts. Pronunciation of some consonants depends on certain rules:

| | |
|---|---|
| c | as the 'k' in 'kit' before a, o and u; as the 'ch' in 'choose' before e and i |
| ch | as the 'k' in 'kit' |
| g | as the 'g' in 'get' before a, o, u and h; as the 'j' in 'jet' before e and i |
| gli | as the 'lli' in 'million' |
| gn | as the 'ny' in 'canyon' |
| h | always silent (ie not pronounced) |
| sc | as 'sk' before a, o, u and h; as the 'sh' in 'sheep' before e and i; |
| z | as the 'ts' in 'lights', except at the beginning of a word, when it's as the 'ds' in 'suds' |

Note that when ci, gi and sci are followed by a, o or u, the 'i' is not pronounced unless the accent falls on the 'i'. Thus the name 'Giovanni' is pronounced jo·*va*·nee, not 'jee·o·*va*·nee'.

A double consonant is pronounced as a longer, more forceful sound than a single consonant. This can directly affect the meaning of a word, eg *sono* (I am), *sonno* (sleep).

## WORD STRESS

Stress is indicated in our pronunciation guide by italics. Word stress generally falls on the second-last syllable (eg spa·*ge*·tee), but when a word has an accent, the stress falls on that syllable, as in città (chee·*ta*), meaning 'city'.

# ACCOMMODATION

| | | |
|---|---|---|
| I'm looking for a ... | *Cerco ...* | *cher*·ko ... |
| guest house | *una pensione* | *oo*·na pen·*syo*·ne |
| hotel | *un albergo* | oon al·*ber*·go |
| youth hostel | *un ostello per* | oon os·*te*·lo per |
| | *la gioventù* | la jo·ven·*too* |

**What is the address?**
| *Qual'è l'indirizzo?* | kwa·*le* leen·dee·*ree*·tso |
|---|---|

**Do you have any rooms available?**
| *Avete camere libere?* | a·*ve*·te *ka*·me·re *lee*·be·re |
|---|---|

**May I see it?**
| *Posso vederla?* | *po*·so ve·*der*·la |
|---|---|

**Where is the bathroom?**
| *Dov'è il bagno?* | do·*ve* eel *ba*·nyo |
|---|---|

| | | |
|---|---|---|
| I'd like (a) ... | *Vorrei ...* | vo·*ray* ... |
| bed | *un letto* | oon *le*·to |
| single room | *una camera* | *oo*·na *ka*·me·ra |
| | *singola* | *seen*·go·la |
| double room | *una camera* | *oo*·na *ka*·me·ra |
| | *matrimoniale* | ma·tree·mo·*nya*·le |
| room with two | *una camera* | *oo*·na *ka*·me·ra |
| beds | *doppia* | *do*·pya |
| room with a | *una camera* | *oo*·na *ka*·me·ra |
| bathroom | *con bagno* | kon *ba*·nyo |
| to share a | *un letto in* | oon *le*·to een |
| dorm | *dormitorio* | dor·mee·*to*·ryo |

| | | |
|---|---|---|
| How much is | *Quanto costa ...?* | *kwan*·to *ko*·sta ... |
| it ...? | | |
| per night | *per la notte* | per la *no*·te |
| per person | *per persona* | per per·*so*·na |

## CONVERSATION & ESSENTIALS

| | | |
|---|---|---|
| Hello. | *Buon giorno.* | bwon *jor*·no |
| | *Ciao.* (inf) | chow |
| Goodbye. | *Arrivederci.* | a·ree·ve·*der*·chee |
| | *Ciao.* (inf) | chow |
| Yes./No. | *Sì./No.* | see/no |
| Please. | *Per favore./* | per fa·*vo*·re |
| | *Per piacere.* | per pya·*chay*·re |
| Thank you. | *Grazie.* | *gra*·tsye |
| You're welcome. | *Prego.* | *pre*·go |

| | | |
|---|---|---|
| Excuse me. | *Mi scusi.* | mee *skoo*·zee |
| I'm sorry. | *Mi scusi./* | mee *skoo*·zee/ |
| | *Mi perdoni.* | mee per·*do*·nee |

**What's your name?**
| *Come si chiama?* | *ko*·me see *kya*·ma |
|---|---|

**My name is ...**
| *Mi chiamo ...* | mee *kya*·mo ... |
|---|---|

**Where are you from?**
| *Da dove viene?* | da *do*·ve *vye*·ne |
|---|---|

**I'm from ...**
| *Vengo da ...* | *ven*·go da ... |
|---|---|

**I (don't) like ...**
| *(Non) Mi piace ...* | (non) mee *pya*·che ... |
|---|---|

**Just a minute.**
| *Un momento.* | oon mo·*men*·to |
|---|---|

# DIRECTIONS

**Where is ...?**
| *Dov'è ...?* | do·*ve* ... |
|---|---|

**Go straight ahead.**
| *Si va sempre diritto.* | see va *sem*·pre dee·*ree*·to |
|---|---|

**Turn left/right.**
| *Giri a sinistra/destra.* | *jee*·ree a see·*nee*·stra/de·stra |
|---|---|

| | | |
|---|---|---|
| at the corner | *al angolo* | al *an*·go·lo |
| at the traffic ligths | *al semaforo* | al se·*ma*·fo·ro |
| behind | *dietro* | *dye*·tro |
| in front of | *davanti* | da·*van*·tee |
| far (from) | *lontano (da)* | lon·*ta*·no (da) |
| near (to) | *vicino (di)* | vee·*chee*·no (dee) |
| opposite | *di fronte a* | dee *fron*·te a |

| | | |
|---|---|---|
| beach | *la spiaggia* | la *spya*·ja |
| bridge | *il ponte* | eel *pon*·te |
| castle | *il castello* | eel kas·*te*·lo |
| cathedral | *il duomo* | eel *dwo*·mo |
| island | *l'isola* | *lee*·so·la |
| market | *il mercato* | eel mer·*ka*·to |
| old city | *il centro* | eel *chen*·tro |
| | *storico* | *sto*·ree·ko |
| palace | *il palazzo* | eel pa·*la*·tso |
| ruins | *le rovine* | le ro·*vee*·ne |
| sea | *il mare* | eel *ma*·re |
| square | *la piazza* | la *pya*·tsa |
| tower | *la torre* | la *to*·re |

LANGUAGE

# EATING OUT

I'd like ..., please.

*Vorrei ..., per favore.* — vo·*ray* ... per fa·*vo*·re

That was delicious!

*Era squisito!* — e·ra skwee·*zee*·to

I don't eat (fish).

*Non mangio (pesce).* — non *man*·jo (*pe*·she)

Please bring the bill.

*Mi porta il conto,* — mee *por*·ta eel *kon*·to

*per favore?* — per fa·*vo*·re

| I'm allergic | *Sono* | *so*·no |
|---|---|---|
| to ... | *allergico/a* ... (m/f) | a·*ler*·jee·ko/a ... |
| dairy produce | *ai latticini* | ai la·tee·*chee*·nee |
| eggs | *alle uova* | a·le *wo*·va |
| nuts | *alle noci* | a·le *no*·chee |
| seafood | *ai frutti di* | ai *froo*·tee dee |
| | *mare* | *ma*·re |

# HEALTH

I'm ill.

*Mi sento male.* — mee *sen*·to *ma*·le

It hurts here.

*Mi fa male qui.* — mee fa *ma*·le kwee

| antiseptic | *antisettico* | an·tee·*se*·tee·ko |
|---|---|---|
| aspirin | *aspirina* | as·pee·*ree*·na |
| condoms | *preservativi* | pre·zer·va·*tee*·vee |
| contraceptive | *contraccetivo* | kon·tra·che·*tee*·vo |
| diarrhoea | *diarrea* | dee·a·*re*·a |
| medicine | *medicina* | me·dee·*chee*·na |
| sunblock cream | *crema solare* | *kre*·ma so·*la*·re |
| tampons | *tamponi* | tam·*po*·nee |

# LANGUAGE DIFFICULTIES

Do you speak English?

*Parla inglese?* — *par*·la een·*gle*·ze

Does anyone here speak English?

*C'è qualcuno che parla* — che kwal·*koo*·no ke *par*·la

*inglese?* — een·*gle*·ze

How do you say ... in Italian?

*Come si dice ... in* — *ko*·me see *dee*·che ... een

*italiano?* — ee·ta·*lya*·no

What does ... mean?

*Che vuol dire ...?* — ke vwol *dee*·re ...

I (don't) understand.

*(Non) Capisco.* — (non) ka·*pee*·sko

Please write it down.

*Può scriverlo, per favore?* — pwo *skree*·ver·lo per fa·*vo*·re

Can you show me (on the map)?

*Può mostrarmelo* — pwo mos·*trar*·me·lo

*(sulla pianta)?* — (soo·la *pyan*·ta)

# NUMBERS

| 0 | *zero* | *dze*·ro |
|---|---|---|
| 1 | *uno* | *oo*·no |
| 2 | *due* | *doo*·e |
| 3 | *tre* | tre |
| 4 | *quattro* | *kwa*·tro |
| 5 | *cinque* | *cheen*·kwe |
| 6 | *sei* | say |
| 7 | *sette* | *se*·te |
| 8 | *otto* | *o*·to |
| 9 | *nove* | *no*·ve |
| 10 | *dieci* | *dye*·chee |
| 11 | *undici* | oon·*dee*·chee |
| 12 | *dodici* | do·*dee*·chee |
| 13 | *tredici* | tre·*dee*·chee |
| 14 | *quattordici* | kwa·*tor*·dee·chee |
| 15 | *quindici* | *kween*·dee·chee |
| 16 | *sedici* | *se*·dee·chee |
| 17 | *diciassette* | dee·cha·*se*·te |
| 18 | *diciotto* | dee·*cho*·to |
| 19 | *diciannove* | dee·cha·*no*·ve |
| 20 | *venti* | *ven*·tee |
| 30 | *trenta* | *tren*·ta |
| 40 | *quaranta* | kwa·*ran*·ta |
| 50 | *cinquanta* | cheen·*kwan*·ta |
| 60 | *sessanta* | se·*san*·ta |
| 70 | *settanta* | se·*tan*·ta |
| 80 | *ottanta* | o·*tan*·ta |
| 90 | *novanta* | no·*van*·ta |
| 100 | *cento* | *chen*·to |
| 1000 | *mille* | *mee*·le |

# QUESTION WORDS

| Who? | *Chi?* | kee |
|---|---|---|
| What? | *Che?* | ke |
| When? | *Quando?* | *kwan*·do |
| Where? | *Dove?* | *do*·ve |
| How? | *Come?* | *ko*·me |

# SHOPPING & SERVICES

| | |
|---|---|
| **I'd like to buy ...** | |
| *Vorrei comprare ...* | vo-*ray* kom-*pra*-re ... |
| **How much is it?** | |
| *Quanto costa?* | *kwan*-to *ko*-sta |
| **I don't like it.** | |
| *Non mi piace.* | non mee *pya*-che |
| **It's too expensive.** | |
| *È troppo caro/a.* | e *tro*-po *ka*-ro/a |
| **I'll take it.** | |
| *Lo/La compro.* | lo/la *kom*-pro |
| **I want to change (money).** | |
| *Voglio cambiare* | vo-lyo kam-*bya*-re |
| *(del denaro).* | (del de-*na*-ro) |

| | | |
|---|---|---|
| **I'm looking for ...** | *Cerco ...* | *cher*-ko ... |
| a bank | *un banco* | oon *ban*-ko |
| the church | *la chiesa* | la *kye*-za |
| the city centre | *il centro* | eel *chen*-tro |
| the market | *il mercato* | eel mer-*ka*-to |
| the museum | *il museo* | eel moo-*ze*-o |
| the post office | *l'ufficio* | loo *fee*-cho |
| | *postale* | po-*sta*-le |
| a toilet | *un gabinetto* | oon ga-bee-*ne*-to |
| the tourist office | *l'ufficio* | loo-*fee*-cho |
| | *di turismo* | dee too-*reez*-mo |

## TIME & DATES

| | | |
|---|---|---|
| **What time is it?** | *Che ore sono?* | ke *o*-re *so*-no |
| **It's (8 o'clock).** | *Sono (le otto).* | *so*-no (le *o*-to) |
| | | |
| in the morning | *di mattina* | dee ma-*tee*-na |
| in the afternoon | *di pomeriggio* | dee po-me-*ree*-jo |
| in the evening | *di sera* | dee *se*-ra |
| today | *oggi* | *o*-jee |
| tomorrow | *domani* | do-*ma*-nee |
| yesterday | *ieri* | *ye*-ree |
| | | |
| Monday | *lunedì* | loo-ne-*dee* |
| Tuesday | *martedì* | mar-te-*dee* |
| Wednesday | *mercoledì* | mer-ko-le-*dee* |
| Thursday | *giovedì* | jo-ve-*dee* |
| Friday | *venerdì* | ve-ner-*dee* |
| Saturday | *sabato* | *sa*-ba-to |
| Sunday | *domenica* | do-*me*-nee-ka |

| | | |
|---|---|---|
| **January** | *gennaio* | je-*na*-yo |
| **February** | *febbraio* | fe-*bra*-yo |
| **March** | *marzo* | *mar*-tso |
| **April** | *aprile* | a-*pree*-le |
| **May** | *maggio* | *ma*-jo |
| **June** | *giugno* | *joo*-nyo |
| **July** | *luglio* | *loo*-lyo |
| **August** | *agosto* | a-*gos*-to |
| **September** | *settembre* | se-*tem*-bre |
| **October** | *ottobre* | o-*to*-bre |
| **November** | *novembre* | no-*vem*-bre |
| **December** | *dicembre* | dee-*chem*-bre |

# TRANSPORT

## PUBLIC TRANSPORT

| | | |
|---|---|---|
| **What time does the ... leave/arrive?** | *A che ora parte/arriva ...?* | a ke *o*-ra *par*-te/a-*ree*-va ... |
| boat | *la nave* | la *na*-ve |
| (city) bus | *l'autobus* | *low*-to-boos |
| (intercity) bus | *il pullman* | eel *pool*-man |
| plane | *l'aereo* | la-*e*-re-o |
| train | *il treno* | eel *tre*-no |

| | |
|---|---|
| **I want to go to ...** | |
| *Voglio andare a ...* | vo-lyo an-*da*-re a ... |
| **The train has been cancelled/delayed.** | |
| *Il treno è soppresso/* | eel *tre*-no e so-*pre*-so/ |
| *in ritardo.* | een ree-*tar*-do |

## EMERGENCIES

**Help!**
*Aiuto!*  a·*yoo*·to
**There's been an accident!**
*C'è stato un incidente!*  che *sta*·to oon een·chee·*den*·te
**I'm lost.**
*Mi sono perso/a.*  mee *so*·no *per*·so/a
**Go away!**
*Lasciami in pace!*  la·sha·mi een *pa*·che
*Vai via!* (inf)  vai *vee*·a

| **Call ...!** | *Chiami ...!* | kee·*ya*·mee ... |
|---|---|---|
| a doctor | *un medico* | oon *me*·dee·ko |
| the police | *la polizia* | la po·lee·*tsee*·ya |

| **I'd like a ...** | *Vorrei un* | vo·*ray* oon |
|---|---|---|
| **ticket.** | *biglietto ...* | bee·*lye*·to ... |
| one-way | *di solo andata* | dee *so*·lo an·*da*·ta |
| return | *di andata e ritorno* | dee an·*da*·ta e ree·*toor*·no |
| 1st class | *di prima classe* | dee *pree*·ma *kla*·se |
| 2nd class | *di seconda classe* | dee se·*kon*·da *kla*·se |

| the first | *il primo* | eel *pree*·mo |
|---|---|---|
| the last | *l'ultimo* | lool·tee·mo |
| platform (two) | *binario (due)* | bee·*na*·ryo (*doo*·e) |
| ticket office | *biglietteria* | bee·lye·te·*ree*·a |
| timetable | *orario* | o·*ra*·ryo |
| train station | *stazione* | sta·*tsyo*·ne |

### PRIVATE TRANSPORT

**Please fill it up.**
*Il pieno, per favore.*  eel *pye*·no per fa·*vo*·re
**I'd like (30) litres.**
*Vorrei (trenta) litri.*  vo·ray (*tren*·ta) *lee*·tree
**Is this the road to ...?**
*Questa strada porta a ...?*  kwe·sta *stra*·da *por*·ta a ...

**(How long) Can I park here?**
*(Per quanto tempo)*  (per *kwan*·to *tem*·po)
*Posso parcheggiare qui?*  po·so par·ke·*ja*·re kwee
**I need a mechanic.**
*Ho bisogno di*  o bee·*zo*·nyo dee
*un meccanico.*  oon me·*ka*·nee·ko
**The car/motorbike has broken down (at ...).**
*La macchina/moto*  la *ma*·kee·na/*mo*·to
*si è guastata (a ...).*  see e gwas·*ta*·ta (a ...)
**I have a flat tyre.**
*Ho una gomma bucata.*  o *oo*·na *go*·ma boo·*ka*·ta
**I've run out of petrol.**
*Ho esaurito la benzina.*  o e·zo·*ree*·to la ben·*dzee*·na

| **I'd like to hire** | *Vorrei* | vo·*ray* |
|---|---|---|
| **a/an ...** | *noleggiare ...* | no·le·*ja*·re ... |
| car | *una macchina* | *oo*·na *ma*·kee·na |
| 4WD | *un fuoristrada* | oon fwo·ree·*stra*·da |
| motorbike | *una moto* | *oo*·na *mo*·to |
| bicycle | *una bici(cletta)* | *oo*·na bee·chee·(*kle*·ta) |

# TRAVEL WITH CHILDREN

| **Is there a/an ...?** | *C'è ...?* | che ... |
|---|---|---|
| **I need a/an ...** | *Ho bisogno di ...* | o bee·*zo*·nyo dee ... |
| baby change room | *un bagno con fasciatoio* | oon *ba*·nyo kon fa·sha·*to*·yo |
| car seat | *un seggiolino per bambini* | oon se·jo·*lee*·no per bam·*bee*·nee |
| child-minding service | *un servizio di babysitter* | oon ser·*vee*·tsyo dee be·bee·*see*·ter |
| children's menu | *un menù per bambini* | oon me·*noo* per bam·*bee*·nee |
| formula (milk) | *latte in polvere* | *la*·te in *pol*·ve·re |
| highchair | *un seggiolone* | oon se·jo·*lo*·ne |
| nappies/diapers | *pannolini* | pa·no·*lee*·nee |
| potty | *un vasino* | oon va·*zee*·no |
| stroller | *un passeggino* | oon pa·se·*jee*·no |

# GLOSSARY

abbazia – abbey
affittacamere – rooms for rent
agora – marketplace, meeting place
agriturismo – farm stay
albergo – hotel
alimentari – grocery shop, delicatessen
anfiteatro – amphitheatre
ara – altar
arco – arch
autostrada – motorway, freeway

badia – abbey
baglio – manor house
bancomat – ATM
belvedere – panoramic viewpoint
benzina – petrol
borgo – ancient town or village; sometimes it's used to mean the equivalent of *via*

cambio – money exchange
camera – room
campanile – bell tower
campeggio – campsite
campo – field
cannolo – pastry shell stuffed with sweet ricotta

cappella – chapel
carabinieri – police with military and civil duties
Carnevale – carnival period between Epiphany and Lent
casa – house
case abusive – literally 'abusive houses'; illegal construction usually associated with the Mafia
cava – quarry
centro – centre
chiesa – church
CIT – Compagnia Italiana di Turismo; Italian national travel agency
città – town, city
clientelismo – system of political patronage
comune – equivalent to municipality or county; town or city council
contrada – district
corso – main street, avenue
cortile – courtyard
Cosa Nostra – Our Thing; alternative name for the Mafia
CTS – Centro Turistico Studentesco e Giovanile; Centre for Student & Youth Tourists

**dammuso** – low-level dwelling made of thick volcanic rock topped by a small whitewashed domed roof
**diretto** – direct; slow train
**duomo** – cathedral

**enoteca** – wine bar, wine shop

**fangho** – mud bath
**faraglione** – rock tower
**ferrovia** – train station
**festa** – festival
**fiume** – river
**fontana** – fountain
**fossa** – pit, hole
**funivia** – cable car

**gola** – gorge
**golfo** – gulf
**grotta** – cave
**guardia medica** – emergency doctor service

**IC** – Intercity; fast train
**interregionale** – long-distance train that stops frequently
**isola** – island

**lago** – lake
**largo** – small square
**latomia** – small quarry
**lido** – beach
**locale** – slow local train; also called *regionale*
**locanda** – inn, small hotel
**lungomare** – seafront road, promenade

**mare** – sea
**mattanza** – ritual slaughter of tuna
**mercato** – market
**molo** – wharf
**monte** – mountain
**municipio** – town hall, municipal offices
**museo** – museum

**Natale** – Christmas

**oratorio** – oratory
**ospedale** – hospital
**osteria** – inn

**palazzo** – palace, mansion
**parco** – park
**Pasqua** – Easter
**passeggiata** – evening stroll
**pensione** – small hotel
**piazza** – square
**piazzale** – large open square
**ponte** – bridge
**porta** – gate, door

**questura** – police station

**reale** – royal
**regionale** – slow local train; also called *locale*
**rifugio** – mountain hut
**riserva naturale** – nature reserve
**rocca** – fortress; rock

**sagra** – festival, generally dedicated to one food item or theme
**sala** – room
**santuario** – sanctuary
**scalinata** – staircase, steps
**spiaggia** – beach
**stazione** – station
**strada** – street, road

**teatro** – theatre
**tempio** – temple
**tonnara** – tuna-processing plant
**torre** – tower
**traghetto** – ferry, boat
**treno** – train

**via** – street, road
**viale** – avenue
**vicolo** – alley, alleyway

# BEHIND THE SCENES

## THIS BOOK

This 5th edition of Lonely Planet's *Sicily* guidebook was updated by Virginia Maxwell and Duncan Garwood. The 4th edition was updated by Vesna Maric, the 3rd edition was updated by Paula Hardy and the 2nd edition was updated by Sally O'Brien. The 1st edition was written by Fionn Davenport. This guidebook was commissioned in Lonely Planet's London office, and produced by the following:

**Commissioning Editors** Joe Bindloss, Paula Hardy

**Coordinating Editors** Susie Ashworth, Carolyn Boicos

**Coordinating Cartographer** Anthony Phelan

**Coordinating Layout Designer** Frank Deim

**Managing Editor** Helen Christinis

**Managing Cartographers** Adrian Persoglia, Herman So

**Managing Layout Designer** Celia Wood

**Assisting Editors** Jackey Coyle, Kristin Odijk, Charles Rawlings-Way

**Assisting Cartographers** Julie Dodkins, Owen Eszeki, Mark Griffiths, Alex Leung, Jolyon Philcox, Brendan Streager, Xavier di Toro

**Cover Research** Naomi Parker, lonelyplanetimages.com

**Internal Image Research** Aude Vauconsant, lonelyplanetimages.com

**Language Content** Laura Crawford

## THE LONELY PLANET STORY

Fresh from an epic journey across Europe, Asia and Australia in 1972, Tony and Maureen Wheeler sat at their kitchen table stapling together notes. The first Lonely Planet guidebook, *Across Asia on the Cheap*, was born.

Travellers snapped up the guides. Inspired by their success, the Wheelers began publishing books to Southeast Asia, India and beyond. Demand was prodigious, and the Wheelers expanded the business rapidly to keep up. Over the years, Lonely Planet extended its coverage to every country and into the virtual world via lonelyplanet.com and the Thorn Tree message board.

As Lonely Planet became a globally loved brand, Tony and Maureen received several offers for the company. But it wasn't until 2007 that they found a partner whom they trusted to remain true to the company's principles of travelling widely, treading lightly and giving sustainably. In October of that year, BBC Worldwide acquired a 75% share in the company, pledging to uphold Lonely Planet's commitment to independent travel, trustworthy advice and editorial independence.

Today, Lonely Planet has offices in Melbourne, London and Oakland, with over 500 staff members and 300 authors. Tony and Maureen are still actively involved with Lonely Planet. They're travelling more often than ever, and they're devoting their spare time to charitable projects. And the company is still driven by the philosophy of *Across Asia on the Cheap*: 'All you've got to do is decide to go and the hardest part is over. So go!'

**Project Managers** Imogen Bannister, Liz Heynes

**Thanks to** Lisa Knights, Wibowo Rusli

# THANKS

## VIRGINIA MAXWELL

Greatest thanks and much love go to Max and Peter, who once again accompanied me on an Italy jaunt for Lonely Planet. Many thanks must also go to my fellow author Duncan Garwood, whose excellent work, support and helpful suggestions were greatly appreciated. In Palermo, *molto grazie* to Patty Marchetti. Thanks to Paula Hardy for giving me the job and to Joe Bindloss for seeing it through to the end. Heartfelt thanks to the long-suffering Imogen Bannister and Herman So.

## DUNCAN GARWOOD

*Grazie* to Claudia Zerbini, Paolo Piano and Giusy Ritto in Catania; Loredana Albani and Giuliana in Syracuse; Vincenzo Grimaudo Cova and Gaetano in Caltagirone; Luigi Napoli and Serenella Bianchini in Agrigento; Diana Brown and Daniela Subba in Lipari; Nino Terrano and Alina Maslowski in Filicudi; Enza Grunno in Enna; Sara Spadaro in Taormina; Francesca Curcuruto in Aci Castello; and Giuseppe Verde in Sciacca. At Lonely Planet, thanks to Paula Hardy for the commission, Herman So for his maps and Laura Stansfeld for her help with the new formatting. Many thanks also to co-author Virginia Maxwell for her support and expert advice, and to David Mills for helping me celebrate my birthday in Catania. On the home front, much love and a heartfelt *grazie* to Lidia and our two boys, Ben and Nick, and my *suocera* Nicla Salvati for her invaluable help.

# OUR READERS

**Many thanks to the travellers who used the last edition and wrote to us with helpful hints, useful advice and interesting anecdotes:**

Sulun Aykurt, Beatriz Alonso Aznar, Sarah Bardell, Melissa Barnard, Adam Bezuijen, Marylou Bosco, Andreanne Bouchard, Boris Bouricius, Sue Bray, Mary Caroe, David Cartwright, Isabelle Caruana-Dingli, Dr Velleda Ceccoli, Sarah Coles, Barbara Conners, Miss VM Conrad, Marcella Croce, Dario Dalla Costa, Elena Dalla Vecchia, Alex De

Jongh, Sabina Spengler De Pertis, Marcel De Vroed, Michael Dempsey, Chris Denys, David Dibden, Andrea Dogliotti, Charlene Doll, Rosy Drohan, Rikki Eckert, Ioannis Eleftheriou, Andrew Feldman, Nicola Fiorilla, Greg Forshaw, Angela Gayton, Clare Gittings, John Glasgow, Ian Govey, Valentina Hartford, Cheryl Hatch, Brenda Hawkins, Fernando Herranz, Amy Huxtable, Maria Ilina, Ronald Jackman, Cori Jones, Felix Jones, Hilary K Josephs, Benjamin K, Katherine Kirby, Frederik Køhlert, Anastasia Kourentzi, Christine Lewis, Fangyan Li, Gerry Maguire, Dominic Maher, Manuela Marchioro, Genevieve Marino, Peter McKallen, Shabnam Merchant, Rosemary Moss, Na Na, George Newton, William Norris, Gaetano Pace, Berti Paola, Marta Papini, Gail Pearce, Elaine Perrone, Lilli Petersen, Anne Pincus, Manuela Pitino, Sona Pivonkova, Andrea Pleasance, Aase Popper, Patrick Pregiato, Susan Prevost, Jacquie Pryor, Margaret Ramskill, Tata Ringberg, Judy Rock, George Rohrmann, Thomas Rubinsky, Barbara Sheerman-Chase, Per Skansberg, Ilan Sluis, Erik Strub, Lindsay Studio, Angela Tagliavia, Sonia Ulliana, Ehud Uri, Marco Vignozzi, Piroska Walsh, Nadia Wanzi, Bob Watson, Anna Wesselink and Julia Wittich-Sauer.

## ACKNOWLEDGMENTS

# INDEX

**INDEX**

INDEX

000 MAP PAGES
000 PHOTOGRAPH PAGES

INDEX

INDEX

## MAP LEGEND

*Note Not all symbols displayed below appear in this guide.*

### ROUTES

Tollway
Freeway
Primary Road
Secondary Road
Tertiary Road
Lane
Unsealed Road
Under Construction

Tunnel
Pedestrian Mall
Steps
Walking Track
Walking Path
Walking Tour
Walking Tour Detour
Pedestrian Overpass

### TRANSPORT

Ferry Route & Terminal
Metro Line & Station
Monorail & Stop
Bus Route & Stop

Train Line & Station
Underground Rail Line
Tram Line & Stop
Cable Car, Funicular

### AREA FEATURES

Airport
Beach
Building
Campus
Cemetery, Christian
Cemetery, Other

Land
Mall, Plaza
Market
Park
Sportsground
Urban

### HYDROGRAPHY

River, Creek
Canal
Water
Swamp
Lake (Dry)

### BOUNDARIES

International
State, Provincial
Suburb
City Wall
Cliff

### SYMBOLS IN THE KEY

**Essential Information**
Tourist Office
Police Station

**Exploring**
Beach
Buddhist
Castle, Fort
Christian
Diving, Snorkelling
Garden
Hindu
Islamic
Jewish
Monument
Museum, Gallery
Place of Interest
Snow Skiing
Swimming Pool
Ruin
Tomb
Winery, Vineyard
Zoo, Bird Sanctuary

**Gastronomic Highlights**
Eating
Cafe

**Nightlife**
Drinking
Entertainment

**Recommended Shops**
Shopping

**Accommodation**
Sleeping
Camping

**Transport**
Airport, Airfield
Cycling, Bicycle Path
Border Crossing
Bus Station
Ferry
General Transport
Train Station
Taxi Rank

**Parking**
Parking

### OTHER MAP SYMBOLS

**Information**
Bank, ATM
Embassy, Consulate
Hospital, Medical
Internet Facilities
Post Office
Telephone

**Geographic**
Cave
Lighthouse
Lookout
Mountain, Volcano
National Park
Picnic Area

---

## LONELY PLANET OFFICES

AUSTRALIA
**Head Office**
Locked Bag 1, Footscray, Victoria 3011
☎ 03 8379 8000, fax 03 8379 8111

USA
150 Linden St, Oakland, CA 94607
☎ 510 250 6400, toll free 800 275 8555
fax 510 893 8572

UK
2nd fl, 186 City Road, London EC1V 2NT
☎ 020 7106 2100, fax 020 7106 2101

CONTACT
talk2us@lonelyplanet.com
lonelyplanet.com/contact

Published by Lonely Planet Publications Pty Ltd
ABN 36 005 607 983
© Lonely Planet 2011
© photographers as indicated 2011
**Cover photograph** Ragusa, Val di Noto, Sicily, SIME/Simeone Giovanni/4Corners. **Internal title page photograph** Tempio della Concordia, Valley of the Temples, Agrigento, Sicily, Diana Mayfield/Lonely Planet Images. Many of the images in this guide are available for licensing from Lonely Planet Images: lonelyplanetimages.com.

MIX
Paper from
responsible sources
FSC™ C021741
www.fsc.org